THE OBJECTIVES OF
MACRO-ECONOMIC POLICY

The Objectives of
Macro-Economic Policy

Ajit K. Dasgupta
Professor of Economics
Sir George Williams University, Montreal

A. J. Hagger
Reader in Economics
University of Tasmania

Macmillan

First published 1971 by
THE MACMILLAN PRESS LTD
London and Basingstoke
Associated companies in New York Toronto
Dublin Melbourne Johannesburg and Madras

SBN 333 12396 4

Printed in Great Britain by
R. & R. CLARK LTD
Edinburgh

Contents

Preface

THIS book is a fairly advanced text in macro-economics written for graduate and final-year undergraduate students. It differs from the general run of advanced texts in this field in a number of ways. In the first place, it has a strong British emphasis: British institutions provide the framework, the problems selected for discussion are British problems, and British empirical research is drawn on wherever possible.

Secondly, it is not a book on macro-economic theory as such. Our central themes are the four great objectives of macro-economic policy – internal balance, external balance, price stability and rapid growth – the measures by which they can be promoted and the possible conflicts between them. A rigorous discussion along these lines requires that the reader possess a fairly sophisticated theoretical equipment, and this we have attempted to provide in the course of the book. But we have not gone beyond this. Thus, while the theoretical content of the book is substantial, it is also deliberately circumscribed. For a comprehensive treatment of macro-economic theory, the student would need to go elsewhere – to R. G. D. Allen's *Macro-economic Theory*, for example. We would justify this approach to the presentation of theory by arguing that most students are unwilling to invest heavily in the acquisition of advanced theoretical tools unless they can see clearly that these tools are indispensable to a proper understanding of the great questions of the day.

Finally, the book has, we hope, a strong empirical flavour. Once again, however, we have made no attempt to be comprehensive. In line with our desire to cater primarily for the needs of British students we have confined our attention to relevant British empirical material, with one or two notable exceptions such as the recent important empirical studies of Jorgenson for the United States.

In short, what we have tried to do is to produce an advanced text in which theoretical, policy and empirical discussions of a macro kind are woven together as tightly as possible within the context of the British economy and British economic institutions.

Inevitably, we have been compelled to make extensive use of notation. We have tried to make this as simple as possible and to avoid double use of symbols wherever confusion appeared likely to result. Nothing is more irritating and distracting than to have to hunt back through several chapters to find the meaning of some symbol, and to minimise the need for this we have adopted the practice of writing key variables in full at fairly regular intervals and inserted a comprehensive list of symbols at the end of the book.

A short reading list has been appended to each chapter. In each case the references which appear have been chosen not only because of their intrinsic worth but also because, by consulting them, the student will find it comparatively easy to build up a substantial bibliography if he wishes to do so.

The book developed from an earlier work by one of us[1] and was substantially written in 1967 while we were working in the Economics Department of the University of Southampton. We were greatly helped by discussions with various members of the Department and we are grateful to them for their assistance. In particular, we are deeply indebted to Mr A. P. Budd who read the manuscript as it developed and suggested many major improvements. We also wish to thank Mrs S. M. Payne and Mr P. J. Rayner of the Economics Department of the University of Tasmania, both of whom worked through large sections of the manuscript and helped to eliminate much error and confusion. The index was prepared by Mr D. W. Challen of the University of Tasmania and our thanks are due to him for his painstaking efforts. Finally we must thank Miss P. Schmidt for her outstanding typing of an extremely difficult manuscript.

A. K. D.
A. J. H.

Sir George Williams University,
Canada,
University of Tasmania,
Australia
1970.

[1] A. J. Hagger, *Price Stability, Growth and Balance* (Melbourne: Cheshire, 1968).

PART ONE

Introduction

1 Macro-Economic Policy Objectives

1.1 Britain's Economic Objectives

The last thirty years have seen a profoundly significant change in the list of agreed macro-economic objectives. Writing in 1931, the Macmillan Committee gave pride of place in their discussion of objectives to the desirability of raising, and then stabilising, the world prices of basic raw materials and foodstuffs, though it recognised that this was as much a matter for international, as for national, action. In the words of the report:

> Thus our objective should be, so far as it lies within the power of this country to influence the international price level, first of all to raise prices a long way above the present level and then to maintain them at the level thus reached with as much stability as can be managed.
>
> We recommend that this objective be accepted as the guiding aim of the monetary policy of this country. . . .[1]

True, other objectives were mentioned in the report, but without elaboration, without emphasis and without conviction. Thus paragraph 280 contained a parenthetical list of monetary policy objectives ('. . . – for example, the maintenance of the parity of the foreign exchanges without unnecessary disturbance to domestic business, the avoidance of the Credit Cycle, and the stability of the price level – . . .'), and paragraph 282 referred in a single sentence to the need to 'promote the stability of output and of employment at a high level'.

The adequacy of the approach embodied in the Macmillan Report was increasingly called in question throughout the late 1930s and the early 1940s, mainly as a result of the experience of the Great Depression and the widespread acceptance of the ideas put forward by

---

[1] *Report of Committee on Finance and Industry*, Cmd 3897 (June 1931) p. 117, paras 275–6.

Keynes in *The General Theory*; and the culmination of this growing dissatisfaction was the publication in 1944 of a path-breaking White Paper.[1] The somewhat bold opening sentences of the Foreword to this paper showed how far the generally accepted view had moved since 1931: 'The Government accept as one of their primary aims and responsibilities the maintenance of a high and stable level of employment after the war. This paper outlines the policy which they propose to follow in pursuit of that aim.' Thus, the maintenance of a high and stable level of employment had now become a 'primary aim' of government. Moreover it was now generally recognised as an aim which had to be consciously pursued through appropriate government policies. The same points were stated with greater emphasis in the body of the paper. For example, after presenting unemployment rates for the period 1858–1938, the paper added: 'If these features which have afflicted our economic life in the past are to be banished, as it is our resolve to banish them, from the future. . . .'[2] Again:

> The Government are prepared to accept in future the responsibility for taking action at the earliest possible stage to arrest a threatened slump. This involves a new approach and a new responsibility for the State. It was at one time believed that every trade depression would automatically bring its own corrective. . . . Experience has shown, however, that under modern conditions this process of self-recovery, if effective at all, is likely to be extremely prolonged and to be accompanied by widespread distress, particularly in a complex industrial society like our own.[3]

All this appears little short of revolutionary when read in conjunction with the Macmillan Report.

The 'maintenance of a high and stable level of employment' has retained the central position among policy objectives, to which it was elevated by the 1944 White Paper, throughout the entire post-war period, and there can be no doubt that it will continue to do so for a long time to come. Nevertheless other objectives have emerged alongside the employment objective (to some extent because of the success of post-war employment policy) and have been given increasing emphasis in recent years. By the end of the 1950s these newer objectives had gained sufficiently wide acceptance for the Radcliffe Committee to be able to list them, along with the employment

---

[1] See *Employment Policy*, Cmd 6527 (May 1944).
[2] Ibid., p. 15.　　　　　　　　　[3] Ibid., p. 16.

objective, as the agreed aims of monetary policy. In the words of the Report:

> We may in summary list the objectives in pursuit of which monetary measures may be used:
> (1) A high and stable level of employment.
> (2) Reasonable stability of the internal purchasing power of money.
> (3) Steady economic growth and improvement of the standard of living.
> (4) Some contribution, implying a margin in the balance of payments, to the economic development of the outside world.
> (5) A strengthening of London's international reserves, implying further margin in the balance of payments.[1]

In the last decade numerous official statements and political manifestos have stressed the importance of the objectives listed by the Radcliffe Committee and the determination of governments (actual and potential) to take whatever steps are necessary to achieve them.

In a White Paper published in 1956 under the title of *The Economic Implications of Full Employment*,[2] the Conservative Government of the day referred to the success of employment policy since the war and added:

> But full employment has brought with it one problem to which we have not yet found a satisfactory solution: yet unless we do find the solution, . . . full employment itself may be threatened. The problem is that of continually rising prices. . . . The purpose of this White Paper is . . . to suggest what will have to be done by the Government and people of this country if reasonable price stability is in future to be maintained.[3]

At a later point in the Paper we read that 'it must be one of our major objectives to maintain in future a much greater degree of price stability than has been achieved in the past ten years'.[4]

Commitment to price stability as a major economic objective was also implicit in the terms of reference of the Council on Prices, Productivity and Incomes: 'Having regard to the desirability of full employment and increasing standards of life based on expanding production and reasonable stability of prices, to keep under review changes in prices, productivity and the level of incomes (including

---

[1] See *Report of Committee on the Working of the Monetary System*, Cmnd 827 (Aug 1959) p. 22.
[2] Cmd 9725 (Mar 1956).   [3] Ibid., p. 2.   [4] Ibid., p. 3.

wages, salaries and profits) and to report thereon from time to time.'[1]

In the opening paragraph of the White Paper, *Prices and Incomes Policy*, price stability was advanced once again as a major economic objective, this time by a Labour Government:

> In the Joint Statement of Intent on Productivity, Prices and Incomes, representatives of the T.U.C. and the employers' organisations have accepted that major objectives of national policy must be:
> to ensure that British industry is dynamic and that its prices are competitive;
> to raise productivity and efficiency so that real national output can increase, and to keep wages, salaries and other forms of incomes in line with this increase;
> to keep the general level of prices stable.[2]

The official economic documents of the last fifteen years also give considerable emphasis to the need both for a viable external situation and for a high rate of economic growth. For example, in the 1956 White Paper already referred to we read: 'The Government is pledged to foster conditions in which the nation can, if it so wills, realise its full potentialities for growth in terms of production and living standards.'[3] The same White Paper also stressed that one of the conditions for realisation by the nation of its 'full potentialities for growth' was a healthy external situation – that the growth and external objectives were inextricably linked:

> The future growth of production in this country must, of course, be affected by what happens in other parts of the world. . . .
> But whatever other countries do, the rate of progress which we shall achieve, and the increase in living standards which we shall attain, will depend mainly on our own enterprise and our own efforts. It is not sufficient that we should have the capacity simply to produce more. We must be able to produce and sell abroad enough exports to pay for essential imports of food and industrial materials and at the same time to meet the cost of our overseas capital commitments and to build up the reserves . . . ; and if we do not export enough, we shall be unable either to support a steady expansion of production at home or to maintain full employment.[4]

Again, the opening sentences of a White Paper published in 1962, also by a Conservative Government, read: 'The Government's policy

[1] *First Report of Council on Prices, Productivity and Incomes* (London: H.M.S.O., 1958) p. 1.
[2] See *Prices and Incomes Policy*, Cmnd 2639 (Apr 1965) p. 5.
[3] See Cmd 9725, p. 10.   [4] Ibid., p. 3.

is to promote a faster rate of economic growth and a more vigorous development of our export trade. This depends on maintaining the strength of the pound and our competitive efficiency, which in turn depend on our ability to keep costs and prices stable.'[1]

The strength of the nation's commitment to the growth objective was again made plain by the establishment in 1962 of the National Economic Development Council, on which the Government, management and trade unions were represented, with objects:

(a) To examine the economic performance of the nation with particular concern for plans for the future in both the private and the public sectors of industry.
(b) To consider together what are the obstacles to quicker growth, what can be done to improve efficiency and whether the best use is being made of our resources.
(c) To seek agreement upon ways of improving economic performance, competitive power and efficiency; in other words, to increase the rate of sound growth.[2]

In the opening paragraphs of its second major report the Council said: 'The first major report of the Council on the growth of the United Kingdom economy to 1966 . . . was seen as establishing a framework which would itself be an important contribution to faster growth. . . . The faster growth programme was accepted by the Council. . . . There was general agreement that faster growth was a major aim of British policy. . . .'[3]

More recently still the Labour Government expressed its firm attachment to the twin aims of rapid growth and a strong external position in the Introduction to *The National Plan*, the opening sentences of which state boldly: 'This is a plan to provide the basis for greater economic growth. An essential part of the Plan is the solution of Britain's balance of payments problem; for growth cannot be maintained unless we pay our way in the world.'[4] A little later we read: 'The task of correcting the balance of payments and achieving the surplus necessary to repay our debts, while at the same time fostering the rapid growth of the economy, is the central challenge. We must succeed if we are to achieve all our objectives of

[1] See *Incomes Policy: The Next Step*, Cmnd 1626 (Feb 1962).
[2] See National Economic Development Council, *Growth of the United Kingdom Economy to 1966* (London: H.M.S.O., 1963) p. viii.
[3] See National Economic Development Council, *The Growth of the Economy* (London: H.M.S.O., 1964) p. 1.
[4] See *The National Plan*, Cmnd 2764 (Sep 1965) p. 1.

social justice and welfare, of rising standards of living, of better social capital, and of a full life for all in a pleasant environment.'[1]

By now enough will have been said to make it clear that both of the major political parties in Britain and, indeed, all major economic groups in the country, are deeply committed to the four macro-economic objectives of a high and stable level of employment, price stability, a high rate of economic growth and a strong balance of payments position. It is these four agreed objectives which form the underlying theme of the present book. Our aim will be to consider these objectives in a systematic way in the context of the British economy and British economic institutions and, wherever possible, to give the discussion a quantitative basis by drawing on the results of relevant British empirical research.

A rigorous discussion along these lines requires a fairly sophisticated theoretical equipment and we have provided this equipment as the need arises. Consequently, the book has a fairly substantial theoretical content. At the same time we have avoided theory for its own sake and have tried to weave the theoretical material into the main argument in a way which makes its relevance to the great issues of the day abundantly clear.

It will be clear already, and we hope that it will become clearer still, that the four objectives are closely interrelated. However, to simplify the exposition we have decided to begin by treating each of them, in turn, in isolation from the rest and only then taking up the problem of interdependence. Accordingly we have devoted Part Two to the employment and balance of payments objectives and Part Three to the price-stability and growth objectives. All questions connected with the interrelationships between the objectives have been held over for discussion in the final part, Part Four.

The rest of this introductory chapter will be devoted to a fairly detailed examination of the objectives themselves in which we shall inquire as to precisely what they mean and why it is that they are widely held to be desirable, not only in Britain but in all advanced industrial countries of the non-Communist world. Before proceeding in this direction, however, we must deal with one point of terminology.

Ever since the 1944 White Paper it has been the common practice (followed by the Radcliffe Committee) to describe the employment objective as the 'maintenance of a high and stable level of employ-

---

[1] See *The National Plan*, Cmnd 2764 (Sep 1965) p. 1.

ment'. However, this is not altogether an appropriate term, because while, since 1944, the authorities have always been concerned to ensure that aggregate demand was sufficient to maintain a high level of employment, they have been equally concerned to ensure that it was not *more than* sufficient for this purpose. The point is well put in the following passage from the 1956 White Paper:

> The Government is pledged to foster conditions in which the nation can, if it so wills, realise its full potentialities for growth in terms of production and living standards. But the Government must no less seek to ensure that the pressure of domestic demand does not reach a level at which it threatens price stability and endangers the balance of payments. To maintain full employment without inflation necessarily involves continual adjustments. At times the pressure of demand will grow too strong and will need curbing; at other times this pressure will be weak, and the economy will need a stimulus. It is the Government's job to keep the pressure right. . . . [1]

We have decided, therefore, to use the term 'maintenance of internal balance' in place of the term 'maintenance of a high and stable level of employment' to describe what has been the central aim of macro-economic policy since the 1944 White Paper. The balance of payments objective we shall describe as 'the maintenance of external balance' or equivalently 'the maintenance of balance of payments equilibrium'. Thus from now on we shall describe the four macro-economic objectives which form our subject matter as: (i) the maintenance of internal balance; (ii) the maintenance of external balance or balance of payments equilibrium; (iii) the achievement of price stability; and (iv) the achievement of a high rate of economic growth. We shall now attempt to clarify these four objectives, beginning with the internal balance objective.

1.2 Internal Balance

Internal balance may be defined as a situation in which aggregate excess demand is zero. This definition, however, immediately raises two questions: (i) What is aggregate excess demand? and (ii) What markets are involved – the commodity markets as a whole, the labour markets as a whole or both market groups? Let us consider these questions in turn.

[1] Cmd 9725, p. 10.

Before we can define *aggregate* excess demand for a group of markets, we must first define excess demand for an individual market. The excess demand which exists in any given market in any given period[1] is defined as the purchases planned in the market during the period, on the basis of the prices announced by sellers at the beginning of the period, *less* the supplies available to the market during the period. This may be positive or negative. Thus if entities plan to purchase 20 units during the period and only 15 units are available for the period, excess demand in the market is 5 units for the period; if planned purchases are 10 and available supplies are 16, excess demand is – 6. The aggregate excess demand which exists for a particular *group* of markets (say the commodity markets as a whole) in the period is then simply the (algebraic) sum of the excess demands of the individual markets comprising the group; or, what is the same thing, the (algebraic) sum of the purchases planned in the market group *less* the (algebraic) sum of the supplies available in the market group. Since the individual excess demands are expressed in varying quantity units (some in tons, others in ounces, others in dozens, others in man-hours and so on) they can be added to get the aggregate excess demand of the group of markets as a whole only if they are first valued in terms of a common set of prices – say, the prices announced at the beginning of the period or the prices realised in the preceding period or in some other earlier period. Thus the aggregate excess demand of a market group for a period is a money value based on a certain set of prices, e.g. £20 million in terms of the prices of period 0.

We have internal balance in any period, then, if aggregate excess demand, as just defined, is zero. But aggregate excess demand in what market group? In the commodity market group, in the labour market group or in both groups combined? How we answer this question

---

[1] The concept of the period is an important one. Underlying the concept are three simplifying assumptions: (i) that each economic entity (household, firm or government) has a fixed 'plan-revision period' (in the sense that the entity revises its spending plans, say, once every month or once every six months or once every year); (ii) that the plan-revision periods of all entities are of the same length; and (iii) that all plan-revision periods are perfectly synchronised so that all spending plans are revised, say, on the first day of each month. These simplifying assumptions enable us to divide time, measured from some fixed starting-point, into an endless succession of plan-revision periods which are of fixed length and which relate to all economic entities – households, firms and governments. Thus whenever we refer, as above, to 'any given period' we shall mean any one of this endless succession of plan-revision periods.

will depend on how we view the relationship between excess commodity demand and excess labour demand. The view most commonly held is that the aggregate excess demand for commodities is always approximately equal to aggregate excess demand for labour, in which case we need concern ourselves with one or the other but not both. There are those, however, who dispute this view and argue that there is no reason whatsoever why labour excess demand should always be equal to commodity excess demand or even why the two should have the same sign, and consequently that our concept of internal balance should embrace both groups of market.[1] Since this is still an open question, it seems that the most sensible course is to adopt the simpler of the two opposing positions for the time being. This we shall do; we shall confine our attention to the commodity markets and say that internal balance exists in any period if aggregate excess demand for commodities is zero, i.e. if aggregate planned purchases of commodities and aggregate available supplies of commodities are equal for the period, when both are valued in terms of some common set of prices.

It will be clear from the discussion of the previous paragraph that zero excess demand for commodities as a whole does not necessarily mean zero excess demand in every one of the individual commodity markets. Thus internal balance, as we have defined it, is consistent with imbalance in some (or in all) of the individual commodity markets.

Our concept is still not quite sharp enough, for there is some ambiguity in the terms 'aggregate planned purchases of commodities' and 'aggregate available supplies of commodities'. By 'aggregate planned purchases of commodities' we shall mean the sum of:

(a) the purchases of commodities which domestic entities in the aggregate desire to make from domestic and foreign producers; and

(b) the purchases which overseas entities in the aggregate desire to make from domestic producers.[2]

---

[1] See in particular Bent Hansen, *A Study in the Theory of Inflation* (London: Allen & Unwin, 1951).

[2] *Desired* purchases must be distinguished from *attempted* purchases. Normally desired and attempted purchases will be one and the same thing. In certain circumstances, however, they will differ. For example, if there is a severe shortage of accommodation an individual may put his name down on several agents' lists: he *desires* to purchase the accommodation provided by one flat, but in order to do so he *attempts* to purchase the accommodation of, say, six flats.

By 'aggregate available supplies of commodities' we shall mean the sum of:

(a) maximum realisable domestic value of production, defined as the maximum domestic value of production of which the existing 'normal' labour force is capable within 'normal' working hours, subject to the limitations imposed by the size of the existing capital stock and the existing industrial distribution of the labour force and the capital stock;[1] and

(b) aggregate realised imports of commodities.

Thus, when we say that internal balance exists in any period, we shall mean that the aggregate value of commodities which domestic entities desire to purchase in the period from domestic and foreign producers *plus* the aggregate value of commodities which overseas entities desire to purchase from domestic producers *equals* the maximum realisable domestic value of production of commodities *plus* aggregate realised imports of commodities.

We shall now present this definition in a more familiar form. We begin by rewriting the internal-balance equality as follows:

Desired domestic purchases of *final* commodities

plus

desired domestic purchases of *intermediate* commodities

plus

desired purchases by overseas entities

EQUALS

maximum realisable value of production

less

maximum realisable value of production of intermediate commodities

less

realised imports of intermediate commodities

plus

maximum realisable value of production of inte mediate commodities

plus

realised imports of intermediate commodities

plus

aggregate realised imports

---

[1] See also section 1.5 below where this concept is more fully discussed.

We next cancel 'desired domestic purchases of intermediate commodities' with 'maximum realisable value of production of intermediate commodities *plus* realised imports of intermediate commodities'. Thus we make the simplifying assumption that zero excess demand in the commodity markets as a whole is always accompanied by zero excess demand in the markets for intermediate commodities. This assumption enables us to write the above equality as:

> Desired domestic purchases of *final* commodities
>
> *plus*
>
> desired purchases by overseas entities
>
> *EQUALS*
>
> maximum realisable domestic *net value added*
>
> *plus*
>
> aggregate realised imports.

Finally, we rewrite this last equality in terms of the familiar social accounting aggregates as:

> Desired consumption expenditure
>
> *plus*
>
> desired gross investment expenditure
>
> *plus*
>
> desired government expenditure
>
> *plus*
>
> desired purchases by overseas entities
>
> *EQUALS*
>
> maximum realisable gross domestic product
>
> *plus*
>
> realised imports.

In view of earlier discussion, all the aggregates appearing in this final equality must be regarded as being valued in terms of the prices of some given period, say period 0, or as being expressed in real terms.

This is the form of the definition of internal balance that we shall work with from now on. If the above equality holds, we shall say that there is internal balance in the period or zero excess demand for commodities. Case A of Table 1.1 represents a situation of internal balance in this sense. If the first half of the equality exceeds the second half we shall say that the situation is one of excess demand for commodities, while in the reverse case we shall describe the situation as one of deficient demand for commodities. Thus case B of Table 1.1 represents a situation of excess demand and case C a situation of deficient demand.

TABLE 1.1

	Case A	Case B	Case C
1. Desired consumption expenditure (£m. in prices of period 0)	72	75	70
2. Desired gross investment expenditure (£m. in prices of period 0)	8	10	5
3. Desired government expenditure (£m. in prices of period 0)	15	18	13
4. Desired expenditure by overseas entities (£m. in prices of period 0)	25	27	22
1+2+3+4	120	130	110
5. Maximum realisable gross domestic product (£m. in prices of period 0)	100	100	100
6. Imports (£m. in prices of period 0)	20	20	20
5+6	120	120	120

The hypothetical figures shown in Table 1.1 also help to explain why the objective of internal balance is regarded as a desirable one. Since imports are £20 million in period 0 prices, the expenditure which is directed towards domestic production is £100 million in case A and £110 million in case B. Thus in case A, expenditure is just sufficient to call forth maximum realisable gross domestic product while in case B it is more than sufficient. Since the maximum realisable gross domestic product is, by definition, the gross domestic product corresponding to full employment of the normal labour force for normal working hours,[1] it follows that expenditure is just sufficient to provide normal full-employment conditions in case A and more than sufficient in case B. On the other hand, in case C the

[1] While this is true of Britain and other advanced economies, it is not true of most of the underdeveloped economies. An important feature of most underdeveloped economies is that the stock of capital equipment is extremely small in relation to the labour force. As a result, the maximum realisable gross domestic product of these economies is the gross domestic product corresponding to full employment of the *capital stock*; the gross domestic product corresponding to full employment of the labour force (and hence the objective of full employment) is normally unattainable.

expenditure which is directed towards domestic production is only £90 million and this is insufficient to call forth normal full-employment conditions. In case C, therefore, there will be less than full employment or 'underemployment' in the period.

We can generalise this by saying that real expenditure will be at least sufficient to provide normal full-employment conditions in any period if the situation is one of internal balance or one of excess demand for commodities, and less than sufficient if the situation is one of deficient demand for commodities. It follows that, to achieve continuous full employment, it is necessary to take either internal balance or excess demand for commodities as a policy objective. But, as we shall see in Chapter 9, excess demand is one of the main sources of rising prices in advanced industrial countries. Thus, while internal balance and excess demand for commodities are equally desirable objectives from the point of view of attaining full employment alone, from the point of view of attaining both full employment and price stability internal balance is definitely to be preferred. In short, internal balance is regarded as a desirable policy objective because it means full employment without the upward pressure on prices which accompanies excess demand.

1.3 External Balance

By external balance or balance of payments equilibrium we shall mean a situation in which the aggregate demand for foreign currencies, in the sense of the aggregate desired purchases of foreign currencies, is neither persistently greater than the available supply of foreign currencies nor persistently less than the available supply, over a run of, say, six to twelve quarters.

Three points should be noted in connection with this definition. The first relates to the 'aggregate demand for foreign currencies' and the 'available supply of foreign currencies', to which the definition refers. These are to be regarded as deseasonalised figures and as adjusted to exclude all contributions arising solely because the balance of payments situation is what it is. For example, the aggregate-demand figures are to be regarded as excluding purchases · of foreign currency by residents in anticipation of exchange devaluation, and the available-supply figures as excluding 'stand-by' credits granted by foreign central banks.

Secondly, it must be understood that, while the definition implies that external balance is absent if the international currency reserves of the country in question are declining (a decline in reserves must reflect excess demand for foreign currencies), it does not necessarily imply that external balance exists if the reserves are stable. A situation in which the reserves are stable but in which they would decline if all import and other direct controls over foreign transactions were removed, e.g. the British situation throughout the 1940s, is not a situation of external balance as we have defined it. It is a situation in which excess demand for foreign currencies exists but is being repressed by the direct controls and so prevented from causing a drain on the international reserves.

Finally, it should be noted that external balance is absent, according to the definition, only if the excess demand, or the deficient demand, for foreign currencies is *persistent* in the sense that the general drift of the international reserves figures is unmistakably downward (in the absence of direct controls) or upward, as the case may be, over a short run of quarters. Thus an isolated decrease in reserves due to some random event, such as a major strike in an export industry, does not constitute absence of external balance on our definition.[1]

As the discussion of the previous section shows, there is a strong case for making internal balance a policy objective because the only alternatives to internal balance are deficient demand for commodities with general unemployment on the one hand, and excess demand for commodities with inflationary pressure on the other; and neither of these is an acceptable alternative. In the case of external balance the position is less straightforward; here the alternatives cannot be completely ruled out. To pursue this point, let us consider separately the case where lack of external balance takes the form of a persistent excess demand for foreign currencies and the case where it consists of a persistent deficiency of demand.

A country which is faced with a persistent excess demand for foreign currencies can do one of three things: (i) it can allow the excess demand to persist and take no steps to protect its international currency reserves; (ii) it can allow the excess demand to persist but impose an import-licensing system accompanied, perhaps, by direct controls over overseas capital payments by residents to protect its

---

[1] The concept of external balance will be further discussed in section 7.1 below, where the short-run concept presented here will be distinguished from the long-run concept.

international reserves; (iii) it can take positive steps to eliminate the excess demand[1] and, if necessary, borrow foreign currency while these are taking effect, i.e. it can make external balance a policy objective.

Now, the essential point is that either the first or the second courses of action may be preferable to the third under certain conditions. The first ('do nothing') certainly involves a risk – the risk that the country's international reserves will disappear altogether. But in any actual situation the risk may or may not be serious, depending on a number of factors such as the size of the country's reserves in the initial situation relative to its trade (or, in the case of an international currency like sterling, relative to its short-term liabilities), the strength of the excess demand for foreign currencies, the likelihood that the excess demand will be eliminated spontaneously within a reasonable time, the likelihood that it will be magnified by specula-tion in favour of exchange devaluation, and so on. If circumstances are favourable and the risk of a total loss of reserves appears to be negligible, 'do nothing' may well be a more sensible course of action than taking positive steps to achieve the external balance objective, especially if these positive steps would be likely to hamper the attainment of one of the other objectives.[2]

The second course of action (imposition of import controls) may also provide an acceptable alternative to the pursuit of external balance under certain conditions. Here it will be necessary to con-sider three main questions: (i) whether, by imposing the controls, the country would be violating either the letter or the spirit of inter-national agreements to which it had subscribed; (ii) the risk of retaliation by, or of damage to good relationships with, other countries; (iii) the probable length of time for which the controls would be needed. If the imposition of the controls can be justified in the light of international agreements, if there is little risk of retaliation and if it seems likely that the controls could be dispensed with in a relatively short time – say two years – there will be little to be said against the 'import controls' alternative and it may well be preferable to the alternative of taking positive steps to eliminate the excess demand for foreign currencies. On the other hand, if one or other of

[1] The nature of these steps will be made clear in Chapter 7.
[2] The British authorities have ruled out the 'do nothing' alternative in the post-war period, mainly because of the chronically low ratio of reserves to short-term liabilities.

these conditions is not met, there will probably be a good case for avoiding the controls altogether and for attempting to eliminate, rather than to repress, the excess demand.

The first and second points listed in the preceding paragraph are obvious enough but the third requires some elaboration. To develop the point it is necessary to consider the arguments which can be advanced against import controls from the point of view of the country which imposes them.

The main argument is that an import-licensing scheme adds to the protection from overseas competition which local industries already receive from the tariff. Moreover, it usually does so in a completely arbitrary way. A typical feature of a licensing scheme is that it gives home production which competes with 'inessential' imports more additional protection than home production which competes with 'essential' imports; and, in general, this pattern of protection will be quite arbitrary in the sense that it will bear no relation to differences in the economic condition of the two industrial groups.

A second argument against import licensing is that it protects existing importing firms from the competition of new firms and so tends to reduce their efficiency.

Thirdly, it is argued that the old importing firms will attempt to exploit the monopoly position which a licensing scheme gives them, either by charging higher prices for imports than would be charged in the absence of the scheme, or by selling unwanted licences to new firms who, presumably, pass on the cost of the licences in the form of higher prices. To the extent that such exploitation occurs, a licensing scheme complicates the attainment of the price-stability objective, partly because it raises the prices of imported raw materials, and partly because it raises money wages by raising the prices of imported consumer goods.[1]

Another argument is that if the overseas *suppliers* of the imports raise their prices in an attempt to appropriate some or all of the monopoly gains which would otherwise accrue to the holders of import licences, the licensing scheme, as well as threatening price stability, will tend to worsen the terms of trade because it will mean an increase in the prices of imports in terms of foreign currency.

Finally, it is argued that an import-licensing scheme suffers from the well-known disadvantages of all direct controls – that they necessitate a substantial administrative organisation, that they offer

[1] See Chapter 9 below for a discussion of these points.

considerable scope for the corruption of public officials and that they involve a significant loss of freedom.

It will be noticed that all of these arguments against import controls presuppose that the controls remain in existence for a considerable time, say, five to ten years; they have little force in relation to a purely temporary scheme – one which exists for, say, less than two years. This brings us back to the main point that import controls may well provide an acceptable alternative to the pursuit of external balance if they are likely to be short-lived. On the other hand, if there is no reason to fear that they will become a more or less permanent feature of the economy, as they did in some countries in the post-war years, it will be better to avoid them altogether and take positive steps to eliminate the excess demand for foreign currencies as soon as possible.

So far we have been considering the alternatives to the pursuit of external balance which exist where there is a persistent excess demand for foreign currencies. Suppose now that the absence of external balance takes the form of a persistent deficiency of demand for foreign currencies, i.e. a persistent upward movement in international currency reserves. What of the alternatives in this case? The only alternative is to do nothing. The main argument against this is that there exists a certain level of reserves beyond which the welfare gain from a further accumulation of reserves (the additional security against unfavourable external developments, such as deterioration in terms of trade, which the additional reserves would give) will be more than offset by the welfare loss (the sacrifice of immediate imports or the failure to increase foreign aid which the further accumulation of reserves would imply), and that, once this level has been reached in the course of the upward movement, action to reverse the movement becomes desirable in the interests of maximum welfare. However, it may well be that the reserves are at such a low level when the upward movement begins that the point where the welfare gain from additional reserves is less than the loss is never, in fact, reached. In this case, the 'do nothing' alternative will be preferable to the pursuit of external balance.

We can sum up this discussion by saying that the case for making external balance a policy objective is not clear-cut because the alternatives to the pursuit of external balance ('do nothing' and import controls) may occasionally be just as, or even more, satisfactory.

1.4 Price Stability

Before attempting to explain what the price-stability objective means, it is important to make clear what it does *not* mean. When we refer to the price-stability objective we do not mean the objective of keeping *individual* prices constant. This is an indefensible objective for a basically private-enterprise economy like the British economy because in such an economy changes in relative prices are the only means by which resources can be shifted from one line of production to another when changes in supply and demand conditions make this desirable from a welfare point of view. Indeed it can be argued that the authorities should aim *both* for price stability and for the greatest possible flexibility of individual prices.

What, then, does price stability mean if it does not mean constancy of individual prices? Briefly it means stability in the general level of prices as measured by some appropriate price index. But this statement is not quite so simple as it seems. In particular, the word 'stability' requires some elaboration. When we say that price stability implies stability of some appropriate price index, we do not mean constancy in the index. Stability in the index is consistent with seasonal movements and also with non-seasonal movements so long as the upward movements and the downward movements roughly cancel each other out. In short, stability of the index requires only that it should not exhibit a clear upward trend.[1]

Even this statement has to be qualified since it is likely that some part of any upward trend in the price index will be a statistical illusion, i.e. will not reflect a genuine upward trend in the general price level. The reason for this is the purely technical difficulty, in constructing price indexes, of making sufficient allowance for continuous improvement in the quality of goods and services of all kinds. The way in which insufficient allowance for quality improvement tends to produce an upward bias in price indexes can be seen from a simple example. Suppose that between any two points of time medical fees double. Suppose that between the same two points of time the quality of medical services also doubles as a result of the

[1] It might well be asked: why not 'a clear upward or *downward* trend'? The answer is that, since governments have assumed responsibility for the maintenance of a high level of employment and have proved themselves capable of carrying out this responsibility, it now seems reasonable to regard persistent downward movements in the general price level as a thing of the past. This point should become quite clear once Chapters 9 and 10 have been read.

increase of medical knowledge and improvements in medical training. Then the true increase in the price of medical services is zero. If, however, one were forced to neglect the quality improvement because of the technical difficulty of taking it into account, one would say that the price of medical services had doubled. The difficulty of allowing for quality improvement is most acute in connection with personal services such as medical services, domestic services and education services. But it is also serious in relation to non-personal services, such as telephone services, the services of rental dwellings and the services of hire-cars, and in relation to durable consumer and producer goods of all kinds.

We can summarise the position now reached by saying that 'price stability' means stability of some appropriate price index in the sense that we can detect no definite upward trend in the index after making proper allowance for the upward bias inherent in all price indexes.

Still one further qualification is required. As we shall see in Chapter 6, the authorities will find it appropriate from time to time to impose heavier indirect taxes on certain goods or to remove subsidies on certain goods as one means of restoring internal balance. Whenever they do so the prices paid for these goods by purchasers will rise. As a result the index used in framing the price-stability objective will also rise, assuming that it is based on prices paid by purchasers rather than on prices received by sellers. But clearly our price-stability concept must be so framed that upward movements in the index which are policy-induced in this way are excluded; otherwise we would have the absurd situation that whenever the authorities deliberately engineered an upward movement in the index in the interests of internal balance, they would be immediately obliged to reverse their action in the interests of price stability.

We can introduce this further qualification by reformulating the concept of price stability in the following way: price stability means absence of a definite upward trend in some appropriate price index after allowance has been made both for the upward bias inherent in price indexes and for upward movements which result from increases of sales taxes or decreases of subsidies. Alternatively we can specify that the index must be one based on the prices received by sellers, not on the prices paid by purchasers,[1] and omit all

[1] An index of the required type would be the implicit deflator of gross domestic product at factor cost, i.e. the index derived by dividing the series for gross

reference to upward movements resulting from sales-tax increases.

Why make price stability, in this sense, an objective of economic policy? Or, putting the question in more familiar terms, why try to avoid inflation?[1] One reason for trying to prevent inflation is that it leads to a redistribution of real income which may well be socially unjust. People whose money income rises less rapidly than the price level will lose relatively in times of inflation, while those whose money income rises more rapidly than the price level will gain. The losers will probably include pensioners, people whose main sources of income are interest or rent payments, professional people such as doctors and lawyers, wage-earners employed by businesses which make it a rule not to pay more than the negotiated rates, and skilled workers. The gainers are likely to include unskilled workers and people whose income consists mainly of dividend payments. While some of this redistribution may be socially desirable, clearly much of it will not be.

The redistributive effects of inflation are not confined to real income; they extend also to real wealth. People or institutions whose wealth consists mainly of assets with a fixed or almost fixed money value, such as bank deposits, government bonds, or private debt of various kinds, will suffer a relative loss of real wealth under infla- tionary conditions while those who hold assets such as ordinary shares and real property which increase in money value as prices rise, or whose liabilities remain fixed in money terms as prices rise, will enjoy a relative gain of real wealth. Once again, while some of this redistribution may be socially just, much of it will not be so.

A second reason for trying to prevent inflation is that the ordinary individual who wishes to save in order to provide an income for his old age or to educate his children or to build a house or otherwise to smooth out anticipated fluctuations in income and consumption is faced with a very serious dilemma. If he invests his savings in a life-assurance policy or in government bonds or if he leaves them with a bank on fixed deposit, he avoids virtually all risk of default; he can be sure that on certain dates in the future certain fixed sums of money will be forthcoming. But by avoiding this risk he incurs

---

domestic product at factor cost in terms of current prices by the series in terms of constant prices.

[1] The reader is warned that 'inflation' is not invariably used, as here, to mean 'absence of price stability'. In particular it should be noted that aggregate excess demand for commodities is sometimes referred to as inflation.

another, the risk that inflation will reduce the real value of these sums of money to such an extent that he will not be able to meet the needs for which the savings have been made. On the other hand, if he invests in company shares or in real property he can reasonably hope to avoid the risks associated with inflation because share prices and property values are likely to rise at least as rapidly as the general price level. But by avoiding this risk he incurs another, unless he happens to have special knowledge about company finance or about the working of the real property market. This is the risk that, even though the prices of shares and property *in general* may rise with inflation, the prices of *his* shares or property may fall, perhaps to nothing, as a result, say, of the bankruptcy of the company whose shares he holds or the establishment of a rubbish tip next to his land, in which case, once again, he would be unable to meet the needs against which he has been saving. Thus, he must take risks which, in the absence of inflation, he could avoid.

In the third place, inflation is undesirable because it encourages a form of speculation which serves no useful purpose, namely speculation on assets such as land and industrial shares whose prices rise with the general price level. Inflation appears to offer large rewards to this type of speculation. Yet the gains will often be more apparent than real because of the rise in the general price level between the date of purchase of the assets and the date of sale. For example, a speculator who buys an asset for £100 and sells it a year later for £105 appears to have added to his wealth by the transaction. But if prices have risen by 5 per cent over the year his gain of real wealth will be zero. In terms of the prices ruling at the date of purchase of the assets he has £100 of wealth when the speculation begins and still has only £100 when it finishes.

Inflation may also lead to balance of payments difficulties. This, of course, is an especially important consideration for countries, like Britain, with a large foreign trade. Inflation can produce balance of payments difficulties both by restricting exports and by stimulating imports. The growth of exports will be checked by rising domestic costs and prices because when domestic costs rise the prices quoted by domestic producers in foreign markets will also rise and this will result in some overseas sales being lost to foreign competitors. By the same token, the growth of imports will be stimulated because the competitive position of domestic producers in the *home* market will be weakened by rising domestic costs and prices.

The extent to which exports will be restricted, and imports stimulated, by inflation will depend on whether inflation is occurring simultaneously in other countries and if so at what pace; the faster prices are rising in other countries the less will be the check to exports, and the stimulus to imports, from domestic inflation and hence the less serious the balance of payments difficulties which inflation will produce.[1]

This leads to the last and possibly the most important reason why inflation needs to be checked, namely that if it is allowed to continue it can eventually become so rapid that practically no one is willing to accept payment in money and there is a virtual collapse of the whole market mechanism. This is a real possibility because once people come to regard inflation as the normal thing they will take steps to protect themselves against it, steps which will most probably help to quicken its pace. For example, one might find the trade unions claiming larger wage increases than they would claim in the absence of inflation to allow for the price rise that they expect to take place before the next wage round. To the extent that they are successful, the index of wage earnings per man and hence the price index will increase more rapidly than would otherwise have been the case. Again one might find businesses deciding to expand their plant now instead of in three years' time, say, because they expect that the cost of the expansion will be a great deal higher then than it is now. By attempting to protect themselves against inflation in this way they will add to the current demand for goods and services, and this will make excess demand and a consequent increase in the pace of inflation more likely.[2]

To sum up, inflation has a number of harmful effects which are serious enough to justify a determined effort to bring it under control.

1.5 Economic Growth

The first step in formulating a concept of economic growth is to decide on a growth 'yardstick'. That is, we must first of all decide on the economic aggregate or aggregates in terms of which economic growth is to be measured. Here there are numerous possibilities, some of the more obvious being: real gross domestic product, real

---

[1] These points will be discussed more fully in Chapter 7 below.
[2] These points will be elaborated in Chapter 9 below.

national income, aggregate real wealth, the aggregate labour force and the aggregate real stock of productive capital. Of these, probably the most widely used is real gross domestic product, partly because in most countries better information is available for this aggregate than for other possible yardsticks such as real net domestic product, aggregate wealth and the aggregate capital stock, and partly because growth in terms of productive inputs, such as the aggregate labour force and the aggregate capital stock, is significant not in itself but only to the extent that it leads to growth in terms of output.

If we adopt real gross domestic product as our yardstick, we can then define 'economic growth' as 'an increase in real gross domestic product' and 'a high rate of economic growth' as 'a high average percentage increase in real gross domestic product'. But the phrase 'high average percentage increase in real gross domestic product' is ambiguous because there are several possible meanings of 'real gross domestic product', several possible meanings of 'average percentage increase' and several possible meanings of 'high'. In order to clarify the growth objective ('a high rate of economic growth'), we must examine these various possibilities in some detail.

Let us begin with 'real gross domestic product'. These words may refer either to a *total* or to an *average* – to real gross domestic product itself or to real gross domestic product per capita or per member of the labour force. This is one source of ambiguity. But ambiguity also arises from a second source, namely from the existence of several quite distinct concepts of real gross domestic product. The first point is clear enough but the second requires further consideration.

There are, in fact, three main concepts of real gross domestic product, namely capacity, potential and realised. By the *capacity gross domestic product* of any period is meant the maximum gross domestic product which could be realised in the period if the economy were at full stretch, that is, if the highest possible percentage of the population, both from the working-age and the retired-age groups were drawn into the labour force, if working hours were put at the upper limit set by the workers' physical endurance, if the unemployment percentage were reduced to the absolute minimum which is technically possible and if shut-downs for maintenance and repairs were held at the minimum needed to keep capital equipment in reasonable working order in the short run.

B

Since the productivity of a given worker or item of capital equipment will vary according to the industry of employment, it is clear
that the capacity concept must involve some assumption about the
industrial distribution of the labour force and the capital stock. The
concept must also be based on some assumption about the maximum
feasible supply of various raw materials, since this will be one of the
factors determining the maximum time for which it is feasible to
operate the existing capital stock. This means, in turn, that some
assumption must be made about the maximum level of raw-material
imports, because the maximum feasible supply of raw materials will
be determined by the maximum level of raw-material imports, once
the distribution of the labour force, and hence the maximum feasible
domestic output of raw materials, is given.

By the *potential gross domestic product* of any period we mean the
maximum gross domestic product which could be realised in the
period, given what might be called 'normal full-employment
conditions' (see section 1.2 above). This implies that there is no
abnormal expansion of the labour force as a result of temporary
recruitment from such groups as pensioners, the physically handi-
capped and married women, that there is no abnormal overtime
working, that no abnormal steps (such as direct labour controls and
attempts to reduce labour turnover) are being taken to lower the
percentage of unemployment which is deemed to be consistent with
'full employment' and that no abnormal working arrangements (for
example, extra shifts, longer intervals between maintenance shut-
downs) are introduced in order to increase the extent to which the
existing capital stock is being utilised. Like the capacity concept, the
potential concept requires some assumption about the industrial
distribution of the (normal) labour force and the capital stock. On
the other hand, it does not require any assumption about the supply
of raw materials, other than that the supply will be sufficient to keep
the normal, employed labour force at work for the normal working
time.[1]

[1] The reader should note that while the terminology to be used in this book
is fairly standard in the American literature, a settled British terminology has not
yet emerged. The terms most commonly found in the British literature are slight
variations on the ones which we have decided to use. Thus in chap. 17 of *Studies
in an Inflationary Economy* (London: Macmillan, 1962) p. 310, fn. 2, Professor
F. W. Paish uses the term 'productive capacity' for what is evidently our 'capacity
gross domestic product'. Again, Godley and Shepherd refer to a concept akin to
our 'potential gross domestic product' either as 'productive potential' or as
'capacity output'. (See W. A. H. Godley and J. R. Shepherd, 'Long-Term Growth

Both the capacity concept and the potential concept are hypothetical in character; they relate to the gross domestic product which *could be* achieved under certain hypothetical conditions. On the other hand, the third concept, *realised gross domestic product*, is actual in character; it represents the gross domestic product which *is, in fact,* achieved in the period.

It appears, then, that the words 'real gross domestic product' can be used in a variety of ways; and the precise meaning one gives to them will depend on how one happens to be viewing the growth objective. Here, it seems, there are two main possibilities: one may be looking forwards (formulating a growth target) or one may be looking backwards (examining the growth record).

Which concept is to be preferred for the purpose of framing a growth target will depend on the circumstances. If the economy is being prepared for some emergency, such as war, interest will be centred on the ultimate productive capacity of the economy rather than on the production which is actually achieved and, hence, in these circumstances, the capacity concept will probably be the most relevant of the three. In more normal times it will be the production actually realised which matters and hence the potential and realised concepts which should be used for the purpose of framing the growth target. Either can be used if internal balance exists and is expected to continue because a target framed in terms of potential gross domestic product will, in effect, be one framed in terms of realised gross domestic product. On the other hand, if internal balance does not exist, or if there is some doubt about its continuance, a target framed in terms of potential product will not necessarily be identical with one framed in terms of realised product and in this case the realised concept will be the more appropriate.

Should the growth target be framed in terms of a total or an average concept? This again will depend on the circumstances. In the case of a poor country which desires growth in order to raise living standards, the only relevant target would be one framed in per capita terms – there would be no point in the country setting a target rate of increase, say, 4 per cent per annum in *total* real realised product because if population were to increase by more than 4 per cent per annum, living standards would decline rather than increase. On the other hand, if growth is desired mainly to enable a war to be fought at some time in the future, there would appear to be a need for a total target as well as a per capita target. A per capita target would still be needed because if capacity product, though increasing in total at the target rate, were to decline per capita, it might prove impossible to achieve the required total level of war production without reducing the goods and services available for civilian purposes below the minimum feasible level. A *total* target would also be needed, however, because while the achievement of a particular rate of increase of capacity product per capita would guarantee the achievement of a particular level of war production per capita, it would not guarantee the achievement of a given *total* level of war production. The same type of reasoning applies where growth is desired mainly to enable a certain desired level of economic aid to be given to underdeveloped countries.

Suppose now that one is looking backwards with an eye on the growth record. Which meaning should be given to 'real gross domestic product' in this situation? Here again it is helpful to distinguish two cases: the case where one's object in examining the growth record is to assess the performance of the authorities in relation to the growth objective, and the case where one is concerned simply to discover what has, in fact, been achieved in the matter of growth over some particular period of time. In the first case, the meaning to be given to 'real gross domestic product' will be determined by the meaning used in framing the growth target. For example, if the growth target for the period has been framed in terms of real capacity gross product per capita, the performance of the authorities responsible for growth can be assessed effectively only by examining the behaviour over the period of the same aggregate. Similarly if the target rate of growth has been fixed in terms of total real realised gross product, one would be bound to use the same aggregate in examining the growth record.

In the second case, the appropriate meaning will depend on the question we wish to answer from our examination of the growth record. For example, if we wish to know how rapidly living standards have increased over some past period, the most relevant interpretation would probably be real realised gross product per capita. Again, if we wish to know how much output has been lost over some past period through failure to attain the internal balance objective, both total real potential product and total real realised product would be relevant.

Earlier we pointed out that our definition of the growth objective ('a high average percentage increase in real gross domestic product') was ambiguous because there were several possible meanings of 'real gross domestic product', 'average percentage increase' and 'high'. Having looked at the first of these three terms, we must now briefly consider the other two. The term 'average percentage increase' is ambiguous because there are several different ways in which the average of the percentage increases of the individual years can be calculated. Of these, it seems that three deserve fairly detailed treatment and the more technically-minded reader will find them discussed in Appendix 1.1.

Finally, by way of clarifying the growth objective, we must consider the word 'high'. This could be taken to mean either 'as high as possible' or 'as high as desirable', each of these meanings, in turn, being capable of a number of different interpretations. However, interpretations of 'high' along these lines can be subsumed under the general heading of 'optimum growth subject to various economic, social and political constraints'. Clarification of 'high' then reduces to examining: (i) the various possible optimising criteria which could be adopted in the growth context; and (ii) the constraints which constitute the major limitations on economic growth.

Problems arise in connection with (i) because the choice of an optimising criterion necessarily involves making ethical judgements of various kinds, and in connection with (ii) both because the effective constraints on growth which apply to a particular country at a particular time may be difficult to identify, and also because the constraints which apply to one country or to one point of time may not apply to another country or another point of time. Since these problems are rather difficult, we have decided not to attempt to discuss them in this introductory chapter. Instead we shall consider them in some detail in Chapters 11 and 12.

To complete our discussion of the growth objective, let us now consider in more detail some of the reasons for desiring a high rate of economic growth which have been touched on in earlier discussion. The advantages of economic growth are most striking in the case of primitive communities where survival itself is continually threatened by famine, plague, disease and natural disasters of various kinds. For such communities economic growth is worth almost any price because it is the one means by which they can hope to achieve a tolerable degree of control over their environment.

In the case of relatively advanced societies such as Britain, the arguments in favour of growth are less decisive but are still quite strong. The main argument is that growth enables the society to achieve many desirable ends with less sacrifice of current consumption than would be necessary in the absence of growth. More leisure, longer and better education, increased security from military attack, more extensive help to poorer countries, better provision for future growth – these are all highly desirable ends. But none of them can be achieved unless a larger volume of current real output is made available for the purpose. Hence, in the absence of growth, none of them can be achieved unless there is a corresponding reduction of current consumption. With growth the required sacrifice of current consumption is reduced because some part of the extra production required for the achievement of these ends can then be obtained from the increment to current real output which constitutes growth, rather than from the existing real output. In fact, if growth is fast enough, the achievement of these and similar ends need involve no sacrifice of current consumption at all. A second reason why an advanced society might desire economic growth is that it helps to reduce social conflict. In the absence of growth, the attempt by any one group to improve its economic position must lead to conflict because if total real output is fixed, one group can have more only if some other group has less. Conflict may still arise if growth is taking place, since the aspirations of the group which is striving for improvement may be growing more rapidly than aggregate real output. But if so it will be less acute than without growth; and it can be avoided altogether provided growth is sufficiently rapid.

1.6 Summary

This book is concerned with the four great macro-economic objectives of internal balance, external balance, price stability and a high rate of economic growth. By internal balance is meant a state of affairs in which aggregate desired real expenditure is equal to real potential gross domestic product plus realised real imports. External balance can be defined as a state of affairs in which there is neither persistent excess demand for foreign currencies nor persistent deficient demand. Price stability is absence of any clear upward movement in some appropriate index of the general price level. Finally, a high rate of economic growth means the optimum growth rate, subject to given economic, social and political constraints, in real gross domestic product.

The case for making external balance a policy objective is not decisive because the alternatives to the pursuit of external balance ('do nothing' and the imposition of temporary import controls) may sometimes be quite as satisfactory, if not more so. The case for the other three objectives is much stronger. Price stability is a desirable objective because inflation (absence of price stability) involves an arbitrary redistribution of income and wealth and creates unnecessary difficulties for the balance of payments. Internal balance is desirable because it gives full employment without the inflationary tendencies which accompany excess demand for commodities. Finally, a high growth rate is worth striving for because it enables a community to gain many important benefits without the sacrifice of current consumption which would otherwise be necessary, and also because it helps to reduce social tensions.

READING LIST

Corden, W. M., 'The Control of Imports: A Case Study', *Manchester School of Economic and Social Studies* (Sep 1958).

Dasgupta, A., 'A Note on Optimum Savings', *Econometrica* (July 1964).

Dow, J. C. R., *The Management of the British Economy 1945–60* (Cambridge University Press, 1964) chap. vi.

Hansen, Bent, *A Study in the Theory of Inflation* (London: Allen & Unwin, 1951) chaps i–iii.

Jaszi, G., 'The Measurement of Aggregate Economic Growth', *Review of Economics and Statistics* (Nov 1961).

Machlup, F., 'Three Concepts of the Balance of Payments and the So-called Dollar Shortage', *Economic Journal* (Mar 1950).

Moffatt, G., 'The Australian Import Licensing System: 1952–1960', *Australian Economic Papers* (Sep 1962).

Pesek, B. P., 'Economic Growth and its Measurement', *Economic Development and Cultural Change* (Apr 1961).

—— 'Growth, Capacity Output and the Output Gap', *Review of Economics and Statistics* (Aug 1963).

The Meaning and Measurement of Economic Growth (Canberra: Commonwealth of Australia, 1964).

Appendix 1.1

CALCULATION OF AVERAGE PERCENTAGE INCREASE OF REAL GROSS DOMESTIC PRODUCT

The two most frequently used methods of calculating the average percentage increase of real gross domestic product over a given set of unit time periods, say a given number of years, may be termed the compound-interest method and the least-squares method.

In the compound-interest method it is assumed that real gross domestic product grew in compound-interest fashion over the interval of time in question, and the compound-interest formula is used to calculate the rate of compound interest implied by the values for the first and last years. This is taken to be the average proportionate increase in real gross domestic product over the period. Thus according to the compound-interest method the average proportionate increase is given by:

$$r = \left[\frac{P_n}{P_0} \right]^{1/n} - 1$$

where r denotes the average proportionate increase, and P_0 and P_n the levels of real gross domestic product for the first and last years, respectively.

Under the least-squares method an equation of the form:

$$P_t = a.b^t$$

where P_t denotes real gross domestic product in year t, and a and b are constants, is fitted to the series for real gross domestic product by the method of least squares. The least-squares estimate of the constant b is then taken to be the average ratio of increase over the period, i.e. r is taken to be given by $r = \hat{b} - 1$ where $\hat{b}$ denotes the least-squares estimate of b.

It seems reasonable to require that any method of calculating the average percentage increase of real gross domestic product should possess two properties. In the first place, since the choice of the time interval for the calculation of the average is necessarily arbitrary, the average should not be highly sensitive to the addition or removal of one or more years at either end of the period – the figure for the period 1950 to 1959, say, should not be noticeably different from the figure for the period 1949 to 1959 or the figure for 1950 to 1960. Secondly, the sum of the real gross domestic product series *which would have been* observed, had real gross product grown in each year at the average percentage rate, should be the same as the sum of the series which is *actually* observed.

The compound-interest method clearly lacks the first property; since the average percentage increase given by this method is based *only* on P_0 and P_n, it must necessarily be highly sensitive to *changes* in P_0 and P_n – that is, it must be highly sensitive to changes in the terminal points of the time interval on which it is based. It also lacks the second property – there is clearly nothing in the method which will ensure equality between the sum of the gross product series actually observed and the sum that would have been observed had real gross product grown in each year at the average percentage rate.

It is worth noting that the method would necessarily possess both properties if real gross product always grew at a *constant* percentage rate. From this it follows that the more nearly constant the observed percentage increases, the more closely the method approximates to one with desirable properties. Since the observed percentage increases in *potential* and *capacity* real gross domestic product are likely to be highly stable, it follows, further, that the compound-interest method is reasonably satisfactory for the purpose of calculating the average percentage increase in either potential real product or capacity real product. Thus there appears to be little wrong with the common practice of calculating the average percentage increase in potential real product by applying the compound-interest formula to two full-employment years or to two years in which realised real product bears approximately the same percentage relationship to potential real product. The method cannot be regarded as satisfactory, however, where the problem is to determine the average percentage increase in *realised* real product, since, in this case, the observed percentage increases are, in general, far from constant.

The least-squares method, unlike the compound-interest method, makes use of all items in the real gross product series. There is, therefore, no reason why the average percentage increase given by this method should be sensitive to changes in the terminal points of the period used to calculate it. On the other hand, the method certainly lacks the second property. In fact, it ensures equality between the sum of the *logarithms* of the real gross products actually observed and the sum of the logarithms which would have been observed had real gross product increased in each year at the least-squares average percentage rate (and been equal in the first year to the least-squares estimate of the constant, a). In other words, it ensures equality between the relevant *products* rather than between the relevant sums.

A third method, recently proposed by Pesek, appears to be superior to both the compound-interest and least-squares method.[1] In this case it is convenient to denote the series of aggregate real gross product by $P_1 \ldots P_n$. Then, as in the least-squares method, an equation of the form

$$P_t = a.b^t$$

is fitted to the series $P_1 \ldots P_n$ and the estimate of b is taken as the average ratio of increase. But instead of choosing b according to the least-squares principle, Pesek's method requires b to be such that the sum of the real gross products actually observed is equal to the sum that would have been observed had real gross product increased each year at the average percentage rate. That is, b is chosen so that:

$$P_1 \sum_{t=0}^{n-1} b^t = \sum_{t=1}^{n} P_t.$$

<hr>

[1] See Boris P. Pesek, 'Economic Growth and its Measurement', *Economic Development and Cultural Change* (Apr 1961) pp. 304–5.

If both sides of this expression are multiplied by b we get:

$$P_1 \sum_{t=1}^{n} b^t = b \sum_{t=1}^{n} P_t.$$

Subtracting the first expression from the second we get:

$$-P_1 + P_1 b^n = (b-1) \sum_{t=1}^{n} P_t$$

or

$$P_1(b^n - 1) = (b-1) \sum_{t=1}^{n} P_t$$

from which it follows that

$$\frac{b^n - 1}{b - 1} = \frac{\sum_{t=1}^{n} P_t}{P_1}.$$

The value of $r = (b-1)$ which satisfies this expression can be easily found from tables of $S_{\overline{n}|i} = [(1+i)^n - 1]/i$. One merely has to locate

$$\frac{\sum_{t=1}^{n} P_t}{P_1}$$

in the body of the tables[1] and read off i for the known value of n. The value of i obtained in this way is the value of $r = b - 1$ which satisfies the expression, as can be seen by putting $(b-1)$ in place of i in $S_{\overline{n}|i} = [(1+i)^n - 1]/i$.

---

[1] These tables can be found, for example, in J. W. Bennett, J. McB. Grant and R. H. Parker, *Topics in Business Finance and Accounting* (Melbourne: Cheshire, 1964).

PART TWO

Internal Balance and External Balance

2 The Consumption Function

2.1 Main Features of Post-Keynesian Macro-theory

This chapter and the following three will be theoretical in character. Our aim in these chapters will be to expound the theoretical work on dynamic, short-run macro-relationships which has been done in recent years in the spirit of Keynes, and to give an account of the British empirical research which bears on this work. By this means we hope to provide a strong theoretical framework for the discussion of the central chapters of this part of the book, namely Chapter 6 on policy in relation to the internal balance objective and Chapter 7 on policy in relation to the objective of external balance.

Unavoidably, certain parts of the discussion will be of a rather detailed kind and may not be easy to absorb on a first reading. To reduce the difficulty we propose to begin by setting out the main features of the body of the work which we wish to expound in the hope that, once having grasped the main general points, the reader will find the detail both more illuminating and easier to assimilate.

One striking feature of post-Keynesian macro-theory is the prevalence of an extremely simple unifying idea – the idea that real expenditure flows are heavily influenced, in the short run, by discrepancies between actual stocks and desired stocks. This idea crops up time and time again. We find it, for example, in a recent study of the short-run consumption function to be discussed in section 3 of the present chapter. In this study it is argued that the 'transitory' component of real consumption expenditure in any period will depend on the size of the discrepancy between the actual and the desired stock of liquid assets. The view that short-run movements in real fixed-capital investment expenditure can be explained largely in terms of a desire to bring the actual stock of fixed-capital equipment into line with the optimum stock, in some sense, also pervades recent work on the determinants of fixed-capital investment, as we shall see in sections 4.1 and 4.2. Again, as will be shown in section 4.3, the discrepancy between the desired and the actual housing stock is an essential element in recent attempts to explain the short-run behaviour of real housing investment. Finally, the discrepancy between actual and desired inventories plays a fundamental part in all modern work on inventory investment. This will become clear in sections 5.1 and 5.2. In fact it is a fair generalisation to say that the short-run macro-relationships which emerge from recent work of the Keynesian variety are invariably 'stock-adjustment' relationships in some important sense.

A second idea which runs through all recent work on short-run macro-relationships is that, when the period is short (say a quarter or a month), the response of the dependent variable in the relationship in question to any given change in some explanatory variable is unlikely to be completed within the period in which the change occurs; on the contrary, for one reason or another, the response is likely to be spread out over a large number of future periods. This notion forms an essential element in the work on the fixed-capital investment function, the inventory investment function and the housing investment function which we shall describe in Chapters 4 and 5, and is also to be found in some recent consumption function studies, as we shall see later on in the present chapter.

One frequently finds this concept of lagged response given mathematical expression by means of a so-called 'distributed-lag' function, i.e. a function which relates the level of the dependent variable in period t to the current level, and all past levels, of the explanatory variable. For example, the starting-point of one recent study of the fixed-capital investment function is the obvious point that if a firm decides in period t to undertake large-scale fixed-capital investment projects, such as the construction of a new factory or the installation of new machines, it will inevitably be forced to spread the *expenditure* associated with these projects over a succession of future periods; some proportion (μ_0) of the expenditure will be undertaken in the current period, some proportion (μ_1) in period ($t+1$), some further proportion (μ_2) in period ($t+2$), and so on. It is then observed that this amounts to saying that the firm's real net fixed-capital investment expenditure in period t will be governed by the expenditure *decided on* in the current period and in a succession of past periods, via a distributed-lag function of the form:

$$i_t^{nf} = \mu_0 {}^* i_t^{nf} + \mu_1 {}^* i_{t-1}^{nf} + \mu_2 {}^* i_{t-2}^{nf} + \mu_3 {}^* i_{t-3}^{nf} + \ldots$$

where i^{nf} denotes expenditure undertaken and $*i^{nf}$ expenditure decided on, and where the μs are a set of non-negative numbers (usually called 'weights') which sum to unity.[1] This expression is then used as a basis for deriving a fixed-capital investment function which, in essence, is a refinement of the well-known acceleration principle.

A device which finds repeated application in the literature is the device of imposing some simple pattern on the weights of a distributed-lag function so as to produce a relationship which is much simpler in form. For example, one frequently finds that the weights are specified as a set of constants which decline geometrically; in this case the distributed-lag function reduces to a relationship in which the current value of the dependent variable is expressed in terms of its value in the previous period and in terms of a *single* value of the explanatory variable. To see this, take a distributed-lag function in which the current value of some variable X is expressed as a weighted sum of the current value, and all past values, of some other variable Y, i.e. a function of the form:

$$X_t = \rho_0 Y_t + \rho_1 Y_{t-1} + \rho_2 Y_{t-2} + \rho_3 Y_{t-3} + \ldots$$

Impose the restriction that the ρs are a set of constants which decline geometrically. Then the above can be written as:

$$X_t = \rho_0 Y_t + \lambda \rho_0 Y_{t-1} + \lambda^2 \rho_0 Y_{t-2} + \lambda^3 \rho_0 Y_{t-3} + \ldots$$

where λ is some positive fraction usually referred to as the 'damping factor'. From this it follows that:

$$\lambda X_{t-1} = \lambda \rho_0 Y_{t-1} + \lambda^2 \rho_0 Y_{t-2} + \lambda^3 \rho_0 Y_{t-3} + \ldots$$

By subtraction we then get:

$$X_t - \lambda X_{t-1} = \rho_0 Y_t$$

which can be rewritten as:

$$X_t = \lambda X_{t-1} + \rho_0 Y_t.$$

If we impose the further restriction that the weights sum to unity, the distributed-lag function reduces to a relationship in which the current value of the dependent variable is a *weighted arithmetic average* of the value of the *dependent* variable in the previous period and the value of the *explanatory* variable in the current period. To

---

[1] It is necessary to impose this restriction because if the firm's investment decisions become stabilised at some fixed level, its investment expenditure must eventually become stabilised at the same level.

see this, suppose that the weights, i.e. the ρs in the above distributed-lag function, sum to unity. Then we have

$$\rho_0 + \lambda\rho_0 + \lambda^2\rho_0 + \lambda^3\rho_0 + \ldots = 1$$

i.e.

$$\frac{\rho_0}{1-\lambda} = 1 \text{ or } \rho_0 = 1 - \lambda.$$

Hence the distributed-lag function can be written as

$$X_t = (1-\lambda)[Y_t + \lambda Y_{t-1} + \lambda^2 Y_{t-2} + \ldots]$$

which, on subtracting λX_{t-1}, gives:

$$X_t = \lambda X_{t-1} + (1-\lambda)Y_t.$$

The 'geometrically declining weight' pattern is a special case of a more general pattern which serves to reduce a distributed-lag function to a relationship in which the current value of the dependent variable is expressed in terms of a finite number of earlier values of the dependent and independent variables. This more general pattern has been extensively used in one recent study of the fixed-capital investment function with which we shall be dealing in section 4.2.

A third prominent feature of post-Keynesian macro-theory is its insistence that all relationships be testable. In line with this requirement, one now finds that whenever a macro-relationship is initially formulated in terms of some non-observable variable, an attempt is made to eliminate this non-observable variable by means of a relationship which links it to an observable variable. For example, in some recent consumption function studies, as we shall see in sections 2.3 and 2.4, one finds an initial formulation of the function in terms of the non-observable 'permanent income'. In these cases a relationship is postulated between permanent income and measured income (e.g. that the permanent income of any period is a weighted arithmetic average of the measured incomes of all past periods) and this relationship is used to replace permanent income by measured income, i.e. to put the function in a testable form. The same device appears in most recent work on the inventory investment function. There the initial formulation typically runs in terms of 'expected sales', and this non-observable is then eliminated by means of a relationship between expected sales and past actual sales, e.g. that the expected sales of any period is a weighted arithmetic average of the sales actually realised in all past periods.

One further prominent feature of post-Keynesian macro-theory is the emphasis placed on what might be called 'the structure' of macro-relationships. Increasingly one finds that the relationship finally proposed and tested is the outcome of a fairly detailed argument in the course of which numerous components have been fitted together, often in an extremely ingenious way. It is no longer regarded as adequate, when formulating a macro-relationship, merely to list the variables which on general common-sense grounds appear reasonable candidates for the role of an explanatory variable and then adopt the lags which seem to give the best fit.

To illustrate the point, reference may be made to a recent British study of the short-run consumption function which will be discussed in detail in the next section. Here the basic idea is that real consumption expenditure, real personal disposable income and real wealth can all be split into two components: a 'transitory' component and a 'permanent' component. This idea is expressed formally by means of three identities. Next the permanent component of real personal disposable income in quarter t is taken to be a weighted arithmetic average of the observed income of quarter t and the permanent income of the preceding quarter. As just explained, this amounts to saying that the permanent income of quarter t is a weighted sum of the observed income of quarter t and all past quarters, the weights having the special property that they decline geometrically and sum to unity (see p. 39 above). A corresponding hypothesis is postulated for permanent wealth. Finally it is postulated that permanent consumption depends linearly on permanent disposable income and permanent wealth, and that transitory consumption is proportional to transitory disposable income. These seven components are then fitted together with great technical skill to give a testable short-run consumption function in which the desired real consumption expenditure of quarter t is linearly dependent on real wealth at the beginning of quarter t, on real disposable income in quarter t and in quarter $(t-1)$ and on real consumption expenditure in quarter $(t-1)$.

The current stress on the need to spell out the structure of all macro-relationships, of which this study is merely one illustration, is highly desirable for two reasons. In the first place, when a macro-relationship is formulated from this standpoint, one is frequently able to specify not only the sign of the parameters but also the range in which they must lie. One is able, therefore, to conduct more powerful tests on the relationship than would have been possible had it been arrived at merely on an intuitive basis. For example, as we shall see in the next section, the authors of the consumption function study just referred to are able to specify, on the basis of their underlying argument, that the coefficient of lagged disposable income in the final relationship is a negative fraction and the coefficient of lagged consumption a positive fraction. The second advantage of this type of approach is that, if the final relationship fails under test, a knowledge of its structure will usually help in the search for something better.

2.2 Plan of Exposition

Having discussed the main general features of the body of work which we aim to expound in this chapter and the following three, we turn to the question of the form which our exposition is to take. In deciding on the best method of exposition we have had two objectives in mind. The first is to provide an account of the work done which is detailed without being overwhelmingly so. The second, equally important, objective is to show how the apparently unrelated contributions of recent years can be fitted together to give a more complete and realistic picture of the short-run workings of the economy as a whole than can be obtained from the simple dynamic Keynesian models which are usually discussed in the elementary texts. In an attempt to achieve both of these objectives, we have decided to give our exposition a somewhat unusual form which will now be outlined.

As our starting-point we shall take the simplest possible short-run macro-dynamic model of the Keynesian variety, namely the model in which aggregate demand is split into two components – desired real consumption expenditure, treated as a lagged function of real gross product alone, and all other expenditure, treated as a datum. We have chosen this model both because of its simplicity and also because it has been widely discussed in the elementary macro-texts. Having set out the model in symbolic form, we shall list its main limitations. Next, we shall single out one of these limitations and attempt to reconstruct the model so as to remove it. To this end, we shall present, and then use, various ideas which have emerged in the recent literature.

We shall then repeat this procedure. The improved version of the basic model will be taken as a new starting-point and attention will be focused on one of the limitations which this model carries over from the basic model. Those ideas from the recent literature on macro-dynamic relationships which appear relevant in this connection will then be expounded and the improved model reconstructed in the light of the exposition. We shall then have a short-run dynamic model which improves on the basic model in *two* respects, while still retaining some of its weaknesses.

We shall continue in this step-by-step fashion until we have presented all of the important recent developments in the field of dynamic short-run macro-relationships, as we see them. From time to time we shall introduce relevant empirical research with special emphasis on British studies. A by-product of the discussion will be a fairly complicated dynamic model which goes some way towards showing the essential short-run interactions between macro-variables in an advanced industrial economy such as the British economy. This final model, and others in the sequence of models which lead up to it, will be of considerable help to us when we come to discuss the instruments for attaining the objectives of internal balance and external balance which are available to the British authorities, and the problems which the authorities face in applying those instruments. This we shall do in Chapters 6 and 7.

In the preceding paragraphs we have used the term 'short-run, dynamic model' on several occasions. Before embarking on the programme just outlined, it seems desirable to consider the meaning of this term a little more closely than we have done so far.

A short-run, dynamic model can be one of two things: (i) a model which is designed to explain the reactions of the unknowns or jointly determined variables to changes in the data *short period by short period* – say, month by month or quarter by quarter, as distinct from, say, year by year or decade by decade; or (ii) a model which is designed to explain the reactions of the unknowns over a *short interval* – say, three to five years, as distinct from, say, fifty years. A model which is short-run in the second sense must necessarily be short-run in the first sense: obviously one cannot analyse the reactions of the jointly determined variables over, say, three years by means of a model in which the period is, say, a decade. However, the converse is not true; for example, one could have a quarterly model designed to explain reactions over a period of ten years. It is important, therefore, that the two meanings of 'short run' should always be kept firmly in mind.

The uses to which our models are to be put in succeeding chapters require that they be short-run in both senses. In constructing these models we shall accordingly think of the period as a quarter and the 'reaction interval' as round about twenty periods or five years. This will affect the character of the relationships at many points.

We are now ready to set down our basic model, which we shall refer to from now on as Model I, in symbolic form. The notation we shall use is as follows:

Y = real gross domestic product (GDP) at factor cost
C = desired real consumption expenditure
D = aggregate demand (aggregate desired real expenditure)
A = aggregate demand *less* desired real consumption expenditure
β_0 and β_1 = unspecified parameters.

In terms of this notation, Model I is:

Desired Consumption Expenditure
$$C_t = \beta_0 + \beta_1 Y_{t-1} \tag{2.1}$$

Components of Aggregate Demand
$$D_t = C_t + A_t \tag{2.2}$$

Demand–Output Relationship
$$Y_t = D_t \tag{2.3}$$

The variable A (aggregate demand *less* consumption demand) is treated as a datum, while C, Y and D are the three variables determined by the model (jointly determined variables).

The main limitations of this model may be listed briefly as follows:

1. Recent research suggests that short-run changes in desired real consumption expenditure cannot be adequately explained solely in terms of changes in lagged income, as postulated by relationship (2.1).

2. Relationship (2.2) makes all real expenditure, apart from real consumption expenditure, a datum. This is unsatisfactory because there are important two-way connections between certain sections of non-consumption expenditure and the variables C, D and Y. It is legitimate to treat a variable as a datum only if it influences other variables in the model but is not, in turn, influenced by them.

3. Aggregate real output does not adjust instantaneously to aggregate demand, as postulated by relationship (2.3).

We shall now concentrate on the first of these three limitations and attempt to reconstruct the model so as to remove it. To help in this task we shall first survey recent work on the short-run consumption function. This will be done in the next three sections. On the basis of the ideas which we shall present there, we shall formulate a short-run consumption function in which the income variable is real disposable income rather than real gross domestic product, as in (2.1), and which refines (2.1) in a number of ways. By introducing real disposable income into our model via the new consumption function, we add a variable which should be treated as a jointly determined variable – that is, which should be determined by the model, not regarded as a datum. To permit this we must add a further relationship. This relationship, which links real personal disposable income and real gross domestic product, is developed in section 2.5. In the final section of the chapter we shall consider the dynamic properties of the revised, four-equation model.

2.3 The Consumption Function: Permanent *versus* Transitory Consumption

Since the war an enormous body of literature has appeared on the consumption function, mainly in the United States. Very little of this is concerned specifically with the short-run consumption function, but what short-run studies there are[1] suggest that quarterly changes in real consumption expenditure cannot be adequately explained solely in terms of changes in income – current or lagged – at least in the case of the United States economy. However, there is no point in ruling out the simple Keynesian consumption function, which at least has

[1] The main recent references are: Gardner Ackley, *Macroeconomic Theory* (New York: Macmillan, 1961) chap. xi; Arnold Zellner, 'The Short-Run Consumption Function', *Econometrica* (Oct 1957); Daniel B. Suits, 'The Determinants of Consumer Expenditure: A Review of Present Knowledge', in *Impacts of Monetary Policy* (Englewood Cliffs, N.J.: Prentice-Hall, 1963); A. Zellner, D. S. Huang and L. C. Chau, 'Further Analysis of the Short-Run Consumption Function with Emphasis on the Role of Liquid Assets', *Econometrica* (July 1965); Z. Griliches, G. S. Maddala, R. Lucas and N. Wallace, 'Notes on Estimated Aggregate Quarterly Consumption Functions', *Econometrica* (July 1962); Richard Stone and D. A. Rowe, 'A Post-War Expenditure Function', *Manchester School of Economic and Social Studies* (May 1962); and Richard Stone, 'Private Saving in Britain, Past, Present and Future', *Manchester School of Economic and Social Studies* (May 1964); J. S. Duesenberry, O. Eckstein and G. Fromm, 'A Simulation of the United States Economy in Recession', *Econometrica* (Oct 1960).

the virtue of simplicity, unless we can find something better to put in its place. The question which arises is: what alternatives have been thrown up by recent research? We shall now present a brief review of the recent short-run studies in an attempt to answer this question.

One idea which runs through much recent work on the short-run consumption function is the idea that the desired real consumption expenditure of any short period, such as a quarter, can be broken down into two independent components – a long-run, or 'permanent', component covering such routine or habitual expenditure as expenditure on food, clothing, cigarettes, petrol and entertainment, and a short-run, or 'transitory', component covering various types of postponable expenditure such as expenditure on new durables, house repairs and overseas travel. Further, since the two components are independent, it must be possible to explain short-run changes in desired real consumption expenditure by finding the determinants of each component in turn and adding the separate effects. This idea is most explicit in the work of Stone and Rowe[1] – the main British work in the field – and it will be convenient to discuss their contribution first.[2]

Stone and Rowe start from the identity:

$$C_t = C_t^1 + C_t^2 \tag{2.4}$$

where C^1 denotes the permanent component of desired real consumption expenditure and C^2 the transitory component. The *permanent* component of real consumption expenditure in any quarter is said to depend linearly on the 'permanent' component of real disposable income in the quarter and on the 'permanent' component of real wealth in the quarter. Thus we have:

$$C_t^1 = \epsilon_1 X_t^1 + \epsilon_2 W_t^1 \tag{2.5}$$

where X^1 denotes the permanent component of real disposable income and W^1 the permanent component of real wealth, and where the ϵs are two constants. On the other hand, the *transitory* component of real consumption expenditure depends linearly on the transitory component of real disposable income alone:

$$C_t^2 = \rho X_t^2. \tag{2.6}$$

---

[1] See preceding footnote.

[2] The set of relationships which we are about to present constitute what Stone refers to in the 1964 paper as the 'basic model'. Several variants of the basic model are also given in this paper (op. cit., pp. 101–4).

The permanent disposable income of any quarter is taken to be a weighted arithmetic average of the *observed* disposable income of the quarter and the permanent income of the preceding quarter, and similarly for permanent wealth. Thus we have:

$$X_t^1 = \lambda X_t + (1 - \lambda) X_{t-1}^1 \tag{2.7}$$

$$W_t^1 = \lambda W_t + (1 - \lambda) W_{t-1}^1 \tag{2.8}$$

where X and W denote, respectively, observed real disposable income and observed real wealth. Note that the same weights are used in both expressions. Finally we have two further identities:

$$X_t = X_t^1 + X_t^2 \tag{2.9}$$

$$W_t = W_t^1 + W_t^2. \tag{2.10}$$

Relationships (2.4) to (2.10) can be put together in the following way to give a fairly simple short-run consumption function. Substitute (2.5) and (2.6) into (2.4) to get:

$$C_t = \epsilon_1 X_t^1 + \epsilon_2 W_t^1 + \rho X_t^2$$

which from (2.9) gives:

$$C_t = \epsilon_1 X_t^1 + \epsilon_2 W_t^1 + \rho X_t - \rho X_t^1. \tag{2.11}$$

Now substitute from (2.7) and (2.8) to get:

$$C_t = \epsilon_1 [\lambda X_t + (1 - \lambda) X_{t-1}^1] + \epsilon_2 [\lambda W_t + (1 - \lambda) W_{t-1}^1] \\ + \rho X_t - \rho[\lambda X_t + (1 - \lambda) X_{t-1}^1].$$

Using (2.11) we can obtain an expression for $(1 - \lambda)C_{t-1}$:

$$(1 - \lambda)C_{t-1} = \epsilon_1(1 - \lambda) X_{t-1}^1 + \epsilon_2(1 - \lambda) W_{t-1}^1 \\ + \rho(1 - \lambda) X_{t-1} - \rho(1 - \lambda) X_{t-1}^1.$$

Subtracting this expression from the expression just derived for C_t gives:

$$C_t - (1 - \lambda)C_{t-1} = \epsilon_1 \lambda X_t + \epsilon_2 \lambda W_t + \rho(1 - \lambda) X_t - \rho(1 - \lambda) X_{t-1}$$

which gives:

$$C_t = \epsilon_2 \lambda W_t + [\epsilon_1 \lambda + \rho(1 - \lambda)] X_t - \rho(1 - \lambda) X_{t-1} + (1 - \lambda)C_{t-1}. \tag{2.12}$$

This is the Stone–Rowe short-run consumption function: desired real consumption expenditure in quarter t is a linear function of real wealth at the beginning of quarter t, real disposable income in quarter

t and in quarter $(t-1)$, and real consumption expenditure in quarter $(t-1)$.

There are two features of this construction which appear to be unsatisfactory. The first is that the view taken about the determination of permanent income appears to be inconsistent with the whole idea of permanent income as that part of the individual's income which reflects his long-run wealth position. This can be seen most easily if equation (2.7) is rewritten, using (2.9), as:

$$X_t^1 - (1-\lambda)X_{t-1}^1 = \lambda X_t^1 + \lambda X_t^2$$

or as:

$$X_t^1 - X_{t-1}^1 = \frac{\lambda}{1-\lambda} X_t^2.$$

According to this expression the change in the permanent component of real disposable income between quarter $(t-1)$ and quarter t is some fixed proportion $[\lambda/(1-\lambda)]$ of the *transitory* component of quarter t – a proposition which seems to rob the permanent-income notion of all meaning.

Equation (2.7) seems to be all the more unsatisfactory when viewed in relation to (2.8). By means of an argument which parallels that just used for permanent income, we find that $(W_t^1 - W_{t-1}^1) = [\lambda/(1-\lambda)]W_t^2$, from which it follows that the marginal permanent wealth–permanent income ratio is given by:

$$\frac{W_t^1 - W_{t-1}^1}{X_t^1 - X_{t-1}^1} = \frac{W_t^2}{X_t^2}.$$

According to this expression, the marginal permanent wealth–permanent income ratio is variable and dependent only on the ratio of transitory wealth to transitory income – a proposition which makes no sense at all.

The second feature of the analysis which calls for comment is the link between transitory consumption and transitory income provided by equation (2.6). This appears to be extremely doubtful in the light of recent work by Suits with United States data.[1] Suits's procedure is to attempt to remove the permanent component from the quarterly figures of both real consumption and real disposable income and then to correlate what remains, i.e. in effect, to correlate transitory consumption and transitory income. Three different devices are used to remove the permanent components from the consumption and

[1] See Suits, op. cit., pp. 36–9.

income figures and, in all cases, the correlation between the transitory components is extremely small. Suits's conclusion is that, for all practical purposes, transitory consumption is independent of transitory income and must be explained in some other way.

On the other hand, it must be pointed out that the Stone–Rowe function gives quite satisfactory statistical results when fitted to the British data. For purposes of fitting, (2.12) is converted into a relationship in which the *personal saving ratio* appears as the dependent variable, by means of the definition: saving ratio $= 1 - C_t/X_t$. In this form, (2.12) and its variants have been fitted by least squares to both annual and quarterly British data in the two papers cited, and the conclusion which emerges is that the hypothesis works well for the British economy in terms of such criteria as correctness of sign of coefficients, statistical reliability of coefficients and predictive ability.

The idea that consumption expenditure and disposable income can be divided into permanent and transitory components also underlies recent work done on the short-run consumption function in the United States, notably the study by Zellner, Huang and Chau.[1] The short-run consumption function to which they are eventually led is:

$$C_t = k_1 X_t^1 + k_2(L_{t-1} - L_t^d) \qquad (2.13)$$

where L and L^d denote, respectively, the actual level and the desired level of liquid assets at the end of the period. It is apparent that the first term $(k_1 X_t^1)$ is to be thought of as the permanent component of desired real consumption expenditure and the second term as the transitory component.[2] Thus (2.13) differs from (2.5)–(2.6) in two respects: the wealth variable plays no part in the determination of the permanent component, and the liquid-asset adjustment variable, rather than transitory income, determines the transitory component.

It is worth noting that before accepting (2.13), Zellner *et al.* examine two possible alternatives to the simple permanent-income hypothesis on which it is based. They are:

permanent component $= k_3(X_t^1 + \beta X_{t-1}^1 + \beta^2 X_{t-2}^1 + \ldots)$ (2.14)

permanent component $= k_4 X_t^1 + k_5 C_{t-1}$ (2.15)

where β in (2.14) is given by: $0 < \beta < 1$. The idea underlying (2.14) is that while the permanent component of desired real consumption

---

[1] See Zellner, Huang and Chau, op. cit.
[2] Cf. ibid., pp. 571, 574.

expenditure is determined by permanent real disposable income alone, the adjustment of permanent consumption to permanent income is not instantaneous as implied by (2.13); rather there is considerable inertia in the adjustment process. A given change in permanent income in quarter t will call forth some part of the desired change in permanent consumption in quarter t, a further part in quarter $(t+1)$, and so on. In other words, on this view, the permanent component of consumption expenditure is linked to the current level, and to past levels, of permanent income by means of a distributed-lag function, i.e. a function of the form:

$$\text{permanent component} = \rho_0 X_t^1 + \rho_1 X_{t-1}^1 + \rho_2 X_{t-2}^1 + \dots$$

where the ρs are a set of parameters.[1]

Relationship (2.14) complicates (2.13) through the addition of an 'inertia', or 'lagged adjustment', effect. On the other hand, (2.15) introduces a 'habit-persistence' effect. The basic idea here is that, because there is a strong element of habit in consumer behaviour, the consumption levels achieved in the past will play an important part in determining the level assumed by the permanent component in the present. One simple way of incorporating this effect is to add a term in C_{t-1} to the relationship governing the permanent component, which is the approach adopted in (2.15).

Both (2.14) and (2.15) are rejected by Zellner *et al.* on statistical grounds in favour of the simpler permanent-income hypothesis embodied in (2.13). Their procedure is to fit three separate relationships to United States quarterly data, namely $C_t = k_1 X_t^1$; $C_t = k_3(X_t^1 + \beta X_{t-1}^1 + \beta^2 X_{t-2}^1 + \dots)$; and $C_t = k_4 X_t^1 + k_5 C_{t-1}$, and then to compare the results in terms of sign and reliability of parameter estimates. What emerges is that the first relationship (the one embodied in (2.13)) does better than either of the other two in terms of the sign and reliability criteria.

Reverting to (2.13), it will be noticed that, as it stands, two of the variables involved, namely X^1 and L^d, are not directly observable. To remedy this deficiency, additional relationships which serve to

---

[1] In (2.14) the ρs take the special form of a set of positive numbers which decline geometrically. It would be natural to impose the restriction that these numbers should add to some positive number lying between zero and unity, thus implying that a change in permanent income which persists indefinitely will cause an ultimate change in permanent consumption of the same sign but of smaller amount. This could be done by requiring that k_3 be equal to $k_1(1-\beta)$ where $0 < k_1 < 1$. Since $0 < \beta < 1$, the sum of the numbers would then be k_1.

link X^1 and L^d to directly observable variables must be introduced. In the case of X^1, two possibilities are considered. They are:[1]

$$X_t^1 = (1 - \xi)(X_t + \xi X_{t-1} + \xi^2 X_{t-2} + \xi^3 X_{t-3} + \ldots) \qquad (2.16)$$

$$X_t^1 = (1 - \xi)[X_t + (\xi + \pi)X_{t-1} + (\xi + \pi)^2 X_{t-2} + (\xi + \pi)^3 X_{t-3} + \ldots] \ (2.17)$$

where $0 < \xi < 1$, $0 < \pi < 1$ and $0 < (\xi + \pi) < 1$.

Let us consider these expressions in turn.

According to relationship (2.16), the permanent component of real disposable income in period t is related to the real disposable income actually realised in period t and in all past periods by means of a distributed-lag function in which the weights decline geometrically and sum to unity (see pp. 12-13 above). Hence it can be reduced to:

$$X_t^1 = (1 - \xi)X_t + \xi X_{t-1}^1.$$

However, this is merely (2.7) in another guise, as can be seen by putting $(1 - \xi) = \lambda$, so that the criticism advanced earlier against (2.7) applies equally to (2.16).

Turn now to (2.17). This expression can be simplified to:

$$X_t^1 = (1 - \xi)X_t + \xi X_{t-1}^1 + \pi X_{t-1}^1.$$

It will be seen that this expression differs from the simplified expression for (2.16) only in the presence of the term πX_{t-1}^1 on the right-hand side. However, this extra term frees $(X_t^1 - X_{t-1}^1)$ from dependence on X_t^2 alone and so frees (2.17) from the criticism levelled at (2.16).

As for the other non-observable variable (L^d), once again two possibilities are considered, namely:

$$L_t^d = \eta X_t^1 \qquad (2.18)$$

$$L_t^d = \eta X_t^1 + \delta i_t \qquad (2.19)$$

where η and δ are, respectively, a positive and a negative constant and i denotes some relevant short-term interest rate.

Using (2.16)–(2.19), we can write (2.13) in four different ways, in terms of observable variables only. Zellner *et al.* fit three of these four versions to United States quarterly data (in two the variables

[1] Zellner *et al.* do not specify any restrictions on ξ and π. However, they must be restricted in the manner indicated if (2.16) and (2.17) are to make sense. For example, if ξ were greater than unity, both (2.16) and (2.17) would imply that X^1 is always negative.

were indentical) find that in all cases k_2 (the coefficient of $(L_{t-1}-L_t^d)$ in (2.13)) is statistically reliable and has the right sign (positive). (In no case could k_1, the coefficient of X_t^1, be estimated separately.) Thus the United States data provide some statistical support for the use of (2.13) as a quarterly consumption function. Zellner *et al.* also find that the coefficient of i_t in (2.19) is statistically unreliable in all cases and conclude from this that (2.18) is to be preferred to (2.19) as a means of transforming L^d into observable variables.

2.4 The Consumption Function: Defence of Living Standards

So far we have been concentrating on aggregate quarterly consumption functions whose starting-point is the distinction between permanent and transitory consumption expenditure and permanent and transitory disposable income. One well-known short-run consumption function which uses a different approach is the Duesenberry–Eckstein–Fromm function.[1] This can be stated as follows:

$$\frac{C_t}{X_{t-1}} = a + b \frac{X_{t-1}}{X_{t-1}^0} + c \frac{C_{t-1}}{X_{t-2}} \tag{2.20}$$

where X_{t-1}^0 denotes the highest level of real disposable income achieved prior to quarter $(t-1)$ and a, b and c are constants.

The essential idea expressed in (2.20) is that in a period of steady exponential growth, desired real consumption expenditure will rise in proportion to real disposable income with the result that the ratio of desired consumption to income will remain constant. On the other hand if growth is checked and the economy enters a period of recession characterised by a continuous absolute decline in income, desired consumption will fall *less* than in proportion to income in each period as consumers attempt to maintain the living standards acquired in the period of steady growth, with the result that the ratio of desired consumption to income will show a steady rise. Thus there is an asymmetry in consumer behaviour as between a period of steady growth in which real income is rising continuously by a more or less constant percentage from quarter to quarter and a period of recession in which real income is falling continuously from quarter to quarter.[2]

---

[1] See Duesenberry, Eckstein and Fromm, op. cit.
[2] Cf. Griliches, Maddala, Lucas and Wallace, op. cit., pp. 491–2.

This proposition can be stated symbolically in the following way:

$$\frac{C_t}{X_{t-1}} = \alpha + \beta \frac{X_{t-1}}{X_{t-1}^0} \tag{2.21}$$

where α is a positive constant and β a negative constant. In conditions of steady exponential growth, $X_{t-1} = (1 + r)X_{t-2}$ and $X_{t-1}^0 = X_{t-2}$ where r is some positive fraction. Hence from (2.21) C_t/X_{t-1} will have a constant value of $[\alpha + \beta(1 + r)]$. On the other hand, if the economy enters a period of recession in which X_{t-1} falls continuously in relation to X_{t-1}^0, $\beta(X_{t-1}/X_{t-1}^0)$ will fall continuously in relation to $\beta(1 + r)$ in numerical terms. Thus, in a recession, C_t/X_{t-1} will rise continuously above its steady-growth value of $[\alpha + \beta(1 + r)]$.

Now (2.20) can be interpreted as (2.21) with a special form of lagged adjustment superimposed. To see this, denote $[\alpha + \beta(X_{t-1}/X_{t-1}^0)]$ by Z_t. Then (2.21) postulates that a given change in Z_t causes an *immediate* adjustment of C_t/X_{t-1}, equal to the full amount of the change in Z_t. Postulate instead that a given change in Z_t causes an *ultimate* adjustment of C_t/X_{t-1}, equal to the full amount of the change in Z_t, but that the adjustment is spread out over an infinite succession of future periods. In other words, postulate that there is a distributed-lag relationship between C/X and Z. Next impose the restriction that the parameters in this distributed-lag relationship are a series of geometrically declining constants which sum to unity. Then we have the following relationship:

$$\frac{C_t}{X_{t-1}} = \lambda \frac{C_{t-1}}{X_{t-2}} + (1 - \lambda)Z_t \tag{2.22}$$

where $0 < \lambda < 1$ (see pp. 39–40 above). On substituting $[\alpha + \beta(X_{t-1}/X_{t-1}^0)]$ for Z_t, this expression gives:

$$\frac{C_t}{X_{t-1}} = \alpha(1 - \lambda) + \beta(1 - \lambda)\frac{X_{t-1}}{X_{t-1}^0} + \lambda\frac{C_{t-1}}{X_{t-2}}$$

which is (2.20) with the constant a replacing $\alpha(1 - \lambda)$, the constant b replacing $\beta(1 - \lambda)$ and the constant c replacing λ.

It is clear from this argument that the constants a and c should be positive, that b should be negative and that c should be less than unity. To test (2.20), therefore, we have merely to fit it to quarterly data and see whether these requirements are met. This has been done recently by Griliches, and an examination of his results[1] shows that

[1] Ibid., pp. 492–4.

the Duesenberry–Eckstein–Fromm quarterly consumption function is highly satisfactory from this point of view.

With this brief survey of recent work on the quarterly aggregate consumption function at our disposal, let us now return to our original question, namely, whether recent research has produced any satisfactory alternatives to the traditional Keynesian short-run consumption function. What emerges from our survey is that, judging only by the usual statistical tests, there are at least three functions – (2.12), (2.13) and (2.20) – which are worth considering as replacements for the consumption function of Model I (relationship (2.1)).

Of the three, (2.12) and (2.13) are preferable to (2.20) on the grounds of simplicity (the ratio form of (2.20) makes it awkward to handle), while (2.13) seems preferable to (2.12) on *a priori* grounds (recall our criticisms of the argument underlying (2.12)). Suppose, then, that we adopt (2.13) as a starting-point and proceed to consider whether we can strengthen it further without introducing too much additional complexity.

It will be recalled that (2.13) is based on the distinction between the permanent component of desired real consumption expenditure and the transitory component. Each of these is explained separately and the separate functions are then added to give the aggregate function. To strengthen (2.13), therefore, we need to improve the explanation of the permanent component, or the explanation of the transitory component, or both. We shall concentrate our attention on the second of these possibilities, since it appears likely to yield the best results.

To begin with, recall that, by definition, the transitory component consists of expenditure of a discretionary or postponable kind, such as expenditure on durables and luxury goods. This being so, we can say that changes in the transitory component will be governed by two main influences: (i) changes in the various consumer attitudes which, between them, determine the strength of the feeling that 'now is a good time to buy'; and (ii) changes in the strength of the financial constraints to which transitory expenditure is subject. If it is to be satisfactory, the function which explains the transitory component must incorporate both these influences. To what extent are they incorporated in the 'transitory' function which enters into (2.13)?

The first is not incorporated at all. To bring it in, one could make the transitory component depend, among other things, on an 'index of consumer attitudes', such as the index published by Katona and his associates since 1954.[1] This is an index based on the replies given by consumers to six questions asked in the periodic attitudinal surveys conducted by the Survey Research Center, namely questions relating to: (i) economic status relative to the preceding year; (ii) personal financial expectations for the coming year; (iii) one-year expectations regarding business conditions; (iv) long-run expectations regarding business conditions; (v) attitude towards buying conditions for household goods and clothing; and (vi) price expectations. For any given survey each respondent is scored two, one or zero on each question according to whether his answer is optimistic, non-committal or pessimistic. The scores of all respondents are then added separately for each question and each of the six score totals is then expressed as a percentage of the corresponding total of the base period (late November 1952). In this way a set of six index numbers are obtained for the survey in question. Finally these component indexes are weighted equally to obtain the overall index for the survey.

The question of the usefulness of the Katona index as an explanatory variable in a transitory function has been examined recently by Mueller by means of a regression analysis, and it seems clear from her results that the index makes a significant contribution to the explanation of movements in the transitory component in the United States.[2]

The second influence (changes in the strength of the financial constraints to which transitory expenditure is subject) is partially incorporated through the liquid-asset adjustment variable. However, it seems desirable that it should be introduced explicitly by means of some variable such as the one included by Stone and Rowe as an amendment to their basic relationship.[3]

[1] See in particular George Katona and Eva Mueller, *Consumer Attitudes and Demand 1950–1952* (University of Michigan, Survey Research Center, Institute for Social Research, 1953); George Katona and Eva Mueller, *Consumer Expectations, 1953–56* (University of Michigan, Survey Research Center, Institute for Social Research, 1956); Eva Mueller, 'Consumer Attitudes: Their Influence and Forecasting Value', in *The Quality and Economic Significance of Anticipations Data* (Princeton University Press, 1960).

[2] See Eva Mueller, 'Ten Years of Consumer Attitude Surveys: Their Forecasting Record', *Journal of the American Statistical Association* (Dec 1963).

[3] The variable introduced by Stone and Rowe was $(\xi_t - \xi_t^*)$ where ξ_t denotes the actual level, and ξ_t^* the 'normal' level, of the percentage down-payment on the hire-purchase of radio and electrical goods, which in their view is a sensitive

Arguing along these lines, we arrive at an aggregate quarterly consumption function of the following form:

$$C_t = k_1 X_t^1 + k_2(L_{t-1} - L_t^d) + k_3 R_t + k_4 N_t$$

where R denotes some index of consumer attitudes which increases when attitudes towards spending become more favourable and vice versa, N some appropriate indicator of changes in the strength of the financial constraints imposed on would-be spenders which rises when monetary conditions become more stringent and vice versa, and k_3 and k_4 a positive, and a negative, constant respectively.

We now have to convert this expression into an expression which runs in terms of observables only, by substituting for X^1 and L^d. For reasons discussed earlier, we prefer (2.17) to (2.16) as a means of dealing with X^1 and (2.18) to (2.19) as a means of dealing with L^d. When these substitutions are made we obtain:

$$C_t = (k_1 - k_2\eta)[(1 - \xi)\{X_t + (\xi + \pi)X_{t-1} + (\xi + \pi)^2 X_{t-2} + \ldots\}] \\ + k_2 L_{t-1} + k_3 R_t + k_4 N_t. \qquad (2.23)$$

To simplify (2.23), we use it to obtain an expression for $(\xi + \pi)C_{t-1}$ and then subtract this expression from (2.23). The result is:

$$C_t = (k_1 - k_2\eta)(1 - \xi)X_t + k_2 L_{t-1} - k_2(\xi + \pi)L_{t-2} + k_3 R_t \\ - k_3(\xi + \pi)R_{t-1} + k_4 N_t - k_4(\xi + \pi)N_{t-1} + (\xi + \pi)C_{t-1}.$$

This expression can be written still more simply as:

$$C_t = \alpha_{10}X_t + \alpha_{11}C_{t-1} + Z^1 \qquad (2.24)$$

where $\alpha_{10} = (k_1 - k_2\eta)(1 - \xi)$, $\alpha_{11} = (\xi + \pi)$ and Z^1 denotes a linear combination of the following variables:

(i) L, the level of liquid assets, lagged one period and lagged two periods;

(ii) N, an index of monetary stringency, current and lagged one period;

(iii) R, an index of consumer attitudes, current and lagged one period.

---

indicator of changes in the strength of the financial constraints to which consumers are subject. The normal level ξ_t^* was defined similarly to permanent income, i.e. by

$$\xi_t^* = \lambda \xi_t + (1 - \lambda)\xi_{t-1}^*.$$

See Stone, 'Private Saving in Britain, Past, Present and Future', op. cit., pp. 82, 103–4.

We propose to treat the variables L, N and R as data throughout the sequence of models to be constructed in this and the following chapters, which means that Z^1 will be taken as a datum throughout. The legitimacy of this will be considered in section 5.5, where the data which remain in the final model will be examined as a whole. While the components of Z^1 are of no interest to us at the present stage, they will become decidedly interesting in Chapter 6 where we consider, among other things, the ways in which the British authorities can manipulate aggregate demand in the interests of maintaining internal balance.

The reader is asked to note that unspecified constants will be denoted throughout the sequence of models in the same manner as in (2.24) – that is, by the symbol α with the appropriate two-number numerical subscript. The first number in the subscript will serve to distinguish the αs in any one relationship from the αs in other relationships, while the second number will distinguish any α in a given relationship from the other αs in that relationship.

2.5 The Disposable Income Function

If we replace the consumption function of Model I (relationship (2.1)) by (2.24), we introduce a new variable which it is desirable to treat as a jointly determined variable, namely X. To make this possible, we must introduce an additional relationship into the model to explain X. Such a relationship could be either: (i) a relationship which shows how X varies in response to changes in Y (real G.D.P. at factor cost) when the income tax and transfer payment structures are held fixed; or (ii) a relationship which shows how X varies in response to changes in Y when the tax and transfer payment structures are allowed to vary also. The additional relationship which we shall introduce to explain X will be of the first type, that is it will be a relationship which shows how X varies when Y varies, on the assumption that the income tax and transfer payment structures remain fixed.

Perhaps the best way to approach the task of formulating a disposable income function of this type is to list the items which intervene between Y and X in the British national accounts. This is done in Table 2.1.

We now consider the way in which the items in this list are likely to vary with gross domestic product, given that the tax and transfer

C

payment structures remain fixed. In the case of *items 3 and 4*, one would expect the variation to be in the same direction, and roughly in the same proportion, as the variation in gross domestic product.

TABLE 2.1

1. *Gross domestic product at factor cost* (Y)
2. *less* Gross trading profits of companies
3. *less* Gross trading surpluses of public corporations
4. *less* Gross profits of other public enterprises
5. *less* Residual error
6. *plus* Dividends and interest
7. *plus* National insurance benefits and other current grants from public authorities
8. *plus* Stock appreciation
9. *Personal income*
10. *less* Payments by persons of U.K. taxes on income
11. *less* National insurance and health contributions
12. *less* Net transfers abroad
13. *Personal disposable income* (X)

Given the structure of taxes on business income, the variation of *items 2 and 6 combined* is also likely to be in the same direction as the variation in gross domestic product. In this case, however, one would expect the variation typically to be *more* than proportional, because the gross trading profits of companies appear to be highly sensitive to changes in gross domestic product in the short run, whereas 'dividends and interest' appears to be comparatively insensitive to short-period changes in gross product, for a given business income-tax structure.[1]

Given the social security structure, *item 7* ('national insurance benefits and other current grants from public authorities') can be expected to move in the opposite direction to gross domestic product and *less* than proportionately, since, given rates of benefit, unemployment benefits move in the opposite direction and roughly in proportion, while the other benefits and grants remain more or less fixed in

[1] The following hypothetical figures may help to illustrate the point. It will be seen that a 20 per cent increase in gross domestic product has been accompanied by a 25 per cent increase (a more than proportional increase) in the gross trading profits of companies. 'Dividends and interest', however, has remained constant. The result is an increase in items 2 and 6 combined of 100 per cent:

	Gross domestic product	Gross trading profits of companies	Dividends and interest	Gross trading profits minus *Dividends and interest* (items 2 and 6 combined)
Quarter 1	100	40	30	10
Quarter 2	120	50	30	20

the face of short-period changes in gross product.[1] Next, we have *items 10 and 11*. Given the personal income-tax and social security structures, one would expect the sum of these items to change in the same direction as gross domestic product, and in view of the progressiveness of the personal income-tax structure, to change more than in proportion. This leaves *items 5, 8 and 12*. These, we can assume, are virtually independent of gross domestic product.

Let us now use this item-by-item discussion to deduce the typical short-run relationship, for a given income tax and social security structure, between real personal disposable income (X) and real G.D.P. at factor cost (Y). For this purpose we shall use the symbol Δ_1 to denote a given increase in real gross domestic product (item 1 of Table 2.1) which takes place in the face of unchanging income tax and transfer payment structures.

We shall also use Δ_2 to denote the corresponding change in item 2 of Table 2.1, and so on down to item 13. Then we have:

$$\Delta_{13} = \Delta_1 - (\Delta_2 + \Delta_3 + \Delta_4 - \Delta_6 - \Delta_7 + \Delta_{10} + \Delta_{11}) - (\Delta_5 - \Delta_8 + \Delta_{12}).$$
$$(2.25)$$

Now the preceding discussion suggests that $(\Delta_2 - \Delta_6)$, Δ_3, Δ_4, Δ_{10} and Δ_{11} will usually be positive, and that Δ_7 will usually be negative, and hence that the first bracket of (2.25) will usually be positive. Also it seems reasonable to assume that it will normally be numerically smaller than Δ_1. Hence, disregarding the second bracket, we can say that Δ_{13} will normally be positive but less than Δ_1, or in other words, that real personal disposable income will usually increase when real gross domestic product increases, the tax and transfer payment structures remaining fixed, but by a smaller absolute amount. This conclusion could be upset if the second bracket, which relates to the items that are independent of gross domestic product, were typically negative *and* numerically large in relation to the first; but there is no reason to think that this is the case.

Granted that X increases when Y increases with fixed tax and

[1] Once again, some hypothetical figures may help to make the point clear. The following table shows a 20 per cent increase in gross domestic product accompanied by a 20 per cent decrease in unemployment benefit (a proportional decrease) and constancy in other benefits. The result is a decrease of 11 per cent in item 7.

	Gross domestic product	Unemployment benefit	Other benefits	Item 7
Quarter 1	100	10	8	18
Quarter 2	120	8	8	16

transfer payment structures, but by a smaller absolute amount, the question arises whether the *proportional* increase in X will usually be larger or smaller than the proportional increase in Y. This question is more complicated and will be explored in Appendix 2.1. The conclusion which emerges is that a given increase in real G.D.P. at factor cost, the income tax and transfer payment structures held fixed, will usually be accompanied by an increase in real personal disposable income which is not only absolutely, but also proportionately, less than the increase in gross product.

The simplest form of relationship to embody these features is one which makes real personal disposable income a linear function of real gross domestic product with a positive vertical intercept and a positive slope of less than unity. The fact that the slope of the function is positive and less than unity means that the absolute increase in real personal disposable income is smaller than the absolute increase in real gross domestic product, while this fact, coupled with the fact that the vertical intercept is positive, means that the elasticity of X with respect to Y is less than unity at all points or, in other words, that the proportional increase in X associated with any given proportional increase in Y is less than the proportional increase in Y.[1] This is the type of relationship that we shall use in our second-stage model. Thus, as well as replacing (2.1) by (2.24) in Model I, we shall add:

$$X_t = \alpha_{20} + \alpha_{21} Y_t \tag{2.26}$$

where α_{20} is positive and α_{21} is positive and less than unity.

As the preceding discussion makes clear, this relationship takes as given the whole income-tax structure (business and personal) and the whole social security structure. For example, an increase in the severity of the *business income*-tax structure will shift the relationship downwards, *ceteris paribus*, because it will mean a lower level of dividends and interest (item 6 of Table 2.1) at any given level of gross domestic product than before. Likewise an increase in the severity of the *personal income*-tax structure will shift the relationship downwards because it will mean a higher level of personal income-tax payments (item 10 of Table 2.1) at any given level of gross product than before. On the other hand, an increase in the liberality

---

[1] The elasticity of a linear function, $X = a + bY$, is:

$$\frac{dX}{dY} \frac{Y}{X} = \frac{bY}{a + bY} = \frac{1}{1 + (a/bY)}.$$

of the *social security* structure will shift the relationship upwards because it will mean a higher level of national insurance benefits (item 7 of Table 2.1) at any given level of gross product than before.

A relationship like (2.26) has extremely important implications. To see what these are within the framework of the simplest possible dynamic model, the reader should add this relationship to Model I with the consumption function rewritten as $C_t = \beta_0 + \beta_1 X_{t-1}$. He will then find that the expression for the deviation of aggregate demand from an initial stationary equilibrium, denoted by d_t, is:

$$d_t = (\beta_1 \alpha_{21}) d_{t-1} + a$$

where a is the permanent increase in non-consumption demand (A) which is assumed to disturb the initial equilibrium. The corresponding expression for the model as it stands is:

$$d_t = \beta_1 d_{t-1} + a.$$

Hence when the new relationship is added, d_t converges on $a/(1 - \beta_1 \alpha_{21})$ as t tends to infinity,[1] whereas with the model as it stands the convergence is on $a/(1 - \beta_1)$. Since α_{21} is less than unity, $(\beta_1 \alpha_{21})$ must be less than β_1 and hence $a/(1 - \beta_1 \alpha_{21})$ must be less than $a/(1 - \beta_1)$. It follows that the effect of introducing the new relationship is to make the change in aggregate demand, which results from a given permanent increase in real non-consumption expenditure, less than it would otherwise be; and the smaller α_{21}, the more powerful this effect.

We can see from this analysis of Model I that a relationship of the form of (2.26) exercises a stabilising influence on aggregate demand, i.e. that it makes aggregate demand less responsive to given changes in the data than would otherwise be the case. Moreover, it does so, essentially, because α_{21} is positive but less than unity, i.e. because the various items which intervene between gross domestic product and personal disposable income react to changes in gross domestic product in such a way that the resulting change in personal disposable income is less, absolutely, than the change in gross domestic product. For this reason, the various institutional arrangements which determine the balance of the response of these items to a change in gross product are commonly referred to as 'built-in stabilisers' and the stabilising influence which they exert as 'built-in' stability.

[1] This assumes that $\beta_1 \alpha_{21} < 1$.

2.6 The Dynamic Properties of Model II

We have now completed the first of our intended revisions of the basic model and, before proceeding, we shall pause to consider the dynamic properties of the revised model which we shall refer to from now on as Model II. This may be set down in formal terms as follows:

Desired Consumption Expenditure

$$C_t = \alpha_{10}X_t + \alpha_{11}C_{t-1} + Z^1 \qquad (2.24)$$

Disposable Income

$$X_t = \alpha_{20} + \alpha_{21}Y_t \qquad (2.26)$$

Components of Aggregate Demand

$$D_t = C_t + A_t \qquad (2.2)$$

Demand–Output Relationship

$$Y_t = D_t \qquad (2.3)$$

There are four jointly determined variables in the system, namely C, X, Y and D. The data consist of the *explicit* data, Z^1 and A, and the *implicit* data, i.e. the variables, institutional arrangements, attitudes, etc., which underlie the first two relationships of the system. Changes in the implicit data will be reflected in changes in the values of the αs in these relationships.

To explore the dynamic properties of the model, we first reduce it to a first-order difference equation in D in the following way. Use (2.2) to replace C_{t-1} in (2.24) by $(D_{t-1} - A_{t-1})$ and (2.26) and (2.3) to replace X_t in (2.24) by $(\alpha_{20} + \alpha_{21}D_t)$. Then substitute for C_t in (2.2). The expression which results is:

$$D_t = \frac{\alpha_{11}}{1 - \alpha_{10}\alpha_{21}}D_{t-1} + \frac{A_t - \alpha_{11}A_{t-1} + Z^1}{1 - \alpha_{10}\alpha_{21}} + \frac{\alpha_{10}\alpha_{20}}{1 - \alpha_{10}\alpha_{21}}. \qquad (2.27)$$

We next derive the solution of this difference equation by standard methods.[1] The solution is:

$$D_t = (D_0 - \bar{D}_0)\left(\frac{\alpha_{11}}{1 - \alpha_{10}\alpha_{21}}\right)^t + \bar{D}_t \qquad (2.28)$$

---

[1] See R. G. D. Allen, *Mathematical Economics* (London: Macmillan, 1956) chap. 6, and W. J. Baumol, *Economic Dynamics*, 2nd ed. (New York: Macmillan, 1959) chap. 9.

where D_0 denotes the level of aggregate demand in some arbitrary initial period and where $\bar{D}_t$ denotes the particular solution (equilibrium path) in period t. The equilibrium time path is determined once time paths have been specified for the explicit data, A and Z^1, and once values have been specified for the four αs.

The character of the time path for D which is generated by (2.28) will depend on the magnitude and sign of $[\alpha_{11}/(1 - \alpha_{10}\alpha_{21})]$. The various possibilities are set out in Table 2.2 below. The question arises whether any of these possibilities can be ruled out by virtue of the restrictions which we have placed already, or which we might decide to place, on the various parameters of which $[\alpha_{11}/(1 - \alpha_{10}\alpha_{21})]$ is composed.

So far the only restrictions placed on these parameters (see pp. 51, 56 and 60 above) are: $0 < \alpha_{11} < 1$; $0 < \alpha_{21} < 1$. Following the usual procedure we shall now place the same restriction on α_{10}, the marginal propensity to consume from disposable income.[1] Together these restrictions ensure that $[\alpha_{11}/(1 - \alpha_{10}\alpha_{21})]$ is positive and enable us to rule out the first two cases listed in Table 2.2. However either of these last two cases is still admissible. The third case will occur if $\alpha_{11} + \alpha_{10}\alpha_{21} > 1$ and the fourth if $\alpha_{11} + \alpha_{10}\alpha_{21} < 1$.

TABLE 2.2

Magnitude and sign of $\dfrac{\alpha_{11}}{1 - \alpha_{10}\alpha_{21}}$	*Nature of time path generated for* $D_t - \bar{D}_t$
$\dfrac{\alpha_{11}}{1 - \alpha_{10}\alpha_{21}}$ negative and $\left\lvert \dfrac{\alpha_{11}}{1 - \alpha_{10}\alpha_{21}} \right\rvert > 1$	$(D_t - \bar{D}_t)$ alternates in sign and $\lvert D_t - \bar{D}_t \rvert \to \infty$ as $t \leftarrow \infty$
$\dfrac{\alpha_{11}}{1 - \alpha_{10}\alpha_{21}}$ negative and $\left\lvert \dfrac{\alpha_{11}}{1 - \alpha_{10}\alpha_{21}} \right\rvert < 1$	$(D_t - \bar{D}_t)$ alternates in sign and $\lvert D_t - \bar{D}_t \rvert \to 0$ as $t \to \infty$
$\dfrac{\alpha_{11}}{1 - \alpha_{10}\alpha_{21}}$ positive and > 1	$(D_t - \bar{D}_t)$ has same sign as $(D_0 - \bar{D}_0)$ and $\lvert D_t - \bar{D}_t \rvert \to \infty$ as $t \to \infty$
$\dfrac{\alpha_{11}}{1 - \alpha_{10}\alpha_{21}}$ positive and < 1	$(D_t - \bar{D}_t)$ has same sign as $(D_0 - \bar{D}_0)$ and $\lvert D_t - \bar{D}_t \rvert \to 0$ as $t \to \infty$

[1] This restriction implies certain restrictions on the parameters k_1, k_2, η and ξ of which α_{10} is composed. It will be recalled that is given by:

$$\alpha_{10} = (k_1 - k_2\eta)(1 - \xi).$$

Hence the restriction $0 < \alpha_{10} < 1$ implies:

$$0 < (k_1 - k_2\eta)(1 - \xi) < 1.$$

Since we have already imposed the restriction $0 < \xi < 1$, we can divide through the above inequality by $(1 - \xi)$ without reversing the direction of the inequality signs. Hence the restriction on α_{10} implies:

$$0 < (k_1 - k_2\eta) < \frac{1}{1 - \xi}.$$

The conclusion we reach, therefore, is that, given reasonable restrictions on the parameters, Model II allows aggregate demand to follow either one of two time paths in response to arbitrary initial conditions. Both paths are monotonic. The first is a path of monotonic explosion away from the equilibrium path – the path defined by the particular solution. The explosion will be in an upward direction if aggregate demand is initially above the equilibrium path $(D_0 > \bar{D}_0)$ and in a downward direction in the reverse case. The second possible path is one of monotonic convergence on the equilibrium path – convergence from below if aggregate demand is initially below the equilibrium path $(D_0 < \bar{D}_0)$ and convergence from above in the reverse case.

By contrast, so long as the usual (positive fraction) restriction is placed on the marginal propensity to consume, Model I allows only one type of behaviour, namely monotonic convergence on the equilibrium path. Thus the modifications which we have introduced into the basic model (simple as they are) suffice to change its dynamic properties in a significant way.

2.7 Summary

The starting-point of this chapter is the simplest possible short-run macro-dynamic model. This is the model in which aggregate demand is split into two components – desired real consumption expenditure, treated as a function of real gross domestic product alone, and desired real non-consumption expenditure treated as a datum – and in which real output is supposed to adjust instantaneously to aggregate demand. We refer to this model as Model I. After surveying the recent literature on the short-run consumption function we replace the consumption function of Model I by one which embodies the main ideas which have emerged from the discussion of the last few years. In this new function desired real consumption expenditure depends on real disposable income, the real consumption expenditure of the previous period and several other variables which we treat as data. To make it possible to to treat the new variable – real disposable income – as a jointly determined variable, we introduce a new relationship which shows how real disposable income responds to changes in real G.D.P. at factor cost when the income-tax and transfer payments structures are held fixed. The dynamic properties of the revised model (Model II) are examined and it is found that they differ significantly from those of Model I. In the case of Model I, given the usual restriction on the marginal propensity to consume, only one type of behaviour is possible for aggregate demand in response to arbitrary initial conditions, namely steady convergence on the equilibrium path. On the other hand, Model II permits aggregate demand to follow either one of two types of monotonic time path – monotonic convergence on the equilibrium path, as in the basic model, or monotonic departure from the equilibrium path. Thus by modifying the basic model in the manner indicated, we introduce the possibility of unstable behaviour in response to arbitrary initial conditions.

READING LIST

Ackley, G., *Macroeconomic Theory* (New York: Macmillan, 1961).
Duesenberry, J. S., Eckstein, O., and Fromm, G., 'A Simulation of the United States Economy in Recession', *Econometrica* (Oct 1960).
Griliches, Z., Maddala, G. S., Lucas, R., and Wallace, N. 'Notes on Estimated Aggregate Quarterly Consumption Functions', *Econometrica* (July 1962).
Katona, G., and Mueller, E., *Consumer Attitudes and Demand 1950–1952* (University of Michigan, Survey Research Center, Institute for Social Research, 1953).
—— and ——, *Consumer Expectations, 1953–56* (University of Michigan, Survey Research Center, Institute for Social Research, 1956).
Mueller, E., 'Consumer Attitudes: Their Influence and Forecasting Value', in *The Quality and Economic Significance of Anticipations Data* (Princeton University Press, 1960).
——, 'Ten Years of Consumer Attitude Surveys: Their Forecasting Record', *Journal of the American Statistical Association* (Dec 1963).
Pearse, P. H., 'Automatic Stabilization and the British Taxes on Income', *Review of Economic Studies*, XXIX (1962).
Stone, R., and Rowe, D. A., 'A Post-War Expenditure Function', *Manchester School of Economic and Social Studies* (May 1962).
——, 'Private Saving in Britain, Past, Present and Future', *Manchester School of Economic and Social Studies* (May 1964).
Suits, D. B., 'The Determinants of Consumer Expenditure: A Review of Present Knowledge', in *Impacts of Monetary Policy* (Englewood Cliffs, N.J.: Prentice-Hall, 1963).
Zellner, A., Huang., D. S., and Chau, L. C., 'Further Analysis of the Short-Run Consumption Function with Emphasis on the Role of Liquid Assets', *Econometrica* (July 1965).
——, 'The Short-Run Consumption Function', *Econometrica* (Oct 1957).

Appendix 2.1

RELATIONSHIP BETWEEN PROPORTIONAL INCREASE IN Y AND CORRESPONDING PROPORTIONAL INCREASE IN X WITH A FIXED TAX AND TRANSFER PAYMENT STRUCTURE

To explore this question we shall need some additional notation. The level of any given item of Table 2.1 at a level of real gross domestic product of Y_0 will be denoted by Π with the number of the item as a subscript,[1] while the proportional increase in the item which is associated with a given increase in real gross domestic product from Y_0 to Y_1, will be denoted by $\hat{\Pi}$ with the number of the item as a subscript. Finally, we shall use k to denote the given proportional increase in gross domestic product. Thus

$$k = \hat{\Pi}_1 = \frac{Y_1 - Y_0}{Y_0}.$$

Then from (2.25) we have:

$$\hat{\Pi}_{13} = \hat{\Pi}_1 \frac{\Pi_1}{\Pi_{13}} - \left(\hat{\Pi}_{2-6} \frac{\Pi_{2-6}}{\Pi_{13}} + \hat{\Pi}_3 \frac{\Pi_3}{\Pi_{13}} + \hat{\Pi}_4 \frac{\Pi_4}{\Pi_{13}} - \hat{\Pi}_7 \frac{\Pi_7}{\Pi_{13}} + \hat{\Pi}_{10+11} \frac{\Pi_{10+11}}{\Pi_{13}} \right)$$
$$- \left(\hat{\Pi}_5 \frac{\Pi_5}{\Pi_{13}} - \hat{\Pi}_8 \frac{\Pi_8}{\Pi_{13}} + \hat{\Pi}_{12} \frac{\Pi_{12}}{\Pi_{13}} \right).$$

Now the item-by-item discussion presented in section 2.5 of the text suggests that we can reasonably expect the following:

$$\hat{\Pi}_3 = \hat{\Pi}_4 = k$$
$$\hat{\Pi}_{2-6} > k$$
$$0 < -\hat{\Pi}_7 < k.$$
$$\hat{\Pi}_{10+11} > k$$

If these relationships hold, we have:

$$\hat{\Pi}_{13} = k \frac{\Pi_1}{\Pi_{13}} - \left((k + a_1) \frac{\Pi_{2-6}}{\Pi_{13}} + k \frac{\Pi_3}{\Pi_{13}} + k \frac{\Pi_4}{\Pi_{13}} + (k - a_2) \frac{\Pi_7}{\Pi_{13}} + (k + a_3) \frac{\Pi_{10+11}}{\Pi_{13}} \right)$$
$$- \left(\hat{\Pi}_5 \frac{\Pi_5}{\Pi_{13}} - \hat{\Pi}_8 \frac{\Pi_8}{\Pi_{13}} + \hat{\Pi}_{12} \frac{\Pi_{12}}{\Pi_{13}} \right)$$

where a_1, a_2 and a_3 are positive constants and $a_2 < k$. This gives:

$$\hat{\Pi}_{13} = k \left(\frac{\Pi_1 - \Pi_3 - \Pi_4 - \Pi_{2-6} - \Pi_7 - \Pi_{10+11}}{\Pi_{13}} \right) - \left(\frac{a_1 \Pi_{2-6} - a_2 \Pi_7 + a_3 \Pi_{10+11}}{\Pi_{13}} \right)$$
$$- \left(\hat{\Pi}_5 \frac{\Pi_5}{\Pi_{13}} - \hat{\Pi}_8 \frac{\Pi_8}{\Pi_{13}} + \hat{\Pi}_{12} \frac{\Pi_{12}}{\Pi_{13}} \right).$$

---

[1] The level of item 2 *less* item 6 corresponding to Y_0 will be denoted by Π_{2-6} and the level of item 10 *plus* item 11 by Π_{10+11}.

It seems reasonable to assume that the first bracket of this expression is less than unity[1] and that the second bracket is positive. Hence, disregarding the final bracket, we can say that $\hat{\Pi}_{13} < k$, i.e. that the proportional increase in real personal disposable income is typically less than the proportional increase in real gross domestic product. This conclusion would be upset if the final bracket, which applies to the items which are independent of gross product, were typically negative and numerically larger than the rest of the expression.

[1] The numerator of this bracket is given by:

$$\Pi_1 - \Pi_3 - \Pi_4 - \Pi_{2-6} - \Pi_7 - \Pi_{10+11} = \Pi_{13} + \Pi_{12} + \Pi_5 - 2\Pi_7 - \Pi_8.$$

3 The External Relationships

3.1 The Demand–Output Relationship

The short-run macro-dynamic model formulated at the end of the previous chapter represents an advance on the simple expository model set out in section 2.2 in that it introduces a considerably more refined consumption function. However, the revised model still retains certain of the defects of the basic model and we must now begin the task of eliminating these further defects.

One of the defects which Model II carries over from Model I is that it postulates an instantaneous adjustment of output to demand via relationship (2.3). In the present chapter we shall concentrate on remedying this weakness. We shall begin this task in the present section by developing a relationship to replace (2.3). This new relationship will bring in a new variable, namely realised real imports, which we shall want to treat as a jointly determined variable. To make this possible, an additional relationship will be needed to explain the short-run behaviour of real imports. Such a relationship will be presented in section 3.2 following an exposition of the modern approach in this area. The third-stage model will then be presented as a whole and its dynamic properties examined.

First, then, we set about the replacement of relationship (2.3). Here there seem to be two main possibilities. The first possibility is to replace $D_t = Y_t$ by a relationship which specifies the structure of the lag of output behind demand. The second is to replace the instantaneous adjustment relationship by one which specifies the extent to which, and the way in which, discrepancies between demand and output are eliminated, while leaving open the question of the precise form of the output–demand lag structure.

Following the first approach, one might replace $D_t = Y_t$ by:

$$Y_t = (1 - \beta)(D_t - M_t) + \beta Y_{t-1} \tag{3.1}$$

where M denotes realised real imports, and $0 < \beta < 1$. In (3.1) the current level of domestic output is expressed as a weighted sum of the current *demand* for domestic output, and the entire sequence of past demands, the weights declining geometrically and summing to unity (see p. 39 above). (3.1) can be regarded as a generalisation of (2.3) which covers the case of a lagged adjustment of output to demand and the case of an open economy. Alternatively (2.3) can be thought of as the special case of (3.1) in which $\beta = 0$ (instantaneous adjustment) and in which $M = 0$ (closed economy).

If the second approach were followed, a satisfactory replacement for $D_t = Y_t$ might be:

$$D_t = Y_t + M_t + U_t \tag{3.2}$$

where U denotes undesired real disinvestment in inventories. This relationship implies that if aggregate demand exceeds the sum of real domestic production and real imports, there will be an undesired real disinvestment in inventories (positive U) equal to the excess. On the other hand, if aggregate demand falls short of the sum of realised real domestic production and realised real imports, there will be an undesired real investment in inventories (negative U) equal to the deficiency.

Relationship (3.2) can be looked at in another way which is also helpful. By definition the variable U is given by:

$U =$ Realised real inventory disinvestment – Desired real inventory disinvestment

or

$U =$ Realised real inventory disinvestment + Desired real inventory investment.

It follows that (3.2) can be rewritten as:

$$D_t - I_t^i = Y_t + M_t + V_t \tag{3.3}$$

where I^i denotes desired real inventory investment and V denotes realised real inventory disinvestment. The implication of (3.3) is that the aggregate demand for final goods and services, other than for purposes of inventory accumulation, is always fully met – either from current domestic production or from imports or from a decumulation of inventories. In this sense there is never an unsatisfied demand for final goods and services.[1] This would appear to be an entirely reasonable proposition for an advanced industrial country like Britain, given normal peace-time conditions, though it would have been seriously at variance with the facts in Britain

[1] This does not mean that there is never *excess* demand, as will be clear from the definition of excess demand given in section 1.2.

during, and immediately after, the war and probably would not be valid for most undeveloped countries even under normal peace-time conditions.

Either of the relationships (3.1) and (3.2) is acceptable as a replacement for (2.3), but we shall use the latter in the models to be presented in this and the following two chapters.

The addition of (3.2) means that the variable M, which does not appear in Model II, is introduced. This variable should be treated as a jointly determined variable rather than as a datum, since there is an obvious two-way connection between M and other variables in the model, such as D and Y. However, to make this possible, we must introduce an additional relationship to explain M. We turn now to the task of developing such a relationship, drawing for the purpose on the main strands of thought which have appeared in the recent literature on the import function.

The use of (3.2) as a replacement for (2.3) brings in a second new variable, in addition to M, namely U (undesired real inventory disinvestment); this should also be treated as a jointly determined variable and in later models this will be done. For the time being, however, we shall treat U as a datum and place only M in the jointly determined category.

3.2 The Import Function

To develop a relationship which explains M (*realised* real imports), we shall proceed in two distinct stages. We shall begin by considering the determinants of *desired* real imports (M^*) and then consider what further explanatory variables need to be introduced to account for the behaviour of *realised* real imports (M).

We shall base our analysis of the determinants of *desired* real imports on the well-known distinction between importables, exportables and non-traded goods. Importables are goods which are imported and which may, or may not, be produced at home as well. For the United Kingdom, tea and motor-cars are examples of importables, the former being an importable which is imported but not produced at home, and the latter an importable which is both imported and produced domestically. Exportables are home-produced goods which are both sold at home and exported. In the case of the United Kingdom, machine tools and television equipment are exportables as are the services of actors and ballet dancers.

Obviously some goods will be *both* importables *and* exportables. For example, in the case of the United Kingdom, motor-cars fall into both categories. Finally, there are non-traded goods. As the name implies, these are goods which are excluded from trade altogether. Examples are housing, road construction and the services provided by public officials.

By definition desired real imports, or import demand, is the demand for importables *as a whole* less the demand for *home-produced* importables. Consequently we can deal with the problem of finding the determinants of desired real imports in two stages. We can begin by considering the determinants of the demand for importables as a whole and then go on to ask what determines the demand for home-produced importables, *given* the demand for importables as a whole. This we shall now do.

We begin with an obvious point, namely, that the demand for importables, like the demand for any other broad class of good, will be largely determined, in the short run, by the level of *aggregate* demand; an increase in aggregate demand will mean an increase, *ceteris paribus*, in the demand for importables, and vice versa.

The *structure* of aggregate demand, meaning by this the division of aggregate demand between the various broad social accounting categories, may also be relevant. Here all depends on whether there are significant differences between the 'importable contents' of the various categories, i.e. whether the value of importables required, directly and indirectly, in the satisfaction of £1 of government demand, say, differs significantly from the value required for the satisfaction of £1 of consumption demand. If such differences exist, then a mere *redistribution* of aggregate demand will produce a change in the demand for importables – either up or down according to the nature of the redistribution. Suppose, for example, that the importable content of government demand is substantially less than that of consumption demand. Then a short-run increase in the ratio between government demand and aggregate demand, offset by an equivalent decrease in the ratio of consumption demand to aggregate demand, would lead to a short-run decrease in the demand for importables, even if the level of aggregate demand were to remain unchanged.

Now one would expect the importable content of inventory investment to be a good deal higher than that of the other main components of aggregate demand, since inventory investment, unlike the other components of aggregate demand, will have a non-traded-goods component of virtually zero, non-traded goods being, by and large, unstorable. What figures there are for the British economy seem to bear this out. In conjunction with the considerations advanced in the preceding paragraph, this point suggests that the level of real inventory investment most probably plays an important part, along with the level of aggregate demand, in explaining short-run changes in the British demand for importables: the higher is real inventory investment, the higher, *ceteris paribus*, is the demand for importables likely to be, and vice versa.

It seems reasonable to suppose that, in the short run, the demand for importables will also depend to a significant extent on the price of importables, relative to the price of exportables and non-traded goods. The theory of consumer behaviour suggests that, *ceteris paribus*, a rise in the relative price of importable consumer goods will lead to some substitution of exportable and/or non-traded consumer goods for importables, and vice versa. Likewise production theory suggests that a rise in the relative price of importable raw materials will cause firms to substitute exportable and/or non-traded raw materials for importables, and vice versa. Hence one would expect that the higher the price of importables as a whole (consumer goods and raw materials combined) relative to the prices of exportables and non-traded goods, the lower the demand for importables, and vice versa.

So far we have been concerned with the determinants of the British demand for importables as a whole. We now ask: what determines the proportion of a *given* British demand for importables which is directed towards home production? The short answer is: the attractiveness of the terms offered to the British purchaser by British producers, relative to the attractiveness of the terms offered by foreign producers. The more attractive, relatively, are the terms offered by British producers, the higher will be the proportion of a given demand for importables which is directed towards British production, and hence the lower, *ceteris paribus*, will be the desired level of real imports, and vice versa.

If we confine our attention to the short run, we can say that 'the terms offered to the British purchaser' have three main elements, namely price, waiting-time for delivery, and credit terms.[1] Hence we

---

[1] If we were interested in the long run we would have to add several more dimensions, e.g. sales effort and after-sales servicing. Such things form an important part of the terms offered but are unlikely to vary substantially in the short run.

can expect that, *ceteris paribus*, the proportion of a given British demand for importables which is met from British production will rise in the short run (desired real imports will fall): (i) if the price of British-made importables falls relative to the price of foreign-made importables in terms of British currency; (ii) if the delivery delay applicable to British-made importables falls relative to the delivery delay applicable to foreign-made importables; and (iii) if the credit terms offered by British producers of importables become more generous relative to those offered by foreign producers, e.g. if the interest rates charged by British producers for trade credit fall relatively, or if the time given for payment is increased relatively.

The analysis presented so far can be summarised in two propositions as follows: (a) in the case of the British economy, the demand for importables as a whole will depend, in the short run, mainly on the level of aggregate demand, the level of real inventory investment and the price of importables relative to the prices of exportables and non-traded goods; (b) the proportion of a given demand for importables which is satisfied by British production will depend, in the short run, on the price of British-made importables relative to the price of foreign-made importables in terms of British currency, on the delivery delay quoted by British producers of importables relative to that quoted by foreign producers and on the relative generosity of the credit terms offered by British producers.

It will be recalled that our task in the present section is to develop a relationship which explains the short-run behaviour of M (realised real imports) for the British economy. Our approach to this task is, first, to list the main determinants of *desired* real imports (M^*) and, second, to consider what additional variables enter into the explanation of M. We have now completed the first of these two stages and we turn to the second.

We shall proceed as follows. First we shall introduce a variable which intervenes between M^* and M, namely the level of import orders M^{**}, and adopt three postulates relating to M^{**} which will enable us to write an expression for M^{**} in terms of M^* and then to convert this expression into an expression for M in terms of M^*. Finally we shall use the list of determinants of M^* just derived to obtain an expression for M in terms of its ultimate determinants.

The three postulates relating to M^{**} are:

   (i) The current level of import orders (M^{**}) depends on the level of import demand (M^*) in the current and all past quarters via a distributed-lag relationship in which the weights decline geometrically and sum to unity. This postulate corresponds to the postulate embodied in the demand–output relationship (3.1).

(ii) The current level of import orders also depends on the current intensity of direct controls over foreign transactions (e.g. import-licensing controls or restrictions on the availability of currency for foreign travel).

(iii) There is a one-quarter delay of import deliveries (M) behind import orders (M^{**}), i.e. it takes one quarter for a variation in the rate of import ordering to be reflected in a variation in the rate of import deliveries. This delay is to be thought of as a shipping delay.

From (i) and (ii) we get:

$$M_t^{**} = [(1-\gamma)\{M_t^* + \gamma M_{t-1}^* + \gamma^2 M_{t-2}^* + \ldots\}] + \rho \xi_t$$

where $0 < \gamma < 1$ and $\rho < 0$. The variable ξ is an indicator of the intensity of direct controls over foreign transactions which takes the value zero when there are no controls in force and becomes increasingly positive as the intensity of the controls increases. Thus, when direct controls are introduced, the variable ξ, in conjunction with the negative coefficient ρ, has the effect of reducing import orders below 'normal', i.e. below the level given by the term in square brackets, the amount of the reduction increasing with the intensity of the controls.

The immediately preceding expression gives:

$$M_t^{**} = \gamma M_{t-1}^{**} + (1-\gamma)M_t^* + \rho \xi_t - \gamma \rho \xi_{t-1}.$$

Also from (iii) we have:

$$M_{t+1} = M_t^{**} \quad \text{and} \quad M_t = M_{t-1}^{**}.$$

Hence we have:

$$M_{t+1} = \gamma M_t + (1-\gamma)M_t^* + \rho \xi_t - \gamma \rho \xi_{t-1}$$

which is equivalent to:

$$M_t = \gamma M_{t-1} + (1-\gamma)M_{t-1}^* + \rho \xi_{t-1} - \gamma \rho \xi_{t-2}.$$

Finally we make use of the argument of the first part of this section to eliminate M^* from the right-hand side of this expression. If we assume that M^* depends linearly on its determinants, as derived above, with a fixed delay of one quarter, we can write the last expression as:

$$M_t = \gamma M_{t-1} + (1-\gamma)[\epsilon_1 D_{t-2} + \epsilon_2 I^i_{t-2}] + Z^2$$

where I^i denotes desired real inventory investment, ϵ_1 and ϵ_2 are positive constants and Z^2 denotes a linear combination of the following variables:

(i) the indicator of the intensity of direct controls over foreign transactions, lagged one period and lagged two periods;

(ii) the price of importables relative to the prices of exportables and non-traded goods, lagged two periods;

(iii) the price of British-made importables relative to the price of foreign-made importables in terms of British currency, lagged two periods;

(iv) the delivery delay quoted by British producers of importables relative to that quoted by foreign producers, lagged two periods;

(v) the credit terms offered to British purchasers of importables by British producers relative to the credit terms offered by foreign producers, lagged two periods.

Thus in the α notation our import function is:

$$M_t = \alpha_{30} M_{t-1} + \alpha_{31} D_{t-2} + \alpha_{32} I^i_{t-2} + Z^2 \tag{3.4}$$

where $\alpha_{30} = \gamma$, $\alpha_{31} = (1-\gamma)\epsilon_1$, $\alpha_{32} = (1-\gamma)\epsilon_2$.

Z^2 will be treated as a datum throughout our sequence of models. The validity of this procedure will be examined in section 5.5. The comment concerning Z^1 made in section 2.4 applies to Z^2 also. Having decided to treat Z^2 as a datum, we need pay no further attention to its precise composition for the time being, though we shall have to do so both in section 5.5 and at certain points in Chapters 6 and 7.

The short-run behaviour of United Kingdom imports has recently been investigated by Godley and Shepherd.[1] Their study is a regression analysis, using quarterly data for the years 1955–64 in which the volume of imports into the United Kingdom is the dependent

[1] See W. A. H. Godley and J. R. Shepherd, 'Forecasting Imports', *National Institute Economic Review* (Aug 1965).

variable. Altogether ten regressions were fitted. The basic equation used was essentially (3.4)[1] and this gave very satisfactory results in the sense that the coefficients of both aggregate demand and real inventory investment were highly reliable statistically and had the right sign. Various modifications of the basic equation were also tried. In one set of four modifications some form of excess demand variable was introduced as an additional explanatory variable. In only one member of this set was the coefficient of the excess demand variable both statistically reliable and correct in terms of sign. In two cases the coefficient had the wrong sign but was not reliable, while in the fourth case the variable had a highly reliable coefficient of the wrong sign. The conclusion which the authors reached was that 'none of these equations suggested any significant tendency for the marginal import propensity to rise when the pressure of demand was high'.[2] In another experiment the basic relationship was modified by the introduction of each of the main components of the aggregate demand variable into the regression separately. The purpose of this was to allow for the possibility of differences in the import contents of the various demand components, other than the one allowed for by the introduction of I^i. However, no very firm conclusions could be drawn from this experiment because of the unreliability of the coefficients of the individual demand components; as one would expect, the high degree of intercorrelation between the various components made it impossible to isolate their separate contributions with any precision. Finally two regressions were run with I^i disaggregated. Broadly speaking, it was found that disaggregation along these lines did little to improve the explanation of aggregate import volume.

It would seem, therefore, that the empirical work of Godley and Shepherd provides strong support for the use of (3.4) in a short-run, macro-dynamic model of the British economy.

[1] See W. A. H. Godley and J. R. Shepherd, 'Forecasting Imports', *National Institute Economic Review* (Aug 1965) Table 1, p. 36. The equation referred to is equation (2) of Table 1. This is identical with (3.4) except that: (i) $(D - I^i)$ and I^i are used as explanatory variables instead of M, D and I^i; (ii) an additional explanatory variable is introduced merely to take care of an inadequacy in the series used for D, namely, that the expenditure estimate of gross domestic product (the series used) invariably differs from the income and output estimates; and (iii) a time trend is introduced to take care of the variables which cause the import function to shift over time – the variables which in our formulation are absorbed in Z^2.

[2] Ibid., p. 37.

3.3 The Dynamic Properties of Model III

Our third-stage model, to be identified from now on as Model III, may now be set down as follows:

Desired Consumption Expenditure
$$C_t = \alpha_{10}X_t + \alpha_{11}C_{t-1} + Z^1 \qquad (2.24)$$

Disposable Income
$$X_t = \alpha_{20} + \alpha_{21}Y_t \qquad (2.26)$$

Components of Aggregate Demand
$$D_t = C_t + A_t \qquad (2.2)$$

Demand–Output Relationship
$$D_t = Y_t + M_t + U_t \qquad (3.2)$$

Realised Imports
$$M_t = \alpha_{30}M_{t-1} + \alpha_{31}D_{t-2} + \alpha_{32}I^i_{t-2} + Z^2 \qquad (3.4)$$

The jointly determined variables are C, X, D, Y and M, while the data of the model are Z^1, A, U, I^i and Z^2. The variables A, U and I^i are 'temporary' data only; in due course we shall extend the model to permit them to be transferred from the category of data to the category of jointly determined variables.

To examine the dynamic properties of Model III, we first reduce the model by substitution. The first three relationships of the model yield the following:

$$D_t = \alpha_{10}(\alpha_{20} + \alpha_{21}Y_t) + \alpha_{11}(D_{t-1} - A_{t-1}) + Z^1 + A_t.$$

With the help of (3.2) we can eliminate Y_t from this expression to get:

$$D_t(1 - \alpha_{10}\alpha_{21}) - \alpha_{11}D_{t-1} + \alpha_{10}\alpha_{21}M_t = \alpha_{10}\alpha_{20} + A_t - \alpha_{11}A_{t-1}$$
$$- \alpha_{10}\alpha_{21}U_t + Z^1.$$

If we now add (3.4) to this expression, our model becomes:

$$D_t(1 - \alpha_{10}\alpha_{21}) - \alpha_{11}D_{t-1} + \alpha_{10}\alpha_{21}M_t = k_1 \qquad (3.5)$$

$$M_t - \alpha_{30}M_{t-1} - \alpha_{31}D_{t-2} = k_2 \qquad (3.6)$$

where k_1 denotes $[\alpha_{10}\alpha_{20} + A_t - \alpha_{11}A_{t-1} - \alpha_{10}\alpha_{21}U_t + Z^1]$ and k_2 denotes $[\alpha_{32}I_{t-2}^i + Z^2]$.

Relationships (3.5) and (3.6) constitute a system of two difference equations in D and M. By using (3.5) to obtain expressions for M_t and M_{t-1} in terms of D_t, D_{t-1} and D_{t-2} and then substituting these expressions into (3.6), one could reduce this system of two difference equations in D and M to a single, second-order difference equation in D. If this were done it would then be possible to analyse the dynamic properties of Model III in the same way as Model II, i.e. by cataloguing every type of dynamic behaviour permitted by the model and the conditions under which each possible behaviour type would emerge. However, we shall not proceed this far. Instead we shall be content with a less general analysis of the type that we shall be forced to employ for the more elaborate models to be presented in later chapters. The structure of these models is such that they cannot be reduced beyond a simultaneous system of difference equations and, as a result, a dynamic analysis of the exhaustive type employed in connection with Model II, will not be feasible. An alternative form of analysis, where a system of difference equations is involved, is to convert the model into numerical form by inserting values for the parameters and then to deduce the character of the time path which, eventually, the numerical system will follow, when started up by arbitrary initial conditions. This is the procedure which we shall use for the later models and we shall now apply it to Model III also.

Lacking econometric estimates for the parameters of the model we shall give them values which seem plausible in the light of the argument used to derive the relationships in which they appear. The parameter values to be used in the dynamic analysis of Model III are: $\alpha_{10}=0\cdot3$; $\alpha_{11}=0\cdot5$; $\alpha_{21}=0\cdot08$; $\alpha_{30}=0\cdot1$; $\alpha_{31}=0\cdot2$. The interested reader will find a comment on the reason for choosing these values in Appendix 5.1.

Given these values of the parameters, the numerical form of Model III is:

$$0\cdot976\,D_t - 0\cdot5\,D_{t-1} + 0\cdot024\,M_t = k_1 \tag{3.7}$$

$$M_t - 0\cdot1\,M_{t-1} - 0\cdot2\,D_{t-2} = k_2. \tag{3.8}$$

[1] For further discussion of dynamic analysis in the simultaneous difference-equation case, see A. S. Goldberger, *Impact Multipliers and Dynamic Properties of the Klein–Goldberger Model* (Amsterdam: North-Holland Publishing Company, 1959) chap. vi.

Details of the solution of this numerical system are set out in Appendix 3.1. The solutions are:

$$D_t = A_{11}(0 \cdot 500)^t + A_{12}(0 \cdot 112)^t + \bar{D}_t \qquad (3.9)$$

$$M_t = A_{21}(0 \cdot 500)^t + A_{22}(0 \cdot 112)^t + \bar{M}_t \qquad (3.10)$$

where $\bar{D}_t$ and $\bar{M}_t$ are the two particular solutions which can be given specific form once time paths have been specified for k_1 and k_2 and where the As are arbitrary constants which can be evaluated once the appropriate initial conditions are specified.

It follows from these expressions that, in the case of Model III, both aggregate demand and real imports will follow a path of monotonic convergence on the equilibrium paths defined by $\bar{D}_t$ and $\bar{M}_t$, respectively, in response to arbitrary initial conditions.

It is of interest to note that, given the values of α_{10}, α_{11} and α_{21} used in the analysis of Model III, the expression $\alpha_{11}/(1 - \alpha_{10}\alpha_{21})$ $= 0 \cdot 512$. Thus, given these values, the time path followed by Model II in response to arbitrary initial conditions is also one of monotonic convergence on the equilibrium path.

3.4 The Export Function

In section 2.2 we listed the main deficiencies of our basic expository model and undertook to remove them one by one in the following chapters. We have now gone some way towards honouring this undertaking in that we have replaced the primitive Keynesian consumption function of Model I (relationship (2.1)) with a more sophisticated relationship based on the results of recent consumption function studies, and the demand–output relationship (relationship (2.3)) with a relationship which is free from the difficulties surrounding (2.3). In the course of making these changes we have introduced two new variables which it seems appropriate to regard as jointly determined variables (variables determined by the model) rather than as data, namely real disposable income and real imports, and we have developed two entirely new relationships ((2.26) and (3.4)) to make this possible.

Despite these improvements, however, the model is still defective because it treats all demand other than consumption demand as a datum. While it may be legitimate to treat some parts of non-consumption demand in this way, there are important components of this aggregate which should be treated, like consumption demand, as jointly determined variables, rather than as variables which are determined outside the model.

What remains to be done, therefore, is to develop relationships which will enable us to transfer non-consumption demand (or at least some parts of it) from the data category to the jointly-determined-variable category. As a first step in this direction, we now extend the definitional relationship (2.2) by breaking up the variable A. The extended relationship is:

$$D_t = C_t + G_t + E_t + I_t$$
$$= C_t + G_t + E_t + (I_t^{gf} + I_t^{gh} + I_t^{ri} + I_t^{ei}) \qquad (3.11)$$

where G denotes desired real government expenditure (government demand), E desired real expenditure by overseas entities (export demand) and I desired real investment expenditure (investment demand) consisting of:

- (i) I^{gf} – desired real expenditure on new fixed-capital equipment (desired real gross fixed-capital investment);
- (ii) I^{gh} – desired real expenditure on new housing (desired real gross housing investment);
- (iii) I^{ri} – desired real expenditure on accumulation of inventories of raw materials and work-in-progress (desired real investment in inventories of raw materials and work-in-progress);
- (iv) I^{ci} – desired real expenditure on accumulation of inventories of finished goods (desired real investment in inventories of finished goods).

In the chapters which follow, we shall develop a series of relationships explaining the four components of I which will enable us to treat the variable I as a jointly determined variable. In the course of carrying out this programme we shall give an account of recent work on the investment function, an area in which progress has been especially rapid in recent years.

The remaining two components of A (G and E) we have decided to treat as data throughout the series of models to be presented in the next two chapters. As far as G is concerned, we shall postpone discussion of the legitimacy of this decision until section 5.5, in line with the practice we have adopted up till now. In the case of E, however, it will be more convenient to deal with the question at this point because the argument of section 3.2 is decidedly relevant to the issue.

In section 5.5 we shall propose a rule or principle for deciding which variables can be properly treated as data and which must be treated as jointly determined variables. This principle is to the effect that it is proper to treat a variable as a datum provided its connection with the jointly determined variables of the model is one-way, or virtually so, i.e. provided the potential datum influences other variables in the model but is not, in turn, influenced by them. In the case of E, an obvious way of applying this principle is to develop an export function for the British economy, using the argument of section 3.2 as a foundation, and then to examine the explanatory variables in this function to see whether there is likely to be any significant feedback to E, via these variables, from the jointly determined variables of Model III. This we shall now do.

The variable E can be regarded as the *rest-of-the-world demand* for imports *from Britain* less any part of this demand which is suppressed by such direct controls over foreign transactions as are in force in the rest of the world. This being so, we should be able to explain E by adapting the analysis of the *British demand* for imports *from the rest of the world* presented in section 3.2. On this basis we reach the conclusion that the main explanatory variables in a function explaining E for the British economy will be: (i) the level of aggregate demand in the rest of the world; (ii) the level of real inventory investment in the rest of the world; (iii) the price of importables in the rest of the world relative to the prices of exportables and non-traded goods; (iv) the price of importables made in the rest of the world relative to the price of importables made in Britain; (v) the delivery delay and credit terms quoted by rest-of-the-world producers of importables relative to those quoted by British producers. These variables between them account for the rest-of-the-world demand for imports from Britain (see p. 73 above). To them must be added a further variable designed to take care of the possibility that some of this demand may be suppressed. This further variable would be: (vi) some indicator of the intensity of direct controls over foreign transactions in force in the rest of the world.

We must now consider whether there is likely to be any significant feedback from Y, D, M, C and X (the jointly determined variables of Model III) to E via these explanatory variables. To the extent that such a two-way connection exists, the case for treating E as a datum is weakened.

It would seem that the feedback via explanatory variables (i), (ii), (iii) and (vi) will be extremely slight – so slight that it can be safely ignored. However, the same cannot be said for explanatory variables (iv) and (v). As we shall see in Chapter 9, the prices of British-made products in general depend closely on D (the level of aggregate demand in Britain). The same is true of the delivery delay quoted by British producers. This being so, there is bound to be a significant feedback to E from the jointly determined variables of Model III, via variables (iv) and (v). Thus our decision to treat E as a datum is not fully justified. It would have been more appropriate, perhaps, to treat E as a jointly determined variable, to introduce an export function containing the explanatory variables listed above, and finally to introduce additional relationships to permit the treatment as, jointly determined variables, of British prices and British delivery delays. We have avoided this more satisfactory approach partly in the interests of manageability and partly because we wish to postpone all discussion of the determinants of British prices until a later stage of the book.

The basis of the above discussion was a function explaining foreign demand for British exports as a whole. It is of interest to note that Steuer, Ball and Eaton have recently employed a function of a broadly similar character in an attempt to explain the foreign demand for *one important class* of British exports, namely machine tools.[1] Their study is a regression analysis using quarterly data. The dependent variable was either foreign orders for British machine tools or the ratio of foreign orders to the total foreign demand for British machine tools, while the explanatory variables were drawn from the following: (i) the total foreign demand for machine tools; (ii) the prices of British, West German and United States machine tools, respectively;[2] (iii) the waiting-times (time elapsing between placing of order and delivery of products) experienced by foreign purchasers of British, West German and United States machine tools, respectively; and (iv) the foreign orders for British machine tools in the immediate past.

A large number of regressions (the exact total is not reported) were fitted between these variables using a variety of time lags and a variety of forms for the relationships, using both current-price and constant-price series for foreign orders of British machine tools and

[1] See M. D. Steuer, R. J. Ball and J. R. Eaton, 'The Effect of Waiting Times on Foreign Orders for Machine Tools', *Economica* (Nov 1966).

[2] West German and United States producers of machine tools are effectively the rest-of-the-world producers of machine tools from the point of view of the United Kingdom. Ibid., p. 390.

total foreign demand for machine tools, and using relationships with, and without, a time trend.[1] Two major results emerge from these regressions. The first is that waiting-times in the United Kingdom and in competitor countries (particularly West Germany) appear to be highly important influences on the short-run behaviour of foreign orders for British machine tools; and the second is 'the failure of prices to make any contribution to the explanation of the flow of new orders for machine tools coming to the U.K.'.[2]

Two comments on these results are in order. In the first place, the poor performance of the price variables does not necessarily mean that relative prices are an unimportant short-run influence on the flow of foreign orders for British machine tools. The price series used in the regressions exhibit virtually no short-run movement and hence the price variables would have been bound to appear as insignificant in the regressions even if, in fact, they are highly important in the real world. In other words, the poor performance of the price variables may simply reflect the lack of short-run movement in the price series during the sample period rather than the insignificance of price as an explanatory variable.[3]

Secondly, suppose that the flow of foreign orders for British machine tools does, in fact, increase whenever the waiting-time experienced by foreign purchasers falls, as suggested by the regressions. This does not necessarily mean that British export demand *as a whole* will also increase. The reason is that the waiting-time experienced by *British* purchasers of British machine tools may *increase* because of the diversion of machine-tool capacity from the home to the foreign market. If this happens there may well be a deterioration in the export performance of those British producers of exportables who use British-made machine tools, to offset the improvement in the export performance of the machine-tool industry itself. Consequently the export performance of British industry as a whole may not improve at all when the waiting-time experienced by foreign purchasers of machine tools falls.[4]

3.5 Summary

One of the defects of the basic expository model (Model I) which is carried over into Model II is that it postulates an instantaneous

---

[1] Ibid., p. 394.   [2] Ibid., p. 395.   [3] Ibid., p. 396.
[4] This point is recognised by Steuer, Ball and Eaton on p. 401.

adjustment of output to demand. We begin the present chapter by removing this defect. Two relationships are presented as possible replacements for the instantaneous-adjustment relationship of Model II. One of these specifies the structure of the lag of output behind demand. The other specifies the way in which, and the extent to which, discrepancies between demand and output are eliminated, while leaving open the precise form of the lag structure. The second is the one finally chosen, though both are satisfactory.

The new relationship introduces the variable M (realised real imports) and the variable U (undesired real inventory disinvestment), neither of which appears in Model II. We decide to treat M as a jointly determined variable in the third-stage model and to make this possible we develop a relationship to explain M. On the other hand, we decide to treat the variable U as a datum in the third-stage model on the understanding that it will be transferred to the jointly determined category, where it belongs, in a later model.

To develop our import function we first consider the determinants of *desired* real imports (M^*). Here our approach is to analyse the determinants of the British demand for importables as a whole (British-produced and foreign-produced) and then to analyse the forces which determine the proportion of this total British demand for importables which is satisfied by foreign production. We then use our list of the determinants of M^* to develop a function which explains M. The import function which is formulated on the basis of these ideas is one in which the current flow of imports in real terms is explained by: (i) the import flow of the previous period; (ii) the level of aggregate demand and the level of desired real inventory investment, two periods previously; (iii) the price of importables relative to the prices of exportables and non-traded goods, the intensity of direct controls over foreign transactions, and several other variables which reflect the relative attractiveness of the terms offered to the British purchaser by British producers of importables.

Our third-stage model (Model III) is formed by removing relationship (2.3) from Model II and replacing it with the demand–output relationship referred to at the beginning of this summary, together with the import function referred to in the previous paragraph. This model reduces to a system of two difference equations in aggregate demand and real imports. On solving this system we find that aggregate demand and real imports will follow a path of monotonic convergence on their equilibrium paths in response to arbitrary initial conditions – a type of dynamic behaviour which is permitted by Model II also.

READING LIST

Adler, J. H., 'United States Import Demand during the Inter-War Period', *American Economic Review* (June 1945).

Ball, R. J., and Marwah, K., 'The U.S. Demand for Imports, 1948–1958', *Review of Economics and Statistics* (Nov 1962).

Chang, T. C., 'The British Demand for Imports in the Inter-War Period', *Economic Journal* (June 1946).

——, 'International Comparison of Demand for Imports', *Review of Economic Studies* (1945–6).

Godley, W. A. H., and Shepherd, J. R., 'Forecasting Imports', *National Institute Economic Review* (Aug 1965).

Goldberger, A. S., *Impact Multipliers and Dynamic Properties of the Klein–Goldberger Model* (Amsterdam: North-Holland Publishing Company, 1959).

Harberger, A. C. 'A Structural Approach to the Problem of Import Demand', *American Economic Association, Papers and Proceedings of the Sixty-Fifth Annual Meeting, American Economic Review*, XLIII (1953), and comments on above by Adler, J. H.

Kemp, M. C., *The Demand for Canadian Imports, 1926–55* (University of Toronto Press, 1962).

Krause, L. B., 'United States Imports, 1947–1958' *Econometrica* (Apr 1962).

Scott, M. F., *A Study of United Kingdom Imports* (Cambridge University Press 1963).

Steuer, M. D., Ball, R. J., and Eaton, J. R., 'The Effect of Waiting Times on Foreign Orders for Machine Tools', *Economica* (Nov 1966).

Appendix 3.1

SOLUTION OF MODEL III

In this appendix we shall first explain the general procedure for solving a system of m linear difference equations in m jointly determined variables $y_1 \ldots y_m$. We shall then apply this procedure to Model III to obtain the solutions for D and M presented in the text.

We begin by setting out the general linear difference-equation system in matrix-operator form as follows:

$$
\begin{bmatrix}
P_{11}(E) & P_{12}(E) & \ldots P_{1\,m}(E) \\
P_{21}(E) & P_{22}(E) & \ldots P_{2\,m}(E) \\
\vdots & \vdots & \vdots \\
P_{m1}(E) & P_{m2}(E) & P_{mm}(E)
\end{bmatrix}
\begin{bmatrix}
y_{1t} \\
y_{2t} \\
\vdots \\
y_{mt}
\end{bmatrix}
=
\begin{bmatrix}
k_1 \\
k_2 \\
\vdots \\
k_m
\end{bmatrix}
\qquad (3.1.1)
$$

Each of the elements in the $(m \times m)$ matrix on the left-hand side of (3.1.1) is a polynomial in E where E is the shift operator, i.e. $E(y_{it}) = y_{i(t-1)}$, $E^2(y_{it}) = y_{i(t-2)}$ and so on. For example, if we treat D as y_1 and M as y_2 in the system of two linear difference equations represented by (3.7) and (3.8), the four elements in the matrix in question would be:

$$P_{11}(E) = 0.976 - 0.5E \qquad P_{12}(E) = 0.024$$
$$P_{21}(E) = -0.2E^2 \qquad P_{22}(E) = 1 - 0.1E.$$

Each of the elements in the $(m \times 1)$ column vector on the right-hand side of (3.1.1) is an expression involving only parameters of the system and variables which it has been decided to treat as data.

To facilitate manipulation by (3.1.1) we shall denote the $(m \times m)$ matrix on the left-hand side of $P(E)$, the $(m \times 1)$ column vector on the left-hand side by y and the $(m \times 1)$ column vector on the right-hand side by k. Then (3.1.1) can be written as:

$$P(E)y = k. \tag{3.1.2}$$

Premultiplying (3.1.2) by $P(E)^{-1}$ we get:

$$y = P(E)^{-1}k. \tag{3.1.3}$$

Using the definition of an inverse we can rewrite (3.1.3) as:

$$y = |P(E)|^{-1}P^*(E)k \tag{3.1.4}$$

where $P^*(E)$ is the adjoint of $P(E)$. Next, multiplying (3.1.4) through by $|P(E)|$, we get:

$$|P(E)|y = P^*(E)k. \tag{3.1.5}$$

Using the definition of a determinant and the fact that the E operator obeys the ordinary rules of algebra, we can write the determinant $|P(E)|$ as a polynomial in E of degree n, the value of n depending on the degree of each of the various polynomials in E which constitute the elements of $P(E)$. That is:

$$|P(E)| = a_0 + a_1E + a_2E^2 + \ldots + a_nE^n \tag{3.1.6}$$

where $a_0 \ldots a_n$ are a set of constants. Hence (3.1.5) can be written as:

$$(a_0 + a_1E + a_2E^2 + \ldots + a_nE^n)y = P^*(E)k. \tag{3.1.7}$$

To see the significance of these manipulations we shall now write (3.1.7) out in full as follows:

$$\begin{aligned}
a_0y_{1t} + a_1y_{1(t-1)} + a_2y_{1(t-2)} + \ldots + a_ny_{1(t-n)} &= k_1^* \\
a_0y_{2t} + a_1y_{2(t-1)} + a_2y_{2(t-2)} + \ldots + a_ny_{2(t-n)} &= k_2^* \\
&\vdots \\
a_0y_{mt} + a_1y_{m(t-1)} + a_2y_{m(t-2)} + \ldots + a_ny_{m(t-n)} &= k_m^*
\end{aligned} \tag{3.1.8}$$

In this expression k_i^* is given by:

$$k_i^* = \sum_{j=1}^{m} P_{ij}^* k_j$$

where P_{ij}^* is the cofactor of the element $P_{ij}(E)$ of $P(E)$. That is, k_i^* is a term involving only parameters of the difference-equation system and current and lagged values of the data.

Now the first of the m expressions in (3.1.8) can be seen to be a linear non-homogeneous difference equation of order n in y_1 alone, the second a linear non-homogeneous difference equation of order n in y_2 alone, and so on. Thus from the ith member of (3.1.8) we can obtain the solution of the difference-equation system (3.1.1) for y_i by standard methods. That is, we have merely to find the roots of the characteristic equation:

$$a_0 x^n + a_1 x^{n-1} + \ldots + a_n = 0 \qquad (3.1.9)$$

and then find the particular solution by specifying a time path for k_i^* on the basis of specified time paths for the data of (3.1.1). The solution for y_i will then take the form:

$$y_{it} = A_{i1}(x_1)^t + A_{i2}(x_2)^t + \ldots + A_{in}(x_n)^t + \bar{y}_{it} \qquad (3.1.10)$$

where $x_1 \ldots x_n$ are the roots of (3.1.9), $\bar{y}_{it}$ is the particular solution and $A_{i1} \ldots A_{in}$ are arbitrary constants to be determined by the specified initial conditions.

Two points which emerge from this discussion should be noted. The first is that since all of the nth-order difference equations in (3.1.8) have the same set of coefficients, they will also have the same characteristic equation, i.e. (3.1.9). Hence the solutions will differ only as regards the particular solutions and the arbitrary As.

Secondly, by comparing (3.1.9) with (3.1.6) we see that the common characteristic equation is, in effect, obtained from $|P(E)|$ simply by replacing a_r with $a_{n-r}(r = 0, 1, \ldots, n)$, substituting x for E and equating the result to zero.

We shall now apply this general procedure to Model III to obtain the solutions for D and M.

We first write the difference-equation system given by (3.7) and (3.8) in matrix operator form as:

$$\begin{bmatrix} \{0 \cdot 976 - 0 \cdot 5E\} & 0 \cdot 024 \\ -0 \cdot 2E^2 & \{1 - 0 \cdot 1E\} \end{bmatrix} \begin{bmatrix} D_t \\ M_t \end{bmatrix} = \begin{bmatrix} k_1 \\ k_2 \end{bmatrix}$$

We next evaluate $|P(E)|$. We have:

$$|P(E)| = \begin{vmatrix} \{0 \cdot 976 - 0 \cdot 5E\} & 0 \cdot 024 \\ -0 \cdot 2E^2 & \{1 - 0 \cdot 1E\} \end{vmatrix} = 0 \cdot 0548E^2 - 0 \cdot 5976E + 0 \cdot 976.$$

Next we use this expression to form the common characteristic equation. This is:

$$0 \cdot 976x^2 - 0 \cdot 5976x + 0 \cdot 0548 = 0.$$

The roots of this equation are:

$$x_1 = \frac{0 \cdot 5976 + \sqrt{[(0 \cdot 5976)^2 - 0 \cdot 2139]}}{2(0 \cdot 976)} = 0 \cdot 500$$

$$x_2 = \frac{0 \cdot 5976 - \sqrt{[(0 \cdot 5976)^2 - 0 \cdot 2139]}}{2(0 \cdot 976)} = 0 \cdot 112.$$

Hence the solutions of the system given by (3.7) and (3.8) are:

$$D_t = A_{11}(0\cdot500)^t + A_{12}(0\cdot112)^t + \bar{D}_t$$
$$M_t = A_{21}(0\cdot500)^t + A_{22}(0\cdot112)^t + \bar{M}_t$$

where $\bar{D}_t$ and $\bar{M}_t$ are the two particular solutions which can be given specific form once time paths have been specified for k_1 and k_2 and where the As are arbitrary constants which can be evaluated once the appropriate initial conditions are specified.

4 The Fixed-capital and Housing Investment Functions

4.1 The Acceleration Principle

In this chapter we shall develop a fixed-capital investment function and a housing investment function. This will enable us to treat two of the components of I which appear in relationship (3.11), namely I^{gf} (desired real gross fixed-capital investment) and I^{gh} (desired real gross housing investment), as jointly determined variables rather than as data and thereby to remedy, to some extent, the weaknesses which remain in Model III. We shall turn to the remaining components of I (I^{ri} and I^{ci}) in the next chapter.

The first two sections of the present chapter will be devoted to a discussion of the fixed-capital investment function and the third section to a discussion of the housing investment function. In the final section we shall reformulate Model III in the light of our discussion and examine the dynamic properties of the new model using a procedure similar to that already applied to Model III.

The fixed-capital investment function which we shall present in the next section will be based largely on recent work by Jorgenson[1] and will be preceded by a discussion of his approach. Since this derives ultimately from the acceleration principle, it may be helpful to begin with a brief account of the arguments underlying the acceleration principle in its simplest form and the main limitations of this relationship as a fixed-capital investment function.

The foundation of the acceleration principle is the idea that, for

[1] The main references are: D. W. Jorgenson, 'Capital Theory and Investment Behaviour', *American Economic Review* (May 1963); D. W. Jorgenson, 'Anticipations and Investment Behaviour', in J. S. Duesenberry, E. Kuh, G. Fromm and L. R. Klein (eds), *The Brookings Quarterly Econometric Model of the United States* (Chicago: Rand-McNally, 1965); D. W. Jorgenson and J. A. Stephenson, 'The Time Structure of Investment Behaviour in United States Manufacturing, 1947–1960', *Review of Economics and Statistics* (Feb. 1967); D. W. Jorgenson and J. A. Stephenson, 'Investment Behaviour in U.S. Manufacturing, 1947–1960', *Econometrica* (Apr 1967).

D

each firm, there is a particular capital stock which is optimum. The problem of deriving the conditions for optimality of the capital stock can be approached in various ways.[1] However, regardless of the approach adopted, the conclusion which emerges is that the firm's optimum capital stock is a function of output and several other variables including the cost of finance to the firm and the business-tax structure. In the usual formulation of the acceleration principle all variables other than output are treated as data so that the optimum capital stock becomes a function of output alone. Finally, the function linking the optimum capital stock with output is given a very simple form: the optimum capital stock is made proportional to output.[2] Thus for the individual firm we have:

$$\bar{k}_t = \beta y_{t-1}$$

where $\bar{k}_t$ is the optimum *real* capital stock of the firm at the beginning of period t (or the end of period $(t-1)$), y_{t-1} the *real* output of the firm in period $(t-1)$ and β is some constant. It should be noted that since $\bar{k}$ is a stock, expressed in £s, and y is a flow, expressed in £s per unit of time, the constant β will be expressed in time units. Thus it differs from the marginal propensity to consume, for example, which is a pure number.

Next it is assumed that the real stock of fixed-capital equipment *actually held* by the firm at the beginning of any period is identical with the optimum stock as at the beginning of the preceding period. This assumption can be expressed as:

$$k_t = \bar{k}_{t-1}$$

where k denotes the actual real fixed-capital stock. Thus, the excess of the optimum over the actual capital stock as at the beginning of the period is given by:

$$\bar{k}_t - k_t = \bar{k}_t - \bar{k}_{t-1} = \beta(y_{t-1} - y_{t-2}).$$

It is assumed, further, that the firm will try to eliminate the whole of this excess during the period. Hence we have:

$$\Delta \bar{k}_t = \beta(y_{t-1} - y_{t-2})$$

---

[1] See, for example, D. W. Jorgenson, 'Anticipations and Investment Behaviour', *op. cit.*, pp. 43–6, and L. M. Koyck, *Distributed Lags and Investment Analysis* (Amsterdam: North-Holland Publishing Co., 1954) pp. 48–73.

[2] The optimum capital stock will be proportional to output, *ceteris paribus*, if the optimum stock is defined as that which maximises net worth subject to a Cobb-Douglas production function. Cf. Jorgenson, 'Anticipations and Investment Behaviour', *op. cit.*, p. 53.

where $\Delta \bar{k}$ denotes the increase in the real fixed-capital stock which is desired between the beginning and the end of the period.

Now, by definition, desired real *net* fixed-capital expenditure is the desired increase in the real capital stock per unit of time. Thus:

$$i_t^{nf} = \frac{\Delta \bar{k}_t}{d} = \frac{\beta}{d}(y_{t-1} - y_{t-2}) = \beta'(y_{t-1} - y_{t-2})$$

where i^{nf} denotes the firm's desired real net fixed-capital expenditure and d the number of time units covered by the period. Since β is expressed in time units, β' must be a pure number whose value varies inversely with the length of the period. For example, suppose that the time unit is taken as one year and that β has a value of four years. Then if the period is one quarter, d would be $\frac{1}{4}$ years and β' would be 16. On the other hand if the period is taken as one year, then d would be one year and β' would be 4. β' is called the 'accelerator' or the 'acceleration coefficient'.

Finally it is assumed that when

$$i_t^{nf} = \beta'(y_{t-1} - y_{t-2})$$

is summed over all firms, a relationship of the same form is obtained for the economy as a whole. Thus we have:

$$I_t^{nf} = v(Y_{t-1} - Y_{t-2})$$

where I^{nf} denotes aggregate desired real *net* fixed-capital investment and where v is a constant – the overall acceleration coefficient. This relationship is called the 'acceleration principle'.

It is clear from this summary of the underlying argument that the acceleration principle is subject to several limitations. To begin with, the basic micro-argument makes use of two highly restrictive assumptions. The first is that the capital stock actually held by the firm at the beginning of the period is optimum in relation to the output of the period before last, i.e. $k_t = \bar{k}_{t-1} = \beta y_{t-2}$. There is, of course, no reason why this should be so; and if it is not so the excess of the optimum over the actual capital stock as at the beginning of the period will no longer be given, as supposed, by the expression:

$$\bar{k}_t - k_t = \beta(y_{t-1} - y_{t-2}).$$

The point is best elaborated with the help of a diagram. In Fig. 4.1 the real stock of fixed-capital equipment held by the firm at the beginning of a period is measured vertically and its real output in the previous period horizontally. The constant β is represented by the slope of the line OF. Hence along OF the firm's capital stock at the beginning of the period will be optimum in relation to its output in

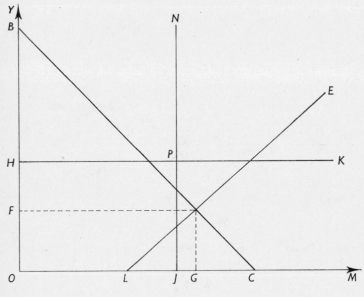

Fig. 4.1

the previous period. Let OB represent y_{t-2} and OD represent y_{t-1}, so that $BD = y_{t-1} - y_{t-2}$. Suppose that at the beginning of period $(t-1)$ the firm's capital stock (k_{t-1}) is not optimum in relation to the output of period $(t-2)$, as assumed by the acceleration principle. To be specific, suppose that k_{t-1} is represented by OA so that the firm has excess capacity of CE at the beginning of period $(t-1)$. In this case, the excess of the optimum stock over the actual stock at the beginning of period t will not be $GL (= \beta BD)$ as assumed by the acceleration principle. On the contrary, the firm will still have excess capacity of GH and will have no incentive to add to its capital stock despite the increase in output.

The second highly restrictive assumption used in the underlying micro-argument is that the whole of the excess of the optimum over the actual capital stock, as at the beginning of the period, will be eliminated immediately, i.e. during the period. However, this represents a most unlikely response on the part of the firm, especially if the period is as short as a quarter or a month. Some minor items of equipment may well be purchased and installed as soon as the increase in output occurs. But in the case of large items of equipment there will probably be some delay before even the final decision to purchase is made, particularly if there is no reasonable certainty that the increase in output is permanent. And once the order for the new equipment has been placed, there is likely to be a further delay while it is constructed and installed. Where the increase in the capital stock includes new buildings as well as new equipment there is the further point that a considerable time will have to be spent in detailed planning before the actual construction of the building can begin.

In addition to these technical reasons, there are good financial reasons why any increase in the capital stock should be widely distributed over time, particularly in the case of small firms. There are three main sources of finance for a firm which wishes to increase its capital stock: (i) funds accumulated from past profits; (ii) funds obtained by borrowing; and (iii) funds obtained by the issue of new shares. For a small firm both (ii) and (iii) suffer from definite limitations. A small firm may well find it difficult to borrow on any terms, particularly if the loan would lead to a substantial increase in its financial leverage or gearing; and, in any case, it may hesitate to use this source of finance unless it feels confident of maintaining the current rate of profit. A new issue of shares may also be difficult for a small firm since the investing public is likely to be both suspicious and ill informed about its profit prospects. Moreover a new share issue may seem unattractive to the existing shareholders if it means a weakening of their hold over the management of the firm, as is particularly likely in the case of a small family firm. For these reasons small firms tend to rely fairly heavily on internally accumulated funds as a source of finance for capital expansion. But this means that, in many instances, an immediate expansion of the firm's capital stock in response to an increase in output will be financially impossible because the funds accumulated from past profits are insufficient to permit it. Even if it wishes otherwise, the firm will have little choice but to undertake the expansion bit by bit as profits are made and the necessary funds accumulated in the shape of depreciation allowances and undistributed profits.

Thus, if an increase in the firm's capital stock does result from an increase in its output, the increase is unlikely to be immediate, as the acceleration principle implies, or even approximately so. Given that the period of the model is short, it is reasonable to suppose that any increase in the capital stock will be spread over many future periods.

So far we have been concentrating on those limitations of the acceleration principle which are inherent in its micro-foundation. A further limitation is inherent in the aggregation of the individual relationships. The acceleration principle assumes that, given a relationship of proportionality at the micro-level, there will also be a relationship of proportionality at the macro-level. But this will be the case only (i) if all firms have the same acceleration coefficient (i.e. have the same capital–output ratio); or (ii) if the distribution of output between firms remains fixed over time.[1] It seems unlikely that either of these conditions will be met.

A fourth limitation of the acceleration principle is that it may be impossible for it to work when real gross domestic product is falling. To pursue this point it is necessary to recall that, by definition, aggregate *net* fixed-capital expenditure is aggregate *gross* fixed-capital expenditure (the aggregate expenditure undertaken on currently produced capital goods) *less* the portion of the gross figure

[1] To see this, take the case of two firms, to be distinguished by means of the superscripts a and b. Then we have:

$$\text{(i)} \quad {}^a i_t^{nf} = {}^a\beta'({}^a y_{t-1} - {}^a y_{t-2}).$$
$$\text{(ii)} \quad {}^b i_t^{nf} = {}^b\beta'({}^b y_{t-1} - {}^b y_{t-2}).$$
$$\text{(iii)} \quad Y_{t-1} = {}^a y_{t-1} + {}^b y_{t-1}.$$
$$\text{(iv)} \quad Y_{t-2} = {}^a y_{t-2} + {}^b y_{t-2}.$$
$$\text{(v)} \quad I_t^{nf} = {}^a i_t^{nf} + {}^b i_t^{nf}.$$

Substituting (i) and (ii) into (v) we get:

$$I_t^{nf} = {}^a\beta'({}^a y_{t-1} - {}^a y_{t-2}) + {}^b\beta'({}^b y_{t-1} - {}^b y_{t-2}).$$

If ${}^a\beta' = {}^b\beta' = v$, this reduces to:

$$I_t^{nf} = v({}^a y_{t-1} + {}^b y_{t-1} - {}^a y_{t-2} - {}^b y_{t-2})$$

or, using (iii) and (iv), to:

$$I_t^{nf} = v(Y_{t-1} - Y_{t-2}).$$

Alternatively, if c is the fixed proportion of output produced by firm a, we have:

$$^a y_{t-1} = c Y_{t-1}; \quad {}^a y_{t-2} = c Y_{t-2}.$$

Then:

$$\begin{aligned} I_t^{nf} &= {}^a\beta' c(Y_{t-1} - Y_{t-2}) + {}^b\beta'(1-c)(Y_{t-1} - Y_{t-2}) \\ &= [{}^a\beta' c + {}^b\beta'(1-c)][Y_{t-1} - Y_{t-2}] \\ &= v(Y_{t-1} - Y_{t-2}) \end{aligned}$$

where v is a constant equal to $[{}^a\beta' c + {}^b\beta'(1-c)]$.

Thus if either of these conditions is met, an aggregate relationship of proportionality will follow from a relationship of proportionality at the micro-level. If neither is met, the aggregate relationship will be non-proportional even though proportionality exists for both firms.

that is required to maintain the existing capital stock intact. Thus, by definition, we have:

$$I_t^{nf} = I_t^{gf} - R_t$$

where R denotes replacement expenditure and I^{gf} gross fixed-capital expenditure. Alternatively we have:

$$I_t^{gf} = I_t^{nf} + R_t.$$

Now negative gross fixed-capital expenditure is impossible. Hence:

$$I_t^{nf} + R_t \geq 0$$

or, in other words:

$$I_t^{nf} \geq -R_t.$$

Thus, by definition, aggregate net fixed-capital expenditure cannot be more negative than $-R$; or, putting it another way, net fixed-capital expenditure, when negative, cannot be numerically greater than R.

Now according to the acceleration principle, when Y falls, i.e. when $(Y_{t-1} - Y_{t-2})$ is negative, I^{nf} will also be negative and numerically equal to $v(Y_{t-1} - Y_{t-2})$. For example, if v is 4 and Y falls by 50, the acceleration principle indicates that I^{nf} will be -200. But this figure may not be possible. It will not be possible, for example, if R is 100; in this case I^{nf} will be -100, not -200 as implied by the acceleration principle.

It is clear, then, that while the acceleration principle *can* work when gross domestic product is falling, as well as when it is rising, there is no guarantee that it will always do so; all depends on the size of the fall in gross domestic product in relation to the current level of replacement expenditure.

The conclusion which emerges from this discussion is that, in its simplest form, the acceleration principle is far from being a satisfactory fixed-capital investment function. On the other hand, the basic idea – that short-run movements in desired fixed-capital investment can be explained in terms of a desire by the firm to bring its actual stock of fixed-capital equipment into line with the optimum stock – is a valuable one. What is required is a fixed-capital investment function which incorporates this idea while, at the same time, avoiding the more serious limitations of the simple acceleration principle. The most prominent recent work in this area – that done by Jorgenson – can be regarded as a move in this direction. In the next section we shall expound Jorgenson's approach and present a fixed-capital investment function which emobodies his ideas.

4.2 Recent Development of the Acceleration Principle

One important feature of Jorgenson's work is that it covers fixed-capital replacement expenditure as well as expenditure on additions to the stock of fixed-capital equipment. Thus it enables us to explain *gross* fixed-capital investment, unlike the acceleration principle which is restricted to *net* fixed-capital investment.

Jorgenson's starting-point is the distinction between investment *expenditure* and investment *decisions*.[1] Suppose that the firm decides in period t to expand its stock of fixed-capital equipment by undertaking such projects as the construction of a new factory or the installation of new machines. If the period is as short as a quarter, as we are supposing, it will not be possible, in general, for the firm to undertake the whole of the expenditure associated with these projects in period t. We assume that some proportion, μ_0, of the total expenditure is undertaken in period t, some proportion, μ_1, in period $(t + 1)$, some proportion, μ_2, in period $(t + 2)$ and so on. This amounts to saying that the real net fixed-capital expenditure which the firm desires to undertake in period t is related to the real net investment expenditure *decided on* in period t, and in all prior periods, by means of a distributed-lag function of the form:

$$i_t^{nf} = \mu_0 * i_t^{nf} + \mu_1 * i_{t-1}^{nf} + \mu_2 * i_{t-2}^{nf} + \mu_3 * i_{t-3}^{nf} + \ldots \qquad (4.1)$$

where $*i^{nf}$ denotes net fixed-capital investment *decisions* and the μs a set of non-negative numbers. The μs must sum to unity, since if the firm's investment decisions become stabilised at some fixed level its investment expenditure must eventually become stabilised at the same level.

Since the expenditure associated with any given decision is spread over a succession of future periods, there must be a backlog of uncompleted projects at the beginning of any period. Now, of the projects decided on in period $(t-1)$, some proportion $(1 - \mu_0)$ will be uncompleted at the beginning of period t. Likewise, of the projects undecided on in period $(t—2)$, some proportion $[1 - (\mu_0 + \mu_1)]$ will be completed at the beginning of period t. In general, of the projects decided on in period $(t - s)$, some proportion $[1 - (\mu_0 + \mu_1 + \ldots + \mu_{s-1})]$

---

[1] Jorgenson uses 'projects' where we use 'decisions'.

will be uncompleted at the beginning of period t. Hence the backlog of uncompleted projects at the beginning of period t will be given by:

$$(1 - \mu_0)^* i_{t-1}^{nf} + [1 - (\mu_0 + \mu_1)]^* i_{t-2}^{nf} + [1 - (\mu_0 + \mu_1 + \mu_2)]^* i_{t-3}^{nf} + \ldots.$$

The next step is to incorporate the fundamental idea of the acceleration principle by supposing that investment *decisions* for any period are designed to eliminate the excess of the optimum fixed-capital stock (at the beginning of the period) over the actual capital stock after allowing for the backlog of uncompleted projects which exists at the beginning of the period.

Thus we have:

$$^* i_t^{nf} = \bar{k}_t - \{k_t + (1 - \mu_0)^* i_{t-1}^{nf} + [1 - (\mu_0 + \mu_1)]^* i_{t-2}^{nf} + \ldots\}. \quad (4.2)$$

The expression in curly brackets represents the sum of: (i) the capital stock in existence at the beginning of period t; and (ii) the capital stock which the firm has already decided to install but which has not yet been installed. The investment *decisions* for the period will be equal to the excess of the optimum capital stock over this sum.

Relationships (4.1) and (4.2) are now combined into a single expression for i^{nf} in terms of $\bar{k}$. The reader who is interested in the detailed manipulations will find them set out in Appendix 4.1. Here we confine ourselves to the result, namely:

$$i_t^{nf} = \mu_0(\bar{k}_t - \bar{k}_{t-1}) + \mu_1(\bar{k}_{t-1} - \bar{k}_{t-2}) + \mu_2(\bar{k}_{t-2} - \bar{k}_{t-3}) + \ldots. \quad (4.3)$$

According to this expression the desired real net fixed-capital investment of the firm in period t will be a weighted arithmetic average of all past changes in the optimum capital stock.

Next we adopt the same hypothesis about $\bar{k}$ as is used in the formulation of the acceleration principle presented earlier, namely that $\bar{k}_t$ is proportional to y_{t-1}, given the cost of capital, the business-tax structure, etc. This enables us to rewrite (4.3) as:

$$i_t^{nf} = \beta\mu_0(y_{t-1} - y_{t-2}) + \beta\mu_1(y_{t-2} - y_{t-3}) + \beta\mu_2(y_{t-3} - y_{t-4}) + \ldots$$

where β is the (micro-) capital–output ratio. Assuming that the form of the relationship is not changed in the aggregation process, we have as our aggregate function:

$$I_t^{nf} = g\rho_0(Y_{t-1} - Y_{t-2}) + g\rho_1(Y_{t-2} - Y_{t-3}) + g\rho_2(Y_{t-3} - Y_{t-4}) + \ldots \quad (4.4)$$

D 2

where g is the overall capital–output ratio and the ρs are the macro-counterparts of the μs, i.e. the ρs are a set of non-negative constants which sum to unity.

We turn now to desired real *replacement expenditure* which we denote by R. Here Jorgenson adopts the simple hypothesis that the desired real replacement expenditure of any period is proportional to the capital stock in existence at the beginning of the period. In terms of symbols his hypothesis is:

$$R_t = \delta K_t \qquad (4.5)$$

where K denotes the aggregate stock of fixed-capital equipment at the beginning of the period and δ is some positive constant, satisfying $0 < \delta < 1$.

Jorgenson justifies the choice of this hypothesis in the following way. Assume that R_t is a weighted arithmetic average of all past levels of real gross fixed-capital investment, thereby allowing for the fact that replacement expenditure generates the need for future replacement expenditure in the same way as does expenditure for expansion of capacity. Assume further that the weights decline geometrically. Then:[1]

$$R_t = \delta I_{t-1}^{gf} + (1 - \delta) R_{t-1} \qquad (4.6)$$

where $0 < \delta < 1$. Now K_{t+1}, the stock of fixed-capital equipment at the *end* of period t, is given by the sum of all prior investment expenditures, net of replacement, that is:

$$K_{t+1} = I_t^{gf} + I_{t-1}^{gf} + I_{t-2}^{gf} + \ldots - R_t - R_{t-1} - R_{t-2} \ldots \qquad (4.7)$$

From (4.7) it follows that:

$$(1 - \delta) K_t = (1 - \delta) I_{t-1}^{gf} + (1 - \delta) I_{t-2}^{gf} + \ldots - (1 - \delta) R_{t-1} - (1 - \delta) R_{t-2} \ldots$$

Subtracting this expression from (4.7) we get:

$$K_{t+1} - (1 - \delta) K_t = I_t^{gf} + \delta I_{t-1}^{gf} + \delta I_{t-2}^{gf} + \ldots - \{ R_t - (1 - \delta) R_{t-1} \} - \{ R_{t-1} - (1 - \delta) R_{t-2} \} - \ldots \qquad (4.8)$$

Now from (4.6) it follows that $R_t - (1 - \delta) R_{t-1} = \delta I_{t-1}^{gf}$; $R_{t-1} - (1 - \delta) R_{t-2} = \delta I_{t-2}^{gf}$; and so on. Hence on substitution in (4.8) we get:

$$K_{t+1} - (1 - \delta) K_t = I_t^{gf}.$$

---

[1] Cf. pp. 39–40 above. Note that R_t depends only on *past* levels of gross fixed-capital investment.

It follows from this that:

$$I_t^{gf} - (K_{t+1} - K_t) = \delta K_t$$

and since the left-hand side of this expression is R_t, we get

$$R_t = \delta K_t$$

which is relationship (4.5). Combining (4.4) and (4.5) and using $I_t^{nf} = I_t^{gf} - R_t$ we get:

$$I_t^{gf} - \delta K_t = g\rho_0(Y_{t-1} - Y_{t-2}) + g\rho_1(Y_{t-2} - Y_{t-3}) + g\rho_2(Y_{t-3} - Y_{t-4}) + \ldots .$$
$$(4.9)$$

To reduce (4.9) to a manageable form we must impose some pattern on the weights. If we make the simplest assumption – that the ρs decline geometrically – we obtain:

$$I_t^{gf} - \delta K_t = g(1 - \tau)(Y_{t-1} - Y_{t-2}) + \tau(I_{t-1}^{gf} - \delta K_{t-1}) \qquad (4.10)$$

where $0 < \tau < 1$. On rearranging (4.10) we obtain the following *gross* fixed-capital investment function:

$$I_t^{gf} = g(1 - \tau)(Y_{t-1} - Y_{t-2}) + \tau I_{t-1}^{gf} + \delta K_t - \tau \delta K_{t-1}.$$

In the α notation this reads:

$$I_t^{gf} = \alpha_{40}(Y_{t-1} - Y_{t-2}) + \alpha_{41}I_{t-1}^{gf} + \alpha_{42}K_t + \alpha_{43}K_{t-1} \qquad (4.11)$$

where $\alpha_{40} = g(1 - \tau)$, $\alpha_{41} = \tau$, $\alpha_{42} = \delta$, $\alpha_{43} = -\alpha_{41}\alpha_{42}$.

The general approach embodied in (4.11) has been extensively tested by Jorgenson in recent years. In his most recent empirical work,[1] Jorgenson has fitted a total of eighteen gross fixed-capital investment functions to United States quarterly data for the period 1947–60. Fifteen of these relate to sub-groups of United States manufacturing industry, e.g. Primary Iron and Steel, Stone, Clay and Glass, and Chemicals and Allied Products, and the remaining three to aggregations of the fifteen sub-groups, namely Total Non-durables, Total Durables and Total Manufacturing.[2]

The argument which Jorgenson uses to derive these functions is essentially the one which has been used to derive (4.11). There are, however, two important complications in Jorgenson's argument

---

[1] See Jorgenson and Stephenson, 'Investment Behaviour in U.S. Manufacturing, 1947–1960', op. cit.

[2] Earlier empirical work was of a more aggregative kind and for this reason provided a less stringent test of the approach underlying (4.11) than the work to be discussed here. Ibid., p. 172.

which are missing from ours and we shall begin our account of his empirical work by explaining these complications. To facilitate this, we now present a brief outline of the structure of Jorgenson's argument.

The first stage in the argument is to demonstrate that *net* fixed-capital investment is a weighted arithmetic average of all past changes in the optimum capital stock, using the reasoning leading up to relationship (4.3) above. Next it is shown that expenditure for the *replacement* of fixed-capital equipment is proportional to the capital stock, the reasoning being that underlying relationship (4.7) above. These two conclusions are then put together to yield the conclusion that the *gross* fixed-capital investment of any period is given by a weighted arithmetic average of all past changes in the optimum capital stock *plus* some positive fraction of the stock of fixed-capital equipment as at the beginning of the period.

The next step is to use a relationship between the optimum capital stock and output to rewrite the gross fixed-capital investment function in terms of past changes in output, rather than past changes in the optimum capital stock. In terms of Jorgenson's notation the relationship used is:

$$K_t^+ = \left(\alpha \frac{p_t}{c_t} \right) Q_t$$

where K^+ is the optimum capital stock, Q is output, p is the price of output, c a function of a number of variables including the proportion of current replacement cost which is allowable for tax purposes, the cost of capital, the proportional rate of change in the price of investment goods and the average rate of tax on business income, and where α is the elasticity of output with respect to the input of capital services, taken to be a constant.[1] Application of this relationship gives a distributed-lag gross fixed-capital investment function of the same form as (4.9) above except that: (i) each output is multiplied by the corresponding p/c ratio; and (ii) the constant α is absorbed into each of the infinite sequence of weights which are attached to the terms in past output change.

Finally, the gross fixed-capital investment function is simplified by assuming a particular pattern for the sequence of weights, namely that the sequence is generated by a so-called rational distributed-lag

[1] This relationship is obtained by maximising the present value of the firm subject to: (i) a Cobb–Douglas production function; and (ii) a relationship giving net investment as gross investment *less* some fixed proportion of the capital stock.

function. This implies that the pattern of the weight sequence is such that the current level of *net* fixed-capital investment can be expressed as a linear combination of a finite number of terms, say $(m+1)$, in past output change and a finite number of past levels, say n, of net fixed-capital investment. In terms of Jorgenson's notation, the pattern of the weight sequence is such that:[1]

$$(I_t - \delta K_t) = \gamma_0 \alpha \left[\frac{p_t}{c_t} Q_t - \frac{p_{t-1}}{c_{t-1}} Q_{t-1} \right] + \cdots$$

$$+ \gamma_m \alpha \left[\frac{p_{t-m}}{c_{t-m}} Q_{t-m} - \frac{p_{t-m-1}}{c_{t-m-1}} Q_{t-m-1} \right] + \omega_1 [I_{t-1} - \delta K_{t-1}] +$$

$$\ldots + \omega_n [I_{t-n} - \delta K_{t-n}].$$

By comparing this expression with (4.10) we see that it gives (4.10) as a special case – the special case of $(m+1) = n = 1$. Thus the geometrically declining weight sequence underlying (4.10) may be regarded as the simplest possible special case of the rational distributed-lag function pattern employed by Jorgenson.

From this account of Jorgenson's argument we see that, essentially, it is the argument of (4.11) with two complications added. In the first place, whereas the argument of (4.11) makes use of a simple linear relationship between the optimum capital stock and output, Jorgenson's argument is based on a relationship in which the optimum capital stock appears as a non-linear function of output, the price of output and the conglomerate variable c. Secondly, whereas we reduce (4.9) to manageable form by imposing a geometrically declining pattern on the weights, $\rho_0, \rho_1, \ldots$, Jorgenson reduces his corresponding relationship by imposing a more complicated weight pattern which embraces ours as a special case.

Before he could use the above expression for $(I_t - \delta K_t)$ for empirical work, Jorgenson had to decide on the value to be allotted to $(m+1)$ and n in each of his eighteen cases. After a certain amount of experimentation it was decided that n should be 2 in each case, that both ω_1 and ω_2 should be non-zero, that $(m+1)$ should be 8, that at most four of the eight coefficients in the sequence $\gamma_0 \ldots \gamma_7$ should be non-zero, and that the chosen non-zero coefficients should themselves form an unbroken sequence.

Within these restrictions there were many possible forms for the

---

[1] δ and K have the same meanings as for us while I corresponds to our I^{gf}. The γs and ωs are constants.

gross fixed-capital investment function of any industry. For example, any one of the following three functions would have been permissible within the restrictions laid down:

$$(I_t - \delta K_t) = \gamma_0 \alpha \left[\frac{p_t}{c_t} Q_t - \frac{p_{t-1}}{c_{t-1}} Q_{t-1} \right] + \omega_1 [I_{t-1} - \delta K_{t-1}] + \omega_2 [I_{t-2} - \delta K_{t-2}]$$

$$(I_t - \delta K_t) = \gamma_3 \alpha \left[\frac{p_{t-3}}{c_{t-3}} Q_{t-3} - \frac{p_{t-4}}{c_{t-4}} Q_{t-4} \right] + \gamma_4 \alpha \left[\frac{p_{t-4}}{c_{t-4}} Q_{t-4} - \frac{p_{t-5}}{c_{t-5}} Q_{t-5} \right]$$
$$+ \omega_1 [I_{t-1} - \delta K_{t-1}] + \omega_2 [I_{t-2} - \delta K_{t-2}]$$

$$(I_t - \delta K_t) = \gamma_5 \alpha \left[\frac{p_{t-5}}{c_{t-5}} Q_{t-5} - \frac{p_{t-6}}{c_{t-6}} Q_{t-6} \right] + \gamma_6 \alpha \left[\frac{p_{t-6}}{c_{t-6}} Q_{t-6} - \frac{p_{t-7}}{c_{t-7}} Q_{t-7} \right]$$
$$+ \gamma_7 \alpha \left[\frac{p_{t-7}}{c_{t-7}} Q_{t-7} - \frac{p_{t-8}}{c_{t-8}} Q_{t-8} \right] + \omega_1 [I_{t-1} - \delta K_{t-1}] + \omega_2 [I_{t-2} - \delta K_{t-2}].$$

Altogether eighteen different lag forms were tried out for each of the fifteen industry groups and the three industry aggregates, the procedure being to fit each of the alternative lag forms to the quarterly data for the industry concerned by the method of single-equation least squares.[1]

At this stage, then, a total of eighteen estimated gross fixed-capital investment functions was available for each of the fifteen industry groups and each of the three industry aggregates. Finally one of these functions was chosen for each industry group, the chosen function being the one which gave the smallest standard error of regression.

By way of example we quote two of the gross fixed-capital investment functions which emerged at the end of this elaborate series of steps – the function for one of the fifteen industry groups (Motor Vehicles and Equipment) and the function for one of the three industry aggregates (Total Manufacturing).[2]

[1] Before this could be done, it was necessary to construct series for the two lagged net investment variables, $(I_{t-1} - \delta K_{t-1})$ and $(I_{t-2} - \delta K_{t-2})$. To permit this, an independent estimate was made of the parameter δ. This estimate was also used in the construction of series for c (current and lagged). It was not used, however, to construct a series for $(I_t - \delta K_t)$, the dependent variable in each of the eighteen functions. Instead the term $(- \delta K_t)$ was transferred to the right side, leaving I_t as the dependent variable and introducing another independent variable, K_t. The coefficient of this independent variable was then estimated along with the coefficients of the terms in past output change and the two terms in lagged net investment. In this way a check was obtained on the extraneous estimate of δ used in the derivation of the series required for the least-squares fit.

[2] See Jorgenson and Stephenson, 'Investment Behaviour in U.S. Manufacturing, 1947–60', op. cit., pp. 193, 199.

Motor Vehicles and Equipment

$$I_t = 0\cdot04142 + 0\cdot00160\left(\frac{p_{t-3}}{c_{t-3}}Q_{t-3} - \frac{p_{t-4}}{c_{t-4}}Q_{t-4}\right)$$

$$+ 0\cdot00316\left(\frac{p_{t-4}}{c_{t-4}}Q_{t-4} - \frac{p_{t-5}}{c_{t-5}}Q_{t-5}\right) + 0\cdot00279\left(\frac{p_{t-5}}{c_{t-5}}Q_{t-5} - \frac{p_{t-6}}{c_{t-6}}Q_{t-6}\right)$$

$$+ 0\cdot00189\left(\frac{p_{t-6}}{c_{t-6}}Q_{t-6} - \frac{p_{t-7}}{c_{t-7}}Q_{t-7}\right) + 1\cdot08317(I_{t-1} + \delta K_{t-1})$$

$$- 0\cdot19562(I_{t-2} - \delta K_{t-2}) + 0\cdot02622K_t.$$

Total Manufacturing

$$I_t = 0\cdot73767 + 0\cdot00299\left(\frac{p_{t-4}}{c_{t-4}}Q_{t-4} - \frac{p_{t-5}}{c_{t-5}}Q_{t-5}\right)$$

$$+ 0\cdot00200\left(\frac{p_{t-5}}{c_{t-5}}Q_{t-5} - \frac{p_{t-6}}{c_{t-6}}Q_{t-6}\right) + 0\cdot00268\left(\frac{p_{t-6}}{c_{t-6}}Q_{t-6} - \frac{p_{t-7}}{c_{t-7}}Q_{t-7}\right)$$

$$+ 0\cdot00370\left(\frac{p_{t-7}}{c_{t-7}}Q_{t-7} - \frac{p_{t-8}}{c_{t-8}}Q_{t-8}\right) + 1\cdot20525(I_{t-1} - \delta K_{t-1})$$

$$- 0\cdot47599(I_{t-2} - \delta K_{t-2}) + 0\cdot01935K_t.$$

The eighteen gross fixed-capital investment functions finally adopted were extensively tested against the quarterly data for 1947–1960. The main test was the usual goodness-of-fit test. In all but one of the eighteen cases the chosen function explained more than 75 per cent of the observed variation in gross fixed-capital investment, while in nine of the eighteen cases it accounted for more than 90 per cent of the observed variation. This is all the more impressive in view of the wide range of behaviour observed in the eighteen gross fixed-capital investment series.

Numerous other tests were carried out in addition to the goodness-of-fit test. Some of these, e.g. the Durbin–Watson test, were of a conventional kind while others, such as the tests for consistency between the internal and external estimates of δ,[1] were comparatively unfamiliar. In general the chosen relationships performed very satisfactorily under these additional tests.

It would seem, therefore, that Jorgenson's most recent empirical

---

[1] See p. 102, n. 1 above.

work provides strong support for the approach to the aggregate gross fixed-capital investment function which has been followed in the present section.

4.3 A Stock-adjustment Housing Investment Function

We shall now proceed to develop a relationship which explains short-run movements in desired real housing investment. For this purpose, as the reader will see, we shall draw on several of the key ideas of previous sections, though we shall not always apply them in quite the same way. As in the case of fixed-capital investment, we shall begin by developing a relationship to explain desired real *net* housing investment and then combine this with a relationship explaining replacement investment to obtain the *gross* housing investment relationship which is our ultimate objective in this section.

The first part of the argument follows much the same pattern as for the case of fixed-capital investment. In particular, it is based on the distinction between investment *expenditure* and investment *decisions*. Suppose that an individual decides in period t to construct a new house for his own occupation or that a firm of developers decides to construct a new block of flats for renting. Obviously, in general, it will not be possible for the individual or firm to undertake the whole of the expenditure on the new house or the new block of flats in period t. We assume that some proportion of the expenditure is undertaken in period t, some proportion in period $(t + 1)$ and so on. On this basis we can then say that the aggregate real net expenditure on new housing which is desired for period t will be related to the expenditure decided on in period t and in all past periods by means of a distributed-lag function in which the parameters are a set of non-negative constants which sum to unity. Thus if we denote real net housing investment *decisions* in period t by $*I_t^{nh}$ and desired real net housing investment *expenditure* by I_t^{nh}, we have:

$$I_t^{nh} = \epsilon_0 * I_t^{nh} + \epsilon_1 * I_{t-1}^{nh} + \epsilon_2 * I_{t-2}^{nh} + \ldots \qquad (4.12)$$

where the ϵs are a set of non-negative numbers which sum to unity.

Again following the pattern of the argument for the fixed-capital case, we assume that the net housing investment decided on in period t is determined by the relationship between (i) the *desired* housing stock as at the beginning of the period; and (ii) the *actual* housing stock *plus* the backlog of partly constructed housing, as at the beginning of the period. However, whereas in the case of fixed-capital investment we supposed that the decisions of period t are designed to eliminate the *whole* of the excess of (i) over (ii), here we suppose that they serve to eliminate *part only* of the excess, say some positive fraction, θ, of the excess.

Reasons for supposing that the adjustment of the actual to the desired stock will not be instantaneous in the case of housing are given by Muth in a recent United States study.[1] The main point is that, in the case of new construction for owner-occupation, the strictly economic considerations will be inextricably bound up with, and partly overborne by, considerations of personal convenience. As Muth puts it: 'It is in the nature of housing decisions that they should be considered carefully, and often moving into new quarters must be meshed with other events – children starting or finishing school, marriage, birth or death of family members, etc.'[2]

Our expression for $*I_t^{nh}$, then, will be of the same form as (4.2) except for the presence of the positive fraction θ. That is, we shall have:

$$*I_t^{nh} = \theta[*K_t^h - \{K_t^h + (1 - \epsilon_0)*I_{t-1}^{nh} + [1 - (\epsilon_0 + \epsilon_1)]*I_{t-2}^{nh} + \ldots\}] \quad (4.13)$$

where $*K^h$ and K^h denote, respectively, the desired stock and the actual stock of houses at the beginning of the period. (We shall have something to say about the determinants of $*K^h$ in a moment.)

We now combine (4.12) and (4.13) into a single expression for I_t^{nh} in terms of $*K^h$, I_{t-1}^{nh} and I_{t-2}^{nh}, using, among other things, the assumption that the ϵs decline geometrically by a damping factor σ. The mechanics follow the same lines as Appendix 4.1 and are set out for the interested reader in Appendix 4.2. The combined expression in question is:

$$I_t^{nh} = \theta(1 - \sigma)(*K_t^h - *K_{t-1}^h) + (1 - \theta + \sigma)I_{t-1}^{nh} + \sigma(\theta - 1)I_{t-2}^{nh} \quad (4.14)$$

where σ is some positive fraction.

The pace of adjustment of the actual to the desired housing stock will not be invariable, even in the short run. In particular it is likely to slacken significantly in the face of an increase in the cost, and/or a decrease in the availability, of housing finance, and vice versa. This amounts to saying that the θ which appears in (4.14) takes the

[1] See R. F. Muth, 'The Demand for Non-Farm Housing', in A. C. Harberger (ed.), *The Demand for Durable Goods* (University of Chicago Press, 1960) pp. 35–6.   [2] Ibid., p. 36.

cost and availability of housing finance as given and changes if either of these variables change.

To complete the development of our net housing investment function, we have now to eliminate from this expression the change in the desired housing stock $(*K_t^h - *K_{t-1}^h)$, which is, of course, non-observable. For this purpose we draw on the work of Muth.[1]

Muth identifies the desired housing stock per capita as at the beginning of period t, with the long-run per capita equilibrium stock which corresponds to the following as data: (i) permanent income per capita; (ii) the housing depreciation rate (depreciation per unit of the housing stock as a ratio of price per unit); and (iii) the housing tax rate (property taxes per unit of the housing stock as a ratio of price per unit). A model of long-run equilibrium in the housing market is then developed in which price, rent, per capita demand for housing services, interest rate on housing loans and required net rate of return on housing services (net return per unit as a ratio of price per unit) are the unknowns, and (i) to (iii) above are the data to which these five variables adjust. Three relationships are proposed. The first is, in effect, a condition of long-run equilibrium in the housing market. If a particular housing stock is to qualify as the long-run equilibrium stock, for specified values of the three data, it must be a stock which house-owners wish to hold at those specified values – by the definition of equilibrium. Hence as a condition of equilibrium we have:

$$\frac{\text{Rent}}{\text{Price}} = \text{Depreciation rate} + \text{Tax rate} + \text{Required net rate of return}.$$

The second relationship explains the equilibrium per capita demand for housing services:

Per capita demand for housing services $= \emptyset$(Rent, Per capita permanent income).

Finally as the third relationship we have:

Required net rate of return $= \psi$(Interest rate on housing loans).

Using the first relationship one can eliminate the rent variable from the second relationship and then use the third relationship to eliminate the required net rate of return. In this way we can obtain:

[1] See R. F. Muth, 'The Demand for Non-Farm Housing', in A. C. Harberger, (ed.), *The Demand for Durable Goods* (University of Chicago Press, 1960) pp. 32–5.

Per capita demand for housing services $= F$(Price, Interest rate, Depreciation rate, Tax rate, Per capita permanent income).

Now assuming, as is natural, that 'one unit of housing services' is defined as 'the quantity of housing services provided by one unit of the housing stock', the demand for housing services and the desired housing stock will always be numerically equal. Hence the expression just derived can be interpreted not only as a long-run equilibrium demand-for-housing services function, but also as a long-run equilibrium housing-stock function, i.e. as a desired-housing-stock function. This, in fact, is the way in which Muth regards it.

On the basis of this argument we now postulate the following:

$$*K_t^h = dX_{t-1}^1 \qquad (4.15)$$

where X^1 denotes permanent income and d denotes some positive constant. It will be evident from the preceding discussion that (4.15) takes as given the following: (i) population; (ii) the long-run equilibrium price of housing; (iii) the long-run equilibrium interest rate on housing loans; (iv) the housing depreciation rate; and (v) the housing tax rate.

Using (4.15) we can replace $(*K_t^h - *K_{t-1}^h)$ in (4.14) by $d(X_{t-1}^1 - X_{t-2}^1)$. This merely replaces one non-observable by another. However, $(X_{t-1}^1 - X_{t-2}^1)$ is a non-observable that we can handle by virtue of our earlier work in connection with the consumption function. It will be recalled that in the course of this work we derived the expression:

$$X_t^1 = (1 - \xi)X_t + \xi X_{t-1}^1 + \pi X_{t-1}^1$$

where ξ and π are two positive fractions (see p. 51 above). Using this expression we can say that:

$$(X_{t-1}^1 - X_{t-2}^1) - (\xi + \pi)(X_{t-2}^1 - X_{t-3}^1) = (1 - \xi)(X_{t-1} - X_{t-2}). \qquad (4.16)$$

This gives us the clue we need. We now proceed as follows. We first use (4.15) to write (4.14) as:

$$I_t^{nh} = \theta(1 - \sigma)d(X_{t-1}^1 - X_{t-2}^1) + (1 - \theta + \sigma)I_{t-1}^{nh} + \sigma(\theta - 1)I_{t-2}^{nh}. \qquad (4.17)$$

Next we use (4.17) to derive an expression for $I_t^{nh} - (\xi + \pi)I_{t-1}^{nh}$, namely:

$$I_t^{nh} - (\xi + \pi)I_{t-1}^{nh} = \theta(1 - \sigma)d\,[(X_{t-1}^1 - X_{t-2}^1) - (\xi + \pi)(X_{t-2}^1 - X_{t-3}^1)]$$
$$+ (1 - \theta + \sigma)[I_{t-1}^{nh} - (\xi + \pi)I_{t-2}^{nh}] + \sigma(\theta - 1)[I_{t-2}^{nh} - (\xi + \pi)I_{t-3}^{nh}]. \quad (4.18)$$

Finally we substitute (4.16) into (4.18) and collect terms to get:

$$I_t^{nh} = [\theta(1 - \sigma)d(1 - \xi)](X_{t-1} - X_{t-2}) + [(\xi + \pi) + (1 - \theta + \sigma)]I_{t-1}^{nh}$$
$$+ [\sigma(\theta - 1) - (\xi + \pi)(1 - \theta + \sigma)]I_{t-2}^{nh} - [\sigma(\theta - 1)(\xi + \pi)]I_{t-3}^{nh}. \quad (4.19)$$

This is our *net* housing investment function. We have now to combine this function with a replacement expenditure function to obtain a *gross* housing investment function. Here we shall adopt the hypothesis which corresponds to the one used earlier to explain desired real fixed-capital replacement (see p. 98 above), namely:

$$R_t^h = \rho K_t^h$$

where R^h denotes desired real replacement expenditure. The justification for this proceeds on exactly the same lines as before. This expression, in conjunction with $I_t^{nh} = I_t^{gh} - R_t^h$, gives

$$I_t^{gh} - \rho K_t^h = \alpha_{50}(X_{t-1} - X_{t-2}) + \alpha_{51}(I_{t-1}^{gh} - \rho K_{t-1}^h) + \alpha_{52}(I_{t-2}^{gh} - \rho K_{t-2}^h)$$
$$+ \alpha_{53}(I_{t-3}^{gh} - \rho K_{t-3}^h)$$

where
$$\alpha_{50} = \theta d(1 - \sigma)(1 - \xi)$$
$$\alpha_{51} = (\xi + \pi) + (1 - \theta + \sigma)$$
$$\alpha_{52} = \sigma(\theta - 1) - (\xi + \pi)(1 - \theta + \sigma)$$
$$\alpha_{53} = \sigma(1 - \theta)(\xi + \pi).$$

This can be rewritten as:

$$I_t^{gh} = \alpha_{50}(X_{t-1} - X_{t-2}) + \alpha_{51}I_{t-1}^{gh} + \alpha_{52}\,I_{t-2}^{gh} + \alpha_{53}I_{t-3}^{gh} + \alpha_{54}K_t^h$$
$$+ \alpha_{55}K_{t-1}^h + \alpha_{56}K_{t-2}^h + \alpha_{57}K_{t-3}^h \quad (4.20)$$

where
$$\alpha_{54} = \rho, \quad \alpha_{55} = -\rho\alpha_{51}, \quad \alpha_{56} = -\rho\alpha_{52}, \quad \alpha_{57} = -\rho\alpha_{53}.$$

This is the relationship explaining the short-run behaviour of real gross housing investment that we set out to derive.

It will be clear from the argument underlying (4.14) and (4.15) that the implicit data for (4.20) are: the cost and availability of housing finance, population, the long-run equilibrium price of housing, the long-run equilibrium interest rate on housing loans, the housing depreciation rate and the housing tax rate.

No empirical work with a relationship like (4.20) has been done in Britain, and indeed it is doubtful whether the available data would permit it. However, Muth has tested a relationship which embodies most of the key elements of (4.20) against annual data for the United States in the study already cited and has obtained highly encouraging results. Muth's procedure is to set up a linear version of the desired-housing-stock function presented earlier (see p. 107 above) and to substitute this into a per capita version of:

$$I_t^{nh} = \theta(*K_t^h - K_t^h)$$

to obtain a linear relationship for per capita net housing investment in terms of long-run price, long-run interest rate, depreciation rate, tax rate, per capita permanent income and per capita housing stock. Finally, this is converted into gross form by means of a per capita version of

$$R_t^h = \rho K_t^h.$$

Thus most of the ingredients of (4.20) are present in the relationship which Muth finally derives.

Muth has fitted his final gross relationship to annual United States data by the method of least squares,[1] and by all the usual statistical criteria the results give strong support to the relationship. All the estimated coefficients have the correct a priori sign. Also, three of the estimated coefficients are at least four times their standard errors while the fourth is at least twice its standard error. Finally, considering that it has been necessary to omit two of the explanatory variables (depreciation rate and tax rate) from the regression because of lack of data, the explained variation is quite high (62 per cent). In fact, the only unfavourable feature of the statistical results is the presence of serial correlation in the disturbances.[2]

4.4 The Dynamic Properties of Model IV

We are now in a position to set out a fourth-stage model – Model IV. This is as follows:

Desired Consumption Expenditure

$$C_t = \alpha_{10} X_t + \alpha_{11} C_{t-1} + Z^1 \tag{2.24}$$

Disposable Income

$$X_t = \alpha_{20} + \alpha_{21} Y_t \tag{2.26}$$

---

[1] See Muth, op. cit., pp. 35–41.   [2] Ibid., pp. 49–50.

Components of Aggregate Demand

$$D_t = C_t + G_t + E_t + I_t^{gf} + I_t^{gh} + I_t^{ri} + I_t^{ci} \qquad (3.11)$$

Demand–Output Relationship

$$D_t = Y_t + M_t + U_t \qquad (3.2)$$

Realised Imports

$$M_t = \alpha_{30} M_{t-1} + \alpha_{31} D_{t-2} + \alpha_{32} I_{t-2}^i + Z^2 \qquad (3.4)$$

Desired Fixed-capital Investment

$$I_t^{gf} = \alpha_{40}(Y_{t-1} - Y_{t-2}) + \alpha_{41} I_{t-1}^{gf} + \alpha_{42} K_t + \alpha_{43} K_{t-1} \qquad (4.11)$$

Desired Housing Investment

$$I_t^{gh} = \alpha_{50}(X_{t-1} - X_{t-2}) + \alpha_{51} I_{t-1}^{gh} + \alpha_{52} I_{t-2}^{gh} + \alpha_{53} I_{t-3}^{gh} + \alpha_{54} K_t^h$$
$$+ \alpha_{55} K_{t-1}^h + \alpha_{56} K_{t-2}^h + \alpha_{57} K_{t-3}^h. \qquad (4.20)$$

The data of this model are Z^1, G, E, I^{ri}, I^{ci}, U, I^i, Z^2, K and K^h, while the jointly determined variables are C, X, D, Y, M, I^{gf} and I^{gh}. The variables I^{ri}, I^{ci}, I^i and U are temporary data only; they will be removed to the jointly determined category in the final model to be presented in the next chapter.

To examine the dynamic properties of Model IV we first reduce the seven relationships, by substitution, to a system of four difference equations in the four jointly determined variables, D, M, I^{gf} and I^{gh}. The reduction proceeds as follows. Relationships (2.24), (2.26) and (3.11) give:

$$D_t = \alpha_{10}(\alpha_{20} + \alpha_{21} Y_t) + \alpha_{11}(D_{t-1} - G_{t-1} - E_{t-1} - I_{t-1}^{gf} - I_{t-1}^{gh} - I_{t-1}^{ri} - I_{t-1}^{ci})$$
$$+ Z^1 + G_t + E_t + I_t^{gf} + I_t^{gh} + I_t^{ri} + I_t^{ci}.$$

Using (3.2) we can eliminate Y from this expression to get:

$$D_t = \alpha_{10}[\alpha_{20} + \alpha_{21}(D_t - M_t - U_t)] + \alpha_{11}(D_{t-1} - G_{t-1} - E_{t-1} - I_{t-1}^{gf}$$
$$- I_{t-1}^{gh} - I_{t-1}^{ri} - I_{t-1}^{ci}) + Z^1 + G_t + E_t + I_t^{gf} + I_t^{gh} + I_t^{ri} + I_t^{ci}.$$

This in turn gives:

$$D_t(1 - \alpha_{10}\alpha_{21}) - \alpha_{11} D_{t-1} + \alpha_{10}\alpha_{21} M_t - I_t^{gf} + \alpha_{11} I_{t-1}^{gf} - I_t^{gh} + \alpha_{11} I_{t-1}^{gh} = k_1$$
$$(4.21)$$

where k_1 denotes: $\alpha_{10}\alpha_{20} - \alpha_{10}\alpha_{21} U_t - \alpha_{11}(G_{t-1} + E_{t-1} + I_{t-1}^{ri} + I_{t-1}^{ci}) + Z^1$ $+ G_t + E_t + I_t^{ri} + I_t^{ci}.$

Using (3.2) once again we can eliminate Y from (4.11) to get:

$$I_t^{gf} - \alpha_{41}I_{t-1}^{gf} - \alpha_{40}(D_{t-1} - D_{t-2}) + \alpha_{40}(M_{t-1} - M_{t-2}) = k_3 \quad (4.22)$$

where k_3 denotes: $\alpha_{42}K_t + \alpha_{43}K_{t-1} - \alpha_{40}(U_{t-1} - U_{t-2})$.

Next using (3.2) and (2.26) we can eliminate X from (4.20) to get:

$$I_t^{gh} - \alpha_{51}I_{t-1}^{gh} - \alpha_{52}I_{t-2}^{gh} - \alpha_{53}I_{t-3}^{gh} - \alpha_{50}\alpha_{21}(D_{t-1} - D_{t-2}) \\ + \alpha_{50}\alpha_{21}(M_{t-1} - M_{t-2}) = k_4 \quad (4.23)$$

where k_4 denotes: $\alpha_{54}K_t^h + \alpha_{55}K_{t-1}^h + \alpha_{56}K_{t-2}^h + \alpha_{57}K_{t-3}^h - \alpha_{50}\alpha_{21}(U_{t-1} - U_{t-2})$.

Finally we rewrite (3.4) as:

$$M_t - \alpha_{30}M_{t-1} - \alpha_{31}D_{t-2} = k_2 \quad\quad\quad (4.24)$$

where k_2 denotes: $\alpha_{32}I_{t-2}^i + Z^2$. Adding this expression to (4.21), (4.22) and (4.23) we have the following system of four difference equations in D, M, I^{gf} and I^{gh}.

$$D_t(1 - \alpha_{10}\alpha_{21}) - \alpha_{11}D_{t-1} + \alpha_{10}\alpha_{21}M_t - I_t^{gf} + \alpha_{11}I_{t-1}^{gf} - I_t^{gh} + \alpha_{11}I_{t-1}^{gh} = k_1. \\ (4.21)$$

$$M_t - \alpha_{30}M_{t-1} - \alpha_{31}D_{t-2} = k_2. \quad\quad\quad (4.24)$$

$$I_t^{gf} - \alpha_{41}I_{t-1}^{gf} - \alpha_{40}(D_{t-1} - D_{t-2}) + \alpha_{40}(M_{t-1} - M_{t-2}) = k_3. \quad (4.22)$$

$$I_t^{gh} - \alpha_{51}I_{t-1}^{gh} - \alpha_{52}I_{t-2}^{gh} - \alpha_{53}I_{t-3}^{gh} - \alpha_{50}\alpha_{21}(D_{t-1} - D_{t-2}) \\ + \alpha_{50}\alpha_{21}(M_{t-1} - M_{t-2}) = k_4. \quad (4.23)$$

The parameter values to be used in the dynamic analysis of Model IV are: $\alpha_{10} = 0\cdot3$; $\alpha_{11} = 0\cdot5$; $\alpha_{21} = 0\cdot08$; $\alpha_{30} = 0\cdot1$; $\alpha_{31} = 0\cdot2$; $\alpha_{40} = 1\cdot36$; $\alpha_{41} = 0\cdot83$; $\alpha_{50} = 0\cdot115$; $\alpha_{51} = 2\cdot130$; $\alpha_{52} = 1\cdot461$; $\alpha_{53} = 0\cdot323$. A comment on these values will be found in Appendix 5.1.

When these values are inserted in the difference-equation system (4.21) to (4.24), we obtain, after a slight rearrangement, the following numerical system:

$$0\cdot976D_t - 0\cdot5D_{t-1} + 0\cdot024M_t - I_t^{gf} + 0\cdot5I_{t-1}^{gf} - I_t^{gh} + 0\cdot5I_{t-1}^{gh} = k_1. \quad (4.25)$$

$$-0\cdot2D_{t-2} + M_t - 0\cdot1M_{t-1} = k_2. \quad\quad\quad (4.26)$$

$$-1\cdot36(D_{t-1} - D_{t-2}) + 1\cdot36(M_{t-1} - M_{t-2}) + I_t^{gf} - 0\cdot83I_{t-1}^{gf} = k_3. \quad (4.27)$$

$$-0\cdot009(D_{t-1} - D_{t-2}) + 0\cdot009(M_{t-1} - M_{t-2}) + I_t^{gh} - 2\cdot130I_{t-1}^{gh} \\ + 1\cdot461I_{t-2}^{gh} - 0\cdot323I_{t-3}^{gh} = k_4. \quad (4.28)$$

Details of the solution of this numerical system are set out in Appendix 4.3. The solution for D is as follows:

$$D_t = A_{11}(1\cdot179)^t \cos\,[24\cdot2t - A_{12}] + A_{13}(0\cdot901)^t + A_{14}(0\cdot685)^t$$
$$+ A_{15}(0\cdot652)^t + A_{16}(0\cdot475)^t \cos\,[7\cdot1t - A_{17}] + A_{18}(-0\cdot356)^t + \bar{D}_t$$

where $\bar{D}_t$ is the particular solution which can be given a specific form once time paths have been specified for the ks, i.e. for the data of the system, and the As are arbitrary constants which can be evaluated once time paths have been specified for the ks, i.e. for the data of the solutions for M, I^{gf} and I^{gh} will be identical with the solution for D except for the particular solution and the arbitrary As.

Each of the solutions will be dominated by the first term, since the absolute value of the pair of complex roots which are incorporated in this term $(1\cdot179)$ exceeds the absolute value of the four real roots $(0\cdot901,\ 0\cdot685,\ 0\cdot652$ and $-0\cdot356)$ and the absolute value of the remaining pair of complex roots $(0\cdot475)$. Thus, eventually, the time path followed by each of the four variables D, M, I^{gf} and I^{gh} in response to arbitrary initial conditions will be one characterised by mildly explosive fluctuations around the particular solution.

4.5 Summary

In the model developed in the previous chapter (Model III) the whole of desired real investment expenditure is treated as a datum. The purpose of the present chapter is to develop two new relationships which make it possible, in part, to remedy this deficiency. These two new relationships are, firstly, a relationship explaining desired real gross fixed-capital investment and, secondly, a relationship explaining desired real gross housing investment. Armed with these relationships we are in a position to transfer gross fixed-capital investment and gross housing investment from the data category to the jointly-determined-variable category.

The fixed-capital investment function which we present is a refined version of the acceleration principle based on the work of Jorgenson and, in the course of developing the function, we give a detailed exposition of his central ideas. The essential ingredients of Jorgenson's approach are: (i) the distinction between fixed-capital investment *decisions* and fixed-capital investment *expenditure*; and (ii) the hypothesis that the fixed-capital investment decisions of any period are designed to eliminate the whole of the excess of the desired stock of fixed-capital equipment as at the beginning of the period, over the sum of the actual stock and the backlog of uncompleted projects. These two ideas form the basis of our housing investment function also, though we employ them with certain important modifications.

The model which emerges when these two new relationships are added to those of Model III consists of seven relationships in the seven jointly determined variables, C, X, D, Y, M, I^{gf} and I^{gh}. This model can be reduced by substitution to a system of four difference equations in the four jointly determined variables, D, M, I^{gf} and I^{gh}. On obtaining the solutions for these variables we find that the model exhibits oscillatory behaviour in response to arbitrary initial conditions and that the oscillations are mildly explosive.

READING LIST

Almon, Shirley, 'The Distributed Lag between Capital Appropriations and Expenditures', *Econometrica* (Jan 1965).

de Leeuw, Frank, 'The Demand for Capital Goods by Manufacturers: A Study of Quarterly Time Series', *Econometrica* (July 1962).

Eckstein, Otto, 'Manufacturing Investment and Business Expectations: Extensions of de Leeuw's Results', *Econometrica* (Apr. 1965).

Greenberg, Edward, 'A Stock-Adjustment Investment Model', *Econometrica* (July 1964).

Jorgenson, D. W., 'Anticipations and Investment Behaviour', in Duesenberry, J. S., Kuh, E., Fromm, G., and Klein, L. R. (eds), *The Brookings Quarterly Econometric Model of the United States* (Chicago: Rand-McNally, 1965).

——, 'Capital Theory and Investment Behaviour', *American Economic Review* (May 1963).

—— and Stephenson, J. A., 'Investment Behaviour in U.S. Manufacturing, 1947–1960', *Econometrica* (Apr 1967).

—— and ——, 'The Time Structure of Investment Behaviour in United States Manufacturing, 1947–1960', *Review of Economics and Statistics* (Feb 1967).

Muth, R. F., 'The Demand for Non-Farm Housing', in Harberger, A. C. (ed.), *The Demand for Durable Goods* (University of Chicago Press, 1960).

Appendix 4.1

DERIVATION OF (4.3) FROM (4.1) AND (4.2)

From (4.2) we obtain

$$*i_t^{nf} = \bar{k}_t - \{k_t + (1 - \mu_0)*i_{t-1}^{nf} + [1 - (\mu_0 + \mu_1)]*i_{t-2}^{nf} + \ldots \}$$

and

$$*i_{t-1}^{nf} = \bar{k}_{t-1} - \{k_{t-1} + (1 - \mu_0)*i_{t-2}^{nf} + [1 - (\mu_0 + \mu_1)]*i_{t-3}^{nf} + \dots\}.$$

Subtracting, we get

$$*i_t^{nf} - *i_{t-1}^{nf} = (\bar{k}_t - \bar{k}_{t-1}) - (k_t - k_{t-1}) - *i_{t-1}^{nf} + \{\mu_0 *i_{t-1}^{nf} + \mu_1 *i_{t-2}^{nf} + \dots\}.$$

Using (4.1) and the fact that $k_t - k_{t-1} = i_{t-1}^{nf}$, we get

$$*i_t^{nf} = \bar{k}_t - \bar{k}_{t-1}.$$

Substituting this and similar expressions into (4.1), we get

$$i_t^{nf} = \mu_0(\bar{k}_t - \bar{k}_{t-1}) + \mu_1(\bar{k}_{t-1} - \bar{k}_{t-2}) + \dots.$$

Appendix 4.2

DERIVATION OF (4.14) FROM (4.12) AND (4.13)

From (4.13) we obtain:

$$*I_t^{nh} = \theta[*K_t^h - K_t^h - \{(1 - \epsilon_0)*I_{t-1}^{nh} + [1 - (\epsilon_0 + \epsilon_1)]*I_{t-2}^{nh} + \dots\}]$$

and

$$*I_{t-1}^{nh} = \theta[*K_{t-1}^h - K_{t-1}^h - \{(1 - \epsilon_0)*I_{t-2}^{nh} + [1 - (\epsilon_0 + \epsilon_1)]*I_{t-3}^{nh} + \dots\}].$$

Subtracting, we get:

$$*I_t^{nh} - *I_{t-1}^{nh} = \theta[(*K_t^h - *K_{t-1}^h) - (K_t^h - K_{t-1}^h) - *I_{t-1}^{nh} + (\epsilon_0 *I_{t-1}^{nh} + \epsilon_1 *I_{t-2}^{nh} + \dots)].$$

Using (4.12) and the fact that $K_t^h - K_{t-1}^h = I_{t-1}^{nh}$, we get:

$$*I_t^{nh} - *I_{t-1}^{nh} = \theta[(*K_t^h - *K_{t-1}^h) - I_{t-1}^{nh} - *I_{t-1}^{nh} + I_{t-2}^{nh}]$$

which can be written as:

$$*I_t^{nh} = \theta(*K_t^h - *K_{t-1}^h) + (1 - \theta)*I_{t-1}^{nh}.$$

Imposing the condition that the ϵs decline geometrically, (4.12) can be written as:

$$I_t^{nh} = (1 - \sigma)*I_t^{nh} + \sigma I_{t-1}^{nh}$$

where σ is some positive fraction.

Substituting the expression for $*I_t^{nh}$ derived above into this expression, we obtain:

$$I_t^{nh} = \theta(1 - \sigma)(*K_t^h - *K_{t-1}^h) + (1 - \theta)(1 - \sigma)*I_{t-1}^{nh} + \sigma I_{t-1}^{nh}.$$

Using (4.12) once again, we get:

$$(1 - \sigma)*I_{t-1}^{nh} = I_{t-1}^{nh} - \sigma I_{t-2}^{nh}$$

which gives:

$$I_t^{nh} = \theta(1 - \sigma)(*K_t^h - *K_{t-1}^h) + (1 - \theta + \sigma)I_{t-1}^{nh} + \sigma(\theta - 1)I_{t-2}^{nh}$$

which is (4.14).

Appendix 4.3

SOLUTION OF MODEL IV

In this appendix we apply the general method for solving a simultaneous system of linear difference equations which was outlined in Appendix 3.1 to Model IV.

The first step is to write (4.25) to (4.28) in matrix-operator form as follows:

$$
\begin{bmatrix}
0{\cdot}976 - 0{\cdot}5E\} & 0{\cdot}024 & \{-1+0{\cdot}5E\} & \{-1+0{\cdot}5E\} \\
0{\cdot}2E^2 & \{1-0{\cdot}1E\} & 0 & 0 \\
1{\cdot}36(E-E^2)\} & \{1{\cdot}36(E-E^2)\} & \{1-0{\cdot}83E\} & 0 \\
0{\cdot}009(E-E^2)\} & \{0{\cdot}009(E-E^2)\} & 0 & \{1-2{\cdot}130E+ \\
& & & 1{\cdot}461E^2 - 0{\cdot}323E^3\}
\end{bmatrix}
\begin{bmatrix}
D_t \\ M_t \\ I^{gf} \\ I_t^{gf}
\end{bmatrix}
=
\begin{bmatrix}
k_1 \\ k_2 \\ k_3 \\ k_4
\end{bmatrix}
$$

Next we find $|P(E)|$. This is given by:

$$|P(E)| = 0{\cdot}976 - 4{\cdot}856E + 10{\cdot}070E^2 - 10{\cdot}841E^3 + 5{\cdot}939E^4 - 0{\cdot}978E^5 \\ - 0{\cdot}575E^6 + 0{\cdot}309E^7 - 0{\cdot}044E^8.$$

From this expression we form the characteristic equation:

$$0{\cdot}976x^8 - 4{\cdot}856x^7 + 10{\cdot}070x^6 - 10{\cdot}841x^5 + 5{\cdot}939x^4 - 0{\cdot}978x^3 - 0{\cdot}575x^2 \\ + 0{\cdot}309x - 0{\cdot}044 = 0.$$

By applying the Lin–Bairstow method[1] we find that this polynomial has four real roots and two pairs of conjugate complex roots as follows:

$$
\begin{aligned}
&x_1 = 1{\cdot}075 + 0{\cdot}484i \\
&x_2 = 1{\cdot}075 - 0{\cdot}484i
\end{aligned}
\Big\} \; \begin{aligned} r &= 1{\cdot}179 \\ \theta &= 24{\cdot}2^0 \end{aligned}
\qquad
\begin{aligned} x_5 &= 0{\cdot}901 \\ x_6 &= 0{\cdot}685 \end{aligned}
$$

$$
\begin{aligned}
&x_3 = 0{\cdot}471 + 0{\cdot}059i \\
&x_4 = 0{\cdot}471 - 0{\cdot}059i
\end{aligned}
\Big\} \; \begin{aligned} r &= 0{\cdot}475 \\ \theta &= 7{\cdot}1^0 \end{aligned}
\qquad
\begin{aligned} x_7 &= 0{\cdot}652 \\ x_8 &= -0{\cdot}356 \end{aligned}
$$

Consequently the solution for D is:

$$D_t = A_{11}(1{\cdot}179)^t \cos [24{\cdot}2t - A_{12}] + A_{13}(0{\cdot}901)^t + A_{14}(0{\cdot}685)^t + A_{15}(0{\cdot}652)^t \\ + A_{16}(0{\cdot}475)^t \cos [7{\cdot}1t - A_{17}] + A_{18}(-0{\cdot}356)^t + \bar{D}_t$$

where $\bar{D}_t$ is the particular solution whose precise character is determined by the time paths specified for the ks and where the As are arbitrary constants which can be evaluated given the appropriate initial conditions. The solution for each of the other jointly determined variables is identical with this except for the particular solution and the arbitrary As, e.g. in the solution for M, $\bar{M}_t$ replaces $\bar{D}_t$ and $A_{21} \ldots A_{28}$ replace $A_{11} \ldots A_{18}$.

---

[1] For details of this method, see R. Beckett and J. Hurt, *Numerical Calculations and Algorithms* (New York: McGraw-Hill, 1967), chap. 3; R. A. Buckingham, *Numerical Methods* (London: Pitman, 1957) chap. 9; and P. Henrici, *Elements of Numerical Analysis* (New York: John Wiley, 1964) chap. 5.

5 Inventory Investment

5.1. Raw-material Inventory Investment

Among the data of Model IV are three variables which were placed in the data category as a temporary measure only, namely I^{ri} (desired real investment in inventories of raw materials and work-in-progress), I^{ci} (desired real investment in inventories of finished goods) and U (undesired real disinvestment in inventories). The main purpose of the present chapter is to develop relationships which will explain these variables and which will enable us to transfer them from the data category to the jointly determined category where they rightly belong.

To this end we shall draw freely on several ideas which have figured prominently in the recent literature on the determinants of inventory investment. Since these ideas are both important and comparatively unfamiliar, we shall present them in some detail even when they have appeared already in a different context in earlier chapters.

We shall begin our discussion by developing a relationship which explains the short-run behaviour of desired real investment in inventories of raw materials and work-in-progress. Modern work in this area usually starts from the proposition that, in planning its investment in inventories of raw materials for any period, a firm will take as its starting-point the excess of the inventory which it *desires* to hold at the beginning of the period over its *actual* inventory at that point of time. However, the firm will not attempt to eliminate the whole of this excess immediately but rather will try to remove it gradually over a succession of future periods. Thus the inventory investment which the firm desires for any period will be equal, not to the excess of desired over actual inventory at the beginning of the period, but to some fraction of that excess.

It will be recalled that a 'partial adjustment' hypothesis of this type was one of the links in the chain of reasoning by which we arrived at our housing investment function in the previous chapter.

In that case the hypothesis was justified by reference to the desire to avoid the personal inconveniences likely to be involved in a rapid adjustment of the actual to the desired housing stock. In the present case, the most direct way of explaining behaviour of the type in question is in terms of the costs which the firm will have to face if it insists on a rapid adjustment of actual inventory to desired inventory, e.g. the costs which will be incurred if the production schedule is altered to ensure a rapid adjustment of the work-in-progress inventory, the premium for rapid delivery which will have to be paid to suppliers of raw materials to effect a rapid build-up of the raw-material inventory and the discounts given by raw-material suppliers for purchase in large lots which will have to be forgone if a rapid run-down of raw-material inventory is insisted on.

An aggregate formalisation of the argument presented so far is:

$$I_t^{ri} = \delta(*K_t^r - K_t^r) \tag{5.1}$$

where $*K^r$ denotes the *desired*, and K^r the *actual*, real inventory of raw materials and work-in-progress held by firms in the aggregate at the beginning of the period and δ is some positive constant satisfying $0 < \delta < 1$.

We have now to consider the determinants of $*K^r$. The inventory of raw materials and work-in-progress which the individual firm desires to hold at the beginning of any period will depend mainly on the level of real output which it plans to produce during the period. Hence we can reasonably postulate that the *aggregate* desired inventory as at the beginning of period t ($*K_t^r$) will be determined mainly by $\hat{Y}_t$, the aggregate output planned for period t.

Apart from $\hat{Y}$, $*K^r$ will be governed in the short run mainly by two factors: (i) the extent of excess demand for commodities, and (ii) the cost of finance. Let us consider these in turn.

There are good reasons for believing that, in the short run, $*K^r$ will vary in the same direction as the excess demand for commodities. In the first place, as excess demand increases, deliveries of raw materials become increasingly uncertain and hence an interruption to production, through the unavailability of some key raw material, becomes increasingly likely. To guard against this possibility many firms will consider it prudent to hold larger inventories of raw materials in relation to output than they would wish to do under more normal supply conditions. Secondly, as the pressure of demand grows, firms which produce to order rather than to stock will be faced with a growing volume of unfilled orders and hence with a growing commitment to their customers in the form of undertakings to deliver at specified future dates. But the mere fact that delivery commitments are growing is likely to make firms more concerned than they otherwise would be about the possibility of a failure to meet their commitments; and this, in turn, may well prompt them to build up their raw-material inventories more in relation to production than they would do otherwise, even if they are experiencing no particular supply difficulties. Finally, as will be made clear in Chapter 9, increasing excess demand means increasing upward pressure on prices, including raw-material prices. Hence, as excess demand grows, the expectation of rising raw-material prices will become more widespread, and so, consequently, will the tendency of firms to hedge against anticipated price increases by carrying larger raw-material inventories in relation to output than they would consider appropriate if prices were stable.

Let us turn now to the second factor, the cost of finance. It can be shown that if the cost of finance to the individual firm increases, the firm will maximise profits by reducing inventories, and vice versa.[1] Thus, to the extent that firms attempt to maximise short-run profits, one can say that $*K^r$ will vary inversely, in the short run, with the overall cost of finance.

In line with this discussion about the determinants of $*K^r$, we shall now adopt the following hypothesis:

$$*K_t^r = \kappa \hat{Y}_t + \epsilon H_t$$

where κ and ϵ are positive constants and where H denotes the excess demand for commodities. It will be clear from the above discussion that this relationship treats the cost of finance as a datum.

If we substitute for $*K_t^r$ in (5.1) we obtain

$$I_t^{ri} = \delta(\kappa \hat{Y}_t + \epsilon H_t - K_t^r). \tag{5.2}$$

We must now eliminate the non-observable variable $\hat{Y}$ from this expression. To this end we shall adopt the hypothesis that the aggregate output planned for period t is a weighted sum of the demand for domestic production in all past periods, the weights declining geometrically and summing to unity. This gives:

[1] According to one well-known formula, the optimum inventory reduction will be approximately equal (in percentage terms) to the percentage increase in the square root of the cost of carrying inventories which results from the increase in the cost of finance.

$$\hat{Y}_t - \mu \hat{Y}_{t-1} = (1-\mu)(D-M)_{t-1} \tag{5.3}$$

where $0 < \mu < 1$ (see pp. 39-40 above).
From (5.2) we get:

$$I_t^{ri} - \mu I_{t-1}^{ri} = \delta\kappa(\hat{Y}_t - \mu \hat{Y}_{t-1}) + \delta\epsilon H_t - \mu\delta\epsilon H_{t-1} - \delta K_t^r + \mu\delta K_{t-1}^r.$$

Finally, on substituting for $(\hat{Y}_t - \mu \hat{Y}_{t-1})$, we get:

$$I_t^{ri} = \mu I_{t-1}^{ri} + \delta\kappa(1-\mu)(D-M)_{t-1} + \delta\epsilon H_t - \mu\delta\epsilon H_{t-1} - \delta K_t^r + \mu\delta K_{t-1}^r.$$

In the α-notation this reads:

$$I_t^{ri} = \alpha_{60} I_{t-1}^{ri} + \alpha_{61} D_{t-1} - \alpha_{61} M_{t-1} + \alpha_{62} H_t + \alpha_{63} H_{t-1} + \alpha_{64} K_t^r + \alpha_{65t}^r K_{-1} \tag{5.4}$$

where $\alpha_{60} = \mu$, $\alpha_{61} = \delta\kappa(1-\mu)$, $\alpha_{62} = \delta\epsilon$, $\alpha_{63} = -\mu\delta\epsilon$, $\alpha_{64} = -\delta$ and $\alpha_{65} = \mu\delta$.

5.2 Finished-goods Inventory Investment

Turning to the finished-goods component of inventory investment, we begin with a 'partial adjustment' hypothesis of the type used in connection with raw-material inventory investment, i.e. we postulate that firms aim to eliminate, during any period, part only of the discrepancy between the inventory of finished goods desired at the beginning of the period and the inventory actually held at the beginning of the period. Thus we have

$$I_t^{ci} = \omega(^*K_t^c - K_t^c) \tag{5.5}$$

where $^*K^c$ denotes the *desired*, and K^c the *actual*, inventory of finished goods at the beginning of the period and ω is a positive fraction.[1]

To this basis we now add the following: (a) that, given the cost of finance, the real inventory of finished goods which a firm desires to hold at the beginning of any period will be some fixed percentage of the sales which it expects to make during the period; (b) that the desired inventory–sales ratio will fall when the cost of finance increases and vice versa; and (c) that the sales which a firm expects to make during the period will depend, in some way, on the sales which it has made in past periods.[2]

[1] The justification for this hypothesis will be clear from the discussion of the preceding section.

[2] Propositions (a) and (c) are readily acceptable. The justification for (b) should be clear from the discussion of the preceding section.

Proposition (a) gives:

$$*K_t^c = n\hat{S}_t$$

where $\hat{S}$ denotes expected sales and n is a positive constant. Substituting this in (5.5) we get:

$$I_t^{ci} = \omega n \hat{S}_t - \omega K_t^c. \tag{5.6}$$

The version of proposition (c) which we shall use is:

$$\hat{S}_t - \beta \hat{S}_{t-1} = (1 - \beta)S_{t-1} \tag{5.7}$$

where $0 < \beta < 1$. This implies that the expected sales in period t is a weighted sum of the sales actually realised in all past periods, the weights declining geometrically as we move back in time and summing to unity (see pp. 39–40 above).

This expression is now used to eliminate the non-observable $\hat{S}_t$ in (5.6). We proceed as follows. From (5.6) we get:

$$I_t^{ci} - \beta I_{t-1}^{ci} = \omega n(\hat{S}_t - \beta \hat{S}_{t-1}) - \omega(K_t^c - \beta K_{t-1}^c).$$

Using (5.7), this can be written as:

$$I_t^{ci} = \beta I_{t-1}^{ci} + \omega n(1 - \beta)S_{t-1} - \omega K_t^c + \beta \omega K_{t-1}^c.$$

If we now replace S (aggregate *realised* sales of finished goods) with D (aggregate *desired* sales of finished goods), this expression becomes:

$$I_t^{ci} = \alpha_{70}I_{t-1}^{ci} + \alpha_{71}D_{t-1} + \alpha_{72}K_t^c + \alpha_{73}K_{t-1}^c \tag{5.8}$$

where $\alpha_{70} = \beta$; $\alpha_{71} = \omega n(1 - \beta)$; $\alpha_{72} = -\omega$; and $\alpha_{73} = \beta \omega$.

5.3 Undesired Inventory Investment

Having developed relationships to explain I^{ri} and I^{ci}, we now turn our attention to U – undesired real disinvestment in inventories. We begin by breaking this up into two components: (i) undesired disinvestment in inventories of finished goods, U^c, and (ii) undesired disinvestment in inventories of raw materials and work-in-progress, U^r. Thus we have:

$$U_t = U_t^c + U_t^r. \tag{5.9}$$

We now consider each component in turn. To explain U_t^c we begin with the definition:

$$*K_{t+1}^c = K_t^c + I_t^{ci} \tag{5.10}$$

which states that the inventory of finished goods which firms in the aggregate desire to hold at the end of any period is equal to the inventory which they actually hold at the beginning of the period *plus* the addition to inventory which they desire to make in the course of the period.

Next the so-called 'buffer stock' principle is used to obtain an expression for $*K_{t+1}^e$ in terms of K_{t+1}^e. As applied to finished goods, the buffer-stock principle postulates that the inventory which firms as a whole actually hold at the end of any period is equal to the inventory which they desire to hold at the end of the period *minus* the excess of actual sales over expected sales in the period. Thus the buffer-stock principle gives:

$$K_{t+1}^e = *K_{t+1}^e - (S_t - \hat{S}_t)$$

which can be rewritten as:

$$*K_{t+1}^e = K_{t+1}^e + (S_t - \hat{S}_t). \tag{5.11}$$

Combining (5.10) and (5.11), we get:

$$(K_t^e - K_{t+1}^e) - (-I_t^{ci}) = S_t - \hat{S}_t. \tag{5.12}$$

Now the left-hand side of (5.12) is *realised* disinvestment in inventories of finished goods in period t *less* desired disinvestment in inventories of finished goods, i.e. undesired disinvestment in inventories of finished goods in period t or U_t^e. Hence:

$$U_t^e = S_t - \hat{S}_t. \tag{5.13}$$

We now use (5.7) to eliminate $\hat{S}$ from this expression. Lagging (5.13) one period, multiplying through by β and subtracting from (5.13), we get:

$$U_t^e - \beta U_{t-1}^e = S_t - \beta S_{t-1} - (\hat{S}_t - \beta \hat{S}_{t-1}). \tag{5.14}$$

On substituting (5.7) we get:

$$U_t^e = \beta U_{t-1}^e + (S_t - S_{t-1}). \tag{5.15}$$

Finally, replacing S by D in (5.15), we get:

$$U_t^e = \beta U_{t-1}^e + (D_t - D_{t-1})$$

which in α-notation is:

$$U_t^e = \alpha_{80} U_{t-1}^e + (D_t - D_{t-1}) \tag{5.16}$$

where $\alpha_{80} = \beta$.

E

We turn now to U^r. We begin with the definition which corresponds to (5.10), namely:

$$*K^r_{t+1} = K^r_t + I^{ri}_t. \tag{5.17}$$

Next we modify the buffer-stock principle to cover the case of raw materials and work-in-progress. An appropriate modification is one which postulates that the inventory which firms in the aggregate actually hold at the end of any period is equal to the inventory which they desire to hold *minus* some proportion of the excess of the actual production of the period over the planned production. Thus we have:

$$K^r_{t+1} = *K^r_{t+1} - p(Y_t - \hat{Y}_t) \tag{5.18}$$

where p is some positive fraction. Combining (5.17) and (5.18), we get:

$$(K^r_t - K^r_{t+1}) - (-I^{ri}_t) = p(Y_t - \hat{Y}_t).$$

The left-hand side of this expression is U^r_t. Hence:

$$U^r_t = p(Y_t - \hat{Y}_t). \tag{5.19}$$

We now use (5.3) to eliminate $\hat{Y}$ from this expression. If we lag (5.19) one period, multiply through by μ and subtract, we get:

$$U^r_t - \mu U^r_{t-1} = p Y_t - p\mu Y_{t-1} - p(\hat{Y}_t - \mu \hat{Y}_{t-1}).$$

Substituting from (5.3) for $(\hat{Y}_t - \mu \hat{Y}_{t-1})$, we get:

$$U^r_t - \mu U^r_{t-1} = p Y_t - p\mu Y_{t-1} - p(1 - \mu)(D - M)_{t-1}$$

which in the α-notation is:

$$U^r_t = \alpha_{90} U^r_{t-1} + \alpha_{91} Y_t + \alpha_{92} Y_{t-1} + \alpha_{93} D_{t-1} - \alpha_{93} M_{t-1} \tag{5.20}$$

where $\alpha_{90} = \mu$, $\alpha_{91} = p$, $\alpha_{92} = -p\mu$ and $\alpha_{93} = -p(1 - \mu)$.

Two pieces of recent British research call for comment at this stage. The first is the study of inventory behaviour in the United Kingdom undertaken by Ball and Drake.[1] Ball and Drake are concerned with the short-run behaviour of *realised* inventory investment. They begin by building up four distinct relationships, each of which purports to explain this variable, from the following six propositions:

(i) that desired inventories are proportional to expected sales;

[1] See R. J. Ball and Pamela S. Drake, 'Stock Adjustment Inventory Models of the United Kingdom Economy', *Manchester School of Economic and Social Studies* (May 1963).

(ii) that actual inventories are equal to desired inventories *minus* the excess of actual over expected sales, i.e. the buffer-stock principle;

(iii) that desired inventory investment is some positive fraction of the excess of desired inventories over actual inventories;

(iv) that desired inventory investment is equal to the change in desired inventories from the previous period *plus* some positive fraction of the excess of desired over actual inventories in the previous period;

(v) that expected sales are equal to actual sales *plus* some fraction of the change in sales from the previous period;

(vi) that expected sales are a weighted sum of current and all past sales with weights which decline geometrically.

All four relationships embody the first two propositions. The first of the four relationships, which Ball and Drake denote by A^F, adds propositions (iii) and (v) to (i) and (ii); the second relationship, denoted by A^N, adds propositions (iii) and (vi); the third relationship, denoted by B^F, adds propositions (iv) and (v), while the fourth relationship, denoted by B^N, adds propositions (iv) and (vi).[1]

Each of the four relationships is fitted to quarterly British data in an attempt to discriminate between them. Since our relationships (5.8) and (5.16) between them embody the four propositions which constitute Ball and Drake's A^N relationship, propositions (i), (iii) and (vi) entering into (5.8) and proposition (ii) entering into (5.16), their empirical results are of some interest.[2] These show that, considering only 'goodness of fit' and 'randomness of residuals', A^N and B^N are superior to A^F and B^F. On the other hand, the sales variable (Y_{t-1} in Ball's notation, S_{t-1} in ours) has the wrong *a priori* sign in A^N whereas none of the other three relationships has coefficients with a wrong sign.[3] However, the significance of this point is diminished by the fact that the estimate of the coefficient in question is very uncertain (roughly equal to its standard error) and that each of the other relationships has at least one estimated coefficient which is uncertain (less than twice its standard error).[4] Ball and Drake also attempt to discriminate between their four relationships by inquiring whether the estimates for the 'structural' parameters (τ, λ and β in

---

[1] Ibid., pp. 87–91.

[2] It can be seen from (5.7) that our formulation of proposition (vi) differs slightly from Ball and Drake's, in that expected sales are a weighted sum of *past* sales only.   [3] Ibid., Table I, p. 94.   [4] Ibid., p. 93.

their notation, β, ω and n in ours) which are implied by the estimates for the coefficients of the relationships (the coefficients are functions of the structural parameters) are more 'sensible' for one or more of the relationships than for the rest. But for various reasons this proves to be impossible.[1] In general, therefore, the results which emerge are somewhat inconclusive. From our point of view they are rendered still less conclusive by the fact that the four relationships in question have been fitted to data for *total* inventories. Their results would have more relevance for our purposes if the four relationships had been fitted to data for investment in inventories of finished goods rather than to data for total inventories.

The second empirical investigation which has some bearing on (5.8) and (5.16) is the much less elaborate study undertaken by Feinstein.[2] He fits to annual British data a relationship which embodies only three of the four propositions from which (5.8) and (5.16) have been built up, namely the propositions (i), (ii) and (iii).[3] Furthermore, like the Ball and Drake relationships, it has been fitted to data for *total* inventories rather than to data for inventories of finished goods, which reduces its relevance still further. Nevertheless it is worth noting, perhaps, that the only two estimates of structural parameters which Feinstein is able to obtain by unscrambling the estimates of his coefficients both have the right sign.[4]

5.4 The Final Model and its Dynamic Properties

To form our final model (Model V), we first add relationships (5.4), (5.8), (5.16) and (5.20) to the relationships comprising Model IV. We then add five definitional relationships to complete the model.

The first of these relates to H (excess demand), a new variable which appears as an explanatory variable in (5.4). The definition of excess demand adopted in Chapter 1 is that excess demand is the excess of D over $(Y^p + M)$ where Y^p denotes real potential gross

---

[1] See R. J. Ball and Pamela S. Drake, 'Stock Adjustment Inventory Models of the United Kingdom Economy', *Manchester School of Economic and Social Studies* (May 1963) pp. 94–101.

[2] See C. H. Feinstein, 'Stockbuilding, Expenditure and the Balance of Payments', *Times Review of Industry* (Dec 1962), and 'Stocks, Sales and Stockbuilding', *Times Review of Industry and Technology* (Mar 1963).

[3] See Feinstein, 'Stocks, Sales and Stockbuilding', op. cit., pp. xiii–xv. It will be seen that a slightly modified form of the buffer-stock principle (proposition (ii)) has been used.

[4] In our notation estimates of ω and n.

domestic product (see section 1.2). Thus we have:

$$H_t = D_t - (Y_t^p + M_t). \tag{5.21}$$

The second and third definitions relate to the new variables K^r and K^c, which appear as explanatory variables in relationships (5.4) and (5.8) respectively. By definition, the inventory of raw materials and work-in-progress held at the beginning of any period is equal to the inventory held at the beginning of the previous period *plus* the realised addition to inventory of the previous period. Now the realised addition to inventory of any period is given by:

Realised investment = Desired investment + (Realised investment
                  − Desired investment)
              = Desired investment + (Desired disinvest-
                  ment − Realised disinvestment).

For period $(t-1)$ the term on the left-hand side of this expression is given by $(K_t^r - K_{t-1}^r)$, while the first and second terms on the right-hand side are given by I_{t-1}^{ri} and $(-U_{t-1}^r)$ respectively. Hence:

$$K_t^r = K_{t-1}^r + I_{t-1}^{ri} - U_{t-1}^r. \tag{5.22}$$

By means of a parallel argument, we get:

$$K_t^c = K_{t-1}^c + I_{t-1}^{ci} - U_{t-1}^c. \tag{5.23}$$

These are the second and third of the definitions that we shall use to close our model.

The fourth definition is:

$$I_t^i = I_t^{ri} + I_t^{ci} \tag{5.24}$$

which merely says that aggregate desired real inventory investment is the sum of its two parts: desired real investment in raw materials and work-in-progress and desired real investment in finished goods.

The fifth and final definition is (5.9), which says that total undesired inventory disinvestment is the sum of its two parts.

We are now ready to set out the final model in our sequence (Model V). This is as follows:

Desired Consumption Expenditure
$$C_t = \alpha_{10}X_t + \alpha_{11}C_{t-1} + Z^1 \tag{2.24}$$

Disposable Income
$$X_t = \alpha_{20} + \alpha_{21}Y_t \tag{2.26}$$

Components of Aggregate Demand

$$D_t = C_t + G_t + E_t + I_t^{gf} + I_t^{gh} + I_t^{ri} + I_t^{ci} \qquad (3.11)$$

Demand–Output Relationship

$$D_t = Y_t + M_t + U_t \qquad (3.2)$$

Realised Imports

$$M_t = \alpha_{30} M_{t-1} + \alpha_{31} D_{t-2} + \alpha_{32} I_{t-2}^i + Z^2 \qquad (3.4)$$

Desired Fixed-capital Investment

$$I_t^{gf} = \alpha_{40}(Y_{t-1} - Y_{t-2}) + \alpha_{41} I_{t-1}^{gf} + \alpha_{42} K_t + \alpha_{43} K_{t-1} \qquad (4.11)$$

Desired Housing Investment

$$I_t^{gh} = \alpha_{50}(X_{t-1} - X_{t-2}) + \alpha_{51} I_{t-1}^{gh} + \alpha_{52} I_{t-2}^{gh} + \alpha_{53} I_{t-3}^{gh} + \alpha_{54} K_t^h \\ + \alpha_{55} K_{t-1}^h + \alpha_{56} K_{t-2}^h + \alpha_{57} K_{t-3}^h \qquad (4.20)$$

Desired Inventory Investment: Raw Materials

$$I_t^{ri} = \alpha_{60} I_{t-1}^{ri} + \alpha_{61} D_{t-1} - \alpha_{61} M_{t-1} + \alpha_{62} H_t + \alpha_{63} H_{t-1} + \alpha_{64} K_t^r + \alpha_{65} K_{t-1}^r \qquad (5.4)$$

Desired Inventory Investment: Finished Goods

$$I_t^{ci} = \alpha_{70} I_{t-1}^{ci} + \alpha_{71} D_{t-1} + \alpha_{72} K_t^c + \alpha_{73} K_{t-1}^c \qquad (5.8)$$

Undesired Inventory Disinvestment: Finished Goods

$$U_t^c = \alpha_{80} U_{t-1}^c + (D_t - D_{t-1}) \qquad (5.16)$$

Undesired Inventory Disinvestment: Raw Materials

$$U_t^r = \alpha_{90} U_{t-1}^r + \alpha_{91} Y_t + \alpha_{92} Y_{t-1} + \alpha_{93} D_{t-1} - \alpha_{93} M_{t-1} \qquad (5.20)$$

Definition of Excess Demand

$$H_t = D_t - (Y_t^p + M_t) \qquad (5.21)$$

Actual Inventory: Raw Materials

$$K_t^r = K_{t-1}^r + I_{t-1}^{ri} - U_{t-1}^r \qquad (5.22)$$

Actual Inventory: Finished Goods

$$K_t^c = K_{t-1}^c + I_{t-1}^{ci} - U_{t-1}^c \qquad (5.23)$$

Components of Desired Inventory Investment

$$I_t^i = I_t^{ri} + I_t^{ci} \qquad (5.24)$$

Components of Undesired Inventory Disinvestment

$$U_t = U_t^r + U_t^c \qquad (5.9)$$

The jointly determined variables are C, X, D, Y, M, I^{gf}, I^{gh}, I^{ri}, I^{ci}, U^r, U^c, H, K^r, K^c, I^i and U, while the data are G, E, Z^1, Z^2, K, K^h and Y^p. Thus provided none of the above data has misclassified (i.e. provided none of the data should properly have been treated as a jointly determined variable), we have a complete model. We shall consider whether or not this proviso has been met in the next section.

We begin our analysis of the dynamic properties of Model V by reducing it, by substitution, to a system of eight linear difference equations in the eight jointly determined variables D, M, I^{gf}, I^{gh}, I^{ri}, I^{ci}, U^c and U^r. The mechanics of this operation are set out in Appendix 5.2. Here we merely set out the result, namely:

$$D_t(1 - \alpha_{10}\alpha_{21}) - \alpha_{11}D_{t-1} + \alpha_{10}\alpha_{21}M_t - I_t^{gf} + \alpha_{11}I_{t-1}^{gf} - I_t^{gh} + \alpha_{11}I_{t-1}^{gh}$$
$$- I_t^{ri} + \alpha_{11}I_{t-1}^{ri} - I_t^{ci} + \alpha_{11}I_{t-1}^{ci} + \alpha_{10}\alpha_{21}U_t^c + \alpha_{10}\alpha_{21}U_t^r = k_1 \quad (5.25)$$

$$M_t - \alpha_{30}M_{t-1} - \alpha_{31}D_{t-2} - \alpha_{32}I_{t-2}^{ri} - \alpha_{32}I_{t-2}^{ci} = k_2 \quad (5.26)$$

$$I_t^{gf} - \alpha_{41}I_{t-1}^{gf} - \alpha_{40}(D_{t-1} - D_{t-2}) + \alpha_{40}(M_{t-1} - M_{t-2}) + \alpha_{40}(U_{t-1}^c - U_{t-2}^c)$$
$$+ \alpha_{40}(U_{t-1}^r - U_{t-2}^r) = k_3 \quad (5.27)$$

$$I_t^{gh} - \alpha_{51}I_{t-1}^{gh} - \alpha_{52}I_{t-2}^{gh} - \alpha_{53}I_{t-3}^{gh} - \alpha_{50}\alpha_{21}(D_{t-1} - D_{t-2})$$
$$+ \alpha_{50}\alpha_{21}(M_{t-1} - M_{t-2}) + \alpha_{50}\alpha_{21}(U_{t-1}^c - U_{t-2}^c)$$
$$+ \alpha_{50}\alpha_{21}(U_{t-1}^r - U_{t-2}^r) = k_4 \quad (5.28)$$

$$I_t^{ri} - (1 + \alpha_{60} + \alpha_{64})I_{t-1}^{ri} + (\alpha_{60} - \alpha_{65})I_{t-2}^{ri} - \alpha_{62}D_t - (\alpha_{61} - \alpha_{62} + \alpha_{63})D_{t-1}$$
$$+ (\alpha_{61} + \alpha_{63})D_{t-2} + \alpha_{62}M_t + (\alpha_{61} - \alpha_{62} + \alpha_{63})M_{t-1}$$
$$- (\alpha_{61} + \alpha_{63})M_{t-2} + \alpha_{64}U_{t-1}^r + \alpha_{65}U_{t-2}^r = k_5 \quad (5.29)$$

$$I_t^{ci} - (1 + \alpha_{70} + \alpha_{72})I_{t-1}^{ci} + (\alpha_{70} - \alpha_{73})I_{t-2}^{ci} - \alpha_{71}(D_{t-1} - D_{t-2})$$
$$+ \alpha_{72}U_{t-1}^c + \alpha_{73}U_{t-2}^c = 0 \quad (5.30)$$

$$U_t^c - \alpha_{80}U_{t-1}^c - (D_t - D_{t-1}) = 0 \quad (5.31)$$

$$U_t^r(1 + \alpha_{91}) + (\alpha_{92} - \alpha_{90})U_{t-1}^r - \alpha_{91}D_t - (\alpha_{92} + \alpha_{93})D_{t-1} + \alpha_{91}M_t$$
$$+ (\alpha_{92} + \alpha_{93})M_{t-1} + \alpha_{91}U_t^c + \alpha_{92}U_{t-1}^c = 0 \quad (5.32)$$

where:
$$k_1 = \alpha_{10}\alpha_{20} + G_t - \alpha_{11}G_{t-1} + E_t - \alpha_{11}E_{t-1} + Z^1$$
$$k_2 = Z^2$$
$$k_3 = \alpha_{42}K_t + \alpha_{43}K_{t-1}$$
$$k_4 = \alpha_{54}K_t^h + \alpha_{55}K_{t-1}^h + \alpha_{56}K_{t-2}^h + \alpha_{57}K_{t-3}^h$$
$$k_5 = -\alpha_{62}Y_t^p + (\alpha_{62} - \alpha_{63})Y_{t-1}^p + \alpha_{63}Y_{t-2}^p.$$

Next we convert (5.25) through (5.32) into a numerical system by using the following values for the αs: $\alpha_{10} = 0 \cdot 3$; $\alpha_{11} = 0 \cdot 5$; $\alpha_{21} = 0 \cdot 08$;

$\alpha_{30} = 0\cdot1$; $\alpha_{31} = 0\cdot2$; $\alpha_{32} = 0\cdot5$; $\alpha_{40} = 1\cdot36$; $\alpha_{41} = 0\cdot83$; $\alpha_{50} = 0\cdot115$; $\alpha_{51} = 2\cdot130$; $\alpha_{52} = -1\cdot461$; $\alpha_{53} = 0\cdot323$; $\alpha_{60} = 0\cdot5$; $\alpha_{61} = 0\cdot013$; $\alpha_{62} = 0\cdot026$; $\alpha_{63} = -0\cdot013$; $\alpha_{64} = -0\cdot2$; $\alpha_{65} = 0\cdot1$; $\alpha_{70} = 0\cdot5$; $\alpha_{71} = 0\cdot15$; $\alpha_{72} = -0\cdot2$; $\alpha_{73} = 0\cdot1$; $\alpha_{80} = 0\cdot5$; $\alpha_{90} = 0\cdot5$; $\alpha_{91} = 0\cdot3$; $\alpha_{92} = -0\cdot15$; $\alpha_{93} = -0\cdot15$. The interested reader will find brief comments on these values in Appendix 5.1. The numerical system which is obtained, after a slight rearrangement, is:

$$0\cdot976D_t - 0\cdot5D_{t-1} + 0\cdot024M_t - I_t^{gf} + 0\cdot5I_{t-1}^{gf} - I_t^{gh} + 0\cdot5I_{t-1}^{gh} - I_t^{ri}$$
$$+ 0\cdot5I_{t-1}^{ri} - I_t^{ci} + 0\cdot5I_{t-1}^{ci} + 0\cdot024U_t^c + 0\cdot024U_t^r = k_1 \quad (5.33)$$

$$-0\cdot2D_{t-2} + M_t - 0\cdot1M_{t-1} - 0\cdot5I_{t-2}^{ri} - 0\cdot5I_{t-2}^{ci} = k_2 \quad (5.34)$$

$$-1\cdot36(D_{t-1} - D_{t-2}) + 1\cdot36(M_{t-1} - M_{t-2}) + I_t^{gf} - 0\cdot83I_{t-1}^{gf}$$
$$+ 1\cdot36(U_{t-1}^c - U_{t-2}^c) + 1\cdot36(U_{t-1}^r - U_{t-2}^r) = k_3 \quad (5.35)$$

$$-0\cdot009(D_{t-1} - D_{t-2}) + 0\cdot009(M_{t-1} - M_{t-2}) + I_t^{gh} - 2\cdot130I_{t-1}^{gh}$$
$$+ 1\cdot461I_{t-2}^{gh} - 0\cdot323I_{t-3}^{gh} + 0\cdot009(U_{t-1}^c - U_{t-2}^c)$$
$$+ 0\cdot009(U_{t-1}^r - U_{t-2}^r) = k_4 \quad (5.36)$$

$$-0\cdot026(D_t - D_{t-1}) + 0\cdot026(M_t - M_{t-1}) + I_t^{ri} - 1\cdot3I_{t-1}^{ri} + 0\cdot4I_{t-2}^{ri}$$
$$- 0\cdot2U_{t-1}^r + 0\cdot1U_{t-2}^r = k_5 \quad (5.37)$$

$$-0\cdot15(D_{t-1} - D_{t-2}) + I_t^{ci} - 1\cdot31I_{t-1}^{ci} + 0\cdot4I_{t-2}^{ci} - 0\cdot2U_{t-1}^c + 0\cdot1U_{t-2}^c = 0 \quad (5.38)$$

$$-(D_t - D_{t-1}) + U_t^c - 0\cdot5U_{t-1}^c = 0 \quad (5.39)$$

$$-0\cdot3(D_t - D_{t-1}) + 0\cdot3(M_t - M_{t-1}) + 0\cdot3U_t^c - 0\cdot15U_{t-1}^c + 1\cdot3U_t^r$$
$$- 0\cdot65U_{t-1}^r = 0. \quad (5.40)$$

Finally we solve the numerical system (5.33) through (5.40). The details of the solution are shown in Appendix 5.3. The solution for D is:

$$D_t = A_{11}(1\cdot388)^t + A_{12}(1\cdot166)^t \cos [23\cdot7t - A_{13}] + A_{14}(1\cdot000)^t$$
$$+ A_{15}(0\cdot943)^t \cos [23\cdot3t - A_{16}] + A_{17}(0\cdot786)^t \cos [38\cdot4t - A_{18}]$$
$$+ A_{19}(-0\cdot566)^t + A_{20}(0\cdot508)^t \cos [49\cdot3t - A_{21}] + A_{22}(-0\cdot309)^t$$
$$+ A_{23}(0\cdot207)^t \cos [50\cdot1t - A_{24}] + \bar{D}_t \quad (5.41)$$

where $\bar{D}_t$ is the particular solution which can be derived once time paths have been specified for the ks and the As are arbitrary constants which can be evaluated given the appropriate initial conditions. The solutions for the other seven jointly determined variables are identical with (5.41) except for the particular solution and the arbitrary As.

It will be recalled that, in moving from Model III to Model IV, we moved from a stable system characterised by monotonic convergence on the equilibrium path to an unstable system in which each of the jointly determined variables eventually follows a mildly explosive cyclical path round equilibrium in response to arbitrary initial conditions. The instability which first appears in Model IV is accentuated as we moved to Model V. This is apparent from (5.41). The second term in this expression generates an explosive cyclical path round $\bar{D}_t$ in response to arbitrary initial conditions, while the fourth and fifth terms generate cyclical paths which are on the borderline of instability. However, the dominant term in the expression is the first, which means that eventually the time paths of D and the other jointly determined variables will be characterised by monotonic explosion.

5.5 The Data of the Model

To justify any economic model, one must justify (i) the choice of relationships; and (ii) the choice of data. As far as Model V is concerned, the choice of relationships has been justified in the course of building up the model step by step from Models I to IV. On the other hand, with one exception, namely the variable E (see pp. 80-2 above), nothing has been said so far to justify the choice of data. We shall now attempt to fill this gap.

We shall begin by explaining the criterion to be used as a basis for deciding whether any particular variable or any particular institutional arrangement, such as the tax structure, can properly be treated as a datum. Our criterion is one which is suggested by the meaning of the word 'datum'. To say that a variable is a datum in any model is to imply that its value in any period is imposed on the model rather than being generated by the model, i.e. the variable is externally given for the purpose of the model. This leads us to the following criterion: It is proper to treat a variable, institutional arrangement, etc., as a datum for the purposes of any model if its current level or state, while determining the current levels of other variables in the model, is not in turn determined by the current levels of other variables; i.e. provided its connection with other variables is a one-way connection or essentially so.

For example, variables, etc., which are fully or largely determined by the authorities, such as government expenditure, the tax and

E 2

transfer payment structure, the exchange rate, the intensity of direct controls over foreign transactions and the stock of money, may be treated as data. Again, in a short-run model one usually feels justified in treating variables like the size of the population, the size of the work force, the stock of fixed-capital equipment and the state of technology as data because the 'feedback' to variables such as these from other variables in the model is likely to be entirely negligible in the short run, even though it may be significant in the long run.

Two points are worth stressing in connection with this criterion. The first point is that while any feature of the real world which remains constant must be treated as a datum, the converse is not true, i.e. it is not the case that a datum is something which remains constant. On the contrary, one of the main tasks of theoretical economics is to postulate *changes* in the data and then to trace the consequences of these changes with the help of the relationships of the model. The second point is that the criterion provides no absolute and final grouping into data and jointly determined variables; some feature of reality which could be treated as a datum in one model would have to be treated as jointly determined in another. For example, while export prices and export volume could be treated as data in an Australian model, it would be preferable to treat them as jointly determined in a British model because, in the British case, export prices and export volume not only influence economic conditions but are also influenced significantly by them. Again, while the state of technology could be taken as given in a short-run model, it would have to be 'explained' in a long-run model.

To apply this criterion we shall divide the data of the model into two groups: (i) the *explicit* data, i.e. the given variables which actually appear in the relationships; and (ii) the *implicit* data, i.e. the given variables, institutional arrangements, etc., which underlie the relationships and determine their precise position and shape.

In the explicit category we have the seven variables E, G, K, K^h, Y^p, Z^1 and Z^2. The first of these has been examined already in the light of our criterion (see pp. 80-2 above), and it remains to consider the rest. Let us begin with G. From the present point of view the essential feature of G is that its value in any period is at the authorities' choice. As we shall see in the next chapter, one of the considerations which may govern their choice is the internal and external economic situation – G is one of the variables which are subject to manipulation by the British authorities in the interests of the four objectives discussed in the opening chapter. Thus the current level of G may be influenced by the current levels of other variables in the model such as D and M. It cannot be said, however, that the current levels of these other variables *determine* the current level of G; the current level of G is fixed by the authorities and they can allow the current levels of other variables to play some part in their decision or not as they choose. Thus, G is a genuine datum in the light of our criterion.

The stock of fixed-capital equipment, K, is certainly dependent on the unknowns via I^{gf}. However, in the short run, the dependence will be weak, since, with a short reaction interval, the addition to K via current investment will be negligible in relation to the level of K (cf. p. 43 above). Consequently the dependence may be safely ignored in a model like Model V which is designed extensively for use in relation to the short run. The same argument holds *mutatis mutandis* for K^h, the stock of housing. Thus both of these variables appear as genuine data in the light of our criterion.

The decision to place Y^p in the data category can be justified along similar lines. Changes in this variable will result from changes in the availability of productive inputs and from changes in the state of technology. Now neither the available stock of productive inputs nor the state of technology are completely independent of the unknowns of our model; for example, both will be influenced by the rate of investment in fixed-capital equipment. However, in the short-run model it seems safe to ignore this dependence because, in the short run, additions to the stock of productive inputs will be insignificant relative to the existing level of the stock and improvements to technology will be negligible relative to the existing state of technology.

We come now to Z^1. By turning back to relationship (2.24), the reader will see that the collection of terms which constitute Z^1 contains three variables, namely, L the level of liquid assets at the end of the period, N some index of monetary stringency and R some index of consumer attitudes (see p. 56 above). The first two of these three variables resemble G in that they are variables which, in the British case, are substantially, if not completely, at the authorities' choice. This is true even though the British authorities have no direct control over these variables as they have over G and must rely on various indirect means, which we shall discuss in the next chapter, if they wish to fix their current values. All that has been said above about the propriety of treating G as a datum applies, therefore, to the variables L and N as well.

The legitimacy of treating R, the index of consumer attitudes, as a datum is more doubtful because, as Katona and his associates freely admit, little is yet known about the origins of short-run changes in consumer attitudes.[1] On the other hand, they are prepared to assert on the basis of present knowledge that 'The economic attitudes of consumers originate in a variety of political and economic developments. It is inadequate to assume that consumer attitudes are merely a reflection of recent trends in, say, incomes or prices and that these can serve as substitutes for data on attitudes; rather it is necessary to measure consumer attitudes and changes in them directly.'[2] This statement and others like it would appear to provide at least some support for our view of R as a variable whose current level determines, but is not, in turn, determined by, the current levels of other variables in our model.

Finally we have Z^2. Reference back to the argument underlying relationship (3.4) shows that Z^2 stands for a collection of terms involving the following variables:

   (i) the British price of importables relative to the prices of exportables and non-traded goods;
  (ii) the price of British-made importables relative to the price of foreign-made importables in terms of British currency;
 (iii) the delivery delay quoted by British producers of importables relative to that quoted by foreign producers;
  (iv) the credit terms offered to British purchasers of importables by British producers relative to the credit terms offered by foreign producers;
   (v) the intensity of direct controls over foreign transactions.

Examination of this list shows that the variables involved in Z^2 fall into three groups:

   (a) those which are clearly genuine data in the light of our criterion;

[1] See George Katona and Eva Mueller, *Consumer Attitudes and Demand, 1950–1952* (University of Michigan, Survey Research Center, Institute for Social Research, 1953) pp. 57–8. A recent study which throws some light on the question is F. Gerrard Adams and Edward W. Green, 'Explaining and Predicting Aggregative Consumer Attitudes', *International Economic Review* (Sep 1965).

[2] Katona and Mueller, op. cit., p. 2.

(b) those which clearly are not genuine data; and
(c) those about which there is some doubt.

In the first group we have variables (ii) and (v) to which everything said above in relation to G applies.[1] In the second group we have variables (i) and (iii). The doubtful variable is (iv). We would consider it proper to treat this variable as a datum if it were clear that the credit terms offered by British producers of importables are determined substantially by the cost and availability of finance in general, because as we shall see in the next chapter, the cost and availability of finance is another variable which in the British case is substantially at choice. Doubt arises simply because so little is known on this point.

The decision to treat (i) and (iii) as data, in defiance of our criterion, was taken partly in the interests of simplicity and partly because we wish to present the relevant theoretical material at a later stage in the book (see Chapters 8 and 9 below).

Let us turn now from the explicit data of our model to the implicit data. Several of the implicit data have been mentioned already in earlier chapters. The main ones are:

(i) the tax and transfer payment structures which underlie (2.26), the disposable income function (see pp. 57–61 above);
(ii) the business tax structure which underlies (4.11), the fixed-capital investment function (see pp. 90–8 above);
(iii) the cost and availability of finance which is a datum for (4.11), (4.20), (5.4) and (5.8), the four investment functions.[2]

In the British case all of these are at the choice of the authorities, or substantially so. The first two are under the authorities' direct control like the variable G, while the third is open to manipulation by various indirect means to be discussed in the next chapter. All three, therefore, would appear to be legitimate data in the light of our criterion.

In addition to the three implicit data listed in the preceding paragraph, all of which emerged in the course of building up the

---

[1] Variable (ii) is at choice because the exchange rate is at choice.

[2] See pp. 97, 108, 118, 119 above. It will be seen from these references that while the *cost* of finance has been mentioned as an implicit datum for all four investment functions, the *availability* of finance has been mentioned only in relation to (4.20), the housing investment function. The reason for this is that the argument underlying the fixed-capital and inventory investment functions is based on the tacit assumption of a perfect capital market. If this assumption is removed, the availability of finance emerges, along with the cost of finance, as one of the variables underlying these functions.

relationships of our model, we must mention one other to which no reference has yet been made, namely the indirect tax structure. From Table 2.1 it will be clear that the indirect tax structure is not a datum underlying (2.26), the disposable income function, because that relationship is one which links personal disposable income and gross domestic product *at factor cost* (see pp. 57–61 above). Where, then, does it enter the picture? The answer is that the indirect tax structure is an implicit datum underlying (2.24), the consumption function; if the indirect tax structure is made more severe, the consumption function will shift downwards, while if it is made less severe the consumption function will shift upwards.

To pursue this point, let us divide real desired consumption expenditure into (a) expenditure on non-durable items; and (b) expenditure on durable items. Consider first the impact effect of an increase in the rate of purchase tax (or a decrease in the subsidy) on some non-durable consumption item, e.g. beer. The increase in the tax rate will lead to an increase in the price of the item to the consumer and hence to a fall in the quantity purchased. But assuming that the elasticity of demand for the item is less than unity, outlay on the item will increase, and with money disposable income, and hence total outlay, unaffected this must mean a decrease in the outlay on other consumer goods. Finally, with no immediate effect on the prices to the consumer of these other consumer goods, this decrease in outlay must mean a decrease in real expenditure also. The conclusion, then, is that real expenditure both on the non-durable item in question and on all other consumer goods in the aggregate will fall, i.e. that the variable C will fall. The effect of the increase in purchase tax must, therefore, be to reduce C at given levels of the explanatory variables of (2.24). Conversely, the effect of a decrease in the rate of purchase tax will be to increase C at given levels of the explanatory variables.

Consider now the case of an increase in the rate of purchase tax on some *durable* consumption item, e.g. domestic refrigerators. The difference between this case and the previous one is that expenditure on the item is postponable and is normally not financed entirely from current income. Once again, the effect will be to reduce real consumption expenditure, but for different reasons. Real expenditure on the durable item in question will fall: (a) because, given the higher price, it will be more difficult to finance expenditure on the item, *ceteris paribus*, than before; and (b) because there will be an incentive to postpone purchase of the item in the hope that the old rate of tax will be restored in the near future.[1] Since the tax increase will have no effect on the rest of real consumption expenditure, real consumption expenditure as a whole must fall. Once again, therefore, the effect of the increase in purchase tax will be to reduce the level of C at given levels of the explanatory variables which enter into (2.24). The argument holds in reverse for the case of a decrease in the rate of purchase tax on some given durable item.

That the indirect tax structure is a legitimate datum on the basis of our criterion will be clear from earlier discussion. Like the direct tax structure and the level of real government expenditure, the indirect tax structure is entirely at choice and hence in no sense is determined by the variables of the model.

5.6 Summary

In the previous chapter we undertook that three variables which had been placed in the data category for the purposes of Model IV would ultimately be treated as jointly determined variables. The variables in question were I^{ri}, I^{ci} and U. The main purpose of the present chapter is to develop relationships which will enable us to honour this undertaking.

We begin by developing two relationships to explain I^{ri} and I^{ci} (desired real investment in inventories of raw materials and work-in-progress and in inventories of finished goods, respectively). Each of these relationships derives from a 'partial adjustment' hypothesis, i.e. a hypothesis which postulates that the individual firm aims to eliminate, during any period, part only of the discrepancy between the inventory desired at the beginning of the period and the inventory actually held at the beginning of the period. We then add two relationships to explain U^r and U^c (undesired disinvestment in inventories of raw materials and work-in-progress and in inventories of finished goods, respectively). Each of these relationships is based on the appropriate version of the so-called buffer-stock principle. As applied to finished goods, this states that the inventory which firms as a whole actually hold at the end of any period is equal to the inventory which they desire to hold at the end of the period *minus* the excess of actual sales over expected sales in the period. As applied

---

[1] This may be quite powerful if it is made clear, when the increase is imposed, that the old rate is to be restored at some specified future date.

to raw materials, the buffer-stock principle postulates that the inventory which firms in the aggregate actually hold at the end of any period is equal to the inventory which they desire to hold *minus* some proportion of the excess of the actual production of the period over the planned production.

Our final model, Model V, is then formed from Model IV by adding the four relationships just discussed to the relationships of Model IV together with five definitional relationships. Altogether, there are sixteen relationships in Model V and sixteen jointly determined variables including I^{ci}, I^{ri}, U^c and U^r.

On exploring the dynamic properties of Model V, we find that it is highly unstable. The dominant term in the solution is one which follows a path of monotonic explosion. In addition, the solution has one strongly explosive cyclical component and two cyclical components which are on the border line of instability.

In the final section of the chapter we attempt to justify the choice of data for Model V. The criterion we use for this purpose is to the effect that it is proper to treat a variable, institutional arrangement, etc., as a datum in any model provided its current level or state, while determining the current levels of other variables in the model, is not in turn determined by the current levels of other variables, i.e. provided its connection with other variables is essentially one-way.

READING LIST

Ball, R. J., and Drake, Pamela S., 'Stock Adjustment Inventory Models of the United Kingdom Economy', *Manchester School of Economic and Social Studies* (May 1963).

Feinstein, C. H., 'Stockbuilding, Expenditure and the Balance of Payments', *Times Review of Industry* (Dec 1962).

——, 'Stocks, Sales and Stockbuilding', *Times Review of Industry and Technology* (Mar 1963).

Johnston, J., 'An Econometric Study of the Production Decision', *Quarterly Journal of Economics* (May 1961).

Lovell, M., 'Manufacturers' Inventories, Sales Expectations, and the Acceleration Principle', *Econometrica* (July 1961).

Metzler, L. A., 'The Nature and Stability of Inventory Cycles', *Review of Economics and Statistics* (Aug 1941).

Modigliani, F., 'Business Reasons for Holding Inventories and their Macroeconomic Implications', in *Problems of Capital Formation: Concepts, Measurement and Controlling Factors*, Studies in Income and Wealth, vol. 19 (National Bureau of Economic Research, Princeton University Press, 1957).

Nevile, J. W., 'Forecasting Inventory Investment', *Economic Record* (June 1963).

Appendix 5.1

PARAMETER VALUES USED IN THE DYNAMIC ANALYSIS
OF MODELS III, IV AND V

In this appendix we comment on the values which have been used for the parameters of relationships (2.24), (2.26), (3.4), (4.11), (4.20), (5.4), (5.8), (5.16) and (5.20) in the analysis of the dynamic properties of Models III, IV and V.

In the course of doing this we make repeated use of a formula which applies whenever the current value of some variable X is determined by the current value and all past values of some other variable Y via a distributed-lag relationship in which the weights decline geometrically. We shall begin by explaining what this formula shows and then give its derivation.

Suppose that stationary equilibrium exists up to period t. Suppose further that in period t there takes place a unit-maintained increase in Y, i.e. that Y rises by unity in period t and stays at its higher level indefinitely. The response of X to this unit-maintained increase in Y will be spread out over a succession of future periods. Let k be some positive integer such that 95 per cent of the ultimate response in X occurs by period $(t+k)$, i.e. within $(k+1)$ periods. Then the formula in question shows k as a function of λ, where λ is the damping factor in the distributed-lag relationship between X and Y.

The derivation of the formula is as follows. The relationship between X and Y is:

$$X_t = \rho_0 Y_t + \lambda \rho_0 Y_{t-1} + \lambda^2 \rho_0 Y_{t-2} + \lambda^3 \rho_0 Y_{t-3} + \dots . \quad (5.1.1)$$

Postulate stationary equilibrium up to period t and a unit-maintained increase in Y in that period. From (5.1.1) it follows that the *ultimate change in* X, consequent on this unit-maintained increase in Y, is given by:

$$\sum_{i=0}^{\infty} (X_{t+i} - X_{t+i-1}) = \rho_0[1 + \lambda + \lambda^2 + \lambda^3 + \dots] = \frac{\rho_0}{1-\lambda}. \quad (5.1.2)$$

It also follows from (5.1.1) that the *change in* X *up to and including period* $(t+k)$ is given by:

$$\sum_{i=0}^{k} (X_{t+i} - X_{t+i-1}) = \rho_0[1 + \lambda + \lambda^2 + \lambda^3 + \dots + \lambda^k] = \frac{\rho_0(1-\lambda^{k+1})}{1-\lambda}. \quad (5.1.3)$$

Hence, using (5.1.3) and (5.1.2), we find that the *proportion of the ultimate change in* X *up to and including period* $(t+k)$ is $(1-\lambda^{k+1})$. For this proportion to be 0·95, we must have:

$$1 - \lambda^{k+1} = 0·95$$

which gives:

$$\lambda^{k+1} = 0·05. \quad (5.1.4)$$

On solving for k, we get:

$$k = \frac{\log 0·05}{\log \lambda} - 1. \quad (5.1.5)$$

This is the formula for k in terms of λ which we seek. Alternatively we can obtain from (5.1.4) a formula for λ in terms of k, namely:

$$\lambda = \text{antilog}\left(\frac{\log 0\cdot05}{k+1}\right). \tag{5.1.6}$$

We shall now take each of the relationships listed in the opening paragraph in turn and comment briefly on the choice of values for the αs in that relationship.

1. *Relationship* (2.24)

(i) $a_{10} = (k_1 - k_2\eta)(1 - \xi)$

The value chosen for a_{10}, the marginal propensity to consume from *observed* disposable income, is in line with the estimates of this parameter which emerge from the quarterly regressions computed from United States data by Zellner *et al*.[1]

(ii) $a_{11} = (\xi + \pi)$

The value chosen for this parameter was also suggested by the quarterly regressions of Zellner *et al*. Note that a_{11} is necessarily a positive fraction, being the damping factor in the distributed-lag relationship between X^1 and X – permanent and observed real disposable income, respectively (see relationships (2.17), (2.23) and (2.24)). The value allotted to a_{11} implies that a given change in observed income will be fully reflected in permanent income within a little more than one year.[2] This can be seen from (5.1.5). Substituting the value allotted to a_{11}, i.e. $0\cdot5$ for λ in this formula, we find that $k = 3\cdot3$. Thus, on the basis of a value of $0\cdot5$ for a_{11}, just under 95 per cent of the ultimate change in permanent income will have occurred by quarter $(t+3)$ and just over 95 per cent by quarter $(t+4)$.

2. *Relationship* (2.26)

(i) a_{21}

The value allotted to a_{21}, the slope of the function relating real personal disposable income to real gross domestic product, reflects parameter estimates used in a recent study by Pearse of the stabilising effectiveness of the 1959 British tax structure.[3] In terms of Pearse's notation, we have used the approximation:

$$\Delta X = \Delta Y(1 - m')(1 - v)$$

---

[1] See A. Zellner, D. S. Huang and L. C. Chau, 'Further Analysis of the Short-Run Consumption Function with Emphasis on the Role of Liquid Assets', *Econometrica* (July 1965) pp. 574–5.

[2] By this we mean that 95 per cent of the ultimate change in permanent income, consequent on the given change in observed income, will have occurred within the stated time. We shall use 'fully reflected' in this sense throughout this appendix.

[3] See R. H. Pearse, 'Automatic Stabilization and the British Taxes on Income', *Review of Economic Studies*, xxix (1962).

where X denotes real personal disposable income, Y real gross domestic product, m' the marginal rate of tax on personal income and v the ratio:

$$\frac{\Delta(\text{company savings before tax})}{\Delta Y}.$$

In Pearse's study[1] a value of $0 \cdot 19$ is used for m', this being the estimated marginal rate of tax on personal income for the 1959 British tax structure, and a value of $0 \cdot 9$ for v. Inserting these values into the approximation gives $\Delta X = 0 \cdot 08 \, \Delta Y$.

3. Relationship (3.4)

(i) $a_{30} = \gamma$

From the argument leading up to (3.4) it can be seen that a_{30} is necessarily a positive fraction since it is the damping factor in the distributed-lag relationship between import orders and import demand. The value allotted to this parameter (i.e. $0 \cdot 1$) implies that import orders adjust fairly rapidly to changes in import demand. If $0 \cdot 1$ is substituted for λ in (5.1.5), we find that $k + 1 = 1 \cdot 30$, implying that a given change in import demand will be fully reflected in import orders within six months.

(ii) $a_{31} = (1 - \gamma)\epsilon_1$; $a_{32} = (1 - \gamma)\epsilon_2$

These parameters, which measure the response of import deliveries to a change in aggregate demand and the response of import orders to a change in the level of real inventory investment, respectively, have been allotted values in line with the least-squares estimates of Godley and Shepherd.[2]

4. Relationship (4.11)

(i) $a_{40} = g(1 - \tau)$; $a_{41} = \tau$

By referring back to section 4.2, the reader will see that a_{40} and a_{41} are given by expressions which involve two parameters, namely g the overall capital–output ratio and τ the damping factor in the distributed-lag relationship between desired real net investment expenditure and the absolute rate of change in real gross domestic product. The values we have used for a_{40} and a_{41} have been obtained by substituting for g and τ in these expressions. For g we have substituted a value of 8 which, given our quarterly period, implies a capital-output ratio of 2 on an annual basis. To evaluate τ we have assumed that it takes four years for a given change in the rate of change in Y to be fully reflected in I^{nf}, i.e. we have solved (5.1.6) for λ with $(k + 1) = 16$. The resulting value for τ is $0 \cdot 83$.

---

[1] Ibid., pp. 129-37.

[2] See W. A. H. Godley and J. R. Shepherd, 'Forecasting Imports', *National Institute Economic Review* (Aug 1965).

5. *Relationship* (4.20)

(i) $a_{50} = \theta d(1 - \sigma)(1 - \xi); \; a_{51} = (\xi + \pi) + (1 - \theta + \sigma);$
$a_{52} = \sigma(\theta - 1) - (\xi + \pi)(1 - \theta + \sigma); \; a_{53} = \sigma(1 - \theta)(\xi + \pi)$

Reference to relationship (4.20) shows that a_{50} through a_{53} are given by expressions involving five parameters, θ, σ, d, ξ and π. The values allotted to a_{50} through a_{53} were derived by allotting values to these five parameters and making the appropriate substitutions.

Let us begin with θ. The parameter θ has the dimensions of $(\text{time})^{-1}$ which means that $1/\theta$ has the dimensions of time (is expressed in time units). This is evident from the fact that the expression in square brackets on the right-hand side of (4.13) is the excess of the desired housing stock over the housing stock which is in existence or which has been decided on, and consequently is expressed in terms of £s, whereas the variable on the left-hand side, being a flow, is expressed in terms of £s per time unit. It follows that $1/\theta$ can be interpreted as the number of periods[1] which will be taken to eliminate the excess of the desired housing stock over the stock which is in existence, or in relation to which decisions have been taken. A value for θ of, say, 0·5 means that the excess will be eliminated over two periods, a value of 0·2 that it will be eliminated over five periods and so on. The value which we have allotted to θ is 0·05. This implies that twenty periods will be required to bring the actual stock of housing into line with the desired stock or, on the basis of a quarterly period, five years.

Turn now to σ. This parameter is the damping factor in the distributed-lag relationship between net housing investment expenditure and net housing investment decisions (relationship (4.12)) and hence necessarily satisfies $0 < \sigma < 1$. We assume that it takes two years for a given change in housing investment decisions to be fully reflected in housing investment expenditure, i.e. we substitute 8 for $(k + 1)$ in (5.1.6). This gives a value for σ of 0·68.

From (4.15) we see that d is the desired ratio between the housing stock and permanent disposable income at the macro-level. We have put this at 3 in terms of annual income. Since we are working with a quarterly period, this means that d has a value of 12.

Finally we have put $(1 - \xi)$ at 0·6. This implies that $\xi = 0·4$ (ξ must satisfy $0 < \xi < 1$), and this implies, in turn, that $\pi = 0·1$ (see comment on a_{11} above).

6. *Relationship* (5.4)

(i) $a_{60} = \mu; \; a_{61} = \delta\kappa(1 - \mu); \; a_{62} = \delta\epsilon; \; a_{63} = -\mu\delta\epsilon; \; a_{64} = -\delta; \; a_{65} = \mu\delta$

From the argument leading up to (5.4) it can be seen that a_{60} through a_{65} are given by expressions involving only four parameters, namely μ, δ, κ and ϵ. The values allotted to a_{60} through a_{65} were derived by allotting values to these four parameters and making the appropriate substitutions. We now comment on the values given to μ, δ, κ and ϵ.

---

[1] Assuming identity between the period and the time unit.

The parameter μ is the damping factor in the distributed-lag relationship between planned domestic production and the demand for domestic production, and hence must satisfy $0 < \mu < 1$. We have given this parameter a value of $0\cdot5$. If this value is substituted for λ in (5.1.5), a value of $3\cdot3$ is found for k. Thus the value allotted to μ implies that a given change in the demand for domestic production will be fully reflected in production plans within five quarters.

The parameter δ was put at $0\cdot2$ in line with the econometric estimates made for the United Kingdom by Ball and Drake.[1] The reciprocal of δ can be interpreted as the number of periods which will be taken to eliminate any discrepancy between the desired inventory of raw materials and work-in-progress and the actual inventory (cf. p. 117 above). Thus, on the basis of a quarterly period, the figure allotted to δ implies that firms in the aggregate will take some fifteen months to bring the actual and the desired raw-material inventories into line.

Both κ and ϵ were given the value $0\cdot13$, in line with Lovell's econometric estimates for the United States.[2]

7. *Relationship* (5.8)

(i) $a_{70} = \beta$; $a_{71} = \omega n(1 - \beta)$; $a_{72} = -\omega$; $a_{73} = \beta\omega$

As will be clear from the argument leading up to (5.8), a_{70} through a_{73} are all composed of three parameters, namely β, ω and n. Accordingly, to obtain values for a_{70} through a_{73} we allotted values to these three parameters and then made the appropriate substitutions.

The values chosen for β, ω and n were: $\beta = 0\cdot5$, $\omega = 0\cdot2$ and $n = 1\cdot5$. All were suggested by the econometric work of Ball and Drake.[3]

The parameter β is the damping factor in the distributed-lag relationship between expected sales and realised sales. The value which we have chosen for this parameter implies that a given change in realised sales will be fully reflected in expected sales within five quarters (see 5.1.5)).

On the basis of a quarterly period, the value allotted to ω implies that firms in the aggregate take some fifteen months to bring the desired inventory of finished goods and the actual inventory into line.

Finally, again on the basis of a quarterly period, the value of $1\cdot5$ adopted for n implies that firms in the aggregate desire to hold inventories of finished goods amounting to about 150 per cent of expected *quarterly* sales or about 38 per cent of *annual* sales.

8. *Relationship* (5.16)

(i) $a_{80} = \beta$

---

[1] See Ball and Drake, op. cit. Note that our δ corresponds with Ball and Drake's λ.

[2] See M. Lovell, 'Manufacturers' Inventories, Sales Expectations and the Acceleration Principle', *Econometrica* (July 1961).

[3] See Ball and Drake, op. cit., pp. 94–101. Note that our β, ω and n correspond, respectively, with Ball and Drake's τ, λ and β.

Reference to (5.16) shows that $a_{80} = \beta$. A comment on the value which we have given to the parameter β appears under 7 (i) above.

9. *Relationship* (5.20)

(i) $a_{90} = \mu$; $a_{91} = p$; $a_{92} = -p\mu$; $a_{93} = -p(1-\mu)$

By returning to the argument underlying (5.20), the reader will see that a_{90} through a_{93} are composed of two parameters, namely, μ and p. A comment on the value allotted to μ will be found under 6 (i) above. Reference back to (5.18) shows that p must satisfy $0 < p < 1$. We have given p a value of 0·3.

Appendix 5.2

DERIVATION OF (5.25)–(5.32)

The sixteen relationships of Model V can be reduced by substitution to a system of eight difference equations in the eight jointly determined variables, D, M, I^{gf}, I^{gh}, I^{ri}, I^{ci}, U^c and U^r.

The reduction proceeds as follows. Relationships (2.24), (2.26) and (3.11) give:

$$D_t = a_{10}(a_{20} + a_{21}Y_t) + a_{11}(D_{t-1} - G_{t-1} - E_{t-1} - I^{gf}_{t-1} - I^{gh}_{t-1} - I^{ri}_{t-1} - I^{ci}_{t-1})$$
$$+ Z^1 + G_t + E_t + I^{gf}_t + I_t + I^{ri}_t + I^{ci}_t.$$

Using (3.2) and (5.9) we can eliminate Y from this expression to get:

$$D_t = a_{10}[a_{20} + a_{21}(D_t - M_t - U^c_t - U^r_t)] + a_{11}(D_{t-1} - G_{t-1} - E_{t-1} - I^{gf}_{t-1} - I^{gh}_{t-1}$$
$$- I^{ri}_{t-1} - I^{ci}_{t-1}) + Z^1 + G_t + E_t + I^{gf}_t + I^{gh}_t + I^{ri}_t + I^{ci}_t.$$

This in turn gives:

$$D_t(1 - a_{10}a_{21}) - a_{11}D_{t-1} + a_{10}a_{21}M_t - I^{gf}_t + a_{11}I^{gf}_{t-1} - I^{gh}_t + a_{11}I^{gh}_{t-1}$$
$$- I^{ri}_t + a_{11}I^{ri}_{t-1} - I^{ci}_t + a_{11}I^{ci}_{t-1} + a_{10}a_{21}U^c_t + a_{10}a_{21}U^r_t = k_1 \quad (5.25)$$

where k_1 denotes $a_{10}a_{20} + G_t - a_{11}G_{t-1} + E_t - a_{11}E_{t-1} + Z^1$.

Using the definition of I^i given by (5.24) we can rewrite (3.4) as:

$$M_t - a_{30}M_{t-1} - a_{31}D_{t-2} - a_{32}I^{ri}_{t-2} - a_{32}I^{ci}_{t-2} = k_2 \quad (5.26)$$

where k_2 denotes Z^2.

Using (3.2) and (5.9) we can eliminate Y from (4.11) to get:

$$I^{gf}_t - a_{41}I^{gf}_{t-1} - a_{40}(D_{t-1} - D_{t-2}) + a_{40}(M_{t-1} - M_{t-2}) + a_{40}(U^c_{t-1} - U^c_{t-2})$$
$$+ a_{40}(U^r_{t-1} - U^r_{t-2}) = k_3 \quad (5.27)$$

where k_3 denotes $a_{42}K_t + a_{43}K_{t-1}$.

Next, using (2.26), (3.2) and (5.9), we can eliminate X from (4.20) to get:

$$I^{gh}_t - a_{51}I^{gh}_{t-1} - a_{52}I^{gh}_{t-2} - a_{53}I^{gh}_{t-3} - a_{50}a_{21}(D_{t-1} - D_{t-2}) + a_{50}a_{21}(M_{t-1} - M_{t-2})$$
$$+ a_{50}a_{21}(U^c_{t-1} - U^c_{t-2}) + a_{50}a_{21}(U^r_{t-1} - U^r_{t-2}) = k_4 \quad (5.28)$$

where k_4 denotes $a_{54}K^h_t + a_{55}K^h_{t-1} + a_{56}K^h_{t-2} + a_{57}K^h_{t-3}$.

Lagging (5.4) one period and subtracting the resulting expression from (5.4), we get:

$$I_t^{ri} - I_{t-1}^{ri} = a_{60}(I_{t-1}^{ri} - I_{t-2}^{ri}) + a_{61}(D_{t-1} - D_{t-2}) - a_{61}(M_{t-1} - M_{t-2}) + a_{62}H_t$$
$$- (a_{62} - a_{63})H_{t-1} - a_{63}H_{t-2} + a_{64}(K_t^r - K_{t-1}^r) + a_{65}(K_{t-1}^r - K_{t-2}^r).$$

Using (5.21) and (5.22) we can eliminate H and K^r from this expression to get:

$$I_t^{ri} - I_{t-1}^{ri} = a_{60}(I_{t-1}^{ir} - I_{t-2}^{ri}) + a_{61}(D_{t-1} - D_{t-2}) - a_{61}(M_{t-1} - M_{t-2})$$
$$+ a_{62}(D_t - Y_t^p - M_t) - (a_{62} - a_{63})(D_{t-1} - Y_{t-1}^p - M_{t-1})$$
$$- a_{63}(D_{t-2} - Y_{t-2}^p - M_{t-2}) + a_{64}(I_{t-1}^{ri} - U_{t-1}^r) + a_{65}(I_{t-2}^{ri} - U_{t-2}^r).$$

This in turn gives:

$$I_t^{ri} - (1 + a_{60} + a_{64})I_{t-1}^{ri} + (a_{60} - a_{65})I_{t-2}^{ri} - a_{62}D_t - (a_{61} - a_{62} + a_{63})D_{t-1}$$
$$+ (a_{61} + a_{63})D_{t-2} + a_{62}M_t + (a_{61} - a_{62} + a_{63})M_{t-1}$$
$$- (a_{61} + a_{63})M_{t-2} + a_{64}U_{t-1}^r + a_{65}U_{t-2}^r = k_5 \qquad (5.29)$$

where k_5 denotes $-a_{62}Y_t^p + (a_{62} - a_{63})Y_{t-1}^p + a_{63}Y_{t-2}^p$.

Lagging (5.8) one period and subtracting the resulting expression from (5.8), we get:

$$I_t^{ci} - I_{t-1}^{ci} = a_{70}I_{t-1}^{ci} - a_{70}I_{t-2}^{ci} + a_{71}(D_{t-1} - D_{t-2}) + a_{72}(K_t^e - K_{t-1}^e)$$
$$+ a_{73}(K_{t-1}^e - K_{t-2}^e).$$

Using (5.23) we can eliminate K^e from this expression to get:

$$I_t^{ci} - (1 + a_{70} + a_{72})I_{t-1}^{ci} + (a_{70} - a_{73})I_{t-2}^{ci} - a_{71}(D_{t-1} - D_{t-2})$$
$$+ a_{72}U_{t-1}^e + a_{73}U_{t-2}^e = 0. \quad (5.30)$$

Rewriting (5.16), we get:

$$U_t^e - a_{80}U_{t-1}^e - (D_t - D_{t-1}) = 0. \qquad (5.31)$$

Finally we use (3.2) and (5.9) to eliminate Y from (5.20), which gives:

$$U_t^r = a_{90}U_{t-1}^r + a_{91}(D_t - M_t - U_t^e - U^r) + a_{92}(D_{t-1} - M_{t-1} - U_{t-1}^e - U_{t-1}^r)$$
$$+ a_{93}D_{t-1} - a_{93}M_{t-1}$$

which we can rewrite as:

$$U_t^r(1 + a_{91}) + (a_{92} - a_{90})U_{t-1}^r - a_{91}D_t - (a_{92} + a_{93})D_{t-1} + a_{91}M_t$$
$$+ (a_{92} + a_{93})M_{t-1} + a_{91}U^e + a_{92}U_{t-1}^e = 0. \quad (5.32)$$

Appendix 5.3

SOLUTION OF MODEL V

In this appendix we apply the method outlined in Appendix 3.1 to obtain the solution of Model V.

The first step is to write (5.33) to (5.40) in matrix-operator form as follows:

$$
\begin{bmatrix}
\{0\cdot976-0\cdot5E\} & 0\cdot024 & \{-1+0\cdot5E\} & \{-1+0\cdot5E\} & \{-1+0\cdot5E\} & \{-1+0\cdot5E\} & 0\cdot024 & 0\cdot024 \\
-0\cdot2E^2 & \{1-0\cdot1E\} & 0 & 0 & -0\cdot5E^2 & -0\cdot5E^2 & 0 & 0 \\
\{-1\cdot36(E-E^2)\} & \{1\cdot36(E-E^2)\} & \{1-0\cdot83E\} & 0 & 0 & 0 & \{1\cdot36(E-E^2)\} & \{1\cdot36(E-E^2)\} \\
\{-0\cdot009(E-E^2)\} & \{0\cdot009(E-E^2)\} & 0 & \{1-2\cdot130E+1\cdot461E^2-0\cdot323E^3\} & 0 & 0 & \{0\cdot009(E-E^2)\} & \{0\cdot009(E-E^2)\} \\
\{-0\cdot026(1-E)\} & \{0\cdot026(1-E)\} & 0 & 0 & \{1-1\cdot3E+0\cdot4E^2\} & 0 & 0 & 0 \\
\{-0\cdot15(E-E^2)\} & 0 & 0 & 0 & 0 & \{1-1\cdot3E+0\cdot4E^2\} & \{-0\cdot2E+0\cdot1E^2\} & \{-0\cdot2E+0\cdot1E^2\} \\
\{-(1-E)\} & 0 & 0 & 0 & 0 & 0 & \{1-0\cdot5E\} & 0 \\
\{0\cdot3(1-E)\} & \{0\cdot3(1-E)\} & 0 & 0 & 0 & 0 & \{0\cdot3-0\cdot15E\} & \{1\cdot3-0\cdot65E\}
\end{bmatrix}
\begin{bmatrix}
D_i \\ M_i \\ I_i^{pf} \\ I_i^{ph} \\ I_i^{z} \\ F_i^{z} \\ U_i^{z} \\ U_i^{z}
\end{bmatrix}
=
\begin{bmatrix}
k_1 \\ k_2 \\ k_3 \\ k_4 \\ k_5 \\ 0 \\ 0 \\ 0
\end{bmatrix}
$$

Next we find $|P(E)|$. This is given by:

$$|P(E)| = 1 \cdot 2662 - 9 \cdot 547E + 31 \cdot 819E^2 - 60 \cdot 850E^3 + 71 \cdot 646E^4 - 49 \cdot 700E^5$$
$$+ 13 \cdot 135E^6 + 9 \cdot 513E^7 - 11 \cdot 469E^8 + 5 \cdot 121E^9 - 0 \cdot 821E^{10}$$
$$- 0 \cdot 228E^{11} + 0 \cdot 142E^{12} - 0 \cdot 028E^{13} + 0 \cdot 002E^{14}.$$

From this expression we form the characteristic equation:

$$1 \cdot 2662x^{14} - 9 \cdot 547x^{13} + 31 \cdot 819x^{12} - 60 \cdot 850x^{11} + 71 \cdot 646x^{10} - 49 \cdot 700x^9$$
$$+ 13 \cdot 135x^8 + 9 \cdot 513x^7 - 11 \cdot 469x^6 + 5 \cdot 121x^5 - 0 \cdot 821x^4 - 0 \cdot 228x^3$$
$$+ 0 \cdot 142x^2 - 0 \cdot 028x + 0 \cdot 002 = 0.$$

By applying the Lin–Bairstow method we find that this polynomial has four real roots and five pairs of complex roots as follows:

$$x_1 = 1 \cdot 388 \qquad\qquad x_9 = -0 \cdot 566$$
$$x_2 = 1 \cdot 068 + 0 \cdot 469i \left.\right\} \; r = 1 \cdot 166 \qquad x_{10} = 0 \cdot 331 + 0 \cdot 385i \left.\right\} \; r = 0 \cdot 508$$
$$x_3 = 1 \cdot 068 - 0 \cdot 469i \left.\right\} \; \theta = 23 \cdot 7^0 \qquad x_{11} = 0 \cdot 331 - 0 \cdot 385i \left.\right\} \; \theta = 49 \cdot 3^0$$
$$x_4 = 1 \cdot 000 \qquad\qquad x_{12} = -0 \cdot 309$$
$$x_5 = 0 \cdot 866 + 0 \cdot 373i \left.\right\} \; r = 0 \cdot 943 \qquad x_{13} = 0 \cdot 133 + 0 \cdot 159i \left.\right\} \; r = 0 \cdot 207$$
$$x_6 = 0 \cdot 866 - 0 \cdot 373i \left.\right\} \; \theta = 23 \cdot 3^0 \qquad x_{14} = 0 \cdot 133 - 0 \cdot 159i \left.\right\} \; \theta = 50 \cdot 1^0$$
$$x_7 = 0 \cdot 616 + 0 \cdot 488i \left.\right\} \; r = 0 \cdot 786$$
$$x_8 = 0 \cdot 616 - 0 \cdot 488i \left.\right\} \; \theta = 38 \cdot 4^0$$

Consequently the solution for D is:

$$D_t = A_{11}(1 \cdot 388)^t + A_{12}(1 \cdot 166)^t \cos [23 \cdot 7t - A_{13}] + A_{14}(1 \cdot 000)^t$$
$$+ A_{15}(0 \cdot 943)^t \cos [23 \cdot 3t - A_{16}] + A_{17}(0 \cdot 786)^t \cos [38 \cdot 4t - A_{18}]$$
$$+ A_{19}(-0 \cdot 566)^t + A_{20}(0 \cdot 508)^t \cos [49 \cdot 3t - A_{21}] + A_{22}(-0 \cdot 309)^t$$
$$+ A_{23}(0 \cdot 207)^t \cos [50 \cdot 1t - A_{24}] + \bar{D}_t$$

where $\bar{D}_t$ is the particular solution whose precise character is determined by the time paths specified for the ks and where the As are arbitrary constants which can be evaluated given the appropriate initial conditions. The solution for each of the other jointly determined variables is identical with this except for the particular solution and the arbitrary As.

6 Stabilisation Policy: The Pursuit of Internal Balance

6.1 Available Instruments

In the first chapter of the book we discussed the four generally accepted objectives of macro-economic policy, namely internal balance, external balance, price stability and a high rate of growth. There we confined ourselves to defining these objectives and indicating the reasons why they are regarded as desirable not only in Britain but in all advanced industrial countries of the Western world. With the theoretical equipment acquired in the preceding four chapters we can now proceed beyond these preliminary questions to the central question of how these four objectives can be attained. In the present chapter we shall use this equipment to consider the problems involved in the attainment of the internal balance objective and in the next chapter we shall use it as a basis for discussing the achievement of external balance. The price-stability objective will be discussed in Chapter 10, after some additional theoretical material has been presented, and the growth objective in Chapters 11–12.

Throughout these chapters, to simplify the exposition, we shall be ignoring possible interdependencies between the four objectives. In the present chapter, for example, we shall discuss the attainment of internal balance without regard to the possibility that steps taken in the pursuit of this objective may affect (either hinder or help) the attainment of the other three. Once each of the objectives has been considered in this simplified way, we shall be in a position to consider the problems which arise because of the interrelationships which exist between them. These problems will occupy us in the last three chapters of the book.

We shall begin our discussion of internal balance policy (or stabilisation policy as it is sometimes called) by defining the basic task which faces the authorities in the pursuit of the internal balance objective. For this purpose we shall return to Model V. This model provides a representation of the free movement over time of certain important aggregates, including aggregate demand (D) and realised real imports (M), subject to various data and various arbitrary initial conditions. We have shown that, given certain plausible values for the parameters of this model, both D and M will behave in an oscillatory fashion in response to arbitrary initial conditions if no attempt is made to manipulate them. On the other hand, in our model, real potential gross domestic product (Y^p) follows a time path which is externally given and which therefore need bear no close relation to the time paths which the model generates for D and M. If the economy is left to itself, therefore, discrepancies will exist over time between ($D - M$) on the one hand and Y^p on the other. The basic task of the authorities, in the pursuit of the internal balance objective, is to change the free movement of D and/or M, whatever that might be, in such a way that these discrepancies are eliminated or at least reduced.[1]

This formulation of the authorities' task raises several major questions. The most important are:

1. What policy instruments can the authorities use for the purpose of managing D and M?
2. How do these instruments work?
3. What techniques are available for manipulating the instruments?
4. How effective are these techniques?
5. How large an impact on D and M can the authorities produce by manipulation of the available instruments?
6. What is the likely lag between any given manipulation of the instruments and the consequent impact on D and M?
7. By what amount should the relevant policy instruments be changed at any point of time?

The purpose of this chapter is to examine each of these questions in turn within the framework of British institutions and in the light of British empirical research. We begin with the question of what policy instruments are available.

For present purposes we define a policy instrument as a datum which is open to manipulation by the authorities and which provides them with a means of managing D and/or M in the interests of internal balance. Our discussion of the data on which Model V is

---

[1] Recall that internal balance exists when there is equality between D and ($Y^p + M$) or between ($D - M$) and Y^p. See section 1.2 above.

based (see pp. 130–5 above) shows that, in this sense of the term, there are three groups of policy instruments available to the British authorities at the present time. They are:

(a) the *fiscal instruments*, consisting of the explicit datum G (real government expenditure) and two implicit data, namely the tax structure and the transfer payment structure;

(b) the *monetary instruments*, consisting of the explicit datum L (the stock of liquid assets) and two implicit data, the cost of finance to firms and individuals and the availability of finance; and

(c) the *import instruments*, consisting of two explicit data, the British price of home-produced importables relative to the British price of foreign-produced importables and the intensity of direct controls over foreign transactions.

Let us suppose that the existing situation is one of excess demand $(D - M > Y^p)$ and that the authorities wish to reduce $(D - M)$ in order to eliminate, or at least reduce, this excess demand. In this case the appropriate manipulations of the policy instruments would be:

Fiscal instruments: decrease in G; increase in severity of tax structure; decrease in liberality of transfer payment structure.

Monetary instruments: decrease in the stock of liquid assets; increase in cost of finance; decrease in availability of finance.

Import instruments: increase in the British price of home-produced importables relative to the British price of foreign-produced importables; decrease in the intensity of direct controls over foreign transactions.

6.2 Nature of Impact

Turning to the second question, we shall now take each of these groups of policy changes in turn and consider the nature of their impact on $(D - M)$ (immediate effect) in the light of Model V. We shall leave it to the reader to reverse the argument to cover the case where the authorities wish to increase $(D - M)$ in a situation of deficient demand.

1. *Fiscal Instruments*

The *decrease in G* will have a direct impact on $(D - M)$ (it is the only one of the changes which will do so), since G is a component of D.

The second member of the fiscal group (the *increase in the severity of the tax structure*) is less straightforward since the nature of the impact will depend on which part of the tax structure is made more severe. There are, in fact, three main possibilities: (i) an increase in the severity of the indirect tax structure; (ii) an increase in the severity of the personal income-tax structure; and (iii) an increase in the severity of the business income-tax structure.

In case (i) the impact of the change in the tax structure will be on C, since the indirect tax structure is a datum for relationship (2.24), the consumption function of Model V (see p. 134 above). Thus in this case the change reduces $(D - M)$ indirectly via an autonomous[1] decrease in C. In case (ii) the impact of the change in the tax structure will be on X, since the immediate effect of a change in the personal income-tax structure is to reduce the level of X corresponding to a given level of Y (see pp. 57–61 above). This follows from the fact that the personal income-tax structure is a datum for the personal disposable income function of Model V (relationship (2.26)). This autonomous decrease in disposable income leads in turn to an *induced* decrease in C via the consumption function and to an induced decrease in I^{gh} via the housing investment function (relationship (4.20)) and thus to a decrease in $(D - M)$ (see p. 108 above). Finally, in case (iii), where it is the business tax structure which is made more severe, the change will work through C, I^{gh} and I^{gf}. An increase in the severity of the business tax structure, like an increase in the severity of the personal tax structure, will cause an autonomous decrease in personal disposable income and, in turn, this will produce an induced decrease in C and I^{gh}. In addition, in this case, the change in the tax structure will lead to an autonomous decrease in I^{gf}, since the business tax structure is a datum for relationship (4.11), the fixed-capital investment function of Model V (see p. 97 above). In case (iii), therefore, the increase in the severity of the tax structure reduces $(D - M)$ indirectly via an induced decrease in C and I^{gh} and an autonomous decrease in I^{gf}.

To sum up, it is clear that the impact of an increase in the severity of the tax structure can take a variety of forms, depending on which part of the structure is changed. Some of these will be more effective than others, either because they work more rapidly and/or because they lead to a greater proportionate decrease in the demand

---

[1] By an 'autonomous' change in an unknown we mean a change produced by a change in some datum (explicit or implicit) as distinct from a change produced by a change in some other unknown. The latter we refer to as an 'induced' change.

component through which they operate and/or because they operate through a demand component which constitutes a larger proportion of aggregate demand.

Finally, we come to the third fiscal change, a decrease in the *liberality of the transfer payment structure*, e.g. by means of a decrease in rates of benefit or a restriction of eligibility for benefit. As will be clear from earlier discussion, this change has exactly the same impact as an increase in the severity of the personal income-tax structure, namely an autonomous decrease in personal disposable income leading to an induced fall in C and I^{gh} via relationships (2.24) and (4.20).

2. *Monetary Instruments*

The impact of a *decrease in the stock of liquid assets* will be on C. It will be recalled that the stock of liquid assets at the end of the previous quarter (or the beginning of the current quarter) appears as an explanatory variable in the consumption function of Model V (relationship (2.24)) with a positive coefficient (see p. 56 above). Thus a decrease in the stock of liquid assets will reduce $(D - M)$ indirectly via an autonomous decrease in C.[1] This effect of the reduction in the liquid-asset stock will be supported by further effects on C and I. We shall return to these further effects shortly.

Let us turn now to the second of the monetary changes – an *increase in the cost of finance*. This will work partly by causing an autonomous decrease in C. Among the explanatory variables of relationship (2.24) is the current value of N, an index which rises when financial conditions become more stringent, either because of an increase in the cost of finance, or because of a decrease in the availability of finance (i.e. an increase in the extent of credit rationing by banks and other lending institutions), or because of some combination of the two. Since this variable appears with a negative coefficient, relationship (2.24) implies that an increase in the cost of finance will lead to an autonomous decrease in C.[2] In addition, this particular monetary

---

[1] From the discussion preceding (2.24), it is apparent that the effect mentioned in the text will be undone since the stock of liquid assets at the beginning of the *previous* quarter also appears as an explanatory variable in the consumption function with a *negative sign*. However, the effect will not be undone completely since the coefficient of the second liquid-asset variable is smaller numerically than that of the first, $(\xi + \pi)$ being a positive fraction.

[2] Once again this effect will be partly undone, since lagged N also appears among the explanatory variables with a positive coefficient. See previous footnote.

change will help to reduce $(D - M)$ by causing an autonomous decrease in I^{gf}, I^{gh}, I^{ri} and I^{ci}, the four components of desired real investment expenditure. This follows from the fact that the cost of finance is an implicit datum for all four investment functions of Model V (relationships (4.11), (4.20), (5.8) and (5.16)) (see p. 133 above).

All that has been said about the effects of an increase in the cost of finance applies, *mutatis mutandis*, to the third member of the monetary group, a *decrease in the availability of finance* (increase in the severity of credit rationing), and the reader will therefore be left to analyse this particular change for himself.

There is one final point before we leave the monetary instruments. It was stated earlier that the first of the three monetary changes (a decrease in the stock of liquid assets) would have effects on C and I in addition to the effect which we analysed in detail. These further effects come about because, as we shall see in section 6.3, a decrease in the stock of liquid assets will make financial conditions more stringent, either by raising the cost of finance or by increasing the extent of credit rationing or both.

3. *Import Instruments*

The specified changes in the import instruments will work primarily through M, the realised level of real imports. As will be clear from the discussion of section 3.2, the British price of home-produced importables relative to the British price of foreign-produced importables and the intensity of direct controls over foreign transactions are two of the explanatory variables in the import function of Model V (relationship (3.4)). It will be clear also from this discussion that the specified changes in these data will produce an autonomous increase in M. Hence the specified changes in the import instruments will help to produce the desired decrease in $(D - M)$ by causing an autonomous increase in M.

6.3 Techniques for Manipulating Instruments

In the preceding sections we listed and classified the various policy instruments which the British authorities can manipulate in the pursuit of the internal balance objective and analysed, with the help of Model V, the nature of the impact on $(D - M)$ of particular changes in those instruments. But we said nothing about the techniques by means of which the manipulations are actually performed, and we must now remedy this omission.

1. *Fiscal Instruments*

The fiscal instruments can be dealt with quite briefly. Let us begin with G, real government expenditure on currently produced goods and services. This has two components – current expenditure and capital expenditure – and the authorities can operate on either or both components in order to effect a reduction in G. Aggregate *current expenditure* can be reduced either directly, by means of a cut in the current expenditure of the central government itself, or indirectly, by means of a cut in the grants for current expenditure which the central government makes to the various local governments. In the case of *capital expenditure* the choice is slightly wider. If the authorities wish to reduce the aggregate real capital expenditure of all governments combined, they can do so, of course, by reducing the capital expenditure of the central government itself (e.g. by reducing expenditure on the construction of main roads, hospitals and universities). Alternatively, they can reduce the capital expenditure of the nationalised industries, since the nationalisation statutes invariably provide that the capital expenditure of the public corporations must be subject to ministerial approval. A third alternative is to reduce the capital expenditure of the local governments. Nearly all of the capital expenditure undertaken by the local governments is financed by borrowing, and no borrowing can be undertaken without the sanction of the appropriate Minister. The central authorities can, therefore, effect a cut in local government capital expenditure simply by withholding the necessary borrowing approval. A cut in local government capital expenditure can also be effected under various statutory provisions, e.g. the provision that acceptance of all housing tenders by the local authorities must be approved by the Minister of Housing, which gives the authorities virtual statutory control over local government housing investment.

In the case of the other two fiscal instruments – the tax structure and the transfer payment structure – the position is equally straightforward. The central authorities have no direct means of increasing the severity of the taxes, such as property rates and licences of various types, which are levied by the local governments, nor of reducing the liberality of the various social service benefits which they provide. Hence if the authorities wish to increase the severity of the tax structure as a whole or to reduce the liberality of the overall transfer payment structure, they can do so only by operating on the tax and transfer payment structure of the central government itself.

2. *Import Instruments*

As the techniques for manipulating the import instruments can also be dealt with fairly briefly, we shall change the order of the previous section and take them next before turning to the more complicated case of the monetary instruments.

As pointed out in section 6.1, the appropriate changes in the import instruments in a situation of excess demand are: increase in the British price of home-produced importables relative to the British price of foreign-produced importables (the home–foreign price ratio); decrease in the intensity of direct controls over foreign transactions. By what means can the British authorities effect these particular changes?

The various techniques which can be used to manipulate the home–foreign price ratio will be discussed in detail in section 7.2. From this discussion it will be seen that, if the authorities wish to increase the home–foreign price ratio as a means of stimulating imports in the interests of internal balance, they can do so in one or more of the following ways: (i) by boosting the rate of increase of the price of home-produced importables, e.g. by removing or reducing existing pressure for wage restraint; (ii) by checking the rate of increase of the price of foreign-produced importables in British currency, e.g. by reducing tariffs or by removing, or reducing the scope of an existing surcharge on imports or an existing import deposit scheme, all of which would be done by decree.

As for the second of the two changes, the authorities can reduce the intensity of any direct controls over foreign transactions which may be in force simply by using the appropriate statutory regulations.

3. *Monetary Instruments*

Having dealt with the techniques which are available for manipulating the fiscal and import instruments, let us now turn to the monetary instruments. Broadly speaking, if the authorities wish to bring about the changes in the monetary instruments specified in the opening section, they can take one or more of the following steps:

(a) reduce the supply of bank credit;
(b) increase bank lending and borrowing rates;

F

(c) reduce the availability of hire-purchase finance;

(d) increase the severity of the business tax structure.[1]

We shall now consider each of these steps in turn. In each case we shall begin by explaining how the step in question will tend to reduce the stock of liquid assets, and/or increase the cost of finance, and/or reduce the availability of finance. We shall then discuss the techniques which the British authorities use when they wish to take that step.

(a) *Reduction of supply of bank credit.* If the authorities reduce the supply of bank credit, in the sense of imposing on the banks a need to reduce the level of advances, they will help to effect the specified changes in the monetary instruments in two quite distinct ways: immediately, by decreasing the availability of bank finance and hence increasing the cost, and decreasing the availability of finance in general, and at one remove, by reducing the stock of money. Take these in turn.

If the banks are placed in the position of having to reduce the level of advances, they will attempt to check the rate of new lending either by increasing the cost of bank finance or by rationing their customers more severely, or by some combination of the two. In the British case, the second alternative (decrease in the availability of bank finance) will usually be the one chosen.[2] This decrease in the availability of bank finance will tend to increase the cost or decrease the availability of finance *in general*. For potential spenders who now find bank finance unobtainable will presumably attempt to obtain finance either (i) by borrowing from some other financial institution, e.g. a hire-purchase company, a building society or a life-assurance company; or (ii) in the case of companies, by issuing securities or shares. To the extent that (i) occurs, the non-bank financial intermediaries will find that there is pressure on the funds which they have available for lending. They will respond to this pressure either by preserving existing loan rates and imposing credit rationing (i.e. by following the example set by the banks) or by raising loan rates to whatever extent is necessary to relieve the

---

[1] Prior to 1959 one further item could have been added to this list: to impose stricter controls over new share issues. See J. C. R. Dow, *The Management of the British Economy*, 1945–60 (Cambridge University Press, 1964) p. 415.

[2] See *Report of the Committee on the Working of the Monetary System*, Cmnd 827 (London: H.M.S.O., 1959) para. 137. From now on this work will be cited more simply as *Radcliffe Report*.

pressure on their loan funds or, most probably, by some combination of rationing and higher loan rates. To the extent that (ii) occurs, the cost of finance will tend to rise because companies which have been denied finance by the banks will be able to obtain it by issuing fixed-interest securities instead, only if they raise their interest rates sufficiently to persuade the holders of idle bank balances to convert them into industrial securities. In short, when bank finance becomes more difficult to obtain, there will either be a generalised increase in the cost of finance, or a reduction in the availability of finance, or both.

A reduction in the supply of bank credit (reduction in the level of bank advances) will help to effect the specified changes in the monetary instruments, then, by decreasing the availability of bank finance. It will also help, at one remove, by reducing the level of bank deposits and hence the stock of money.

A reduction in the stock of money will help to produce the desired changes in the monetary instruments, both directly and indirectly. As for the direct effect, given desired transactions balances, a reduction in the stock of money will mean a fall in the level of idle money balances and hence, *ceteris paribus*, a fall in the stock of liquid assets, of which the stock of idle money constitutes the main component. Thus one of the desired changes in the monetary instruments (a reduction in the stock of liquid assets) will emerge as a direct result of a reduction in the stock of money.

The other two specified monetary changes (increase in the cost of finance and decrease in the availability of finance) will also follow a reduction in the stock of money, but in this case there will be an intervening variable, namely the average yield on government securities. According to the theory of security yields outlined in Appendix 6.1,[1] a fall in the stock of money will lead, *ceteris paribus*, to a rise in the general level of security yields. This, in turn, can be expected to increase the cost of finance and/or reduce the availability of finance in several different ways. One consequence of the rise in yields will be that government securities become more attractive to the life-assurance offices and the pension funds. Broadly speaking, these institutions aim at a distribution of their funds between government securities, private securities, shares, mortgages, etc.,

[1] This is a straightforward extension of Keynesian liquidity preference theory designed primarily to allow for the existence of assets other than money and bonds.

which gives them sufficient income to cover their actuarial commitments but which, at the same time, minimises risk. This being so, they can be expected to switch funds from private securities, shares and mortgages to government securities when the yield on government securities increases because, by doing this, they can secure a portfolio which is less risky but which still produces the required minimum income. But such a rearrangement of their portfolios will tend to decrease the funds which they have available for investment in new issues of shares and private securities and in mortgage loans, and hence to increase the pressure on these funds. This increased pressure on available funds will lead the life offices and pension funds either to raise lending rates or to ration would-be borrowers or both. Moreover, these effects will be generalised as those individuals and firms who are diverted from the life offices and pension funds try to obtain finance elsewhere.

Secondly, an increase in the average bond yield means a decrease in the market price of bonds and hence an increase in the capital loss suffered by any holder of bonds who sells them instead of holding them to maturity. For this reason we can expect an increase in the level of bond yields to make holders of bonds less willing than before to sell them in order to finance expenditure. For example, firms which are holding accumulated funds in bonds will be less willing than before to sell them in order to finance investment expenditure. The same will be true of individuals who have been saving in order to finance durable consumption expenditure and who are holding their accumulated savings in the form of bonds. Thus some firms and individuals who would have used 'internal finance' prior to the rise in yields will now attempt to obtain finance from a commercial bank or some other financial institutions. Consequently there will be increased pressure on the loan funds which these institutions have available and this will have the result of increasing the cost and/or reducing the availability of finance.

Finally, an increase in the average yield on government bonds must lead, more or less immediately, to a comparable rise in the yield on long-term private bonds, since the two types of security are highly substitutable. As a result, companies which borrow direct from the public by issuing long-term fixed-interest securities will be forced to pay more than before for their funds following a rise in bond yields.

To sum up, a reduction in the supply of bank credit will work to bring about the desired changes in the monetary instruments in two distinct ways: (i) immediately, by decreasing the availability of bank finance; and (ii) at one remove, by reducing the stock of money. A *decrease in the availability of bank finance* will mean that potential spenders will be diverted from the banks to other sources of finance and this diversion will lead to an increase in the cost, and a decrease in the availability of finance in general. A *decrease in the stock of money* will produce a decrease in the stock of liquid assets directly and an increase in the cost, and a decrease in the availability of finance indirectly, by increasing the yield on long-term government securities. An increase in security yields will tend to increase cost and decrease availability in three main ways. In the first place, it will lead the life offices and pension funds to switch funds from private securities and mortgages to government securities. Secondly, it will make holders of securities less willing than before to sell them to finance expenditure. Finally, it will lead a comparable rise in the yield on long-term private bonds.

Having explained how a reduction in the supply of bank credit works, we turn to the next question: What techniques are available to the authorities should they wish to effect a reduction in the supply of bank credit? To force a reduction in the supply of bank credit the British authorities can make use of one or more of the following techniques. They can:

(i) make open-market sales of bonds (OM);
(ii) produce a 'budget surplus' (BS);
(iii) make an official request for restraint in bank lending (OR);
(iv) call for 'special deposits' from the commercial banks (SD);
(v) engage in funding (F).

Open-market sales is the traditional technique for reducing the supply of bank credit, though it has not been used in the post-war period.[1] The way in which it works or is supposed to work is well known. When the authorities sell bonds to the customers of the commercial banks, both the deposits of the commercial banks and their cash holdings with the Bank of England fall by the amount of the sale, with the result that their cash ratios also fall. If the bonds are sold to the banks themselves, deposits remain the same and cash holdings with the Bank of England fall by the amount of the sale. Hence cash ratios fall once again. To restore their cash ratios, the

[1] See *Radcliffe Report*, para. 430.

commercial banks will attempt to reduce their deposits by reducing their advances.[1]

The *budget surplus* technique is, in effect, an extension of the technique of making open-market sales. The essential point here is that government payments to customers of the commercial banks (whether for currently produced goods and services or not) will cause the banks' deposits, and their cash holdings with the Bank of England, to increase by equal amounts, and hence tend to raise their cash ratios.[2] On the other hand, government receipts from customers of the banks (whether from taxation or from the sale of physical or paper assets to the banks' customers) will reduce the banks' deposits and their cash holdings with the Bank of England by equal amounts, and so tend to reduce their cash ratios.[3] It follows that by creating a budget surplus, in the sense of arranging government finance so that cash receipts of all types exceed cash outlays of all types, the authorities can force a net reduction in the cash ratios of the commercial banks.[4] The sequence of events from here on is exactly the same as that described in connection with open-market sales and need not be repeated.

The *official request* is a post-war device. In section 4 of the Bank of England Act, 1946, the Bank was given power to 'request information from and make recommendations to bankers, and . . . if so authorised by the Treasury, issue directions to any banker for the purpose of securing that effect is given to any such request or recommendation'. This power permits the authorities to instruct the commercial banks about advance policy and, in particular, to direct them to reduce advances whenever this appears desirable as a means of achieving internal balance. However, formal instructions under this section of the Bank of England Act have never, in fact, been issued. Instead the authorities have preferred an informal procedure under which, from

[1] The reader is reminded that this is the way in which open-market sales *purport* to work. Whether they in fact work in this way is altogether another question which will be discussed in the next section.

[2] If government payments are made to the banks themselves, the banks' cash holdings with the Bank of England will increase while their deposits will remain unchanged. Once again, therefore, there will be a tendency for cash ratios to rise.

[3] Government receipts from the banks themselves will cause the banks' cash holdings to fall and will leave their deposits unchanged. Hence they will tend to reduce the banks' cash ratios in this case too.

[4] It should be noted that the term 'budget surplus' is being used here to mean an excess of cash receipts over cash disbursements. It is therefore quite a different concept from the more familiar one of an excess of tax collections over expenditure on currently produced goods and services.

time to time, they advise the banks of their wishes in rgard t*o loan
ceilings and loan priorities and request the banks' co-operation in
carrying out these wishes. 'Official requests' have been issued on
numerous occasions in the twenty years since the end of the war,
both by Labour and Conservative Chancellors, and were particularly
prominent after 1955.[1]

The *special deposits* technique is the newest of the five, having
originated as recently as 1958. In that year the Bank of England
negotiated an agreement with the commercial banks under which the
Bank could call for special deposits from the commercial banks,
whenever it wished to do so, on the understanding that the banks
would not reckon these special deposits as part of their liquid assets.
Thus when the Bank makes a call for special deposits, the cash holdings of the commercial banks are immediately reduced by the amount
of the call and, since deposits are unaffected, their cash ratios fall.
To restore their ratios the banks will take the various steps already
discussed in connection with the open-market sales device, i.e. they
will attempt to reduce deposits by reducing advances. In fact the only
difference between the special deposits technique and the technique
of open-market sales, as far as method of operation is concerned, is
that open-market sales reduce the cash ratios of the banks by
effecting an equal reduction in both cash holdings and deposits,
whereas a call for special deposits reduces their cash ratios by
effecting a reduction in cash holdings only.

Finally there is the technique of *funding*. A funding operation is
one which increases the average maturity of the national debt in the
hands of the banks and the non-bank public, without changing its
size, e.g. a sale of bonds by the Bank of England coupled with non-
replacement by the Treasury of an equivalent amount of maturing
Treasury bills. Like a call for special deposits, a funding operation
causes a reduction in the supply of bank credit by producing a change
in the structure of the banks' assets. As a result of the funding,
the banks' illiquid assets increase (in the form of bonds), and
their liquid assets decrease (in the form of Treasury bills), by an
equal amount. Thus while their *cash* ratios are unaffected, their
liquid-asset ratios fall; and to restore them to their original level the
banks will attempt, as in the case of open-market sales and a call

[1] See J. H. Karenken, 'Monetary Policy', in R. E. Caves, *Britain's Economic
Prospects*, a Brooking's Institution Study (London: Allen & Unwin, 1968)
pp. 68–103, and Dow, *op. cit.*, pp. 235–42.

for special deposits, to reduce their deposits by reducing their advances.[1]

(b) *Increase of bank lending and borrowing rates.* At the outset of the present section we set out four steps which the authorities could take in order to increase the cost of finance and/or decrease the availability of finance. We have now dealt with the first of these four steps – to reduce the supply of bank credit – and we turn to the second. This is to effect an increase in bank lending and borrowing rates. Once again we shall begin our discussion by explaining how an increase in the lending and borrowing rates of the banks will help to achieve the desired increase in cost and decrease in availability and then consider the various techniques which the authorities can use in order to bring about an increase in bank lending and borrowing rates.

An increase in bank *lending* rates will increase the cost of finance directly and will also work indirectly to increase cost and/or decrease availability. Some individuals or firms who would otherwise have borrowed from a bank will now seek a cheaper loan from some other financial institution or, in the case of firms, will make a new issue of shares or fixed-interest securities. The result will be a generalised increase in the cost of finance or a decrease in its availability (cf. p. 154 above). Thus a rise in overdraft rates has the same type of indirect effect as a decrease in the supply of bank credit which is engineered by one of the five techniques discussed in the preceding subsection. In both cases the *modus operandi* is a diversion of would-be borrowers from the banks to some other source of finance.

An increase in bank *borrowing* rates (rates paid on interest-bearing deposits) will have no direct effect on the cost of finance but may well have a significant indirect effect, either on cost or availability or both. A rise in bank deposit rates will make lending to the banks more attractive than before, relative to other forms of short-term lending, e.g. lending to hire-purchase companies and building societies. Consequently if the hire-purchase companies, building societies, etc., do not raise their borrowing rates, they will lose funds to the banks and so will be forced to ration their customers, i.e. there will be a decrease in the availability of finance. On the other hand, if these institutions follow the banks' example and raise borrowing rates so

---

[1] Once again this is a somewhat idealised picture. For further discussion, see section 6.4.

as to avoid the need for further rationing, they will have to raise lending rates as well and this will mean an increase in the cost of finance.

We turn now to available techniques. The traditional technique for raising bank *lending* rates is to increase Bank Rate. By increasing Bank Rate the Bank of England signals its desire for an increase in bank *overdraft* rates and the commercial banks always respond readily to the signal because they know that the Bank of England can always impose its wishes if they fail to do so, e.g. by open-market operations coupled with back-door lending at penal rates.

A rise in Bank Rate also leads automatically to a rise in bank *borrowing* rates. By convention the rate of interest on deposit accounts is fixed by reference to Bank Rate and is usually Bank Rate *less* 2 per cent.[1]

(c) *Reduction of availability of hire-purchase finance.* The third step which the authorities can take if they wish to bring about the changes in the monetary instruments specified in the opening section of this chapter is to reduce the availability and/or increase the cost of hire-purchase finance. By this means they can reduce the availability, and increase the cost of finance in general, both directly and also indirectly by diverting potential borrowers from the hire-purchase companies to other sources of finance (cf. p. 154 above).

Turning to techniques, the main way in which the British authorities can reduce the *availability* of hire-purchase finance is through their statutory power over the provisions in hire-purchase contracts. By using this power to raise the minimum down-payment and lower the maximum repayment period,[2] the authorities, in effect, restrict the new lending which the hire-purchase companies are prepared to undertake at existing rates of interest, i.e. they impose a tighter rationing of hire-purchase finance. This technique was first introduced in 1952 and has been used frequently since then.[3]

Should they wish to effect an increase in the *cost* of hire-purchase finance, the authorities can make use of the 'official request' technique mentioned earlier. By means of an 'official request' to the banks the authorities can make it more difficult for the hire-purchase companies to obtain bank finance. If their access to bank finance is

---

[1] See *Radcliffe Report*, para. 131.
[2] These can be varied by the President of the Board of Trade under statutory regulation.   [3] See Dow, op. cit., pp. 246–7.

F 2

restricted in this way, the hire-purchase companies will be forced to increase their direct borrowing from the public in order to maintain lending at existing levels. But to obtain additional finance by way of direct deposits from the public they will have to raise the rates which they offer on these deposits and, in turn, the rates at which they lend. The end result, therefore, will be an increase in the cost of hire-purchase finance.

(d) *Increase in severity of business tax structure.* The fourth and final step which the authorities can take to effect the specified monetary changes is to increase the severity of the business tax structure.

An increase in the severity of the business tax structure will reduce the supply of internal business finance and cause some firms which would otherwise have used internal funds for financing investment expenditure to seek some form of external finance instead. This will increase the pressure on the funds which the banks, insurance companies, etc., have available for lending and lead either to an extension of existing credit rationing, or an increase in the cost of finance, or both. An increase in the severity of the business tax structure will, therefore, work in two distinct ways: directly, by reducing the incentive to invest, and indirectly, by reducing the supply of internal finance and, in turn, the availability of finance in general.

As for available techniques, the authorities can increase the severity of the business tax structure simply by passing the appropriate legislation, e.g. legislation which increases rates of profits tax, legislation which withdraws or reduces depreciation allowances, legislation which withdraws or reduces initial allowances.

6.4 Effectiveness of Techniques

We have now discussed the first three of the seven questions listed in the opening section of the chapter and we turn to the fourth. In the preceding section we described the techniques which the British authorities use in order to manipulate the fiscal, monetary and import instruments which constitute the basis of stabilisation policy. The question we now consider is: how effective are these techniques? Given that the authorities wish to produce certain specified changes in the instruments, are the techniques which they have available sufficiently powerful to enable them to do so? There is little to be said in answer to this question as far as the fiscal and import instruments are concerned, and we shall therefore dispose of them first. We shall then turn to the monetary instruments where the question is rather more involved.

1. *Fiscal Instruments*

As far as the fiscal instruments are concerned, the answer emerges fairly clearly from the discussion of the preceding section. We saw there that the central government can reduce its own real expenditure by decree and that it has the necessary statutory power to effect a cut in the capital expenditure of the nationalised industries if it wishes to do so. Moreover it has financial and statutory powers which permit it to manipulate local government expenditure, both current and capital. It would seem, therefore, that the British authorities have virtually full control over the variable G and that there is no purely technical difficulty in the way of their reducing G by any desired amount in the interests of internal balance, though, of course, there may be serious political and other difficulties.

Much the same appears to be true of the other two fiscal instruments – the tax structure and the transfer payment structure. As pointed out in the preceding section, the authorities can change the central government tax and transfer payment structure in whatever way they wish, simply by passing the necessary legislation; and by manipulating the structures of the central government they can change the overall structures of the central and local governments combined, to any desired extent. This is subject to the qualification that, since the local government tax and transfer payment structures are beyond the control of the central authorities, a change in the central government tax or transfer payment structures could conceivably be offset by a change in the opposite direction in the local government structures. But since these play a comparatively small part in determining the overall structures and, in any case, offer little scope for significant change in the short run, this qualification is unimportant.

2. *Import Instruments*

The techniques for manipulating the import instruments can also be dealt with quite briefly. These are effective enough when the situation is one of excess demand. In the reverse situation, however, they give the authorities only limited control over the two import instruments. In a situation of deficient demand the appropriate changes in the import instruments would be: reduction in home–foreign price ratio; increase in intensity of direct controls over foreign transactions. At first glance it would appear that the authorities have ample statutory power to bring about these changes. For example, they have the power to impose an import surcharge, to raise tariffs and to impose or intensify direct controls over foreign transactions. However, while these statutory powers are available on paper, they cannot be freely used to promote internal balance because of the obligations which the British Government has assumed under international agreements such as the I.M.F. and GATT agreements. For example, an increase in tariffs or an intensification of direct controls over foreign transactions aimed solely at eliminating deficient demand would be incompatible with Britain's membership of GATT.

3. *Monetary Instruments*

Doubts also arise in connection with the *monetary instruments*. It will be recalled that, in the previous section, we listed four steps which the authorities could take in order to bring about the changes in the monetary instruments specified in the opening section as appropriate in a situation of excess demand: (i) reduce the supply of bank credit; (ii) increase bank lending and borrowing rates; (iii) reduce the supply of hire-purchase finance; and (iv) increase the severity of the business tax structure. We also discussed the various techniques by means of which these steps could be implemented. There seems to be little reason to doubt the effectiveness of the techniques discussed under headings (ii), (iii) and (iv) – the Bank Rate technique and the statutory and other means of reducing the supply of hire-purchase finance and the supply of internal business finance. The five techniques introduced under heading (i), however, are much more dubious. There has been a great deal of discussion about the effectiveness of these five techniques in recent years and we shall now try to give a brief account of the main points which have emerged from this discussion.

It was pointed out in the previous section (see pp. 157–9 above) that three of the five techniques in question, the technique of open-market operations (OM), the technique of special deposits (SD) and the budget-surplus technique (BS), are intended to force a reduction in the supply of bank credit via a reduction in the cash ratios of the commercial banks. However, if the banks happen to be operating with cash ratios which are above the conventional minimum, e.g. if they are in the process of moving to a new equilibrium following a disturbance caused by favourable developments in the balance of payments, there is no guarantee that a given reduction in their cash ratios will put pressure on them to reduce advances; it may merely serve to mop up their 'excess cash'.

The same type of argument can be used in relation to the funding technique (F). As explained in the previous section (see pp. 159–60 above), this technique is meant to force a reduction in the supply of bank credit via a reduction in the banks' liquid-asset ratios. However, if the banks happen to be operating with excessive liquid-asset ratios, the application of this technique may merely serve to mop up 'excess liquidity'; there need be no pressure whatsoever to reduce advances.

Against this it can be argued that there will always be some reduction in cash or liquid-asset ratios which will bring the necessary pressure to bear on the banks, and that if the techniques in question are applied vigorously enough it will always be possible to achieve this particular reduction. Hence, if these techniques fail to work for the particular reason under discussion, this is not because they are ineffective but rather because the authorities are unwilling to face up to the difficulties, genuine or otherwise, which a correct application of the techniques might involve.

Assume now that the banks are always in equilibrium (i.e. that they are always working with the conventional minimum cash and liquidity ratios), thus putting on one side the difficulty just discussed. Even so, it is argued, the OM, BS, SD and F techniques may fail because when the banks' cash ratios (or, in the case of F, their liquid-asset ratios) are reduced, they may decide to restore their cash ratios or liquid-asset ratios as the case may be, not by reducing their advances but by reducing some other form of illiquid asset. In particular they may decide to sell bonds instead of reducing advances.

It has been argued frequently in recent years that the banks are, in fact, unlikely to react in the manner just described provided that concurrent steps are taken to raise bond yields (lower bond prices). In these circumstances, it is said, the banks would prefer to suffer the loss of income involved in reducing advances rather than suffer the capital loss which would now face any holder of bonds who sold them prior to maturity. However, while this view was widely held in the 1950s under the label of the 'availability doctrine' or the 'Roosa effect',[1] recent theoretical and empirical work in the United States has raised doubts about its validity.[2]

We come now to one of the most lengthy and important controversies in the post-war monetary literature, namely the controversy between the advocates of the 'old-orthodoxy' and the 'new-orthodoxy'.[3] The old-orthodoxy group are supporters of OM. The new-orthodoxy group claim that OM is likely to be ineffective for reasons which resemble those just considered (we shall discuss them in detail shortly) and advocate funding as the best alternative to OM.

We shall begin our account of this controversy by attempting to explain the substance of the criticism which is advanced by the new-orthodoxy group against the OM technique.[4] Since this criticism consists of urging that the traditional account of the *modus operandi* of OM, to which the old orthodoxy subscribes, is defective, the reader may find it helpful to have the traditional view restated at the outset in rather more detail than in the previous section (see pp. 157–158 above).

In the traditional (old-orthodox) account of the *modus operandi* of the OM technique, the banks respond to the fall in their cash ratios, which the Bank of England produces by the open-market sale of securities, by reducing their advances. The essence of the old-orthodox view can be seen from the following four hypothetical balance sheets relating to the commercial banks as a whole.

---

[1] It appears to have been accepted by the Radcliffe Committee. See *Radcliffe Report*, para. 146.

[2] Cf. A. D. Tussing, 'Can Monetary Policy Influence the Availability of Credit?', *Journal of Finance* (Mar 1966) and the further references given there.

[3] This controversy has now been raging for something like ten years and has produced a substantial literature. The following discussion relies heavily on a hitherto unpublished survey of this literature by Mr A Budd. Lack of space prevents us from giving a complete bibliography, but the most important references would seem to be: R. S. Sayers, 'The Determination of the Volume of Bank Deposits, England 1955–56', *Banca Nazionale del Lavoro Quarterly Review* (Dec 1955); W. M. Dacey, 'The Floating Debt Problem', *Lloyds Bank Review* (Apr 1956); A. W. Jasay, 'Liquidity Ratios and Funding in Monetary Control', *Oxford Economic Papers* (Oct 1956); W. M. Dacey, 'Treasury Bills and the Money Supply', *Lloyds Bank Review* (Jan 1960); R. L. Crouch, 'A Re-examination of Open-Market Operations', *Oxford Economic Papers* (Aug. 1963); D. T. Coppock and N. J. Gibson, 'The Volume of Deposits and the Cash and Liquid Assets Ratios', *Manchester School* (Sep 1963); W. T. Newlyn, 'The Supply of Money and its Control', *Economic Journal* (June 1964); R. L. Crouch, 'The Inadequacy of "New Orthodox" Methods of Monetary Control', *Economic Journal* (Dec 1964).

[4] The controversy has been in terms of OM, though it is relevant to BS and SD also.

Open-market Operations: Old-orthodox View

I(a)		
Liabilities	*Assets*	
Deposits 1000	Cash	80
	Other liquid assets	220
	Illiquid assets	700
1000		1000

II(a)		
Liabilities	*Assets*	
Deposits 990	Cash	70
	Other liquid assets	220
	Illiquid assets	700
990		990

III(a)		
Liabilities	*Assets*	
Deposits 875	Cash	70
	Other liquid assets	220
	Illiquid assets	585
875		875

IV(a)		
Liabilities	*Assets*	
Deposits 875	Cash	70
	Other liquid assets	192·5
	Illiquid assets	612·5
875		875

Balance sheet I(a) shows an initial equilibrium with the cash ratio at 8 per cent and the liquid-asset ratio at 30 per cent. Balance sheet II(a) shows the position after OM has been applied – a sale of bonds worth 10 to the customers of the banks has reduced both cash and deposits by 10 and reduced the cash ratio below the conventional 8 per cent minimum. In balance sheet III(a) we see the reaction envisaged by the old orthodoxy: the banks restore their cash ratio to 8 per cent by reducing both advances (illiquid assets) and deposits by 115. This leaves the liquid-asset ratio higher than 30 per cent, and to reduce it to the conventional minimum they are obliged to reduce Treasury bills or other liquid assets by 27·5 and increase advances by an equal amount, thus reaching the final position shown in balance sheet IV(a). The ultimate fall in advances is therefore 8·75 times the open-market sale, while the fall in the money stock is 12·5 times the open-market sale.

Let us now consider the objections advanced by the new orthodoxy against this view. Earlier in this section we drew attention to the possibility that the banks may respond to a fall in their cash ratios by reducing their holdings of bonds rather than by reducing advances. The advocates of the new orthodoxy stress still another possibility. Their argument is that when faced with the fall in their cash ratios, which results from the application of the OM technique, the commercial banks will react not by reducing advances, but by calling in loans from the discount market. Since the discount houses will repay the banks by rediscounting Treasury bills with the Bank of England, this amounts to saying that the OM technique is ineffective because, when faced with the reduction in their cash ratios, the banks will react, not by reducing their advances, but by replenishing their cash holdings.

The essence of this new-orthodox argument can be stated in terms of the four balance sheets set out below. In the new-orthodox view, balance sheets I(a) and II(a) above are acceptable but balance sheets III(a) and IV(a) would have to be amended. As they see it, the position would be as follows:

Open-market Operations: New-orthodox view

I(b)

Liabilities		Assets	
Deposits	1000	Cash	80
		Other liquid assets	220
		Illiquid assets	700
	1000		1000

II(b)

Liabilities		Assets	
Deposits	990	Cash	70
		Other liquid assets	220
		Illiquid assets	700
	990		990

III(b)

Liabilities		Assets	
Deposits	990	Cash	80
		Other liquid assets	210
		Illiquid assets	700
	990		990

IV(b)

Liabilities		Assets	
Deposits	1000	Cash	80
		Other liquid assets	220
		Illiquid assets	700
	1000		1000

In balance sheet III(b) we see the reaction to the reduction in cash ratios which is envisaged by the new orthodoxy: cash returns to 80 and other liquid assets falls to 210 as the banks replenish their cash holdings by calling in loans from the discount houses. With cash at 80 the banks can now expand deposits to their original level. The final position is shown in balance sheet IV(b). (This assumes that the banks achieve the expansion of deposits from stage III to stage IV by increasing their holding of other liquid assets by 10, e.g. by buying Treasury bills from their customers rather than by increasing illiquid assets by 10, their object being to restore their liquid-asset ratio to 30 per cent.) Thus OM has been completely ineffective in the sense that there has been no reduction at all, either in the money stock or in the level of advances.

The advocates of the old orthodoxy reply to this criticism by reaffirming their belief that the picture given in balance sheets I(a), II(a), III(a) and IV(a) is substantially correct and directing their attack on the tacit assumption underlying the new-orthodox position, namely that when the discount houses are asked by the commercial banks to repay their loans they will do so by rediscounting Treasury bills with the Bank of England. According to the old-orthodoxy this is an unacceptable assumption. Their view is that so long as Bank Rate is a genuinely penal rate (in effect so long as the authorities really want OM to work), the discount houses will try to find some way of repaying the banks which does not involve borrowing from the Bank of England. Two possible alternatives are suggested by the adherents of the old orthodoxy. In the first place the discount houses could borrow direct from the public. Secondly, they could reduce their holding of Treasury bills, by buying fewer bills at the next weekly tender than mature on that day, and then use the extra cash gained in this way to repay the banks.

In the first case, so the argument runs, new-orthodox balance sheets I(b) to IV(b) would have to be replaced by I(c) to IV(c). These are as follows:

I(c)

Liabilities		Assets	
Deposits	1000	Cash	80
		Other liquid assets	220
		Illiquid assets	700
	1000		1000

II(c)

Liabilities		Assets	
Deposits	990	Cash	70
		Other liquid assets	220
		Illiquid assets	700
	990		990

III(c)

Liabilities		Assets	
Deposits	980	Cash	70
		Other liquid assets	210
		Illiquid assets	700
	980		980

IV(c)

Liabilities		Assets	
Deposits	875	Cash	70
		Other liquid assets	192·5
		Illiquid assets	612·5
	875		875

When the discount houses borrow 10 from the public in order to repay the banks, all that happens is that the deposits of one group of the banks' customers (the discount houses) rise by 10 while the deposits of another group (the members of the public from whom the discount houses are borrowing) fall by 10 – aggregate deposits and cash holdings remain unchanged. Then when the discount houses use the funds borrowed from the public to repay the banks, both deposits and other liquid assets fall by 10 (balance sheet III(c)). Thus if the discount houses follow the first of the two alternatives mentioned above, neither the cash ratio nor the liquid-asset ratio will be at their conventional minimum levels after the discount houses have repaid their loans, and to reach equilibrium the banks will have to reduce advances (or sell bonds) and sell Treasury bills (balance sheet IV(c)).

As regards the second alternative, it must be assumed, so the old orthodoxy argues, that the bills not taken up by the discount houses are taken up by the customers of the banks: the alternative assumption that they are taken up by the Bank of England, in the interests of the Treasury (to avoid the rise in the bill rate which must occur if the public are to be induced to take them up), is illegitimate because it amounts to the assumption that the authorities do not wish OM to work.[1] In this event, however, balance sheets III(c) and IV(c) must apply once again. When the banks' customers buy rejected Treasury bills to the value of 10, the banks' cash holdings and deposits will both fall by this amount as cheques are drawn in favour of the Treasury. However, the fall in cash holdings will be exactly offset by a rise in cash holdings as the discount houses repay their loans to the banks with cheques drawn in their favour by the Treasury. Cash holdings will therefore be unaffected by the repayment of the loans by the discount houses which means that III(c) will be the intermediate balance sheet once again. And, of course, if III(c) is the intermediate balance sheet, IV(c) must be the final balance sheet.

It will be observed that balance sheet IV(c) is identical with balance sheet IV(a). We thus reach the conclusion that if the discount houses refrain from borrowing from the Bank of England in order to repay their loans to the banks and instead adopt one or other of the alternatives in question, the final result will not be the one predicted by the new orthodoxy but the one predicted in the traditional account of the OM technique.

Thus it would seem that an essential issue in the controversy between the new and the old orthodoxy relates to the behaviour of the discount houses. Are they optimisers, and if so what do they optimise and under what constraints? Presumably there will be one

---

[1] It would make no sense, of course, to assume that the rejected bills are taken up by the banks themselves, since that would mean that the banks deliberately reduce 'other liquids' by calling in loans from the discount houses and then immediately restore them to their original level by purchasing additional Treasury bills.

set of answers to these questions that would imply recourse to the Bank of England even with a genuinely penal Bank Rate, and another set that would lead one to predict the adoption of some alternative course of action such as the two examined in detail above. If the first set of answers were shown to be correct, the picture presented by the new orthodoxy would have to be accepted and the OM technique dismissed as ineffective. On the other hand, if the second set of answers were to be supported by the evidence, the traditional picture of the working of OM would remain entirely valid and there would be no reason to doubt the effectiveness of this technique.

The technique for controlling the supply of bank credit which the supporters of the new orthodoxy favour in place of OM, BS and SD is funding. Their view of the *modus operandi* of funding is the one sketched earlier (see pp. 159–60 above). That is, they see funding as an operation which works by changing the structure of the banks' assets in such a way that liquid assets form a smaller proportion, and illiquid assets a higher proportion, of total assets than before. Assuming an initial equilibrium, this change in asset structure will mean that the banks' liquid-asset ratios are now below the conventional minimum and to restore them the banks will be obliged to reduce advances.

The new-orthodox viewpoint on funding can be summed up by means of the following four hypothetical balance sheets:

Funding: New-orthodox View

	I(d)				II(d)	
Liabilities	*Assets*			*Liabilities*	*Assets*	
Deposits 1000	Cash	80		Deposits 1000	Cash	80
	Other liquid assets	220			Other liquid assets	210
	Illiquid assets	700			Illiquid assets	710
1000		1000		1000		1000

	III(d)				IV(d)	
Liabilities	*Assets*			*Liabilities*	*Assets*	
Deposits 966·7	Cash	80		Deposits 966·7	Cash	77·3
	Other liquid assets	210			Other liquid assets	212·7
	Illiquid assets	676·7			Illiquid assets	676·7
966·7		966·7		966·7		966·7

Balance sheet I(d) shows an initial equilibrium with the cash ratio at 8 per cent and the liquid-asset ratio at 30 per cent. Balance sheet II(d) shows the effect of a funding operation which reduces other liquid assets (in the shape of Treasury bills) by 10 and increases illiquid assets (in the shape of bonds) by 10. In balance sheet III(d) we see the reduction in advances (and deposits) which has the effect of restoring the liquid-asset ratio to 30 per cent. However, the cash ratio is now above the 8 per cent conventional minimum and to reduce it to 8 per cent the banks will reduce cash by 2·7 and increase other liquid assets by the same amount, e.g. by making additional loans of 2·7 to the discount houses which the latter use to reduce their debt to the Bank of England. The final equilibrium is shown in balance sheet IV(d). Both advances and deposits have fallen as a result of the funding of 10, whereas they would have remained unchanged if an open-market sale of 10 had been used instead (see balance sheet IV(b)). Funding is, therefore, the more effective technique according to the new-orthodox view.

The old-orthodox reply to this argument is to ask why, at stage III, the banks must reduce advances and deposits in order to restore their liquid-asset ratios to 30 per cent? Why could they not increase liquid assets by 10 and deposits by 10, as at stage IV in the OM case (see balance sheets III(b) and IV(b)), and then reduce illiquid assets (and deposits) by 10 by reducing advances? If this were done, balance sheet I(d) would be reinstated and the only effect of the funding would be to reduce advances by the amount of the funding; there would be no change in the stock of money. Alternatively, the old orthodoxy would argue that if it is impossible for the banks to acquire additional liquid assets at stage III in the funding case, it must also be impossible for them to do so at stage IV in the OM case. Hence, if balance sheets III(d) and IV(d) are correct, balance sheet IV(b) must be incorrect and would have to be revised so that it became identical with IV(d).

The adherents of the old orthodoxy would ask another question also. The new orthodoxy tacitly assumes that in a funding operation it is the *banks* which acquire the additional bonds and the *banks* which lose the Treasury bills. What happens (1) if the *customers* of the banks lose the Treasury bills while the banks acquire the bonds, and (2) if the *banks* lose the bills and their *customers* acquire the bonds?

In case (1) balance sheet II(d) would have to be amended. When the customers of the banks lose the Treasury bills, both cash and deposits rise by 10, and when the banks acquire the bonds, cash falls by 10 and illiquid assets rise by 10. After the funding operation, therefore, the combined balance sheet would be II(e), not II(d).

II(e)

Liabilities		Assets	
Deposits	1010	Cash	80
		Other liquid assets	220
		Illiquid assets	710
	1010		1010

Now, however, both the cash ratio and the liquid-asset ratio are below the conventional minimum, and to restore equilibrium the banks would reduce both advances and deposits by 10. In other words, balance sheet I(d) would be reinstated and the only effect of the funding would be a reduction in advances equal to the funding.

In case (2) balance sheet II(d) would have to be amended once again. When the customers of the banks acquire the bonds, both deposits and cash fall by 10. When the banks lose the bills, cash rises by 10 and other liquid assets falls by 10. Hence after the funding operation the combined balance sheet would be II(f), not II(d).

II(f)

Liabilities		Assets	
Deposits	990	Cash	80
		Other liquid assets	210
		Illiquid assets	700
	990		990

Now II(f) is identical with III(b). Hence the final balance sheet must be IV(b), not IV(d). In other words, the funding of 10 will have been no more effective than a (new-orthodox) OM of 10 in reducing the stock of money.

These old-orthodox counter-arguments appear to be perfectly legitimate, and it would seem that the new-orthodox faith in funding as an instrument for reducing the supply of bank credit is misplaced. This does not reflect on their claim that OM (and implicitly BS and SD) are ineffective. But, as pointed out earlier, the validity of this claim cannot be tested until more is known about the behaviour of the discount houses.

Up till now in our discussion of the effectiveness of the available techniques for manipulating the monetary instruments we have been concerned with the possibility that the OM, BS, SD and F techniques, for one reason or another, may fail to achieve their primary object of reducing the supply of bank finance. We now turn to another difficulty which applies to the official-request technique (OR) as well, namely that even if they succeed in reducing the supply of bank finance, they may contribute very little to the reduction of the supply of finance in general because the reduction in bank finance to which they lead may itself provoke an offsetting increase in the supply of some other type of finance. One possibility is that a reduction in the supply of bank finance may lead to an increase in the supply of 'internal finance'. That is, firms which are finding it difficult to obtain all the finance they need from the banks may meet the difficulty by a temporary reduction in their transactions and/or precautionary money holdings. Another possibility is that a reduction in the supply of bank credit may stimulate an offsetting increase in the supply of trade credit.

The latter possibility was the subject of extensive empirical investigation by Brechling and Lipsey in the early 1960s.[1] Some three or four years earlier, the Radcliffe Committee had expressed the view that a restriction of bank credit was most likely to stimulate an expansion of trade credit.[2] On the other hand, Dow had come to the conclusion that trade credit was unlikely to expand, and might well contract, when the supply of bank finance was reduced.[3] One of the main purposes of the investigation undertaken by Brechling and Lipsey was to settle this question.

Brechling and Lipsey (B. & L.) began by deriving two linear regressions for each of a sample of 75 firms: the regression of G_i (the gross credit given by the ith firm to its customers) on S_i (the sales of the ith firm) and the regression of T_i (the gross credit taken by the ith firm from its suppliers) on P_i (the purchases of the ith firm). In all cases the regressions were based on annual data for the years 1950 to 1959. Next the regression of G_i on S_i was used to calculate a series of residuals, denoted by g_i, for each of the 75 firms and the regression of T_i on P_i to derive a series of residuals denoted by t_i. The g_i

---

[1] See F. P. R. Brechling and R. G. Lipsey, 'Trade Credit and Monetary Policy', *Economic Journal* (Dec 1963).

[2] See *Radcliffe Report*, paras 297–311.

[3] See Dow, op. cit., pp. 313–14, 321–4.

residual series was taken to indicate the 'abnormal' movement in G_i, i.e. the movement which could not be explained by movements in S_i. Similarly the t_i residual was taken to indicate the abnormal movement in T_i – the movement which could not be accounted for by movement in P_i. Finally, both residual series were summed over the 75 firms to obtain a series for g and t, the abnormal movement in the gross credit given by the 75 firms as a whole, and the abnormal movement in gross credit taken by the 75 firms as a whole, respectively.

The series for g and t over the ten-year period were then plotted alongside four indicators of the restrictiveness of monetary policy, namely the yield on Consols, the yield on Treasury bills, the ratio between the stock of money and gross domestic product and the ratio of bank advances to gross domestic product. From an inspection of these charts, it was concluded that trade credit shows a definite tendency to expand when monetary policy becomes more restrictive, and vice versa.

In the second stage of the investigation an attempt was made to assess the quantitative significance of this conclusion. The question asked was: Does the expansion of trade credit which occurs when bank finance is curtailed constitute a major limitation of the OM, BS, SD, OR and F techniques or are the offsetting movements in trade credit so small that they can safely be ignored? To answer this question it was necessary to derive series for the *net* abnormal credit given and taken by the 75 firms in the aggregate. To this end the ith firm was assumed to be a net giver of abnormal credit in a particular year if $g_i > t_i$ in that year, and the amount of the abnormal net credit given by the firm was measured by $(g_i - t_i)$. On the other hand the ith firm was taken to be a net taker of abnormal credit if $t_i > g_i$, and the amount of the abnormal net credit taken by the firm was measured by $(t_i - g_i)$. By aggregating over all firms in all years it was then possible to obtain two series – one showing the aggregate net credit given by the firms in the sample and the other aggregate net credit taken by the firms in the sample. In a closed system of firms, the series for aggregate net credit given and taken would be identical. The fact that these two series were not identical for the sample of 75 firms was attributed by B. & L. to sampling error rather than to the absence of a closed system among the population of firms as a whole, and this led them to base further work on the arithmetic mean of the two sample series.

Having derived an abnormal net credit series for the 75 firms as a whole in this way, B. & L. next expressed this series as a percentage of the income generated by the 75 firms and assumed that the resulting series of percentages applied to the economy as a whole.

Finally, the series for abnormal net credit as a percentage of income generated was compared with four other series relating to the economy as a whole, namely (i) new capital issues as a percentage of income; (ii) change in bank advances as a percentage of income; (iii) change in building societies' advances as a percentage of income; and (iv) change in public borrowing as a percentage of income. The series of abnormal net credit to income percentages proved to be of the same order of magnitude as the other four percentage series (if anything slightly larger), and on this basis B. & L. came to the conclusion that the extension of trade credit was potentially a very powerful frustrator of monetary policy.[1]

From this brief summary of their work it would seem that there is little reason to doubt B. & L.'s conclusion that the supply of trade credit tends to increase whenever the monetary authorities take action to reduce the supply of bank credit. On the other hand, their conclusion about the quantitative significance of the offset appears to lack a proper foundation. The main weakness of their approach to this question is that the four 'reference series', with which the series of percentages of abnormal net credit to income generated are compared, are of doubtful relevance. To assess the significance of trade credit expansion as an offset to monetary policy, one would need to find some way of comparing the expansion of trade credit with the reduction of bank credit which provokes it,[2] and this B. & L. do not appear to have done.

The main conclusions of the present section can now be summarised as follows. We set out in this section to assess the effectiveness of existing techniques for manipulating the various policy instruments

---

[1] It should be noted that B. & L. also compared a series showing the percentage of *inflationary* abnormal net credit to income with the four reference series, but were not inclined to attach much weight to this comparison because of doubts about the reliability of their inflationary abnormal net credit series. This was derived by reducing the $(g_i - t_i)$ of the givers of abnormal credit to the extent of any abnormal decrease in stocks and the $(t_i - g_i)$ of the takers of abnormal net credit to the extent of any abnormal increase in money or financial assets and then proceeding as before.

[2] See the attack on B. & L.'s work by White and their reply: W. H. White, 'Trade Credit and Monetary Policy: A Reconciliation', *Economic Journal* (Dec 1964), and R. G. Lipsey and F. P. R. Brechling, 'Trade Credit and Monetary Policy: A Rejoinder', *Economic Journal* (Mar 1966).

and for this purpose we took the fiscal instruments, the import instruments and the monetary instruments in turn. As regards the fiscal instruments and the import instruments our conclusions were straightforward: with existing techniques the fiscal instruments appear to be well within the authorities' control whereas, given membership of such international organisations as I.M.F. and GATT, there is little the authorities can do to manipulate the import instruments in the interests of the internal balance objective. In the case of the monetary instruments our answers were less direct. The Bank Rate technique and those techniques which purport to work via changes in the supply of hire-purchase finance probably make a useful contribution, but the remaining monetary techniques are somewhat unreliable. OM, BS, SD and OR are likely to work well provided the commercial banks' cash and liquidity ratios are at minimum levels, provided the banks can be dissuaded from selling bonds instead of reducing advances when their cash and liquidity ratios fall below minimum levels, and provided the discount houses avoid borrowing from the Bank of England when asked by the commercial banks to repay loans. In the absence of some or all of these favourable conditions, however, they will be comparatively ineffective techniques for effecting the desired changes in the monetary instruments. Nor, when conditions are unfavourable to the use of these techniques, is funding likely to prove an acceptable substitute. In addition, there is the further problem that even when they do work, there is a decided possibility that their contribution will be nullified, to some extent, by an expansion of trade credit.

It would appear, therefore, that the control over policy instruments which existing techniques give to the British authorities is by no means complete. But it is reasonably adequate and there is little reason to believe that stabilisation policy will fail solely because the authorities lack the ability to produce any desired set of changes in the fiscal, import and monetary instruments.

6.5 Scale of Impact

In the previous section we were concerned with the degree of control which the British authorities have over the main policy instruments. The question asked there was whether, given existing techniques, the authorities can implement, say, a 2 per cent increase in the cost of finance or a 1 per cent decrease in government expenditure or a 3 per cent increase in severity of the tax structure if they wish to do so in order to reduce aggregate demand. In the present section, on the other hand, we shall take their ability to manipulate the policy instruments for granted and turn to another question, namely: What is the maximum impact on $(D-M)$ which the British authorities can hope to produce, given a range of variation in the policy instruments such as that experienced in the post-war period? It is not possible yet to give a detailed answer to this question, since much of the basic empirical work on the British economy that would be needed for a detailed analysis still remains to be done. There are several recent British studies, however, which throw a good deal of light on some aspects of the question, and our main object in this section is to give a brief review of four of these studies. Having done this, we shall then attempt to make a rough estimate of the order of magnitude of the changes in $(D-M)$ which seem feasible in Britain with existing techniques for manipulating the policy instruments.

The first study to be considered is one undertaken by Dow with the object of estimating the impact on consumption demand of the various changes in the British tax structure which were made between 1945 and 1960.[1] This study was based largely on information given in the *Financial Statement*, a document which is issued with every budget. Among other information, the *Financial Statement* contains a forecast of the total change in central government revenue which will result in a 'full year' from the various changes in the tax structure which are being proposed in the budget. This forecast total is classified in the *Financial Statement* by type of tax; and Dow's first step was to reclassify each of the forecast totals for the 1945–60 period by type of effect rather than by type of tax. Specifically, each of the forecast totals was split into five main categories: change in tax on personal income; change in tax on personal expenditure; change in tax on personal capital; change in tax on non-personal (i.e. company) income; and change in tax on non-personal expenditure. The 'personal income' category was then further subdivided according to the type of income affected, the categories used being:
Change in tax on income from employment:
  lower ranges
  upper ranges.
Change in tax on dividends, interest and trading incomes.

[1] See Dow, op. cit., pp. 146–209.

As an example, take the autumn budget of 1945. The *Financial Statement* accompanying this budget forecast that the total change in central government revenues which would result from the proposed changes in the tax structure would be − £385 million in a 'full year'. This total was reclassified by Dow as follows:[1]

TABLE 6.1

Change in tax on income from employment:		
lower ranges	− 157	
upper ranges	− 54	
	——	− 211
Change in tax on dividends, interest and		− 81
trading incomes		——
Change in tax on personal income		− 292
Change in tax on personal expenditure		− 10
Change in tax on personal capital		Nil
Change in tax on non-personal income		− 83
Change in tax on non-personal expenditure		Nil
		——
Total forecast tax change		− 385

Dow's next step was to make 'what are no more than guesses'[2] about the marginal propensities to consume which apply to changes of the first three types. The guesses were:

Type of tax change	*Marginal propensity to consume*
Tax on income from employment:	
lower ranges	1·0
upper ranges	0·67
Tax on dividends, interest and trading income	0·5
Tax on personal expenditure	0·8
Tax on personal capital	0·1

That is, it was assumed that an increase in the yield from taxes levied on employment income of, say, £10 million would lead to an equal reduction in consumption demand if the reduction in income were concentrated in the lower income groups, and a reduction of £6·7 million in consumption demand if the reduction were concentrated in the upper income groups. An increase of £10 million in the yield of tax on *non*-employment income was assumed to cause a still smaller reduction in consumption demand, namely £5 million. Finally, an increase of £10 million in the tax yield was assumed to result in a reduction in consumption demand of £8 million in the case

<hr />

[1] Ibid., pp. 198–9.   [2] Ibid., p. 197.

of taxes on personal expenditure and £1 million in the case of taxes on personal capital.

The final step was to apply these marginal propensities to the figures in Table 6.1 and to the corresponding figures for each of the other budgets under review. For the budget dealt with in Table 6.1 the result was an increase in consumption demand of £242 million which was calculated as follows:

$$\text{Increase in consumption demand} = (157 \times 1 \cdot 0) + (54 \times 0 \cdot 67)$$
$$+ (81 \times 0 \cdot 5) + (10 \times 0 \cdot 8) = 242.$$

The complete set of figures is shown in Table 6.2.[1] These figures suggest that, in the British case, a change in consumption demand of as much as £300 million per annum in terms of present-day prices is entirely practicable in political terms through the use of the tax instrument alone.

TABLE 6.2

Budget	Change in consumption demand (£m.)	Budget	Change in consumption demand (£m.)	Budget	Change in consumption demand (£m.)
Oct 1945	+242	1950	+37	Oct 1955	−59
1946	+87	1951	−84	1956	+10
1947	−8	1952	+176	1957	−70
Nov 1947	−120	1953	+128	1958	+52
1948	+42	1954	+3	1959	+215
1949	+38	1955	+90	1960	−4

We turn now to a second study which is relevant to our present problem. This is the econometric study of the impact on consumer durable spending of variations in the direct hire-purchase controls (see section 6.2 above), undertaken recently by Ball and Drake.[2] The starting-point of the study is an econometric relationship which explains the quarterly behaviour of real consumer-durable expenditure for the British economy. After much experimentation, Ball and Drake decided on the following linear relationship:

$$(C_d)_t = A + 0 \cdot 253\, Y_t + 0 \cdot 907 N_t - 0 \cdot 051 \sum_{i=1954}^{t-1} (C_d)_i$$

where C_d denotes expenditure on consumer durables in constant prices, Y disposable income deflated by the price of consumer

[1] See Dow, op. cit., pp. 198–9.
[2] See R. J. Ball and Pamela S. Drake, 'The Impact of Credit Control on Consumer Durable Spending in the United Kingdom, 1957–1961', *Review of Economic Studies*, xxx (1963).

durables, N new hire-purchase credits issued and A the constant term in the relationship together with a collection of dummy seasonal variables and their coefficients.[1] On the usual statistical tests this relationship is fairly satisfactory. The overall fit is good, all coefficients have the right sign and the coefficients of all variables other than the seasonals are at least twice their standard errors. In fact the only real statistical difficulty appears to be the presence of a rather high degree of serial correlation.

Next Ball and Drake derive a relationship which explains the quarterly behaviour of N. Again after considerable experimentation, the following relationship, estimated from quarterly data by the method of two-stage least squares, is finally accepted as the most satisfactory from a statistical point of view:

$$N_t = B + 0.410(C_d)_t - 1.727d_t - 0.049D_{t-1} - 11.20(M_3)_t$$

where d denotes 'the minimum average deposit rate' (a weighted average of the minimum deposit percentages prescribed by the authorities under the hire-purchase regulations),[2] D the outstanding hire-purchase debt deflated by the price of consumer durables, M_3 'the average minimum monthly payment'[3] and B the constant term and the terms involving the dummy seasonal variables. Once again this relationship appears to be satisfactory on the basis of the usual statistical tests.

Finally, the two fitted relationships are treated as a pair of simultaneous equations in the unknowns $(C_d)_t$ and N_t and solved for $(C_d)_t$. The solution is:

$$(C_d)_t = A' + 0.403 Y_t - 0.081 \sum_{i=1954}^{t-1} (C_d)_i - 0.071D_{t-1} - 2.493d_t - 16.20(M_3)_t$$

where A' is an expression in A and B.

[1] The above relationship was derived from quarterly British data for the period 1957 (III) to 1961 (IV) by the method of two-stage least squares. The dummy seasonal variables are merely a device for coping with the seasonal element in quarterly data, and as they are of no interest in the subsequent discussion we have decided to suppress them in the interests of simplicity. The interested reader can find them written out in full in Ball and Drake, op. cit., p. 185.

[2] This variable assumes a zero value for years in which the regulations are not in force. Ibid., p. 194.

[3] This is an index of the real burden of hire-purchase payments and is given by:

$$\frac{[100 - \text{minimum average deposit rate}] \text{ (per cent)}}{\text{maximum average contract length (months)}}.$$

As already explained, the minimum average deposit rate is a weighted average of the prescribed minimum deposit precentages. Similarly the maximum average

This expression can be used to derive quantitative conclusions about the impact on real durable-goods spending of changes in prescribed mlnimum deposit rates and prescribed maximum contract lengths. For example, taking the expression at its face value, one can say that, *ceteris paribus*, an increase in the minimum average deposit rate from zero to 33 per cent (the range of variation actually observed) will reduce $(C_d)_t$ by about £82 million per quarter (33 × 2·493 = 82·269) in terms of 1954 prices[1] or by about 28 per cent of the average value of $(C_d)_t$ observed during the sample period.[2] Again, given a minimum average deposit rate of 6 per cent (the mean value observed in the sample period), a decrease in the maximum average contract length from 36 months to 24 months (an *increase* in M_3 from $(100 - 6)/36 = 2·6$ to $(100 - 6)/24 = 3·9$) would reduce $(C_d)_t$ by about £21 million per quarter in 1954 prices ($1·3 \times 16·20 = 21·06$) or by a little over 7 per cent of the mean value for the sample period.

These and similar conclusions must be treated with some caution for a number of reasons which the authors are at pains to point out. In particular it must not be overlooked that they involve the assumption of given real disposable income. Nevertheless they suggest that if the authorities increase minimum deposit rates and reduce maximum contract lengths simultaneously, as they have normally done in the past, they should be able to reduce consumer durable spending by something like £80 million per quarter in terms of present-day prices by more or less normal use of the hire-purchase instrument.

We turn, finally, to two questionnaire studies undertaken for the Radcliffe Committee by the Association of British Chambers of Commerce (A.B.C.C.) and the Federation of British Industries (F.B.I.) respectively. For reasons to be explained shortly, these studies are less illuminating than the two examined so far. Nevertheless they are worth considering in some detail for the light they throw on the likely impact of the monetary instruments.

The A.B.C.C. survey was conducted in March 1958. In that month 16,000 copies of a questionnaire drawn up by A.B.C.C. were sent to

---

contract length is a weighted average of the prescribed maximum lengths of contract, three years being taken as the maximum contract length where none was prescribed.

[1] All the value variables involved in the relationships for $(C_d)_t$ and N_t were expressed in 1954 prices for the purpose of the fitting.

[2] The assumption that M_3 remains fixed which underlies this calculation implies that the reduction in the minimum average deposit rate is offset by an increase in the maximum average contract length.

72 affiliated Chambers of Commerce with a request that they post the questionnaire to all, or a representative sample, of their members. In the event 3600 completed questionnaires were returned to A.B.C.C. from 68 of the 72 individual Chambers of Commerce.[1]

Of the eleven questions included in the questionnaire, two are especially relevant in the present connection, namely, questions 2 and 3. These are reproduced in Tables 6.3 and 6.4, together with a summary of the replies given in the 3404 questionnaires finally analysed.[2]

TABLE 6.3

Question	Percentage of respondents*		
	Answering yes	Answering no	Not answering
2. Have you since September 1957 experienced:			
(i) a reduction (other than seasonal) in your turnover	53	46	1
(ii) a reduction (other than seasonal) in your stocks and/or work in progress	37	60	3
(iii) reduced	24	59	17
or (iv) postponed fixed investment projects?	32	56	12

Source: *Memoranda*, pp. 91, 92.

* Note that in this table and in Tables 6.4, 6.5 and 6.6 the term 'respondent' refers to a firm whose completed questionnaire was analysed. For example, in the case of the present table the number of respondents is 3404.

One is tempted to conclude from these results that the monetary measures of September 1957 probably had a substantial impact on investment demand in Britain. According to Table 6.4, 4 per cent of the respondents gave 'the increased cost of borrowing' as the principal reason for the observed reduction in turnover and/or reduction in inventories and/or reduction in fixed-capital investment and/or postponement of fixed-capital investment. Another 5 per cent listed 'greater difficulty in obtaining finance' as the principal reason and a further 12 per cent listed either 'tightness of money among your customers' or 'hire-purchase restrictions'. Thus something like 20 per cent of the respondents attributed the change in their output and/or investment demand since September 1957 directly or indirectly to the

[1] See *Committee on the Working of the Monetary System: Principal Memoranda of Evidence*, vol. 2 (London: H.M.S.O., 1960) p. 88. Henceforth this publication will be cited as *Memoranda*.

[2] Some 5 per cent of the completed questionnaires were not analysed because of inadequacies in the replies.

TABLE 6.4

Question	Percentage of respondents ticking *as* principal reason*
3. If the answer to any of the questions in 2 above is *Yes* please number in order of importance the principal considerations [(i) to (ix)] below which have affected the decisions recorded.	
(i) a general slackening of business	30
(ii) tightness of money among your customers	11
(iii) hire-purchase restrictions	1
(iv) the increased cost of borrowing	4
(v) greater difficulty in obtaining finance (restrictions on bank credit; capital issues control)	5
(vi) increased competition	2
(vii) an altered assessment of trading prospects	2
(viii) cuts in the investment programme of the Government, public authorities, and nationalised industries	3
(ix) any other cause (please specify)	2

Source: *Memoranda*, pp. 91, 92.

* Note that while the question asked for a ranking of reasons in order of importance, only the *principal* reason was tabulated. It should also be noted that 40 per cent of the 3404 respondents whose questionnaires were analysed failed to answer this question.

monetary measures which were taken at that time. On the face of it, this suggests that the impact of the measures was considerable.

However, it is doubtful whether the results shown in Tables 6.3 and 6.4 will really bear this much weight or indeed whether any very definite conclusion can be drawn from them at all.

One basic difficulty is that the original sample was not 'scientifically' chosen; the Chambers of Commerce affiliated to A.B.C.C. were apparently given a completely free hand in deciding which firms were to receive the questionnaire. Moreover the effective response rate, in the sense of the percentage of returns analysed, was very low (a little over 20 per cent) and the non-response may well have introduced a serious bias in the results.[1] To add to the non-response difficulty, many of the firms who 'responded', in the sense that their questionnaires were analysed, failed to answer particular questions. In the case of question 3, for example, 40 per cent of the respondents failed to give an answer.[2]

In addition to these statistical difficulties there are serious diffi-

---

[1] Cf. *Radcliffe Report*, para. 453.   [2] See *Memoranda*, p. 92.

culties of interpretation. For example, were the 4 per cent who gave
'increased cost of borrowing' as the principal reason (Table 6.4)
giving it as the principal reason for the reduction in their turnover or
the principal reason for the postponement of fixed-capital investment
projects? Again, of the 30 per cent opposite (i) in Table 6.4, how
many were attributing a reduction in turnover to a general slacken-
ing of business, and how many were attributing a postponement of
fixed-capital investment projects to this particular cause?

A further difficulty is that the first question was so framed that
firms which actually increased stocks and fixed-capital investment
projects, but by less than they would have done in the absence of the
monetary measures, were bound to answer 'No' to the first question
and hence to be excluded from the second. Thus part, and perhaps an
important part, of the impact of the monetary measures on investment demand was not recorded.

A final limitation, and for our purposes a most serious one, is that
the tables give no *quantitative* information. What we should have
liked to know was not merely *whether* a particular firm felt the
impact of the measures but also *to what extent* it did so.

We turn now to the F.B.I. survey which was designed, among other

TABLE 6.5

Question	Percentage * of respondents answering yes in relation to two financial years ending		
	1953	1955	1957
Supply of Funds			
(ii) In any of the periods indicated [two financial years ending 1953, 1955 and 1957] did the difficulty of raising extra money outside the firm (including both the cost of borrowing and the administrative difficulties involved) cause you to:			
(a) reduce your stocks?	4	6	11
(b) decide against raising your stocks?	4	8	12
(c) decide to postpone fixed investment which you would otherwise have under-taken?	5	9	2
(d) reduce your general level of trading?	1	3	4
(e) decide against raising your general level of trading?	3	5	7
(f) take any other action?	1	1	2

Source: *Memoranda*, p. 119.

* The percentages appearing in this table have been calculated from the
absolute numbers given in *Memoranda* on the basis of a total of 1595.

G

things, to determine the impact of monetary measures on investment decisions during the period 1951–7. In this case the questionnaire was sent to all manufacturing members with the instruction that subsidiary companies which had no responsibility for investment and borrowing decisions should not complete it. Of a maximum response of about 5000 returns, 1595 returns (or about 32 per cent of the maximum) were analysed.[1]

The F.B.I. questionnaire covered a great deal of interesting ground, but only three of the questions seem to be immediately relevant, namely question (ii) under the heading 'Supply of Funds' and questions (i) and (ii) under the heading 'Interest Rates'. These questions are reproduced in Tables 6.5 and 6.6, together with a summary of the replies.

TABLE 6.6

	Percentage* of respondents	
Question	*Answering yes*	*Answering no*
Interest Rates		
(i) Does your judgement of the profitability of new investment vary from time to time according to the prevailing rate of interest?	37	51
(ii) Was the rise in Bank Rate from 3 to 4½ per cent during January and February 1955 a *major* factor in taking your business decisions? If so, did it cause you to:	11	84
(a) modify the market expectations for your product?	5	—
(b) defer an investment decision or substantially reduce an investment project because of its effect on costs?	4	—
(c) defer an investment decision or substantially reduce an investment project because you considered it to be a danger signal?	3	—
(d) reduce or defer raising your stocks of purchased goods because of its effect on costs?	6	—
(e) reduce or defer raising your stock of purchased goods because you considered it to be a danger signal?	4	—
(f) take any other action?	2	—

Source: *Memoranda*, p. 120.

* The percentages appearing in this table have been calculated from the absolute numbers given in *Memoranda* on the basis of a total of 1595.

As before, the immediate impression given by these tables is that monetary measures probably had a fairly substantial impact on

[1] See *Memoranda*, p. 118.

investment demand during the 1950s – at least in terms of the number of firms affected. For example, Table 6.5 shows that during the two financial years ending 1957, 25 per cent of the respondents reduced (or at least did not raise) inventory investment and/or fixed-capital investment because of the difficulty of raising the required finance. Again, it appears from Table 6.6 that the rise in Bank Rate during January and February 1955 was a *major* factor in investment and other decisions for something over 11 per cent of respondents. Moreover, in this case one is more inclined to take the figures at their face value than in the case of the A.B.C.C. survey. For one thing the non-response problem seems to have been much less serious in the F.B.I. than in the A.B.C.C. survey. Also the questionnaire was much more tightly framed and one has little difficulty in knowing what the figures actually mean.

Taking the results of the two surveys together, it is hard to escape the conclusion that the impact of monetary measures on investment demand was far from negligible during the 1950s. However, any figure for the reduction in demand that might have been achieved in any actual case can be little better than a guess, and there is good reason to prefer the guess of the Radcliffe Committee to any other. After reviewing the evidence put before them on this point by the A.B.C.C., F.B.I. and others, the Committee came to the following conclusion:

> In relation to the present size of the national income, and having regard to the kind of margin that becomes debatable when the Chancellor of the Exchequer weighs up the position at Budget time, we should look upon a minimum effect of the order of £100 mn. over a year as an adjustment worth seeking. We have tried to decide whether any of the measures which we have been reviewing has had effect of this order. . . . While we have no statistics firm enough to warrant any assurance, we find it difficult, on such evidence as we have received, to believe that any of the changes in interest rates have by themselves had an impact of this order of magnitude. The squeeze on bank advances in 1955–56 perhaps would, if the impact could be measured, qualify by this criterion. . . . [1]

Let us now return to the question posed at the outset of the present section. Suppose that the authorities limit themselves to the range of variation of the policy instruments which has been observed in the

---

[1] See *Radcliffe Report*, para. 471.

post-war period and which, presumably, is practicable in political terms. What is the maximum impact on $(D-M)$ which can be hoped for?

Dow's study suggests that the authorities could probably reduce consumption demand by as much as £300 million per year in terms of present-day prices by the use of the tax instrument, while the study of Ball and Drake seems to indicate that a further reduction of the same order of magnitude might well be achievable by use of direct hire-purchase controls. If we accept the Radcliffe Committee's guess about the likely impact of the monetary instruments on investment demand, we should add to these figures a reduction in investment demand of, say, £150 million as the contribution of the monetary instruments (£100 million on account of decreased availability of finance and £50 million on account of increased cost). Reduction in government expenditure would make some contribution but it would probably not be large. According to Dow, 'The government no longer hopes to alter public investment by more than £50 million in the course of a year or so: but no post-war attempt to cut it has probably succeeded in affecting public investment more severely.'[1] Finally, something would have to be added to account for the reduction in investment demand that could be achieved by means of the tax instrument. As we saw earlier, changes in the severity of the business tax structure affect investment demand both directly via the incentive to invest and indirectly via the availability of finance (see p. 162 above). As regards the latter, Dow has estimated that, in the 1945–60 period, changes in the business tax structure have produced changes in the supply of internal finance of as much as £250 million in either direction.[2] The associated changes in investment demand can only be guessed at, and Dow's guess is that 'tax changes had an effect on investment much less than one to one'.[3] It would seem that the most that could be added in on this count would be, say, £100 million. Putting these figures together we reach the conclusion that, without going outside the range of variation of the policy instruments experienced in the post-war period, the British authorities could probably reduce aggregate demand by about £900 million in terms of present-day prices if all available instruments were brought to bear. The effect on $(D-M)$ would be something less than this – say, about £800 million.

We have been talking throughout in terms of a situation of excess

[1] See Dow, op. cit., p. 221.   [2] Ibid., p. 208.   [3] Ibid., p. 292.

demand. Would the figure of £800 million just arrived at be applicable in the reverse situation – where the problem was to increase $(D-M)$? There seems to be little reason to doubt that it would. One would have to reckon on a smaller contribution from the monetary instruments because, while a decrease in the availability of finance will certainly reduce demand, an increase in the availability of finance will do nothing, of itself, to increase demand; its role is rather to make possible increases in expenditure which are desired because of other changes. On the other hand it is presumably a good deal easier, politically, to reduce the severity of the tax structure than it is to increase it, and a good deal easier to raise government expenditure (especially current expenditure) than to cut it, so that more could be expected from the fiscal instruments. Thus the two situations will be asymmetrical only if the larger contribution from the fiscal instruments is insufficient to outweigh the smaller contribution from the monetary instruments, and there is no reason why this should be the case.

What scale of impact does our figure of £800 million represent? To answer this question we must put the figure in some sort of perspective. The most relevant comparison is with *potential* gross domestic product. Actual domestic product in current prices is now running at about £28,500 million and potential product is probably nearer about £30,000 million. Thus, in effect, the conclusion we have come to in this section is that the authorities should be able to raise or lower $(D-M)$ by as much as $2\frac{1}{2}$ to 3 per cent of potential gross domestic product without resorting to unfamiliar ranges or variation in the policy instruments. Thus it would seem reasonable to say that if stabilisation policy were to run into difficulties in Britain, it would not be because the impact of changes in the policy instruments was too weak.

6.6 Timing of Impact

The aspect of stabilisation policy considered in the preceding section was the *magnitude* of the impact on $(D-M)$ of changes in the various policy instruments. In this section we shall consider another aspect, namely the *timing* of the impact.

For various reasons to be discussed shortly, the impact of any given change in the policy instruments is likely to lag some time behind the particular discrepancy between Y^p and $(D-M)$ which it was designed to offset. As a result a policy change, which would have tended to move the economy towards balance in the absence of the lag, may have the effect of driving it further from balance in the presence of the lag. Put another way, a policy change which would have been stabilising if properly timed may, in the event, be *de*stabilising, i.e. may widen the discrepancy between Y^p and $(D-M)$ instead of narrowing it. The reason for this is that by the time the impact of the policy change is felt, the relationship which exists between Y^p, D and M may be very different from the one to which the policy change was directed because the economy will have moved under its own steam during the interval. Suppose, for example, that the free movement of the economy is, indeed, of the character deduced for Model V – that, if left to itself, the economy will follow an oscillatory path in response to arbitrary initial conditions. Suppose further that the authorities take steps to offset a deficiency of demand which arises in the course of the down phase of one of these oscillations. The lag may be such that by the time the impact of these steps is felt, the economy will have moved from the down phase of the oscillation into the up phase. In this event the deficiency of demand will have become smaller by the time the impact is felt than it was when the policy change was initiated; it may even have been turned into an excess demand. Consequently, at best, the policy change will be inappropriate as regards magnitude. At worst, it will be inappropriate as regards direction. How important is this problem likely to be in the case of the British economy? Before one could give a firm answer to this question one would need to know, for each of the main policy instruments, how long the lag is likely to be in the British case. Unfortunately, the research needed to provide this information has not yet been carried out and the best we can do is to give a tentative answer based partly on rough guesses and partly on work done recently in other countries.

As a start it is helpful to divide the total lag associated with any given policy instrument into three parts: (1) the lag between the emergence of the discrepancy between Y^p and $(D-M)$ and the recognition of the need to offset this discrepancy by manipulation of the policy instrument, or the *recognition lag*; (2) the lag between the recognition of the need for a change in the instrument and the implementation of the change, or the *implementation lag*; and (3) the lag between the change in the instrument and its impact on $(D-M)$, or the *impact lag*.

1. *The Recognition Lag*

From its very nature the length of the recognition lag must be the same for all policy instruments. No attempt to measure this part of the total lag has yet been made for the British economy. However, a recent United States study[1] suggests that it averaged about four months in that country over the period 1946–61 and there is little reason to expect the British figure to be noticeably different.

By contrast, the length of the implementation lag is likely to vary considerably as between the various policy instruments. Accordingly, we shall now present an item-by-item discussion of the various instruments, first as regards the length of the implementation lag and then as regards the length of the impact lag.

2. *The Implementation Lag*

The implementation lag will be virtually zero for the *ratio between the British price of home-produced and foreign-produced importables*, since, in the case of this instrument, nothing more than an announcement by the authorities of a new exchange rate is required to effect a change. It will also be very short for the *cost of finance*. In this case, too, a change can be implemented by decree – by the announcement of a new Bank Rate.

In the case of the *tax and social security structures*, the time required to implement a change will depend on: (i) the time required by the authorities to pass the necessary legislation and issue fresh instructions to the tax-collecting or social security agents concerned (e.g. all employers in the case of a change in personal income-tax rates, the appropriate retailers in the case of a change in rates of purchase tax on certain durable items and all post offices in the case of a change in, say, the old-age pension); and (ii) the time required by these agents to put the new instructions into effect. If the policy change in question consists of a change in the *indirect* tax structure (i) is virtually zero, and the sum of (i) and (ii) should then be no more than, say, one month. No time is required to pass the necessary legislation in this case because, since the 1961 budget, the British authorities have been able to manipulate the indirect tax structure by regulation – specifically to raise or reduce purchase tax, and all main customs duties, by up to 10 per cent. In all other cases the sum of (i) and (ii) is likely to be at least two months and it may be a good

[1] See R. Fels, 'The Recognition-Lag and Semi-Automatic Stabilizers', *Review of Economics and Statistics* (Aug 1963).

deal longer if the authorities are not prepared to implement the change through an extraordinary budget,[1] since then (i) can be as much as twelve months.

Most of what has just been said about the tax and social security structures applies equally to the *intensity of direct controls over foreign transactions*. In the case of this instrument also, the length of the implementation lag will depend on the time required by the authorities to pass the necessary legislation and to issue fresh instructions to the appropriate officials, and on the time required by these officials to revise administrative procedures in the light of the new instructions. Provided the changes are reasonably simple, this should not exceed about two months.

We have seen that the implementation lag is virtually zero for the cost of finance. This will be true for the *availability of finance* also, to the extent that the authorities rely on the hire-purchase regulator to effect the change, since in this case tighter credit rationing can be imposed simply by Board of Trade decree. On the other hand, the lag may be substantial for this particular instrument if the change in availability is effected primarily through reduction in the supply of bank credit. This is particularly true where a *decrease* in availability is called for. To begin with, there will be some delay while the necessary instructions about the more restrictive advance policy are prepared in the head offices of the banks and circulated to branch managers. There will, presumably, be further delay while these instructions are put into effect. But even if they are put into effect immediately at the branch level, there will sometimes be a considerable delay before the growth of bank advances is checked to the desired extent. The reason for this is that while the banks can effectively regulate the granting of *new* overdraft limits, they find it difficult to cancel, or even substantially reduce, the unused portions of existing overdraft limits. If these are abnormally high in relation to advances, the banks' attempts to restrict the granting of new overdraft limits will not be reflected in a reduction in the rate of growth of bank advances, and hence in the availability of finance, for a considerable time – possibly from four to six months. Thus, where the authorities rely primarily on the OM, BS, SD, OR and F techniques to effect a reduction in the availability of finance, the implementation lag may be quite long – as much as six to nine months.

---

[1] Extraordinary budgets were introduced on only three occasions in the period 1945–60, namely in October 1945, November 1947 and October 1955.

The discussion of the preceding paragraph is relevant to the *stock of liquid assets* also, since the main way of manipulating this particular monetary instrument is by operating on the supply of bank credit.

We come, finally, to the fiscal instrument, *real government expenditure*. Here the length of the implementation lag will vary considerably according to whether the desired change is a decrease or an increase, and also according to the way in which the change is implemented.

Suppose, to begin with, that the authorities wish to *decrease G*. In this case the quickest way of implementing the change will be to adjust the works programme of the central government so that the projects which are now scheduled for early commencement are smaller than those which are nearing completion. The implementation lag associated with this procedure will depend mainly on the time needed to make the necessary adjustment to the works programme and should not exceed more than, say, one month. A somewhat slower method of effecting the decrease will be to curtail some of the central government projects which are already under way. Here the implementation lag will consist of the time which must elapse before the authorities can decide which projects should be slowed down *plus* the time which must elapse before this decision can be translated into an actual decrease in expenditure. Once again the first part of the lag should not be more than a few weeks. On the other hand, the second part may be fairly substantial because a major public works project cannot be suddenly curtailed without considerable waste and considerable hardship to the members of the work force who are engaged on it. A figure of three or four months for the total implementation lag seems a reasonable estimate for this method. A still slower method of bringing about the decrease in *G* will be by reducing the funds which the local governments have available for capital expenditure by use of the loan-sanction technique (see p. 152 above). The implementation lag associated with this method of reducing *G* will again consist of several components. The first part of the lag will be the time required to bring about the reduction in local government borrowing, once the need to reduce local government capital expenditure has been recognised. This will depend on the extent of the administrative delay involved in dealing with local government borrowing applications and could, perhaps, be put at two months. On top of this there will be some lapse of time between the reduction in funds for capital expenditure and the reduction in expenditure itself. This will vary from a few weeks to a few months,

G 2

depending on whether the reduction in expenditure is effected by a revision of the works schedule for the coming months or by a curtailment of projects which are already under way. Thus, the total implementation lag for this method will range from, say, three months to about seven months. Probably the slowest method of all will be to bring about the reduction in G by means of a reduction in central government current expenditure. It would seem that the only way in which the central government can substantially reduce its current expenditure is by reducing its commitments in such fields as health, education, social services and research – the scope for 'economy' in the narrow sense appears to be extremely limited. If this is so, the implementation lag for this method can hardly be less than, say, eighteen months.

Suppose now that the need is for an *increase* in G. In this case, too, a rescheduling of central government works will probably be the quickest method of implementing the change, with an implementation lag of no more than a few weeks. However, there are two other methods which will probably be almost as rapid: the method of speeding up central government works which are already under way and the method of increasing central government current expenditure. Probably the slowest method will be by increasing the funds which are available to the local government to finance capital expenditure, with a minimum lag of, say, three months.

To sum up the present discussion we can say that, where the need is to decrease G, the implementation lag will vary considerably according to the method used to effect the decrease. The minimum lag is likely to be about one month and the maximum about eighteen months. Where the need is to increase G, the range is likely to be much smaller – from a minimum of about one month to a maximum of about three months.

3. *The Impact Lag*

We come finally to the third part of the lag, the impact lag. In the case of one of the instruments, the fiscal instrument G, the impact lag will be zero. This follows from the fact that the instrument is a *component of D* so that the impact on $(D-M)$ of a change in the instrument must be immediate. This argument cannot be applied to any of the other instruments, however, since unlike G they are not, themselves, part either of D or of M. For example, the monetary instruments influence $(D-M)$ via two components of D, namely C and I; they are not, themselves, part either of D or of M.

Our object in this section is to form an estimate of the size of the impact lag for each of the instruments, apart from G. For this purpose we shall make use of the relationships of Model V and the values used for the αs in the dynamic analysis of that model. We shall begin with the two import instruments: the intensity of direct controls over foreign transactions (the 'direct controls' instrument) and the ratio between the British price of home-produced and foreign-produced importables (the 'relative price' instrument).

(a) *Import instruments*. To estimate the impact lag for the two import instruments, we make use of the import function of Model V which we repeat, for the reader's convenience, in a slightly modified form:

$$M_t = \alpha_{30} M_{t-1} + \alpha_{31} D_{t-2} + \alpha_{32} I^i_{t-2} + (1-\gamma)\epsilon_3 P_{t-2} + \rho \xi_{t-1} - \gamma \rho \xi_{t-2} + {}^*Z^2$$
$$(6.1)$$

where P denotes the price of British-made importables relative to the price of foreign-made importables in terms of British currency, and ${}^*Z^2$ is Z^2 after the removal of the term in P and the terms in ξ, the indicator of the intensity of direct controls over foreign transactions (see p. 75 above).

We begin with the *direct-controls instrument*. We postulate stationary equilibrium up to period 0 and a policy-induced, maintained increase in the intensity of direct controls of an amount d in that period, i.e. $\xi_{-1} - \xi_{-2} = 0$; $\xi_0 - \xi_{-1} = d$; $\xi_1 - \xi_0 = 0$. We also postulate that the remaining data involved in the import function remain fixed, i.e. ${}^*Z^2 = $ constant. Finally, since we are interested only in the impact effect of a change in the instrument, we rule out secondary effects via the jointly determined variables D and I, by postulating that these variables remain fixed after the change in the direct-controls instrument. On this basis (6.1) generates the following sequence, in which m_t denotes $(M_t - M_{t-1})$:

$$m_0 = 0$$
$$m_1 = \alpha_{30} m_0 + \rho d = \rho d$$
$$m_2 = \alpha_{30} m_1 - \gamma \rho d = \rho d[\alpha_{30} - \gamma] = 0 \text{ (since } \alpha_{30} = \gamma) \text{ (see p. 75 above)}.$$
$$m_3 = \alpha_{30} m_2 = 0$$
$$m_4 = \alpha_{30} m_3 = 0$$
$$\vdots$$
$$m_t = \alpha_{30} m_{t-1} = 0.$$

From this sequence we see that the whole of the change in M, consequent on the postulated change in the direct-controls instrument, has occurred by period 1. With a quarterly period, therefore, the impact lag for this instrument is three months.

We turn now to the second import instrument, the *relative-price instrument*. Using (6.1) once again, we see that a maintained increase in this instrument of an amount p, which impinges on a stationary equilibrium, will generate the following sequence, in the absence of secondary effects:

$$m_0 = m_1 = 0$$
$$m_2 = (1 - \gamma)\epsilon_3 p$$
$$m_3 = \alpha_{30}m_2$$
$$m_4 = \alpha_{30}m_3 = (\alpha_{30})^2 m_2$$
$$\vdots$$
$$m_t = \alpha_{30}m_{t-1} = (\alpha_{30})^{t-2} m_2.$$

This sequence differs from the first sequence in that the general term in the sequence never falls to zero. In other words the postulated increase in the relative-price instrument is still affecting imports after any finite number of periods, however large; the full impact of the change is never realised. To estimate the impact lag in this case, therefore, we adopt a convention to the effect that the full impact on M of the postulated change in the instrument is realised in the period in which the change in M, from the initial equilibrium, reaches 95 per cent of the ultimate change. We then calculate for period 0 the proportion of the ultimate change in M which has been realised by that period and similarly for period 1, period 2, etc. If we find that the proportion reaches 0·95 in period 5, say, then we put the impact lag for the instrument under discussion at six quarterly periods or eighteen months.

The calculations referred to in the preceding paragraph we shall call the *time-form of the response* for the relative-price instrument. They are shown in Table 6.7. The entries in this table have been calculated from the following formula, using the value 0·1 for α_{30}:[1]

$$\frac{\sum\limits_{t=0}^{T} m_t}{\sum\limits_{t=0}^{\infty} m_t} = \left(\frac{m_2\{1 - (\alpha_{30})^{T-1}\}}{1 - \alpha_{30}} \right) \div \left(\frac{m_2}{1 - \alpha_{30}} \right) = 1 - (\alpha_{30})^{T-1}.$$

---

[1] It will be recalled that this was the value which we allotted to this parameter for the purpose of the dynamic analysis of Models III to V. See Appendix 5.1.

TABLE 6.7

Time-form of Response for Relative Price Instrument

Value of T

	0	1	2	3	4
$1 - (\alpha_{30})^{T-1}$	0	0	0·9	0·99	0·999

It will be seen from Table 6.7 that 95 per cent of the ultimate change in M, consequent on the postulated change in the relative-price instrument, is achieved when $T = 3$. Accordingly, we put the impact lag for the relative-price instrument at twelve months.

(b) *Monetary instruments.* We turn now to the monetary instruments: the stock of liquid assets (the 'liquid-asset' instrument) and the cost and availability of finance to private firms and individuals (the 'cost and availability' instruments).

We saw earlier that the impact of a variation in the *liquid-asset instrument* is on C (see p. 150 above). Accordingly, to measure the impact lag for this instrument we turn to the consumption function of Model V (relationship (2.24)). For convenience this is repeated below in a slightly modified form:

$$C_t = \alpha_{10}X_t + \alpha_{11}C_{t-1} + k_2 L_{t-1} - k_2(\xi + \pi)L_{t-2} + {}^*Z^1 \qquad (6.2)$$

where ${}^*Z^1$ is Z^1 after the removal of the two terms in L (see p. 56 above).

As before we postulate stationary equilibrium up to period 0 and a maintained increase in the liquid-asset instrument of an amount l at some point in that period, i.e. $L_{-1} - L_{-2} = 0$; $L_0 - L_{-1} = l$; $L_1 - L_0 = 0$.[1] We also postulate that the remaining data involved in the consumption function remain fixed, i.e. ${}^*Z^1 = $ constant. Secondary effects via the jointly determined variable X are ruled out. On this basis (6.2) generates the following sequence, in which c_t denotes $(C_t - C_{t-1})$:

$c_0 = 0$

$c_1 = \alpha_{11}c_0 + k_2 l = k_2 l$

$c_2 = \alpha_{11}c_1 - k_2(\xi + \pi)l = 0$ (since $\alpha_{11} = (\xi + \pi)$) (see p. 56 above)

$c_3 = \alpha_{11}c_2 = 0$

$c_4 = \alpha_{11}c_3 = 0$

$\vdots$

$c_t = \alpha_{11}c_{t-1} = 0.$

---

[1] Recall that L is the stock of liquid assets at the *end* of the period. See p. 49 above.

From this sequence we see that the whole of the change in C, consequent on the postulated change in the liquid-asset instrument, occurs in period 1. In other words, the impact lag for this particular instrument is three months.

The liquid-asset instrument and the import instruments have two features which are of some importance as far as the analysis of impact lags is concerned. The first is that they work through a *single* relationship – the import function in the case of the two import instruments and the consumption function in the case of the stock of liquid assets. The second feature is that they work by *changing the level of some variable* (explicit datum) in the relationship concerned – a component of Z^2 in the case of the import instruments and a component of Z^1 in the case of the liquid-asset instrument.

The two monetary instruments to which we now turn, *the cost and availability of finance*, differ from the import instruments and the liquid-asset instrument in both of these respects. In the first place, as we have seen (see pp. 150–1 above), they work through five relationships – the consumption function and the four investment relationships – rather than through a single relationship. Secondly, only in the case of the consumption function do they work by changing the level of some explicit datum. In the case of the investment relationships they work by changing the *coefficients of the explanatory variables*, rather than by changing the variables themselves.

To take account of the first point, we shall apply the approach used in connection with the import instruments and the liquid-asset instrument, to the consumption function and to each of the four investment relationships in turn. This will give us a separate estimate of the impact lag for each of the components of $(D-M)$ which are affected by a change in the cost and availability instruments. These separate estimates will then be averaged to obtain an estimate of 'the' impact lag for these two monetary instruments.

We begin with consumption expenditure. As a first step we rewrite the consumption function (2.24) as:

$$C_t = \alpha_{10}X_t + \alpha_{11}C_{t-1} + k_4N_t - k_4(\xi + \pi)N_{t-1} + {}^*Z^1 \qquad (6.3)$$

where ${}^*Z^1$ is now Z^1 after the removal of the terms in N (see p. 56 above).

We postulate stationary equilibrium up to period 0 and a maintained increase in N of an amount n in period 0 consequent on the postulated change in the cost and availability instrument, i.e.

$N_{-1} - N_{-2} = 0$; $N_0 - N_{-1} = n$; $N_1 - N_0 = 0$. Assuming that the remaining data involved in the consumption function remain fixed and secondary effects via X are ruled out, (6.3) generates the following sequence where n_t denotes $(N_t - N_{t-1})$:

$$c_0 = k_4 n$$
$$c_1 = \alpha_{11} c_0 - k_4(\xi + \pi)n = 0 \text{ (since } \alpha_{11} = (\xi + \pi))$$
$$c_2 = \alpha_{11} c_1 = 0$$
$$c_3 = \alpha_{11} c_2 = 0$$
$$\vdots$$
$$c_t = \alpha_{11} c_{t-1} = 0.$$

Thus the whole of the change in C occurs in period 0, i.e. the impact lag for the cost and availability instruments is zero.

We deal next with fixed-capital investment expenditure. To estimate the impact lag of the cost and availability instruments for this component of D, we make use of relationship (4.11):

$$I_t^{gf} = \alpha_{40}(Y_{t-1} - Y_{t-2}) + \alpha_{41} I_{t-1}^{gf} + \alpha_{42} K_t + \alpha_{43} K_{t-1}. \qquad (4.11)$$

Once again suppose that stationary equilibrium exists up to period 0 and that there is some policy-induced change in the cost and/or availability of finance in that period. Since both the cost and availability of finance are implicit data for (4.11), the change in question will twist the relationship in some way, i.e. it will have the effect of changing one or more of its coefficients (see p. 133 above). We postulate that α_{40} changes to α'_{40}, α_{41} to α'_{41} and so on. Finally, since we are concerned only with the impact effect of the change in the instruments, we rule out secondary effects by postulating that Y and K remain fixed at the stationary equilibrium levels which exist up to period 0. On these assumptions (4.11) generates the following sequence in which i_t^{gf} denotes $(I_t^{gf} - I_{t-1}^{gf})$ and $\bar{I}^{gf}$ and $\bar{K}$ denote the stationary equilibrium levels of I^{gf} and K, respectively:

$$i_0^{gf} = (\alpha'_{41} - \alpha_{41})\bar{I}^{gf} + [(\alpha'_{42} - \alpha_{42}) + (\alpha'_{43} - \alpha_{43})]\bar{K}$$
$$i_1^{gf} = \alpha'_{41} i_0^{gf}$$
$$i_2^{gf} = \alpha'_{41} i_1^{gf} = (\alpha'_{41})^2 i_0^{gf}$$
$$\vdots$$
$$i_t^{gf} = \alpha'_{41} i_{t-1}^{gf} = (\alpha'_{41})^t i_0^g.$$

From this sequence we see that, in this case, the time-form of the response is given by:

$$\frac{\sum\limits_{t=0}^{T} i_t^{qf}}{\sum\limits_{t=0}^{\infty} i_t^{qf}} = 1 - (\alpha'_{41})^{T+1}.$$

Values of this expression, using the value 0.83 for α'_{41},[1] are shown in the first row of Table 6.8. It will be seen from Table 6.8 that the ratio of the cumulated change to the ultimate change reaches 0.95 when $T = 15$. Hence the cost and availability instruments are estimated to have an impact lag of four years as far as the fixed-capital investment component of D is concerned.

TABLE 6.8

Time-form of Response for Cost and Availability Instruments:
Fixed-capital Investment and Inventory Investment

Value of T

	0	1	2	3	4	5	10	14	15
$1 - (\alpha_{41})^{T+1}$	0·17	0·31	0·43	0·53	0·61	0·67	0·87	0·94	0·95
$1 - (\alpha'_{60})^{T+1}$	0·50	0·75	0·88	0·94	0·97				
$1 - (\alpha_{70})^{T+1}$	0·50	0·75	0·88	0·94	0·97				

We turn now to inventory investment in raw materials and inventory investment in finished goods. If the reader starts with relationships (5.4) and (5.8) and follows an argument which parallels exactly that given above for fixed-capital investment, he will see that, in the case of inventory investment in raw materials, the time-form of the response is given by $1 - (\alpha'_{60})^{T+1}$, while in the case of inventory investment in finished goods, it is given by $1 - (\alpha'_{70})^{T+1}$ where α'_{60} is the value of the coefficient of I_{t-1}^{ri} in (5.4) after the postulated change in the cost and/or availability instruments and α'_{70} is the new value of the coefficient of I_{t-1}^{ci} in (5.8). Using values of 0.5 for both α'_{60} and α'_{70} (the values used in the dynamic analysis of model V), he will then see that the time-form of the response for inventory investment in raw materials (inventory investment in finished goods) is as set out in the second (third) row of Table 6.8. From these calculations it will be seen, in turn, that the impact lag for the cost and availability

[1] This is the value used for this coefficient in the dynamic analysis of Models IV and V. See Appendix 5.1.

instruments is estimated to be fifteen months as regards both inventory investment in raw materials and inventory investment in finished goods.

The last component of D to be considered is real housing investment. In this case an analysis of the familiar type based on the housing investment function of Models IV and V (relationship (4.20)) would require quite extensive computations. Since, as already explained, the figure for the impact lag of the cost and availability instrument is to be found by averaging the separate impact lags for consumption expenditure and the four components of investment expenditure, and since the housing investment lag will have a comparatively small weight in this average, we have decided that it would not be worth while undertaking these computations.[1] Instead in the final calculation we shall include an arbitrary figure of five years for the housing investment lag. A comparison between the arguments underlying (4.20) and (4.11) shows that, while both types of investment are subject to a distributed lag of expenditure behind decisions, housing investment involves, on top of this, a lag in the adjustment of the actual housing stock to the desired housing stock. It suggests, therefore, that the impact lag associated with the cost and availability instruments will probably be a little longer in the case of the housing investment component than in the case of the fixed-capital investment component. Thus the figure of five years which we have decided to allot to the former appears quite plausible in the light of the figure of four years which we have already calculated for the latter.

The estimates of the impact lag for the cost and availability instruments which we have derived in this section are:

Consumption expenditure	0 months
Fixed-capital investment	48 months
Inventory investment in raw materials and work-in-progress	15 months
Inventory investment in finished goods	15 months
Housing investment	60 months

To form an estimate of 'the' impact lag for the cost and availability instruments we take a weighted average of these figures, the weight for each figure being the approximate proportion which the expenditure aggregate concerned bears to aggregate private expenditure in

[1] The reader who is interested in the mechanism of a computation based on (4.20) will find it outlined in Appendix 6.2.

the case of the British economy.[1] The resulting figure is three months.

(c) *The fiscal instruments.* We come finally to the two fiscal instruments – *the tax structure* and *the transfer payment structure.* We shall refer to these as the 'tax instruments'.

Like the cost and availability instruments, the tax instruments work through more than one relationship (see p. 144 above). Accordingly, to estimate the impact lag for these instruments, we shall proceed as with the cost and availability instruments, i.e. we shall apply our method of estimation to each of the relevant relationships in turn.

We begin with consumption expenditure. Here our first step is to rewrite the consumption function (relationship (2.24)) as:

$$C_t = \alpha_{10}\alpha_{20} + \alpha_{10}\alpha_{21} Y_t + \alpha_{11} C_{t-1} + Z^1. \tag{6.4}$$

This is (2.24) after substitution of (2.26). We now postulate stationary equilibrium up to period 0 and a change either in the tax structure or in the transfer payment structure in that period, with Z^1 constant. Secondary effects via Y are ruled out. We suppose, to begin with, that the postulated change in structure consists of a change either in the *personal income-tax structure, the business income-tax structure or the transfer payment structure.* From earlier analysis (see p. 133 above) we know that in all these cases the change will be reflected in new values for the coefficients of the disposable income function. Let the new values be α'_{20} and α'_{21}. Then (6.4) will generate the following sequence, in which c_t denotes $(C_t - C_{t-1})$ and $\overline{Y}$ the stationary equilibrium level of Y:

$$c_0 = \alpha_{10}(\alpha'_{20} - \alpha_{20}) + \alpha_{10}(\alpha'_{21} - \alpha_{21}) \overline{Y}$$
$$c_1 = \alpha'_{11} c_0$$
$$c_2 = (\alpha'_{11})^2 c_0$$
$$\vdots$$
$$c_t = (\alpha'_{11})^t c_0.$$

Suppose now that the postulated change in structure is a change in the *indirect tax structure.* In this case the change will be reflected in new values for the coefficients of the consumption function (see pp. 134–5 above). Evidently the sequence generated by (6.4) will be the same as the above except for c_0, which will now be given by:

$$c_0 = \alpha_{20}(\alpha'_{10} - \alpha_{10}) + \alpha_{21}(\alpha'_{10} - \alpha_{10}) \overline{Y} + (\alpha'_{11} - \alpha_{11})C$$

---

[1] The weights used were 0·78, 0·16, 0·01, 0·01 and 0·04 respectively.

where α'_{10} and α'_{11} are the new values for the coefficients of the consumption function and C is the stationary equilibrium of C. This being so, the time-form of the response for a change in the indirect tax structure will be exactly the same as for a change in the personal income-tax structure, the business income-tax structure or the transfer payment structure. It follows that, for *any* change in the tax or transfer payment structure, the time-form of the response will be given by:

$$\frac{\displaystyle\sum_{t=0}^{T} c_t}{\displaystyle\sum_{t=0}^{\infty} c_t} = 1 - (\alpha'_{11})^{T+1}.$$

Values of this ratio calculated on the basis of a value of 0·5 for α'_{11}[1] are shown in Table 6.9. It will be seen that the ratio reaches 0·95 when $T=4$. On this basis we put the impact lag for a change in the tax and transfer payment structure at fifteen months as far as consumption expenditure is concerned.

TABLE 6.9

Time-form of Response for Tax Instruments:
Consumption Expenditure

Value of T

	0	1	2	3	4
$1 - (\alpha'_{11})^{T+1}$	0·50	0·75	0·88	0·94	0·97

We turn now to fixed-capital investment. A change in tax structure which involves the *business tax structure* will work through the fixed-capital investment function (relationship (4.11)) as well as through the consumption function, since the business tax structure is one of the implicit data for this relationship (see p. 133 above). A change in the business tax structure will be reflected in new values for the coefficients of (4.11) in exactly the same way as will a change in the cost and availability of finance. Hence the analysis presented above for the latter instrument (see pp. 199–200 above) is fully applicable to the present case also. Accordingly, we can say from the results of this analysis that, as far as fixed-capital investment is concerned, the tax instrument will have an impact lag of four years.

By taking a weighted average[2] of the impact lags estimated above

[1] This is the value used in the dynamic analysis of Models III to V. See Appendix 5.1.

[2] The weights used were 0·83 for consumption expenditure and 0·17 for fixed-capital investment expenditure.

for consumption expenditure and fixed-capital investment expenditure, we obtain a figure of twenty-one months for 'the' impact lag of the tax instrument.[1]

4. *The Total Lag*

The series of rough estimates made in this section are brought together in Table 6.10.

TABLE 6.10

Lag (months)

Instrument	Recognition*	Implementation	Impact	Total
Fiscal				
Government expenditure	4	1 to 18	0	5 to 22
Tax and transfer payment structure	4	1 to 2	21	26 to 27
Monetary				
Stock of liquid assets	4	0 to 9	3	7 to 16
Cost and availability of finance	4	0 to 9	3	7 to 16
Import				
Intensity of direct controls	4	2	3	9
Relative price	4	0	12	16

* See p. 191 above.

For what they are worth, these figures suggest that, whatever instrument is used to offset a discrepancy between $(D-M)$ and Y^p, there is likely to be a considerable lag between the emergence of the discrepancy and the impact of the instrument. At best the lag is likely to be of the order of six months and at worst something like two years. A lag of this magnitude constitutes a major problem for stabilisation policy in Britain, since it makes destabilising policy changes a real possibility.

6.7 Size of Change in Instruments

We come now to the last of the seven questions raised at the outset of the present chapter: *By how much* should the instruments be changed from time to time in the interests of the internal balance

---

[1] We must rule out the possibility that a change in tax structure will have an impact via housing investment as well as via consumption expenditure and fixed-capital investment expenditure (cf. p. 149 above) because our method of estimating impact lags involves the assumption that the postulated policy change impinges on a stationary equilibrium and because the disposable income variable appears in (4.20) as a rate of change.

objective? For example, suppose that the authorities have decided that aggregate demand should be restricted and have selected government expenditure, the stock of liquid assets and the cost of finance as the instruments to be used for this purpose. Should they reduce government expenditure and the stock of liquid assets by, say, 1 per cent and $\frac{1}{2}$ per cent respectively, and increase the cost of finance by 3 percentage points, or would more appropriate figures be 2 per cent, 3 per cent and 5 percentage points? The question is a difficult one and so far no really satisfactory way of answering it has been proposed. Some useful work has been done in recent years on clarifying the problem, however, and some interesting suggestions have been made as to how it might be solved. In this section we shall confine ourselves to presenting a brief outline of these recent contributions.

We said a moment ago that the question of appropriate magnitudes of change in the instruments is a difficult one, and it may be helpful to indicate, at the outset, why this should be so. There are two main reasons. In the first place, before one can say what change in the instruments is appropriate at any point of time, one must know what the state of the economy will be when the impact of the change is felt. Evidently this requires: (i) that one should know at what point of time the impact will be felt, i.e. that one should know what the implementation and impact lags are for the chosen instruments; and (ii) that one should have some means of determining the path which the economy will take between the point of time in question and the point of time at which the impact will be felt. Since both of these are very large requirements, the question of appropriate magnitudes of change is bound to be a difficult one.

Turning to the second reason, there is one very important preliminary point which must be discussed. This is that when the authorities change one or more of the policy instruments they affect the levels of the key variables D and M over all future time – not merely at the point of impact. The point can be clarified in terms of Model V. As will be clear from the dynamic analysis of that model (see pp. 124–9 above) the time paths followed by D, M and the other jointly determined variables in the model can be split, conceptually, into two components: an equilibrium path and a deviation from that equilibrium path. The character of the first component is determined once time paths have been specified for the ks; and since these are merely expressions involving the explicit data of the model, it is the time paths specified for the explicit data which ultimately determine the character of the equilibrium path. The value of the second component is determined by the structure of the model – by the values of the α-coefficients. Now when the authorities change any one of the instruments they must affect one or both of these components and hence change the entire future time path of D and M and of the system generally. For example, if a change is made in either the fiscal instrument G or the monetary instrument L, new time paths are specified for these data and hence for k_1, which involves both G and L.[1] Consequently these changes in the instruments would change the character of the equilibrium paths of D, M and the other jointly determined variables. As a second example, a change in the cost and/or availability of finance or in the tax structure will be reflected in new values for certain of the α-coefficients, i.e. in a change in the structure of the model. These changes in the instruments, therefore, would mean a change in the size, and perhaps in the character, of the second component.

When the instruments are changed, then, the entire future time path of the system is affected. The values of the variables D and M will now be different over all future time from what they would have been in the absence of the change in the instruments. Consequently the discrepancy between $(D-M)$ and Y^p will also be different over all future time.

It follows from this discussion that, in deciding what magnitude of change in the instruments is appropriate at any point of time, the authorities must consider the effect of their actions not only at the point of impact but also beyond this point. For it may well be that a particular change in the instruments which is appropriate in terms of its effect on the discrepancy between $(D-M)$ and Y^p at the point of impact may be quite inappropriate in the light of the effect on this discrepancy at later points of time. And it is this need to consider the question of appropriate magnitude of change in the instruments in a fully dynamic setting which constitutes the second main reason why the question is such a difficult one.

The point that we have been making in the last few paragraphs was first recognised in the literature several years ago. But it was only comparatively recently that the next step was taken and suggestions for a fully dynamic approach to the question of the appropriate magnitude of change in the instruments put forward. In a moment

---

[1] For the definition of k_1, see p. 127 above.

we shall give a brief account of one of these suggestions. However, since it stems, in part, from the pioneering work of Phillips, we shall first summarise his contribution.[1]

Let us begin by outlining the two dynamic models which form the basis of Phillips's analysis. Both can be regarded as slight extensions of our Model I, the simple model which forms the starting-point of the sequence of models developed in Chapters 2 to 5 (see p. 44 above).

The relationships of the simpler of the two models (the 'multiplier' model) can be outlined in literary terms as follows:

1. Aggregate demand at time t is split into two components: (i) desired real consumption expenditure; and (ii) all other expenditure.
2. Desired real consumption expenditure at time t is taken to be proportional to real gross domestic product at time t.
3. Real gross domestic product at time t depends on the level of aggregate demand at time t and at all earlier points of time via a relationship in which the influence of past aggregate demand on current output declines steadily as one proceeds back in time from time t. In fact, the demand–output relationship of the present model is the continuous-analysis, closed-economy equivalent of relationship (3.1). The jointly-determined variables are consumption demand, aggregate demand and real gross domestic product, while non-consumption demand is treated as a datum.

As will be clear from the above, the model is set up for continuous analysis as distinct from the period analysis employed in Chapters 2 to 5. Thus the variables relate to *time t*, not to *period t*. Apart from this the present model differs from Model I only in the absence of a lag in the adjustment of consumption to income and the presence of a lag in the adjustment of output to demand.

The second of the two models (the 'multiplier–accelerator' model) extends the first model in two directions. In the first place aggregate demand is now split into *three* components: (i) desired real consumption expenditure; (ii) desired real investment expenditure; and (iii) all other expenditure. Secondly, a relationship is introduced to

[1] See A. W. Phillips, 'Stabilization Policy in a Closed Economy', *Economic Journal* (June 1954) and 'Stabilization Policy and the Time-Forms of Lagged Responses', *Economic Journal* (June 1957); and R. G. D. Allen, *Macro-Economic Theory* (London: Macmillan, 1967) pp. 350–62.

explain desired real investment expenditure. This is the continuous-analysis version of the relationship developed in Chapter 4 to explain real net fixed-capital investment expenditure, namely relationship (4.4), i.e. it is a relationship which postulates that desired real investment expenditure at time t depends on the rate of change of output at time t and at all previous points of time with the weight of past output-change declining monotonically as one moves back in time from time t.

The problem which Phillips poses, and which he investigates with the help of these models, may be formulated as follows. Assume that prior to time 0 stationary equilibrium exists. The demand–output relationship incorporated in the models is such that in stationary equilibrium aggregate demand and real gross domestic product must be equal at all points of time. Thus prior to time 0 we have D and Y constant and equal. Assume, further, that the constant level of Y which exists prior to time 0 is equal to the potential level, Y^p. Thus, the stationary equilibrium which exists prior to time 0 is one characterised by a continuous equality between D and Y^p, i.e. by continuous internal balance, given the closed-economy assumption.

We suppose that this state of stationary equilibrium with internal balance is disturbed at time 0 by a once-for-all decline in the autonomous element of aggregate demand and that the authorities decide to intervene with the object of restoring the desirable condition which existed prior to time 0. It is assumed that this intervention consists of manipulating the fiscal instrument G according to some rule or combination of rules. Three rules are considered. These are referred to as proportional stabilisation policy, integral stabilisation policy and derivative stabilisation policy. In the case of *proportional stabilisation policy*, G is equated at each point of time after time 0 with some fixed proportion of the deficiency in Y, at that point of time, in relation to the desired level – the level existing prior to time 0. With *integral stabilisation policy* the level of G is equated at each point of time after time 0 with a fixed proportion of the *cumulative* deficiency in Y from time 0 to that point of time. Finally, in the case of *derivative stabilisation policy*, G is equated at each point of time after time 0 with some fixed proportion of the absolute rate of change of Y at that point of time.

The object of the analysis is twofold: (i) to compare the time path of Y after time 0 in the absence of any form of stabilisation policy (the 'unregulated' time path) with the desired level of Y; (ii) to compare the time path of Y after time 0 in the presence of a stabilisation policy comprising some combination of the above three rules (the 'regulated' time path) with the desired level of Y. The first of these two objects is pursued in terms of the models as outlined above; these are the appropriate forms for the purpose since they make no provision for any form of official intervention. The second of the two objects is pursued in terms of the models as already outlined with two extra variables and two extra relationships tacked on to allow for the application of a stabilisation policy based on the three rules.

The first of the extra variables is G, the desired (and realised) level of real government expenditure at time t, which is introduced as a further component of aggregate demand. The second additional variable is P, the *planned* level of real government expenditure at time t. The existence of an implementation lag and an impact lag is allowed for by making the realised level of government demand at time t depend on the level planned for time t and all previous points of time with the weight of past planned levels declining monotonically as one moves back in time from time 0. This is the first of the two additional relationships. The second is a relationship governing P which allows P to be fixed according to any combination of the three stabilisation policy rules outlined above.

What emerges from the analysis is that both the unregulated time path and the regulated time path can take many different forms depending on the values of the parameters in the basic model, on the combination of stabilisation policy rules which the authorities decide to employ and on the size of the parameters (the proportionality factors) in these rules. Until these details are specified, little can be said about whether the regulated time path is superior to the unregulated, in relation to the situation existing prior to time 0, and, if it is superior, about the extent of its superiority.

We referred earlier to recent suggestions for a fully dynamic treatment of the problem of what is the appropriate magnitude of change in the instrument at any point of time, i.e. a treatment of the problem which recognises that any change in the instruments will affect the whole of the future time path of the system and hence will have implications for internal balance, not only at the point of impact, but over all future time. We now briefly consider these suggestions.[1]

[1] Some references are: J. K. Sengupta and D. Walker, 'On the Empirical Specification of Optimal Economic Policy for Growth and Stabilization under a

As will be clear from our outline of his work, Phillips's approach was to specify a particular time-form for official intervention in advance, and then to examine the implications of this specified time-form for internal balance within the framework of two simple dynamic models. The essential feature of the more recent approach is that what is specified in advance is not the time-form for official intervention, as in Phillips, but the optimising criterion or objective function which that time-form must satisfy: the time-form for official intervention is the *outcome* of the analysis, not the starting-point.

In outline the procedure is as follows, though there are numerous minor variations on the theme.

1. It is assumed: (i) that the only instrument to be used for stabilisation purposes is the fiscal instrument, G, as in Phillips; (ii) that at each point of time there is some desired level of G which the authorities specify – presumably on the basis of allocational considerations; (iii) that at each point of time there is some desired level of real gross domestic product which the authorities specify on the basis of internal-balance considerations.

2. An objective function is formulated in terms of the actual levels of Y and G over some specified future time interval and the corresponding desired levels. Usually this objective function takes the form of a time integral, over a specified future time interval, of some function of the deviations of the actual Ys from the desired Ys and the deviations of the actual Gs from the desired Gs; commonly a weighted average of the squared deviations of the actual Ys from the desired Ys and the actual Gs from the desired Gs is used as the function to be integrated.

3. The problem of finding the appropriate variations in the government expenditure instrument over a specified future time interval is then formulated as a time-optimisation problem. Specifically, the problem posed is to find a path for the instrument G over the specified future time interval such that the objective function is minimised subject to the constraints

Macro-Dynamic Model', *Manchester School of Economic and Social Studies* (Sep 1964); J. K. Sengupta, 'Optimum Economic Policy for Stabilization with a Quadratic Criterion Function', *Zeitschrift für die Gesamte Staatswissenschaft* (Oct 1965); J. K. Sengupta, 'A Simple Generalization of the Phillips-Type Model of Economic Stabilization', *Zeitschrift für die Gesamte Staatswissenschaft* (Oct 1966); K. A. Fox, J. K. Sengupta and E. Thorbecke, *The Theory of Quantitative Economic Policy with Applications to Economic Growth and Stabilization* (Amsterdam: North-Holland Publishing Co., 1966) chap. 8.

imposed by some dynamic model with arbitrary initial conditions and specified time paths for the explicit data. In most
applications, one of the two Phillips models outlined above, or
some simple modification of one of these models, has been used.
In any event the model which provides the constraint has
usually been simple enough to make it possible to solve the
time-optimisation problem by standard calculus-of-variations
techniques, though in some cases it has been necessary to apply
the newer Pontryagin techniques.

The most striking feature of the approach outlined in the preceding
paragraph is that it treats the problem of determining the appropriate
magnitudes of change in the instruments as a problem which is
essentially dynamic in character. To this extent it represents a considerable advance. Nevertheless, at the present stage of development the approach suffers from two limitations which should be
noted.

In the first place, the constraints imposed on the optimisation
process are still of an extremely simple kind. As will be clear from
earlier discussion, the constraining model is never much more
realistic than our Model I. Also the time paths specified for the
explicit data are invariably rudimentary, e.g. commonly the explicit
data are taken to be constant at zero. Whether the approach would
still be feasible if reasonably realistic constraints were imposed (e.g.
if the constraining model were more like Model V than Model I) is
open to doubt.

Secondly, so far there has been no progress beyond the case of a
single instrument – real government expenditure. This is not a
particularly interesting case because, in practice, it is common for
some combination of instruments to be used and also because
nowadays the government expenditure instrument is out of favour
(cf. p. 188 above). It remains to be seen whether the approach is
sufficiently flexible to accommodate more interesting cases than the
one so far examined.

6.8 Summary

The policy instruments through which the British authorities manage
D and/or M in the interests of internal balance fall into three groups,
namely:

(i) the *fiscal instruments*, consisting of the explicit datum G (real

government expenditure) and two implicit data, namely the
tax structure and the transfer payment structure;

(ii) the *monetary instruments*, consisting of the explicit datum L
(the stock of liquid assets) and two implicit data, the cost of
finance to firms and individuals and the availability of
finance; and

(iii) the *import instruments*, consisting of two explicit data, the
British price of home-produced importables relative to the
British price of foreign-produced importables and the inten-
sity of direct controls over foreign transactions.

Many different techniques are used to manipulate these instruments. Some of these work in a direct and obvious way, e.g. the use
of tax legislation to alter the tax structure, the use of Board of Trade
regulations to alter the availability of hire-purchase finance, the use
of Bank Rate to change the cost of bank finance and the issuing of
an 'official request' by the Bank of England to the commercial banks
to change the level and composition of bank advances. Others of the
available techniques, e.g. the use of open-market operations to
change the cost and availability of finance, work indirectly and in
ways which are sometimes far from obvious. Several of the available
techniques have serious limitations, but taken as a whole they appear
to be reasonably effective and to give the authorities a large measure
of control over the policy instruments.

An important consideration is the order of magnitude of the impact
on D and/or M which the authorities can hope to produce by
manipulation of the available policy instruments. By piecing together
various recent quantitative studies we are able to throw some light
on this point. Our conclusion is that by using all available instruments the authorities can produce an impact on $(D-M)$ of something
like 3 per cent of real potential gross domestic product without
departing from ranges of variation in the instruments which post-war
experience has shown to be acceptable in political terms.

The timing of the impact of changes in the instruments is of interest
as well as the magnitude of the impact. To help illuminate this aspect
of stabilisation policy, we make a rough estimate for each instrument
of the total lag between the need for a change in the instrument and
the impact of the change on D and/or M. We do this by dividing the
total lag into three parts (the recognition lag, the implementation lag
and the impact lag) and making a separate estimate for each of these
three components. These estimates are extremely rough but, for what

they are worth, they imply that at best the total lag may be something like six months while at worst it may be of the order of two years. This suggests that there is a real possibility that stabilisation policy may in fact be destabilising in its effects.

In the final section of the chapter we turn to the problem of determining the precise magnitude of the changes in the instruments which it is appropriate to make at any point of time. This has been recognised as an essentially dynamic problem since the work of Phillips on proportional, integral and derivative stabilisation policies, but only recently have positive suggestions been made for solving the problem within a dynamic framework. A brief account of one of these suggestions is given and the conclusion is drawn that, while it represents an important advance, it still requires development in certain directions.

READING LIST

Ball, R. J., and Drake, Pamela S., 'The Impact of Credit Control on Consumer Durable Spending in the United Kingdom, 1957–1961', *Review of Economic Studies* (1963).

Balopoulos, E. T., *Fiscal Policy Models of the British Economy* (Amsterdam: North-Holland Publishing Co., 1967).

Brechling, F. P. R., and Lipsey, R. G., 'Trade Credit and Monetary Policy', *Economic Journal* (Dec 1963).

Bristow, J. A., 'Taxation and Income Stabilization', *Economic Journal* (June 1968).

Coates, J. B., 'Trade Credit and Monetary Policy: A Study of the Accounts of 50 Companies', *Oxford Economic Papers* (Mar 1967).

Coppock, D. T., and Gibson, N. J., 'The Volume of Deposits and the Cash and Liquid Assets Ratios', *Manchester School* (Sep 1963).

Cramp, A. B., 'The Control of Bank Deposits', *Lloyds Bank Review* (Oct 1967).

Crouch, R. L., 'A Re-examination of Open-Market Operations', *Oxford Economic Papers* (June 1963).

—— 'The Inadequacy of "New Orthodox" Methods of Monetary Control', *Economic Journal* (Dec 1964).

Dacey, W. M., 'The Floating Debt Problem', *Lloyds Bank Review* (Apr 1956).

——, 'Treasury Bills and the Money Supply', *Lloyds Bank Review* (Jan 1960).

Dow, J. C. R., *The Management of the British Economy, 1945–60* (Cambridge University Press, 1964).

Fels, R., 'The Recognition-Lag and Semi-Automatic Stabilizers', *Review of Economics and Statistics* (Aug 1963).

Jasay, A. E. de, 'Liquidity Ratios and Funding in Monetary Control', *Oxford Economic Papers* (Sep 1956).

Karenken, J. H., 'Monetary Policy', in Caves, R. E., *Britain's Economic Prospects*, a Brookings Institution Study (London: Allen & Unwin, 1968).

Musgrave, R. A., and Musgrave, P. B., 'Fiscal Policy', in Caves, *Britain's Economic Prospects*.

Newlyn, W. T., 'The Supply of Money and its Control', *Economic Journal* (June 1964).

Phillips, A. W., 'Stabilization Policy in a Closed Economy', *Economic Journal* (June 1954).

——, 'Stabilization Policy and the Time-Forms of Lagged Responses', *Economic Journal* (June 1957).

Report of the Committee on the Working of the Monetary System, Cmnd 827 (London: H.M.S.O., 1959).

Sayers, R. S., 'The Determination of the Volume of Bank Deposits, England 1955–56', *Banca Nazionale del Lavoro Quarterly Review* (Dec 1955).

Sengupta, J. K., and Walker, D., 'On the Empirical Specification of Optimal Economic Policy for Growth and Stabilization under a Macro-Dynamic Model', *Manchester School of Economic and Social Studies* (Sep 1964).

Turvey, R., *Interest Rates and Asset Prices* (London: Allen & Unwin, 1960).

Tussing, A. D., 'Can Monetary Policy Influence the Availability of Credit?' *Journal of Finance* (Mar 1966).

Appendix 6.1

THE DETERMINATION OF THE YIELD ON GOVERNMENT BONDS[1]

The model we shall use to explain how the average yield on government bonds is determined is based on a two-sector classification of entities: the central government and the banking system constitute the first sector (labelled the 'monetary sector'), while all other entities constitute the second sector (labelled the 'private sector'). In addition, the model employs a fourfold classification of the assets owned by the private sector as a whole: the assets of the private sector as a whole are divided into money, short-term government bonds, long-term government bonds and real or physical assets, e.g. farms, factories, houses. It is assumed that the private sector as a whole has no liabilities of any sort to the monetary sector so that the wealth and aggregate assets of the private sector are identical.

We define 'one bond' as that amount of bonds which gives the owner a claim to an income of £1 per annum. The quantity of government bonds held by the private sector (B) is then identical with the aggregate income to which the owners of these bonds are entitled. Since the price of 'one bond' (F) multiplied by B gives the market value of the bonds held by the private sector, the average yield on government bonds must be given by $B/BF = 1/F$. In other words the price of one bond is the reciprocal of the average yield on bonds.

Similarly we define 'one physical asset' as that amount of physical assets which gives the owner an income of £1 per annum, so that the quantity of physical assets held by the private sector (R) is identical with the aggregate income accruing to the private sector from the ownership

---

[1] This appendix relies heavily on Ralph Turvey's *Interest Rates and Asset Prices* (London: Allen & Unwin, 1960).

of physical assets. The market value of the private sector's stock of physical assets is given by RQ where Q is the price of 'one physical asset'.

Given our assumptions, the wealth of the private sector as a whole (W) is given by:

$$W = M + BF + RQ \qquad (6.1.1)$$

where M is the nominal money stock.[1]

We now introduce relationships designed to explain, respectively, the demand for money and the demand for government bonds on the part of the private sector as a whole. (For simplicity we assume linearity and ignore the constant term.) The demand-for-money function of the private sector we take to be:

$$D_M = \beta_{10}W + \beta_{11}F + \beta_{12}Q + \beta_{13}Y^* + \beta_{14}\frac{S}{B} \qquad (6.1.2)$$

where D_M denotes the demand for money, Y^* gross national product in current prices, and S the quantity of short-term government bonds held in the private sector.[2]

We take it that the βs in this equation satisfy the following inequalities:

$$0 < \beta_{10} \leqslant 1$$
$$\beta_{11} > 0$$
$$\beta_{12} > 0$$
$$\beta_{13} > 0$$
$$\beta_{14} < 0.$$

The first inequality reflects the assumption that money is 'superior' as regards wealth ($\beta_{10} > 0$) and also the assumption that a given increase in wealth will produce an increase in the demand for money which is no larger than the increase in wealth ($\beta_{10} \leqslant 1$). The second and third inequalities reflect the assumption that money, bonds and physical assets are 'substitutes' so that a rise in the yield (fall in the price) of either bonds or physical assets will result in a fall in the demand for money from the private sector. The sign of β_{13} can be justified by means of the argument that, *ceteris paribus*, the aggregate private demand for money will be higher, the higher is transactions demand, and that, in the short run, the transactions demand will be higher, the higher is money gross national product. Finally, we can justify the sign of β_{14} by arguing that, *ceteris paribus*, the higher is S/B the greater will be the quantity of short-term bonds ('near-money') held by the private sector and hence the smaller will be its demand for money.

The demand for bonds from the private sector is given by:

$$D_B = \beta_{20}W + \beta_{21}F + \beta_{22}Q. \qquad (6.1.3.)$$

It should be noted that D_B is the *monetary*, not the quantitative, demand for bonds. Writing the equation in this way helps enormously to simplify

---

[1] This ignores the possibility that some of the money stock will be held in the monetary sector, e.g. currency held by the commercial banks.

[2] Using the same device as before, we can identify this with the aggregate income to which the owners of these securities are entitled.

later algebraic manipulations. On the other hand it raises a minor difficulty. Had we taken quantitative demand as the dependent variable, we could have been quite definite about the sign of β_{21}: we could have said $\beta_{21} < 0$. As the equation stands, however, we can say nothing definite about the sign of β_{21}. If the elasticity of demand for bonds with respect to the price of bonds is less than unity β_{21} will be positive; otherwise it will be negative. Because of this indefiniteness about the sign of β_{21}, some of the conclusions to be drawn from the model will be less clear-cut than they would have been otherwise.

The signs of the remaining βs cause no trouble. They will be:

$$\beta_{20} > 0$$
$$\beta_{22} > 0.$$

The first of these inequalities reflects the assumption that bonds as well as money are superior with respect to wealth and the second the assumption that real physical assets are substitutes for bonds as well as for money.

We now add two relationships which impose equality between the private sector's demand for money (bonds) and the stock of money (bonds) which is actually held by the private sector. These relationships are:

$$D_M = M \tag{6.1.4}$$

$$D_B = BF. \tag{6.1.5}$$

By substituting these two relationships into (6.1.2) and (6.1.3) we can eliminate D_M and D_B and emerge with a set of three relationships in the variables M, B, R, Y^*, S/B, F, Q and W. These three relationships enable us to express any three of the variables in terms of the remaining five. In particular they enable us to find expressions for F, Q and W in terms of M, B, R, Y^* and S/B. The expression for F is the one which is of particular interest since our object is to find the determinants of the average yield on government bonds and F is the reciprocal of this average yield. The expression for H is:

$$F = \frac{M[\beta_{22}(1 - \beta_{10}) + \beta_{12}\beta_{20} + \beta_{20}R] - Y^*(\beta_{13}\beta_{22} + \beta_{13}\beta_{20}R) + [(S/B)(-\beta_{14}\beta_{22} - \beta_{14}\beta_{20}R)]}{(\beta_{11}\beta_{22} - \beta_{12}\beta_{21}) + B[\beta_{12}(1 - \beta_{20}) + \beta_{10}\beta_{22} + \beta_{10}R] + R(\beta_{11}\beta_{20} - \beta_{10}\beta_{21}).} \tag{6.1.6}$$

We require that the numerator and denominator of this expression have the same sign, since negative F is impossible on economic grounds. If we assume that $\beta_{21} < 0$ and that β_{20} is not only positive but less than unity, then we can say that every term in the denominator and hence the denominator as a whole is positive. The numerator must then be positive also and we can proceed to draw the following comparative-statical, *ceteris paribus*, conclusions:

(i) A decrease in the quantity of money (M) will cause F to fall, i.e. the average yield on government bonds to rise, and vice versa. This must be so since the coefficient of M is necessarily positive, given the restrictions imposed on the βs.

(ii) An increase in the average maturity of the central government's debt to the private sector (decrease in S/B) will cause F to fall (the average yield to rise) and vice versa, since the coefficient of S/B is necessarily positive.

(iii) An increase in the quantity of government bonds held by the private sector (B) will cause F to fall (the average yield to rise) and vice versa, since the coefficient of B is necessarily positive.

(iv) An upward shift in the demand-for-money function which results either from an increase in β_{11} or in β_{13} will cause F to fall (the average yield to rise) and vice versa. This follows because an increase in β_{11} will produce an increase in the first and last terms in the denominator of (6.1.6) and hence in the denominator as a whole and because an increase in β_{13} will raise the coefficient of Y^* and hence reduce the numerator of (6.1.6) as a whole.

(v) An upward shift in the demand-for-money function due to a fall in the numerical value of β_{14} will cause the average yield to rise and vice versa, since it will reduce the numerator of (6.1.6).

(vi) A downward shift in the demand-for-bonds function resulting from an increase in the numerical value of β_{21} (still assuming it to be negative) will cause the average yield to rise, since it will produce an increase in the denominator of (6.1.6), and vice versa.

The model of bond-yield determination presented and analysed above is best regarded as a straight extension of the Keynesian model. The Keynesian model consists simply of a demand-for-money function in which the explanatory variables are F and Y^* and a relationship imposing equality between the stock of money and the demand for money from the private sector. Our model extends this: (i) by introducing three additional explanatory variables into the demand-for-money function, namely W, Q and S/B; and (ii) by adding three more relationships, namely (6.1.1), (6.1.3) and (6.1.5).

As for (i), the introduction of Q and S/B is required by a widening of the simplifying assumptions. In the Keynesian model it is assumed that the private sector can hold its wealth in only one of *two* forms: money and some undated bond issued either by the Government or by some firm. On the other hand, in our model the assumption is that the private sector can hold wealth in any one of *four* forms: money, long-term government bonds, short-term government bonds and physical assets. This being so, both Q and S/B must appear as explanatory variables in the demand-for-money function. On the other hand, the introduction of W seems to be called for whatever the simplifying assumptions. The size of an individual's wealth must be relevant to his demand for a particular asset since it imposes a limitation within which he must operate when deciding how much of the asset he wishes to hold. In fact the position of wealth in relation to asset demand is strictly analogous to the position of income in relation to commodity demand: in the case of asset demand the individual faces a wealth constraint, whereas in the case of commodity demand he faces an income constraint.

Turn now to the additional relationships. The first (the wealth definition) follows naturally from the inclusion of wealth as an explanatory variable in

H

the demand-for-money function; a Keynesian model with wealth in the demand-for-money function could use a relationship of this type ($W = M + BF$) just as easily as the wider model now proposed. On the other hand, the inclusion of the second and third of the new relationships is possible only because of the widening of assumptions. For suppose we had retained the Keynesian assumptions and modified the Keynesian model only by adding W to the demand-for-money function and introducing $W = M + BF$ as an extra relationship. The introduction of a demand-for-bonds function and an equilibrium condition for the bond market would then have been inappropriate, since the demand for bonds would have been determined already by the wealth definition and the demand-for-money function, while the equilibrium condition for the bond market would have been derivable, by subtraction, from the wealth definition and the relationship $D_M = M$.[1]

While our model is more elaborate than the Keynesian model, it is still extremely simple. One way of extending it would be to allow for certain important financial assets which are now completely neglected – in particular, shares. This could be done most easily by introducing the price of these assets, e.g. the price of shares, as additional explanatory variables in both the demand-for-money and the demand-for-bonds functions. (The wealth definition would be unaffected by the introduction of shares, since shares do not form part of the assets of the private sector as a whole.) A second possibility would be to introduce further disaggregation – either of the sectors or of the assets or of both. Examples of the first are a division of the monetary sector into, say, the central government and its authorities (e.g. the Bank of England) on the one hand and the commercial banks on the other hand, and a division of the private sector into, say, financial intermediaries, other firms and individuals. Examples of the second are a division of real assets into, say, land and other real property and a subdivision of long-term government securities into, say, those with more than five and those with less than five years to maturity. These and other possible extensions would doubtless suggest further ways in which the British authorities can manipulate the average yield on British Government bonds.

Appendix 6.2

OUTLINE OF COMPUTATION OF IMPACT LAG FOR COST AND AVAILABILITY OF FINANCE: HOUSING INVESTMENT COMPONENT

In this case the computation would be based on relationship (4.20).

$$I_t^{gh} = a_{50}(X_{t-1} - X_{t-2}) + a_{51}I_{t-1}^{gh} + a_{52}I_{t-2}^{gh} + a_{53}I_{t-3}^{gh} + a_{54}K_t^h$$
$$+ a_{55}K_{t-1}^h + a_{56}K_{t-2}^h + a_{57}K_{t-3}^h. \quad (4.20)$$

---

[1] For the same reasons the inclusion of a demand-for-real-assets function and an equilibrium condition for the real assets market would have been innappropriate in the case of our extended Keynesian model.

As before we would postulate stationary equilibrium up to period 0 and a policy-induced change in the cost and/or availability of finance in that period. The effect of this change would be to twist the housing relationship, since the cost and availability of finance are part of the implicit data which underlie this relationship (see p. 133 above). We would write the new values of the coefficients of the relationship as a'_{50} a'_{51}, etc. Finally, we would rule out the secondary effects of the postulated change by assuming that all explanatory variables in (4.20), apart from the lagged I^{gh} variables, are kept at their original stationary equilibrium levels.

On this basis (4.20) generates the following sequence in which i^{gh} denotes $I_t^{gh} - I_{t-1}^{gh}$ and $\bar{I}^{gh}$ and $\bar{K}^h$ denote the stationary equilibrium levels of I^{gh} and K^h respectively:

$$i_0^{gh} = [(a'_{51} - a_{51}) + (a'_{52} - a_{52}) + (a'_{53} - a_{53})]\bar{I}^{gh} + [(a'_{54} - a_{54})$$
$$+ (a'_{55} - a_{55}) + (a'_{56} - a_{56}) + (a'_{57} - a_{57})]\bar{K}^h$$

$$i_1^{gh} = a'_{51}i_0^{gh} \tag{6.2.1}$$

$$i_2^{gh} = a'_{51}i_1^{gh} + a'_{52}i_0^{gh} \tag{6.2.2}$$

$$i_3^{gh} = a'_{51}i_2^{gh} + a'_{52}i_1^{gh} + a'_{53}i_0^{gh} \tag{6.2.3}$$
$$\vdots \qquad\qquad\qquad\qquad \vdots$$

$$i_t^{gh} = a'_{51}i_{t-1}^{gh} + a'_{52}i^{gh} + a'_{53}i_{t-3}^{gh}. \tag{6.2.4}$$

To estimate the time-form of the response for housing investment, we would first derive the solution of (6.2.4). This solution would be an expression of the form:

$$i_t^{gh} = A_1(x_1)^t + A_2(x_2)^t + A_3(x_3)^t \tag{6.2.5}$$

where A_1, A_2 and A_3 are arbitrary constants and x_1, x_2 and x_3 are the roots of the characteristic equation:

$$x^3 - a'_{51}x^2 - a'_{52}x - a'_{53} = 0. \tag{6.2.6}$$

To find the solution it would be necessary to specify values for the coefficients a'_{51}, a'_{52} and a'_{53}. Once this has been done it would be possible to find actual values for x_1, x_2 and x_3 in (6.2.5) by solving the third-degree polynomial (6.2.6). It would also be possible to evaluate A_1, A_2 and A_3. To do this we would solve the following equations which are based on (6.2.1), (6.2.2) and (6.2.3) as initial conditions:

$$A_1x_1 + A_2x_2 + A_3x_3 = k_1i_0^{gh}$$
$$A_1(x_1)^2 + A_2(x_2)^2 + A_3(x_3)^2 = k_2i_0$$
$$A_1(x_1)^3 + A_2(x_2)^3 + A_3(x_3)^3 = k_3i_0^{gh}$$

where k_1, k_2 and k_3 are given by:

$$k_1 = a'_{51}$$
$$k_2 = (a'_{51})^2 + a'_{52}$$
$$k_3 = (a'_{51})^3 + 2a'_{51}a'_{52} + a'_{53}.$$

The solutions for A_1, A_2 and A_3 would take the form:

$$A_1 = k_1' i_0^{gh}$$
$$A_2 = k_2' i_0^{gh} \qquad (6.2.7)$$
$$A_3 = k_3' i_0^{gh}$$

where k_1', k_2' and k_3' are constants depending on x_1, x_2 and x_3 and on k_1, k_2 and k_3, i.e. constants depending ultimately on the values specified for a_{51}', a_{52}' and a_{53}'.

Together, relationships (6.2.5) and (6.2.7) imply that the *numerator* of the time-form of the response would be given by:

$$\sum_{t=0}^{T} i_t^{gh} = i_0^{gh} + \sum_{t=1}^{T} i_t^{gh}$$

$$= i_0^{gh} \left[1 + \sum_{t=1}^{T} \{ k_1'(x_1)^t + k_2'(x_2)^t + k_3'(x_3)^t \} \right]$$

$$= i_0^{gh} \left[1 + k_1'(1 - x_1^T) \left(\frac{x_1}{1 - x_1} \right) + k_2'(1 - x_2^T) \left(\frac{x_2}{1 - x_2} \right) \right. \qquad (6.2.8)$$

$$\left. + k_3'(1 - x_3^T) \left(\frac{x_3}{1 - x_3} \right) \right].$$

Relationships (6.2.5) and (6.2.7) also imply that the *denominator* of the time-form of the response is given by:[1]

$$\sum_{t=0}^{\infty} i_t = i_0^g + \sum_{t=1}^{\infty} i_t$$

$$= i_0^{gh} \left[1 + \sum_{t=1}^{\infty} k_1'(x_1)^t + k_2'(x_2)^t + k_3'(x_3)^t \right] \qquad (6.2.9)$$

$$= i_0^{gh} \left[1 + k_1' \left(\frac{x_1}{1 - x_1} \right) + k_2' \left(\frac{x_2}{1 - x_2} \right) + k_3' \left(\frac{x_3}{1 - x_3} \right) \right].$$

Hence the two relationships in question imply that the time-form of the response is given by the ratio between (6.2.8) and (6.2.9). From the foregoing it is evident that this would be calculable once a_{51}', a_{52}' and a_{53}' had been specified.

---

[1] This assumes that x_1, x_2 and x_3 are real numbers lying between 0 and $+1$.

7 Balance of Payments Policy: The Pursuit of External Balance

7.1 Short-run Balance and Long-run Balance

In this chapter we shall use the theoretical material presented earlier, especially the material of Chapter 3, as a basis for discussing the attainment of the second of our four objectives – the objective of external balance. As in the previous chapter we shall assume for simplicity that external balance is being pursued as an isolated objective. This will permit us to leave over for later discussion the question of the possible interrelationships between this objective and the other three.

We shall begin by expanding our earlier discussion of the meaning of external balance. In section 1.3 we said that *short-run* external balance (or short-run balance of payments equilibrium) exists if the aggregate demand for foreign currencies is neither persistently greater than the available supply nor persistently less than the available supply, over a short run of quarters (say about six to twelve quarters), after both the demand figures and the supply figures have been adjusted to exclude influences which are purely seasonal, or speculative, in character. We must now distinguish between short-run external balance, defined in this way, and *long-run* external balance.

While there is no generally accepted concept of long-run balance, a concept which would probably command wide acceptance among British economists, on the grounds of its relevance to the British situation, is the following: long-run external balance (or long-run balance of payments equilibrium) exists if, on the average over several years (say a decade), the surplus on current account is just sufficient, in the absence of long-term direct controls over foreign transactions, to provide for the desired long-term capital outflow *plus* an appropriate level of foreign aid *plus* an appropriate increase in the ratio between international reserves and short-term liabilities to the rest of the world. Long-run external balance in this sense is a desirable objective for Britain because it implies that over a run of good and bad years the ratio of Britain's reserves to her short-term liabilities, which is generally agreed to be too low, is being raised without recourse to a reduction in foreign aid or to permanent direct controls over foreign transactions or to drastic measures to increase the reserves such as the compulsory acquisition of financial and other assets held abroad by British residents, all of which would be un-desirable from a world point of view.

A country which experiences repeated short-run disequilibria in its balance of payments will usually be found to be suffering from a long-run disequilibrium as well – typically the one is merely a reflection of the other. However, the two types of disequilibrium do not necessarily go together. It is quite possible for short-run dis-equilibrium to occur intermittently over a run of years in which there is a long-run balance. Likewise it is perfectly possible for a long-run disequilibrium to be masked for a time either by short-run policy measures or by fortuitous temporary events such as favourable movements in the terms of trade or abnormally low capital outflow in certain years, i.e. it is perfectly possible for short-run balance to accompany long-run disequilibrium.

In the rest of this chapter we shall be concerned with the measures which the British authorities can take, and do take from time to time, to promote the objective of external balance, and we shall base our discussion on the distinction between short-run and long-run balance which has been developed in this introductory section. From now on we shall frequently make use of the convenient, though not very precise, terms 'deficit' and 'surplus'. By 'short-run deficit' we shall mean a short-run disequilibrium in the balance of payments (or an absence of short-run balance) in which an excess of aggregate demand for foreign currencies persists over a short run of quarters, and by 'short-run surplus' a disequilibrium in which the available supply is persistently in excess of the aggregate demand. By 'long-run deficit' we shall mean a long-run balance of payments disequilibrium in which the current account balance is insufficient, averaged over a run of good and bad years, to provide for desired long-term foreign investment and an appropriate amount of foreign aid, and for a contribution to the improvement of the ratio of reserves to short-term liabilities without recourse to permanent direct controls over foreign transactions; and by 'long-run surplus' a long-run disequilibrium characterised by an average level of the current account balance which is more than sufficient for those purposes.

In the next section we shall discuss the steps which the British authorities can take to deal with a short-run deficit in the balance of payments, and in sections 7.3 and 7.4 the more fundamental steps which are needed to eliminate a long-run deficit. With some minor qualifications, the problems of eliminating a short-run and a long-run *surplus* are symmetrical with the corresponding deficit problems, and we shall therefore not discuss them in detail. It will be left to the interested reader to reverse the argument of sections 7.2 to 7.4 to cover these two cases if he wishes to do so.

7.2 Short-run Deficit

In section 1.3, it was pointed out that the authorities have three alternatives open to them when faced with a short-run balance of payments deficit: (i) they can do nothing in the hope that the deficit will look after itself; (ii) they can impose direct controls over foreign transactions while the deficit persists; or (iii) they can take positive steps to eliminate the deficit, or, in other words, make external balance a policy objective.[1] It was also suggested that, in some circumstances, there may be a strong case for adopting either of the first two alternatives in preference to the third. 'Do nothing' may be preferable to elimination of the deficit if the country's foreign currency reserves are ample in relation to its trade or its short-term liabilities when the deficit first becomes apparent, and if there is good reason to believe that the deficit will be short-lived. Repressing the excess demand for foreign currencies by means of import licensing or some other form of direct controls over foreign transactions may be preferable if the controls conform with the country's international obligations, if there is little danger of retaliation and if the controls are likely to be short-lived. Suppose, however, that circumstances are such that alternative (iii) – positive steps to eliminate the deficit – is the preferred alternative, e.g. because the reserves are dangerously small so that alternative (i) has to be ruled out and because it appears that it may be difficult to justify the controls in the international

[1] The reader is reminded that (ii) and (iii) are quite distinct. The imposition of direct controls over foreign transactions, of itself, contributes nothing to the elimination of a deficit (excess demand for foreign currencies). It is a means of repressing excess demand for foreign currencies, not a means of removing this excess demand. Cf. p. 16 above.

forum so that alternative (ii) is unsatisfactory. In this case the authorities will have to make the further decision as to the nature of the 'positive steps'. In the British case, the steps chosen on any actual occasion will be some combination of the following three:

1. Restrict aggregate demand.
2. Depress the home–foreign price ratio.
3. Increase short-term interest rates.

Our main object in the present section is to discuss each of the above three steps in some detail. In each case we shall be concerned with three questions: (i) how can it be implemented?; (ii) how does it work?; and (iii) what are its limitations?

1. *Demand Restriction*

We begin with the first of the three steps – restriction of aggregate demand. By this, we mean the imposition of a check on the rate of increase of aggregate demand and the subsequent removal of this check once the short-run deficit has been eliminated – the procedure which is sometimes given the illuminating label 'stop–go'. The first of the three questions raised above (how can stop–go be implemented?) has already been discussed in detail in Chapter 6 and there is nothing further to add at this point. We turn, therefore, to the second question: how does stop–go work?

Here we must begin by explaining what we mean by 'work'. By definition, the short-run deficit which has to be eliminated is a state of persistent excess demand for foreign currencies. This being so, the task facing the authorities is to find ways of keeping the aggregate demand for foreign currencies at a lower level, quarter by quarter, while the disequilibrium persists, than it would have been otherwise and/or of keeping the available supply of foreign currencies at a higher level. Thus when we raise the question of how a particular measure will work, in the context of a short-run balance of payments deficit, we are really asking: how will the measure contribute to a reduction in the aggregate demand for foreign currencies and/or to an increase in the available supply of foreign currencies, quarter by quarter, in the short period over which the deficit continues?

As far as stop–go is concerned, two distinct answers have been given to this question in relation to the British economy. In the first place it has been said that temporary demand restriction will work by causing the desired volume of Britain's imports to be lower, quarter by quarter, than it would have been otherwise and hence, given the prices of her imports in terms of foreign currency, by causing Britain's demand for foreign currency to pay for imports to be lower. It has also been said that temporary demand restriction will work by causing the volume of Britain's exports to be higher than it would have been otherwise and hence, given the foreign-currency prices of her exports, by causing the supply of foreign currency which becomes available to Britain from the sale of exports to be higher also. We shall now consider each of these answers in turn.

(a) *Demand restriction and imports.* To provide a framework for consideration of the first point, we return to the discussion of section 3.2 above on the determinants of M^*, the demand for imports into Britain (see pp. 70–2 above)[1]. The conclusion reached there was that, in the case of the British economy, the main determinants of desired real imports are as set out in the following list, in which the 'plus' or 'minus' at the end of an item is the sign of the partial derivative of desired real imports with respect to the determinant concerned:

  (i) the level of aggregate demand in Britain ($+$);
 (ii) the level of real inventory investment in Britain ($+$);
(iii) the price of importables in Britain relative to the prices of exportables and non-traded goods ($-$);
(iv) the price of British-made importables relative to the price of foreign-made importables, both prices in terms of British currency ($+$);
 (v) the delivery delay quoted by British producers of importables relative to the delivery delay quoted by foreign producers of importables ($+$);
(vi) the generosity of the credit terms offered by British producers of importables relative to the credit terms offered by foreign producers ($-$).

What can be said, in the light of the foregoing, about the effect of temporary demand restriction on the demand for imports by British residents? What emerges is that there are three main ways in which temporary demand restriction will contribute towards a lower level of import demand, quarter by quarter, than would have occurred otherwise.

---

[1] Note that while M (realised imports) is the relevant concept for internal balance, M^* (desired imports) is the relevant concept for external balance. This follows ultimately from the way in which internal and external balance are defined.

H 2

In the first place, since aggregate demand will be lower in each period than it would have been in the absence of the policy change, import demand must also be lower than otherwise by virtue of item (i).

Secondly, since aggregate demand will be lower than otherwise, the rate of increase of money wage earnings will also be lower. This means, in turn, that the rate of increase of British prices will be lower[1] and this, in turn, that the price of British-made importables will be lower relative to the price of foreign-made importables in terms of British currency (given the rate of increase of foreign prices) than would otherwise have been the case. Consequently, imports must be lower than otherwise by virtue of item (iv).

Finally, it can be argued that since aggregate demand will be lower in each period, the delivery delay quoted by British producers of importables will also be lower in each period, relative to that quoted by foreign producers, and hence that import demand will be lower than otherwise by virtue of item (v). The basis of this argument is the point that the relative delivery delay applying to any single importable good, e.g. motor-cars, at any point of time will depend primarily on the pressure of demand for the British product relative to the pressure of demand for the foreign product. For example, if the pressure of demand for British-made motor-cars falls relative to the pressure of demand for European-made motor-cars, the relative delivery delay will also fall and vice versa. This being so, the relative delivery delay applying to importables *as a whole* will vary in the same direction as relative excess demand. Now a policy of temporary demand restriction means that excess demand in Britain will be lower absolutely in each period than it would have been and hence, given excess demand in the rest of the world, that it will be lower relatively also. Consequently, temporary demand restriction must mean a lower relative delivery delay, and via this a lower demand for imports by British residents, than would otherwise have been the case.

(b) *Demand restriction and exports.* Having considered the suggestion that temporary demand restriction will work by causing the desired volume of imports to be lower than it would have been, we turn now to the second possibility that it will work by causing the volume of exports to be higher.

We begin our discussion of this suggestion with the obvious point that a temporary restriction of aggregate demand in Britain will not

[1] See Chapter 9 for a full discussion of this point.

increase the volume of British exports unless it provides British firms with an incentive to expand their sales in foreign markets. Will it do so? This question can be examined properly only within the framework of a model of the exporting firm, and the model we shall use is one proposed some years ago by R. J. Ball.[1]

The main features of Ball's model are as follows:

(i) The firm is a price-maker (or quantity-taker), i.e. it fixes prices and supplies whatever is demanded at the fixed price, subject to the restriction that the marginal cost of producing the output required to permit the full satisfaction of demand shall not exceed the fixed price.

(ii) The price fixed in the foreign market may or may not be the same as the price fixed in the domestic market.

(iii) The firm maintains a certain minimum level of exports 'either because it is desired to maintain goodwill in the foreign market or perhaps from the fear that if exports fall below that minimum the firms may incur such official displeasure that uncongenial policies restricting the home market may follow'.[2]

(iv) The domestic market is given prior claim to the firm's output, i.e. given the minimum level of exports the firm sells as much as it can in the domestic market.

(v) Subject to the prior claim of the domestic market the firm sells as much as possible in the export market over and above the minimum (see (iii)).

Some arithmetic examples will now be given to help clarify this model.

Example 1 (both domestic and foreign demand fully satisfied)

Domestic price	10
Foreign price	15
Minimum exports	200
Domestic demand	1000
Foreign demand	500
Marginal cost at output of 1500	8

In this case the firm's cost conditions are such that it can meet both the domestic demand and the foreign demand without violating the marginal cost condition of (i). It will therefore produce 1000 units for

---

[1] See R. J. Ball, 'Credit Restriction and the Supply of Exports', *Manchester School of Economic and Social Studies* (May 1961). Actually in this article Ball puts forward *two* models of the exporting firm – the 'price discrimination' model and the 'fixed-price' model. The model we have adopted is the 'fixed-price' model which is the one Ball apparently prefers (ibid., pp. 166–8). The discussion which follows makes extensive use of Ball's work. [2] Ibid., p. 164.

the domestic market and 500 for the foreign market; both the home demand and the foreign demand will be fully satisfied.

Example 2 (domestic demand fully satisfied; unsatisfied foreign demand)

Domestic price	15
Foreign price	10
Minimum exports	200
Domestic demand	1000
Foreign demand	500
Marginal cost at output of 1100	9
Marginal cost at output of 1200	10
Marginal cost at output of 1500	15

If the firm were to produce 1500 units in order to satisfy both the domestic and foreign demand in full, it would be violating the marginal cost restriction in the foreign market. It will avoid this by producing 1200, of which 1000 will go to the domestic market, thereby fully satisfying the domestic demand, and 200 (the minimum level of exports) to the foreign market, leaving an unsatisfied foreign demand of 300.

Example 3 (unsatisfied demand in both domestic and foreign markets)

Domestic price	10
Foreign price	15
Minimum exports	200
Domestic demand	1000
Foreign demand	500
Marginal cost at output of 1000	10
Marginal cost at output of 1200	15
Marginal cost at output of 1500	17

In this final example there will be unsatisfied demand in both the domestic and the foreign market, because if the firm were to produce 1500 in order to satisfy fully both the domestic and the foreign demand, it would be violating the marginal cost restriction in both markets. The policy chosen in this case will be to produce 1000, of which 800 will go to the home market (leaving an unsatisfied demand of 200) and the remainder (the 200 minimum) to the foreign market, leaving an unsatisfied foreign demand of 300.

So much for the model itself. Let us now postulate a temporary restriction of aggregate demand in Britain which shifts the domestic demand curve for the firm's product to the left. We assume that the firm's cost conditions are unaffected by the demand restriction and that neither the domestic price nor the foreign price is altered. The question we now ask is: will the firm's sales in the export market be higher following the demand restriction than they would have been otherwise?

It is clear that, given the above model of the exporting firm, the answer will be 'yes' on some occasions and 'no' on others. Suppose, for example, that the situation depicted in example 2 is the situation that would have existed in the absence of the demand restriction and that the situation which exists following the restriction is the same except that domestic demand is 900 instead of 1000. Then export sales will be 300 with the demand restriction as compared with 200 otherwise. This is a case where the answer to our question would be 'yes'. Suppose, on the other hand, that the situation that would have existed in the absence of the demand restriction is the situation depicted in example 3 and, as before, that the situation which exists following the restriction is the same except that the domestic demand is 900 instead of 1000. Then export sales will be 200 with the demand restriction and 200 in the absence of the demand restriction. In this case the answer to our question would be 'no'. Here the effect of the demand restriction would be to make the unsatisfied domestic demand less than it would have been by 100, not to make export sales more than they would have been.

The conclusion which emerges from this analysis is that the proposition that temporary demand restriction will contribute to an expansion of export volume, by providing domestic firms with an incentive to expand export sales, is a dubious one. It may have this effect in any actual case or it may not. All depends on the cost conditions facing exporting firms, on the prices which have been set in the home and foreign markets, on the conditions of demand in the home and foreign markets and on the extent of the reduction in domestic demand for the firm's product consequent on the demand restriction. Further than that one cannot go.

A necessary condition for the success of temporary demand restriction as a means of increasing export volume is that it should provide British firms with an incentive to expand export sales. What we have just argued is that there is some doubt as to whether this necessary condition will be met in general. We turn now to another question, namely whether the condition in question is also sufficient. We can certainly say that demand restriction will not increase export volume *unless* it provides British firms with an incentive to expand export sales. Can we also say that demand restriction will increase export volume *so long as* it provides British firms with this incentive? Clearly, no. British exporting firms may *wish* to expand sales in export markets following a reduction in the demand for the product at home, but obviously they will not be able to do so unless there was previously some unsatisfied demand in foreign markets[1] or unless there is an increase in foreign demand as a result of the demand restriction in Britain. Thus, to assess the effectiveness of demand restriction as a means of increasing export volume, we need to inquire not only whether it is likely to increase the supply of British exports but also whether it is likely to increase the overseas demand for them.

The best way to approach this question is to return to the discussion of section 3.4 about the export demand function for the British economy. The conclusion of this discussion was that the function explaining export demand for the British economy will contain six main explanatory variables, namely[2]

   (i) the level of aggregate demand in the rest of the world (+);

   (ii) the level of real inventory investment in the rest of the world (+);

   (iii) the price of importables in the rest of the world relative to the prices of exportables and non-traded goods (−);

   (iv) the price of rest-of-world importables produced in the rest of the world relative to the price of rest-of-world importables produced in Britain (+);

   (v) the delivery delay and credit terms quoted by rest-of-world producers of rest-of-world importables relative to those quoted by British producers (+);

   (vi) the intensity of direct controls over foreign transactions in the rest of the world (−).

With this list of explanatory variables before us we can see that there are two main ways in which temporary demand restriction in

---

[1] Suppose, for example, that the situation depicted in example 1 is the situation that would have existed in the absence of the demand restriction, and the situation with the restriction is the same except that the domestic demand is 900 instead of 1000. Then the exporting firm in question would have an incentive to expand sales in the export market by 100. But it will not be able to do so because foreign demand was fully satisfied before the demand restriction was applied.

[2] The sign appearing at the end of each item in the following list is the sign of the relevant partial derivative.

Britain is likely to raise the overseas demand for British exports. In the first place, as argued earlier in this section, one of the effects of demand restriction in Britain will be to cause the waiting-time quoted to foreign purchasers by foreign producers to be higher relative to the waiting-time quoted by British producers than it would have been otherwise. For this reason demand restriction will have a favourable effect on the overseas demand for British exports via item (v). Secondly, as pointed out already and as will be argued in detail in Chapter 9, there is good reason to suppose that demand restriction in Britain will normally check the rate of increase of British prices by checking the rate of increase of average wage and salary earnings. It will therefore tend to raise the price of rest-of-world importables made in the rest of the world relative to the price of rest-of-world importables made in Britain and hence tend to increase the overseas demand for British exports via item (iv).

We can sum up the present discussion by saying that, while there are good reasons for believing that temporary demand restriction in Britain will tend to increase the overseas demand for British exports, there is some doubt about whether, as a general rule, it will provide British exporting firms with an incentive to meet this increased demand, and hence doubt about its effectiveness as a measure for increasing the volume of British exports in the short run.

So far we have been considering the short-run effect of demand restriction on the volume of exports at the *a priori* level. We turn now to an empirical study of this question made recently by Ball, Eaton and Steuer (B.E.S.).[1] The problem which B.E.S. set themselves was to determine whether changes in the level of excess demand in Britain have a significant effect on the export performance of British manufacturing industry. Two approaches to this problem were adopted. The first approach took the form of a quarterly regression analysis using as explanatory variables an indicator of excess demand (the assumption being that excess demand is the only important short-run influence on export performance) and a group of variables designed to take care of the long-run influences on the level of manufacturing exports. The second approach differed only in that the long-run influences were incorporated in a purely mechanical way by using a time variable in the regression analysis.

---

[1] See R. J. Ball, J. R. Eaton and M. D. Steuer, 'The Relationship between United Kingdom Export Performance in Manufactures and the Internal Pressure of Demand', *Economic Journal* (Sep 1966).

A large number of regressions were calculated from the first approach. In some of these regressions the dependent variable was the level of British manufactured exports, in others it was the percentage change in British manufactured exports and in others again it was the ratio of British manufactured exports to world trade in manufactures. Some of the regressions were linear in form, others were linear in terms of logarithms. In some cases deseasonalised data were used and in others the problem of seasonality in the quarterly data was dealt with by introducing dummy seasonal variables into the regressions. Thus the regressions which followed on the first approach were a highly varied group. In view of this, the uniformity of the results is impressive. Broadly speaking, B.E.S. found that the excess demand variable made no significant contribution to the explanation of export performance when the only explanatory variables included with it were world demand and relative prices.[1] On the other hand, when three variables (world demand, relative prices and the United Kingdom share in world output) were added to the excess-demand variable to take care of the longer-run influences, the coefficient of the excess-demand variable was generally significant and of the right *a priori* sign (negative), but tended to be unstable over time.[2] B.E.S. considered these results somewhat indecisive and were reluctant to base any firm conclusions about the short-run influence of demand reduction on export performance on them.

The second approach also gave rise to a large number of quarterly regressions. Once again these exhibited considerable variety as regards dependent variable, form of equation, etc. In spite of this variety, the excess-demand variable repeatedly emerged with a highly significant negative coefficient. Thus the regressions based on the second approach gave much stronger support to the view that British export performance is likely to improve when the pressure of demand falls than did the regressions based on the first approach.

Let us now summarise the discussion presented so far in the present section. One of the actions which the British authorities can take in order to correct a short-run disequilibrium in the balance of payments is to impose a temporary check on the growth of aggregate demand.

[1] See R. J. Ball, J. R. Eaton and M. D. Steuer, 'The Relationship between United Kingdom Export Performance in Manufactures and the Internal Pressure of Demand', *Economic Journal* (Sep 1966). pp. 507, 509.
[2] Ibid., pp. 509–10.

This will contribute to the restoration of balance by causing the volume of imports to be smaller than otherwise. It may also help by causing the volume of exports to be higher. While this appears somewhat doubtful in the light of *a priori* argument based on a simple model of the exporting firm, it has recently been given quite strong empirical support in a study by Ball, Eaton and Steuer.

(c) *Limitations of demand restriction.* Before leaving the topic of demand restriction, we shall briefly consider its main limitations as a means of correcting a short-run balance of payments deficit.

One important limitation of demand restriction is that it is likely to be a considerable time before its beneficial effects on the external situation are felt. We have seen already that demand restriction works mainly by causing import demand to be lower than it would be otherwise. However, this lowering of import demand will have no effect, of itself, on the demand for foreign currencies to pay for imports, which is what really matters. The demand for foreign currencies will fall: (i) only after the lower import demand has been translated into a lower volume of import orders; (ii) only after this lower volume of import orders, in turn, has been translated into a lower volume of import deliveries; and (iii) only after this lower volume of import deliveries, in turn, has been translated into a lower level of import payments.

As for (i), it will be recalled that we postulated in earlier discussion (see p. 73 above) that the current level of import orders depends on the level of import demand in the current period and all past periods via a distributed-lag relationship in which the weights decline geometrically and sum to unity. It was also suggested that a plausible value for the damping factor in this relationship might be 0·1 – a value which implies that it takes about six months for a given change in import demand to be fully reflected in a change in import orders (see p. 78 above). As regards (ii), we have postulated in earlier argument that, in the British case, it takes one quarter for a variation in the rate of import ordering to be reflected in a variation in the rate of import deliveries (see p. 74 above). On this basis and allowing one quarter to cover (iii), it can be seen that it may well be twelve months or so before demand restriction makes a significant impact on the short-run balance of payments deficit.

A second limitation of demand restriction is that while contributing to the attainment of external balance, it may hinder the attainment of internal balance. Here the essential point is that when the authorities restrict aggregate demand they also restrict $(D - M)$, given that the marginal propensity to import is less than unity.[1] Consequently, if the internal situation is one of balance or deficient demand for commodities, the application of demand restriction in the interests of external balance will mean either the emergence of deficient demand or the intensification of deficient demand, as the case may be, and hence will be undesirable from the point of view of the internal balance objective. Only if the internal situation is one characterised by excess demand for commodities will the restriction of aggregate demand promote both objectives simultaneously. However, the question of the interrelationship between internal balance and external balance is a fairly complicated one and, for a detailed treatment, the reader must wait until Chapter 14.

2. *Reduction of Home–Foreign Price Ratio*

(a) *Available devices.* Instead of, or in addition to, restricting aggregate demand, the authorities may decide to depress temporarily the home–foreign price ratio as a means of eliminating the short-run deficit, where the term 'home–foreign price ratio' is an abbreviation for 'the price of British-made importables relative to the price of foreign-made importables in terms of British currency'. We shall now consider this possibility in detail. As with demand restriction we shall be concerned with three questions: (i) how can this particular step be implemented? (ii) how does it work? (iii) what are its limitations? In this case the second question requires only brief treatment and we shall therefore deal with it first.

As we saw earlier in this section, the desired volume of imports into Britain depends directly on the home–foreign price ratio: the higher is the home–foreign price ratio, given the other determinants of import demand, the larger is the desired volume of imports. It follows that depressing the home–foreign price ratio will work (contribute to a reduction in the demand for foreign currencies) by reducing the level of import demand and hence reducing the demand for foreign currency to pay for imports.

Turning to the question of implementation, we first note that the home–foreign price ratio will fall so long as the rate of increase of the British-currency price of home-produced importables is less than the rate of increase of the British-currency price of foreign-produced

---

[1] This was the assumption made in the dynamic analysis of Models III to V (see p. 78 above).

importables.[1] It follows that, if the British authorities wish to depress the home–foreign price ratio, they must either: (a) check the rate of increase of the British-currency price of home-produced importables; and/or (b) boost the rate of increase of the British-currency price of foreign-produced importables.

Suppose, to begin with, that the authorities decide on alternative (a), i.e. to depress the home–foreign price ratio by checking the rate of increase of the price of home-produced importables. What action can they take? The main possibility is to try to bring about a temporary 'freeze' on average wage and salary earnings. This will help to check the rate of increase of the price of home-produced importables by easing the upward pressure on price exerted by rising unit labour cost.[2] There are three instances of action of this type on the part of the British authorities in the post-war period – the 'wage-freeze' of 1948–50, the 'pay-pause' of 1961–2 and the 'standstill on incomes' of 1966–7. Each of these episodes will be discussed in detail in section 10.2.

If the authorities opt for alternative (b), i.e. if they decide to depress the home–foreign price ratio by boosting the rate of increase of the price of foreign-produced importables in terms of British currency, they have a choice between imposition of a temporary surcharge on imports and introduction of an import-deposit scheme. The way in which these devices serve to boost the rate of increase of the British-currency price of foreign-produced importables is well known and we shall therefore confine ourselves to a brief recapitulation.

First, take the *temporary surcharge on imports*. As the name implies, this consists of the imposition of a special levy on selected imports on top of any regular levies, such as import duty, to which they may already be subject. It will have the effect, therefore, of raising the British-currency price of all foreign-produced importables on which it is imposed (except where it provokes the foreign producer to reduce his price in terms of foreign currency, at least in proportion to the surcharge) and hence will serve to boost the rate of increase of the British-currency price of foreign-produced importables in the period in which it is introduced.

Let us turn now to the second device – the *import-deposit scheme*.

---

[1] A reduction in the home–foreign price ratio does not require that the British price level should *fall*.

[2] See Chapter 9 for a full discussion of this point.

Under such a scheme, an importer is required to lodge a deposit equal to some prescribed percentage of the value of the goods being imported with the customs authorities before he can remove the goods from the port area. This deposit, which bears no interest, is then repaid to the importer after a prescribed interval. The immediate effect of the scheme is to impose an additional interest cost on the importer – the interest which he loses if he uses his own funds to finance the deposits and the interest which he pays if he obtains the necessary funds by borrowing. Presumably he will pass on this extra cost. Hence the final effect of the scheme is to raise the British-currency price of imported goods and hence to stimulate the rate of increase of the British-currency price of foreign-made importables in the period in which it is introduced.

Each of these devices has been used on one occasion in the post-war period. A temporary import surcharge was introduced in Britain in October 1964 as a short-term balance of payments measure. A charge of 15 per cent was to be levied on all imports regardless of origin, with the exception of foodstuffs, unmanufactured tobacco and basic raw materials, in addition to the normal customs duty. The charge was reduced to 10 per cent in April 1965 and was abolished altogether in November 1966. An import-deposit scheme came into force in November 1968 and is still operating at the time of writing. Initially, the scheme was restricted almost entirely to manufactured goods amounting to about one-third of total imports and required a 50 per cent deposit, repayable in 180 days.

A third possible way of boosting the rate of increase of the price of foreign-made importables in British currency is by means of a devaluation of the pound. However, in the short-run context, devaluation is a theoretical, rather than a practical, possibility.[1] There are two main reasons for this.

In the first place, under the I.M.F. agreement to which Britain subscribes, all but minor devaluations require the approval of the Fund and it is unlikely that this approval would be forthcoming if the devaluation were being proposed as a means of eliminating a purely short-run deficit.

Secondly, as a short-run weapon, devaluation suffers from the serious disadvantage that its use as a means of eliminating short-run

[1] The two post-war devaluations of sterling – in 1949 and 1967 – are to be regarded as attempts to deal with a *long*-run balance of payments deficit (see section 7.3 below).

deficits would virtually guarantee that these deficits would be larger, and hence more difficult to handle, than they would have been otherwise. For if the emergence of a deficit invariably gave rise to a widespread belief in the imminence of devaluation, as it would do if devaluation were included in the authorities' short-run armoury, speculative activity of a type that would greatly intensify the deficit would be bound to develop. For example, individuals and firms with bank deposits in Britain would send them out of the country with the intention of making an easy capital gain by bringing them back again when the expected devaluation finally occurred. Again, any British resident who had a payment to make overseas would make the payment as quickly as possible because by delaying it he would be running the risk that the amount of the payment would increase in terms of British currency as a result of the devaluation. Similarly, any overseas resident who had a payment to make in Britain would delay the payment for as long as possible in the hope that the payment would be reduced in terms of his own currency by the expected devaluation. The combined effect of these speculative activities and others of a similar nature would be to make the deficit much more serious than if there had been no question of a devaluation because the authorities were known to be unwilling even to contemplate it as a short-run weapon.

(b) *Limitations of available devices.* We turn now to the question of the limitations of the various devices for depressing the home–foreign price ratio which were discussed in the preceding subsection. In view of the remarks which we have just made about devaluation, to the effect that it is a theoretical but not a practical possibility in the short-run context, we shall confine our attention to the remaining three devices, namely the wage-freeze, the temporary import surcharge and the import-deposit scheme. Devaluation will be taken up again in the relevant (long-term) context in the next section.

At the outset we make a general point which applies to all three devices, namely that, like demand restriction, they contribute to the elimination of a short-run deficit only after a considerable lapse of time because, again like demand restriction, their immediate impact is on import demand, not on import payments. Only when the lower import demand has been translated into a lower volume of import orders, and this in turn into a lower volume of import deliveries, will there be any beneficial effects from the wage freeze, the import surcharge or the import-deposit scheme, whichever it may be.

Having made this general point, we shall now take each of the three devices in turn and discuss the limitations which are specific to that particular device.

(i) *Wage-freeze.* In the case of the British economy the main difficulty associated with the wage-freeze approach to the problem of the home–foreign price ratio is that the authorities may find it very hard to put a wage-freeze into effect. In a country like Britain it is not feasible for the authorities to impose a wage-freeze by legislation, as they can a temporary import surcharge or an import-deposit scheme. What they must do is to persuade the leaders of labour and management that a freeze is necessary and rely on them to win general acceptance for the freeze from the members of their organisations. Statutory power can help, perhaps, by reassuring those who are doing their best to implement the freeze that they will not suffer as a result. But in the end a freeze can be implemented only if most trade unionists and employers are willing to accept it voluntarily. British experience, summarised in section 10.2, would appear to indicate that they are unlikely to do so except in a period of acute external difficulty. In the British context, the wage-freeze must be regarded as a crisis weapon, not as one which can be brought into play whenever steps have to be taken to eliminate a short-run deficit. In this respect it differs from the temporary surcharge and the import-deposit scheme and also from demand restriction.

(ii) *Import surcharge.* The temporary import surcharge is subject to three main limitations as a means of depressing the home–foreign price ratio. In the first place, its effect is once-and-for-all: the imposition of a surcharge stimulates the rate of increase of the British-currency price of foreign importables in the period in which it is imposed but it has no effect on the rates of increase of subsequent periods. In this respect it differs from the wage-freeze, which has a depressing effect on the rate of increase of the price of home-produced importables for as long as it remains in force.

A second limitation of the surcharge is that its favourable effect on the home–foreign price ratio via the rate of increase of the price of foreign-made importables may be nullified, to some extent, by an unfavourable effect via the rate of increase of the price of British-made importables. There are two main ways in which this unfavourable effect may arise. In the first place, the surcharge may boost the rate of increase of the price of British-made importables by raising the cost of the imported materials which are used in their manufacture.

Secondly, it may have the same effect by raising the money wages which British producers of importables have to pay through its tendency to raise the cost of imported necessities such as tea, butter and tobacco. One of the ways of minimising this difficulty would be to exclude industrial materials and essential foodstuffs from the scope of the surcharge, as was done when the surcharge was imposed in October 1964.[1]

The third limitation of the import surcharge is that it may provoke retaliation by other countries, in which case its positive contribution to the elimination of the deficit on the import side will be offset by a negative contribution on the export side. The authorities can minimise the danger of retaliation by making the surcharge fairly small, as they did in October 1964. But of course, the smaller the surcharge the smaller its contribution to the elimination of the deficit; and the question which has to be faced is whether a surcharge which is small enough to avoid retaliation contributes enough to the solution of the problem of short-run balance for its use to be warranted, especially in view of the bad feeling between Britain and her trading partners to which, inevitably, it will give rise.

A recent econometric study of the 1964 surcharge by Johnston and Henderson (J. & H.) has shed some light on this question.[2] In outline the procedure followed by J. & H. is as follows. The first step is to set up an import function. The explanatory variables in this function are designed to take care of all 'normal' influences on the level of British imports but make no allowance for the influence (direct or indirect) of an import surcharge. Next the function is estimated from quarterly British data for the period 1955 (I) to 1964 (III) by ordinary least squares. The estimated function is then used to predict the level of imports for each of the first seven quarters beyond the sample period, i.e. for the last quarter of 1964, all four quarters of 1965 and the first two quarters of 1966, the prediction being made, in each case, by substituting the values of the explanatory variables observed for the quarter in question into the estimated import function. Finally the 'forecast error' (actual imports minus predicted imports) is calculated for each forecast.

The seven quarters for which predictions are made cover almost the entire surcharge period; and since the function generating the

---

[1] See p. 236 above.
[2] See J. Johnston and M. Henderson, 'Assessing the Effects of the Import Surcharge', *Manchester School of Economic and Social Studies* (May 1967).

predictions makes no allowance for the depressing effects of the surcharge, one would expect to find that the predictions are, in general, too high, i.e. one would expect to find a systematic tendency for the forecast error to be negative. Assuming that this proves to be the case, one can then use the forecast errors as a basis for estimating the magnitude of the depressing effect exerted on imports by the surcharge.[1] This J. & H. do.

So much for the broad approach of the study. The procedure described in the last paragraph was applied by J. & H., after much experimentation, to three distinct import functions. All three functions show a systematic tendency for negative forecast errors, thus supporting the view that the surcharge worked and that it worked in the right direction. On the other hand, all three functions suggest that the effect of the surcharge was extremely slight. By taking the algebraic total of the forecast errors to the end of 1965, J. & H. find that the 'import saving' attributable to the surcharge to the end of 1965 was £127 million for one function, £123 million for another and £156 million for the third. Thus it would appear that the import saving attributable to the surcharge to the end of 1965 was only of the order of 1 to 2 per cent of the total import bill for those five quarters.[2]

The J. & H. study raises serious doubts, therefore, as to the efficacy of a surcharge of the severity and coverage of that imposed in October 1964. Whether it would have been possible for the authorities to go further than they did on that occasion without provoking retaliation is difficult to say. It is worth noting, however, that, mild as it was, the surcharge led to strong protests from Britain's trading partners, particularly from members of the EFTA group.

(iii) *Import-deposit scheme.* As regards the third device – the introduction of an import-deposit scheme – all that needs to be said is that the first two of the three limitations attached to the import surcharge apply to the import-deposit scheme as well. Like the import surcharge the import-deposit scheme suffers from the limitation that its contribution is once-for-all and from the further limitation that it tends to raise the rate of increase of the price of British-made importables as well as foreign-made importables. The argument required to justify these statements parallels that used in connection with the

---

[1] If there proves to be no systematic tendency for negative forecast errors, the conclusion must be either that the surcharge had no effect or that its effect was perverse.

[2] See Johnston and Henderson, op. cit., pp. 100 ff.

import surcharge and it will be left to the reader to spell it out for himself.

We shall now sum up this discussion about the possibility of eliminating a short-run deficit through a reduction in the home–foreign price ratio. If the authorities decide to adopt this particular approach, they can implement their decision by employing one or more of the following devices: (i) a temporary wage-freeze; (ii) a temporary import surcharge; (iii) an import-deposit scheme. The first of these devices helps to reduce the home–foreign price ratio by checking the rate of increase of British prices, while the second and third contribute by boosting the rate of increase of foreign prices in British currency. The main limitation of the temporary wage-freeze is that it is not easy to put it into effect. By contrast, the second and third devices can be introduced without any difficulty at all; in both cases it is merely a matter of passing a simple piece of legislation. Their limitations are of a different kind. As far as the temporary import surcharge is concerned, there are three main limitations, namely that its effect is once-for-all, that it will tend to raise the price of British-made importables as well as the price of foreign-made importables and that it may well provoke retaliation. The first two of these limitations apply to the import-deposit scheme also.

3. *Increase of Short-term Interest Rates*

The third step which the British authorities can, and do, take if they set out to eliminate a short-run deficit is to raise short-term interest rates. This step may be taken in isolation or in conjunction with one or both of the other two steps which have been discussed already – demand restriction and depression of the home–foreign price ratio. As before, there are three questions to be asked about this third step, namely (i) how can it be implemented? (ii) how does it work? and (iii) what are its limitations? The answer to the first question has been given already in Chapter 6 and we turn, therefore, to the second question.

An increase in the short-term interest rates ruling in London works by increasing the attractiveness of holding short-term funds in London relative to other financial centres and decreasing the relative attractiveness of short-term borrowing in London[1] and hence causing

----

[1] This assumes that the postulated increase in the short-term rate ruling in London does not produce a corresponding increase either in the short rates ruling in other financial centres or in the cost of exchange cover or in both. In any actual

some movement of short-term funds into London and some shifting of short-term borrowing from London to other financial centres. Whereas the two steps discussed so far – demand restriction and depression of the home–foreign price ratio – work through items in the *current* account, this third step operates via the *capital* account.

As regards the third question, manipulation of interest rates may well be a useful short-run balance of payments instrument when the long-run balance of payments position is healthy, but is not likely to be particularly effective in the face of a substantial long-run deficit in the balance of payments. The reason is that, in such a situation, fear of a devaluation of sterling will be widespread; and many owners of short-term funds who would otherwise have considered it worth while to move them to London in order to obtain a higher rate of interest will be deterred from doing so because of the fear that devaluation will impose a capital loss many times greater than the income gain. Admittedly, there is the possibility of avoiding this danger of capital loss by selling sterling in the forward exchange market. However, this possibility is not likely to affect their calculations to any significant extent because, if they fear the possibility of devaluation, presumably they will also fear the possibility that an intensification of restrictions on the movement of capital by non-residents will result in a nullification of forward exchange contracts.

Evidence submitted to the Radcliffe Committee indicated that while the British authorities have made some use of the interest-rate weapon in recent years, they consider that the lack of confidence in sterling has been such as to render it largely ineffective.[1]

7.3 Long-run Deficit: Stop-gap Measures

In evidence before the Radcliffe Committee, Treasury witnesses said 'that they were now inclined to assume that resources should be found for a surplus on current account averaging about £450 mn. a year in the early 1960s'[2] to provide for an appropriate level of foreign aid, for desired long-term investment abroad and for a steady

---

situation these assumptions may not hold: the short rates ruling in other financial centres may well rise in response to a rise in the London rate if the countries concerned are themselves experiencing balance of payments difficulties, while the cost of exchange cover could also rise if the rise in London rates were to weaken foreigners' confidence in the pound and strengthen their belief in the likelihood of devaluation.

[1] See *Radcliffe Report*, paras 695–702.   [2] Ibid., para. 630.

improvement in the relationship between reserves and short-term liabilities. The Radcliffe Committee apparently regarded this figure as the most authoritative estimate available at the time, and it still seems to provide the best starting-point for a consideration of Britain's long-run balance of payments position. If we accept it, we find it difficult to escape the conclusion that in the 1960s Britain was experiencing a substantial long-run deficit in the balance of payments, according to the definition of this term put forward in section 7.1. For, in the period 1960–7, the current account balance was in surplus in only three years and the average deficit was around £115 million.[1] Admittedly there is scope for juggling with the balancing item and possibly for some transfer of items from the current account to the capital account, and this might well produce a more favourable impression than is gained by examining the current account balances as they are presented in the official estimates. But it is hard to believe that the basic conclusion (that Britain faced a substantial long-run balance of payments deficit in the 1960s) would be upset.

Various measures for eliminating Britain's long-run external deficit will be considered in the next section. Most of these measures were set in train in the 1960s, but since none of them was likely to produce quick results, it was argued, at various levels, that some form of 'stop-gap' measure was also required – a measure which would prevent further deterioration in the long-run situation while the fundamental corrective measures were taking effect. Three main candidates for this stop-gap role have been widely discussed in recent years. They are:

1. Medium-term demand restriction.
2. Medium-term import licensing and exchange control.
3. Devaluation.

We shall now consider each of these in turn.

1. *Medium-term Demand Restriction*

By 'medium-term demand restriction' we mean a reduction in aggregate demand relative to real potential gross domestic product, which lasts for just as long as is required to enable the slow-acting corrective measures to produce their full effect on the long-run situation. This may be as much as three to five years. Thus we have in mind something very different from the 'stop–go' type of demand

---

[1] See *United Kingdom Balance of Payments, 1968* (London: H.M.S.O., 1968) p. 7.

restriction dealt with in section 7.2 in connection with the short-run balance of payments problem.

The demand restriction which meets the needs of the long-term external situation may imply only *disinflation*, i.e. it may merely mean a smaller excess demand for commodities over the period concerned than would have existed otherwise. In this case it will be desirable from the internal point of view, as well as the external, and will probably be a better stop-gap measure than either import licensing or devaluation. On the other hand, it could mean *deflation* over the period concerned, either because there is no excess demand to be eliminated or because the long-run deficit is such that a demand restriction which merely eliminates excess demand will fail to do the job which is required. In this case, the demand restriction stop-gap is subject to two serious disadvantages.

In the first place, in the circumstances envisaged, it involves general unemployment over a considerable period with resulting hardship for many members of the labour force and their families. In addition it involves a welfare loss for the community as a whole, since it means that, over a period of perhaps three to five years, the level of aggregate output is below the level which could have been achieved had full use been made of available productive resources.

Secondly, when demand restriction means deflation rather than disinflation, it is likely to conflict with the fundamental corrective measures and so delay the solution of the long-run problem. We shall return to this question in the next section, but the essential point is that the measures concerned depend for their success both on a high rate of investment in fixed-capital equipment and on a willingness to abandon restrictive practices, and neither of these is likely to be generated by a long period of deflation.

2. *Medium-term Import Licensing*

The second main stop-gap measure, medium-term import licensing and exchange control, is subject to difficulties of a rather different kind. Import licensing gives added protection to domestic producers of importables, it puts existing importing firms in a monopoly position, it may cause a deterioration in the terms of trade, it is costly to administer and it involves both a loss of freedom for the consumer and the possibility of administrative corruption. Some of this is also true of exchange control (direct control over foreign capital movements by British residents and over expenditure abroad by British tourists). In particular it could be argued that exchange control means heavy administrative costs, that it tends to foster administrative corruption and that it places an undesirable limit on individual freedom. These difficulties were considered at length in Chapter 1; the conclusion reached there was that they are not likely to be particularly serious unless the controls remain in force for a considerable time. Thus how we view this alternative will depend on the length of time covered by 'medium-term'. If 'medium-term' means, say, no more than two to three years, there would appear to be little reason to reject it on purely economic grounds. On the other hand, if it will be necessary to keep the controls in force for, say, five to six years to give the fundamental correctives sufficient time to work, the case against this form of stop-gap is fairly strong – though it could be argued that, if 'medium-term' means five to six years, the case against the demand restriction alternative would be even stronger.

3. *Devaluation*

This brings us to the third main candidate for the stop-gap rule – devaluation. We shall be concerned only with the technical aspects of devaluation – with how it works and how well it works. Of course, the devaluation discussion ranges far beyond this into questions of a political and moral nature.[1] We propose to ignore these wider aspects of the problem, though the economist frequently pronounces on them and may well be justified in doing so (cf. pp. 381–2 below).

(a) *Devaluation and imports*. The traditional view of devaluation is that it fulfils the stop-gap role in two main ways: firstly by depressing import payments, in terms of foreign currency, and secondly by stimulating export receipts, in terms of foreign currency. On the import side the argument is familiar and we shall confine ourselves to a brief restatement.

Since devaluation consists of reducing the number of units of foreign currency which exchange for one unit of British currency, it must have the effect of raising the prices of all foreign-made importables in terms of British currency, except in those unlikely cases where the foreign producer reduces his price, in terms of his own currency, at least in proportion to the devaluation. For example, suppose that

---

[1] See also D. J. Coppock, 'The Alleged Case against Devaluation', *Manchester School of Economic and Social Studies* (Sep 1965) pp. 295–300, and *Radcliffe Report*, paras 708–22.

the authorities move the sterling exchange rate from $U.S. 2·4 = £1 sterling to $U.S. 2 = £1 sterling. Take a foreign-made article which can be landed in Britain for $U.S. 4·8 prior to the devaluation. This article will sell in Britain for £2 sterling prior to the devaluation. After the devaluation it will sell for something in excess of £2 sterling unless the foreign producer of the article reponds to the devaluation by reducing the price of the article in terms of his own currency by at least one-sixth, i.e. by at least $U.S. 0·8. It may well be that the foreign producer will make no reduction at all in price in terms of his own currency following the devaluation. In this case the article in question will sell in Britain for £2·4 sterling after the devaluation (4·8/2) – a rise of 20 per cent on the pre-devaluation price.

It will be the case, then, that the prices of all foreign-made importables will rise more, in terms of British currency, in the period in which a devaluation takes place than they would have done in the absence of the devaluation. Thus devaluation will boost the rate of increase of the denominator of the home–foreign price ratio in the period in which it takes place[1] and hence will tend to reduce this ratio. According to the theory of the import function presented in Chapter 3 and summarised in section 7.2 (see p. 225 above), this will mean a reduction in import demand and this, in turn, will mean a reduction in the demand for foreign currency to pay for imports. Thus, on the import side at least, there is good reason to suppose that devaluation does what it is intended to do.

(b) *Devaluation and exports.* We now take up the second part of the traditional view – that devaluation also contributes by stimulating export receipts – using Ball's model of the exporting firm, presented earlier in the chapter, as a framework.

Suppose, to begin with, that the exporting firm reduces its overseas price in proportion to the devaluation, i.e. that the devaluation has no effect on the relationship between the home price and the export price in terms of British currency. This is the usual assumption; and if the two prices are cost-based in some way, it is a sensible one. In this case the devaluation has the effect of reducing the home–foreign price ratio in the rest of the world; and according to the theory of the export function presented in section 3.4 and restated earlier in the chapter, this will result in an increase in the demand for British exports. Presumably, British firms will meet this extra demand; it

---

[1] This is subject to the qualification about price reduction in terms of foreign currency mentioned in the preceding paragraph.

would be foolish of them to reduce their overseas prices unless they intended to do so, since this would represent a pointless sacrifice of profits on their part. Given that the extra overseas demand generated by the price reductions is met by British exporters, the devaluation will mean not only an increase in the *demand* for exports but also an increase in the *actual volume* of exports. However, since by assumption the overseas price has been reduced in terms of foreign currency, this increase in export volume will not necessarily mean an increase in export receipts in terms of foreign currency. All depends on the size of the price elasticity of overseas demand. If this exceeds unity, export receipts will increase in terms of foreign currency as a result of the devaluation, whereas if the elasticity is less than unity, export receipts will fall in terms of foreign currency.

Suppose now that the exporting firm leaves the foreign price unchanged in terms of foreign currency so that it rises in terms of British currency in proportion to the devaluation. There are then two possibilities: (i) the home price may be left unchanged; or (ii) the home price may be raised in proportion to the devaluation so as to preserve the old relationship between the export price and the home price in terms of British currency.

In the first case, our model predicts that the volume of export sales will increase if some foreign demand was unsatisfied prior to the devaluation, but not otherwise (cf. examples 2 and 3, p. 228 above). In the second case, the volume of export sales will not increase unless there was unsatisfied foreign demand prior to the devaluation, but even then it may not increase: the existence of unsatisfied foreign demand is a necessary, but not a sufficient, condition for an increase in the volume of export sales in this case. Consider the following numerical examples:

	(1) Prior to devaluation	(2) After 10 per cent devaluation	(3) After 25 per cent devaluation
Domestic price	10	11	12·5
Foreign price (British currency)	15	16·5	18·75
Minimum exports	200	200	200
Domestic demand	1000	950	800
Foreign demand	500	500	500
Marginal cost at output of 1000	10	10	10
Marginal cost at output of 1050	11	11	11
Marginal cost at output of 1100	12·5	12·5	12·5
Marginal cost at output at 1150	14	14	14
Marginal cost at output of 1200	15	15	15
Marginal cost at output of 1250	16·5	16·5	16·5

Prior to the devaluation (column 1) there will be an unsatisfied foreign demand of 300 and an unsatisfied home demand of 200. After a 25 per cent devaluation (column 3), the domestic demand will be satisfied and there will be unsatisfied foreign demand of 200, i.e. the volume of export sales will rise by 100 as a result of the devaluation. On the other hand, after a 10 per cent devaluation (column 2,) there will be an unsatisfied home demand of 100 and an unsatisfied foreign demand of 300, i.e. no change in the volume of export sales following the devaluation.

To sum up, we can say that if exporting firms do not reduce their export prices in terms of foreign currency, the volume of British exports (and hence export receipts in terms of foreign currency) will not fall as a result of the devaluation and may rise. Export volume and export receipts will certainly rise if home prices are left unchanged and if there was unsatisfied foreign demand prior to the devaluation. They *may* rise if home prices are increased and if there was unsatisfied foreign demand prior to the devaluation, but need not do so.

(c) *Devaluation and the current account balance.* The upshot of the discussion so far is that while import payments are certain to fall in terms of foreign currency following a devaluation, export receipts may rise or fall or remain unchanged. Thus, while it is likely that the total impact of the devaluation on the current account balance will be favourable, it is by no means certain that this will be so.

Attempts to narrow the area of doubt take two main forms. One approach is to use a world trade model to derive the condition which must be satisfied if devaluation is to improve the current account balance of the devaluing country and then to judge on the basis of plausible values of the parameters involved in this condition whether or not devaluation is likely to be successful. Fairly simple conditions of this type have been derived and have been widely accepted and taught. However, in a recent contribution, Pearce has shown that even in the simplest model the correct condition is extremely complex,[1] and his analysis suggests that progress along this particular route is likely to be slow.

The second approach concentrates on the import side, where the *direction* of the effect is reasonably certain, and involves an attempt to measure the *size* of the effect. The best-known British study of this

[1] See I. F. Pearce, 'The Problem of the Balance of Payments', *International Economic Review* (Jan 1961).

type is the one undertaken recently by Scott.[1] We shall not enter into the details of Scott's calculations, which are particularly complicated. However, in view of the importance of his study, we propose to give a brief general account of the methods used and conclusions reached as they relate to the question in hand.

As explained earlier, devaluation helps on the import side of the current account balance by raising the price of foreign-produced importables in terms of British currency and so reducing import volume. To measure the contribution of devaluation on the import side, therefore, one must know the elasticity of demand for imports with respect to their price in terms of home currency. One of the main objects of Scott's study is to measure this elasticity for Britain. His procedure is to estimate the elasticity separately for three groups of British imports, namely food, materials and manufactures, and then to combine these three group elasticities to obtain the price elasticity of demand for British imports as a whole. We shall begin by out-lining his work on manufacturing imports,[2] which is the most novel part of the study, both as regards methods and as regards conclusions. We shall then deal rather more briefly with the work on imports of food and imports of materials and finally consider the implications of the results as a whole.

Scott begins his study of manufacturing imports by setting up log-linear demand functions for imported manufactures and home-produced manufactures respectively. The following notation is used:

M = volume of imported manufactures

P_c = volume of home-produced manufactures for sale on the home market.

$\bar{M}$ = British-currency price of imported manufactures, including duty[3]

$\bar{P}_c$ = British-currency price of home-produced manufactures

$\overline{G - H}$ = British-currency price of non-manufactures

Y = real income.

The demand functions are:[4]

$$\Delta \log M = \bar{m}_M \Delta \log \bar{M} + \bar{p}_M \Delta \log \bar{P}_c + \overline{g - h}_M \Delta \log \overline{G - H} + y_M \Delta \log Y \quad (7.1)$$

---

[1] See M. FG. Scott, *A Study of United Kingdom Imports* (Cambridge University Press, 1963).   [2] Ibid., pp. 77–85, 158–70.

[3] Note that we have simplified Scott's notation by using $\bar{M}$ for the British-currency price of imported manufactures instead of $\bar{M}M^*$. In Scott's notation, $\bar{M}$ denotes the British-currency price *excluding* duty and M^* the duty.   [4] Ibid., p. 162.

I

$$\Delta \log P_c = \overline{m}_P \Delta \log \overline{M} + \overline{p}_P \Delta \log \overline{P}_c + \overline{g - h}_P \Delta \log \overline{G - H}$$
$$+ y_P \Delta \log Y \quad (7.2)$$

where the coefficients of the explanatory variables are the respective partial elasticities, e.g. the coefficient of the home price of imported manufactures in the import-demand function $(\overline{m}_M)$ is the partial elasticity of British demand for imported manufactures with respect to their British-currency price.

Next Scott imposes the following restrictions on the coefficients of the demand functions:

$$\overline{m}_M + \overline{p}_M + \overline{g - h}_M = 1 \quad \text{and} \quad \overline{m}_P + \overline{P}_P + \overline{g - h}_P = 1 \quad (7.3)$$

$$\overline{g - h}_M = \overline{g - h}_P \quad \text{and} \quad y_M = y_P. \quad (7.4)$$

The first restriction implies that if the British-currency prices of imported manufactures, domestically produced manufactures and non-manufactures all change by some given percentage (real income remaining constant), neither the demand for imported manufactures nor the demand for home-produced manufactures will be affected. The second restriction implies that a given percentage change in either the British-currency price of non-manufactures or real income will affect the demand for imported manufactures and home-produced manufactures to the same proportionate extent.

It can be shown that together these two restrictions imply that movements in the *relative* demand for imported and home-produced manufactures are governed only by movements in relative price. The exact relationship is:[1]

$$\Delta \log \left(\frac{M}{P_c}\right) = \sigma \Delta \log \left(\frac{\overline{M}}{\overline{P}_c}\right) \quad (7.5)$$

where $\sigma = \overline{m}_M - \overline{m}_P$. It follows that if a period can be found in which the two restrictions were substantially met and in which there was no unsatisfied demand either for imported manufactures or for domestically produced manufactures, it will be possible to estimate σ by:

$$\sigma = \frac{\Delta \log M - \Delta \log P_c}{\Delta \log \overline{M} - \Delta \log \overline{P}_c}.$$

---

[1] Combining (7.3) and (7.4), we get:
$$\overline{m}_M - \overline{m}_P = \overline{p}_M - \overline{p}_P = (\text{say}) \ \sigma.$$
Subtracting (7.2) from (7.1) and using (7.4), we obtain:
$$\Delta \log M - \Delta \log P_c = (\overline{m}_M - \overline{m}_P) \Delta \log \overline{M} + (\overline{p}_M - \overline{p}_P) \Delta \log \overline{P}_c$$
$$= \sigma (\Delta \log \overline{M} - \Delta \log \overline{P}_c).$$

In Scott's view, 1930–5 was such a period and he proceeds to estimate σ from the above formula using the data for the two terminal years of this period. To obtain an estimate of $\overline{m}_M$ – the parameter of interest – he imposes a further restriction, namely:

$$\frac{\overline{m}_P}{\overline{p}_M} = \frac{M\overline{M}}{P\overline{P}} = r$$

where $M\overline{M}/P\overline{P}$ is the ratio between the outlay on imported manufactures and the outlay on domestic manufactures. Knowing σ he is then able to obtain an expression for $\overline{m}_M$ in terms of σ, $\overline{g - h}_M$ and r.[1]

Scott argues not only that 1930–5 is an appropriate period for the application of the above procedure, but also that it is the *only* one which is appropriate. Other periods have to be ruled out either because they are characterised at some point by unsatisfied demand for imports (in which case estimates of the elasticity obtained by his method will reflect changes in the availability of imports as well as price changes) or because the recorded changes in relative demands and relative prices are small enough to be attributable entirely to errors of measurement (in which case estimates obtained by Scott's or any other method would reflect nothing other than measurement error).

The price elasticity which finally emerges from Scott's calculations is – 7.[2] This is considerably higher than previous estimates obtained by least squares. However, Scott argues that the latter are bound to be low because of the extremely small movements in relative price over the sample period. As he puts it: 'The least-squares technique is likely to be misleading in these circumstances, since small divergences in relative prices can easily occur on account of errors in

[1] We have:
$$\sigma = \overline{m}_M - \overline{m}_P$$
$$= \overline{m}_M - r\overline{p}_M$$
$$= \overline{m}_M + r(\overline{m}_M + \overline{g - h}_M)$$
$$= \overline{m}_M(1 + r) + rg - h_M.$$
See Scott, op. cit., pp. 84, 161.

[2] Ibid., pp. 162, 167–8. The figure which emerges from the calculations just described is – 6·2. This is a partial elasticity and hence is based on the assumption of no change in the home price of domestic manufactures. Scott argues that a change in the home price of imported manufactures is not likely, in fact, to be accompanied by a constant price of domestic manufactures, but on the contrary is likely to induce a change in the opposite direction. The upward adjustment of the price elasticity from – 6·2 to – 7 represents an attempt to allow for this repercussion on the price of domestic manufactures.

measurement and chance concentrations of influences on particular types of goods. *These* divergences will accordingly *not* be accompanied by large quantity movements, and the "best fit" will therefore not be given by an equation with a high price elasticity.'[1]

We turn now from manufactures to the other two groups – food and materials. Here Scott's treatment is more conventional and his conclusions less startling. For the food group two estimates of the import price elasticity are presented, one based on the assumption that imported food and home-produced food are perfect substitutes and the other based on the assumption of imperfect substitutability between the two.[2] On the first assumption there is no demand for imported food as such and the import price elasticity can be obtained simply by taking a log-linear regression of total domestic food consumption on price and other relevant explanatory variables. This has been done in a number of studies of the demand for food in the United Kingdom and Scott derives his first estimate of the import price elasticity from the results of these studies.[3] If substitutability is imperfect, two demand functions are required, one for imported food and one for domestically produced food. The procedure followed in the case of manufactures is thus applicable and Scott uses it to derive his second elasticity estimate. The figure obtained in this way is -0.83.[4]

To estimate the elasticity for the third group – materials – Scott takes a log-linear regression of imports of materials on the price of imported materials and other relevant variables.[5] The elasticity which emerges (the estimated coefficient of the price of imported materials in the regression) is -0.2.[6]

The estimates for each group are brought together in the second column of Table 7.1, where they are described, following Scott, as 'best guesses'. Since these 'best guesses' are rather uncertain, Scott gives upper and lower limits for each which are set out in the first and third columns of the table.[7]

We turn now to the implications of these results for the devaluation question. If a weighted average of the three best guesses is taken, using 1957 imports as weights, a figure of -1.5 is obtained for the

---

[1] See Scott, op. cit., p. 176 (italics in original).
[2] Ibid., p. 94.   [3] Ibid., p. 97.   [4] Ibid., p. 100.
[5] This procedure assumes that imported materials and home-produced materials are perfect substitutes.
[6] See Scott, op. cit., pp. 133–46.
[7] Ibid., pp. 100, 145, 162.

price elasticity of demand for British imports as a whole.[1] Taken at its face value, this means that a 1 per cent devaluation which has no effect on import prices in terms of foreign currency will lead to a fall

TABLE 7.1

Price Elasticity Import category	Lower limit	Best guess	Upper limit
Manufactures	− 4	− 7	− 13
Food	− 0·67	− 0·83	− 0·99
Materials	0	− 0·2	− 0·6

of 1·5 per cent in the volume of British imports and hence to a fall of 1·5 per cent in Britain's total payments for imports in terms of foreign currency. This is a substantial effect. If the calculation of the combined price elasticity is based on the lower limits instead of the best guesses it would be around − 1·0, which still represents a sizeable effect.

Scott's estimates suggest that devaluation may have a substantial impact on the export side of the current account as well as on the import side. Assuming that the rest of the world's price elasticity of demand for imported manufactures is much the same as Britain's, it would appear from Scott's estimates that the price elasticity of demand for British manufactured exports could be of the order of − 7; and since British exports consist almost entirely of manufactured goods, much the same figure will apply to exports as a whole. Thus, if British manufacturers reduce their export prices in terms of foreign currency following a devaluation, as is usually assumed (cf. p. 246 above), it appears likely that the consequent reduction in her foreign currency payments for imports will be reinforced by a substantial increase in her foreign currency receipts from exports.

The broad conclusion which emerges from Scott's work, therefore, is that devaluation is almost certain to have a favourable initial impact on Britain's current account balance. However, to assess the usefulness of devaluation as a stop-gap measure, one must look beyond the impact effect and consider the possibility that the *secondary* consequences of devaluation will be such as to offset the favourable impact effect.

[1] See Scott, op. cit., Table 12, p. 49. The figure of − 0·6 used for the elasticity of the food group in this calculation is the best guess (− 0·83) after adjustment for the repercussion of the postulated change in the price of imported food on the price of home-produced food (ibid., p. 95).

The main point to be considered in this connection is that, in the absence of offsetting action, devaluation is likely to start up inflationary sequences in Britain which will tend to raise the home–foreign price ratio and hence cancel out some of the favourable impact of the devaluation.

One effect of the devaluation will be to raise the price of imported materials in terms of British currency. This will mean an increase in the unit costs of British producers and this, in turn, will mean an increase in the price of British goods. This increase in the price of British goods can be expected to lead to an increase in the general level of money wages in Britain because it will mean an increase in the wage-earner's cost of living. In turn, this increase in money wages will mean a further increase in the unit costs of British producers and hence in the price of British goods, and so on. Thus, the devaluation will initiate a continuous upward movement in the price of British goods through its effect on the price of imported materials.

A second effect of the devaluation will be to raise the British price of imported foodstuffs and other finished consumer goods. This will increase the cost of living of British workers directly and so will lead to pressure for increased money wages. This increase in money wages will mean an increase in the general level of unit cost in Britain and this, in turn, will lead to a rise in the price of British goods. This will lead to further wage increases which, in turn, will result in further price increases, and so on.[1]

Thus devaluation is likely to initiate inflationary price rises in Britain along two distinct routes; and if the initial gain to the current account is not to be lost, the authorities may need to accompany the devaluation with some type of anti-inflationary measure, such as a wage stop or demand restriction.

(d) *Devaluation: another view.* To conclude our discussion of devaluation, we shall now briefly consider a suggestion put forward recently by Pearce to the effect that the main contribution of devaluation to the solution of the long-term balance of payments problem may well be different from that which the advocates of devaluation usually envisage.[2] In outline, Pearce's argument is as follows. If internal balance exists both in the devaluing country (the home country) and in the rest of the world prior to the devaluation, and if it is to be maintained in the face of an improvement in the current

[1] Chapter 9 will contain a more rigorous discussion of these points.
[2] See Pearce, op. cit., pp. 26–8.

account balance of the devaluing country, there must be a reduction in real gross domestic expenditure in the devaluing country and an offsetting increase in the rest of the world. This follows from the fact that internal balance is defined by the condition:[1]

$$\text{Gross domestic expenditure} = Y^p + (M - E)$$

and from the fact that the exports of the devaluing country are the imports of the rest of the world; and it holds whether the devaluation is 'successful' or not. The success or otherwise of the devaluation is relevant to the size of the cut in demand in the home country but not to whether it is required.

The reduction in real domestic expenditure in the devaluing country will reduce the demand for both traded goods (exportables and importables) and non-traded goods. But whereas, in the case of traded goods, the reduction of home demand will be offset by an increase in overseas demand following the expansion of real domestic expenditure in the rest of the world, in the case of non-traded goods there will be no offset to the reduction of home demand. Consequently, there will be unemployment in the non-traded-goods sector[2] unless demand is diverted from the traded-goods sector via a fall in the price of non-traded goods relative to the price of traded goods.[3] Now devaluation produces a fall in the price of non-traded goods relative to the price of traded goods because, while it has no effect on the price of non-traded goods, it raises the price (in home currency) of foreign-produced importables and possibly the home price of exportables as well. Devaluation is required, therefore, not because of its effect on the current account balance, which may well be adverse, but because it enables an improvement in the current account balance of the devaluing country to be reconciled with internal balance both in the devaluing country and in the rest of the world and also with the avoidance of unemployment in the devaluing country due to a misdirection, as distinct from an inadequate level, of real domestic expenditure. In short, '*it may be that the success of exchange depreciation as a policy rests more upon its power to reduce*

---

[1] This is a rearrangement of: $D = Y^p + M$.

[2] Since the internal balance condition is satisfied by hypothesis, this would be due to a misdirection of demand rather than to an inadequacy of demand.

[3] To prevent this from leading to unemployment in the traded-goods sector, it may be necessary for the expansion of real gross domestic expenditure in the rest of the world to be accompanied by a rise in the relative price of non-traded goods.

the price of non-traded goods relative to those traded than upon its power to affect the real terms of trade.[1]

Suppose that a decision is made in favour of devaluation, either on the traditional grounds that it will bring about a quick, even though limited, improvement in the external position and so provide a breathing-space while more fundamental measures take effect, or on the grounds suggested by Pearce that it will reduce the hardship which would otherwise follow the demand reduction which must accompany the improvement in the external position. The question which then arises is : how large should the devaluation be ? No precise answer can be given to this question, of course, without some know-ledge of the size of the long-run deficit with which policy has to deal. What can be said, however, is that there is a strong case for avoid-ing a small devaluation, regardless of the scale of the external problem. The reason is that if the original devaluation is a small one, the belief that further devaluation is to follow is bound to be wide-spread. Consequently, as soon as short-run balance of payments difficulties emerge following the devaluation, speculative activities of a kind that will greatly intensify the short-run problem are in-evitable with the result that much more severe doses of the measures discussed in section 7.2 are likely to be required than otherwise would be the case (cf. pp. 236–7 above).[2]

On the other hand, it is probably true that the larger the original devaluation, the greater the likelihood that Britain's trade com-petitors will also devalue in an attempt to preserve their competitive position in export markets. To the extent that they do so, some of the gain that might have accrued to Britain from the devaluation will be cancelled out.

We shall now try to sum up this discussion of possible stop-gap measures. The virtue of medium-term demand restriction is that it is certain to work provided it is carried far enough. However, it involves unemployment with its attendant hardship and a cumulative loss of output which may be quite substantial if 'medium-term' means something like five years. It also tends to complicate the task of finding a genuine solution to the long-run problem. Medium-term import licensing can also be relied on to work. Again a price has to be

---

[1] Pearce, op. cit., p. 28 (italics in original).

[2] Much of the short-run balance of payments difficulty which Britain has experienced since the war has been attributable to speculative activity of this type. See *Radcliffe Report*, pp. 233–6, and J. C. R. Dow, *The Management of the British Economy, 1945–1960* (Cambridge University Press, 1964) pp. 89–90, 95–8.

paid in the form of undesirable side effects, particularly side effects of an allocational character. However, the price is unlikely to be as high as that exacted by demand restriction, especially if 'medium-term' means a period as short as, say, two to three years. As for devaluation, it now seems reasonably certain in the light of recent empirical work that the impact effect will be substantial in the British case. But this does not mean that devaluation is certain to work. For one thing there is the possibility of retaliation. This is much more likely to occur in the case of devaluation than in the case of demand restriction and import licensing because retaliation will not involve an obvious cost to the retaliating country in the case of devaluation as it will in the case of demand restriction and import licensing. Secondly, there is the point that devaluation is bound to start up inflationary sequences which will undermine the favourable impact effect to some extent unless appropriate offsetting action is taken.

Of the three possibilities, therefore, medium-term import licensing appears to be the most satisfactory, given that the fundamental corrective measures will produce most of their effect inside about three years. If this condition does not hold, devaluation may be preferable. Medium-term demand restriction appears to be the least desirable alternative whatever the period covered by 'medium-term'.

7.4 Long-run Deficit: Corrective Measures

In section 7.1 we defined a long-run balance of payments deficit, in the British context, as a situation in which, on the average over a long run of years, the current account balance is insufficient, without direct control over foreign transactions, to provide for the desired level of long-term foreign investment, for an appropriate level of foreign aid and for a reasonably rapid improvement in the ratio of reserves to short-term liabilities. If the desired average level of foreign aid and the desired rate of improvement in the reserves–liabilities ratio are taken as given, and if more or less permanent direct controls over foreign transactions are ruled out, it follows from this definition that the measures which can be used by the British authorities to correct a long-run deficit are of two kinds:

1. Measures, other than import licensing, designed to increase the long-run average level of the current account balance.
2. Measures, other than exchange controls, designed to reduce the average desired level of long-term foreign investment.

We shall now consider each of these possibilities in turn. In effect, what we shall be doing is to describe the policy package which successive British Governments have adopted to deal with Britain's long-term balance of payments problem.

1. *Current Account*

(a) *Government expenditure overseas.* The most direct way of increasing the average current account balance open to the British authorities is to bring about a continuous reduction in the overseas current expenditure of the central government itself. If foreign-aid grants are excluded, the only effective means of doing this is through a continuous reduction in military expenditure overseas. This can be achieved, to some extent, by eliminating wasteful expenditure and by improving the efficiency of overseas military bases. However, no substantial reduction in Britain's military expenditure overseas seems possible without a scaling-down of her international commitments; and since this is bound to take a considerable time, no dramatic results can be expected from this particular measure in the medium run.

(b) *Export promotion.* In common with most governments, the British Government now provides a great deal of direct assistance to British exporters. This takes a variety of forms. For example, the Board of Trade provides free advice to exporters on all aspects of selling abroad and gives financial and other support to overseas 'trade fairs', 'British Weeks' and similar activities designed to advertise British products abroad. Again, through an autonomous government department, the Export Credits Guarantee Department, the Government provides exporters with insurance against many of the risks involved in selling overseas which are not normally covered by commercial insurers, e.g. insolvency of the buyer, imposition of new import-licensing restrictions in the buyer's country, action on the part of the buyer's government which delays payment to the exporter, and so on. The Export Credits Guarantee Department also assists in the financing of exports by guaranteeing loans made by British banks and other financial institutions to overseas purchasers of British products, particularly long-term loans for the purchase of large capital goods. As a further example one might mention the tax concessions which are available to exporters in the form of a refund of some of the indirect taxation borne by exports.

Thus, a second way in which the authorities can help to raise the average current account balance is by continuously extending these types of direct assistance to exporters and also by making exporters better informed about the help which is available to them at any one time.

(c) *Competitive position of British firms.* The third and most important way of improving the average level of the current account balance in the long run is by strengthening the long-run competitive position of British firms. By strengthening the competitive position of *im*portable producers the authorities will help to check the long-run growth of import volume, while by strengthening the competitive position of *ex*portable producers they will help to stimulate the long-run growth of export volume. Either way they will help to raise the long-run average level of the current account balance.

By 'the competitive position of British firms' is meant the attractiveness of the terms which British firms offer to purchasers relative to the attractiveness of terms offered by their foreign rivals – foreign rivals in the home market in the case of importable producers and foreign rivals in overseas markets in the case of exportable producers. To 'strengthen' the competitive position of British firms, then, is to make the terms which they offer relatively more attractive. This can be done in a variety of ways: by a relative improvement in quality in the widest sense; by a relative improvement in after-sales services; by a relative reduction in delivery delay; and by a relative reduction in price. Thus the policy measures that we are now concerned with are measures directed towards achieving a long-run relative improvement in the quality of British products and in the after-sales service offered by British firms and a long-run reduction in relative delivery delay and in relative price. We propose to concentrate on the last of these (long-run reduction in relative price), not because the terms relating to quality, after-sales service and delivery delay are unimportant but rather because they constitute a part of the total terms offered which cannot be easily influenced by policy action in the long run.

To produce a long-run decrease in the prices quoted by British firms, relative to those quoted by their foreign rivals, the authorities must check the long-run rate of increase of British prices – the rate of increase of foreign prices is, of course, beyond their control. This, in turn, requires a check to the rate of increase of unit production costs or to the rate of increase of profit margins or both. As regards the first, there is one important source of increase in the unit production costs of British firms which is beyond the control of the British authorities, namely increase in the unit cost of imported materials. However, the main source of increase can certainly be stopped up by policy action. We refer to increase in unit labour cost. To check the long-run rate of increase in unit labour cost (wage and salary earnings per man ÷ output per man), the authorities must either check the rate of increase of money wage and salary earnings per man or stimulate the rate of increase of output per man or both.

To sum up the discussion so far, we can say that if the British authorities wish to effect a long-run decrease in the prices quoted by British firms relative to those quoted by their foreign rivals, as a means of strengthening the competitive position of British firms and so of raising the average level of the current account balance, they must do one or more of the following: (i) check the rate of increase of the profit margins of British firms over the long run; (ii) check the long-run rate of increase of money wage and salary earnings per man in Britain; (iii) stimulate the long-run rate of increase of output per man in Britain. Policy directed towards (i) and (ii) has now become known as 'prices and incomes policy' and will be the subject of detailed discussion in Chapter 10. Here we shall confine ourselves to a brief discussion of some of the measures which the British authorities can adopt (and which, to a large extent, they have already adopted) to raise the rate of increase of British productivity over the long run.

There are six main sources of long-term increase in labour productivity, namely: (i) increase in fixed-capital input per unit of labour input; (ii) improvement in the quality of fixed-capital input; (iii) improvement in the quality of labour input; (iv) increase of knowledge relevant to production; (v) decrease in the extent of restrictive practices; (vi) fuller realisation of economies of scale. If the authorities are to raise the long-run rate of increase of labour productivity as a means of strengthening the competitive position of British firms, they must find ways of exploiting these sources of increase. What are the possibilities?

To *raise the fixed-capital input* accompanying each unit of labour input the authorities must obviously stimulate investment in fixed-capital equipment. The analysis of section 4.2 suggests that the most effective way of doing this is to ensure, by appropriate management of aggregate demand, that real gross domestic product is kept on a rapidly rising long-run path.

To stimulate improvement in *the quality of the fixed-capital input*, the authorities must attempt to narrow the gap between the existing technology and the best-known technology. One way of doing this is by reducing the average age of the stock of fixed capital. This, in turn, requires an increase in the ratio of fixed-capital investment to the stock of fixed capital. Thus stimulation of fixed-capital investment by means of a rapidly rising gross domestic product is relevant in this connection also. Another way of narrowing the gap between the existing and the best-known technology is to encourage those forms of new capital inflow which bring up-to-date technology into Britain with them, particularly inflow associated with the establishment of subsidiaries of technologically advanced overseas firms, in this country.

An obvious way of stimulating *improvement in the quality of labour input* is by increasing the length and raising the quality of education. A less obvious way is by improving the health of the labour force through an extension of public health activities, through the provision of cheap, nutritional food in schools and industrial canteens, through an increase in the level of medical and other social service benefits and through an increase in the size and quality of the housing stock. The last of these requires that housing investment be stimulated, and from the analysis of section 4.3 it would appear that the best way of providing the necessary stimulus to private housing investment is to ensure that disposable income is kept on a rapidly rising long-run path by appropriate management of aggregate demand.

An *increase of knowledge relevant to production* requires an extension of technical research in the usual sense and also of research into organisational and managerial problems. The authorities can help to bring this about directly, by extending the research of this type being done in government research establishments, and indirectly, by encouraging technical and managerial research in industrial laboratories and universities through the provision of finance, the granting of tax concessions and other similar means.

One way of *reducing the scope of restrictive practices* is by means of restrictive practices legislation of the type now in force in the United Kingdom and in most advanced industrial countries. In addition, however, it is necessary to remove the fear of loss of income and employment which constitutes the main reason for the existence of these practices. This can be done only by ensuring through appropriate management of demand that full employment and rising incomes are generally regarded as the normal state of affairs.

Finally, the authorities can help to *promote a fuller realisation of economies of scale* partly by undertaking studies designed to discover where, and to what extent, unexploited scale economies exist and partly by encouraging various forms of industrial reorganisation which will enable known economies to be realised, e.g. mergers and standardisation of products.

It will be recalled that, in the previous section, we observed that one disadvantage of medium-term demand restriction as a stop-gap measure is that it conflicts to some extent with the corrective measures and so delays the solution of the long-run external problem. We can now see why this is so. The elimination of the long-run deficit in the British balance of payments requires, among other things, a strengthening of the competitive position of British firms. This requires, among other things, a higher long-run rate of increase of labour productivity in Britain. But, as our brief discussion of the sources of productivity increase makes clear, this will be difficult to achieve if aggregate demand is so managed that real gross domestic product is kept below the potential level, and allowed to rise only slowly within the limits set by the growth of potential gross product, over a period of, perhaps, three to five years – which is what the 'medium-run demand reduction' alternative implies. From the point of view of long-run productivity increase, what is required is the exact opposite of this – a situation in which real gross domestic product is kept rising at a rapid rate on, or if necessary above, the potential gross product path and in which there is no uncertainty about future income and employment.

2. *Capital Account*

At the outset of the present section we said that, in order to correct a long-run deficit in the balance of payments, the authorities must do one (or both) of two things: they must either take steps to increase the average level of the current account balance, or they must take steps to reduce the average desired level of net long-term capital outflow. We have now dealt with the first and it remains to consider the second.

The authorities can reduce the average desired level of net long-term capital outflow either directly, by reducing *official* long-term investment overseas, or indirectly, by altering the tax structure so as to make *private* long-term investment overseas less attractive than before. The first of these two possibilities is straightforward but the second requires some elaboration. To illustrate the sorts of tax changes which may help to reduce the average level of private long-term investment overseas, we shall refer to the changes made in the budget of April 1965.

There were three main changes in the 1965 budget. In the first place, there was a revision in the company-tax arrangements. Prior to the 1965 budget, resident British companies were liable for income tax at the standard rate of 8s. 3d. in the £, on all profits, and for profits tax at the rate of 15 per cent. In the 1965 budget this was changed in two ways. Firstly, income tax on distributed profits was now to be paid by the dividend-receiver himself rather than by the company. Secondly, the two taxes on company profits were replaced by a single tax known as corporation tax. The rate of corporation tax was originally fixed at 35 per cent, this being the rate which, it was estimated, would produce the same yield as the 15 per cent profits tax *plus* income tax at the standard rate on undistributed profits. Later the rate was raised to 40 per cent.

One of the results of the introduction of the corporation tax was to create a bias against the earning of overseas profits. To see how this came about, it must be recalled that under the so-called 'double-tax arrangements' a British company which earns profits overseas can offset the tax which it pays on these profits to the overseas government concerned, against its tax liability to the British Government. This means that the tax burden applying to profits earned overseas will be the same as (heavier than) that applying to profits earned in Britain if the liability for tax on these profits to the British Government exceeds (falls short of) the liability to the overseas government. Under the company-tax arrangements which operated prior to the 1965 budget, the liability for British tax was usually the greater of the two, i.e. the tax burden applying to profits earned by British companies overseas was usually the same as that applying to profits earned in Britain. After the 1965 budget this was no longer the case. Since the rates of tax levied on profits by overseas governments usually exceeded the maximum rate of corporation tax, the tax burden applying to profits earned overseas (the foreign tax liability) was now normally greater than that applying to profits earned in Britain (the British corporation tax). Thus, a bias against overseas profits was introduced into the tax structure and presumably this led some British companies to expand their British operations more, and their foreign operations less, than they would have done otherwise. To this extent the tax change tended to depress the average level of direct overseas investment and, *ceteris paribus*, the level of Britain's net long-term capital outflow.

A second tax change announced in the 1965 budget related to the relief for underlying tax granted to United Kingdom residents receiving dividends from abroad. Prior to the 1965 budget a United Kingdom resident who received dividends on shares held in a foreign company was not required to pay the full British income tax on these dividends, since he was given rebate for the profits tax already paid by the foreign company to the foreign government concerned, i.e. he was given relief in respect of the 'underlying tax'. Under the revised company-tax arrangements just discussed, this was a more favourable position than that of a United Kingdom resident receiving dividends from a British company because, under the new company-tax arrangements, such a United Kingdom resident was to be given no credit for the corporation tax paid by that company to the British Government. Thus the revised company-tax arrangements created a tax bias in favour of portfolio investment overseas. To remove this bias the Chancellor withdrew the relief from underlying tax hitherto granted to United Kingdom residents receiving dividends from abroad, and announced that he would attempt to renegotiate the relevant double-tax agreements to permit its withdrawal in the remaining cases. The effect of this particular tax change was therefore to make the average level of overseas portfolio investment, and hence the level of long-term capital outflow as a whole, less than it would have been otherwise.

Finally, the 1965 budget removed the tax bias in favour of the Overseas Trade Corporations which had previously been exempt from profits tax and enjoyed special concessions not granted to other companies in relation to income tax. The effect was to reduce the long-term capital outflow associated with the Overseas Trade Corporation scheme below what it would have been otherwise.

If the average level of net long-term capital outflow is reduced, either directly, or indirectly through tax changes of the type just described, the size of the current account balance which is required, on average over a long run of years, to provide for long-term capital outflow, foreign aid and an improvement to the ratio of reserves to short-term liabilities, will also be reduced. To that extent, the long-run balance of payments deficit will fall. On the other hand, the reduction in long-term capital outflow may itself reduce the average current account balance: and to the extent that it does so the long-run deficit will rise. The 'net' decrease in the long-run deficit may therefore be less than the 'gross' decrease if this particular approach is employed. This point is likely to assume maximum importance in the case where the reduction in the average level of long-term capital outflow takes the form of a reduction in the average level of *direct overseas investment*, and we shall concentrate on this case from now on.

The essence of the problem can be brought out in the following way. Suppose that the reduction in the average level of long-term capital outflow is effected by making direct overseas investment in all future years £100 less than it would have been otherwise. Consider the first year of the new policy, year 0. The reduction of £100 in direct overseas investment in that year will have an *initial* effect on the current account balance (an effect which is confined to the year in question) and a series of *continuing* effects (effects which are felt in all subsequent years).

The initial effect will take the form of a reduction of £x in British machinery exports in year 0 compared with what they would have been otherwise. The idea here is that some of the £100 of forgone direct overseas investment would have been used by the overseas subsidiaries concerned to purchase machinery from Britain and that these purchases will no longer take place.

The main continuing effects may be listed as follows:

(i) The decrease of £100 in direct investment coupled with the decrease of £x in exports will mean either an increase of £$(100 - x)$ in reserves in year 0 or an increase of £$(100 - x)$ in overseas assets or a decrease of £$(100 - x)$ in overseas liabilities, compared with the alternative position. If we assume that some combination of the second and third possibilities eventuates, there will be a reduction of £y per year in the net interest payable overseas in all subsequent years.

(ii) Assuming that all of the after-tax profits that would have been earned on the £100 of forgone direct overseas investment would have been repatriated, net profits received from abroad will be less than they would have been by £p per year in all subsequent years.

(iii) There will be a reduction of £z per year in all subsequent years in British exports (visible and invisible). This will take the form partly of a reduction in exports of materials, components and other input items, partly of a reduction in exports of finished goods and partly of a reduction in services.

The effects of the new policy in the first five years of its operation can now be summarised in tabular form as follows:

TABLE 7.2

	(1) Reduction in direct investment overseas ('gross' reduction in deficit)	(2) Reduction in current account balance	(3) (1)–(2) 'net' reduction in deficit
Year 0	100	x	$(100 - x)$
Year 1	100	$x + (z + p - y)$	$100 - (x + z + p - y)$
Year 2	100	$x + 2(z + p - y)$	$100 - (x + 2z + 2p - 2y)$
Year 3	100	$x + 3(z + p - y)$	$100 - (x + 3z + 3p - 3y)$
Year 4	100	$x + 4(z + p - y)$	$100 - (x + 4z + 4p - 4y)$

From this table we can see that, on the average of the first five years, the 'gross' decrease in the external deficit is £100 per annum. On the other hand, the 'net' decrease is:

$$100 - \frac{(5x + 10z + 10p - 10y)}{5}.$$

The second term in this expression could conceivably be negative, but this does not seem at all likely, i.e. it seems clear that, on the average of the first five years, the 'net' effect of the new policy will be less than the 'gross' effect.

It is also clear from the above argument that the gap between the gross effect and the net effect must grow with time, so that if we were to take averages over, say, ten years instead of five years, the new policy would appear in a still less favourable light.

To obtain some idea of the quantitative significance of the point under discussion, one needs estimates of x, z, p and y. The most recent estimates are those found in the two Reddaway reports,[1] which are based on information relating to the period 1955–64 supplied by British manufacturing companies with overseas subsidiaries. We shall now give a brief account of these estimates.

The estimate for x was £11. This was obtained by using the questionnaire replies to substitute in the formula:

[1] See W. B. Reddaway, in collaboration with J. O. N. Perkins, S. J. Potter and C. T. Taylor, *Effects of U.K. Direct Investment Overseas: An Interim Report* (Cambridge University Press, 1967) (to be cited as *Interim Report*), and W. B. Reddaway, in collaboration with S. J. Potter and C. T. Taylor, *Effects of U.K. Direct Investment Overseas: Final Report* (Cambridge University Press, 1968) (to be cited as *Final Report*).

$$x = 100 \left[\frac{\text{Hypothetical annual reduction in purchases of British capital goods by subsidiaries consequent on operation under non-British ownership}}{\text{Observed annual increase in net operating assets}} \right].$$

The figure for the denominator in this expression was obtained, of course, direct from the questionnaire replies. The numerator represents the annual purchases of British capital goods actually made by the subsidiaries over the ten-year period *less* the annual purchases which they *would have* made had they been operating under some form of non-British ownership. The figure for the first term in the numerator was obtained direct from the questionnaire replies. To obtain the figure for the second term it was assumed:

(i) that had the subsidiaries not been operating under British ownership during the decade in question, they would have been operating at the same level under some other form of ownership – either with 100 per cent local capital, or with 100 per cent overseas non-British capital, or with some combination of local and overseas capital, i.e. that there would have been 100 per cent 'substitute production';

(ii) that had the subsidiaries embodied entirely *local capital* instead of being in British ownership, they would have reduced their purchases of British-made capital goods hardly at all; and

(iii) that had the subsidiaries embodied entirely *non-British overseas capital* instead of being in British ownership, they would have reduced their purchases of British capital goods virtually to zero. These assumptions enabled the researchers to say, for each subsidiary, that the hypothetical reduction in purchases of British-made capital goods consequent on expansion at the observed rate under non-British ownership was somewhere between zero and the purchases which it actually made in the relevant ten-year period, the exact position in the range depending on the mix of local, and overseas non-British, capital which the subsidiary would have embodied in the alternative situation. Having fixed the purchases of each subsidiary for the alternative situation on this basis, the hypothetical figure for the subsidiaries as a whole was found by straight addition of the individual figures.[1]

[1] For further details, see *Interim Report*, chap x and appendix E. The estimate given in *Interim Report* was £9, but this was raised to £11 in *Final Report*. See *Interim Report*, p. 127, and *Final Report*, pp. 233–4, 346.

For y (the annual reduction in net interest payable overseas consequent on the reduction of £100 in direct overseas investment in year 0), an estimate of a little under £2¾ was obtained, by applying a rate of 3 per cent to £89, i.e. £$(100 - x)$.[1]

To estimate p (the annual reduction in net profits received from abroad consequent on the £100 reduction in direct overseas investment in year 0), the *accounting* post-tax rate of profit on the total net operating assets of the subsidiaries as a whole was determined for the 1955–64 period. This rate was then adjusted from an accounting (historical-cost) basis to a replacement-cost basis and a further adjustment was made to eliminate inventory profits. The figure arrived at in this way was a little over £5¼[2].

To estimate z (the *continuing* annual reduction in British exports consequent on the £100 reduction in direct overseas investment in year 0), visible exports and invisible exports were considered separately. The continuing effect on *visible* exports (input items and finished goods) was estimated by means of the same procedure, in particular by use of the same assumptions, as employed to estimate the initial effect – the reduction in exports of capital goods in year 0 itself. The figure which emerged was £1. To estimate the continuing effect on invisible exports, separate estimates were made for 'freight, etc.', 'management fees, royalties, etc.', 'licensing fees' and 'other'. By and large these estimates were little better than guesses, e.g. the 'freight, etc.' item was estimated simply by taking a figure of 5 per cent of the continuing effect on visible exports. When combined, these separate estimates gave a figure of £½. The estimate for z itself was therefore £1½.[3]

Earlier we presented a formula showing the average 'net' decrease in the external deficit which would follow an annual reduction of £100 in direct overseas investment. This formula related to the first five years of the new policy. By substituting the Reddaway estimates for x, z, p and y in this formula, we reach the conclusion that, on the average of the first five years of the new policy, the 'net' decrease in the external deficit would be £81 as compared with a 'gross' decrease of £100. Substitution in the corresponding formula for the first *ten* years of the new policy shows that the average 'net' decrease would be £71, i.e. about 30 per cent less than the gross decrease. These

[1] See *Final Report*, pp. 276–8, 346.
[2] See *Interim Report*, pp. 96–9, and *Final Report*, pp. 272–5, 346.
[3] See *Interim Report*, chap. xii and appendix E, and *Final Report*, p. 346.

figures suggest that efforts to correct Britain's long-run balance of payments deficit by reducing the desired level of direct overseas investment may be a good deal less helpful than would appear at first sight.

Moreover, the list of effects presented above, and the Reddaway arithmetic which parallels them, is by no means complete. For example, the calculations take no account of the fact that the reductions in direct investment overseas, while improving the British long-run balance of payments position, will worsen the long-run balance of payments position of the overseas countries concerned, unless the 'substitute production' is financed 100 per cent by non-British, foreign capital. This deterioration in the external position of the recipient countries may lead them to take steps to reduce their imports; and in this event British exports would suffer both directly and also indirectly through the adverse consequences of the import-restricting measures on the external position of third countries. If proper account were to be taken of this and other similar effects of a reduction in British direct investment overseas, the approach to the restoration of the long-run external balance via the capital account would probably appear even less effective than it does on the basis of the Reddaway calculations as they stand. In fact, if may well be that reduction of long-term overseas investment is best regarded less as a corrective measure than as a stop-gap which is to be retained only until the corrective measures have taken effect.

7.5 Summary

To correct a *short-run* balance of payments deficit, the British authorities must take one or more of the following steps: (1) restrict aggregate demand; (2) depress the home–foreign price ratio; and (3) reduce short-term interest rates. Steps (1) and (2) work by reducing the demand for foreign currency to pay for imports and, in the case of (2), by increasing the receipts of foreign currency from the sale of exports. By contrast, step (3) works through capital account items.

Step (2) can be implemented in one or more of the following three ways: (i) by means of a temporary wage-freeze; (ii) by means of a temporary import surcharge; (iii) by means of an import-deposit scheme. All three approaches have been tried by the British authorities in the post-war period.

To eliminate a *long-run* deficit the authorities must take measures of a more fundamental kind. It follows from the definition of 'long-run deficit' that the measures taken must be designed: (1) to increase the long-run average level of the current account balance; and/or (2) to reduce the long-run average level of net capital outflow. In the first group would appear measures aimed at reducing the long-run average level of government spending abroad, measures designed to improve the long-run competitive position of British producers and measures designed to extend the scope and quality of direct government assistance to British exporters. The second group would cover changes in the tax structure designed to weaken the incentive for British residents to undertake portfolio and direct investment overseas.

Since none of the corrective measures discussed in the preceding paragraph are likely to produce quick results, it may be necessary to support them by some 'stop-gap' measure designed merely to prevent a further deterioration in the long-run position while they are taking effect. The three main candidates for the role are: (1) medium-run demand restriction; (2) medium-run import controls; and (3) devaluation. The main disadvantage of (1) is that it may involve unemployment with its attendant hardship and waste of resources, while (2) suffers from the limitation that it has undesirable allocational effects which may be significant if the controls remain in force for a considerable time. The difficulty with (3) is that it invites retaliation and may therefore fail to work.

Of the three, import controls are probably the most satisfactory alternative if it seems likely that the correctives will start to 'bite' in a fairly short time – say about two to three years. Otherwise, devaluation has the strongest claim despite doubts about its efficacy.

READING LIST

Ball, R. J., 'Credit Restriction and the Supply of Exports', *Manchester School o Economic and Social Studies* (May 1961).
——, Eaton, J. R., and Steuer, M. D., 'The Relationship between United Kingdom Export Performance in Manufactures and the Internal Pressure of Demand', *Economic Journal* (Sep 1966).
Cooper, R. N., 'The Balance of Payments', in Caves, R. E., and Associates, *Britain's Economic Prospects* (London: Allen & Unwin, 1968).
Coppock, D. J., 'The Alleged Case against Devaluation', *Manchester School of Economic and Social Studies* (Sep 1965).

Johnston, J., and Henderson, M., 'Assessing the Effects of the Import Surcharge', *Manchester School of Economic and Social Studies* (May 1967).

Manser, W. A. P., 'The Reddaway Report – Not the Last Word on Foreign Investment', *Westminster Bank Review* (Aug 1967).

Pearce, I. F., 'The Problem of the Balance of Payments', *International Economic Review* (Jan 1961).

Perkins, J. O. N., 'The Reddaway Report and Australia', *Australian Economic Papers* (Dec 1967).

Reddaway, W. B., in collaboration with Perkins, J. O. N., Potter, S. J., and Taylor, C. T., *Effects of U.K. Direct Investment Overseas: An Interim Report* (Cambridge University Press, 1967).

——, in collaboration with Potter, S. J., and Taylor, C. T., *Effects of U.K. Direct Investment Overseas: Final Report* (Cambridge University Press, 1968).

Scott, M. FG., *A Study of United Kingdom Imports* (Cambridge University Press, 1963).

PART THREE

Price Stability and Economic Growth

8 The Inflationary Process: Market-Clearing Approach

8.1 Introduction

We come now to the third of our four objectives, the objective of price stability. This was defined in Chapter 1 in a negative way as absence of a persistent upward movement in some appropriate price index. Our ultimate aim in this chapter and the next two is to consider what steps the British authorities can take to promote price stability in this sense. Before we can do this, however, we must clearly have some explanation of how the persistent upward movements in the price level, which constitute absence of price stability, actually come about. One explanation of this phenomenon will be examined in the present chapter and an alternative explanation, which seems more satisfactory for the British economy, in the next. Both of these explanations are strictly short-run in character, i.e. they purport to account for a continuous upward movement in the chosen price index short period by short period (say, month by month or quarter by quarter) over a short reaction interval (say, two or three years), rather than, say, year by year over twenty years (see section 2.2).

8.2 The Keynesian Model of the Inflationary Process

The explanation of the inflationary process to be discussed in this chapter may be termed the Keynesian explanation, since the underlying model is a simple adaptation of the familiar Keynesian 'multiplier' model – Model I of Chapter 2. Our first task is to present this model and to consider its relationships in detail. Before undertaking this task, however, we shall give a brief outline of the Keynesian explanation so that its essential features will be clear at the outset. An initial stationary equilibrium is postulated in which there is equality between aggregate demand and real G.D.P. (gross domestic product) and in which real G.D.P. is at the capacity level.[1] It is assumed that this equilibrium is disturbed by a once-for-all autonomous increase in aggregate demand. It is then shown that the resulting excess of aggregate demand over real G.D.P. will give rise to a cumulative upward movement in G.D.P. in terms of current prices. *Real* G.D.P., however, will remain fixed after the disturbance, since, by assumption, it is already at the capacity level when the disturbance occurs, and since capacity real G.D.P. can be taken as fixed over a short reaction interval. In this way a continuous upward movement in the ratio of G.D.P. in current prices to G.D.P. in constant prices is demonstrated. In other words, it is shown that the implicit G.D.P. deflator will exhibit a definite upward trend: absence of price stability is accounted for.

For a more detailed, formal treatment of the Keynesian explanation, we begin by considering the model on which the whole explanation rests.[2]

First, take the *simplifying assumptions*. The main assumptions are:
  (i) that the economy is closed;
  (ii) that there is no government fiscal activity;
  (iii) that no inventories are held.

Let us turn next to the *relationships*. The relationships of the model are as follows:

$$P_t = \frac{Y_t^*}{Y_t} \tag{8.1}$$

$$C_t^* = a + b Y_{t-1}^* \tag{8.2}$$

$$I_t^* = I_t P_{t-1} \tag{8.3}$$

$$Y_t^* = C_t^* + I_t^*. \tag{8.4}$$

Here, C^* and I^* denote, respectively, desired consumption expenditure and investment expenditure in terms of current prices, Y^* realised G.D.P. at factor cost in terms of current prices, Y realised G.D.P. at factor cost in terms of constant prices, I desired investment expenditure in terms of constant prices and P the implicit deflator of G.D.P. at factor cost (cf. p. 21, n. 1 above) – the price index whose upward movement we wish to explain. Let us consider these relationships in turn.

The first relationship defines the price index whose movement is to

---

[1] See section 1.5 above for the definition of capacity gross domestic product.
[2] This is not the only 'Keynesian' model which has appeared in the literature. Others will be found in the references given at the end of the chapter.

be explained as the implicit deflator of G.D.P. at factor cost. The second relationship is the current-price version of the real consumption function of the Keynesian multiplier model (relationship (2.1)). It implies that consumers are subject to 'money illusion' in the sense that desired real consumption expenditure falls in the course of the inflationary process even though real G.D.P. remains fixed. We can see this without difficulty if we divide through by P_{t-1}. We then get:

$$\frac{C_t^*}{P_{t-1}} = \frac{a}{P_{t-1}} + b\frac{Y_{t-1}^*}{P_{t-1}} = \frac{a}{P_{t-1}} + bY_{t-1}.$$

If we assume that consumers fix desired expenditure for period t on the assumption that prices in period t will be the same as in period $(t-1)$, we can identify the left-hand side of this expression with the desired real consumption expenditure of period t. According to the expression, this equals a constant (bY_{t-1}) plus an amount (a/P_{t-1}) which declines as the price index rises. In other words, the expression implies that desired real consumption expenditure will show a continuous decline in the course of the inflationary process, despite the constancy of real G.D.P.

The third relationship defines the desired real investment expenditure of period $t(I_t)$ as the desired investment expenditure of period t in current prices (I_t^*) divided by the price index for period $(t-1)$. It implies, therefore, that in fixing desired expenditure in current prices for period t, investors act on the assumption that prices ruling in period $(t-1)$ will continue into period t.

Finally, relationship (8.4) embodies a view about price determination. The nature of this view becomes clear if we divide through by P_{t-1}. We then obtain:

$$\frac{Y_t^*}{P_{t-1}} = \frac{C_t^* + I_t^*}{P_{t-1}}.$$

Since $Y_t^* = Y_t P_t$, this can be written as:

$$\frac{Y_t P_t}{P_{t-1}} = \frac{C_t^* + I_t^*}{P_{t-1}}.$$

Finally, dividing through by Y_t, we get:

$$\frac{P_t}{P_{t-1}} = \frac{C_t^* + I_t^*}{P_{t-1}} \frac{1}{Y_t}. \tag{8.5}$$

Relationship (8.5) implies that the ratio of the price index in period t to the price index in period $(t-1)$ is equal to the ratio of aggregate demand in period $t[(C_t^* + I_t^*)/P_{t-1}]$ to real G.D.P. in period $t(Y_t)$.[1] Put another way, the implication is that the ratio of increase in prices between period $(t - 1)$ and period t is equal to the ratio between the claims which are made on output in period t and the output which is available to meet those claims. Thus if the claims on output are, say, 10 per cent greater than output in period t, the price index will rise by 10 per cent in the period. On the other hand, if there is no excess of claims on output over available output, there will be no price rise. Prices rise if and only if claims on output are in excess of the output which is available to meet those claims. In short, (8.5) (and hence (8.4)) implies either that all prices are 'auction-market' prices or that they behave as if they were.

Alternatively, the point can be made in terms of the concept of unsatisfied demand. The general definition of the unsatisfied demand of any period (UD) is:

$$(UD)_t = (D_t - I_t^i) - (Y_t + M_t + V_t)$$

where V_t denotes realised real inventory disinvestment (cf. p. 69 above).[2] For the special case of a closed economy with no inventories (see assumptions (i) and (iii) above), this takes the simple form:

$$(UD)_t = D_t - Y_t = \frac{C_t^* + I_t^*}{P_{t-1}} - Y_t. \tag{8.6}$$

Dividing (8.6) through by Y_t, we get an expression for *relative* unsatisfied demand, i.e. unsatisfied demand as a proportion of real G.D.P., namely:

$$\frac{(UD)_t}{Y_t} = \frac{C_t^* + I_t^*}{P_{t-1}} \cdot \frac{1}{Y_t} - 1.$$

Now returning to (8.5) and using this expression for relative unsatisfied demand, we find that:

$$\frac{P_t - P_{t-1}}{P_{t-1}} = \frac{C_t^* + I_t^*}{P_{t-1}} \cdot \frac{1}{Y_t} - 1 = \frac{(UD)_t}{Y_t}. \tag{8.7}$$

This expression (and hence 8.4)) implies that $(P_t - P_{t-1})/P_{t-1}$ will be positive in any period, i.e. that prices will rise if and only if unsatisfied demand is positive in the period, and further that the price rise, in

---

[1] See assumptions (i) and (ii) above. Note that both aggregate demand and real G.D.P. are expressed in initial equilibrium prices.

[2] Unsatisfied demand must be distinguished from *excess* demand (H), which is defined by: $H_t = D_t - (Y_t^p + M_t)$.

percentage terms, will be equal to the relative unsatisfied demand of the period.

So much for the relationships of the model. The data of the model are I and Y. The treatment of Y as a datum is justified because it can be assumed that Y remains fixed from period 0 onwards.[1] This assumption, in turn, is justified because we are assuming that real G.D.P. is already at the capacity level when the disturbance to the initial equilibrium occurs and because we are dealing with a short reaction interval over which capacity product can be taken as fixed. The treatment of I as a datum is more questionable; we shall consider it further in section 8.4.

8.3 The Inflationary Process

Let us postulate an initial equilibrium in which real G.D.P. is at capacity level. Suppose that this equilibrium is disturbed in period 0 by a once-for-all increase in I; I rises to a higher level in period 0 and stays at this higher level in all subsequent periods. Then, according to the model set out in the previous section, the result will be a continuous upward movement in Y^*. But, as already explained, Y can be assumed to remain fixed at the initial equilibrium level from period 0 onwards. Hence the continuous upward movement in Y^* must also mean a continuous upward movement in the relevant price index P, by virtue of (8.1). That is, the shock must produce an inflationary process. We shall now justify these statements by means of a simple algebraic argument.

Relationships (8.2) to (8.4) give:

$$Y_t^* = a + b Y_{t-1}^* + I_t^* = a + b Y_{t-1}^* + I_t P_{t-1}.$$

Using (8.1) we can write this expression as

$$Y_t^* = a + b Y_{t-1}^* + \left(\frac{I_t}{Y_{t-1}}\right) Y_{t-1}^*. \tag{8.8}$$

Since the price index, along with all other variables, is constant in the initial equilibrium, we have for all periods up to period 0: $Y_t^* = Y_{t-1}^* = Y_{t-1} = \bar{Y}$ where $\bar{Y}$ is some constant. We also have I_t constant at, say, $\bar{I}$. Hence (8.8) implies for the initial equilibrium:

$$\bar{Y} = a + b \bar{Y} + \left(\frac{\bar{I}}{\bar{Y}}\right) \bar{Y} = a + b \bar{Y} + \bar{I}. \tag{8.9}$$

[1] All variables which remain fixed are genuine data (cf. section 5.5 above).

Subtracting (8.9) from (8.8), we get:

$$y_t^* = by_{t-1}^* + \left(\frac{I_t}{Y_{t-1}}\right)Y_{t-1}^* - \bar{I}$$

where y^* denotes $(Y^* - \bar{Y})$ or the deviation of Y^* from its initial equilibrium level. Since $Y_{t-1}^* = y_{t-1}^* + \bar{Y}$, the above expression can be written as:

$$y_t^* = by_{t-1}^* + \frac{I_t}{Y_{t-1}}(y_{t-1}^* + \bar{Y}) - \bar{I}$$

or as:

$$y_t^* = \left(b + \frac{I_t}{Y_{t-1}}\right)y_{t-1}^* + \left[\frac{I_t}{Y_{t-1}}\bar{Y} - \bar{I}\right]. \tag{8.10}$$

With the help of (8.10) it is a simple matter to trace the development of Y^*, expressed in terms of deviations from the initial equilibrium level, for period 0 and subsequent periods. For period 0 and subsequent periods, I_t/Y_{t-1} is, by hypothesis, equal to some positive constant $\bar{I}/\bar{Y}$ where $\bar{I}$ is the higher level of I which obtains from period 0 onwards. Let us denote this constant by j. The square bracket in (8.10) is also a positive constant for period 0 and subsequent periods. Denote this constant by i. Then (8.10) gives:

$$y_0^* = (b+j)y_{-1}^* + i = i$$
$$y_1^* = (b+j)y_0^* + i = i\{1 + (b+j)\}$$
$$y_2^* = (b+j)y_1^* + i = i\{1 + (b+j) + (b+j)^2\}$$
$$\vdots$$

Since $(b+j)$ is positive, it is clear from this sequence that all deviations are positive and that each is larger than the one before. In other words, the sequence shows that G.D.P. in current prices will move upwards continuously from its initial equilibrium level as a result of the shock. But given constant Y, this means that P (the implicit deflator of G.D.P.) will also move upwards continuously – there will be an inflationary process.

It is also clear that, given $(b+j) < 1$, y_t^* will converge on $i/[1-(b+j)]$, which means that Y_t^* will converge on $\bar{Y} + i/[1-(b+j)]$, the new equilibrium level. Thus the inflationary process will peter out as long as b is less than $(1-j)$. Now:

$$1 - j = 1 - \frac{\bar{I}}{\bar{Y}}.$$

Hence the inflationary process will peter out as long as the marginal propensity to consume (b) is less than the proportion of real G.D.P. which consumers wish to claim from period 0 onwards.

Another interesting result is that the 'full-employment' multiplier (the ratio between the increase in equilibrium Y^* associated with an increase in I which occurs when Y is at capacity level, and the increase in I) is larger than the 'underemployment' multiplier (the ratio between the increase in equilibrium Y associated with an increase in I which occurs when Y is below capacity, and the increase in I). The full-employment multiplier is given by $1/[1-(b+j)]$, while the underemployment multiplier is given by $1/(1-b)$,[1] which is less than $1/[1-(b+j)]$ because $j>0$.

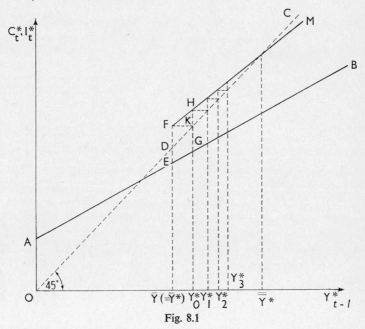

Fig. 8.1

Let us now consider the foregoing in terms of a simple diagram (Fig. 8.1). This makes use of a rearrangement of (8.4), which is obtained by subtracting Y_{t-1}^* from both sides, namely:

$$Y_t^* - Y_{t-1}^* = (C_t^* + I_t^*) - Y_{t-1}^*. \qquad (8.11)$$

---

[1] This assumes that the marginal propensity to consume is the same for the real (underemployment) consumption function as for the money (full-employment) consumption function.

K

On the vertical axis of Fig. 8.1 we measure C_t^* and I_t^*, while on the horizontal axis we measure Y_{t-1}^*. The initial equilibrium level of G.D.P. is represented by $O\,\overline{Y}(=O\,\overline{Y}^*)$. The line AB represents the consumption function (relationship (8.2)). Hence the distance DE measures $\overline{I}$, desired investment expenditure in both constant and current prices in the initial equilibrium. *Real* desired investment expenditure is assumed to rise in period 0 to $\overline{\overline{I}}$, which we represent by FE, and to remain at this level in all subsequent periods. Hence the constant j is represented by $FE/O\,\overline{Y}$.

Relationship (8.11) is now used to locate Y_0^*. This relationship gives:

$$Y_0^* - \overline{Y} = C_0^* + I_0^* - \overline{Y}.$$

Now the right-hand side of this expression is represented by the distance FD. Hence to find Y_0^* we merely measure this distance along the horizontal axis from $\overline{Y}$.

Having located Y_0^*, we can now locate Y_1^* in the same way. The distance GY_0^* represents C_1^*, while $I_1^* = (I_1/Y_0)Y_0^* = (\overline{\overline{I}}/\overline{Y})Y_0^*$ is represented by HG, which is given by

$$HG = \frac{FE}{O\,\overline{Y}} \cdot OY_0^*.$$

Hence by a further application of (8.11) we find that $(Y_1^* - Y_0^*)$ is represented by HK. This enables us to locate Y_1^* by measuring along a distance HK from Y_0^*. By repeated application of this procedure we can locate as many items as we wish in the sequence for Y^*. Two more, Y_2^* and Y_3^*, are shown. Evidently there is convergence on $\overline{\overline{Y}}^*$, the new equilibrium value of G.D.P. in current prices, which is found by dropping a perpendicular from the point of intersection of FM (representing $C_t^* + I_t^*$) and OC. The reason for the convergence is that the slope of AB which represents the constant b is less than $[1 - (FE/O\,\overline{Y})]$, which represents the constant $(1-j)$.

It follows from the definition of unsatisfied demand presented earlier (relationship (8.6)) and from the preceding discussion that some demand will remain unsatisfied throughout the inflationary process. To show this, we first use the definition of unsatisfied demand, together with (8.4), to get:

$$(UD)_t = \frac{Y_t^* - P_{t-1}Y_t}{P_{t-1}}.$$

Now using $Y_t = Y_{t-1}$ (see p. 276 above) and (8.1), we obtain:

$$(UD)_t = \frac{Y_t^* - Y_{t-1}^*}{P_{t-1}}.$$

It follows from this expression that unsatisfied demand will be positive from period 0 onwards, since, as we know from the preceding discussion, $Y_t^* > Y_{t-1}^*$ from period 0 onwards.

The question which arises from this conclusion is: whose expenditure plans are frustrated – consumers' or investors' or both? The answer is that both groups fail to achieve the real expenditure which they set out to achieve. This is because, in the case of both groups, the monetary outlay which is undertaken in period t is sufficient to give the real expenditure desired for the period only if prices remain the same in period t as in period $(t-1)$. In fact, however, prices rise in period t, with the result that the real expenditure which consumers and investors actually achieve is less than the real expenditure which they set out to achieve. In fact the price index rises in period t to whatever level is necessary to bring aggregate *realised* real expenditure into equality with real available supplies (realised G.D.P. in constant prices). This is clear from the fact that the realised expenditure of period t, in initial equilibrium prices, is $(C_t^* + I_t^*)/P_t$, which equals available supplies in initial equilibrium prices (Y_t^*/P_t) by virtue of relationship (8.4).

It should be noted, however, that, provided the process is convergent, the discrepancy between the desired and the realised real expenditure narrows continually for both groups, because, given convergence, P_t/P_{t-1} tends to unity as t tends to ∞ and hence C_t^*/P_t and I_t^*/P_t tend to C_t^*/P_{t-1} and I_t^*/P_{t-1} respectively. In fact, in the new equilibrium, if it were ever reached, both groups would be realising their expenditure plans in full. As a result of money illusion (see section 8.2 above), consumers would have reduced their claims on current output sufficiently to make room for the larger claims of investors; prices would have stopped rising; and the source of the frustration of expenditure plans would therefore have been removed. Thus the function of the inflationary process would have been to reconcile the claims on current output of the two groups of spenders.

8.4 Limitations of the Keynesian Explanation

As the preceding discussion makes clear, the Keynesian explanation views inflation as a phenomenon associated with a situation in which no increase in real available supplies is possible, because real G.D.P. has reached capacity level; inflation occurs, essentially, because an increase in aggregate demand impinges on a situation of this type. In other words, the underlying view is that inflation is a feature of *abnormal* economic situations, particularly wars and their aftermaths.[1]

In the light of post-war experience this is seen to be far too narrow a view. For example, the Australian situation in the late 1950s was not one characterised by unsatisfied demand; it is even doubtful whether there was appreciable excess demand in Australia in those years. Yet prices rose by about 16 per cent between 1955 and 1962 or by about 2 per cent per annum. Again, the sharp inflation in the United States in 1955–7 occurred in a situation in which there was little sign of excess demand, let alone unsatisfied demand, and some evidence that demand was actually deficient.[2] In short, the lesson of post-war experience is that inflation is by no means confined to abnormal economic situations but rather that it is something which is likely to occur whenever the economy is in the vicinity of internal balance. The main limitation of the Keynesian explanation, then, is the narrowness of its foundations.

A second limitation is its treatment of desired real investment expenditure as a datum. This might not be inappropriate if an inflationary situation and a situation of unsatisfied demand were synonymous, because where extensive unsatisfied demand exists, as in war or post-war situations, there is likely to be some scheme for the licensing of investment expenditure which would effectively establish a one-way connection between this variable and the three unknowns of the model, i.e. which would justify its treatment as a datum. Since inflation and unsatisfied demand are not synonymous, however, one cannot legitimately assume that quantitative controls over investment expenditure are present, which means that one cannot ignore the likely effects of the inflationary process on the desired level of real investment expenditure.

Finally, as noted in section 2.3, post-war experience in the United States suggests that we cannot explain short-run movements in consumer outlay adequately by means of a consumption function in

[1] The first, and classic, version of the Keynesian explanation was presented by Keynes himself in a pamphlet entitled *How to Pay for the War* which was, in effect, an exercise in war-time economics.

[2] C. L. Schultze, 'Recent Inflation in the United States', *Study of Employment, Growth, and Price Levels*, Study Paper No. 1 (Washington, 1959) chap. 5.

which consumption expenditure in current prices depends only on national income in current prices. The use of such a consumption function in the Keynesian explanation constitutes a third important limitation of this line of approach.

It seems, then, that the Keynesian explanation does not provide a particularly strong theoretical framework for the discussion of anti-inflationary policy and that we shall need to look for something better before attempting to consider the price-stability objective in the British context. One possible alternative will be examined in the next chapter.

8.5 Summary

Inflation can be explained in terms of a model which is a simple adaptation of the Keynesian multiplier model. An initial equilibrium is postulated in which aggregate demand is equal to real G.D.P. and in which real G.D.P. is at the capacity level. It is also postulated that this equilibrium is disturbed by a once-for-all autonomous increase in aggregate demand. The excess of aggregate demand over real G.D.P. which results from the disturbance gives rise to a cumulative upward movement in G.D.P. *in terms of current prices* via a mechanism which resembles the mechanism of the Keynesian multiplier model. However, since it has been assumed that *real* G.D.P. is already at the capacity level when the disturbance occurs and that the reaction interval is short, it can also be assumed that real G.D.P. must remain fixed in the course of the cumulative upward movement of G.D.P. in terms of current prices. Consequently, there must be a cumulative upward movement in the ratio of G.D.P. in current prices to G.D.P. in constant prices, i.e. there must be a cumulative upward movement in the implicit G.D.P. deflator.

According to this explanation, inflation occurs because an autonomous increase in aggregate demand impinges on a situation in which real G.D.P. has reached capacity level and hence cannot be increased to meet the increase in aggregate demand. In other words, inflation is a manifestation of unsatisfied demand and hence is a phenomenon associated with abnormal economic situations, particularly wars and their aftermaths. However, this view of inflation is untenable in the light of post-war experience, which shows that inflation is by no means confined to situations characterised by unsatisfied demand and that it can even occur when there is a substantial deficiency of demand. For this and other reasons, the Keynesian explanation is not particularly satisfactory and an alternative explanation is required.

READING LIST

Brown, A. J., *The Great Inflation 1939–1951* (Oxford University Press, 1955).

Goodwin, R. M., 'The Multiplier', in Harris, S. E. (ed.), *The New Economics* (New York: Alfred A. Knopf, 1948).

Keynes, J. M., *How to Pay for the War* (London: Macmillan, 1940).

Koopmans, T., 'The Dynamics of Inflation', *Review of Economics and Statistics* (May 1942).

Smithies, A., 'The Behaviour of Money National Income under Inflationary Conditions', *Quarterly Journal of Economics* (Nov 1942).

Turvey, R., 'Period Analysis and Inflation', *Economica* (Aug 1949).

9 The Inflationary Process: The Administered-pricing Approach

9.1 Introduction

A prominent feature of the model of the inflationary process analysed in the previous chapter is that it explains the continuous upward movement in the general price level without reference to the way in which individual prices are actually fixed. The price equation of that model merely says that the percentage increase in the price index in any period is equal to the excess of aggregate demand over real gross domestic product in the period, as a percentage of real gross domestic product. This could be taken to mean that prices are fixed so as to clear the market. But it could also be taken to mean that prices are fixed with some quite different objective in view (e.g. so as to secure a particular absolute profit margin or a particular relative profit margin) and that the result is *as if* market-clearing were the rule. There is thus a definite view as to the *results* of price fixation, but none as to the methods.

By contrast, the model which we shall develop in the present chapter embodies a quite specific hypothesis about the method used to fix individual prices, namely that price is raised whenever variable cost per unit of output increases, the new price being fixed by adding some margin (possibly, but not necessarily, the same margin as before) to the new unit variable cost to cover fixed costs and to provide a profit. For example, if unit variable cost increases from 50p to 80p and the profit margin remains constant at, say, 25 per cent of unit variable cost, price would be raised, according to this hypothesis, from $62\frac{1}{2}$p per unit to £1 per unit.

9.2 The Price and Wage Equations

Our first task in this section is to use the pricing hypothesis just outlined to develop an aggregate price equation. This price equation will form the central relationship of a complete model which will be presented later in this section and used to analyse the inflationary process in the next section.

Perhaps the best way to begin is to consider a firm which makes only one product and which fixes the price of this product by the method outlined in the previous section. We shall suppose that the firm takes time to raise its price when faced with an increase in unit cost, and to make the argument as concrete as possible we shall assume a fixed delay of one period. The following symbols will be used:

p = price per unit
l = variable labour cost per unit
n = variable non-labour cost per unit
v = total variable cost per unit (i.e. $v = l + n$)
k = relative net revenue per unit *plus* one (i.e. $[(p-v)/v] + 1$ or the profit margin *plus* one).

In terms of these symbols, the relationship between the firm's price, variable cost per unit and profit margin is:

$$p_t = v_{t-1}k_t \tag{9.1}$$

where
$$k_t = \frac{p_t - v_{t-1}}{v_{t-1}} + 1 = \frac{p_t}{v_{t-1}}.$$

From this expression it follows that the *proportional rate of increase* in the firm's price is given by:

$$\dot{p}_t = \dot{v}_{t-1} + \dot{k}_t \tag{9.2}$$

where the dot stands for 'proportional rate of increase'. This is an approximate expression which gives good results so long as $\dot{v}_{t-1}$ and $\dot{k}_t$ are small, as will be the case if the period is short – say a quarter.[1]

[1] From (9.1) we have:

$$\dot{p}_t = \frac{v_{t-1}k_t - v_{t-2}k_{t-1}}{v_{t-2}k_{t-1}}$$

$$= \frac{v_{t-1}k_t - v_{t-1}k_{t-1} + v_{t-1}k_{t-1} - v_{t-2}k_{t-1}}{v_{t-2}k_{t-1}}$$

$$= \frac{v_{t-1}[k_t - k_{t-1}] + k_{t-1}(v_{t-1} - v_{t-2})}{v_{t-2}k_{t-1}}$$

$$= \left(\frac{v_{t-1}}{v_{t-2}}\right)\dot{k}_t + \dot{v}_{t-1}$$

$$= (1 + \dot{v}_{t-1})\dot{k}_t + \dot{v}_{t-1}$$

$$= \dot{v}_{t-1} + \dot{k}_t + \dot{v}_{t-1}\dot{k}_t.$$

Variable cost per unit can be broken up into two components: (i) variable labour cost per unit; and (ii) variable non-labour cost per unit. Thus:

$$v_{t-1} = l_{t-1} + n_{t-1}. \tag{9.3}$$

From this expression it follows that:

$$\dot{v}_{t-1} = \epsilon_1 \dot{l}_{t-1} + \epsilon_2 \dot{n}_{t-1} \tag{9.4}$$

where ϵ_1 denotes l_{t-2}/v_{t-2} and ϵ_2 denotes n_{t-2}/v_{t-2}, i.e. $\epsilon_1(\epsilon_2)$ is the ratio of unit labour cost (unit non-labour cost) to unit variable cost in period $(t-2)$.[1] Clearly $\epsilon_1 + \epsilon_2 = 1$. Substituting (9.4) into (9.2), we get:

$$\dot{p}_t = \epsilon_1 \dot{l}_{t-1} + \epsilon_2 \dot{n}_{t-1} + \dot{k}_t. \tag{9.5}$$

The final form of our expression for $\dot{p}$ is obtained by manipulating the first term in (9.5). We have:

$$l_{t-1} = \frac{w_{t-1}}{o_{t-1}} \tag{9.6}$$

where w denotes wage earnings per man or per man-hour and o denotes output per man or per man-hour. From this it follows that:

$$\dot{l}_{t-1} = \dot{w}_{t-1} - \dot{o}_{t-1}. \tag{9.7}$$

Once again this is an approximation which gives good results provided that $\dot{o}_{t-1}$ is small.[2] Substituting (9.7) into (9.5), we get:

$$\dot{p}_t = \epsilon_1(\dot{w}_{t-1} - \dot{o}_{t-1}) + \epsilon_2 \dot{n}_{t-1} + \dot{k}_t. \tag{9.8}$$

If $\dot{v}_{t-1}$ and $\dot{k}_t$ are both small, the final term in this expression will be small enough to be neglected, since it will be the product of two small numbers. For example, if $\dot{v}_{t-1} = 0.02$ and $\dot{k}_t = 0.01$ (rates of increase of 2 per cent and 1 per cent respectively in variable cost per unit and in the ratio of price to variable cost per unit), the final term will be 0.0002. When $\dot{v}_{t-1}\dot{k}_t$ is omitted, the above expression for $\dot{p}_t$ reduces to (9.2).

[1] From (9.3) we have:

$$\dot{v}_{t-1} = \frac{v_{t-1} - v_{t-2}}{v_{t-2}} = \frac{(l_{t-1} + n_{t-1}) - (l_{t-2} + n_{t-2})}{v_{t-2}}$$

$$= \frac{(l_{t-1} - l_{t-2}) + (n_{t-1} - n_{t-2})}{v_{t-2}}$$

$$= \frac{l_{t-1} - l_{t-2}}{l_{t-2}} \cdot \frac{l_{t-2}}{v_{t-2}} + \frac{n_{t-1} - n_{t-2}}{n_{t-2}} \cdot \frac{n_{t-2}}{v_{t-2}}$$

$$= \epsilon_1 \dot{l}_{t-1} + \epsilon_2 \dot{n}_{t-1}.$$

[2] The derivation of (9.7) is as follows. From (9.6) we have:

$$l_{t-1} = \frac{(w_{t-1}/o_{t-1}) - (w_{t-2}/o_{t-2})}{(w_{t-2}/o_{t-2})}$$

This expression is an approximation which gives good results so long as all the relevant proportional rates of increase are small. An interesting special case of (9.8) is the case of constant profit margins. If we denote the profit margin by u, we have, from the definition of k:

$$k_t = 1 + u_t.$$

It follows that:

$$\dot{k}_t = \frac{(1 + u_t) - (1 + u_{t-1})}{(1 + u_{t-1})}$$

$$= \left(\frac{u_t - u_{t-1}}{u_{t-1}}\right)\left(\frac{u_{t-1}}{1 + u_{t-1}}\right)$$

$$= \dot{u}_t\left(\frac{u_{t-1}}{1 + u_{t-1}}\right).$$

Hence if profit margins are constant ($\dot{u}_t = 0$), we have $\dot{k}_t = 0$ and (9.8) reduces to the first two terms.

The aggregate price equation which we shall employ is the analogue of (9.8) for the economy as a whole, namely:

$$\dot{p}_t = \beta_1(\dot{W}_{t-1} - \dot{O}_{t-1}) + \beta_2\dot{M}_{t-1} + \dot{K}_t. \tag{9.9}$$

In this expression P is the implicit deflator of gross domestic product at factor cost, as in the previous chapter, W is an index of money wage earnings per man in the economy as a whole, O an index of output per man in the economy as a whole, M an index of the cost of imported materials per unit of output in the economy as a whole,

---

$$\dot{l}_{t-1} = \frac{(w_{t-1}/o_{t-1}) - (w_{t-2}/o_{t-1}) + (w_{t-2}/o_{t-1}) - (w_{t-2}/o_{t-2})}{(w_{t-2}/o_{t-2})}$$

$$= \frac{\dfrac{1}{o_{t-1}}(w_{t-1} - w_{t-2}) + w_{t-2}\left(\dfrac{1}{o_{t-1}} - \dfrac{1}{o_{t-2}}\right)}{w_{t-2}/o_{t-2}}$$

$$= \frac{o_{t-2}}{o_{t-1}}\dot{w}_{t-1} + \left(\frac{o_{t-2} - o_{t-1}}{o_{t-1}}\right)$$

$$= \frac{o_{t-2}}{o_{t-1}}\dot{w}_{t-1} - \left(\frac{o_{t-1} - o_{t-2}}{o_{t-2}}\right) \cdot \left(\frac{o_{t-2}}{o_{t-1}}\right)$$

$$= (\dot{w}_{t-1} - \dot{o}_{t-1})\frac{o_{t-2}}{o_{t-1}}$$

$$= (\dot{w}_{t-1} - \dot{o}_{t-1})\left(\frac{1}{\dot{o}_{t-1} + 1}\right).$$

If $\dot{o}_t$ is small, then $1/(\dot{o}_{t-1} + 1)$ will be very close to unity which means that $\dot{l}_{t-1}$ will be closely approximated by $(\dot{w}_{t-1} - \dot{o}_{t-1})$.

and K an index of the ratio of price to unit variable cost in the economy as a whole.

A few observations on this aggregate price equation are in order. Firstly, since the only variable non-labour cost at the level of the economy as a whole is imported materials, the macro-analogue of $\dot{n}$ is $\dot{M}$. Secondly, since the coefficients β_1 and β_2 are the macro-counterparts of the coefficients ϵ_1 and ϵ_2, they can be interpreted as the contributions of labour cost and imported materials cost, respectively, to aggregate variable cost in the economy as a whole, i.e. as two positive numbers which sum to unity.[1] On a strict interpretation β_1 and β_2 would be treated as variables, but we shall simplify by treating them as constants. Finally, it should be noted that, in the special case of constant profit margins, $\dot{K}_t = 0$ and the price equation consists of the first two terms only.

Having developed an aggregate price equation, we now propose a set of relationships to explain $\dot{W}$, the proportional rate of increase in money wage earnings per man. Together with (9.9) these relationships will constitute our model of the inflationary process.

We begin with the definition:

$$\dot{W}_t = \dot{W}_t^r + (\dot{W}_t - \dot{W}_t^r) \qquad (9.10)$$

where $\dot{W}^r$ denotes the proportional rate of increase in nationally negotiated wage rates per man. The second term on the right-hand side of this expression (i.e. the excess of the proportional rate of increase of wage earnings per man over the proportional rate of increase of negotiated wage rates per man) is usually known as the 'wage-drift', and we shall employ this term.

We next adopt hypotheses to explain each of the two components of $\dot{W}$. As regards the first component, our hypothesis is that the proportional rate of increase in negotiated wage rates per man depends on: (i) the proportional rate of increase in price ($\dot{P}$) in the recent past; and (ii) the current level of excess demand, H. More precisely we postulate that, given H, $\dot{W}^r$ will be higher, the higher is lagged $\dot{P}$, and that, given lagged $\dot{P}$, $\dot{W}^r$ will be higher, the higher is H. As regards the second component, we postulate that the wage-drift depends positively on the current level of excess demand. Taken together with (9.10), these hypotheses imply that $\dot{W}_t$ is an increasing function of lagged $\dot{P}$, given H, and an increasing function of H, given

[1] Cf. the definition of ϵ_1 and ϵ_2 following (9.4).

lagged $\dot{P}$. We embody this proposition in the following linear relationship:

$$\dot{W}_t = \xi_1 \dot{P}_{t-1} + \xi_2 H_t \qquad (9.11)$$

where the ξs are positive constants.

Of the six variables appearing in relationships (9.9) and (9.11) ($\dot{P}$, $\dot{W}$, $\dot{O}$, $\dot{M}$, $\dot{K}$ and H), we propose to treat four as data, namely $\dot{O}$, $\dot{M}$, $\dot{K}$ and H. The remaining two variables, $\dot{P}$ and $\dot{W}$, we shall take as jointly determined. Thus, given that the data are correctly classified, we have a complete model of the inflationary process, i.e. a model which contains enough information to explain a continuous upward movement in prices.

9.3 Inflationary Mechanisms

According to the model presented in the preceding section, there are several different ways in which an inflationary process can occur in an advanced industrial country like the United Kingdom. To facilitate the description of these processes, we shall set out the model as a whole at this point.

$$\dot{P}_t = \beta_1(\dot{W}_{t-1} - \dot{O}_{t-1}) + \beta_2 \dot{M}_{t-1} + \dot{K}_t \qquad (9.9)$$

$$\dot{W}_t = \xi_1 \dot{P}_{t-1} + \xi_2 H_t. \qquad (9.11)$$

One way in which an inflationary sequence can emerge is through a rise in the price of imported materials. Postulate an initial situation in which $\dot{W}$, $\dot{O}$, $\dot{M}$ and $\dot{K}$ are zero, so that $\dot{P}$ is zero also (prices are constant), and in which H is zero. Postulate also that $\dot{M}$ becomes positive for one period and then returns to its original zero value, i.e. that the unit cost of imported materials rises to a new level in some period and stays at this new level thereafter. (From now on we shall refer to this type of disturbance as a 'maintained increase'.) Then according to (9.9), if all else remains unchanged, $\dot{P}$ will become positive in the period following this maintained increase in the unit cost of imported materials, i.e. prices will rise in the period following the disturbance. In the next period, according to (9.11), this positive $\dot{P}$ will give rise to a positive $\dot{W}$ even though H remains at zero, i.e. wage earnings per man will rise. In the period after that, the positive $\dot{W}$ will give rise to a positive $\dot{P}$ even though $\dot{O}$, $\dot{M}$ and $\dot{K}$ continue at zero, i.e. prices will rise again. We stop our description at this point, but enough has been said to show that the maintained increase in the unit cost of imported materials will give rise to a continuous upward movement in prices and wage earnings per man, i.e. to an inflationary sequence.

The process just described can be set out schematically in the following way.

1. Maintained Rise in the Unit Cost of Imported Materials

$$\overset{+}{\dot{M}} \longrightarrow \overset{+}{\dot{P}} \longrightarrow \overset{+}{\dot{W}} \longrightarrow \overset{+}{\dot{P}} \longrightarrow \ldots .$$
$$\quad (9.9) \qquad (9.11) \qquad (9.9)$$

In this scheme the 'plus' sign above a variable indicates that the variable is positive while the horizontal arrow stands for 'leads to'. The number in brackets under the arrow indicates which of the two equations of our model produces the result which immediately follows. Thus the above scheme reads: an initial positive rate of increase in the unit cost of imported materials leads to a positive rate of increase in prices via relationship (9.9), which in turn leads to a positive rate of increase in wage earnings per man via relationship (9.11) and so on.

The same type of schematic representation will now be used to describe five further inflationary processes which are possible within the framework of our model. It is to be understood in all cases that the initial situation on which the disturbance impinges is one in which $\dot{W}$, $\dot{O}$, $\dot{M}$ and $\dot{K}$ are zero and in which excess demand is zero.

2. Maintained Fall in Output per Man

$$\overset{-}{\dot{O}} \longrightarrow \overset{+}{\dot{P}} \longrightarrow \overset{+}{\dot{W}} \longrightarrow \overset{+}{\dot{P}} \longrightarrow \ldots .$$
$$\quad (9.9) \qquad (9.11) \qquad (9.9)$$

3. Maintained Rise in Profit Margins

$$\overset{+}{\dot{K}} \longrightarrow \overset{+}{\dot{P}} \longrightarrow \overset{+}{\dot{W}} \longrightarrow \overset{+}{\dot{P}} \longrightarrow \ldots .$$
$$\quad (9.9) \qquad (9.11) \qquad (9.9)$$

4. Temporary Rise in Excess Demand

$$\overset{\uparrow}{H} \longrightarrow \overset{+}{\dot{W}} \longrightarrow \overset{+}{\dot{P}} \longrightarrow \overset{+}{\dot{W}} \longrightarrow \overset{+}{\dot{P}} \longrightarrow \ldots .$$
$$(9.11) \qquad (9.9) \qquad (9.11) \qquad (9.9)$$

5. *Maintained Autonomous Rise in Prices*

$$\overset{+}{\dot{P}} \longrightarrow \overset{+}{\dot{W}} \longrightarrow \overset{+}{\dot{P}} \longrightarrow \overset{+}{\dot{W}} \longrightarrow \overset{+}{\dot{P}} \longrightarrow \ldots$$
$$\;\;(9.11)\qquad (9.9)\qquad (9.11)\qquad (9.9)$$

6. *Maintained Autonomous Rise in Wage Earnings per Man*

$$\overset{+}{\dot{W}} \longrightarrow \overset{+}{\dot{P}} \longrightarrow \overset{+}{\dot{W}} \longrightarrow \overset{+}{\dot{P}} \longrightarrow \ldots$$
$$\;\;(9.9)\qquad (9.11)\qquad (9.9)$$

In the case of process 2, the initial disturbance is a maintained *fall* in output per man, denoted by $\dot{O}$ with a *minus* sign on top in place of the plus sign. Process 3 is initiated by a maintained increase in profit margins. Process 4 is initiated by a temporary rise in excess demand, i.e. excess demand is assumed to rise to a positive level in some period and then to revert to its original zero level thereafter. As in the case of processes 1, 2 and 3, the disturbance here is a one-period disturbance. However, in the case of $\dot{M}$, $\dot{O}$ and $\dot{K}$, a one-period disturbance implies a *permanent* increase in level since these variables are rates of increase, whereas in the case of H, which is a level, not a rate of increase, a one-period disturbance implies a *temporary* increase in level.[1] In the case of process 5 the disturbance is a maintained *autonomous* rise in prices, by which we mean a maintained increase in prices which occurs other than via (9.9). An example is a rise in prices which results when a price-freeze is terminated. Finally, process 6 is initiated by a maintained autonomous rise in wage earnings per man, this being a maintained increase in wage earnings which occurs without any prior change in the explanatory variables of (9.11). One example is a rise in wage earnings which results from an increase in the prices of imported consumer goods following a devaluation or the imposition of an import surcharge. A second example is a rise in wage earnings which occurs when the prices of necessities rise following an increase in the severity of the indirect tax structure.[2] A third example is a rise in wage earnings which arises because the representatives of the trade unions adopt a more militant

---

[1] It will be seen that this difference between process 4 and the first three processes is reflected in a difference in notation. In the case of process 4 the initial disturbance is indicated by $\overset{\uparrow}{H}$, not $\overset{+}{H}$.

[2] Neither of these price changes will be reflected in the index P which, by definition, is the implicit deflator of gross domestic product at factor cost (see p. 290 above).

attitude at national wage negotiations, this increase in militancy being unconnected with any prior change in prices or with any increase in the tightness of the labour market.

In any actual inflation, of course, it is likely that two or more of the six processes just described will be operating at once. Moreover there are likely to be continuous inflationary disturbances rather than the one-period disturbances postulated above, e.g. a continuous rise in the unit cost of imported materials ($\dot{M}$ positive in a *succession* of periods, not merely in a single period). Any actual inflation, therefore, is likely to be a fairly complicated phenomenon and it will not be easy to isolate the contributions being made to the observed price rise by the various data of our model.

9.4 Empirical Studies: The Model as a Whole

In the remainder of this chapter we shall discuss a number of recent empirical studies which are relevant to the model developed in section 9.2 and used in section 9.3. We shall begin by giving a brief account of a study undertaken some years ago by Dicks-Mireaux in which he used econometric techniques to estimate a model closely resembling our own.[1] Other empirical studies which are concerned with particular sections of the model, rather than with the model as a whole, will be discussed in later sections.

After a considerable amount of experimentation with alternative explanatory variables and lag structures, Dicks-Mireaux finally adopted the following two-equation model in which $\dot{P}$ and $\dot{W}$ are the jointly determined variables and $\dot{M}$, $\dot{O}$ and H are data:

$$\dot{P}_t = a + b\dot{W}_t + c\dot{M}_{t-\frac{1}{4}} + d\dot{O}_t \tag{9.12}$$

$$\dot{W}_t = e + f\dot{P}_t + g\dot{P}_{t-1} + hH_{t-\frac{1}{4}}. \tag{9.13}$$

The non-integral lag which appears in each of these equations requires some explanation. The variable $\dot{M}_{t-\frac{1}{4}}$ denotes the proportional rate of change of the unit cost of imported materials as between year t lagged three months and year $(t-1)$ lagged three months. For example, if year t is the year 1958, $\dot{M}_{t-\frac{1}{4}}$ will be the proportional rate of change in the unit cost of imported materials between the twelve months ending September 1957 and the twelve months ending

[1] See L. A. Dicks-Mireaux, 'The Interrelationship between Cost and Price Changes, 1946–1959: A Study of Inflation in Post-War Britain', *Oxford Economic Papers* (Oct 1961).

September 1958. Similarly $H_{t-\frac{1}{4}}$ is the level of excess demand in year t lagged three months.

The main points of difference between the Dicks-Mireaux model and the model constituted by (9.9) and (9.11) may be summarised as follows:

1. Both $\dot{P}_t$ and $\dot{P}_{t-1}$ appear as explanatory variables in the Dicks-Mireaux wage equation (9.13), whereas only the latter appears in (9.11).

2. $\dot{W}$ and $\dot{O}$ are unlagged in (9.12), whereas both are lagged one period in (9.9).

3. $\dot{M}$ appears with a non-integral lag in (9.12) and with an integral lag in (9.9).

4. H is unlagged in (9.11) and appears with a non-integral lag in (9.13).

5. In (9.9) the coefficient of $\dot{O}$ is numerically equal to the coefficient of $\dot{W}$ and opposite in sign, whereas in (9.12) there is no restriction of the coefficient of $\dot{O}$.

6. In the case of (9.12) and (9.13) there is no restriction on the intercepts, whereas the intercepts of (9.9) and (9.11) are restricted to zero.

7. $\dot{K}$ is not among the explanatory variables of (9.12), whereas it appears with a coefficient of unity in (9.9). The most straightforward interpretation of the omission of $\dot{K}$ from (9.12) is that (9.12) is based on the assumption of constant profit margins (see p. 291 above).

Since these differences are all of a fairly minor character, an examination of the estimated version of (9.12) and (9.13) should help to throw further light on our own model, quite apart from its intrinsic interest. Accordingly we shall now proceed with such an examination.

After experimenting with various methods of estimation, Dicks-Mireaux finally adopted the following numerical relationships, derived from annual data for the years 1946–59, as giving 'the best description of the short-term changes in the wage/price mechanism'.[1]

$$\dot{P}_t = 2\cdot47 + 0\cdot27\dot{W}_t + 0\cdot21\dot{M}_{t-\frac{1}{4}} - 0.54\dot{O}_t \qquad (9.14)$$

$$\dot{W}_t = 3\cdot90 + 0\cdot30\dot{P}_t + 0\cdot16\dot{P}_{t-1} + 2\cdot78H_{t-\frac{1}{4}}. \qquad (9.15)$$

Several aspects of these relationships deserve comment. In the first place, all the coefficients of (9.12) and (9.13), with the exception

---

[1] Dicks-Mireaux, op. cit., p. 281. (9.14) and (9.15) are, respectively, (7) and (6) of Dicks-Mireaux rewritten in our notation and without the random disturbances.

of the coefficient of $\dot{P}_{t-1}$ in (9.13), are 'well determined' in the usual sense that the estimate of the coefficient is at least twice the estimate of its standard error.

Secondly, it will be observed that the coefficients of $\dot{W}$, $\dot{M}$ and $\dot{O}$ in (9.14) have the properties which we should expect them to have on the basis of the argument underlying the price equation of our own model (relationship (9.9)). This argument shows that: (i) the coefficients of $\dot{W}$ and $\dot{M}$ in (9.9), namely β_1 and β_2, are positive numbers lying between zero and unity, since they represent, respectively, the proportion of labour cost and the proportion of imported materials cost to aggregate variable cost in the economy as a whole; and (ii) that β_1 and β_2 sum to unity. It will be seen that the coefficients of $\dot{W}$ and $\dot{M}$ in (9.14) reproduce these properties to the extent that both are positive numbers lying between zero and unity. They do not sum to unity as required, but this is not to be expected since they are no more than estimates of the true coefficients – estimates which are subject to sampling error. As for $\dot{O}$, the coefficient of $\dot{O}$ in (9.9) is $-\beta_1$. The coefficient of $\dot{O}$ in (9.14) reproduces this property in part, in that it is a negative number which is smaller numerically than unity. It is not equal numerically to the coefficient of $\dot{W}$ in (9.14), but once again this is not to be expected in view of the fact that the numerical coefficients appearing in (9.14) are estimates of the true coefficients only.

Thirdly, taken at their face value, the estimated coefficients imply: (i) that if the rate of increase of money wage earnings per man rises by one point (e.g. from 3 per cent per annum to 4 per cent per annum), the rate of increase of prices will rise by just over one-quarter of one point; (ii) that if the rate of increase in the unit cost of imported materials rises by one point, the rate of increase of prices will again rise by a little less than one-quarter of one point; (iii) that if the rate of increase of output per man *falls* by one point, the rate of increase of prices will rise by about a little over one-half of one point; (iv) that if the rate of increase of prices rises by one point, the rate of money wage earnings per man will rise by something less than one-half of one point; and (v) that if the level of excess demand rises by one point,[1] the rate of increase of prices will rise by nearly three points.

Fourthly, the estimated coefficient imply that the inflationary

[1] The excess-demand variable used in the fitting of (9.15) is *relative* excess demand, i.e. excess demand as a percentage of employment.

process is stable. By substituting (9.15) into (9.14) we see that the system reduces to the following non-homogeneous first-order difference equation:

$$\dot{P}_t = 0\cdot047\dot{P}_{t-1} + A \tag{9.16}$$

where A is given by:

$$A = 3\cdot839 + 0\cdot817H_{t-\frac{1}{4}} + 0\cdot228\dot{M}_{t-\frac{1}{4}} - 0\cdot588\dot{O}_t.$$

The solution of this difference equation is:

$$\dot{P}_t = (\dot{P}_0 - \bar{\dot{P}}_0)(0\cdot047)^t + \bar{\dot{P}}_t \tag{9.17}$$

in which $\bar{\dot{P}}$ is the particular solution (equilibrium path) determined by the time paths specified for the data, H, $\dot{M}$ and $\dot{O}$. This expression implies that $\dot{P}_t \to \bar{\dot{P}}_t$ as $t \to \infty$, given an arbitrary value of $(\dot{P}_0 - \bar{\dot{P}}_0)$. In other words the implication is that the rate of increase of prices will tend towards the equilibrium path determined by the time paths specified for the data of the system, in response to arbitrary initial conditions.

Finally, it will be seen that, unlike (9.9) and (9.11), both (9.14) and (9.15) have sizeable positive intercepts. Taken at face value the estimates imply that prices will rise by nearly $2\frac{1}{2}$ per cent per annum even if wage earnings, imported materials cost and productivity are constant, and that wage earnings will rise by nearly 4 per cent per annum even though prices are constant and excess demand is zero.[1] One possible reaction to these large intercepts is to say that the relationships have been misspecified, and that the intercepts merely reflect the coefficients of omitted explanatory variables. Dicks-Mireaux conducts an interesting test of one form of this hypothesis which asserts that the intercepts should really be allocated over the coefficients attached to lagged values of the existing explanatory variables.

As far as the price equation is concerned, the manner in which he conducts this test is as follows. His starting-point is the supposition that the 'long-run' coefficients of the $\dot{W}$ variable, the $\dot{M}$ variable and the $\dot{O}$ variable, which we shall denote by b', c' and d', respectively, satisfy the restrictions: (i) $b' = -d'$; (ii) $b' + c' = 1$.[2] These restrictions imply that an increase of one point in the rate of increase of unit labour cost (regardless of whether it rises from the wage-earnings

---

[1] The observations on $\dot{P}$, $\dot{W}$, $\dot{M}$ and $\dot{O}$ used to fit (9.14) and (9.15) were *percentage* rates of increase, not *proportionate* rates of increase.

[2] These, of course, are the restrictions which apply to the coefficients of (9.9) (see pp. 290–1 above).

side or the productivity side) coupled with a one-point increase in the rate of increase of unit material cost will lead, in the long run, to a one-point increase in the rate of increase of prices. In other words, if the rate of increase of unit costs *as a whole* increases by one point, the rate of increase of prices will increase by one point also in the long run, i.e. in the long run cost increases are fully passed on so that long-run profit margins are constant.

From an examination of British data for the period 1946–59, he concludes that plausible values for $b' (= -d')$ and c' are 0·74 and 0·26, respectively. Each of these long-run coefficients is then distributed (somewhat arbitrarily) over year t and the four preceding years on the assumption that the coefficient for any year will be smaller, the further removed is the year from year t. Thus the numerical relationship (9.14) is rewritten so that it contains five wage variables ($\dot{W}_t$, $\dot{W}_{t-1}$, $\dot{W}_{t-2}$, $\dot{W}_{t-3}$, $\dot{W}_{t-4}$) whose coefficients sum to 0·74, five materials-cost variables whose coefficients sum to 0·26 and five productivity variables whose coefficients sum to $-0·74$. At the same time the intercept is reduced to $-0·6$. The new numerical price equation is then used to predict the rate of change of prices for the United Kingdom for each of the years 1951–9 and the predictions are compared with the actual figures. Since the agreement between the actual and predicted values proves to be quite close, Dicks-Mireaux is prepared to accept the hypothesis that the large value of the intercept in (9.14) is a reflection merely of omission from the list of explanatory variables of lagged values of $\dot{W}$, $\dot{M}$ and $\dot{O}$.

The same type of test is applied to the wage equation (9.13). In this case the supposition is that the long-run coefficient for the $\dot{P}$ variable is unity, i.e. that an increase of one point in the rate of increase of prices will lead, in the long run, to a one-point increase in the rate of increase of wage earnings per man. This long-run coefficient is then distributed over year t and the four preceding years. Thus the new numerical wage equation is a transformation of (9.13) in which $\dot{P}_{t-2}$, $\dot{P}_{t-3}$ and $\dot{P}_{t-4}$ are added to $\dot{P}_t$ and $\dot{P}_{t-1}$ as explanatory variables, the coefficients of the five $\dot{P}$ variables summing to unity. At the same time the value of the intercept is reduced to a figure of 1·9. The coefficient of $H_{t-\frac{1}{4}}$ is left unchanged. The new numerical wage relationship is then used, as before, to predict the rate of increase of wage earnings per man in the years 1951–9. In this case the predictions are not particularly successful. Accordingly, Dicks-

Mireaux is led to doubt the hypothesis that the large positive intercept in (9.13) reflects the omission of lagged values of $\dot{P}$ from the
list of explanatory variables, while recognising that the results are
far from conclusive.

Of the two tests just described, the test on the price equation
appears to be the more conclusive. This test suggests that the total
response of price to changes in unit cost is likely to be spread out
over a considerable time interval. In the next section we describe
some further empirical work on the price equation which points
in the same direction.

9.5 Empirical Studies: The Price Equation

Examination of the micro-argument underlying the price equation
of our model (see section 9.2) shows that it embodies, *inter alia*, two
propositions:

(i) that the full effect on price of an increase in cost is felt in the
period following the cost increase:

(ii) that the response of price to an increase in unit labour cost
which results from an *increase in earnings per man* is the same
as the response of price to an increase in unit labour cost
which results from a *decrease in output per man*.

In this section we shall examine a recent British study by R. R.
Neild[1] which is relevant to both of these propositions.

Neild's study relates to manufacturing, other than food, drink
and tobacco, and is designed to test three distinct short-run price
equations for this part of the manufacturing sector. We shall begin by
setting out these price equations in terms of the following symbols:[2]

p = index of prices in the non-food manufacturing sector

l = index of unit labour cost in the non-food manufacturing
sector

m = index of unit material cost in the non-food manufacturing
sector.

All three equations take the following general form:

$$p_t = \alpha_0 + \alpha_1[\beta_1\{(1 - \lambda)(l_t + \lambda l_{t-1} + \lambda^2 l_{t-2} + \ldots)\}$$
$$+ \beta_2\{\mu_0 m_t + \mu_1 m_{t-1} + \mu_2(1 - \lambda)(m_{t-2} + \lambda m_{t-3} + \lambda^2 m_{t-4} + \ldots)\}]$$

$$(9.18)$$

[1] See R. R. Neild, *Pricing and Employment in the Trade Cycle* (Cambridge
University Press, 1963).
[2] This differs slightly from the notation used by Neild.

where $\beta_1 + \beta_2 = 1$; $0 < \lambda < 1$; $\mu_0 + \mu_1 + \mu_2 = 1$ and α_0 and α_1 are positive constants. The first of the two expressions in curly brackets will be recognised as a weighted arithmetic average of the current value and all past values of the index of unit labour cost (with geometrically declining weights), while the second of the two expressions in curly brackets is evidently a weighted arithmetic average of the current value and all past values of the index of unit material cost, given the restriction that $\mu_0 + \mu_1 + \mu_2 = 1$. Thus the term in square brackets is a weighted sum of two terms, the first of which reflects the current level and past levels of the index of unit labour cost and the second of which reflects the current level and past levels of the index of unit material cost. It can be thought of as an index which reflects both the current level, and also the past history, of unit cost as a whole. According to relationship (9.18), the price index depends linearly on this rather complex unit-cost index.

Relationship (9.18) implies that in a stationary equilibrium situation the following relationship holds:

$$\bar{p} = \alpha_0 + \alpha_1 \beta_1 \bar{l} + \alpha_1 \beta_2 \bar{m} \qquad (9.19)$$

where the bar over a variable indicates the stationary equilibrium value of that variable.[1] It follows from (9.19), in turn, that $\alpha_1 \beta_1$ measures the 'long-run' or eventual increase in the price index consequent on a one-point increase in the index of unit labour cost, given the index of material cost. Similarly $\alpha_1 \beta_2$ measures the long-run increase in the price index consequent on an increase of one point in the index of unit material cost, given the index of unit labour cost.[2]

All three of the short-run price equations which Neild examines,

---

[1] This uses $\mu_0 + \mu_1 + \mu_2 = 1$ and $0 < \lambda < 1$.

[2] Each of these long-run response coefficients can also be obtained by taking the limit of the corresponding short-run response coefficient. Take $\alpha_1 \beta_1$, for example. The short-run coefficient which measures the *immediate* increase in the price index following a unit increase in the index of unit labour cost, which occurs in period t, is: $\alpha_1 \beta_1 (1 - \lambda)$. The short-run coefficient which measures the increase up to period $(t + 1)$ is: $\alpha_1 \beta_1 (1 - \lambda)(1 + \lambda)$. The short-run coefficient which measures the increase up to period $(t + 2)$ is: $\alpha_1 \beta_1 (1 - \lambda)(1 + \lambda + \lambda^2)$. In general, the short-run coefficient which measures the increase up to period $(t + i)$ is: $\alpha_1 \beta_1 (1 - \lambda)(1 + \lambda + \lambda^2 + \dots + \lambda^i)$. This can be seen by assuming a stationary equilibrium up to period t and using (9.18) to find an expression for $p_{t+i} - p_{t+i-1}$. By taking the limit of the short-run coefficient as $i \to \infty$, and remembering that $0 < \lambda < 1$, we find that the long-run coefficient is:

$$\lim_{i \to \infty} \alpha_1 \beta_1 (1 - \lambda)(1 + \lambda + \lambda^2 + \dots + \lambda^i) = \alpha_1 \beta_1.$$

then, take the form of (9.18). The differences between them lie in the hypothesis which they embody about the effect on pricing decisions of changes in labour productivity. In the case of the first of the three equations (equation A), the index of unit labour cost l is replaced throughout (9.18) by w/o where w denotes the index of wage earnings per man and o the index of output per man. In the second and third equations (equations B and C), l is replaced throughout (9.18) by w/o' where o' denotes the *trend value* of the index of output per man. Equation B differs from equation C only in the form which is given to this trend value. Thus, equations B and C imply that purely short-run movements in productivity have no effect on price. In particular, they imply that there will be no increase in price when productivity declines in a recession as a result of the hoarding of labour. A long-run increase in productivity due to technical progress will be passed on in the form of a lower price, but otherwise productivity change is irrelevant to price determination.

We are now in a position to show the connection between the three short-run price equations tested by Neild and the simpler price equation used in our model. In summary the position is as follows:

1. All three of Neild's equations permit the full effect of a cost increase on price to be widely distributed over time, whereas (9.9) requires that the full effect be felt in the period following the cost increase (see proposition (i) above).

2. Equations B and C distinguish between changes in output per man which originate in technical progress and those which reflect purely short-run influences such as changes in the level of activity, whereas equation A and (9.9) suggest that price will be fully adjusted to changes in output per man, whatever its origin (see proposition (ii) above). This amounts to saying that in equations B and C a distinction is made between increases in the unit labour-cost index which reflect increases in earnings per man and those which reflect decreases in output per man, whereas no such distinction is made in equation A and in (9.9).

To test the competing hypotheses about the effect on pricing decisions of changes in productivity, i.e. to test equation A against equations B and C, Neild first reduces (9.18) to a much simpler form in the following way. From (9.18) we get:

$$\lambda p_{t-1} = \lambda\alpha_0 + \alpha_1[\beta_1\{(1-\lambda)(\lambda l_{t-1} + \lambda^2 l_{t-2} + \ldots)\} + \beta_2\{\lambda\mu_0 m_{t-1}$$
$$+ \lambda\mu_1 m_{t-2} + \mu_2(1-\lambda)(\lambda m_{t-3} + \lambda^2 m_{t-4} + \ldots)\}].$$

When this expression is subtracted from (9.18) we get:

$$p_t - \lambda p_{t-1} = \alpha_0(1-\lambda) + \alpha_1\beta_1(1-\lambda)l_t + \alpha_1\beta_2\mu_0 m_t$$
$$+ \alpha_1\beta_2(\mu_1 - \lambda\mu_0)m_{t-1} + \alpha_1\beta_2\{\mu_2(1-\lambda) - \lambda\mu_1\}m_{t-2}.$$

This, in turn gives:

$$p_t = b_0 + b_1 l_t + b_2 m_t + b_3 m_{t-1} + b_4 m_{t-2} + b_5 p_{t-1} \qquad (9.20)$$

where:
$$b_0 = \alpha_0(1-\lambda)$$
$$b_1 = \alpha_1\beta_1(1-\lambda)$$
$$b_2 = \alpha_1\beta_2\mu_0$$
$$b_3 = \alpha_1\beta_2(\mu_1 - \lambda\mu_0)$$
$$b_4 = \alpha_1\beta_2\{\mu_2(1-\lambda) - \lambda\mu_1\}$$
$$b_5 = \lambda.$$

Neild estimates (9.20) from quarterly data by ordinary least squares for the periods 1950–60 and 1953–60 (i.e. including and excluding the years of the Korean war). For equation A, l is replaced in (9.20) by w/o, for equation B, l is replaced by $w/(1\cdot025)^t$, i.e. it is assumed that the trend rate of growth of output per man is constant at $2\frac{1}{2}$ per cent per annum, and for equation C, $w/(1+\rho)^t$ is used in place of l, i.e. the trend rate of growth is assumed to be constant, but the value of the constant is left to be determined by the estimation process rather than being imposed in advance.

The estimates of equation A for the two periods are then compared with the estimates of equation B and C for the two periods. The coefficients of the unit labour-cost variable together with their standard errors are shown in the table below.

TABLE 9.1

Equation Period	A $l = w/o$	B $l = w/(1\cdot025)^t$	C $l = w/(1+\rho)^t$
1950–60	0·009 (0·029)	0·197 (0·031)	0·153 (0·031)
1953–60	0·026 (0·046)	0·141 (0·025)	0·059 (0·018)

The two estimates of equation A are then compared with the two estimates of equation B and the two estimates of equation C. This comparison shows that equations B and C are more satisfactory than equation A on the usual statistical criteria. In particular both the B equations and the C equations give a much better fit than the corresponding A equations. Moreover, both the B equations and the C equations provide a much firmer estimate for the coefficient of the unit labour-cost variable than the corresponding A equations. This is evidenced by the fact that in both B equations the estimated coefficient is roughly six times the estimated standard error and in both C equations more than three times. On the other hand, the estimated coefficient is only about one-half of its estimated standard error for one of the two A equations and only one-third for the other (see Table 9.1).

We shall now attempt to summarise our discussion of Neild's study. The main object of the study is to discriminate between three aggregate price equations which differ only as regards the role which they allot to productivity change. The first equation embodies the usual view that a decline in output per man, whatever its origin, tends to raise price, and an increase in output per man to lower price. On the other hand, the second and third equations imply that changes in productivity affect price only to the extent that they originate in technical progress, i.e. only to the extent that they are long-run in character. Changes in productivity which are short-run in character, in the sense that they reflect the hoarding of labour in a downturn and its dishoarding in the ensuing upturn, have no effect on price according to this equation. Since the second and third of the three equations give the better performance under econometric test, the study supports the view of the role of productivity change in price determination which they embody against the more traditional view embodied in the first equation and also in our equation (9.9).

9.6 Empirical Studies: Negotiated Wage Rates

It will be recalled that the wage-earnings equation of our model is made up from two components:
  (i) a hypothesis relating to the determinants of the rate of increase of negotiated wage rates; and
  (ii) a hypothesis relating to the determinants of the wage-drift.
In the present section we review a group of studies which are relevant to (i). We begin with the well-known study of Dicks-Mireaux and Dow[1] (D.D.M.) in which the authors test a more elaborate version

---

[1] See L. A. Dicks-Mireaux and J. C. R. Dow, 'The Determinants of Wage Inflation: United Kingdom, 1946–56', *Journal of the Royal Statistical Society*, series A, CXXII (2) (1959).

of the hypothesis advanced in section 9.2 above to explain the rate of change of negotiated wage rates.

The hypothesis developed by D.D.M. is based on two simplifying assumptions of an institutional character, namely (a) that each of the separate bargaining groups in the labour force has an annual wage settlement which always occurs in the same quarter of the year; and (b) that the same number of workers are affected by new wage settlements in all four quarters.

A wage-rate function is proposed for quarter t which relates to the workers whose annual settlement takes place in quarter t and which explains the rate of increase in the wage rates negotiated in the quarter over the rates negotiated for the workers concerned at the previous annual settlement four quarters earlier. To set out this function we shall use the following notation:

w = wage-rate index

P = retail price index

d = measure of the level of excess demand for labour[1]

f = measure of the 'pushfulness' of the trade unions.

In terms of this notation the wage-rate function proposed for quarter t is:

$$\frac{w_t}{w_{t-4}} = A\left(\frac{P_t}{P_{t-4}}\right)^\alpha d_t^\beta f_t^\gamma \qquad (9.21)$$

where A, α, β and γ are constants.

We now proceed to show how D.D.M. build their hypothesis as to the determinants of the rate of increase of negotiated wage rates on the above foundations. Denote the ratio of increase in the *overall* index of negotiated wage rates between quarter t and the corresponding quarter a year earlier by (W_t^r/W_{t-4}^r). We can regard $(W/_t^t W_{t-4}^r)$ as the average of four separate ratios of increase:

(i) the ratio of increase in the rates negotiated in quarter t over the rates applying to the workers concerned in quarter $(t-4)$;

(ii) the ratio of increase in the rates negotiated in quarter $(t-1)$ over the rates applying to the workers concerned in quarter $(t-4)$;

(iii) the ratio of increase in the rates negotiated in quarter $(t-2)$ over the rates applying to the workers concerned in quarter $(t-4)$; and

[1] d is given by $d = 1 + (E/V)$ where E denotes labour excess demand and V employment. d will be greater than unity in any quarter if excess demand is positive and less than unity if excess demand is negative.

(iv) the ratio of increase in the rates negotiated in quarter $(t-3)$ over the rates applying to the workers concerned in quarter $(t-4)$.

Now (i) is given by w_t/w_{t-4}. Also (ii) is given by w_{t-1}/w_{t-5} since, by assumption, rates are negotiated only once a year, and the ratio of increase in rates between quarter $(t-1)$ and quarter $(t-4)$ must be the same as the ratio of increase between quarter $(t-1)$ and quarter $(t-5)$ Similarly (iii) and (iv) are given by w_{t-2}/w_{t-6} and w_{t-3}/w_{t-7}. Hence W_t^r/W_{t-4}^r can be regarded as some average of w_t/w_{t-4}, w_{t-1}/w_{t-5}, w_{t-2}/w_{t-6} and w_{t-3}/w_{t-7}. By virtue of assumption (b) above, that the same number of workers are affected by each quarterly settlement, an unweighted average will be appropriate. If we use an unweighted *geometric* average we have:

$$\frac{W_t^r}{W_{t-4}^r} = \left(\frac{w_t}{w_{t-4}} \cdot \frac{w_{t-1}}{w_{t-5}} \cdot \frac{w_{t-2}}{w_{t-6}} \cdot \frac{w_{t-3}}{w_{t-7}} \right)^{\frac{1}{4}}. \qquad (9.22)$$

If we now substitute for the ws from (9.21) we get:

$$\frac{W_t^r}{W_{t-4}^r} = \bar{A} \left(\frac{\bar{P}_t}{\bar{P}_{t-4}} \right)^{\alpha} \bar{d}_t^{\beta} \, \bar{f}_t^{\gamma} \qquad (9.23)$$

where $\bar{A}$ is a constant and

$$\frac{\bar{P}_t}{\bar{P}_{t-4}} = \left(\frac{P_t}{P_{t-4}} \cdot \frac{P_{t-1}}{P_{t-5}} \cdot \frac{P_{t-2}}{P_{t-6}} \cdot \frac{P_{t-3}}{P_{t-7}} \right)^{\frac{1}{4}}$$

$$\bar{d}_t = (d_t \cdot d_{t-1} \cdot d_{t-2} \cdot d_{t-3})^{\frac{1}{4}}$$

$$\bar{f}_t = (f_t \cdot f_{t-1} \cdot f_{t-2} \cdot f_{t-3})^{\frac{1}{4}}.$$

The variable explained by (9.23) is the ratio of increase in the wage-rate index between quarter t and *the corresponding quarter one year earlier*. On the other hand, the dependent variable in our wage-rate hypothesis ($\dot{W}_t^r$) is the rate of increase in the wage-rate index between quarter t and *the previous quarter*. Hence the two hypotheses are not immediately comparable. However, a D.D.M.-type relationship which has $\dot{W}_t^r$ as the dependent variable can be derived without difficulty and, to bring out the connection between the D.D.M. hypothesis and our own, we shall do this before proceeding to a consideration of D.D.M.'s test of (9.23).

Reasoning along D.D.M. lines, we can say that the rate of increase in the wage-rate index between quarter t and the previous quarter ($\dot{W}_t^r$) will be some function, say g, of the ratio of increase between quarter t and the previous quarter in the wage rates of those workers whose wages are renegotiated in quarter t. But by the annual-settlement assumption, the ratio of increase between quarter t and the previous quarter in the wage rates of those workers whose wages are renegotiated in quarter t will be identical with w_t/w_{t-4}. Hence we have:

$$\dot{W}_t^r = g\left(\frac{w_t}{w_{t-4}}\right) \tag{9.24}$$

where g is some function.

Using (9.21) we can replace w_t/w_{t-4} in (9.24) by a function of P_t/P_{t-4}, d_t and f_t. Thus, reasoning along D.D.M. lines, we arrive at:

$$\dot{W}_t^r = \phi(P_t/P_{t-4}, d_t, f_t). \tag{9.25}$$

Evidently the hypothesis embodied in (9.25) is very similar to the hypothesis advanced in section 9.2 which makes $\dot{W}_t^r$ depend on: (i) the lagged rate of increase of price, as compared with the previous quarter; and (ii) the current pressure of labour excess demand. The differences between the two hypotheses are:

1. The price variable in (9.25) is the *ratio* of increase in prices between quarter t and quarter $(t-4)$, whereas the price variable in our hypothesis is the *rate* of increase in prices between quarter $(t-1)$ and quarter $(t-2)$.
2. The trade union pressure variable is included as an explanatory variable in (9.25) and does not appear in our relationship.
3. In the case of (9.25) the form of the function is unspecified, whereas a linear form is specified for our relationship.

In view of the similarity between the two hypotheses, the results of D.D.M.'s empirical work with (9.23) are of considerable interest. To test (9.23), D.D.M. first apply a logarithmic transformation which converts it into the linear relationship:

$$\log\left(\frac{\dot{W}_t^r}{\dot{W}_{t-4}^r}\right) = \log \bar{A} + \alpha \log\left(\frac{\bar{P}_t}{\bar{P}_{t-4}}\right) + \beta \log \bar{d}_t + \gamma \log \bar{f}_t. \tag{9.26}$$

Relationship (9.26) is then estimated by applying ordinary least squares to quarterly observations on the logs of the variables, the sample period being 1946 (IV) to 1956 (IV). The fitted relationship proves to be highly satisfactory on the usual statistical tests. Each of the estimates of coefficients is several times its estimated standard error, the overall fit of the relationship is good and, on the basis of the Durbin–Watson test, there is no evidence of first-order serial correlation in the disturbance term.[1]

We turn now to a series of three studies by Hines[2] which are closely related to the D.D.M. study just discussed. In these studies Hines is concerned with two basic questions, namely whether (i) trade union pressure and (ii) the level of unemployment are significant determinants of the rate of change of money wage rates. We shall now present an outline of Hines's approach to these questions, together with a summary of his main findings.

Take first the question of the role of trade union pressure. As we have seen, this question was considered in the D.D.M. study, one of the explanatory variables in D.D.M.'s basic wage-rate function (relationship (9.21)) being a measure of the pushfulness of the trade unions. However, as Hines points out, D.D.M.'s treatment of the question was not altogether satisfactory. To obtain their measure of pushfulness, D.D.M. first rated each of the years covered by their study for pushfulness on the basis of a five-point scale ranging from 'marked restraint' to 'marked pushfulness', and then used these annual ratings to construct a quarterly series. Hence their measure of pushfulness was entirely subjective.[3] Hines proposes an alternative measure, based on trade union membership, which avoids this difficulty. His starting-point is the same as D.D.M.'s – that since trade union 'militancy' (the equivalent of D.D.M.'s 'pushfulness') is an attitude and hence is not directly measurable, it is necessary to find some variable which is highly correlated with militancy to act as a proxy. The proxy he suggests, however, is an objective one. His argument is that when the unions are in a militant frame of mind they 'increase their membership as a proportion of the labour force, i.e. they run successful membership campaigns. Thus the rate of change of unionisation depends on the degree of militancy.'[4] This leads him to select ΔT as a quantitative proxy for militancy, where

[1] See Dicks-Mireaux and Dow, op. cit., Table 8, line 7, p. 159.

[2] See A. G. Hines, 'Trade Unions and Wage Inflation in the United Kingdom 1893–1961', *Review of Economic Studies* (Oct 1964) (to be cited henceforth as 'Trade Unions'); A. G. Hines, 'Wage Inflation in the United Kingdom 1948–1962: A Disaggregated Study', *Economic Journal* (Mar 1969) (to be cited as 'Wage Inflation'); and A. G. Hines, 'Unemployment and the Rate of Change of Money Wage Rates in the United Kingdom 1862–1963: A Reappraisal', *Review of Economics and Statistics* (Feb 1968) (to be cited as 'Unemployment').

[3] See Dicks-Mireaux and Dow, op. cit., pp. 160–1, and Hines, 'Trade Unions', p. 224.

[4] See Hines, 'Wage Inflation', p. 68.

ΔT denotes the absolute change in trade union membership as a proportion of the labour force, and to investigate the relationship between the rate of change of money wage rates and ΔT as the best way of testing the hypothesis that militancy is an independent determinant of changes in money wage rates.

The relationship between the rate of change of money wage rates and ΔT is investigated by Hines both at the level of the economy as a whole and also at the industry level. In his macro-study,[1] Hines experiments with a set of three relationships which are as follows:

$$\text{(i)} \quad \Delta W_t = a_1 + b_1 T$$
$$\text{(ii)} \quad \Delta W_t = a_2 + b_2 \Delta T \qquad (9.27)$$
$$\text{(iii)} \quad \Delta W_t = a_3 + b_3 T + c_3 \Delta T$$

where ΔW denotes the percentage rate of change of money wage rates[2] and T the *level* of trade union membership expressed as a proportion of the labour force. This set of relationships is fitted by ordinary least squares to annual British data for five separate periods: 1893–1912, 1921–38, 1949–61, 1921–61 (excluding 1939–48) and 1893–1961 (excluding 1913–20 and 1939–48). The coefficient of ΔT has the right sign and is considerably more than twice its standard error in every one of the ten regressions in which it appears.[3]

In his micro-study,[4] Hines works with annual data for twelve British industries for the years 1948–62. His procedure is to estimate for each industry and for the aggregate a relationship in which the dependent variable is the percentage rate of change in the index of money wage rates and the explanatory variable is either current ΔT or lagged ΔT. The method of estimation used is ordinary least squares. The most successful relationships are the thirteen in which current ΔT appears as the explanatory variable. In all of these thirteen cases the estimated coefficient has the right sign and in nine of the thirteen cases the estimated coefficient is more than twice its standard error.[5]

The results of these two studies appear to give strong support to the hypothesis that trade union militancy is an important determinant of the rate of change of money wage rates.

[1] See Hines, 'Trade Unions'.   [2] ΔW corresponds to $100\dot{W}$ in our notation.

[3] See Hines, 'Trade Unions', Table 1, p. 228. The coefficient of T has the right sign in seven of the ten regressions in which it appears but is more than twice its standard error in only two of these seven regressions.

[4] See Hines, 'Wage Inflation'.

[5] See Hines, 'Wage Inflation', Table 1. Note that the figures in this table show the estimated coefficient as a proportion of its standard error (see p. 70, n. 1).

We turn now to the question of the part played by the level of unemployment in the determination of the rate of change of money wage rates. Interest in this question derives largely from the pioneering study of Phillips,[1] and it may be helpful to begin with a brief account of his work.

The proposition which Phillips advanced was that, in the case of the United Kingdom, the unemployment percentage is the key determinant of the rate of change of money wage rates. He arrived at this proposition by arguing: (i) that the rate of change of money wage rates is a function of the level of excess demand for labour; and (ii) that the unemployment percentage (the number of unemployed as a percentage of the labour force) is a satisfactory proxy for labour excess demand. Together these two propositions imply that the rate of change of money wage rates is a function of the unemployment percentage.

Phillips proposed a particular non-linear form for the postulated relationship between the rate of change of money wage rates and the unemployment percentage, namely:

$$\Delta W_t + a = b(U_t)^c \tag{9.28}$$

where ΔW and U denote, respectively, the percentage rate of change of money wage rates and the unemployment percentage, and where a, b and c are three constants.[2] Using annual British data for the years 1861–1913 Phillips also estimated the three constants in the relationship, obtaining the numerical relationship:

$$\Delta W_t + 0.900 = 9.638(U_t)^{-1.394}.$$

This can be written in the alternative form:

$$\Delta W_t = -0.900 + \frac{9.638}{(U_t)^{1.394}}. \tag{9.29}$$

The implications of (9.29) are as follows:

(a) As the unemployment percentage approaches zero, the rate of increase of money wage rates becomes infinite ($\Delta W_t \rightarrow \infty$ as $U_t \rightarrow 0$).

[1] See A. W. Phillips, 'The Relation between Unemployment and the Rate of Change of Money Wage Rates in the United Kingdom', *Economica* (Nov 1958).
[2] We are using Hines's notation in the interests of comparability.

(b) As the unemployment percentage increases, the rate of increase of money wage rates falls and reaches zero when the unemployment percentage is 5·5.[1]

(c) For unemployment percentages in excess of 5·5 the rate of increase of money wage rates is negative, i.e. money wage rates decline. However, money wage rates never decline by more than 0·9 per cent per annum no matter how large the unemployment percentage becomes ($\Delta W_t \to -0.900$ as $U_t \to \infty$).

Using (a), (b) and (c), we see that the graphical representation of (9.29) is that given in Fig. 9.1.

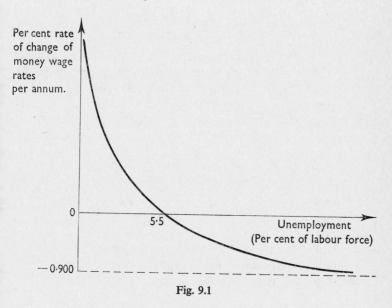

Fig. 9.1

A curve which shows the relationship between the rate of change of money wage rates and the unemployment percentage and which has the general properties of the curve depicted in Fig. 9.1 is nowadays referred to as a 'Phillips curve'.

---

[1] With $\Delta W_t = 0$, (9.29) gives:

$$\log 0.900 = \log 9.638 - 1.394 \log U_t$$

which in turn gives

$$\log U_t = \frac{\log 9.638 - \log 0.900}{1.394}.$$

From this expression we obtain: $U_t = 5.479$.

The work which Hines has done on the relationship between the rate of change of money wage rates and the level of unemployment stems directly from this work of Phillips and comprises studies both at the macro-level and at the industry level. In the main macro-study,[1] his procedure is to fit three different versions of the Phillips relationship to annual British data for the years 1893–1912, 1920–39 and 1949–61, using ordinary least squares. More precisely, the three relationships which are estimated for each of the three periods in question are of the form:

$$\text{(i)} \quad \Delta W_t = a + b(U_t)^{-1}$$
$$\text{(ii)} \quad \Delta W_t = a + b(U_t)^{-1} + c\Delta T_t + d\Delta P_{t-\frac{1}{2}} \qquad (9.30)$$
$$\text{(iii)} \quad \Delta W_t = a + b(U_t)^{-1} + c\Delta T_t + d\Delta P_{t-\frac{1}{2}} + e\Delta U_t$$

where ΔP denotes the percentage rate of change of prices[2] and ΔU the absolute rate of change of the unemployment percentage. By referring to (9.28) we see that the first of these relationships is the basic Phillips relationship with an *a priori* restriction on the parameter c (the value of c is specified in advance to be -1), while the second and third relationships are straightforward extensions of the basic relationship. For the period 1893–1912, the coefficient of the U variable is well determined (is considerably more than twice its standard error) in all three relationships. For the period 1920–39, on the other hand, the coefficient has the wrong sign in two of the three relationships and is less than twice its standard error in all three, while for the period 1949–61 the coefficient is less than twice its standard error in two of the three relationships.[3]

In another macro-study,[4] Hines experimented with yet a fourth version of the Phillips relationship, namely:

$$\Delta W_t = a + bU_t + c\Delta T_t + dT_t + e\Delta P_{t-\frac{1}{2}}. \qquad (9.31)$$

This relationship is a modification of (9.30) (ii). The most important point of difference is that the unemployment percentage enters linearly into (9.31), whereas it enters non-linearly into (9.30) (ii). In addition, both the level of the trade union membership proportion and its absolute rate of change enter (9.31) as explanatory variables, whereas only the latter appears in (9.30) (ii). In the macro-study in

---

[1] See Hines, 'Unemployment', pp. 62–7.
[2] On the meaning of the non-integral lag, see p. 295 above.
[3] See Hines, 'Unemployment', Table 1.
[4] See Hines, 'Trade Unions', pp. 239–42, 246.

question, Hines fitted (9.31) by ordinary least squares to annual British data for five separate periods: 1893–1912, 1921–38, 1949–61, 1921–61 (excluding 1939–48) and 1893–1961 (excluding 1913–20 and 1939–48). Only one of the five estimations, the estimation based on the years 1893–1912, gave a coefficient of U which was more than twice its standard error.[1] An estimation for the period 1921–61 (excluding 1939–48) was also done by the method of two-stage least squares. In this case the coefficient of U was less than twice its standard error once again.[2]

Hines has investigated the relationship between the rate of change of money wage rates and the unemployment percentage at the industry level also. Here his procedure is to estimate six alternative wage-rate relationships for each of twelve industry groups, using ordinary least squares and annual data for the period 1948–62. The dependent variable is the percentage rate of change of money wage rates in all six relationships. The list of explanatory variables varies from relationship to relationship, but in the case of five of the six relationships the explanatory variables include the unemployment percentage.[3] Thus, in all, there are sixty post-war regressions involving the unemployment percentage. In only ten of these does the unemployment variable show up as important on the criterion of an estimated coefficient in excess of twice its standard error.[4] Moreover, in the case of seven of the twelve industries there were no regressions in which the coefficient of the unemployment percentage was well determined.

Taken together, the results of these three studies give strong support to the view that, while the level of unemployment was probably a key determinant of the rate of change of money wage rates in Britain in the nineteenth century and in the early part of the twentieth century, it has ceased to have any real significance since the end of the Second World War.

We pointed out at the beginning of our discussion of the Phillips curve that the theoretical basis of the curve consisted of two propositions: (i) that the rate of change of money wage rates is dependent on the level of excess demand for labour; and (ii) that the unemployment percentage can be used as a proxy for labour excess demand.

[1] Ibid., p. 246.   [2] Ibid., p. 240.

[3] The unemployment percentage enters linearly in all cases. See Hines, 'Wage Inflation', p. 75, n. 3.

[4] Ibid., Table III. Note once again that the figures in this table show the estimated coefficient as a proportion of its standard error.

L

This being so, if we accept Hines's conclusion that there has been no significant relation between the rate of change of money wage rates and the unemployment percentage in Britain since the end of the Second World War, we are forced to conclude that one or both of these propositions are untenable as far as the post-war British economy is concerned. In view of the work of Dicks-Mireaux and Dow (see pp. 307–8 above), there appears to be little justification for rejecting proposition (i). Hence we are led to suspect proposition (ii), i.e. to suspect that the unemployment percentage may no longer be a satisfactory proxy for labour excess demand in the case of the British economy.

A possible explanation of the apparent failure of the unemployment percentage as a proxy for labour excess demand in the post-war period is as follows. Denote the actual level of employment by E, the desired level of employment by $\bar{E}$, the *number* of registered unemployed by U^* and the labour force by L where all four variables relate to the end of the period. Suppose that the following relationships hold between E, $\bar{E}$ and U^*:

$$(E_t - E_{t-1}) = k(\bar{E}_t - E_{t-1}) \tag{9.32}$$

$$U^*_t - U^*_{t-1} = s(L_t - L_{t-1}) + r(E_t - E_{t-1}) \tag{9.33}$$

where k, s and r are three constants which satisfy: $0 < k \le 1$; $0 < s < 1$; $-1 < r < 0$. Both of these relationships appear plausible. According to (9.32) the increase in the level of employment between the beginning and the end of period t will be proportional to the excess of desired employment as at the end of the period over actual employment as at the beginning of the period, i.e. (9.32) is a 'partial-adjustment' hypothesis of the type introduced in earlier chapters (see p. 116 above). In (9.33) a linear relationship is postulated between the change in the number of registered unemployed, the change in the labour force and the change in employment. This relationship implies that, with a constant labour force, a given decrease in employment will be reflected in a smaller increase in the level of registered unemployed, since some of the new unemployed will fail to register. Likewise the relationship implies that, with a constant level of employment, a given increase in the labour force will be reflected in a smaller increase in the level of registered unemployed, since some of the new entrants to the labour force who are unable to obtain employment will fail to register.

Substituting (9.32) into (9.33), we get:

$$U_t^* - U_{t-1}^* = s(L_t - L_{t-1}) + rk(\bar{E}_t - E_{t-1})$$

$$\therefore \quad U_t^* - U_{t-1}^* = -s[(\bar{E}_t - L_t) - (\bar{E}_{t-1} - L_{t-1})] + [s(\bar{E}_t - \bar{E}_{t-1}) + rk(\bar{E}_t - E_{t-1})].$$

Now $U_t^* = L_t U_t$ where U is the unemployment percentage. Hence:

$$U_t - U_{t-1}\frac{L_{t-1}}{L_t} = -s\left[\frac{\bar{E}_t - L_t}{L_t} - \frac{\bar{E}_{t-1} - L_{t-1}}{L_{t-1}}\cdot\frac{L_{t-1}}{L_t}\right]$$
$$+ \left[\frac{s(\bar{E}_t - \bar{E}_{t-1}) + rk(\bar{E}_t - E_{t-1})}{L_t}\right].$$

Since $L_t/L_{t-1}\simeq 1$ given that the period is short, we have:

$$U_t - U_{t-1}\simeq -s\left[\frac{\bar{E}_t - L_t}{L_t} - \frac{\bar{E}_{t-1} - L_{t-1}}{L_{t-1}}\right] + \left[\frac{s(\bar{E}_t - \bar{E}_{t-1}) + rk(\bar{E}_t - E_{t-1})}{L_t}\right].$$
$$(9.34)$$

Now the term in the first square bracket on the right-hand side of (9.34) is the change in the relative excess demand for labour. Consequently for the unemployment percentage to be a satisfactory proxy for labour excess demand, it would be necessary for the term in the second square bracket to be zero – the change in the unemployment percentage would then be negatively proportional to the change in the relative excess demand for labour. And since the term in question will not be zero, in general, it follows that, given (9.32) and (9.33), the unemployment percentage will not be a satisfactory proxy for labour excess demand except in very special circumstances.

The second term on the right-hand side of (9.34) will be zero if $k = 1$ and $s = -r$, for if $k = 1$, (9.32) gives $\bar{E}_{t-1} = E_{t-1}$. One can say, therefore, that the use of the unemployment percentage as a proxy for labour excess demand involves assuming that actual employment adjusts instantaneously to desired employment ($k = 1$) and that the degree of failure to register for employment is the same among new members of the labour force as among old ($s = -r$).

To sum up this discussion of Hines's work, we can say that he has made a twofold contribution to the study of the determinants of the rate of change of negotiated wage rates. In the first place he has established the importance of trade union militancy or pushfulness as an explanatory variable in the wage-rate function. Secondly he has shown that, as far as the British economy is concerned, the Phillips curve was, essentially, a nineteenth-century phenomenon and that, for all practical purposes, it no longer exists. This does not mean that labour excess demand can be dismissed as an explanatory variable in the British wage-rate function, but rather that it is badly represented by the unemployment percentage.

9.7 Empirical Studies: Wage-drift

We turn now from the determinants of the rate of increase of negotiated wage rates to the determinants of the wage-drift. The most detailed British study of this question is the study undertaken by Judith Marquand[1] which follows the same lines as the pioneering Swedish study of Hansen and Rehn,[2] and we shall begin by presenting an account of her work.

Marquand begins by formulating a simple hypothesis about the determinants of wage-drift and for this purpose lists the main ways in which wage-drift (a discrepancy between the rate of increase of wage earnings and the rate of increase of negotiated wage rates) can arise. In the first place, the rate of increase of wage earnings can deviate from the rate of increase of wage rates because of changes in the extent of overtime working. Secondly, wage-drift can arise because of changes in productivity. This connection is most obvious in the case of industries characterised by piece-work. When the productivity of piece-workers increases for any reason, there will be an increase in piece-workers' earnings; and since this increase in earnings takes place at unchanged piece-work rates, the increase in productivity will be reflected in wage-drift. Finally, and most obviously, wage-drift can arise because employers pay wage rates which are higher than those negotiated at the national level as a means of maintaining, or perhaps increasing, their labour force.

In the light of this list of the main sources of wage-drift, Marquand proposes a hypothesis to explain wage-drift. To set out this hypothesis, Marquand uses the following notation:

---

[1] See J. Marquand, 'Earnings-Drift in the United Kingdom 1948–57', *Oxford Economic Papers*, n.s. (Feb 1960).

[2] See B. Hansen and G. Rehn, 'On Wage Drift: A Problem of Money-wage Dynamics', in *25 Economic Essays in Honour of Erik Lindahl* (Stockholm: Ekonomisk Tidskrift, 1956).

d = wage-drift[1]
h = hours worked
p = productivity, measured as change in output per man
v = unfilled vacancies (an indicator of excess demand)
q = gross profits per man-hour.

In terms of this notation, the hypothesis is:

$$d_t = \alpha h_t + \beta p_t + \gamma v_t + \delta p_t \qquad (9.35)$$

where α, β, γ and δ are four positive constants.

The variables h and p are introduced to take care of wage-drift arising from the first and second of the three sources listed above, respectively, and the variables v and q to take care of wage-drift arising from the third source. The idea underlying the latter is that the higher is excess demand, the greater will be the difficulty of obtaining a labour force of sufficient size and quality and hence the greater the *incentive* for employers to pay their workers at higher than negotiated rates. On the other hand, the higher is the profit level, the greater will be the *ability* of employers to pay in excess of the negotiated rates.

Marquand has submitted the wage-drift hypothesis set out in (9.35) to two tests – a signs-of-change test and a correlation test – the data for both tests being annual British data for the years 1948–57 for each of sixteen industrial groups. The signs-of-change test is designed to test one aspect of the hypothesis, namely the positive signs of the four coefficients, rather than the hypothesis as a whole. For the purposes of this test the data for the sixteen separate industries are pooled and the signs of change between successive years are determined for each of the variables in (9.35). The signs of change are then compared, year by year, for various pairs of the variables, e.g. d and h, d and v, and so on, and for each pair the number of like signs and the number of unlike signs is counted. From the results of these counts it is concluded that, as postulated by (9.35), a positive association exists between d and each of the explanatory variables. The test is also performed on the pooled data for the eight industries which showed the most rapid increases in production over the sample period and the eight industries which showed the least rapid increases. Here the results are less conclusive. For the first group of eight industries there is definite evidence of positive association

---

[1] Note that Marquand uses the term 'earnings-drift' where we use 'wage-drift' and reserves the term 'wage-drift' for earnings-drift (our wage-drift) after elimination of the contribution of changes in overtime.

between d and h and d and p but not between d and v and d and q. For the second group of industries there is evidence of a positive association between d and h and d and v but not between d and the other two explanatory variables.

The correlation test consists of the calculation, for each of the sixteen industry groups, of various simple correlation coefficients between the variables entering (9.35), together with various first-order, second-order and third-order partial coefficients. An examination of these calculations suggests that the positive association between wage-drift and the four explanatory variables in (9.35), which is confirmed by the main signs-of-change test is not particularly strong. As an example, take the second-order and third-order partial correlations between wage-drift and unfilled vacancies, and between wage-drift and output per man. Only seven of the sixteen industries show a second-order partial coefficient between d and v which differs significantly from zero at the 5 per cent level, and only eight a second-order coefficient between d and p which is significant at this level. Of the sixteen industries only four show a third-order partial coefficient between d and v which is significant at the 5 per cent level and only three a third-order coefficient between d and p which is significant at this level.[1]

To sum up, we can say that from the standpoint of our wage equation (9.11), the most significant conclusion to emerge from Marquand's study is that, at the level of the individual industry, there is some evidence of a positive association between wage-drift and labour excess demand but little to suggest that the association is a particularly strong one.

Another important study of determinants of wage-drift in the United Kingdom is the study undertaken some years ago by the O.E.E.C. and reported in *The Problem of Rising Prices*.[2] Unlike Marquand's study, the O.E.E.C. study is concerned only with the determinants of wage-drift in the major British industries as a whole. The study takes the form of a regression analysis in which the dependent variable is six-monthly wage-drift adjusted for changes in overtime.[3] Several regressions are tried, the explanatory variables in each case being drawn from a list of nine. In addition to the

---

[1] See Marquand, op. cit., Appendix 4, p. 104.

[2] See W. Fellner, M. Gilbert, B. Hansen, R. Kahn, F. Lutz and P. de Wolff, *The Problem of Rising Prices* (Paris: Organization for European Economic Co-operation, 1961) pp. 432–6, 449–50.   [3] Ibid., p. 449.

variables investigated by Marquand in her study of wage-drift in specific industries, the list of explanatory variables includes certain interesting new variables, among which is the 'wage-round', i.e. the number of workers affected by wage-rate changes in the current six-monthly period. The most successful regressions are two in which six-monthly wage-drift is explained by this particular variable – on its own in one regression and together with the excess demand for labour in the other. In the notation used in the study the regressions in question are:

$$WD = 1 \cdot 09 - 0 \cdot 0001135 WR \qquad (9.36)$$

$$WD = 1 \cdot 97 - 0 \cdot 0002457 WR + 0 \cdot 0004783 DL \qquad (9.37)$$

where WD denotes wage-drift, WR wage-round and DL labour excess demand.

It will be observed that the wage-round variable appears with a negative sign in both regressions. Thus the regressions imply that, other things being equal, the wage-drift of any six-monthly period will be smaller, the larger is the number of workers whose wage rates have been renegotiated in the period. This, in turn, suggests that part of the wage-drift which takes place after any wage-bargaining session is consolidated into negotiated rates at the next bargaining session. In other words, the regressions suggest that, to some extent, wage-drift and increases in negotiated rates are alternatives.

An attempt is made in the study to assess the order of magnitude of this consolidation on the basis of the parameter estimates of (9.36) and (9.37) above. Regression (9.36) implies that if *no* workers are affected by changes in negotiated rates in a particular six-monthly period, the wage-drift of the period will be 2·2 per cent per annum ($2 \times 1 \cdot 09$) while the corresponding figure for regression (9·37) is 4·0 per cent per annum ($2 \times 1 \cdot 97$).[1] On the other hand, when *all* workers are affected by changes in negotiated rates in a particular six-monthly period, the wage-drift of the period will be only 0·7 per cent per annum.[2] These figures suggest that anything between two-thirds and four-fifths of 'inter-bargain' wage-drift would be consolidated into negotiated rates in any period if all workers were to receive increases in negotiated rates.

[1] This assumes zero excess demand for labour.
[2] It is not clear from the study whether this figure comes from regression (9.36) or regression (9.37).

In the O.E.E.C. study the quantitative significance of consolidation is assessed by measuring the reduction in wage-drift in a situation in which all workers are covered by a new wage settlement as compared with a situation in which none are so covered. Another possible approach to the measurement problem is to consider the extent to which earnings rise, rather than the extent to which wage-drift falls, in response to an increase in negotiated rates. This is the approach followed by Dicks-Mireaux and Shepherd (D.M.S.) in another important British study.[1]

The procedure adopted by D.M.S. is to estimate from annual data for manufacturing industry the following relationship:

$$e_t = \alpha_0 + \alpha_1 w_t + \alpha_2 d_t \qquad (9.38)$$

where e is the twelve-month percentage change in weekly wage earnings adjusted for changes in hours worked, w is the twelve-month percentage change in weekly wage rates and d is the average level of labour excess demand during the twelve months over which the changes in earnings and rates have been measured. Two methods of estimation were applied to the data, namely two-stage least squares and ordinary least squares. The coefficient of w was estimated at 0·59 by the first method and at 0·63 by the second method,[2] which suggests that, given the level of d, an increase of one point in the rate of increase of the wage-rate index will be reflected in an increase of a little under two-thirds of one point in the rate of increase of the wage-earnings index or by a reduction of about one-third of a point in wage-drift. Thus the D.M.S. study suggests that consolidation is an important phenomenon in the United Kingdom, though a good deal less important than would appear from the O.E.E.C. study discussed above.

9.8 Implications of Empirical Studies

To conclude the chapter, we shall now make a brief assessment of the model presented in section 9.2 in the light of the results of the empirical studies discussed in sections 9.4 to 9.7.

The study by Dicks-Mireaux, which we discussed in section 9.4, indicates that our model is along the right general lines, and this assessment stands when the results of the more detailed studies

[1] See L. A. Dicks-Mireaux and J. R. Shepherd, 'The Wages Structure and Some Implications for Incomes Policy', *National Institute Economic Review* (Nov 1962).   [2] Ibid., p. 48, Table 10.

discussed in sections 9.5 to 9.7 are taken into the reckoning. These studies suggest that the broad structure of the price and wage equations which comprise the model is sound and that the model constitutes a satisfactory framework for the discussion of policy against inflation. On the other hand, the studies in question point to various ways in which the detail of price and wage equations could be improved, albeit at the cost of some added complexity. For example, the results of Neild's study provide grounds for arguing that it might be more appropriate to represent the response of the price index to changes in the various unit-cost indexes by means of some form of distributed lag rather than by the simple one-period delay embodied in our equation (9.9). Also from Neild's study there is reason to believe that we could improve the price equation by incorporating in it the distinction between long-run changes in productivity, which reflect technical progress, and short-run changes which reflect variations in the level of activity. The studies of the determinants of changes in money wage rates by Dicks-Mireaux and Dow and by Hines suggest that we could improve our wage-rate equation by adding some proxy for trade union pushfulness, such as Hines's ΔT, to the two explanatory variables which appear already. Finally, the studies of the determinants of wage-drift discussed in the early part of the present section, though somewhat inconclusive, give grounds for the belief that excess demand is not the only important determinant of wage-drift. None of these possible amendments is unimportant, and it will be necessary to keep them in mind when we come to discuss anti-inflation policy in the next chapter within the framework of the model comprised by (9.9) and (9.11).

9.9 Summary

The Keynesian model of the inflationary process contains no hypothesis about the way in which individual prices are fixed. An alternative model which overcomes the main limitations of the Keynesian model can be constructed by adopting a specific hypothesis about price fixation, namely that price is raised whenever variable cost per unit of output increases, the new price being fixed by adding some margin – possibly, but not necessarily, the same margin as before – to the new unit variable cost to cover fixed costs and to provide a profit. From this starting-point an aggregate price equation is developed which makes the proportionate rate of increase of the price index depend directly on the lagged proportionate rate of increase of the index of wage and salary earnings per man, the lagged proportionate rate of increase of the index of unit imported materials cost and the current proportionate rate of increase of the index of profit margins, and inversely on the lagged proportionate rate of increase of the index of output per man. A complete model of the inflationary process is then devised by adding to the price equation a money-wage equation which specifies that the proportionate rate of increase of the index of wage and salary earnings per man depends on the lagged proportionate rate of increase of the price index and the current level of excess demand. The unknowns in this two-equation model are the proportionate rate of increase of the price index and the proportionate rate of increase of the index of wage and salary earnings per man, while the explicit data are the level of excess demand, the proportionate rate of increase of the index of unit imported materials cost, the proportionate rate of increase of the index of profit margins and the proportionate rate of increase of the index of output per man.

This model implies that there are six basic ways in which an inflation can develop: by means of a maintained rise in the unit cost of imported materials; by means of a maintained fall in output per man; by means of a maintained rise in profit margins; by means of a temporary rise in excess demand; by means of an autonomous rise in prices; and by means of an autonomous rise in wage earnings per man.

In recent years there have been several British empirical studies which bear on this model. The most important of these studies are examined in detail in the chapter and, in the final section, the model is assessed in the light of them. The conclusion which emerges is that the broad structure of the model is sound and that it constitutes a satisfactory framework for the discussion of anti-inflation policy in the British context, though the details of the price and wage equations could possibly be improved at the cost of some added complexity.

READING LIST

Brown, A. J., *The Great Inflation, 1939–1951* (London: Oxford University Press, 1955).

Dicks-Mireaux, L. A., and Dow, J. C. R., 'The Determinants of Wage Inflation:

United Kingdom, 1946–56', *Journal of the Royal Statistical Society*, series A, CXXII (2) (1959).

——, 'The Interrelationship between Cost and Price Changes, 1946–1959: A Study of Inflation in Post-war Britain', *Oxford Economic Papers*, n.s. (Oct 1961).

—— and Shepherd, J. R., 'The Wages Structure and Some Implications for Incomes Policy', *National Institute Economic Review* (Nov 1962).

Dow, J. C. R., 'Analysis of the Generation of Price Inflation: A Study of Cost and Price Changes in the United Kingdom, 1946–54', *Oxford Economic Papers*, n.s. (Sep 1956).

—— and Dicks-Mireaux, L. A., 'The Excess Demand for Labour: A Study of Conditions in Great Britain, 1946–56', *Oxford Economic Papers*, n.s. (Feb 1958).

Eckstein, O., and Wilson, T. A., 'The Determination of Money Wages in American Industry', *Quarterly Journal of Economics* (Aug 1962).

Fellner, F., Gilbert, M., Hansen, B., Kahn, R., Lutz, F., and de Wolff, P., *The Problem of Rising Prices* (Paris: Organization for European Economic Co-operation, 1961).

Gillion, C., 'Wage-Rates, Earnings and Wage-Drift', *National Institute Economic Review* (Nov 1968).

Hansen, B., and Rehn, G., 'On Wage Drift: A Problem of Money-wage Dynamics', in *25 Economic Essays in Honour of Eric Lindahl* (Stockholm: Ekonomisk Tidskrift, 1956).

Hines, A. G., 'Trade Unions and Wage Inflation in the United Kingdom 1893–1961', *Review of Economic Studies* (Oct 1964).

——, 'Unemployment and the Rate of Change of Money Wage Rates in the United Kingdom 1862–1963: A Reappraisal', *Review of Economics and Statistics* (Feb 1968).

——, 'Wage Inflation in the United Kingdom 1948–1962: A Disaggregated Study', *Economic Journal* (Mar 1969).

Klein, L. R., and Ball, R. J., 'Some Econometrics of the Determination of Absolute Prices and Wages', *Economic Journal* (Sep 1959).

Knowles, K. G. J. C., and Winsten, C. B., 'Can the Level of Unemployment Explain Changes in Wages?', *Bulletin of the Oxford University Institute of Statistics* (Feb 1959).

Lipsey, R. G., 'The Relation between Unemployment and the Rate of Change of Money Wage Rates in the United Kingdom, 1862–1957: A Further Analysis', *Economica*, n.s. (Feb 1960).

—— and Steuer, M. D., 'The Relation between Profits and Wage Rates', *Economica*, n.s. (May 1961).

Marquand, J., 'Earnings-drift in the United Kingdom, 1948–57', *Oxford Economic Papers*, n.s. (Feb 1960).

Neild, R. R., *Pricing and Employment in the Trade Cycle* (Cambridge University Press, 1963).

Paish, F. W., *Studies in an Inflationary Economy: The United Kingdom, 1948–1961* (London: Macmillan, 1962).

Phelps Brown, E. H., 'Wage Drift', *Economica* (Nov 1962).

Phillips, A. W., 'The Relation between Unemployment and the Rate of Change of Money Wage Rates in the United Kingdom, 1861–1957', *Economica*, n.s. (Nov 1958).

10 Anti-inflation Policy: The Pursuit of Price Stability

10.1 Introduction

In Chapters 6 and 7 we discussed various policy questions relating to the objectives of internal balance and external balance within the framework of the theoretical material presented in Chapters 2 to 5. In the present chapter we turn to the third of the four macro-objectives considered in the first chapter of the book – the objective of price stability. As in Chapters 6 and 7 our aim will be to consider the ways in which this objective can be attained, and to do this, moreover, within a fairly tight theoretical framework. In this case the theoretical background for our discussion will be the model developed in the preceding chapter. It seems fair to say that this model, or a model which resembles it very closely, underlies all contemporary discussion of policy in relation to the price-stability objective.

The starting-point of our discussion is the price equation of the model, which we repeat for the reader's convenience at this point:

$$\dot{P}_t = \beta_1(\dot{W}_{t-1} - \dot{O}_{t-1}) + \beta_2 \dot{M}_{t-1} + \dot{K}_t \tag{9.9}$$

where P is the implicit deflator of gross domestic product at factor cost, W is an index of money wage earnings per man in the economy as a whole, O is an index of output per man in the economy as a whole, M is an index of the cost of imported materials per unit of output in the economy as a whole, K is an index of the ratio of price to unit variable cost in the economy as a whole and β_1 and β_2 are two positive constants. The dot indicates 'proportional rate of increase'.

The task of anti-inflation policy can be thought of as that of making $\dot{P}$ less than otherwise by suitable manipulation of the various magnitudes which enter into (9.9). Of these, the constants β_1 and β_2 and the rate of increase of the index M are largely beyond the authorities' control and, for all practical purposes, $\dot{P}$ can be reduced below what it would otherwise be in only one of three ways:

(i) by reducing $\dot{W}$ below what it would otherwise be;
(ii) by raising $\dot{O}$ above what it would otherwise be; and
(iii) by reducing $\dot{K}$ below what it would otherwise be.

This much is fairly common ground. There is general agreement that (i), (ii) and (iii) represent the desired results. Where the parties to the debate about anti-inflation policy differ is in relation to the means of achieving these results. There are two broad approaches to the problem which are quite distinct, though by no means mutually exclusive.

The first approach is to use direct persuasion (backed, perhaps, by legal sanctions) at all relevant points – to attempt to persuade the parties to wage negotiations to exercise more restraint than they would have done if left to themselves (item (i) above), to try to persuade firms to adopt new practices which will raise their productivity (item (ii)), and to attempt to persuade price-makers to increase price by less than they would have done otherwise or to reduce price when otherwise they would have left it unchanged (item (iii)). The second approach is to use the instruments of economic policy discussed in Chapter 6 to so restrict aggregate demand that the level of $\dot{W}$ (the rate of increase of wage earnings per man) is less than it would have been otherwise (item (i)).

The first approach is often dubbed the 'cost-inflation' approach and the second the 'demand-inflation' approach. We shall not use these terms, because we believe them to have been the source of great confusion. The terms we shall use are, for the first, the 'prices and incomes policy' (P.I.P.) approach and for the second the 'demand-restriction' (D.R.) approach. We shall consider the P.I.P. approach, in the British context, in the next four sections. Section 10.6 will deal with the D.R. approach.

10.2 P.I.P. Approach: Post-war Development

The P.I.P. approach to the control of inflation has been tried on several different occasions in the United Kingdom over the post-war period, and we shall begin our discussion of this approach by giving a brief account of the various phases through which it has passed. These may be distinguished as follows:

1. Phase 1: 1948–50.
2. Phase 2: 1956.
3. Phase 3: 1961–2.
4. Phase 4: 1962–4.
5. Phase 5: 1965–6.
6. Phase 6: 1966–7.
7. Phase 7: 1967–.

1. *Phase 1: 1948–50*

The P.I.P. approach was first tried by the Attlee Labour Government over the period 1948–50, when the United Kingdom was faced with serious balance of payments difficulties. The first phase of the P.I.P. approach became known as the 'wage-freeze' and, as this name suggests, the emphasis in this phase was mainly on wage restraint. In effect, what the authorities set out to do was to make $\dot{W}$ equal to zero as a means of temporarily depressing the home–import price ratio and so checking the growth of import payments (see p. 235 above).

To implement the freeze the authorities relied primarily on exhortation. In the White Paper which initiated the freeze,[1] the Government stated quite bluntly that 'In present conditions ... there is no justification for any *general* increase of individual money incomes'[2] and pressed this view on 'all those engaged in negotiations or decisions which might result in an increase in wages or other personal incomes'.[3] In addition to such exhortation the Government undertook, in the above-mentioned White Paper, to set a good example in any wage negotiations in which it might itself be directly concerned, and made the veiled threat that if, in spite of its appeals, wages were increased, 'there can be no presumption ... that the resulting costs will be taken into account in settling controlled prices'.[4] But it shied clear of any attempt to bolster the voluntary approach by means of legislation giving the authorities some form of statutory power over wage decisions.

2. *Phase 2: 1956*

In the second phase of the P.I.P. approach the authorities stressed the need for price restraint as well as for wage restraint, i.e. they attempted to make both $\dot{K}$ and $\dot{W}$ less than they would otherwise

---

[1] See *Statement on Personal Income, Costs and Prices*, Cmd 7321 (Feb 1948).
[2] Ibid., p. 3 (italics in original).   [3] Ibid., p. 4.   [4] Ibid.

have been. Once again they avoided legislation and relied on direct persuasion to achieve the desired results. This took the form of a series of informal discussions between the Conservative Government of the day and leaders of labour and management on the question of wage and price restraint, coupled with public appeals for restraint of a very general kind to both sides of industry. As an example of the latter, we quote the following passage from a White Paper published in March 1956:

> This is the dilemma which confronts the country. If the prosperous economic conditions necessary to maintain full employment are exploited by trade unions and business men, price stability and full employment become incompatible. The solution lies in self-restraint in making wage claims and fixing profit margins and prices, so that total money income rises no faster than total output. In the absence of such self-restraint, it may seem that the country can make a choice . . . between full employment and continually rising prices, or price stability secured with some danger to the level of employment that might otherwise have been achieved.[1]

These efforts appear to have carried weight with the leaders of management and they may well have contributed something towards the exercise of price restraint in 1956 and subsequent years. On the other hand, they made no real impression on the trade union leaders[2] and in the late 1950s the trade union movement remained actively hostile to any suggestion that absence of wage restraint was the main cause of the inflationary developments of those years.

3. Phase 3: 1961–2

The third phase of the P.I.P. approach, known generally as the 'pay-pause', resembled the first in that, in effect, it was an attempt to make W equal to zero as a means of remedying a critical external situation. The pay-pause was initiated in a statement on 25 July 1961 by the then Conservative Chancellor, Mr Selwyn Lloyd. Mr Lloyd's statement was extremely brief and somewhat half-hearted. After drawing attention to the critical external situation, the Chancellor added:

> In my view, there must be a pause [in wage and salary increases] until productivity has caught up and there is room for further advances. It is not possible in any general statement to cover every particular case. Where commitments have already been entered into, they should be met.

---

[1] See The Economic Implications of Full Employment, Cmd 9725 (Mar 1956) p. 11.

[2] See Economist, 4 Aug 1956, pp. 388 and 426, and 25 Aug 1956, p. 616.

Subject to this, however, a pause is essential as a basis for continued prosperity and growth. In those areas for which the Government have direct responsibility we shall act in accordance with this policy. The Government ask that the same lines should be followed elsewhere both in the private sector and in those parts of the public sector outside the immediate control of the Government.[1]

As will be clear from this quotation, on this occasion, as on the occasion of the wage-freeze, the authorities relied on exhortation of the private sector, strengthened by the pledge of a good example in the public sector, to achieve the desired results. Once again there was no question of the authorities assuming statutory power in relation to wage decisions.

There is general agreement that the pay-pause had little effect on the level of W. The Government certainly fulfilled the Chancellor's undertaking to implement the pause in those wage negotiations in which it was itself concerned. For example, wage and salary increases which were granted to civil servants and workers in the National Health Services after the beginning of the pause in July 1961 were not implemented until after the formal end of the pause on 31 March 1962. Also certain awards of the Civil Service Arbitration Tribunal and the Industrial Court were held in abeyance as a result of government intervention. On the other hand, there is little evidence that the Government's example was followed to any appreciable extent in the private sector and in those parts of the public sector over which the Government had no immediate control.

4. *Phase 4: 1962–4*

In phase 4, as in phases 1 and 3, the emphasis, in the main, was on wage restraint: the objective was a lower W than would otherwise have been achieved. On this occasion, however, there was one important new feature. In phases 1 and 3 the target rate of increase in money wage and salary earnings per man over the economy as a whole, or the 'wage norm' as it was later to be called, was put at zero. In phase 4, on the other hand, the norm was put at 2 to $2\frac{1}{2}$ per cent per annum. The argument for choosing this figure was that since it is 'a condition of reasonable price stability that increases in incomes should keep in step with the growth of production', and since in recent years 'national production per head has risen by about 2 to

---

[1] See H.C. Deb, 25 July 1961, pp. 222–3.

2½ per cent a year', it is necessary for the achievement of price stability 'that the increase of wages and salaries . . . should be kept within this figure during the next phase'.[1]

As on all previous occasions, the Government relied on exhortation to achieve the desired results: 'It is for employers and employees to work out the application of the considerations set out above to individual cases. . . . The Government ask, however, that all negotiations affecting wages and salaries in 1962 should reflect these considerations'.[2] However, this and similar appeals fell on deaf ears. This was no surprise. For, in January 1962, the Trades Union Congress had been invited by the Conservative Government of the day to help formulate proposals for wage restraint in the post-pay-pause period. This invitation had been rejected and the Government had been obliged to proceed without trade union support.[3]

5. *Phase 5: 1965–6*

As will be clear from the foregoing, the trade union movement displayed little enthusiasm for prices and incomes policy during the 1950s and early 1960s when Conservative Governments were in power. This attitude changed with the election of the second post-war Labour Government in October 1964, and in December 1964 representatives of the Trades Union Congress joined representatives of the Government and the employers' organisations in signing the *Joint Statement of Intent on Productivity, Prices and Incomes* which ushered in the fifth phase of the P.I.P. approach. This new phase was marked by several interesting developments, of which four deserve attention.

In the first place, there was a return to the emphasis on price restraint, as well as wage restraint, which had first appeared in phase 2 and which had been played down in phases 3 and 4.

Secondly, prime responsibility for the implementation of prices and incomes policy was given to a new organisation, known as the National Board for Prices and Incomes (N.B.P.I.), which was set up by the Government in April 1965. The Board was to be an investigating body; the intention was that, on a reference from the Government, the Board would conduct an investigation to see whether a specified price increase or a specified wage increase was justified and would then make its findings and recommendations known to the

---

[1] See *Incomes Policy: The Next Step*, Cmnd 1626 (Feb 1962) p. 4.
[2] Ibid., p. 5.   [3] Ibid., p. 4.

parties concerned. There was to be no compulsion on the parties concerned in an investigation to accept the Board's recommendations. It was hoped that government persuasion backed by the pressure of public opinion would be enough to ensure that most of the Board's recommendations were put into effect.

A third important development in phase 5 related to the general character of the statements setting out the price and wage criteria, i.e. the type of behaviour which the authorities would regard as desirable by those concerned with fixing prices and money wages. Whereas in earlier phases these had been couched in the most general terms, in phase 5 they became quite detailed and specific in character.

The criteria for *price* behaviour were set out in paragraphs 9 and 10 of a White Paper entitled *Prices and Incomes Policy*,[1] in the following way:

9. To keep the general level of prices stable, it is vital that price increases should be avoided where possible and that prices should be reduced wherever circumstances permit. Enterprises will not be expected to raise their prices except in the following circumstances:
  (i) if output per employee cannot be increased sufficiently to allow wages and salaries to increase at a rate consistent with the criteria for incomes . . . without some increase in prices, and no offsetting reductions can be made in non-labour costs per unit of output or in the return sought on investment;
 (ii) if there are unavoidable increases in non-labour costs such as materials, fuel, services or marketing costs per unit of output which cannot be offset by reductions in labour or capital costs per unit of output or in the return sought on investment;
(iii) if there are unavoidable increases in capital costs per unit of output which cannot be offset by reductions in non-capital costs per unit or in the return sought on investment;
 (iv) if, after every effort has been made to reduce costs, the enterprise is unable to secure the capital required to meet home and overseas demand.
10. Enterprises will be expected to reduce their prices in the following circumstances:
  (i) if output per employee is increasing faster than the rate of increase in wages and salaries which is consistent with the criteria for incomes . . . and there are no offsetting and unavoidable increases in non-labour costs per unit of output;
 (ii) if the costs of materials, fuel or services per unit of output are falling and there are no offsetting and unavoidable increases in labour or capital costs per unit of output;
(iii) if capital costs per unit of output are falling and there are no

[1] See *Prices and Incomes Policy*, Cmnd 2639 (Apr 1965).

offsetting and unavoidable increases in non-capital costs per unit of output;

(iv) if profits are based on excessive market power.[1]

The White Paper, *Prices and Incomes Policy*, also set out *criteria* for *wage* behaviour. These consisted of: (i) a norm for wage and salary increases; and (ii) a list of the circumstances justifying pay increases in excess of the prescribed norm. As in phase 4, the norm was fixed, in the interests of price stability, at a figure equal to the average annual percentage increase in output per head which seemed likely over the next few years. The figure actually prescribed was 3 to $3\frac{1}{2}$ per cent per annum, this being the average annual increase in output per head which had been predicted for the period 1964–70 and which was being used at the time in drawing up the National Plan.[2]

Those involved in negotiations for wage and salary increases were urged to keep within the prescribed norm except where exceptional treatment was required in the national interest. The circumstances in which pay increases in excess of the norm would be justified, in the Government's view, were listed in paragraph 15 of *Prices and Incomes Policy* as follows:

15. Exceptional pay increases should be confined to the following circumstances:
   (i) where the employees concerned, for example by accepting more exacting work or a major change in working practices, make a direct contribution towards increasing productivity in the particular firm or industry. Even in such cases some of the benefit should accrue to the community as a whole in the form of lower prices;
  (ii) where it is essential in the national interest to secure a change in the distribution of manpower (or to prevent a change which would otherwise take place) and a pay increase would be necessary and effective for this purpose;
 (iii) where there is general recognition that existing wage and salary levels are too low to maintain a reasonable standard of living;
  (iv) where there is widespread recognition that the pay of a certain group of workers has fallen seriously out of line with the level of remuneration for similar work and needs in the national interest to be improved.[3]

We come now to the fourth of the important developments in the P.I.P. approach which characterised phase 5, namely the increasing

---

[1] Ibid., p. 7.
[2] See *The National Plan,* Cmnd 2764 (Sep 1965).   [3] Ibid., p. 8.

emphasis given to the need for productivity increase. In earlier phases the authorities had tended to think of prices and incomes policy as a means of reducing $\dot{W}$ and $\dot{K}$. Now they saw it as a means of increasing $\dot{O}$ as well (cf. p. 325 above). This new emphasis on the importance of productivity increase as a factor making for price stability was largely attributable to the N.B.P.I. In its first General Report, covering the period from its inception in April 1965 up to July 1966, the Board stated that it had endeavoured to make recommendations of two kinds in reply to each of the references made to it, whether it was a reference relating to incomes or prices. The first kind were recommendations concerned with whether a proposed increase in price or money incomes was justified in the light of the criteria laid down in *Prices and Incomes Policy*. The second kind were recommendations concerned with ways of increasing productivity in the industry concerned, the ground for the latter type of recommendation being that 'the only source for increased incomes which will not lead to increases in prices is improved productivity'.[1]

6. *Phase 6: 1966–7*

Phase 6 began with a White Paper entitled *Prices and Incomes Standstill*[2] in which the Government announced that the 'country needs a breathing space of twelve months in which productivity can catch up with the excessive increases in incomes which have been taking place'[3] and went on to propose: (i) that the six months from July to December 1966 should be regarded as a period of 'standstill' in which, as far as possible, there should be no increases either in prices or in money wages; and (ii) that the six months from January to June 1967 should be regarded as a period of 'severe restraint' in which some increases in prices and wages would be justified but in which all those who were involved in fixing prices and money wages would be expected to exercise exceptional restraint. Thus phase 6 resembled phases 1 and 3 in that it was a period of temporary 'freeze'. A further point of resemblance was that, as on the two earlier occasions, the freeze emerged against the background of a difficult external situation. However, the differences between the 1966 freeze and those of phases 1 and 3 appear to be more important than the similarities, and to these we now turn.

[1] See National Board for Prices and Incomes, *General Report, April 1965 to July 1966*, Cmnd 3087 (Aug 1966) pp. 10–11.
[2] See *Prices and Incomes Standstill*, Cmnd 3073 (July 1966).   [3] Ibid., p. 2.

The first point of difference is the obvious one that, whereas on the two earlier occasions the freeze applied to money wages only, in 1966 the freeze applied to *prices* as well as money wages. On this occasion an enterprise was required to notify the appropriate authorities before making any increase in price and was expected to delay the proposed increase until their written permission had been obtained.

Secondly, the exceptional circumstances which would be held to justify a price or wage increase were spelled out in much greater detail in the case of the 1966 freeze than on the two previous occasions. *Price* increases were to be regarded as justified, in the period of standstill and in the subsequent period of severe restraint, where there had been a marked increase, that could not be absorbed in:

the costs of imported materials or in costs arising from changes in supply for seasonal and other reasons, or which are due to action by the Government, such as increased taxation; or where an enterprise finds itself faced by increased costs which it is unable to restrain, and which are too large to absorb fully, such as the cost of bought-in components forming a large part of its total costs. There may also be exceptional circumstances in which without some increase in price the receipts of an enterprise are not adequate to enable it to maintain efficiency and undertake necessary investment.[1]

In the case of *money wages*, limited increases would be justified: (i) where it could be shown that they would lead to an increase in productivity which served the national interest as well as the interests of the workers and managements concerned; and (ii) where they were essential to improve the standard of living of the lowest-paid worker. Only in the most exceptional cases would increases be justified to attract or retain manpower, or to correct an anomaly.[2]

Finally, the 1966 freeze differed from those of 1948–50 and 1961–2 in that it was backed by wide statutory powers. These were embodied in Part IV of the *Prices and Incomes Act, 1966,* and could be brought into operation by an Order in Council subject to confirmation by both Houses of Parliament. They were to lapse automatically twelve months after receiving the Royal Assent unless previously revoked by Order in Council. This legislation gave the Government 'power to make orders . . . directing that specified

[1] See *Prices and Incomes Standstill: Period of Severe Restraint,* Cmnd 3150 (Nov 1966) p. 4. [2] Ibid., pp. 6–7.

prices or charges, or specified rates of remuneration, shall not be increased from the date of the order without Ministerial consent. A temporary standstill could therefore be imposed where necessary on both prices and charges and on levels of remuneration. . . . It will also give power to reverse where necessary unjustified price or pay increases implemented since 20 July 1966.'[1]

The Government expressed the hope 'that severe restraint will be observed on a voluntary basis' and gave the assurance that 'The Government will use their statutory powers for the sole purpose of ensuring that the voluntary support of the majority is not undermined by the actions of a few'.[2] The hope was fulfilled: 'The success of the standstill and of the period of severe restraint so far has been due largely to the voluntary acceptance by management and unions and by the public generally of the national need for restraint and willingness to sacrifice immediate personal benefit in the interest of the whole community. Only in a relatively small number of cases has it been necessary to make Orders under Part IV of the Prices and Incomes Act, 1966, restricting particular prices or the pay of particular groups of workers.'[3]

7. Phase 7: July 1967–

The current phase of the P.I.P. approach has been marked by two major developments. In the first place there have been important changes in the legislative position. The wide statutory powers conferred by Part IV of the *Prices and Incomes Act, 1966*, lapsed on 11 August 1967. Prior to this, however, the Government had activated Part II of the Act which required notification to the Government of proposed price and wage increases and which gave the Government power to delay a proposed increase in price or money wages for up to seven months subject to its being referred to the N.B.P.I. The 1967 Act was, in turn, succeeded by the *Prices and Incomes Act, 1968*, which prolonged the powers of the 1967 Act to the end of 1969 and extended the Government's power to delay a proposed increase in price or pay from six months to eleven months, subject, as before, to its being referred for investigation to the N.B.P.I. The 1968 Act also empowered the Government to require

---

[1] See *Prices and Incomes Standstill*, pp. 7–8.
[2] See *Prices and Incomes Standstill: Period of Severe Restraint*, p. 3.
[3] See *Prices and Incomes Policy after 30th June, 1967*, Cmnd 3235 (Mar 1967) p. 2.

réductions in existing prices where these were recommended by the N.B.P.I.

The second main development since July 1967 has been the return to the criteria of phase 5 which were abandoned during the standstill and the period of severe restraint (see pp. 330–1 above). The criteria for prices were restored in July 1967,[1] while those for money wages were restored in March 1968.[2]

10.3 P.I.P. Approach: Establishment of Criteria

As will be clear from the historical survey given in the previous section, there are two main problems associated with the P.I.P. approach to the control of inflation. The first is to establish the criteria which are to govern increases in prices and money incomes. The second is to see that these criteria are followed by those who are responsible for fixing prices and for negotiating wage settlements.

The problem of establishing criteria can itself be broken down into a number of sub-problems. Of these, the most critical and interesting is the problem of fixing the norm for the average annual percentage increase in money wages and salaries per man-hour, and we shall be concentrating exclusively on this problem in the present section.

There are two main ways of approaching this problem. One approach is to fix the norm in some completely arbitrary way. In particular, the authorities may simply declare a wage and salary freeze, i.e. arbitrarily put the norm at zero, as the British authorities did in 1948, 1961 and 1966, as a means of meeting an acute short-run balance of payments problem. This approach is unlikely to succeed, and indeed is unlikely to be tried, except for short periods and only then in the face of some national crisis which, by common consent, demands drastic action on the part of the authorities. The alternative approach, which is appropriate if the object of the prices and incomes policy is to reduce the rate of increase of prices in the longer run, is to derive a rule for the establishment of the wages norm which has some rational basis in terms of a generally accepted model of the inflationary process. It is this approach that we shall be exploring in the present section. Our main

[1] Ibid., pp. 3–4.
[2] See *Productivity, Prices and Incomes Policy in 1968 and 1969*, Cmnd 3590 (Apr 1968) pp. 7–8.

object will be to discuss several alternative rules for fixing the norm and to assess their usefulness in connection with the P.I.P. approach.

The simplest rule for fixing the norm is to require that, for the future period in question, the average annual percentage increase in wage and salary earnings per man-hour be equal to the average annual percentage increase in real G.D.P. per man-hour which is expected for that period. We shall refer to this rule as the *productivity* rule. As will be clear from the historical account of the previous section, this is the rule which the British authorities have followed whenever they have prescribed a non-zero norm. If we denote the norm given by the productivity rule by $\dot{W}^{(1)}$ and the expected average annual percentage increase in real G.D.P. per man-hour by $\dot{O}^*$, we can state the productivity rule symbolically as:

$$\dot{W}^{(1)} = \dot{O}^*. \tag{10.1}$$

The basis of the productivity rule is clear from (9.9). If the norm given by this rule is followed, then, on average, there will be no upward pressure on the price level, via rising unit labour cost, so that rising unit imported materials cost and rising profit margins will be the only remaining sources of inflationary pressure.

With the help of (9.9) we can derive a formula showing the percentage increase in prices which would occur, at rates of increase in the O, M and K indexes equal to the expected average, if the norm prescribed by the productivity rule were adhered to. We denote this hypothetical rate of inflation by $\dot{P}^{(1)}$. To obtain the required formula for $\dot{P}^{(1)}$ we have merely to substitute in (9.9) $\dot{W}^{(1)}$, as given by (10.1), for $\dot{W}_{t-1}$, $\dot{O}^*$ for $\dot{O}_{t-1}$, $\dot{M}^*$ for $\dot{M}_{t-1}$ and $\dot{K}^*$ for $\dot{K}_t$ where $\dot{M}^*$ and $\dot{K}^*$ are, respectively, the expected average annual percentage increase in the M index and the K index. The formula which emerges is:

$$\dot{P}^{(1)} = \beta_2 \dot{M}^* + \dot{K}^*. \tag{10.2}$$

A second possible rule, which we shall refer to as the *price-stability* rule, is, in effect, a simple extension of the productivity rule. The price-stability rule requires that, for the future period in question, the average annual percentage increase in wage and salary earnings per man-hour be such that, on average, there will be no upward pressure on the price level from *any* source. That is, the rule gives a rate of increase in money wage and salary earnings per man-hour ($\dot{W}^{(2)}$) such that the price index will be constant at rates of increase in the O, M and K indexes equal to $\dot{O}^*$, $\dot{M}^*$ and $\dot{K}^*$, the average rates which are expected for the period for which the norm is being fixed. A symbolic statement of this rule can be derived from (9.9) by substituting $\dot{W}^{(2)}$ for $\dot{W}_{t-1}$, $\dot{O}^*$ for $\dot{O}_{t-1}$, $\dot{M}^*$ for $\dot{M}_{t-1}$, $\dot{K}^*$ for $\dot{K}_t$ and zero for $\dot{P}_t$, and then solving for $\dot{W}^{(2)}$. The resulting expression is:

$$\dot{W}^{(2)} = \dot{O}^* - \frac{1}{\beta_1}(\beta_2\dot{M}^* + \dot{K}^*) = \dot{O}^* - \frac{1}{\beta_1}\dot{P}^{(1)}. \qquad (10.3)$$

It follows from the definition of the price-stability rule that the expression for $\dot{P}^{(2)}$, the hypothetical rate of inflation that would follow adherence to the rule, given rates of increase in the O, M and K indexes equal to $\dot{O}^*$, $\dot{M}^*$ and $\dot{K}^*$ respectively, is as follows:

$$\dot{P}^{(2)} = 0. \qquad (10.4)$$

A third possible rule for establishing the wage and salary norm is to require that the average annual percentage increase in the index of average wage and salary earnings, in the future period in question, be equal to the average annual percentage increase in G.D.P. per man-hour which is expected for that period, *plus* the percentage increase in prices which would occur in the period if the productivity rule were adhered to, i.e. if there were no upward pressure on the price level from rising unit labour cost. We shall refer to this rule as the *productivity-plus-prices* rule. A symbolic statement of this rule is:

$$\dot{W}^{(3)} = \dot{O}^* + \dot{P}^{(1)}. \qquad (10.5)$$

We now derive a formula for $\dot{P}^{(3)}$, the hypothetical rate of inflation which would follow if the norm defined by the productivity-plus-prices rule were followed, given rates of increase in the O, M and K indexes equal to $\dot{O}^*$, $\dot{M}^*$ and $\dot{K}^*$ respectively. As before, we do this by substituting in (9.9) $\dot{W}^{(3)}$, as given by (10.5), for $\dot{W}_{t-1}$, $\dot{O}^*$ for $\dot{O}_{t-1}$, $\dot{M}^*$ for $\dot{M}_{t-1}$ and $\dot{K}^*$ for $\dot{K}_t$. The formula which emerges is:

$$\dot{P}^{(3)} = \dot{P}^{(1)}(1 + \beta). \qquad (10.6)$$

A fourth possible rule is to require that the average annual percentage increase in average wage and salary earnings be equal either to the figure prescribed by the productivity rule or to $\dot{P}^{(1)}$ (the rate of price increase which would follow adherence to the productivity rule), whichever is the larger. We shall refer to this rule as the *modified-productivity-plus-prices* rule. Formally the rule is as follows:

$$\text{(a)} \quad \dot{W}^{(4)} = \dot{O}^* \qquad \dot{O}^* \geqslant \dot{P}^{(1)}$$
$$\text{(b)} \quad \dot{W}^{(4)} = \dot{P}^{(1)} \qquad \dot{O}^* < \dot{P}^{(1)}. \tag{10.7}$$

Using (10.7), the formula for $\dot{P}^{(4)}$, the hypothetical rate of inflation which would occur at rates of increase in the O, M and K indexes equal to the expected average if the norm prescribed by the rule were adhered to, can be obtained in the same way as before. The formula is:

$$\text{(a)} \quad \dot{P}^{(4)} = \dot{P}^{(1)} \qquad\qquad\qquad \dot{O}^* \geqslant \dot{P}^{(1)}$$
$$\text{(b)} \quad \dot{P}^{(4)} = \beta_1[\dot{P}^{(1)} - \dot{O}^*] + \dot{P}^{(1)} \qquad \dot{O}^* < \dot{P}^{(1)}. \tag{10.8}$$

It will be seen from (10.1), (10.3) and (10.5) that the price-stability rule and the productivity-plus-prices rule are identical with the productivity rule if $\dot{P}^{(1)} = 0$, i.e. if $\dot{M}^* = \dot{K}^* = 0$ or if $\dot{K}^* = -\beta_2 \dot{M}^*$. From (10.7) it will be seen that the modified-productivity-plus-prices rule is also identical with the productivity rule, if $\dot{P}^{(1)} = 0$ and $\dot{O}^* > 0$, for then part (a) of (10.7) applies.

The above four rules are by no means the only possibilities, but we shall confine our attention to them. To assess these rules and others like them, one needs to ask two questions: (i) How effective are they in promoting price stability? (ii) How fair are they in terms of distributive shares? We intend to do this. First, however, we shall use (10.1) to (10.8) to derive expressions for $\dot{W}B^{(i)}$ ($i = 1, \ldots, 4$) where $\dot{W}B^{(i)}$ denotes the percentage increase in the index of the *real* wage bill that would follow adherence to the norm prescribed by rule i at rates of increase of the O, M, K and N indexes equal to $\dot{O}^*$, $\dot{M}^*$, $\dot{K}^*$ and $\dot{N}^*$ respectively. (N is an index of man-hours worked.) These four expressions will assist in the assessment of the rules from the point of view of equity. Since the index of the real wage bill is given by WN/P, each of these expressions will take the form:[1]

$$\dot{W}B^{(i)} = \dot{W}^{(i)} + \dot{N}^* - \dot{P}^{(1)}. \tag{10.9}$$

The expressions for $\dot{W}B^{(i)}$ can be easily derived by appropriate substitution into (10.9) from (10.1) to (10.8). The latter expressions are assembled for the reader's convenience in the second and third

[1] The right-hand side of this expression is an approximation for the percentage increase in the index of the real wage-bill that would follow adherence to the norm specified by rule i, given rates of increase of the O, M, K and N indexes, equal to $\dot{O}^*$, $\dot{M}^*$, $\dot{K}^*$ and $\dot{N}^*$ respectively. See section 9.2 above, p. 288, n. 1 and p. 289, n. 2.

columns of Table 10.1, and in the final column we show the desired expression for the $\dot{W}B^{(i)}$.

TABLE 10.1

(1) Rule	(2) $\dot{W}^{(i)}$	(3) $\dot{P}^{(i)}$	(4) $\dot{W}B^{(i)}$
1. Productivity	$\dot{O}^*$	$\dot{P}^{(1)}$	$(\dot{O}^* + \dot{N}^*) - \dot{P}^{(1)}$
2. Price stability	$\dot{O}^* - \dfrac{1}{\beta_1}\dot{P}^{(1)}$	zero	$(\dot{O}^* + \dot{N}^*) - \dfrac{1}{\beta_1}\dot{P}^{(1)}$
3. Productivity-plus-prices	$\dot{O}^* + \dot{P}^{(1)}$	$\dot{P}^{(1)}(1 + \beta_1)$	$(\dot{O}^* + \dot{N}^*) - \beta_1\dot{P}^{(1)}$
4. Modified productivity-plus-prices:			
(a) $\dot{O}^* > \dot{P}^{(1)}$	$\dot{O}^*$	$\dot{P}^{(1)}$	$(\dot{O}^* + \dot{N}^*) - \dot{P}^{(1)}$
(b) $\dot{O}^* < \dot{P}^{(1)}$	$\dot{P}^{(1)}$	$\beta_1[\dot{P}^{(1)} - \dot{O}^*] + \dot{P}^{(1)}$	$(\dot{O}^* + \dot{N}^*) - [\beta_1\dot{P}^{(1)} + \dot{O}^*(1 - \beta_1)]$

We turn now to an assessment of the rules. We begin with an assessment from the point of view of price stability. From column 3 of Table 10.1 the following conclusions can be derived directly.[1] First, if $\dot{P}^{(1)} = 0$, all four rules give price stability. Second, if $\dot{P}^{(1)} > 0$, the ranking of the rules on the basis of the rate of inflation, from smallest to largest, is as follows:

If $\dot{O}^* > \dot{P}^{(1)}$
1. Price stability.
2. Productivity; modified-productivity-plus-prices.
3. Productivity-plus-prices.

If $\dot{O}^* < \dot{P}^{(1)}$
1. Price stability.
2. Productivity.
3. Modified-productivity-plus-prices.
4. Productivity-plus-prices.

Third, if $\dot{P}^{(1)} < 0$, the ranking is as follows:
1. Productivity-plus-prices.
2. Productivity; Modified-productivity-plus-prices.
3. Price stability.

We turn now to an assessment from the point of view of equity. From column 4 of Table 10.1 the following conclusions can be drawn. First, if $\dot{P}^{(1)} = 0$, all four rules gives the same result for the percentage increase in the index of real wage-bill, namely $(\dot{O}^* + \dot{N}^*)$. Since $(\dot{O}^* + \dot{N}^*)$ is an approximation to the expected average annual

---

[1] We are assuming that $\dot{O}^* > O$, i.e. that labour productivity is always expected to increase.

percentage increase in real G.D.P., we can say that, when $\dot{P}^{(1)} = 0$, all four rules imply that, at rates of change in the relevant indexes equal to the average expected for the period of the norm, the share of wage-earners in G.D.P. will remain fixed. Second, when $\dot{P}^{(1)} > 0$, all four rules imply a decline in the wage-share.[1] If the rules are ranked on the basis of the magnitude of the decline in the wage-share, from smallest to largest, the ranking is as follows:

If $\dot{O}^* > \dot{P}^{(1)}$	If $\dot{O}^* < \dot{P}^{(1)}$
1. Productivity-plus-prices.	1. Productivity-plus-prices.
2. Productivity; modified-productivity-plus-prices.	2. Modified-productivity-plus-prices.[2]
3. Price stability.	3. Productivity.
	4. Price stability.

Third, when $\dot{P}^{(1)} < 0$ all four rules imply an increase in the wage-share. If the rules are ranked on the basis of the magnitude of the increase, from largest to smallest, the ranking is as follows:

1. Price stability.
2. Productivity;
   modified-productivity-plus-prices.
3. Productivity-plus-prices.

We shall now attempt an overall assessment of the four rules, based on the conclusions reached in the preceding paragraphs. It would appear that the best all-round performer of the four is the productivity rule. The price-stability rule is superior to the productivity rule from the price-stability viewpoint if $\dot{P}^{(1)} > 0$ but is inferior from this viewpoint when $\dot{P}^{(1)} < 0$ and is decidedly inferior from the equity viewpoint when $\dot{P}^{(1)} > 0$. Likewise the productivity-plus-prices rule ranks ahead of the productivity rule from the standpoint of equity when $\dot{P}^{(1)} > 0$. On the other hand, it is inferior from this standpoint when $\dot{P}^{(1)} < 0$, and is also inferior from the standpoint of price stability when $\dot{P}^{(1)} > 0$. The modified-productivity-plus-prices rule ranks ahead of the productivity rule only from the equity standpoint, and even then only in the case when $0 < \dot{O}^* < \dot{P}^{(1)}$, which appears a rather unlikely case when the formula for $\dot{P}^{(1)}$ is examined.[3]

---

[1] Recall that $0 < \beta_1 < 1$.
[2] Note that with $\dot{O}^* < \dot{P}^{(1)}$ we have:
$$\beta_1 \dot{P}^{(1)} + \dot{O}^*(1 - \beta_1) < \beta_1 \dot{P}^{(1)} + \dot{P}^{(1)}(1 - \beta_1) = \dot{P}^{(1)}.$$
[3] Suppose $\dot{O}^* = 0 \cdot 03$ per annum, $\dot{K}^* = 0$ and $\beta_2 = 0 \cdot 2$. Then the inequality $0 < \dot{O}^* < \dot{P}^{(1)}$ implies: $\dot{M}^* > 0 \cdot 15$ per annum.

The all-round superiority of the productivity rule can be highlighted by saying that, while it never earns the first rank, its rank, with one unimportant exception, is never below 2, the exception being the third ranking which it earns from the equity standpoint in the rather unlikely event that $0 < \dot{O}^* < \dot{P}^{(1)}$.

10.4 P.I.P. Approach: Implementation of Criteria

At the outset of the previous section we said that the problems associated with the P.I.P. approach fall into two main groups: those concerned with the establishment of criteria for prices and incomes and those concerned with the implementation of these criteria. Having considered the first group, we turn now to the second. Implementing the criteria for prices and incomes raises two main problems. The first is to persuade the leaders of the trade unions and the employers' organisations to endorse the criteria. The second is to find ways of backing up this endorsement. We shall now consider these two problems in turn.

A necessary condition (though not a sufficient one) for success in implementing the criteria for prices and incomes is that the criteria should be accepted by the leaders of the employers' organisations and by the leaders of the trade unions. For this to happen, the leaders of organised labour and management must be: (i) convinced of the need to avoid inflation; (ii) able to see that the proposed criteria will contribute to this end; (iii) satisfied that the proposed criteria are fair; and (iv) confident that they can gain rank-and-file support for their endorsement of the proposed criteria. We shall now take each of these four requirements in turn and briefly consider the circumstances which will be conducive to its fulfilment.

It would appear that the first requirement is likely to be met only in times of national crises. British experience suggests that it will be comparatively easy for the authorities to convince the leaders of organised labour and management of the need to avoid inflation if stable prices can be represented as an essential part of a plan to meet some national emergency such as a war or a balance of payments crisis. It also suggests, however, that this initial hurdle may be quite difficult to overcome in more normal times when the only arguments which the authorities can advance in support of the need for price stability are arguments which are not likely to appeal very strongly to the ordinary man, e.g. the argument that without price stability the country's price level will get out of line with that of its trading competitors over the long run.

As for the second requirement, it would seem obvious that the leaders of organised labour and management will be better able to see a connection between the criteria they are being asked to endorse and the objective of price stability if the criteria have some rational basis in terms of a simple model of the inflationary process, than if they are essentially arbitrary. This being so, it would appear that one development which will make an important contribution to the fulfilment of the second requirement is the adoption of some rule for establishing the wage norm of the type discussed in the previous section, since the main characteristic of such rules is that they follow quite logically from a particularly simple model of the inflationary process.

The third requirement for endorsement of the criteria is that the leaders of management must be satisfied that the prices criteria are fair, while the leaders of labour must be satisfied about the fairness of the wages criteria. Starting with the *prices* criteria, an obvious point is that the leaders of management are unlikely to be satisfied that the prices criteria are fair if these imply that cost increases which result from wage increases in excess of the norm are 'avoidable' and hence that they should not be passed on in higher prices. They might well argue that there are two parties involved in the wage bargain and that both must be held responsible if the wages norm is violated. As for the wages criteria, it can be argued that it will be difficult to convince the trade union leaders of the fairness of a rule for establishing the wages norm unless this involves compensation for price increases for which labour is in no way responsible, i.e. price increases which result from causes other than wage increases in excess of the norm, such as an increase in the cost of imported materials, an increase in profit margins in violation of the price criteria or an increase in the severity of indirect taxation. It may well be that, to win the support of the trade union leaders for the prices and incomes criteria, the authorities will have to adopt a rule for establishing the wages norm which concedes this point, e.g. the productivity-plus-prices rule or the modified-productivity-plus-prices rule, even though the rule is less than satisfactory from the price-stability point of view.

This brings us to the fourth requirement for securing union and management endorsement of the criteria, i.e. that, having accepted the criteria themselves, the leaders of organised labour and management should be confident of the ability to win rank-and-file support for their action.

As far as the *trade union* leaders are concerned, there are two circumstances which will contribute materially to the development of this confidence. The first is the adoption of a wage rule which is relatively simple. For example, the union leaders would be more likely to endorse a set of wages criteria if the wages norm derives, let us say, from the productivity rule than if it derives from the price-stability rule, because, while the former is fairly easy to explain, the latter is somewhat technical and would not be easily grasped by the ordinary trade union member.

We said a moment ago that the authorities may be well advised to base the wages norm on a rule which gains high marks from the point of view of equity even though it is less than satisfactory from the point of view of price stability, if, in so doing, they greatly increase the chances of endorsement of the criteria by the union leaders. What we are now saying is that, in choosing a wage rule, there may be a case for stressing simplicity as well as equity. A rule which is both manifestly fair from the workers' point of view and also very simple in conception may be the best rule to adopt in the end, even though it may not be particularly satisfactory when judged from the standpoint of its direct contribution to the achievement of price stability. For example, the productivity-plus-prices rule, which is a poor rule on the price-stability criterion, may nevertheless be the best of the four rules discussed earlier, simply because the chances of union endorsement of the criteria would be higher with this rule than with any of its rivals.

The second circumstance which will help to give the trade union leaders confidence in their ability to gain mass support for their endorsement of the criteria is the presence of a Labour Government. For the ordinary trade union member will be less suspicious of proposals for wage restraint which emanate from a Labour Government than he will be of proposals made by a Conservative Government and hence more ready to support his leaders' endorsement of the proposals in the former case than in the latter. This is borne out by the British experience described in section 10.2. Strong union support for the prices and incomes criteria was forthcoming in 1948–50 and also in the years following the *Joint Statement of Intent* in 1964, in both of which periods a Labour Government was in power. By contrast, the unions opposed outright all of the attempts to establish prices and incomes criteria which were made by Conservative Governments in the years between 1951 and 1964 (see pp. 325–9 above).

As regards the *leaders of management*, one consideration which is likely to carry considerable weight is whether or not the large public enterprises are to be expected to follow the prices criteria. Management leaders are likely to be more confident of winning their members' support for an endorsement of the proposed prices criteria if these impose exactly the same discipline on the public business sector as on the private business sector than if they place public businesses in a more favourable position than private businesses.

So far, in this section, we have been concerned with the problem of securing endorsement of the proposed criteria for prices and incomes from the leaders of the employers' organisations and the leaders of the trade unions. Unless the authorities can solve this problem, there is little chance that the criteria will be implemented. On the other hand, the authorities may well succeed in solving the problem and still fail to have the criteria implemented. Success in obtaining the support of organised labour and management provides no guarantee of successful implementation; it merely makes it possible. The question which now arises, therefore, is what further action the authorities could take to see that the criteria are implemented, once they had secured the support of the leaders of organised management and labour for those criteria.

One way in which the authorities could back up the endorsement of the criteria by the leaders of organised labour and management would be by means of legislation. To be useful, this legislation would have to require notification of all proposed increases in prices and wages, but beyond this could take any one of a number of forms. One form would be legislation which required, in addition to notification, that no price or wage increase take place without permission from the appropriate authority. A second possible form would be legislation which gave the authorities power to delay any proposed price or wage increase for a specified period while some independent body determined whether or not it was in line with the criteria which had been laid down. The decision of this authority would then be legally enforceable. A third type would be legislation which gave the authorities some power of delay subject to investigation by an independent body but which put compliance with the recommendations of this body on a voluntary basis. If this type of legislation were adopted, the authorities would have to rely on the pressure of public opinion to enforce compliance with the recommendations of the investigating body and this pressure would be forthcoming only if the investigating body had acquired considerable prestige and only if its recommendations were widely publicised.

As pointed out in section 10.2, legislation of the first of these three types was introduced in the United Kingdom in 1966 and, in the following year, was replaced by legislation of the third type under which the authorities had a power of delay of six months subject to the proposed increase being referred to the N.B.P.I. The attitude of the British authorities to legislation of this type has been that it is useful only when there is general support for the criteria and that its main contribution is to ensure that this general support is not eroded by the anti-social behaviour of a small minority of employers or workers. In the words of one of the White Papers, statutory power should be used 'to deter the selfish minority who are not prepared to co-operate and, no less important, to reassure those who are observing the policy laid down . . . that they will not be penalised for doing so'.[1]

A second way in which the authorities could support the endorsement of the criteria by the leaders of organised labour and management is by means of demand restriction. This could help in two directions: (i) by checking wage-drift; and (ii) by checking hidden price increases in violation of the prices criteria. Let us consider these in turn.

Suppose that the trade union leaders give their support to the criteria. There is then a good chance that the rate of increase of *negotiated wage rates* will be kept in line with the wages norm. However, what is required is that the rate of increase of *average earnings* should be kept in line with the norm. Hence, having secured an appropriate rate of increase of negotiated rates, the authorities will still face the problem of keeping the rate of increase of average earnings in line with the rate of increase of negotiated rates, i.e. the problem of checking wage-drift. Now the empirical work surveyed in section 9.7 suggests that there is a positive association between wage-drift and excess demand. To the extent that this is so, a policy of demand restriction should contribute something to a solution of the wage-drift problem and hence give some backing to the endorsement

---

[1] See *Prices and Incomes Standstill*, Cmnd. 3073, (July 1966) p.8.

M

of the prices and wages criteria by the leaders of organised labour and management.

How far would this policy of demand restriction need to be taken in order that it should make a significant impact on the wage-drift problem? Obviously this would depend on the strength of the link between excess demand and wage-drift. However, it would also depend on the extent to which wage-drift was being pushed up by forces other than excess demand. In this connection one important factor would be the tightness of the norm itself. For the tighter the norm, the more severe would be the restriction on negotiated increases; and from the empirical work surveyed in section 9.7 it would appear that the more severely negotiated increases were limited, the larger would be the wage-drift. In short, the tighter the norm, the greater would be the residual wage-drift problem and the greater the degree of demand restriction which would be required to back up the endorsement of the criteria by the leaders of labour and management.

A policy of demand restriction might lend support in yet another way. Price-makers who wish to raise their price in violation of the prices criteria, while still appearing to conform with the criteria, have several courses of action open to them. One is to reduce quality while quoting the same price. Another is to withdraw, or reduce, discounts and gifts of various kinds while quoting the same price. There are numerous other devices of this type which enable price-makers to increase effective price while keeping nominal price constant. Since price-makers will be in a better position to employ such devices when there is a measure of excess demand than when aggregate demand is in rough balance with available supply, or is deficient, it follows that a policy of demand restriction might help to check hidden price increases and, in this way, contribute to the implementation of the prices criteria.

A third way of backing up the endorsement of the criteria by the leaders of labour and management would be to expand efforts to increase productivity, such as those made by the N.B.P.I. (see p. 332 above). For the higher the rate of increase of productivity, the higher would be the wages norm under any conceivable wage rule; and the higher the norm, the less incentive would workers have to attempt to secure wage increases in excess of the norm by individual bargaining at the workshop level.

Finally, the authorities might be able to back up the endorsement of the criteria by giving employers some financial incentive not to pay their workers at rates in excess of those dictated by the wages norm. An example of this type of approach can be drawn from the 1948 'wage-freeze'. On this occasion, the authorities made it clear that increased labour costs, which could be attributed to wage payments in excess of the norm, might not be taken into account in settling controlled prices and in this way ensured that employers had a strong financial incentive to resist pressure for excessive wage increases (see p. 326 above).

10.5 The Effectiveness of the P.I.P. Approach

To determine how effective the P.I.P. approach has been over any period in which it has been tried, it is not enough to examine the actual behaviour of prices and money incomes in the period in relation to the targets laid down under the policy. For suppose it transpired that the rates of increase of prices and incomes exceeded the targets set by the authorities. One could not conclude from this that the policy had failed, since other factors, e.g. excess demand, may have been working against the policy, and had they not been doing so the target rates of increase of prices and money incomes might well have been achieved. Suppose one found, on the other hand, that prices and money incomes had risen in line with the targets. One would not be justified in concluding that the policy had succeeded because other factors, e.g. falling import prices, may have been supporting the policy and these other factors may have been responsible for the achievement of the target rates of increase of prices and money incomes.

In its Third General Report, the N.B.P.I. proposed two alternative ways of determining the effectiveness of the P.I.P. approach which avoid these difficulties.[1] The starting-point of both these methods is the econometric work of Dicks-Mireaux which we discussed in section 9.4. It will be recalled that both of Dicks-Mireaux's numerical relationships were derived from annual data for the years 1946–59 (see p. 296 above). The Board argued that in these years the P.I.P. approach existed only in a very rudimentary form – the main development of the approach occurred after 1964. This being so, one way of testing for the effectiveness of the P.I.P. approach in the

[1] See National Board for Prices and Incomes, *Third General Report, August 1967 to July 1968*, Cmnd 3715 (July 1968) pp. 63–7.

United Kingdom would be to re-estimate the Dicks-Mireaux price and wage equations using data for a period which included the years after 1964. If the P.I.P. approach has been effective, one would expect to find that the new estimates of at least some of the coefficients in the price and wage equations were smaller than those derived by Dicks-Mireaux on the basis of data for years in which no well-developed P.I.P. approach existed, since the whole purpose of the approach is to make the rate of change of prices and money wages less responsive to general economic conditions than they would have been otherwise. This, in fact, is the first of the two methods which the Board proposed. To apply the method, both the Dicks-Mireaux price equation and the Dicks-Mireaux wage equation[1] were re-estimated by the two-stage least-squares method (the method used by Dicks-Mireaux) from data for the years 1946–66.

Comparison of the two sets of equations showed that, while the coefficients in the re-estimated price equation were much the same as in the original price equation, there was a significant difference between the estimated coefficients in the two wage equations. In the original wage equation the estimated coefficient of the excess demand variable was 2·78 (see p. 296 above). In the re-estimated wage equation, however, the estimate of this coefficient was only 1·44, i.e. only about one-half as large as in the original equation. Thus, the results of the test were consistent with the view that the application of the P.I.P. approach in the years following 1964 was effective in that it reduced substantially the responsiveness of money wages to excess demand.

The second method of testing the effectiveness of the P.I.P. approach also started from the Dicks-Mireaux price and wage equations. In this case two additional explanatory variables were introduced into each equation and the enlarged equations were then re-estimated from data for the years 1946–66. Both of the new explanatory variables were dummy variables. The first was a variable taking a value of unity in years when a fairly loose prices and incomes policy was being implemented and zero in all other years, while the second was a variable taking a value of unity in years when a fairly tight policy was in operation and zero in all other years. If the P.I.P. approach had been effective in the United Kingdom, one would expect to find both variables appearing in the re-estimated price and

---

[1] The wage equation differs from the Dicks-Mireaux equation in that $\dot{P}_{t-1}$ is excluded. See p. 296 above.

wage equations with negative coefficients. This, indeed, is the case as far as the wage equation is concerned. In the re-estimated wage equation both variables appeared with coefficients of round about −1, suggesting that in years in which the approach was being tried, whether on a voluntary or a non-voluntary basis, the rate of increase of money wages was about 1 percentage point less, at a given level of excess demand and a given rate of past inflation, than it was in years in which the approach was not being followed in either form. On the other hand, in the re-estimated price equation, both of the dummy variables appeared with positive coefficients, suggesting that as far as prices are concerned, the direct effect of employing the P.I.P. approach was perverse. These results have to be treated with considerable caution, however, because in all four cases the estimated coefficient of the dummy variable was less than twice its standard error.

Another assessment of the effectiveness of the P.I.P. approach in Britain was made recently by Smith as part of the Brookings study.[1] Smith used the second of the two methods just described, but in a much more elaborate way. Whereas in the N.B.P.I. study only one estimation was run for wages and one for prices, in the Brookings study twelve estimations were run for wages and sixteen for prices. Also, in the N.B.P.I. study only two dummy variables were used according to whether a fairly loose or a fairly tight incomes policy was implemented, whereas the Brookings study six dummy variables were used, one for each of the first six phases of incomes policy distinguished in section 10.2. The justification for using the six different dummies was that the prices and incomes policy took a distinct form in each of the six phases in question. Only by associating a separate dummy variable with each phase could a separate measure of effectiveness be obtained for each form of the policy.

To describe Smith's study we shall make use of his notation, which is as follows:

W = a wage index
P_r = an index of retail prices
U = average unemployment percentage
R = an index of industrial output per employee
P_m = an index of import prices
$I_1, \ldots, I_6$ = a series of dummy variables.[2]

[1] See D. C. Smith, 'Incomes Policy', in R. E. Caves and Associates, *Britain's Economic Prospects* (London: Allen & Unwin, 1968) pp. 140–4.
[2] The dummy variable I_1 was given a non-zero value for each period in the

All of the twelve *wage* estimations took the form:

$$\dot{W}_t = a + bU_t^{-1} + c\dot{P}_{r(t)} + e\dot{P}_{r(t-1)} + f_1 I_1 + f_2 I_2 + f_3 I_3 + f_4 I_4 + f_5 I_5 + f_6 I_6 \quad (10.10)$$

where the dot indicates 'annual proportional rate of increase'. In three of the twelve the series used for $\dot{W}$ was derived from a quarterly index of weekly wage rates (W_w), in three others from a quarterly index of hourly wage rates (W_h), in three others from a six-monthly index of hourly earnings including overtime (W_{ei}) and in three others from a six-monthly index of hourly earnings excluding overtime (W_{ex}).

Of the three estimations based on W_w, two were done by ordinary least squares and one by two-stage least squares. In one of the two ordinary least-squares estimations so-called 'regular' dummy variables were used, while in the other 'proportional' dummy variables were used. In the two-stage least-squares estimation, regular dummies were employed.[1] The same applies *mutatis mutandis* to each of the other three groups of three estimations.

Of the sixteen price estimations, twelve took the form:

$$\dot{P}_{r(t)} = g + h\dot{W}_t + j\dot{P}_{m(t-1)} + k\dot{R}_t + m_1 I_1 + m_2 I_2 + m_3 I_3 + m_4 I_4 + m_5 I_5 + m_6 I_6. \quad (10.11)$$

In three of these the series used for $\dot{W}$ was derived from W_w, in three others from W_h, in three others from W_{ei} and in three others from W_{ex}. In each group of three, two estimations were done by ordinary least squares (one with regular dummies and one with proportional dummies) and one by two-stage least squares.

The four remaining price equations had the same form as (10.11) except that the dependent variable was $\dot{P}_{w(t)}$ (the rate of increase of wholesale prices) instead of $\dot{P}_{r(t)}$, while $\dot{P}_{m(t)}$ replaced $\dot{P}_{m(t-1)}$ in the list of explanatory variables. In two of the four cases the series used for $\dot{W}$ was based on W_{ei} and in two others on W_{ex}. One of the two based on W_{ei} used regular dummies and the other proportional dummies, and similarly in the other group of two. All four estimations were done by ordinary least squares.

---

years 1948–50 and a zero value otherwise. Similarly I_2, I_3, I_4, I_5 and I_6 were given non-zero values in the years 1956, 1961–2, 1962–4, 1965–6 and 1966–7, respectively, and zero values otherwise.

[1] When a regular dummy is used, it is implied that the incomes policy was more effective at the beginning of the period concerned than at the end. On the other hand when a proportional dummy is used it is implied that the effectiveness of the policy increased over the period concerned in proportion to the length of time for which it had been operating. See Smith, op. cit., pp. 140–1.

All regressions which used a *wage-rate* index (i.e. W_w or W_h) were based on quarterly data (first quarter 1948 to second quarter 1967) and the rates of increase used were rates of increase for the quarter in question over four quarters earlier. Similarly in all regressions which used a *wage-earnings* index (i.e. W_{ei} or W_{ex}), the estimation was based on six-monthly data (first half 1948 to first half 1967) and the rates of increase of W and P were rates of increase for the six-monthly period in question over two six-months earlier.

In Table 10.2 we summarise the results of the various estimations just described by showing, for each dummy variable, the number of estimations in which the estimated coefficient of that dummy variable was 'well determined' in the usual sense of being at least twice its estimated standard error. For example, from row 1 of the table we find that the estimated coefficient of I_1 was well determined: (i) in all of the six estimations in which the series used for $\dot{W}$ was derived from a wage-rate index; (ii) in only two of the six wage estimations in which the series used for $\dot{W}$ was derived from a wage-earnings index; (iii) in only eight of the sixteen price estimations.

From this table conclusions about the effectiveness of the various phases of the P.I.P. approach can be drawn quite readily. To draw conclusions about the *indirect* effectiveness of the approach in any given phase – its effectiveness in restraining the rate of increase of prices via the rate of increase of money wages – we must consider the entries in the first two columns of the table for the dummy variable corresponding to the phase. For the purpose of assessing the *direct*

TABLE 10.2

Dummy variable	Dependent variable (1) $\dot{W}_w$; $\dot{W}_h$	(2) $\dot{W}_{ei}$; $\dot{W}_{ex}$	(3) $\dot{P}_r$; $\dot{P}_w$
(1) I_1 (1948–50)	6	2	8
(2) I_2 (1956)	0	0	8
(3) I_3 (1961–2)	3	0	3
(4) I_4 (1962–4)	1	0	0
(5) I_5 (1965–6)	4	6	1
(6) I_6 (1966–7)	4	1	1

effectiveness of the approach in any given phase – its effectiveness in restraining the rate of increase of prices directly rather than through money wages – we must examine the entries in the appropriate row of the third column of this table.

The main conclusions which emerge from the table and from the estimates of the coefficients of the dummy variables given in Smith's study, are as follows:

1. In phase 1 the policy appears to have been very effective in restraining the rate of increase of money wage rates. This is suggested by the fact that the estimated coefficient of I_1 was 'well determined' in all of the six wage estimations in which the dependent variable was the rate of increase of a wage-rate index. The estimated coefficient of I_1 was round about -0.02 in all these estimations, which suggests that the annual rate of increase of money wage rates was reduced by about 2 percentage points as a result of the policy. Whether the policy was quite as successful in reducing the rate of increase of money wage *earnings* in this phase is open to doubt, since of the six wage estimations in which the dependent variable was the rate of increase of a wage-earnings index, the estimated coefficient of I_1 was more than twice its standard error in only two cases. The fact that the estimated coefficient of I_1 was well determined in eight of the sixteen price estimations may suggest that the prices and incomes policy made a worth-while *direct* contribution to price stability in phase 1. However, examination of Smith's calculations shows that in all of these eight cases the estimated coefficient had the 'wrong' (i.e. positive) sign.[1] If anything, therefore, the direct contribution of the policy was perverse in this phase.

2. In phase 2 the P.I.P. approach appears to have had no significant effect on the course of wage rates or wage earnings (see row 2, columns 2 and 3 of Table 10.2). On the other hand, as far as direct effectiveness is concerned the evidence is somewhat more favourable. The estimated coefficient of I_2 in the price equation was 'well determined' in eight of the sixteen estimations, though in three of these the sign was wrong.

3. In phases 3 and 4 the policy appears to have had no worth-while effect – either direct or indirect – on the rate of price increase (see rows 3 and 4).

4. In phase 5 the policy appears to have had a perverse effect on money wage earnings. The estimated coefficient of the dummy variable I_5 was more than twice its estimated standard error in all six of the wage estimations in which the dependent variable was the rate of increase of a wage-earnings index, and in all of these six cases the estimated coefficient had a value round about $+0.02$. Thus, taken at face value, the estimated coefficients suggest that the

---

[1] See Smith, op. cit., pp. 142–4.

rate of increase of wage earnings may have been some 2 per cent per annum *higher* because of the prices and incomes policy. On the other hand, the policy may have had the desired effect on wage rates; in the case of the six wage estimations in which the dependent variable was the rate of increase of a wage-rate index, there were four cases in which the estimated coefficient of I_5 was more than twice its standard error and in three of these four cases the estimated coefficient was round about -0.01. Thus, in three of the four cases, the estimated coefficient had the 'right' sign, and suggested that a reduction in the annual rate of increase of wage rates of about one percentage point could be attributed to the policy. There is little sign that the policy had any direct effect on the rate of price increase in this phase.

5. In phase 6 the policy appears to have restrained the rate of increase of money wage rates but not the rate of increase of money wage earnings. Of the six wage estimations in which the dependent variable was the rate of increase of a money wage-rate index, there were four in which the estimated coefficient of I_6 was more than twice its standard error. In three of these four cases the estimated coefficient was a little over -0.01 in absolute value and in the fourth case was a little over -0.02. Thus the evidence suggests that in 1966–7 the policy may have been responsible for reducing the annual rate of increase of money wage rates by between 1 and 2 percentage points. On the other hand, of the six estimations in which the dependent variable was the rate of increase of a money wage-earnings index, there was only one case in which the estimated coefficient of I_6 was more than twice its standard error, which suggests that the policy had no significant effect on the rate of increase of money wage earnings in the 1966–7 period. In this phase, as in the preceding phase, there is little to suggest that the policy had any worth-while direct effect on the rate of price increase.

The conclusions presented in the preceding paragraphs can be briefly summarised as follows. There is little in the Brookings evidence to suggest that the P.I.P. approach can help to reduce the rate of increase of prices directly. On the other hand, the study suggests that it can help indirectly, by reducing the rate of increase of money wages. Whether or not it will do so in any actual case will depend mainly on the extent to which the unions trust the Government which is attempting to carry out the policy, on how vigorously the policy is applied and on the nature of the circumstances in which it is

M 2

applied. On the evidence of the Brookings study, if conditions are right, a reduction in the annual rate of increase of money wages per man of as much as 2 percentage points can be expected from a vigorous application of the P.I.P. approach.

10.6 The D.R. Approach

In section 10.1 we argued, on the basis of our price equation (relationship (9.9)), that the task of anti-inflation policy is to find ways of achieving one or more of three results: (i) a lower $\dot{W}$ than otherwise; (ii) a higher $\dot{O}$ than otherwise; and (iii) a lower $\dot{K}$ than otherwise. We also distinguished two possible approaches to this task. The first approach, which we termed the P.I.P. (prices and incomes policy) approach, is to attempt to achieve all three of the above results by means of some form of direct persuasion. This is the approach which we have been considering in the last four sections. The second approach, the D.R. (demand-restriction) approach, is to attempt to achieve the first of the three results by means of demand restriction via the fiscal, monetary and import instruments discussed in Chapter 6. To this approach we now turn.

The difference between the P.I.P. approach, in so far as it relates to (i) above, and the D.R. approach can be illustrated diagrammatically by means of Fig. 10.1. This is based on relationship (9.11) which we repeat for the reader's convenience:

$$\dot{W}_t = \xi_1 \dot{P}_{t-1} + \xi_2 H_t \qquad (9.11)$$

where $\dot{W}$ denotes the proportional rate of increase in money wage earnings per man, $\dot{P}$ the proportional rate of increase in the general price level, and H the level of excess demand and where ξ_1 and ξ_2 are two constants.

With a given rate of inflation (say $\dot{P}^*$), (9.11) can be represented on a diagram with $\dot{W}$ on the vertical axis and H on the horizontal axis, as a family of straight lines passing through the origin, each member of the family corresponding to a given degree of trade union 'pushfulness' (cf. pp. 304–8 above). Two members of the family are shown in Fig. 10.1, namely OK and OJ. Along OJ the unions are less militant than along OK. Let the degree of pushfulness be such that OK applies and let the level of excess demand be OE. Then $\dot{W}$ will be OB. If the P.I.P. approach were being followed, the authorities would leave excess demand at *OE* and attempt to *shift* the wage change–excess demand curve to *OJ*, say, by moderating the pushfulness of the unions. By this means they would reduce $\dot{W}$ from *OB* to *OA*. On the other hand, if the D.R. approach were being followed the

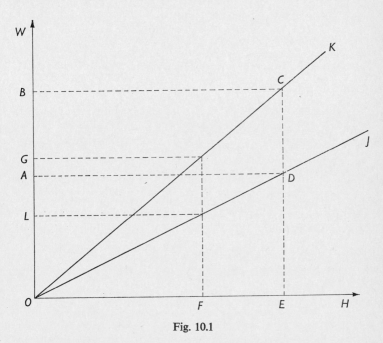

Fig. 10.1

authorities would leave the wage change–excess demand curve at *OK* and *move down* the curve by restricting aggregate demand and hence reducing excess demand – say from *OE* to *OF*. By this means they would reduce $\dot{W}$ from *OB* to *OG*. Of course, there is no reason why the authorities should follow one approach to the exclusion of the other. If both approaches were being followed, the authorities would shift the wage change–excess demand curve downwards and then move down the new curve by means of demand restriction. The result would be to lower $\dot{W}$ from *OB* to *OL*.

Two main questions arise in connection with the D.R. approach. They are:

(i) If the D.R. approach is used alone to achieve price stability what will be the resulting unemployment percentage? In other words, what will be the cost of price stability in terms of unemployment, if price stability is achieved by means of D.R. alone?

(ii) Will D.R. tend to *raise* $\dot{P}$ as well as lower it?

We shall now consider each of these questions in turn.

There have been two well-known attempts to determine the unemployment percentage required for price stability for the British economy in recent years – one by Phillips and one by Paish.

Phillips's estimate[1] is based on his fitted relationship between the rate of increase of money wage rates and the unemployment percentage – relationship (9.29). He assumes: (i) that the only source of upward pressure on the price level is rising unit labour cost; and (ii) that the rate of increase of money wage earnings is equal to the rate of increase of money wage rates – that wage-drift is zero. On these assumptions, according to relationship (9.9), price stability requires that the rate of increase of money wage rates should be equal to the rate of increase of productivity. Phillips assumes a rate of increase of productivity of 2 per cent per annum. Hence to achieve price stability in Britain, he argues, it will be necessary to achieve an average rate of increase of wage rates of 2 per cent per annum. Finally, to determine the unemployment percentage which would be associated with this rate of increase of money wage rates, Phillips uses (9.29). With $\Delta W = 2$, (9.29) gives:[2]

$$\log U_t = \frac{\log 9 \cdot 638 - \log 2 \cdot 900}{1 \cdot 394}$$

which, in turn, gives $U_t = 2 \cdot 367$. His conclusion, then, is that to achieve price stability in Britain by D.R. alone (if there were no concurrent attempt to shift the Phillips curve to the left), it would be necessary to carry it to the point where unemployment was a little less than $2\frac{1}{2}$ per cent of the labour force.

We turn now to the estimate made by Paish.[3] Underlying Paish's estimate is a highly personal definition of 'inflation'. Paish rejects the usual definition of inflation in terms of the rate of increase of some appropriate price index – the definition we adopt (see section 1.4

---

[1] See A. W. Phillips, 'The Relation between Unemployment and the Rate of Change of Money Wage Rates in the United Kingdom', *Economica* (Nov 1958) p. 299.

[2] Note that the dependent variable in (9.29) is the percentage rate of increase in the index of weekly wage rates.

[3] See F. W. Paish, *Rise and Fall of Incomes Policy* (London: Institute of Economic Affairs, 1969) pp. 19–43.

above) – and substitutes a definition which runs in terms of the relationship between the rate of increase of money incomes and the rate of increase of real potential gross domestic product (Paish's term is 'productive potential'). In his own words: 'The definition of inflation must therefore be a condition in which incomes are rising faster, not than the current rise in real national income, but than the *maintainable* rise. Apart from the effects of changes in the terms of trade and in net income from foreign investments, this is the same thing as the maintainable rise of output, or, as it is sometimes called, the rise of productive potential.'[1]

Given this definition of inflation, to estimate the cost of price stability in terms of unemployment one must determine the un-employment percentage at which the rate of rise of productive potential and the rate of rise of money incomes are equalised. Paish does this by: (i) calculating, for each of the years 1952 to 1968, the rate of increase of productive potential over the previous year and the rate of increase of income from employment over the previous year; (ii) noting the years in which the two rates were approximately equal; and (iii) observing the unemployment percentage for those years.[2] The conclusion which emerges is as follows: 'A comparison of Charts 3A and 3B shows that in the only years, 1958 and 1967, in which the rate of rise of income from employment slowed down to equality with the rate of growth of productive potential the percent-age of unemployment was about $2\frac{1}{2}$ per cent. So long as the growth of productive potential is maintained at about its present rate, this seems to be the lowest level of unemployment which is, in the long run, compatible with an absence of inflation.'[3] Thus Paish's con-clusion is the same, broadly speaking, as Phillips's.

Neither of the two estimates just discussed is entirely acceptable. Phillips's estimate is suspect because it is firmly based on the Phillips curve; and, as we have seen, the validity of this curve for the post-war British economy has been called into question by the recent work of Hines (see pp. 308–14 above). Paish avoids difficulties of this sort, but the usefulness of his estimate is limited by the somewhat eccentric definition of inflation on which it is based. In view of this, we propose now to provide a rough check on the order of magnitude of the figure obtained by Phillips and Paish, using as a foundation

[1] Ibid., p. 20 (italics in original).
[2] Ibid., Table V, p. 30, and Table IX, p. 42.
[3] Ibid., p. 43.

the Dicks-Mireaux econometric relationships discussed in section 9.4 above and repeated below.

$$\dot{P}_t = 2 \cdot 47 + 0 \cdot 27 \dot{W}_t + 0 \cdot 21 \dot{M}_{t-\frac{1}{2}} - 0 \cdot 54 \dot{O}_t \qquad (9.14)$$

$$\dot{W}_t = 3 \cdot 90 + 0 \cdot 30 \dot{P}_t + 0 \cdot 16 \dot{P}_{t-1} + 2 \cdot 78 H_{t-\frac{1}{4}}. \qquad (9.15)$$

We shall proceed as follows. We shall postulate a moving equilibrium in which all rates of increase are constant and use the price equation (relationship (9.14)) to find the equilibrium level of $\dot{W}$ which is consistent with price stability ($\dot{P}=0$) and with specified equilibrium levels of $\dot{M}$ and $\dot{O}$. Having calculated this value of $\dot{W}$ from the price equation, we shall then turn to the wage equation (relationship (9.15)) and find the value of H (relative excess demand) which is consistent with this value of $\dot{W}$ and with price stability. Finally we shall translate this value of H into an unemployment percentage. This will be the unemployment percentage which is consistent with price stability according to the Dicks-Mireaux relationships.

Starting with the price equation, then, we specify that in the postulated moving equilibrium the rate of increase in the unit cost of imported materials is zero (imported materials cost is constant) and the rate of increase of output per man is 2 per cent per annum.[1] On this basis the price equation gives a value of $-5 \cdot 15$ per cent per annum as the equilibrium value of $\dot{W}$ which is consistent with price stability. This figure is obtained by suppressing time subscripts throughout (9.14), substituting zero for $\dot{P}$ and $\dot{M}$ and 2 for $\dot{O}$ and then solving for $\dot{W}$. Turning now to the wage relationship, we find that with this value of $\dot{W}$ the value of H which is consistent with price stability is $-4 \cdot 36$. This figure is found by suppressing time subscripts throughout (9.15), substituting $-5 \cdot 15$ for $\dot{W}$ and zero for $\dot{P}$ and then solving for H. Finally, we make use of (9.34) to translate the figure of $-4 \cdot 36$ for H into an unemployment percentage. We proceed by dropping the second term in (9.34), putting $s = 0 \cdot 4^2$ and assuming that an unemployment percentage of 1 per cent corresponds to a relative excess demand of zero.[3] On this basis (9.34) gives:

$$U_t - 1 = -0 \cdot 4 \left(\frac{\bar{E}_t - L_t}{L_t} \right).$$

[1] This is the figure on which Phillips's calculation is based. See p. 356 above.
[2] Cf. C. Gilleon, 'Wage-Rates, Earnings, and Wage-Drift', *National Institute Economic Review* (Nov 1968) p. 53.
[3] Cf. Paish, op. cit., Table VIII, p. 41.

Substituting $-4\cdot36$ for $[(\bar{E}_t - L_t)/L_t]$, we find that the unemployment percentage which corresponds to a value of -4.36 for H is $2\cdot74$.

Thus the figure for the cost of price stability in terms of unemployment which emerges from our rough calculation varies only slightly from the figures calculated by Phillips and Paish. Thus while we find their methods unacceptable, we have a fair degree of confidence in their results.

We turn now to the second of the two questions which arise in connection with the D.R. approach – whether demand restriction will have effects which tend to raise the rate of inflation and hence which work against its favourable effect via a reduction in the rate of increase of money wages. In this connection there appear to be two main possibilities: (i) that demand restriction will check the rate of increase of productivity; (ii) that demand restriction will stimulate trade union pushfulness. In the event of (i) being realised, the D.R. approach would tend to raise $\dot{P}$ directly via the price equation (cf. relationship (9.9)), while if (ii) were to result the D.R. approach would tend to raise $\dot{P}$ indirectly via the wage equation.

On the first possibility, we begin by noting that demand restriction may check the rate of increase of productivity both in the short run and also in the long run. The *short-term* effects are by now reasonably well known. If the rate of growth of aggregate demand is checked by policy action, as a means of promoting price stability, a short-run decline in the rate of growth of aggregate output will almost certainly follow (cf. relationship (3.2), pp. 68–9 above). This, in turn, will mean a short-run decline in the rate of growth of employment. However, post-war experience shows that the decline in the rate of growth of employment is usually less than the decline in the rate of growth of output, i.e. that demand restriction usually leads to a short-run decline in labour productivity. The main reasons why the check to employment tends to be less than the check to output in the face of demand restriction have been summarised as follows: 'Part of a firm's labour force represents an overhead, not closely adjustable in the short-run to the level of output. Firms may also be reluctant to discharge labour since this would worsen labour relations, or entail the disbandment of work teams. Difficulty may be expected in finding labour again, particularly skilled grades, should demand later rise.'[1]

As for the *long-term* effects, one could argue that, by checking the

[1] See J. C. R. Dow and L. A. Dicks-Mireaux, 'Price Stability and the Policy of Deflation', *National Institute Economic Review* (May 1959) p. 20.

growth of output, demand restriction will tend to depress the level of real investment in fixed-capital equipment (cf. relationship (4.11)) and that this, in turn, will tend in various ways to check the long-term growth of productivity. Some of the recent work on the sources of economic growth which we shall discuss in Chapter 12 lends considerable support to this line of argument. Nevertheless it has yet to be fully confirmed and in the meantime the long-term effects of demand restriction on the growth of productivity remain somewhat uncertain.

The distinction made above between the short-run and the long-run productivity effects of demand restriction is of some importance in view of Neild's study (see section 9.5 above). Suppose that it were indeed the case, as Neild's results suggest, that only long-run productivity movements are relevant to pricing decisions. Then the argument that demand restriction will tend to raise $\dot{P}$ by checking the growth of productivity would be somewhat dubious because then the 'growth of productivity' referred to would have to be the long-run productivity growth and, as we have seen, the long-run productivity effects of demand restriction are somewhat uncertain. On the other hand, suppose that the more common view embodied in (9.9.) – the view that prices tend to rise in the face of productivity decline whether it be short-run or long-run in character – were the correct one. Then the argument in question would be substantial because then the 'growth of productivity' referred to could be either short-run productivity growth or long-run, and the short-term productivity effects of demand restriction are both powerful and reasonably certain even if there is doubt about the long-term effects.

The second of the two possibilities raised above is that demand restriction may tend to raise $\dot{P}$, by stimulating trade union pushfulness. This possibility has been explored recently by Hines.[1] Hines's procedure was to estimate a relationship in which the dependent variable was ΔT (his index of pushfulness) and the explanatory variables were U and ΔU (the unemployment percentage and the absolute rate of change in the unemployment percentage). The relationship was estimated by ordinary least squares from annual British data for five separate periods, namely 1893–1912, 1921–38, 1949–61, 1921–61 (excluding 1939–48) and 1893–1961 (excluding 1913–20 and 1939–48). Now if the unions do, in fact, become more pushful in the face of demand restriction (i.e. growing unemploy-

---

[1] See A. G. Hines, 'Trade Unions and Wage Inflation in the United Kingdom 1893–1961', *Review of Economic Studies* (Oct 1964).

ment), one would expect the estimated coefficient of ΔU in the relationship in question to have a positive sign. In none of Hines's five estimations was this the case.[1] In view of these results we are inclined to dismiss the argument that demand restriction will make the unions more militant and, in this way, stimulate $\dot{P}$.

The discussion of the present section may be summed up as follows. If the authorities were to attempt to achieve price stability in Britain by means of the D.R. approach alone, unemployment of the order of $2\frac{1}{2}$ per cent of the labour force would be the likely result. In arriving at this figure no allowance is made for the possibility that demand restriction may have unintended adverse price-*raising* effects. To the extent that such effects exist, the cost of price stability in terms of unemployment would be higher still. Of the two possible adverse effects examined, one has been dismissed, namely the effect via trade union pushfulness. The other – the effect via productivity – has been admitted, though we remain somewhat uncertain as to the weight to be attached to it.

The broad conclusion which emerges from the discussion of the present chapter is that the attainment of price stability calls for some combination of the P.I.P. and D.R. approaches. Use of the P.I.P. approach alone is unsatisfactory because, if post-war British experience is any guide, this approach is too weak to stop inflation on its own, however vigorously it is applied. Use of the D.R. approach alone is also unsatisfactory but for a different reason. There is little doubt that the D.R. approach is capable of doing the whole job of stopping inflation, provided it is carried far enough. However, recent research suggests that, in the case of the British economy, 'far enough' may well be to the point where some $2\frac{1}{2}$ per cent of the labour force is unemployed. Unemployment of this magnitude would represent a serious waste of resources and would involve substantial personal hardship for many members of the labour force and their dependants. The obvious compromise is to get as much as possible from the P.I.P. approach, without relying on it entirely, and then to use demand restriction to do the rest of the job.

10.7 Summary

The task of anti-inflation policy can be thought of as that of making $\dot{P}$ less than otherwise in one or more of the following three ways:

[1] Ibid., pp. 233–4.

(i) by reducing $\dot{W}$ below what it would otherwise be; (ii) by raising $\dot{O}$ above what it would otherwise be; (iii) by reducing $\dot{K}$ below what it would otherwise be. There are two approaches to this task. The first approach (the P.I.P. approach) involves the use of direct persuasion to change the behaviour patterns of those engaged in wage and price decisions in a way which is conducive to price stability, e.g. to persuade the parties to wage negotiations to exercise more restraint than they would have done otherwise. The second approach (the D.R. approach) involves restricting aggregate demand with a view to making $\dot{W}$ less than it would have been otherwise.

Examination of the development of the P.I.P. approach in the post-war period suggests that there are two types of problem associated with this approach: (i) problems of formulating the 'price and wage criteria', i.e. the patterns of price and wage behaviour which are desirable from the point of view of price stability; and (ii) problems of implementing these criteria. Of the problems in the first group, only one is discussed, namely the problem of devising a rule for setting the wage norm – the desirable level of $\dot{W}$. Four such rules are examined. Of these the one which appears to be the best all-found performer, both from the standpoint of price stability and the standpoint of equity, is the 'productivity' rule: $\dot{W} = \dot{O}^*$ where $\dot{O}^*$ is the expected average percentage rate of increase in real G.D.P. per man-hour.

In the second group of problems associated with the P.I.P. approach – problems of implementation – we find two of special interest: (i) how to persuade the leaders of management and labour to endorse the criteria; and (ii) how to back up this endorsement. As regards the first, it seems that if endorsement is to be achieved, the leaders of organised labour and management must be convinced of the need to avoid inflation, able to see that the proposed criteria will contribute to this end, satisfied that the proposed criteria are fair, and confident that they can gain rank-and-file support for their endorsement of the proposed criteria. As regards the second problem, the main ways of backing up endorsement of the criteria are by means of legislation, by means of demand restriction, by promoting productivity increase and by giving employers some form of financial incentive not to pay their workers at rates in excess of the norm.

In recent years extensive econometric work, using the dummy-variable device, has been undertaken with the object of measuring the effectiveness of the P.I.P. approach in Britain since the war. The broad conclusion which emerges from this work is that, while the direct contribution of the P.I.P. approach to a reduction in $\dot{P}$ is likely to be negligible, its indirect contribution via $\dot{W}$ may be quite significant, given favourable conditions and determination on the part of the authorities to make the policy work.

In the final section of the chapter we consider briefly the second way of approaching the task of anti-inflation policy – the demand-restriction (D.R.) approach. The crucial question here is how far the restriction of aggregate demand would have to be carried if price stability were to be achieved by this means alone. Of recent attempts to answer this question, the most notable are those of Phillips and Paish. Their work suggests that, in the case of the British economy, to achieve price stability it would be necessary to carry demand restriction to the point where something like $2\frac{1}{2}$ per cent of the labour force was unemployed.

READING LIST

Incomes Policy: The Next Step, Cmnd 1626 (Feb 1962).
National Board for Prices and Incomes, *General Report, April 1965 to July 1966*, Cmnd 3087 (Aug 1966).
——, *Second General Report, July 1966 to August 1967*, Cmnd 3394 (Aug 1967).
——, *Third General Report, August 1967 to July 1968*, Cmnd 3715 (July 1968).
Paish, F. W., *Rise and Fall of Incomes Policy* (London: Institute of Economic Affairs, 1969).
—— and Hennessy, J., *Policy for Incomes?* (London: Institute of Economic Affairs, 1967).
Phillips, A. W., 'The Relation between Unemployment and the Rate of Change of Money Wage Rates in the United Kingdom', *Economica* (Nov 1958).
Prices and Incomes Policy, Cmnd 2639 (Apr 1965).
Prices and Incomes Policy after 30th June, 1967, Cmnd 3235 (Mar 1967).
Prices and Incomes Standstill, Cmnd 3073 (July 1966).
Prices and Incomes Standstill: Period of Severe Restraint, Cmnd 3150 (Nov 1966).
Smith, D. C., 'Incomes Policy', in Caves, R. E., and associates, *Britain's Economic Prospects* (London: Allen & Unwin, 1968).

11 Optimum Economic Growth

11.1 Introduction

In this chapter and the next we shall discuss the last of the four objectives of macro-economic policy with which the book is concerned. This is the objective of a high growth rate. As we shall see, the analysis of growth as an objective of economic policy involves problems which are both more fundamental and less familiar than those we have yet encountered, and for this reason the discussion of these chapters will differ from the discussion so far in several important respects. We shall start with a brief look at three of these differences.

The first point of difference concerns the role of ethical judgements. In the discussion of Chapters 6, 7 and 10 on the attainment of the objectives of internal and external balance and price stability, the question of ethical judgements did not arise explicitly. The problem of choosing between different methods of attaining a given objective was discussed in terms of 'efficiency' considerations alone, i.e. in terms of the likely impact of changes in particular policy instruments on 'target' variables such as D and M. This approach to economic policy is valid provided it can be assumed that the effects of a particular policy in areas which naturally involve ethical judgements, e.g. the distribution of income, can be neglected, either because these effects are known to be negligible or because the Government can be relied on to take care of such areas by whatever means are appropriate. In the case of policy issues of the sort dealt with in earlier chapters, this assumption is a reasonable one and the exclusion of ethical judgements is therefore not difficult to accept. On the other hand, in the case of the policy issues which arise in connection with the growth objective, ethical judgements can hardly be avoided. For example, growth policy is inextricably bound up with the choice of a rate and pattern of investment. But this choice is itself bound up with the question of the distribution of consumption as between generations. Hence, it necessarily involves ethical (or 'value') judgements of a most fundamental kind. The literature on the theory of optimal economic growth which has developed in the last decade or so differs from the mainstream of Keynesian macro-economics in that it recognises the importance of such ethical judgements by formulating them explicitly in a 'social welfare function'. One of the main objectives of this chapter is to analyse some of the basic conceptual difficulties which arise in the application of social welfare functions, and to bring to bear on our discussion of British growth policy such insights as it may provide.

The second main point of difference, which indeed arises from the first, concerns the possibility of testing. In Chapter 2 it was pointed out that one of the main features of short-run Keynesian macro-economic theory which nowadays forms the basis for discussion of the internal balance and external balance objectives, is an insistence that all relationships be testable. As will be clear from Chapter 9, the theory of the inflationary process, which underlies contemporary discussion of the price-stability objective, possesses the same characteristic. When we turn to the theory which provides the framework for discussion of the growth objective, however, we find that the principle of testability, while still applicable to some extent, is subject to definite limitations. In some discussions of the growth objective the basic model will involve only technical and behavioural relationships relating the rate of growth to other observable economic variables. An example would be the model used for an investigation of how far the relatively slow growth rate of the United Kingdom since the war, compared with other Western European countries, could be attributed to a lower ratio of investment to gross domestic product, to an unfavourable sectoral distribution of investment, to a lower rate of technical progress and so on. In such cases the principle of testability continues to hold. But there will be other discussions of the growth objective in which ethical judgements are involved as well as technical and behavioural relationships, and in these cases 'testing' in the ordinary sense of the word will not be possible. Take, for example, a discussion concerned with the 'right' things to aim at in growth policy. Here the basic model would be a model of planned growth in which ethical judgements were involved in some way. On the question of testing, one could argue that since the object of the underlying model was to help to provide better understanding of, and stronger support for, certain growth targets, the model, if successful, could be expected to be self-fulfilling. If accepted, such an argument would give the model 'testability' of a sort but it would not be testability in the sense in which the word is customarily used.

Thirdly, there is a difference in the time-scale underlying the discussion. In discussing the objectives of internal balance, external balance and price stability it was convenient to work with a short-run dynamic model. In Chapter 2 two meanings of the term 'short-run dynamic model' were distinguished. In the first sense the term referred to a model in which the reactions of the jointly determined variables to changes in the data were regarded as occurring short period by short period, e.g. month by month or quarter by quarter, rather than year by year or decade by decade. In the second sense it referred to a model in which the reactions of the jointly determined variables were regarded as occurring over a short total time interval, i.e. as a model with a short time horizon. The models which we developed as a framework for discussing internal balance, external balance and price stability were short-run dynamic models in both these senses. When it comes to an analysis of the growth objective, however, a short-run model in either or both of the above senses is no longer appropriate. As far as the first sense of 'short-run' is concerned, year-by-year changes in output, consumption, etc., constitute the natural time-scale of analysis in considering problems of growth. As regards the second sense of 'short-run', there is no one time horizon that clearly commends itself as providing the appropriate time-scale for analysis in dealing with growth problems. Indeed, one of the crucial difficulties associated with the theory of optimal economic growth is that the time horizon over which we choose to compare alternative types of policy may make a substantial difference to our decision as to what the 'best' policy is. The relevant time horizon thus becomes, in a certain sense, part of the problem to be solved rather than simply part of the data.

11.2 Choice of the Optimum Growth Rate

In Chapter 1 we devoted considerable effort to clarifying the objective of a high growth rate (see pp. 24–30 above). We pointed out that the term 'a high growth rate' could be taken to mean 'a high average percentage increase in real gross domestic product'. However, this was not the end of the matter because there proved to be various possible meanings of 'gross domestic product' and various possible meanings of 'average percentage increase' between which a choice had to be made before the growth objective could be said to be clearly defined. Also there was the problem of the precise meaning to be given to 'high'. Here our contribution was to say that 'high' could be interpreted to mean 'optimum subject to constraints of an economic, social or political character'. Thus, at the end of our discussion we had defined the growth objective as the achievement of that average percentage increase (in, say, the 'compound interest' sense) in real gross domestic product (in, say, the 'realised' sense) which is optimum given various economic, social and political constraints.

The question which now arises is whether it is possible to find this optimum growth rate; if it is not possible the definition will not be a particularly useful one for policy purposes. This question has been the subject of much discussion, particularly since the end of the Second World War, and the main object of the present chapter is to give a brief survey of some of the leading contributions which have been made to the discussion.

Most modern work on the problem of deriving the optimum growth rate (the 'optimum growth problem') takes as its starting-point an early article by Ramsey,[1] and the main object of the present section is to outline what might be called the Ramsey approach. For this purpose we shall make use of the following notation:

Y = aggregate real output at time t
K = aggregate real capital stock at time t
L = labour employed at time t
I = aggregate real investment expenditure at time t
C = aggregate real consumption expenditure at time t
U = social welfare at time t.

It will be observed that all of our variables, flows as well as stocks, relate to 'time t', not to 'period t', i.e. they are regarded as continuous functions of time. They are defined in this way because, for the first time, we shall be making use of the 'continuous' form of dynamic analysis as distinct from the 'period-analysis' form used exclusively up to this point. In accordance with the usual convention we shall denote the first time derivatives of our variables by means of the above symbols with one dot on top and the second time derivatives by means of these symbols with two dots on top.[2]

---

[1] See F. P. Ramsey, 'A Mathematical Theory of Saving', *Economic Journal* (Dec 1928).
[2] To avoid possible confusion we would stress that the meaning of the 'one-dot' symbol in this chapter is different from its meaning in Chapters 9 and 10. In the

Ramsey's contribution was to show that, given a set of highly simplified assumptions, the optimum growth problem could be formulated as the problem of choosing the capital stock at each point of time in such a way as to give the right allocation of output between consumption and savings at that point of time, this being the allocation which maximised welfare over some finite time interval. We shall begin by listing the assumptions which Ramsey used in terms of the above notation.

1. There is a single good which can either be consumed directly or used as a capital good, i.e. as a means of producing itself. Real gross domestic product (G.D.P.) at time t can be identified with Y, the output of this single good at time t.

2. The output of the good at time t depends on the amount of the good which is used as capital at time t and on the amount of labour employed at time t.

3. The form of this dependence is given by a production function: $Y = f(K, L)$ which is assumed to remain unchanged over time, i.e. technical progress is absent.

4. Labour employed is assumed to grow at a given constant proportionate rate g from a given level, L_0, at time 0, i.e. $L = L_0 e^{gt}$ where L_0 and g are given.

5. There is no depreciation of capital equipment.

6. Social welfare at time t depends on the amount of the single good which is used for consumption.

7. The form of this dependence is given by a social welfare function, $U = u(C)$, which is assumed to remain unchanged over time.

8. Social welfare at any point of time is independent of its level at any other point of time and social welfare at different points of time is additive.

In the light of assumptions 6–8, a natural way to define the optimum time path of real G.D.P. is to say that it is that time path which makes aggregate social welfare over some specified time horizon a maximum, subject to the various economic constraints imposed by assumptions 1–5. If we can determine this particular time path of real G.D.P., we shall have solved the optimum growth problem. For once the optimum time path of real G.D.P. has been determined, the

---

present chapter the symbol denotes the first time derivative of the variable concerned, whereas in Chapters 9 and 10 it denotes the proportionate rate of increase of the variable.

optimum average percentage rate of increase of real G.D.P. will have been determined also, whatever method of averaging is used. Broadly speaking there are two main approaches to the problem of determining the optimum growth path of real G.D.P. thus defined. One possibility is to try to determine this path directly. The other approach is to try to determine the optimum growth path of some other variable in the first instance and then to use this to determine the optimum growth path of real G.D.P. If the second, indirect approach is used, a natural variable to select as 'choice function' is K, the capital stock at time t. As indicated above, this is, in fact, the usual procedure in applications of the Ramsey approach. We shall begin by presenting the indirect approach, using K as a choice function, and then outline the direct approach.

Our initial formulation of the optimum growth problem, then, is: To find K, regarded as a function of t, such that:

$$\int_0^T u(C)dt \tag{11.1}$$

is maximised subject to:

$$Y = C + I \tag{11.2}$$

$$Y = f(K, L) \tag{11.3}$$

$$I = \frac{dK}{dt} = \dot{K} \tag{11.4}$$

$$L = L_0 e^{gt} \tag{11.5}$$

$$K(0) = \overline{K}_0; \; K(T) = \overline{K}_T \tag{11.6}$$

where $K(0)$ and $K(T)$ are the values of K at time 0 and at time T, respectively, and $\overline{K}_0$ and $\overline{K}_T$ are given.[1]

Relationships (11.2)–(11.5) are genuine economic constraints. By contrast (11.6), which specifies the initial and terminal value of the capital stock, is a constraint imposed merely to facilitate the application of standard mathematical methods, as will be seen below. The two statements appearing in (11.6) are known as 'boundary conditions'.

---

[1] It should be noted that Ramsey himself worked in terms of an infinite time horizon (see Ramsey, op. cit., p. 547). We have specified a finite time horizon, running from time 0 to time T, merely to simplify the exposition. See also section 11.4.

The solution proceeds as follows. Using (11.2), (11.3) and (11.4), and recognising that (11.5) gives L as a function of t alone (L_0 and g are data), we write the function $u(C)$ as a function of K, $\dot{K}$ and t. We have:

$$u(C) = u(Y - I) = u\{f(K, L) - \dot{K}\} = \phi(K, \dot{K}, t). \tag{11.7}$$

Hence the above formulation of the optimum growth problem can be rewritten as:

To find K, regarded as a function of t, such that:

$$\int_0^T \phi(K, \dot{K}, t)dt \tag{11.8}$$

is maximised subject to:

$$K(0) = \overline{K}_0; \; K(T) = \overline{K}_T.$$

In this form the problem appears as the so-called 'fundamental problem' in the calculus of variations, the solution of which is well known.[1] It transpires that the maximising K must satisfy the Euler–Lagrange condition:

$$\frac{\partial \phi}{\partial K} = \frac{d}{dt}\left(\frac{\partial \phi}{\partial \dot{K}}\right). \tag{11.9}$$

This is a necessary condition which corresponds to the first-order condition for a maximum in the ordinary calculus and is supplemented by second-order conditions designed to ensure that the K which satisfies (11.9) is one which makes (11.7) a maximum, not a minimum. The second-order conditions for a maximum in the calculus of variations involve some mathematical complexity and different versions of these have been provided by Jacobi and Weierstrass. We shall not discuss them here, except to point out that under the usual curvature assumptions made in economic theory (diminishing marginal 'utility', diminishing marginal factor-productivity), the second-order conditions associated with the optimum growth problem will normally hold for a growth path which satisfies the Euler–Lagrange condition.

Inspection of (11.9) shows that it is a second-order differential equation in K and in its first and second time derivatives. The optimum growth problem thus reduces to the problem of finding the solution of this differential equation. Given a specific form for the production function (11.3) and the social welfare function (11.1), the

[1] For a treatment of this problem see R. G. D. Allen, *Mathematical Analysis for Economists* (London: Macmillan, 1967) pp. 521–33.

problem can be solved in principle, though of course there may be considerable practical difficulty in finding the solution of the differential equation if the form of either the production function or the social welfare function is at all complicated.[1]

The Euler–Lagrange condition (11.9) can be given various economic interpretations, two of which are of interest. From (11.7) we have:

$$\frac{\partial \phi}{\partial K} = u'(C)\frac{\partial f}{\partial K}$$

$$\frac{\partial \phi}{\delta \dot{K}} = -u'(C).$$

Hence (11.9) can be written as:

$$u'(C)\frac{\partial f}{\partial K} = \frac{d}{dt}(-u'(C)).$$

This, in turn, gives:

$$\frac{1}{u'(C)}\frac{d}{dt}(u'(C)) = -\frac{\partial f}{\partial K}. \tag{11.10}$$

The expression $u'(C)$ is the marginal 'utility' of consumption, which means that the left-hand side of (11.10) is the proportionate rate of change in the marginal utility of consumption. The expression $\partial f/\partial K$ is the marginal physical product of capital. Thus the version of the Euler–Lagrange condition given by (11.10) yields the conclusion that the maximising K must be such that the proportionate rate of change of the marginal utility of consumption at any point of time is numerically equal to the marginal product of capital at that point of time. This has been called 'the Ramsey rule for optimum growth'.

Alternatively, the Ramsey rule can be written in the equivalent form:

$$u'(C) = \frac{B - u(C)}{\dot{K}} \tag{11.11}$$

where B is a constant (see Appendix 11.1 for details). In this form the rule states that the optimum growth path of K is such that the marginal 'cost' of saving (i.e. the marginal utility of consumption) at any point of time is equated with its marginal future benefit at that point of time.

To help elucidate the preceding discussion, we shall now derive

[1] The boundary conditions would be used to determine the two arbitrary constants of integration in the solution.

the Euler–Lagrange condition for the case where the production and social welfare functions take particularly simple forms, namely:

$$f(K, L) = aK + bL \tag{11.12}$$

$$u(C) = \log C. \tag{11.13}$$

By following through (11.7) we see that, given (11.12) and (11.13), the function $\phi(K, \dot{K}, t)$ is given by:

$$\phi(K, \dot{K}, t) = \log (aK - \dot{K} + bL_0 e^{gt}). \tag{11.14}$$

Hence $\dfrac{\partial \phi}{\partial K}$ and $\dfrac{d}{dt}\left(\dfrac{\partial \phi}{\partial \dot{K}}\right)$ are given by:

$$\frac{\partial \phi}{\partial K} = u'(C)\,\frac{\partial f}{\partial K} = a(aK - \dot{K} + bL_0 e^{gt})^{-1} \tag{11.15}$$

$$\frac{d}{dt}\left(\frac{\partial \phi}{\partial \dot{K}}\right) = \frac{d}{dt}[-u'(C)] = \frac{d}{dt}[-(aK - \dot{K} + bL_0 e^{gt})^{-1}]$$
$$= (aK - \dot{K} + bL_0 e^{gt})^{-2}(a\dot{K} - \ddot{K} + bgL_0 e^{gt}). \tag{11.16}$$

The Euler–Lagrange condition, therefore, is:

$$a(aK - \dot{K} + bL_0 e^{gt}) = a\dot{K} - \ddot{K} + bgL_0 e^{gt}. \tag{11.17}$$

Finally, collecting terms in $\dot{K}$ and K we get:

$$\ddot{K} - 2a\dot{K} + a^2 K = (g - a)bL_0 e^{gt}. \tag{11.18}$$

This is a second-order differential equation in K and its first two time derivatives, whose solution is as follows:

$$K = (B + At)e^{at} + \frac{bL_0 e^{gt}}{(g - a)} \tag{11.19}$$

where B and A are arbitrary constants to be determined by the boundary conditions. This expression gives the optimum growth path for the capital stock in terms of the given magnitudes a, L_0, g and b. To find the optimum growth path for real G.D.P. we have merely to substitute (11.19) in (11.12) to get:

$$Y = aK + bL = (B' + A't)e^{at} + \frac{gbL_0 e^{gt}}{(g - a)} \tag{11.20}$$

where $B' = aB$ and $A' = aA$ are arbitrary constants to be determined by the terminal values of Y.

In the foregoing we have derived the optimum growth path for real G.D.P. indirectly via the optimum growth path for K. Instead we can derive the optimum real G.D.P. path directly. The argument is as follows.

Using (11.2) to (11.5), we have:

$$u(C) = u(Y - I) = u(Y - \dot{K}) = u\left(Y - \frac{1}{\partial f/\partial K}\left[\dot{Y} - \frac{\partial f}{\partial L}\dot{L}\right]\right)$$

$$= u\left(Y - \frac{1}{\partial f/\partial K}\left[\dot{Y} - \frac{\partial f}{\partial L}gL_0e^{gt}\right]\right). \quad (11.21)$$

Since $\partial f/\partial K$ and $\partial f/\partial L$ are functions of K and L where K and L are functions of t, (11.21) gives:

$$u(C) = F(Y, \dot{Y}, t). \quad (11.22)$$

Thus, our first formulation of the optimum growth problem (see p. 370 above) is equivalent to the following:

To find Y, regarded as a function of t, such that:

$$\int_0^T F(Y, \dot{Y}, t)dt \quad (11.23)$$

is maximised subject to:

$$Y(0) = \overline{Y}_0; \quad Y(T) = \overline{Y}_T$$

where $\overline{Y}_0$ and $\overline{Y}_T$ are specified values for Y at time 0 and time T respectively, which are obtained from: $\overline{Y}_0 = f(\overline{K}_0, L_0)$; $\overline{Y}_T = f(\overline{K}_T, L_0e^{gT})$. Once again our problem reduces to the fundamental problem of the calculus of variations. The maximising Y will be given by the Euler-Lagrange condition:

$$\frac{\partial F}{\partial Y} = \frac{d}{dt}\left(\frac{\partial F}{\partial \dot{Y}}\right). \quad (11.24)$$

This is a second-order differential equation in Y and its first two time derivatives, the solution of which gives the optimum growth path for real G.D.P. directly.

Returning to the special case defined by (11.12) and (11.13), we find that the function $F(Y, \dot{Y}, t)$ is given by:

$$\log\left(Y - \frac{1}{a}[\dot{Y} - bgL_0e^{gt}]\right) \quad (11.25)$$

Hence $\partial F/\partial Y$ and $\partial F/\partial \dot{Y}$ are given by:

$$\frac{\partial F}{\partial Y} = \left(Y - \frac{1}{a}[\dot{Y} - bgL_0e^{gt}]\right)^{-1} \quad (11.26)$$

$$\frac{\partial F}{\partial \dot{Y}} = -\frac{1}{a}\left(Y - \frac{1}{a}[\dot{Y} - bgL_0e^{gt}]\right)^{-1}. \qquad (11.27)$$

From (11.27) it follows that the right-hand side of (11.24) is given by:

$$\frac{d}{dt}\left(\frac{\partial F}{\partial \dot{Y}}\right) = \frac{1}{a}\left(\dot{Y} - \frac{1}{a}\ddot{Y} + \frac{1}{a}bg^2L_0e^{gt}\right)\left(Y - \frac{1}{a}[\dot{Y} - bgL_0e^{gt}]\right)^{-2}. \quad (11.28)$$

Hence the Euler–Lagrange condition is:

$$\left(Y - \frac{1}{a}[\dot{Y} - bgL_0e^{gt}]\right) = \frac{1}{a}\left(\dot{Y} - \frac{1}{a}\ddot{Y} + \frac{1}{a}bg^2L_0e^{gt}\right). \quad (11.29)$$

This expression can be reduced to:

$$\ddot{Y} - 2a\,\dot{Y} + a^2 Y = (g-a)bgL_0e^{gt}. \qquad (11.30)$$

Relationship (11.30) is a second-order differential equation in Y and its first two time derivatives whose solution is:

$$Y = (B' + A't)e^{at} + \frac{gbL_0e^{gt}}{(g-a)} \qquad (11.31)$$

where B' and A' are two arbitrary constants to be determined by the terminal values of Y. This expression gives the optimum growth path for Y and is seen to be identical with the earlier expression (11.20).

In recent years work on the pure theory of optimum economic growth has consisted largely of extensions and specialisations of the Ramsey approach. In particular the theory has been extended to take into account such complications as technical progress, the existence of a number of sectors in the economy between which capital may not be shiftable, an infinite time horizon and time preference. Attention has also been drawn to the fact that the classical calculus of variations yields only interior maxima and hence that the maximising solution may not exclude decumulation (i.e. may not ensure $\dot{K} \geq 0$, for all t). Also, alternative techniques of optimisation such as dynamic programming and the Pontryagin maximum principle are being used increasingly for the derivation of optimum growth paths.

The welfare-maximising approach to economic growth has played an important part in clarifying the nature of planning. In particular, the spirit underlying the approach, namely that high growth rates are not to be prized as such but must be judged in the light of their effects on the welfare of the members of the society concerned, is one which those connected with formulating growth policy, whether in developed or in developing countries, can ill afford to ignore. On the other hand, if we are interested in the theory of optimal growth not merely as a conceptual framework for thinking about growth but also as a technique for the analysis of specific policies affecting the growth of an actual economy, such as the British economy, several far-reaching difficulties arise. Of these, two appear to be crucial. One is concerned with the social welfare function which is to be maximised; the other with the length of the time period over which maximisation is to extend. We shall discuss these problems in turn in the next two sections of the chapter.

11.3 The Choice of a Welfare Function

It is now generally agreed that the choice of the welfare function to be maximised necessarily involves ethical judgements. That this general agreement exists is largely due to the work of Arrow[1] and our first task in this section is to give an outline of his contribution. Our second task is to consider the question which the economist must face once he accepts the necessity for ethical judgements, namely whether he can legitimately choose a welfare function which embodies his own ethical judgements and if not whether there are any acceptable alternatives.

The question which Arrow set out to investigate may be stated briefly as follows. Suppose that society consists of n individuals. Assume that each individual has an ordering of social states and further that the ordering is *complete* in the sense that, for each pair of alternatives, either the individual prefers one to the other or is indifferent between them. Finally, assume that each individual's ordering is *transitive*, i.e. that if the individual prefers x to y (is indifferent between x and y) and prefers y to z (is indifferent between y and z) then he also prefers x to z (is indifferent between x and z). Define a *social welfare function* as a rule which gives, for each set of n individual orderings of alternative social states, a corresponding social ordering. The question, then, is: Does a social welfare function exist?

Arrow begins his attack on this question by specifying certain conditions which the social welfare function should satisfy if it is to be accepted as a reasonable method of aggregation. The basic

[1] See K. J. Arrow, *Social Choice and Individual Values* (New York: Wiley, 1951).

condition is that social choice should have the same rational structure as individual choice, i.e. that the social ordering which is to determine social choice should be complete and transitive. To this condition are added five others which may be listed as follows.

Condition 1

First, among all the alternative social states there is a set of at least three alternatives such that all logically possible individual orderings over the set are admissible in the sense that they are orderings for which the social welfare function yields a complete and consistent social ordering. A short way of expressing this condition is to say that there is at least one 'free triple' among admissible alternatives. As Arrow observes, the purpose of this condition is to ensure that '*for some sufficiently wide range of sets of individual orderings, the social welfare function give rise to a true social ordering*',[1] i.e. to make the method applicable in a wide range of contexts. If the 'free triple' condition were relaxed, the social welfare function could be made trivial, e.g. by being restricted to choices over only a few highly selected sets of possible individual preference orderings. The existence or otherwise of such a social welfare function would not be of much interest from the point of view of welfare economics.

Condition 2

Secondly, there is a non-negative association between individual orderings and social choice, i.e. 'if one alternative social state rises or remains still in the ordering of every individual without any other change in those orderings, we expect that it rises, or at least does not fall, in the social ordering'.[2] This condition is self-explanatory and, along with conditions 4 and 5 below, is part of the consumers' sovereignty requirement.

Condition 3

Arrow's third condition states that the social ordering of a set of alternatives should depend only on the *orderings by individuals over this set* and not on the existence or ordering of alternatives outside this set. This condition is known in the literature as the 'independence of irrelevant alternatives' and again has strong intuitive appeal. One of the less obvious consequences of this condition is to rule out cardinal utility for individuals, for the condition requires *inter alia*

[1] Arrow, op. cit., p. 25. (Italics ours.) [2] Ibid.

that the social orderings of a set of alternatives should depend only on individual *orderings* of these alternatives (and not, for example, on their preference intensities).

Condition 4

The fourth condition requires that the social welfare function must not be 'imposed'. According to Arrow's definition, a social welfare function is said to be imposed when there is some pair of alternatives x and y such that society can never express a preference for y over x, irrespective of individual preferences, for example even if all individuals prefer y to x. Imposed social welfare thus makes some preference orderings taboo. To this extent it offends the principle of consumers' sovereignty and hence goes against the spirit of Arrow's exercise.

Condition 5

The final condition is similar in nature to condition 4 and requires that the social welfare function must be non-dictatorial, i.e. social orderings should not be determined solely by the preferences of a particular individual member of society. Thus, the condition requires that there should be no individual such that whenever he strictly prefers x to y, society strictly prefers x to y, regardless of other individuals' preferences.

These five conditions, which together represent the requirements for collective rationality and consumers' sovereignty, have considerable intuitive appeal. Using them as a starting-point, Arrow reached the conclusion that a social welfare function does not exist by showing that there can be no social welfare function (method of arriving at a social ordering) such that the five conditions are satisfied simultaneously. This conclusion has become known as the *Possibility Theorem*.

While Arrow's Possibility Theorem had a profound influence on the subsequent development of welfare economics, later discussion showed that the theorem itself, as originally stated, was false. A counter-example by Blau[1] showed up a technical flaw in Arrow's proof and led to the reformulation of the conditions under which the Possibility Theorem holds. The five original conditions were replaced by four as follows. First, a social ordering can be obtained from any logically possible set of individual orderings. In other

[1] J. H. Blau, 'The Existence of Social Welfare Functions', *Econometrica* (Apr 1957).

N

words, all triples, rather than just one, as in the original formulation, are required to be free. Secondly, if all individuals strictly prefer x to y, the social ordering must show a preference for x over y. The other two conditions are the 'independence of irrelevant alternatives' and 'non-dictatorship' which are the same as conditions 3 and 5 respectively in the older version of the theorem. The new Possibility Theorem then states that these four conditions are mutually inconsistent, i.e. that there exists no method of reaching a consistent and complete social ordering of alternatives, which satisfies the four conditions, from individual orderings alone.

The relevance of the amended Possibility Theorem depends on how much intuitive appeal the new conditions possess. Now, conditions 3 and 4 ('independence of irrelevant alternatives' and 'non-dictatorship') are taken over unaltered from the older version. Clearly both these would be regarded by most people as part of their concept of collective rationality and hence as desirable conditions for a reasonable social welfare function to fulfil. Condition 2, which can be interpreted as a weaker version of the Pareto optimality principle, would certainly command wide consent also. As regards condition 1, the case seems to be rather different. The requirement that all triples be free is indeed much stronger than the requirement that at least one triple be free. However, Rothenberg argues persuasively that, as far as the theoretical significance of the Possibility Theorem is concerned, the difference between the two versions of condition 1 is really much less than would appear.[1] As he points out, Blau's counter-examples to Arrow's original theorem work 'because they call on ordering principles that apply to only a few alternatives instead of all'.[2] On the other hand, unless many alternatives are affected, the question of social choice, for all practical purposes, remains essentially unsolved. 'If many alternatives are included, in contrast, the intuitive sense of the limitations is probably not very different from the organizing force of principles which restrict orderings on all issues.'[3] Rothenberg concludes that in the context of this discussion, the impact of the new Possibility Theorem differs very little from that of the old. This conclusion is strengthened by the consideration that, whether we are discussing the old or the amended version of the Possibility Theorem, the set of conditions of 'reasonableness' imposed on the social welfare function cannot, even re-

---

[1] J. F. Rothenberg, *The Measurement of Social Welfare* (Englewood Cliffs, N.J.: Prentice-Hall, 1961).   [2] Ibid., p. 30.   [3] Ibid.

motely, be regarded as exhaustive. Indeed, the discussion following Blau's counter-example focused attention on how weak Arrow's original conditions were! As amended by Blau, they still leave out a great many requirements on social ordering that intuition would suggest. If these were included, the Possibility Theorem would apply *a fortiori*.

The Possibility Theorem creates a genuine impasse for welfare economics. For it asserts that a social ordering which is complete and consistent and which satisfies certain relatively weak common-sense criteria of rationality cannot, in general, be derived from individual preference orderings alone. Not surprisingly, several possible ways of escaping from the impasse have been suggested, and of those we shall now consider three.[1]

The first suggestion is to drop the requirement that the social ordering be transitive. However, this suggestion has drastic implications not all of which have been realised by its proponents. In particular, it means that social choice ceases to be independent of the order in which we take up pair-wise the alternatives for comparison. In effect, this 'solution' amounts to abandoning the search for collective rationality altogether.

The second suggested avenue of escape is to relax the condition of 'independence of irrelevant alternatives'. This enables one to use cardinal indicators of utility, rather than merely *orderings*, for individual preferences. If, in fact, individuals are assumed to have cardinal welfare functions and if these are interpersonally comparable, a social ordering can be found by aggregating these in some way.

The problem of finding a rationale for cardinal welfare has been approached in two main ways. One developed by Armstrong[2] proceeds from the assumption of a 'perception threshold' for the individual. This implies that a consumer's indifference as between two alternatives can be attributed to his failure to discriminate between them and hence that such indifference is naturally an intransitive relationship. From this approach one can derive a cardinal index of welfare. The other main approach to cardinal utility is the approach developed by von Neumann and Morgenstern.[3] They

[1] For variants of this proposal, see M. C. Kemp, 'Arrow's General Possibility Theorem', *Review of Economic Studies*, vol. 21 (1953–4).

[2] W. E. Armstrong, 'Uncertainty and the Utility Function', *Economic Journal* (Mar 1948).

[3] J. von Neumann and O. Morgenstern, *Theory of Games and Economic Behaviour*, 2nd ed. (Princeton: Princeton University Press, 1947).

showed that a complete individual ordering, unique up to a linear transformation, follows from a fairly plausible set of axioms which, essentially, describe the individual's attitude to risk. From this approach one is able to derive the individual's utility function. Both of these methods of cardinalising welfare involve serious theoretical difficulties which have been much discussed.[1] In the last analysis, these difficulties arise from the arbitrariness involved in making the individual's utility indices, however derived, comparable so that they can be aggregated into an index of *social* welfare. This is, in essence, the old problem of the impossibility of interpersonal comparisons of welfare. In the context of our discussion it is well at this stage to remember Graaff's[2] comment on the problem of interpersonal comparisons. He pointed out that 'economists do not really mean that interpersonal comparisons are "impossible". All they mean is that they cannot be made without judgements of an essentially ethical nature.'[3] This underlies our emphasis on the role of ethical judgements in the choice of economic policies.

There is yet a third way of escaping from the impasse created by the Possibility Theorem. This makes use of the consideration that at a given time and in a stable society the preference orderings of individuals are likely to reflect a shared culture and hence to show certain similarities among themselves. If these similarities are sufficiently strong, various methods, notably the method of simple majority decisions, would provide a complete and consistent social welfare function with acceptable properties. Indeed, much of the recent literature on the existence of a social welfare function has been concerned with a more precise formulation of such similarities between individual preference orderings, and with stating the conditions under which they are sufficient, i.e. lead to a social ordering with desirable characteristics. One case where the degree of similarity between the individual preference orderings is clearly sufficient for this purpose is when they are identical; the social ordering can then be taken to be the same. However, unanimity is a pretty strong condition and has little empirical relevance. Discussion of the problem in its more general form has centred largely on variants of the 'single-peakedness condition'. A set of individual orderings is said to be single-peaked if there is some basic ordering of the alternatives

---

[1] See, for example, Rothenberg, op. cit.

[2] J. de V. Graaff, *Theoretical Welfare Economics* (Cambridge University Press, 1957).   [3] Ibid., p. 8.

such that in passing from one alternative to the next in this ordering each individual rises monotonically to the peak of his preferences and then falls monotonically, i.e. such that the map showing the direction of preference of each individual over all alternatives appears geometrically, as single-peaked. It has been proved that, provided the single-peakedness condition holds, the method of majority decisions will be transitive and will indeed provide an acceptable social welfare function. However, the interpretative significance of this proposition is subject *inter alia* to the following limitations. First, it can be shown that the single-peakedness condition implies the absence of *any* free triple among admissible alternatives. Hence it violates the first condition of both Arrow's and Blau's versions of the Possibility Theorem. Intuitively this is not particularly surprising, for the purpose of the free-triple condition was to make the range of situations to which the social welfare function can apply as wide as possible. The rationale of postulating similarities between individual orderings, of which the single-peakedness condition is a particular example, on the contrary, is to make this range narrower. Secondly – and this is crucial – the single-peakedness condition is unlikely to hold. It is the less likely to be satisfied, the greater the complexity of choice being considered. In a society where the number of dimensions that each alternative carries is very large, the single-peakedness condition is unlikely to be of much empirical interest. Largely because of this, recent research has shifted to investigating less demanding forms of similarity between individual preference orderings as a basis for a social welfare function. While such attempts may turn out to be fruitful in the long run, as yet they do not appear to have brought us any nearer the goal of being able to derive a meaningful social ordering from individual preferences.

To sum up, although much ingenuity has been spent no thinking up ways of escaping from the implications of the Possibility Theorem, no genuine escape route can yet be said to have emerged. Hence, the explicit introduction of ethical judgements into any social welfare function to be used for deriving an optimum growth path appears inevitable.

This brings us to the problem raised at the outset of this section. Given that the social welfare function necessarily involves ethical judgements, in what way should the economist who sets out to use optimum growth theory in the formulation of policy approach his task ?

One possible approach would be to use a social welfare function which incorporates his own ethical judgements. The ethical judgements of the economist are indeed often particularly relevant for planning decisions because, *inter alia*, he may be expected to have special knowledge about the economic structure within which such judgements are to be made effective. Nevertheless, there are other members of the community whose claims to special knowledge may also be deemed equally legitimate. Moreover, in decisions with far-reaching social consequences, claims based on specialist knowledge are themselves likely to be regarded with suspicion, at least under political democracy. Hence basic ethical judgements which may underlie the economist's approach to policy decisions will be serious claimants for social use only if they happen to be widely shared in the community at large. This may not necessarily be the case.

A second possible approach would be for the economist to follow through his optimum growth exercise on the basis of some specified ethical judgement (A) without necessarily committing himself to this particular judgement. What he would then be doing would be to work out the implications of A for optimum growth, i.e. to derive the optimum growth path (B) which would follow *if* one accepted A. Someone who happened to accept A could then recommend B on the basis of the work done by the economist.

Clearly, this approach has a certain intellectual appeal. As Little puts it : 'The economist can, of course, investigate what follows from any set of value premises he likes to choose. If the value premises are made explicit and are not hidden, the result will be informative and interesting – and cannot be misleading. So long as there are some people who would be prepared to accept the stated premises, the result cannot be entirely useless.'[1] Nevertheless, it is important to realise that such a procedure is incomplete in that it leaves the problem of the choice of the ethical judgement itself hanging in the air. After all, if one is discussing the consequences of a particular ethical judgement, one can adopt the judgement of those in power, or of one's peers or indeed any judgement whatever. It is thus legitimate to ask why the economist has taken A, rather than some other ethical judgement, as his starting-point. This suggests that our second possible reaction to the implications of the Possibility Theorem cannot be demarcated altogether from the first and hence that it cannot entirely escape the difficulties associated with it.

[1] See I. M. D. Little, *A Critique of Welfare Economics* (London: Oxford University Press, 1950) p. 83.

A third possible approach, which may indeed be described as a logical outcome of the second, would be to regard the choice of a social welfare function as a first step towards setting up a meaningful dialogue between professional economists and the community as a whole. On this view, the optimum growth models discussed by the economist are useful to the extent that they stimulate decision-makers throughout the economy – trade unions, business managers and consumers as well as local and central government officials – to examine the decisions facing them in the light of the basic preference orderings set for the economy as a whole. In turn, their reactions should have a feedback effect on the original specification of social welfare. An iterative process may thus ensue which, ideally, should converge towards some kind of a consensus. In a country like Britain with a pluralistic structure of social organisation and a largely decentralised economy, this would appear to be a natural approach. But it suffers from the difficulty that the terms in which the economist's optimum growth models are expressed do not readily lend themselves to meaningful interpretation by members of the community in general.[1]

A further possible approach would be to argue that in an area such as optimum growth where the problems involved are fundamental, complex and generally unfamiliar, to take the choice of a particular welfare function as one's point of departure may well be inappropriate. Rather the optimum growth theorist should see his task as that of spelling out the consequences of adopting *different* welfare functions – in particular of working out the alternative time paths of consumption implied by these different welfare functions – and thus enabling essentially political decisions to be made on a more rational basis than would otherwise be possible.

Clearly this has implications for the level of aggregation at which planning models are formulated. The one-sector or two-sector models usually discussed in the theoretical literature on optimal economic growth have the disadvantage that people may not be able to relate the implications of adopting different preference functions to their ordinary day-to-day experience of a multi-commodity world. On the other hand, too much detail may be self-defeating. A model with a

---

[1] Cf. A. K. Sen, 'On Optimising the Rate of Saving', *Economic Journal* (Sep 1961) p. 481: 'I must confess, however, that the possibility of a lively political debate on such questions as "should we maximise the logarithm of consumption?" appears to me to be limited.'

few hundred variables and several thousand possible alternatives can hardly provide a basis for a meaningful dialogue on optimum growth policies. Rather, it may well lead to what has sometimes been described as an 'information death': one is killed by too much detail. Here, as elsewhere, it would be necessary to steer a middle course.

11.4 Choice of a Time Horizon

At the end of section 11.2 we said that there were two crucial difficulties associated with the Ramsey-type approach to optimum growth – one relating to the welfare function which is to be maximised, the other to the length of the time period over which maximisation is to extend. The first of these difficulties was discussed in the preceding section and we turn now to the second.

In some contexts it may be legitimate to regard the time horizon as being given from outside, for example by some political agency. In others, the choice of the relevant time horizon naturally appears as an essential part of the planning problem which the economist must examine. The basic choice is then between some finite time horizon and an infinite time horizon.

The most obvious reason for preferring an infinite time horizon is that with a finite horizon the particular time period chosen is necessarily arbitrary; such arbitrariness can be avoided by setting the end of the planning horizon indefinitely far off into the future. There are certain difficulties associated with the use of an infinite time horizon, however, two of which we shall now discuss.

The first concerns changes in production possibilities and tastes. In most applications of the Ramsey approach an existing production function is projected unchanged into the future. Where the attempt to incorporate technical progress is made, the procedure is to assume a known and steady rate of progress, which does not basically alter the structure of the problem. In a finite-time model, where the planning horizon is not too long, the neglect of technical progress may be defended as a first approximation. With an infinite time horizon, however, such a defence is difficult to sustain. A way out of the difficulty would be to build uncertainty as to future improvements in productive possibilities into the optimising model as one of its crucial features. However, little theoretical work in this direction seems to have been done as yet.

A second difficulty, which has attracted some attention in recent years, relates to the problem of whether an optimum path exists in models using an infinite time horizon. Deriving an optimum growth path for a model with an infinite time horizon is equivalent to maximising the integral $I = \int_0^\infty u(x)dt$, where u denotes a (given) index of valuation, and $x = x(t)$, the rate of consumption at time t, represents the function subject to choice. Hence the problem of whether an optimum growth path exists is equivalent to the problem of whether I converges. Chakravarty,[1] following earlier work by Samuelson and Solow,[2] states the problem formally in the following way:

> The economic significance of formulating the choice problem as one of maximizing $\int_0^\infty Udt$ arises from the possible ordering that the functional imposes on alternative infinite programs. But if the total utility associated with any feasible infinite program is infinitely large, because $\int_0^\infty Udt$ does not converge, then there is no possibility of introducing any order on the policy space through such mappings from the policy to the utility space.[3]

One way out of the difficulty is to postulate 'bliss', i.e. an upper bound on the time-rate of utility, as Ramsey did. The problem then reduces to one of minimising the sum of deviations from bliss; and this sum converges.[4] However, even without the Ramsey assumption, there are various ways in which an ordering relation can be defined on divergent programmes, though these are more complex, mathematically, than simple convergence.[5]

To sum up, it would seem that while, in principle, an infinite time horizon is the more appropriate assumption for the analysis of optimum growth paths, the difficulties to which it gives rise are such that, at least for the time being, the use of a finite time horizon may be the only practical possiblity.

If the finite time horizon is used, two important problems have to be faced. The first concerns the exact length of the horizon. This will be influenced necessarily by technical–administrative considerations. Sensitivity analysis, i.e. analysis of the extent to which the optimum

[1] S. Chakravarty, 'The Existence of an Optimum Savings Program', *Econometrica* (Jan 1962).

[2] P. A. Samuelson and R. M. Solow, 'A Complete Capital Model Involving Heterogeneous Capital Goods', *Quarterly Journal of Economics* (Nov 1956).

[3] Chakravarty, op. cit., p. 181.

[4] See Ramsey, op. cit., p. 369, n. 1 above.

[5] See A. Dasgupta, 'A Note on Optimum Savings', *Econometrica* (July 1964).

growth path varies in response to changes in the time horizon, can help to reduce the arbitrariness involved. Secondly, there is the problem of specifying the terminal boundary condition (see p. 369 above). This defines the level of some economic variable that must be attained at the end of the relevant horizon. There may indeed be a choice as between alternative formulations of the terminal condition. A formulation which has much to commend it on intuitive grounds is one in terms of the capital stock. The state of terminal equipment such as factories, forests, mines and minerals represents the economic legacy of a finite-horizon planning model in an obvious way. Indeed if we interpret maximisation of welfare over the chosen horizon literally, i.e. if we regard those demarcated by the horizon as the only ones in whose welfare we are interested, it is reasonable to require that physical capital should be exhausted by the end of the horizon, i.e. that the relevant value of terminal equipment is zero. However, few exponents of a finite-horizon approach would be prepared to take such an extreme stand. Their view rather is that the maximisation of welfare over the chosen horizon should be constrained by the need for making *some* provision for the post-horizon period.[1]

Alternatively, the terminal condition can be set in terms of consumption rather than of the capital stock. One particular device that has found wide econometric application is that of stipulating the *level* of consumption at the end of the horizon and its *rate of growth* from that time onwards.

A completely different approach to the time-horizon problem has recently been suggested by Inagaki, who argues that while the life of a nation is indeed infinite, that of a government or decision-making authority is finite. Hence, in the decision-making context a nation is properly identified with an infinite sequence of finite governments. Accordingly, the problem of optimum growth is no longer regarded as one of maximising a welfare function but as that of selecting a group-decision rule, e.g. the Ramsey rule (see p. 371 above), which is acceptable to all successive governments (populations) of the nation concerned. The implications of this approach for growth policy remain to be worked out.[2]

It would seem that if the optimising approach to the formulation

[1] Cf. Graaff, op. cit., p. 97: 'Unless it is firmly believed that the Day of Judgement will coincide with the horizon, terminal equipment should be positive.'

[2] See M. Inagaki, *Optimal Economic Growth: Shifting Finite versus Infinite Time Horizon* (Amsterdam: North-Holland Publishing Company, 1969).

of the growth objective is to be fruitful, it should satisfy two main requirements. The first, which emerged from the discussion of section 11.3 (see p. 383 above), is that the theoretical model used should be capable of spelling out in some detail the consequences of adopting particular value judgements. This requirement implies that the exploratory aspect of optimising models is crucially important. As Koopmans observes, optimisation and exploration 'have to be engaged in simultaneously, with the latter serving to guide and strengthen the former'.[1]

The second requirement concerns the relationship between theory and available information. If optimum growth theory is to be more than an empty economic box, it is clearly necessary that the optimising model should not make demands on statistical information which it is impossible to fulfil, and that it should be framed so as to enable such information as is available to be utilised to the best advantage. To quote Koopmans again, 'Rather than searching for a largely invisible optimal path, one may have to look for a good rule for choosing the next stretch of the path with the help of all information available at the time'.[2]

In the light of this discussion, an approach which commends itself is one based on the input–output model. Since the input–output model focuses attention on the production of goods by means of other goods – all goods being regarded potentially as intermediate goods – it allows the repercussions, both direct and indirect, of a particular policy throughout the economy to be spelled out in detail. Thus, it fits in well with the first requirement. As far as the second requirement is concerned, fairly reliable input–output tables are now available for most developed countries. Moreover, the more well-developed versions of the input–output model are ideally suited to the utilisation of information on technical change in particular sectors and can thus be geared to future values of technical coefficients as well as to current values. Because of these advantages of the input–output model and the inherent difficulties in choosing and applying a 'social welfare function' to a complex economy, the input–output technique has played a central role in quantitative growth planning in a number of advanced countries, including Holland, Norway and the United Kingdom.

One of the most ambitious and sophisticated applications of this

[1] T. C. Koopmans, 'Objectives, Constraints and Outcomes in Optimal Growth Models', *Econometrica* (Jan 1967 p. 12).   [2] Ibid., p. 12.

approach is the work being done by Stone and his colleagues on the Cambridge Growth Project. We shall now attempt to present a brief account of the assumptions, methods and conclusions of the Cambridge Growth Project and to place these in the wider context of the theory of optimum economic growth.

11.5 The Cambridge Growth Model: Basic Model

The main purpose of the Cambridge Growth Project in its present phase is to explore in detail the implications of particular growth assumptions. Suppose that a particular growth target were to be postulated for consumption expenditure and for the other elements of final demand for, say, a decade ahead. Then it would be important to know what the shape of the economy would have to be, at the end of the decade, if this growth target were to be achieved. For example, one would wish to know what level of output would be required for each industry, what aggregate capital stock would be required, how the capital stock and the labour force would have to be distributed between industries, what the level and composition of imports would have to be, and so on. It is with questions of this type that the Cambridge Growth Project is concerned. As the members of the Project put it: 'the main purpose . . . is to find out where and how we are likely to run into difficulties as we try to increase the rate of growth'.[1] In another place they say that they are concerned to 'investigate alternative goals expressed mainly in terms of the growth of consumption. People who are concerned with day-to-day problems are naturally more interested in the immediate path which the economy should take. But in our view a discussion of the desirable goal comes first, because one cannot choose a path unless one knows where one is going.'[2]

The basis of all their work is a model of the input–output variety. The purpose of this section and the next four sections is to give an account of this model and to show how it can be used to provide information of the type indicated in the opening paragraph of this section.[3] Since the model is fairly elaborate, we propose to set it out

---

[1] See R. Stone and A. Brown, *A Computable Model of Economic Growth* (London: Chapman & Hall, for the Department of Applied Economics, University of Cambridge, 1962) p. 28.   [2] Ibid., p. 88.

[3] It must be emphasised that the Cambridge model is a working model which is subject to revision in the light of performance. The account which we shall present is based on Stone and Brown, op. cit., and R. Stone, 'A Demonstration

in stages. In this section we shall deal with the central relationships of the model which we shall refer to as the 'basic model'. We shall then introduce the remaining relationships, step by step, in sections 11.6–11.9. In section 11.10 we shall outline some calculations which have been made recently with the model and in the final section of the chapter we shall present a brief commentary on the Cambridge model as a whole.

As already indicated, the Cambridge model is essentially a highly sophisticated version of the input–output model. Accordingly, it may be helpful to begin by considering the simplest possible version of this model. For this purpose we shall use the following notation:

q_s = output of commodity s in year t

q_r = output of commodity r in year t

f_s = final demand for commodity s in year t

q_{sr} = output of commodity s used as a current input (raw material) in the production of commodity r in year t

a_{sr} = output of commodity s used as a current input in the production of commodity r in year t per unit of output of commodity r.

In terms of this notation, the simplest possible input–output model is as follows:

$$q_s = \sum_{r=1}^{n} q_{sr} + f_s \qquad s = 1, 2, \ldots, n \qquad (11.32)$$

$$q_{sr} = a_{sr} q_r \qquad r, s = 1, 2, \ldots, n. \qquad (11.33)$$

The first of these blocks of n relationships says, for each of the n commodities produced by the economic system, that the entire output of the commodity in any period is used either as a current input, i.e. raw material, in the manufacture of other commodities, or for the purpose of satisfying final demand, while the second block of $(r \times s)$ relationships merely reproduces the definition of a_{sr}. By substitution from (11.33) to (11.32) we can reduce the model to the following set of n relationships:

$$q_s = \sum_{r=1}^{n} a_{sr} q_r + f_s \qquad s = 1, 2, \ldots, n. \qquad (11.34)$$

Model for Economic Growth', *Manchester School of Economic and Social Studies* (Jan 1962).

This set of relationships can be conveniently expressed in matrix form. For this purpose we define the following matrices:

$$q = \begin{bmatrix} q_1 \\ q_2 \\ \vdots \\ q_n \end{bmatrix} \quad f = \begin{bmatrix} f_1 \\ f_2 \\ \vdots \\ f_n \end{bmatrix} \quad A = \begin{bmatrix} a_{11} \dots a_{1r} \dots a_{1n} \\ \vdots \quad \vdots \quad \vdots \\ a_{s1} \dots a_{sr} \dots a_{sn} \\ \vdots \quad \vdots \quad \vdots \\ a_{n1} \dots a_{nr} \dots a_{nn} \end{bmatrix}$$

Using these matrices we can write (11.34) as:

$$q = Aq + f. \tag{11.35}$$

This gives the following expression for the output vector q:

$$q = (I - A)^{-1}f = B^{-1}f \tag{11.36}$$

where I is the unit matrix and $B = (I - A)$. From (11.36) it would be possible, given the matrix of input–output coefficients A, to determine the amount which each industry would need to produce in some year t (elements of the q vector) if a specified final bill of goods for that year (elements of the f vector) were to be met. It would be a matter simply of inverting the matrix $(I - A)$ and post-multiplying the resulting matrix by the vector f.

The input–output model of (11.36) is designed for the case where the specification of the bill of goods takes the simple form of a list of the output levels required to satisfy final demand in year t. A more complicated specification is as follows: (a) the output levels required to satisfy consumption demand in year t; and (b) the proportionate rates of growth in these levels from year t onwards. The basic Cambridge model can be regarded as an extension of the model of (11.36) which enables this more complicated case to be handled.

We shall now set out the basic Cambridge model using the symbols a_{sr}, q_s, A and q already introduced *plus* the following:[1]

---

[1] We shall be formulating the model in terms of 'commodities', but it could equally well be formulated in terms of 'industries'. For example, we could define q_s as the output of industry s rather than the output of commodity s. In numerical work with the model (see section 11.10) the Cambridge group use 31 industries. They also use 31 commodities, namely the 31 principal products of the 31 industries. The 31 commodities are given the same names as the 31 industries but the output of a commodity is not the same as the output of the industry with the same name. This is because the output of industry s consists of more than the output of its principal product, and because some of the output of the principal product of industry s comes from other industries.

e_s = output of commodity s required for purposes of consumption in year t

v_s = output of commodity s required for purposes of capital accumulation in year t

K_{sr} = output of commodity s used as a capital input in the production of commodity r per unit of output of commodity r

r_s = constant proportionate rate of growth in e_s in all years after year t

e = column vector of order n with e_s in row s

v = volumn vector of order n with v_s in row s

K = square matrix of order n with K_{sr} in row s, column r

$\hat{r}$ = diagonal matrix of order n with r_s in row s, column s

Δ = first-difference operator (to be explained)

E = shift operator (to be explained).

In terms of this notation, the basic Cambridge model consists of the following three matrix equations:

$$\begin{aligned} q &= Aq + e + v \\ &= B^{-1}e + B^{-1}v \end{aligned} \tag{11.37}$$

$$v = K\Delta q \tag{11.38}$$

$$Ee = (I + \hat{r})e \tag{11.39}$$

The first of these relationships corresponds to (11.35) for the elementary input–output model. In the first form it merely says that the entire output of commodity $s(q_s)$ is used either as a current input in the production of commodities $(\sum_{r=1}^{n} a_{sr}q_r)$, or for purposes of capital accumulation (v_s) or to satisfy final consumption demand for commodity $s(e_s)$. In the second form it says that the output of commodity s is the sum of two parts: (i) the output which is required, directly and indirectly, to satisfy final consumption demand as a whole $(\sum_{r=1}^{n} f^{sr}e_r)$[1] and (ii) the output which is required, directly and indirectly, to satisfy final demand for purposes of capital accumulation as a whole $(\sum_{r=1}^{n} f^{sr}v_r)$.

The significance of (11.38) can be seen once the expression Δq is understood. Placing the first-difference operator Δ in front of the q vector has the effect of transforming each element in the vector into a

[1] f^{sr} is the element in row s, column r, of B^{-1}.

first difference, i.e. the element in row s of the vector Δq denotes, not the output of commodity s in period t but the *change* in the output of commodity s between period $(t-1)$ and period t. Thus the sth relationship in the block of n expressed by (11.38) reads:

$$v_s = \sum_{r=1}^{n} K_{sr}\Delta q_r \qquad (11.40)$$

where Δq_r denotes the change in q_r between period $(t-1)$ and period t. Reference back to the definition of K_{sr} shows that the typical item in the sum on the right-hand side of (11.40) is that part of the output of commodity s which is absorbed by the producers of commodity r for purposes of capital accumulation in period t. Hence (11.38) merely says that the final demand for commodity s for purposes of capital accumulation is the sum of the final demands of the producers of the n individual commodities.

Finally, relationship (11.39) is readily understood once it is realised that placing the shift operator E in front of the e vector merely pushes each of the elements in this vector forward one year so that the element in row s becomes the output of commodity s required to satisfy consumption demand for commodity s in year $(t+1)$ instead of year t. Thus the sth relationship in the block of n expressed by (11.39) imposes the requirement that the output of commodity s which is used to satisfy the consumption demand for that commodity is $(100\ r_s)$ per cent greater in year $(t+1)$ than in year t.

Returning to the simple input–output model of (11.34), it will be recalled that, having set out the model in matrix form, we proceeded to solve it for q in terms of f. The purpose of this manipulation was to obtain an expression enabling us to determine the output vector which would be required to meet a specified bill of goods, expressed in the form of a vector of the output levels required to satisfy final demand, in some specified future year, given the input–output matrix A. We now follow a similar procedure for the more elaborate input–output model of (11.37), (11.38) and (11.39). In this case, we solve the model for q in terms of e and $\hat{r}$ to obtain an expression corresponding to (11.36). Given the matrices K and A, this expression will enable us to determine the output vector which would be required to meet a specified bill of goods in some specified future year (year 0, say) when this takes the form of: (a) a vector of the output levels required to satisfy consumption demand in year 0; and

(b) a vector of the proportionate rates of growth which are to apply to the elements of consumption demand from year 0 indefinitely. The mechanics of the solution are considerably more complicated in this case than in the simple input–output case and we deal with them in Appendix 11.2. It will be seen from this appendix that the solution is given by:

$$q = B^{-1} \left\{ \sum_{i=0}^{\infty} [KB^{-1}]^i \hat{r}^i \right\} e. \tag{11.41}$$

It will also be clear from the appendix that in practice a reasonable approximation to the solution can be obtained by considering only the first four or five terms in the infinite sum.

The successive terms on the right-hand side of (11.41) have a natural economic interpretation which is of interest. The first term in the series, corresponding to $i = 0$, is:

$$B^{-1}e.$$

From (11.37) we know that this is the output required to deliver the specified consumption vector in year 0. The second term, corresponding to $i = 1$, is:

$$B^{-1}KB^{-1}\hat{r}e.$$

From (11.37) once again, we know that $B^{-1}\hat{r}e$ is the output required to enable the increment of consumption $\hat{r}e$ to be delivered in year 1 and all subsequent years. Thus the second term in the sequence is the output required in year 0 to provide the capital accumulation which is required in year 0 to enable the increment of consumption $\hat{r}e$ to be delivered in year 1 and all subsequent years. The third term corresponding to $i = 2$, is:

$$B^{-1}KB^{-1}KB^{-1}\hat{r}^2e.$$

Reasoning in the same way as before, we find that $B^{-1}KB^{-1}\hat{r}^2e$ is the output required in year 1 to provide the capital accumulation which is required in year 1 to enable the increment of consumption $\hat{r}^2e$ to be delivered in year 2 and all subsequent years. Hence the third term in the sequence is the output which is required in year 0 to increase the capital stock enough in year 0 to provide the capital accumulation required in year 1 to ensure that the increment of consumption $\hat{r}^2e$ is delivered in year 2 and all subsequent years.

We stop the discussion with the third term. However, enough has been said to show that the output vector given by (11.41) is one which ensures (as it must) that the specified consumption vector is delivered in year 0 and that the increments to consumption in subsequent years are those which are required to keep each element in the consumption vector growing exponentially.

11.6 The Cambridge Growth Model: Consumption and Price Equations

In this section we carry our exposition of the Cambridge model a stage further by adding to the basic model a block of n consumption functions and a block of n price equations. The effect of this extension of the basic model is that the e vector is now determined by the model itself whereas in the basic model it is given externally. To write the new relationships we shall use the following additional notation:

p_s = price of commodity s in year t

y_s = direct factor cost of commodity s per unit of output in year t

μ = aggregate real expenditure on consumption in year t (a scalar)

p = column vector of order n with p_s in row s

$\hat{p}$ = diagonal matrix of order n with p_s in row s, column s

y = column vector of order n with y_s in row s.

In this notation the consumption functions of the Cambridge model are as follows:

$$\hat{p}e = \hat{p}b^* + b(\mu - p'b^*) \tag{11.42}$$

where b^* and b are column vectors of constants. This is a block of n relationships, one for each commodity. The typical relationship – the relationship for commodity s – is:

$$p_s e_s = p_s b_s^* + b_s(\mu - \sum_{s=1}^{n} p_s b_s^*). \tag{11.43}$$

The implications of (11.42) become clear from an examination of (11.43). Dividing through by p_s we see that the parameter b_s^* represents the 'committed purchases of commodity s', i.e. the purchases which consumers make whatever the price situation. Hence the expression $(\mu - \sum_{s=1}^{n} p_s b_s^*)$ represents total consumption expenditure (μ) *less* total committed expenditure, i.e. total uncommitted expenditure.

Thus (11.43) says that total expenditure on commodity s consists of two parts: the committed expenditure on commodity s; and some proportion b_s of total uncommitted expenditure. The first part is independent of the price situation whereas the second part varies according to the structure of relative prices, given the parameters μ and b_s.

We turn now to the n price equations. These are obtained as follows. We begin with the relationship:

$$p = y + A'p. \tag{11.44}$$

This says that the price of each commodity (p_s) is equal to the cost of its primary inputs per unit of output (y_s) *plus* the cost of its intermediate inputs per unit of output $(\sum\limits_{r=1}^{n} a_{rs}p_r)$. From (11.44) we obtain:

$$p = (I - A')^{-1}y. \tag{11.45}$$

These are the n price equations of the Cambridge model.

As things now stand, the model consists of the basic model (11.37), (11.38) and (11.39), together with the consumption functions (11.42) and the price equations (11.45). Given certain data, one could determine from these relationships the output vector required to meet a specified bill of goods in some specified future year (year 0). The bill of goods would now take the form of: (a) a specified level of aggregate consumption expenditure, μ; and (b) a vector of the proportionate rates of growth which are to apply to the elements of consumption demand from year 0 onwards (the diagonal elements of $\hat{r}$). This is simpler than the bill of goods which applies in the case of the basic model in that the specification of aggregate real consumption expenditure replaces the specification of the individual purchases of the n commodities. Thus the elaboration of the model has made possible the simplification of the bill-of-goods specification. The data needed to determine the required output vector would be: (i) the vector y for year 0; (ii) the matrix A; (iii) the matrix K; (iv) the vector b^*; and (v) the vector b. Given (i) and (ii), one could determine the price vector, p, for year 0 from (11.45). Given (iv) and (v) one could then determine the e vector for year 0 from (11.42) on the basis of the specified μ. Finally, with the e vector available and given (ii) and (iii), one could determine the q vector for year 0 from (11.41) on the basis of the specified $\hat{r}$.

11.7 The Cambridge Growth Model: Production Functions

We come now to the third stage of our exposition of the Cambridge growth model in which we present relationships which enable the vector y to be determined by the model instead of being imposed from outside. For this purpose we introduce the following notation:

l_s = input of labour into production of commodity s

k_s = input of capital into production of commodity s

l = column vector of order n with l_s in row s

k = column vector of order n with k_s in row s

ω = wage rate (a scalar)

π = profit rate (a scalar)

λ = labour force (a scalar).

Assuming a common wage rate and profit rate in all industries, we write:

$$\hat{q}y = \omega l + \pi k = \omega(l + \frac{\pi}{\omega}k) = \omega(l + \alpha^{-1}k) \qquad (11.46)$$

where α denotes ω/π and $\hat{q}$ denotes a diagonal matrix with q_s in row s, column s. This block of equations says, for each commodity, that total direct factor cost is the sum of total labour cost and total capital cost. Premultiplying by $\hat{q}^{-1}$ we get:

$$y = \omega\hat{q}^{-1}l + \pi\hat{q}^{-1}k \qquad (11.47)$$

which says that direct factor cost per unit of output is equal to labour cost per unit of output *plus* capital cost per unit of output.[1] Relationship (11.47) is our starting-point. We now derive an expression for k in terms of l and a further expression for l in terms of q, which, together with (11.47), effectively determine y given ω and α, q being already determined by the rest of the model.

The first step is to impose the first-order conditions for profit maximisation:

$$\frac{\partial q_s}{\partial l_s} \bigg/ \frac{\partial q_s}{\partial k_s} = \frac{\omega}{\pi} = \alpha. \qquad (11.48)$$

Next a set of production functions is introduced from which an expression for the ratio of marginal physical products can be derived for substitution in (11.48). The production function introduced for

---

[1] Since $\hat{q}$ is a diagonal matrix with q_s in row s, column s, $\hat{q}^{-1}$ will be a diagonal matrix with q_s^{-1} in row s, column s.

commodity s is the constant-returns version of the C.E.S. production function, namely:

$$q_s = a_s[(1 - d_s)(l_s)^{-c_s} + d_s(k_s)^{-c_s}]^{(-c_s)^{-1}} \quad (11.49)$$

where a_s, d_s and c_s are parameters.[1] With this production function the marginal physical products are given by:

$$\frac{\partial q_s}{\partial l_s} = (1 - d_s)(a_s)^{-c_s}(q_s)^{(c_s+1)}(l_s)^{-(c_s+1)}$$

$$\frac{\partial q_s}{\partial k_s} = d_s(a_s)^{-c_s}(q_s)^{(c_s+1)}(k_s)^{-(c_s+1)}.$$

On substituting these expressions into (11.48) we get:

$$\frac{(1 - d_s)}{d_s} \frac{(l_s)^{-(c_s+1)}}{(k_s)^{-(c_s+1)}} = \alpha$$

which gives the following expression for k_s:

$$k_s = \left\{\left(\alpha\frac{d_s}{1 - d_s}\right)^{(1+c_s)^{-1}}\right\} l_s. \quad (11.50)$$

The term in braces *is* the optimal capital–labour ratio for commodity s. Hence we have:

$$k = \hat{h}l \quad (11.51)$$

where $\hat{h}$ is a diagonal matrix with the optimal capital–labour ratio for commodity s in row s, column s. This is the expression for k in terms of l to which we referred above. We turn now to the expression for l in terms of q to which we also referred. This is derived by substituting (11.50) for k_s in the production function (11.49). The required expression is:

$$l_s = \left[a_s^{-1}\left\{(1 - d_s) + d_s\left(\frac{\alpha d_s}{1 - d_s}\right)^{-c_s(1+c_s)^{-1}}\right\}^{(c_s)^{-1}}\right]q_s. \quad (11.52)$$

The term in square brackets is the optimal labour–output ratio. Hence we can write

$$l = \hat{g}q \quad (11.53)$$

[1] The Cambridge group have had second thoughts about the production function. See R. Stone, *The Model in its Environment: A Progress Report* (London: Chapman & Hall, for the Department of Applied Economics, University of Cambridge, 1964) pp. 33–5.

where $\hat{g}$ is a diagonal matrix with the optimal labour–output ratio for commodity s in row s, column s.

Since q is already determined by the rest of the model, relationships (11.47), (11.51) and (11.53) effectively determine y, given α, ω and the parameters of the production functions. Using $\lambda = \sum_{s=1}^{n} l_s$, and the q_s determined by the rest of the model, it is possible to compute α from (11.52). Hence (11.47), (11.51) and (11.53) effectively determine y given ω, λ and the parameters of the production functions.

The position now reached can be summarised as follows. Postulate a bill of goods for year 0 in the form of a specified level of aggregate real consumption expenditure, μ, and a vector of the proportionate rates of growth which are to apply to the elements of consumption demand from year 0 onwards (the diagonal elements of $\hat{r}$). Assume that the following are also given for year 0: (i) the matrix A; (ii) the matrix K; (iii) the vector b^*; (iv) the vector b; (v) the scalars λ and ω; (vi) the parameters of the production functions. Then taken together, (11.41), (11.42), (11.45), (11.47), (11.51) and (11.53) enable us to determine the outputs of the n commodities which would have to be delivered in year 0 to enable the bill of goods to be met.

In practice the calculations would proceed as follows. A set of prices would be assumed for year 0 and these would be used to fix μ (the aggregate *real* consumption expenditure in year 0) in terms of year 0 prices. With μ and p thus fixed, the e vector for year 0 would be determined from (11.42) using the given b^* vector and the given b vector. Then with the e vector fixed, the q vector would be determined from (11.41) on the basis of the specified $\hat{r}$ and the given K and A matrices. With the q vector thus fixed, and with λ given, both α and the l vector could be determined from (11.53) and with these fixed the k vector could be determined from (11.51). The y vector would then be determined from (11.47) on the basis of the calculated q, l and k vectors, the calculated α and the given ω. Finally, with the y vector available, the p vector would be calculated from (11.45) using the given A matrix. It would then be a matter of comparing the calculated price vector with the price vector assumed at the outset. Should they happen to coincide, the calculations would be complete and the q vector sought would be the one determined from (11.41) in the manner described above. In general, however, the two price vectors will differ and a second cycle of calculations, starting from the price vector calculated in the first cycle, would be undertaken. This would give a second estimate of the q vector. In turn, this would be improved and so on. Enough iterations would be undertaken to bring the assumed and the calculated price vectors into line, and the q vector sought would be the one which emerged from the final cycle of calculations.[1]

Once the structure of output implied by the specified bill of goods had been determined in this manner, other information of great importance could also be derived. In particular, it would be possible to derive from (11.53) the distribution of the given labour force which would have to be achieved if the specified bill of goods were to be met. Once this had been worked out, it would then be possible to determine from (11.51) both the total capital input implied by the bill of goods and the distribution among industries. Thus, when the calculations had been completed there would be a considerable amount of information available about 'where and how we are likely to run into difficulties as we try to increase the rate of growth'.

11.8 The Cambridge Growth Model: Balance of Payments

As presented so far, the Cambridge growth model relates to a closed economy; and to complete our exposition we must explain how the balance of payments comes into the picture. We begin with a general account and follow this up with a more detailed formal treatment.

The first point to note is that in the full Cambridge model there is a balance of payments constraint in the form of a pre-assigned balance of trade. Exports and imports must be such that in the year t the excess of the former over the latter is equal to this pre-assigned figure. The level of British exports in year t is taken as given, as in most studies involving the British balance of payments. Any adjustment, therefore, falls on imports; imports must be such in year t that they fall short of exogenous exports by an amount equal to the pre-assigned trade balance.

A crucial distinction is drawn between 'complementary' and 'competitive' imports. The former consist of goods which cannot be, or are not normally, produced in Britain. The latter are goods which are produced in Britain but are also imported from abroad and hence compete directly with products of British industry. For

[1] The A and K matrix would be changed from one cycle of calculations to the next in the light of the p vector generated by the previous cycle. See Stone, 'A Demonstration Model for Economic Growth', pp. 8–10 and p. 408 below.

purposes of classification, imports are defined to be complementary (competitive) if their volume during the 1950s amounted to more than (less than) the corresponding domestic production. Accordingly the major agricultural imports and most of the imports of raw materials used in British industry are classified as complementary, while most imports of manufactured products are treated as competitive.

In so far as they are intermediate goods, *complementary* imports are treated like all other inputs in an input–output scheme, i.e. it is assumed that the amount of any particular complementary import required in the production of any specified commodity will be proportional to the output of that commodity. Thus, British imports of crude oil are assumed to move proportionately to the level of output of the British mineral-oil refinery industry; imports of foodstuffs are taken to move in proportion to the total output of the food-processing industry, and so on.

The role of *competitive* imports in the Cambridge model is quite different. Essentially, this class of import serves as the residual item which bears the burden of the adjustment involved in meeting the balance of payments constraint. The level of any given competitive import is assumed to depend on the 'residual' available, given the level of exports, the level of complementary imports and the pre-assigned level of the balance of trade. In other words, competitive imports are adjusted on a sliding scale depending on the exigencies of the trade balance. This scale itself is worked out so as to reflect the variability of competitive imports in response to short-term fluctuations in domestic demand.

With these preliminary points disposed of, the way in which the Cambridge growth model brings the balance of payments into the picture can now be described. We start with a certain bill of goods including now a set of final demands for purposes of export. The problem is to derive the pattern of imports which is implied by the structure of production needed to meet this bill of goods and by the requirement of an acceptable trade balance. Complementary imports for purposes of final demand are determined once the bill of goods has been specified. The given level of exports and the pre-assigned trade balance then determine, between them, the *sum* of the two remaining classes of imports, namely: (i) complementary imports required for intermediate use; and (ii) competitive imports. The division of this sum between the two components is then determined by the bill of goods: the amount left over for complementary imports of raw materials, after competitive imports have been fixed, must be sufficient to support the level of domestic production which is required, given the level of competitive imports, to permit the delivery of the bill of goods.

The essential features of the above discussion can be worked into the model built up in the three preceding sections in the following way.

First, relationship (11.37) must be extended to read:

$$q = Aq + e + v + x - m \qquad (11.54)$$

where x denotes a column vector whose elements are the given export levels and m the column vector whose elements are the levels of competitive imports. This relationship has the same interpretation as (11.37) except that here export demand is recognised as an element of final demand and competitive imports as a source from which final demand can be met.

Next, three new relationships must be added to the model. For this purpose we introduce the following new notation:

β = pre-assigned trade balance (a scalar)

n = column vector of complementary imports for intermediate use

i = unit vector, i.e. column vector of 1's

a_1, a_2, a_3 = column vectors of parameters

$\hat{a}_3$ = diagonal matrix of order n with elements of a_3 along the leading diagonal.

The three relationships in question are:

$$\beta = i'x - i'm - i'n \qquad (11.55)$$

$$m = a_1 + a_2 i'm \qquad (11.56)$$

$$n = \hat{a}_3 q. \qquad (11.57)$$

The first of these new relationships expresses the balance of payments constraint. The term $i'x$ is a scalar denoting the value of exports, $i'm$ a scalar denoting the value of competitive imports and $i'n$ a scalar denoting the value of complementary imports. Hence (11.55) merely says that the excess of exports over imports must be some pre-assigned figure.[1] The second of the new relationships makes

[1] It should be noted that (11.55) 'works' only if the elements of the x, m and n vectors are money values. If the elements of the x vector, say, were in physical units, the operation would be impossible because it would involve the summation

the value of each competitive import a linear function of the total value of competitive imports. Finally (11.57) shows the relationship between complementary imports into each commodity and the output of that commodity.

To find the expression for q given by the extended model, we first eliminate m from (11.54). Substituting (11.55) and (11.57) into (11.56) we get the following expression for m:

$$m = a_1 + a_2(i'x - i'\hat{a}_3 q - \beta).$$

When this expression is substituted into (11.54) we get:

$$q = Aq + e + v + x - a_1 - a_2 i'x + a_2 a_3' q + a_2 \beta$$

which gives:

$$q - Aq - a_2 a_3' q = e + v + (I - a_2 i')x + a_2 \beta - a_1.$$

This expression can be written as:

$$q = B^{*-1}v + B^{*-1}(e + Cx + a_2\beta - a_1) \qquad (11.58)$$

where $B^* = (I - A - a_2 a_3')$ and $C = (I - a_2 i')$. Using this expression, together with (11.38) and (11.39), we can obtain an expression for v in terms of e, $\hat{r}$ and x and hence for q in terms of these magnitudes (cf. Appendix 11.2). With this expression taking the place of (11.41), with a specified x vector included in the bill of goods and with β, a_1, a_2 and a_3 added to the list of data, the whole of the procedure for finding the q vector implied by the specified bill of goods, which was described at the end of the previous section (see pp. 398–9 above), continues to apply. Now, however, the q vector which finally emerges is one which satisfies the balance of payments constraint, as well as permitting delivery of the bill of goods.

Once the q vector has been found, the vector of complementary imports, n, can be obtained from (11.57). Using (11.55) one can then find the aggregate value of competitive imports and, in turn, the vector of competitive imports from (11.56).

---

of n items expressed in different units. This means in turn that (11.54) works only if the elements of the q, v and e vectors are money values. Thus at this point we must define our 'volume' vectors a little more precisely than has been necessary hitherto; the element in row s of the output vector q must now be defined as the value of the output of commodity s in year t expressed in the prices of some base year and similarly for the v, e, x, m and n vectors. It should also be noted that in (11.55) complementary imports for purposes of final demand are assumed to be zero.

11.9 Cambridge Growth Model: Simplified Version

In this section we shall describe a simplified version of the model set out in sections 11.5 to 11.8. Essentially this simpler model consists of the 'basic model' set out in section 11.5 with the external relationships presented in section 11.8 tacked on. The relationships of the model are as follows:

$$q = Aq + h + v + x - m \tag{11.59}$$

$$v = K\Delta q + \hat{k}\Delta q = (K + \hat{k})\Delta q \tag{11.60}$$

$$E^\theta f^* = (I + \theta \hat{r}^*)f^* \qquad (\theta = 0, 1, 2, \ldots) \tag{11.61}$$

$$f^* = h + x \tag{11.62}$$

$$\beta = i'x - i'm - i'n - z \tag{11.63}$$

$$m = a_1 + a_2 i'm \tag{11.64}$$

$$n = \hat{a}_3 q. \tag{11.65}$$

The new symbols appearing in these relationships are defined as follows:

h = column vector of outputs required to satisfy exogenous domestic final demand in year t

k_s = addition to stocks of commodity s per unit of additional output of commodity s

$\hat{k}$ = diagonal matrix with k_s in row s, column s

f^* = column vector of outputs required to satisfy exogenous final demand (domestic and foreign) in year t

r_s^* = constant absolute rate of growth in f^* in all years after year t

$\hat{r}^*$ = diagonal matrix with r_s^* in row s, column s

z = value of complementary imports into final demand.

As pointed out earlier, in essence the above version of the model is the basic model with the addition of the external relationships. However, both sets of relationships have been modified before being put together and we shall comment on the modifications before proceeding.

In the first place, (11.59) differs from (11.37), as extended by (11.54), in that the vector h replaces the vector e. The former vector covers *all* domestic final demand other than v and is treated as *exogenous*, whereas the latter covers only final domestic demand for purposes of *private consumption* and is treated as *endogenous*. Thus, there are two changes from (11.54) to (11.59) – consumption demand becomes exogenous instead of being determined by the model, and the elements of final domestic demand, other than e and v, which are excluded from (11.54), e.g. the final demand of the public sector, are introduced and treated as exogenous along with consumption demand.

Secondly, there is an important difference between (11.60) and (11.38). In (11.38) v_s is the final demand for commodity s by industry s and by the other industries for purposes of capital extension. In (11.60), on the other hand, v_s includes, as well, the final demand for commodity s by industry s for purposes of stock-building, this element of v_s being related to the change in the output of commodity s by a factor of proportionality, k_s.

Thirdly, (11.61) modifies (11.39) in one important respect. Whereas (11.39) imposes the restriction that the *consumption* demand for each commodity grows *exponentially*, (11.61) imposes the restriction that the *exogenous final* demand as a whole grows *linearly*.

Finally, the balance of payments constraint (11.63) differs from (11.55) in that it allows for complementary imports into final use as well as into intermediate use.

To solve the above model for q, we must find expressions for v and m in terms of the exogenous vectors h and x, the matrices of parameters A, K, $\hat{k}$, a_1, a_2, a_3 and $\hat{r}^*$, and the scalars z and β, for substitution in (11.59). We begin with the expression for v.

To eliminate v from (11.59) we must find an expression for Δq in terms of h, x and the various matrices of parameters. We proceed as follows. Applying the first difference operator to (11.59) we get:

$$\Delta q = A\Delta q + \Delta h + \Delta v + \Delta x - \Delta m. \qquad (11.66)$$

It can be shown[1] that (11.59)–(11.62) imply:

$$q = B^{-1}[I + KB^{-1}\hat{r}^*]f^*.$$

From this and (11.61) it follows that $\Delta^2 q = 0$, where 0 is the null vector, and hence that $\Delta v = (K + \hat{k})\Delta^2 q = 0$. Also from (11.63)–(11.65) we have:[2]

$$\Delta m = a_2(i'\Delta x - a_3^1\Delta q - \Delta z). \qquad (11.67)$$

---

[1] See R. Stone and J. A. C. Brown, 'Output and Investment for Exponential Growth in Consumption', *Review of Economic Studies*, XXIX (1962) pp. 244–5.

[2] From (11.64) we get:

$$\Delta m = a_2 i'\Delta m.$$

Substituting for $i'\Delta m$ from (11.63) we get:

$$\Delta m = a_2(i'\Delta x - i'\Delta n - \Delta z - \Delta \beta).$$

Setting $\Delta \beta = 0$ in this expression (the pre-assigned balance of trade remains fixed) and using (11.65) we get:

$$\Delta m = a_2(i'\Delta x - i'\hat{a}_3\Delta q - \Delta z) = a_2(i'\Delta x - a_3\Delta q - \Delta z).$$

Hence from (11.66) we have:

$$\Delta q = A\Delta q + \Delta h + \Delta x - a_2(i'\Delta x - a_3'\Delta q - \Delta z).$$

This can be simplified to:

$$\Delta q = B^{*-1}(\Delta h + C\Delta x + a_2\Delta z) \qquad (11.68)$$

where $B^* = [I - A - a_2a_3']$ and $C = (I - a_2i')$. This is the desired expression for Δq. Substituting this expression in (11.60) we obtain the following expression for v, for substitution in (11.59), namely:

$$v = (K + \hat{k})B^{*-1}(\Delta h + C\Delta x + a_2\Delta z). \qquad (11.69)$$

To eliminate m from (11.59) we substitute the following expression, obtained by substituting (11.63) and (11.65) into (11.64):

$$m = a_1 + a_2i'x - a_2a_3'q - a_2(z + \beta). \qquad (11.70)$$

Hence the solution for q, obtained by substituting (11.69) and (11.70) in (11.59), is:

$$q = B^{*-1}\{h + Cx + a_2(z + \beta) - a_1 + (K + \hat{k})B^{*-1}[\Delta h + C\Delta x + a_2\Delta z]\}. \qquad (11.71)$$

Given information on the parameters of the system, relationship (11.71) enables us to find the structure of production which will have to be achieved in year 0 to permit delivery of a specified bill of goods of the form:

(a) a vector of the outputs required to satisfy exogenous final domestic demand in year 0 (h vector);

(b) a vector of the outputs required to satisfy export demand in year 0 (x vector);

(c) a vector of the absolute growth rates in exogenous final domestic demand which are to apply indefinitely from year 0 on (Δh vector);

(d) a vector of the absolute growth rates in export demand which are to apply from year 0 on indefinitely (Δx vector).

The required information on the parameters of the system would be:

(i) the coefficient matrices A, K, $\hat{k}$, a_1, a_2 and a_3;

(ii) the value of complementary imports into final demand in year 0 (z scalar);

(iii) the absolute growth rate which is to apply to complementary imports into final demand from year 0 onwards (Δz scalar);

(iv) the balance of payments constraint β.

11.10 Cambridge Growth Model: Some Numerical Results

In the previous five sections we have explained the structure of the Cambridge model and the way in which it could be used to work out the implications of a specified bill of goods, given the necessary information about the parameters of the system. To make this discussion more concrete, we shall now refer briefly to some preliminary calculations which have been made for the British economy with the help of the model. The aim of these calculations was to derive the structure of production which would have to be achieved in Britain in 1970 to permit the delivery of a particular bill of goods in that year. To explain the calculations, therefore, we must begin by outlining the procedure used to derive the 1970 bill of goods. This we shall now do.

The model used to make the calculations was the simplified version discussed in the preceding section,[1] not the full model presented in sections 11.5 to 11.8, i.e. the required structure of production was determined by substituting in (11.71). Hence to derive the bill of goods it was necessary to derive: (a) an h vector for 1970; (b) an x vector for 1970; (c) a Δh vector for 1970; and (d) a Δx vector for 1970. We shall consider the derivation of components (a) and (c) first and then take components (b) and (d).

To derive the h vector for 1970, exogenous final domestic demand was first broken up into five categories, namely: (i) private consumption expenditure; (ii) expenditure on investment in consumer durables and dwellings; (iii) public consumption expenditure; (iv) public social capital investment expenditure; and (v) expenditure on the replacement of industrial fixed assets. The next step was to estimate the total of each of these categories for 1970 in terms of 1960 prices. The method used in each case was to make some reasonable assumption about the growth rate which would apply over the 1960–70 decade and then to apply this rate to the known figure for 1960. In the case of the first two categories two estimates, referred to as 'projection A' and 'projection B', were made, the latter being based on a slightly higher assumed growth rate than the former. The following table shows, for each category, the percentage increase over the decade 1960–70 which was implied by the estimated 1970 total.

[1] See A. Brown, *Exploring 1970: Some Numerical Results* (London: Chapman & Hall, for the Department of Applied Economics, University of Cambridge, 1965) pp. 40–2.

TABLE 11.1

Category	*Estimated percentage increase, 1960-70*	
	Projection A	*Projection B*
(i) Private consumption expenditure	38	44
(ii) Investment in consumer durables and dwellings	46	55
(iii) Public consumption expenditure	40	–
(iv) Public investment in social capital	187	–
(v) Replacement expenditure	16	–

Source: Brown, op. cit., Tables II.1, II.3, II.4, II.5 and II.6.

The next step was to convert these category totals into demands for individual commodities, expressed as money values in 1960 prices. In the case of category (v) this was done directly. In the case of categories (i)–(iv), however, the conversion was carried out in two stages. In the first stage the category totals were broken down into their 'natural' components. In the case of categories (i) and (ii) this was a set of consumers' commodity categories or a 'shopping list', while in the case of categories (iii) and (iv) the natural components were a set of 'purposes' such as police and justice, military and civil defence and health. These natural components were then allocated to the various relevant industrial commodity categories. For example, 'expenditure on women's clothing' which was an item in the 'shopping list' was allocated, at the second stage, to four industrial commodity categories: leather and clothing, textiles, trade and transport.

At this point, then, five separate components of the 1970 h vector were available, namely the sub-vectors for each of the above five categories of exogenous final domestic demand. To obtain the h vector itself, it was merely a matter of summing these five components. In the case of categories (i) and (ii) the allocation of category totals to industrial commodities described above was done for both projections. Thus the end point of the operation was not a single h vector for 1970 but two alternative h vectors – a projection A vector and a projection B vector.

The Δh vector for 1970 was derived on the basis of the same five-fold division of exogenous final domestic demand as the h vector. An assumption was made about the total annual increase in each of these five categories, in terms of 1960 money values, which would apply from 1970 onwards. Each of these five expenditure increments was then converted into a set of increments of demand for individual commodities in the manner described above in connection with the h vector.

Turning now to the x and Δx vectors, the procedure used to obtain the x vector was to assume that aggregate exports would grow, in real terms, at the rate of 5 per cent per annum between 1960 and 1966 and at a somewhat smaller rate between 1966 and 1970, so that over the decade as a whole the average rate of increase would be 4·1 per cent per annum. This assumption, together with the known figure for aggregate exports in 1960, permitted calculation of a figure for aggregate exports in 1970, in terms of 1960 prices. The final step was to allocate this figure directly to the various industrial commodity categories to obtain the x vector for 1970. The Δx vector was then derived by comparing corresponding elements of the x vector for 1960 and 1970 and making a reasonable assumption about the likely annual increase in each element from 1970 onwards.

Having explained the procedure used to derive the bill of goods for 1970, we next comment on the methods used to obtain information about the parameters of the system, namely the matrices A, K and $\hat{k}$, the vectors a_1, a_2, a_3, and the scalars z, Δz and β. All the components of the calculations (i.e. all the magnitudes needed for substitution in (11.71)) will then have been dealt with and we shall be ready to consider some of the results which emerged.

Broadly speaking, the method used to derive the A matrix (matrix of *current* input–output coefficients) for 1970 was as follows.[1] First the matrix for 1960 was derived from the known matrix for 1954 by adjusting the elements of the 1954 matrix so that they agreed with the known marginal totals for 1960. The adjustments in question were based on two assumptions. The first was that changes in current input–output coefficients reflect: (i) price changes; (ii) 'substitution effects' which operate on the coefficients in a particular row; and (iii) 'fabrication effects' which operate on the coefficients in a particular column. The second assumption was that (ii) and (iii) operate uniformly over rows and columns respectively. Next a provisional 1970 matrix was obtained, either by direct estimation of coefficients or, where this was not possible because of lack of reliable up-to-date information, by projecting the trends in coefficients implied by a comparison of the actual 1954 matrix and the estimated 1960 matrix. Finally, the provisional 1970 matrix was discussed with experts in the different industries and adjustments made subjectively in the light of their comments.

Next we consider the derivation of the matrix K – the matrix of

[1] See Stone, *The Model in its Environment*, pp. 48–50.

capital input–output coefficients – for 1970. Here the first step was to derive the Δq vector for 1970 by substitution in (11.68). (This required knowledge of the a_2 and a_3 vectors and the Δz scalar for 1970, the derivation of which has yet to be explained.) Next, an incremental capital–output ratio was applied to each element in this Δq vector to obtain, for each commodity, the capital extension that would be undertaken in 1970 by the industry producing that commodity. The incremental capital–output ratios in question were based on a study of the relationships between capital stock and output in British industry in the 1950s.[1] Finally, each of the capital extension figures so obtained was allocated over commodities on the basis of the known commodity distribution of capital extension in each industry in 1960.[2]

Turn now to the diagonal matrix $\hat{k}$. It will be recalled that the element in row s, column s, of this matrix (the off-diagonal elements are zero) is the addition to stocks of commodity s held in the productive system per unit of additional output of commodity s. A rough estimate of this figure for 1970 was obtained by dividing the amount of commodity s held in stock in 1960 by the output of commodity s in 1960, i.e. the *marginal* stock–output ratio for 1970 was estimated by means of the *average* stock–output ratio for 1960.[3]

As for the methods used to derive the scalars z and Δz and the vectors a_1, a_2 and a_3 for 1970, it appears that the only available information is of a very general kind. Thus, as regards z, we are told that the 'amount of complementary imports of final products is determined by our analysis of consumers' demand and our projections of government expenditure'.[4] On the a_1, a_2 and a_3 vectors we have the comment:

Complementary intermediate imports are estimated by fixed coefficients applied to the outputs of the various using industries. . . . These coefficients are based on post-war trends and at present are very rough, because the classification of imports has only been carried out for the three years 1948, 1954 and 1960.

Individual groups of competitive imports . . . are treated as linear functions of the total amount of money available for competitive imports as a whole. These coefficients are roughly assessed on the basis of recent experience.[5]

---

[1] See G. Pyatt, *Capital, Output and Employment, 1948–1960* (London: Chapman & Hall, for the Department of Applied Economics, University of Cambridge, 1964).   [2] See Brown, *Exploring 1970*, p. 34.
[3] Ibid., p. 32.   [4] Ibid., p. 55.
[5] See Stone, *The Model in its Environment*, p. 48.

O

Finally we come to the scalar β. Since β is the pre-assigned trade balance for 1970, it can be any figure which appears to be relevant to the British situation. In fact two alternative values were given to β for the purposes of the calculations, namely (i) $\beta = 0$; (ii) $\beta = £200$ million.[1]

We come now to the calculations themselves. As already indicated, these comprise the elements of the q vector (the structure of output

TABLE 11.2

	Domestic output in 1970			
	A(i)		B(ii)	
	1960 (£m.)	Percentage increase over 1960	1960 (£m.)	Percentage increase over 1960
Commodities	(1)	(2)	(3)	(4)
1. Agriculture, etc.	1906	23	1954	26
2. Coal-mining	827	2	852	5
3. Mining and quarrying n.e.s.	239	59	248	65
4. Food processing	2601	13	2657	16
5. Drink and tobacco	831	19	856	23
6. Coke ovens, etc.	241	3	248	6
7. Mineral-oil refining	1102	115	1171	129
8. Chemicals n.e.s.	3414	72	3552	79
9. Iron and steel	3205	54	3304	59
10. Non-ferrous metals	1148	59	1217	69
11. Engineering and electrical goods	6492	68	6672	73
12. Shipbuilding, etc.	503	11	505	12
13. Motors and cycles	3053	82	3162	89
14. Aircraft	941	54	984	61
15. Railway locomotives, etc.	251	24	,253	25
16. Metal goods n.e.s.	2308	63	2393	69
17. Textiles	2698	29	2862	37
18. Leather, clothing, etc.	1478	42	1560	50
19. Building materials	612	40	626	44
20. Pottery and glass	265	22	276	27
21. Timber, furniture, etc.	876	56	913	63
22. Paper, printing, etc.	2054	42	2153	49
23. Rubber	424	44	442	50
24. Other manufacturing	691	95	737	108
25. Construction	4586	51	4672	54
26. Gas	538	44	564	51
27. Electricity	1689	118	1802	132
28. Water	173	76	177	81
29. Transport and communications	4036	33	4146	37
30. Distributive trades	5076	41	5311	48
31. Services n.e.s.	6671	65	7009	73
Total	60,929	50	63,278	56

[1] See Brown, *Exploring 1970*, p. 9.

which would have to be achieved in 1970 to permit delivery of the specified bill of goods in that year); and they were made by substituting the h, Δh, x and Δx vectors for 1970 in (11.71) together with the 1970 versions of the A, K and $\hat{k}$ matrices, the a_1, a_2 and a_3 vectors and the scalars z, Δz and β. In fact four sets of calculations were made, two using the 'projection A' h vector and two using the 'projection B' h vector (see p. 406 above). Of the two using the 'projection A' h vector, one used (i) $\beta = 0$ and the other used (ii) $\beta = £200$ million (see p. 410 above); and similarly for the two using the 'projection B' h vector. Only two of these four sets of calculations have been published, namely the A(i) calculations and the B(ii) calculations. The first set embodies the least ambitious assumptions of the four, since it uses the weaker of the two sets of assumptions about the growth, during the 1960s, of exogenous final domestic demand in combination with the smaller of the two pre-assigned balance of trade figures. By contrast the B(ii) calculations embody the more ambitious assumptions of the four sets, since they combine the stronger assumptions about the growth of exogenous demand in the 1960s with the larger of the two figures for β. The two sets of calculations in question are summarised in Table 11.2.[1] The most striking feature of the table is the wide range of increases over the decade 1960–70 which the figures imply. For example, the required output of electricity in 1970 is 118 per cent higher than in 1960 in A(i) and 132 per cent higher in B(ii). On the other hand the required output of coal-mining is only 2 per cent higher than in 1960 in A(i) and 5 per cent higher in B(ii).

The vector of competitive imports of commodities for 1970 was also calculated both on the basis of the calculated A(i) q vector and also on the basis of the calculated B(ii) q vector, the formula used for the purpose being (11.70). These calculations are also of interest and are presented in Table 11.3.[2]

In Table 11.4 we present a further set of calculations which have been derived from the initial set of 'commodity' calculations. These comprise the increases in *industrial* output, as distinct from *commodity* output (see p. 390, n. 1 above), over the 1960–70 decade which are implied by the 1970 bill of goods. For purposes of comparison the table also shows the observed increases in industrial output over the 1950–60 decade.[3]

It will be clear from the table that, in the case of several industries,

[1] Ibid., pp. 38–9.   [2] Ibid., pp. 38–9.   [3] Ibid., p. 44.

the required growth rate implied by the calculations for the 1960–70 decade differs very little from the growth rate actually achieved in the preceding decade. This is true for example, of agriculture, forestry

TABLE 11.3

Competitive imports in 1970

	A(i)		B(ii)	
Commodities	1960 (£m.)	Percentage increase over 1960	1960 (£m.)	Percentage increase over 1960
1. Agriculture, etc.	345	13	345	13
2. Coal-mining	1	..	1	..
3. Mining and quarrying n.e.s.	29	107	27	93
4. Food processing	578	27	578	27
5. Drink and tobacco	58	346	52	300
6. Coke ovens, etc.	2	..	2	..
7. Mineral-oil refining	161	11	145	0
8. Chemicals n.e.s.	355	72	329	60
9. Iron and steel	45	− 48	31	− 64
10. Non-ferrous metals	89	22	59	− 19
11. Engineering and electrical goods	422	51	371	33
12. Shipbuilding, etc.	21	250	19	37
13. Motors and cycles	148	164	105	88
14. Aircraft	51	− 16	27	− 56
15. Railway locomotives, etc.	0	..	0	..
16. Metal goods n.e.s.	76	41	64	19
17. Textiles	240	36	214	21
18. Leather, clothing, etc.	139	108	126	88
19. Building materials	16	23	15	15
20. Pottery and glass	38	124	36	112
21. Timber, furniture, etc.	78	44	72	33
22. Paper, printing, etc.	167	42	157	− 33
23. Rubber	11	22	6	..
24. Other manufacturing	63	54	48	22
25. Construction	0	..	0	..
26. Gas	0	..	0	..
27. Electricity	0	..	0	..
28. Water	0	..	0	..
29. Transport and communications	27	29	25	19
30. Distributive trades	5	..	3	..
31. Services n.e.s.	426	31	367	13
Total	3589	38	3224	24

and fishing; coke ovens, etc.; chemicals n.e.s.; pottery and glass; and paper, printing and publishing. In the case of several other industries, however, a significantly higher growth rate would be required in the 1960–70 decade than was achieved between 1950 and 1960. Examples are: mining and quarrying; iron and steel; engineering and electrical goods; railway locomotives and rolling stock; metal goods n.e.s.; and leather, clothing, footwear. For some industries a noticeably smaller growth rate would be called for, notably mineral-oil refining and aircraft.

TABLE 11.4

Industries	Percentage increase in output			Annual rate of growth of output percentage		
	1950–60	1960–70 A(i)	B(ii)	1950–60	1960–70 A(i)	B(ii)
1. Agriculture, etc.	24	23	26	2·2	2·1	2·3
2. Coal-mining	– 11	3	6	– 1·2	0·2	0·6
3. Mining and quarrying n.e.s.	44	59	65	3·7	4·6	5·0
4. Food processing	33	12	14	2·9	1·1	1·3
5. Drink and tobacco	28	19	23	2·5	1·7	2·1
6. Coke ovens, etc.	18	11	15	1·7	1·0	1·4
7. Mineral-oil refining	364	114	127	15·4	7·6	8·2
8. Chemicals n.e.s.	77	71	78	5·7	5·4	5·8
9. Iron and steel	39	56	61	3·3	4·4	4·8
10. Non-ferrous metals	47	57	66	3·9	4·5	5·1
11. Engineering and electrical goods	51	68	73	4·1	5·2	5·5
12. Shipbuilding, etc.	– 1	13	14	– 0·1	1·2	1·3
13. Motors and cycles	106	78	85	7·2	5·8	6·2
14. Aircraft	159	57	64	9·5	4·5	5·0
15. Railway locomotives, etc.	– 43	26	28	– 5·6	2·3	2·5
16. Metal goods n.e.s.	33	64	70	2·9	4·9	5·3
17. Textiles	– 5	29	37	– 0·5	2·5	3·2
18. Leather, clothing, etc.	14	42	50	1·3	3·5	4·1
19. Building materials	30	41	44	2·6	3·4	3·7
20. Pottery and glass	24	23	27	2·2	2·1	2·4
21. Timber, furniture, etc.	25	56	63	2·2	4·4	4·9
22. Paper, printing, etc.	55	42	49	4·4	3·5	4·0
23. Rubber	}54	42	48	}4·3	3·5	3·9
24. Other manufacturing		97	110		6·8	7·4
25. Construction	22	51	54	2·0	4·1	4·3
26. Gas	0	42	49	0·0	3·5	4·0
27. Electricity	116	117	132	7·7	7·7	8·4
28. Water	16	76	81	1·5	5·7	5·9
29. Transport and communications	22	33	37	2·0	2·9	3·2
30. Distributive trades	28	42	48	2·5	3·5	3·9
31. Services n.e.s.	33	65	73	2·9	5·0	5·5
Total	32	50	56	2·8	4·1	4·4

The increase in aggregate domestic output over the 1960–70 decade which is implied by the calculations has important implications for the growth in overall labour productivity. On the reasonable assumption that the labour force will grow by 7 per cent over the decade, the increase of 50–56 per cent in aggregate domestic output which is implied by the calculations gives a required growth rate in labour productivity of between 3·4 and 3·8 per cent per annum over the ten years, which is high by the standard of recent British experience.

Finally it should be noted that no calculations are presented for the industrial distribution of the labour force and the capital stock in 1970. Such calculations were not possible within the framework of the simplified model; only the full model could have generated information on these points.

11.11 The Cambridge Project: Assessment

So far we have been concerned with the structure of the Cambridge model and with its main applications. We proceed to a commentary on the approach as a whole. Our first comment concerns the treatment of the balance of payments. Let us take exports first. It is of some interest to compare the treatment of British exports in the Cambridge Project with our own discussion in Chapter 3. We pointed out there that the level of British exports to the rest of the world in the short run should be analysed in terms of a function including the following as the main explanatory variables: the rest-of-the world aggregate demand, the rest-of-the-world real inventory investment, the price of importables in the rest of the world relative to prices of exportables and non-traded goods, and the delivery delay and credit terms quoted by the rest-of-the-world producers of importables relative to those by British producers. In the longer-run context with which the Cambridge model is primarily concerned, these variables – with the exception of rest-of-the-world real inventory investment – would still appear to be the main determinants of British exports. The treatment of exports as exogenous is clearly inappropriate, and indeed is regarded by the authors as such. They point out, for example, that a proper estimation of British exports would involve data on world incomes, British prices in relation to world prices and so on. The reason for using the simple 'market research' approach despite its obvious limitations is essentially a practical one: it makes calculations manageable.[1] Indeed, Stone regards this part of his model as only a stop-gap, to be replaced in due course by a more sophisticated demand analysis of the type applied to private consumers' expenditure (see pp. 394–5 above).

[1] We have used a similar justification ourselves (see Chapter 3, p. 82).

The treatment of imports in the Cambridge model, which rests on the distinction between competitive and complementary imports, is subject to similar limitations. The point at issue here is not simply the arbitrary procedure used to distinguish between competitive and complementary items of imports; after all, any statistical classification must be arbitrary in some degree. The point rather is that in making such a very rigid distinction one tends to obscure the implications of import substitution for growth policy.[1] If the model is to provide guidance for import policy, a detailed specification of the chief explanatory variables that influence the level of British imports would appear to be called for.

At this stage, we may profitably look back at our own discussion of the short-run import function (see pp. 70–6 above). We suggested there that it would be convenient to approach the problem in two stages, the first stage being concerned with the demand for importables as a whole (rather than imports as such), the second with the proportion of a given demand for importables which is satisfied by British domestic production. As far as the first stage is concerned, our analysis suggested that the short-run demand for importables would depend on the level of aggregate demand, the level of real inventory investment and the price of importables relative to the prices of exportables and non-traded goods. As for the second stage, our conclusion was that the proportion of a given British demand for importables which is satisfied by British production would depend, in the short run, on the prices of British-made importables relative to those of foreign-made importables in terms of British currency, and on the credit terms and delivery delays quoted by British producers of importables relative to those quoted by foreign producers. In a long-run analysis of the type being undertaken by the Cambridge group, the answers would no doubt be somewhat different. For example, the long-run demand for importables would probably be influenced much more by the level of aggregate demand, less by relative prices and hardly at all by inventory investment. Similarly, it is

[1] In practice, the rigidity of the distinction between complementary and competitive imports is softened by bringing in other criteria as well. 'Many types of imports vary considerably within a narrow range but for one reason or another we would not wish to see them move outside that range. For example, we probably would not wish to see a substantial fall in agricultural imports, even though with the kind of policies which were adopted during the last war it would be physically possible to replace many of them with British farm products.' Stone and Brown, *A Complete Model of Economic Growth*, p. 58. In other words, some items are treated as complementary rather than competitive on 'social' or political grounds.

probable that differences in credit and delivery terms would play a relatively insignificant role in determining the long-run proportion of the total British demand for importables to be satisfied by British production. However, while the factors themselves might vary in importance, a broadly similar analysis would still appear to be relevant.

It may be argued that the Cambridge Growth Project is not intended primarily as a planning model for the analysis of balance of payments policies for the British economy, but rather as a device for deriving a 'technically feasible' growth solution, in the sense of a structure of output for any specified bill of goods which is both internally consistent and compatible with a pre-assigned trade balance, and hence that the above comments are not necessarily valid criticisms of the Cambridge Project itself. However that may be, they serve to draw attention to the wide gap that still remains between short-run, specific policy models, on the one hand, and long-run growth models on the other.

The next comment relates to the treatment of technical change. The matrices A and K, which summarise the current and capital input–output coefficients, respectively, embody the technological assumptions of the model. Thus, assuming A and K constant throughout is equivalent to assuming that there is no technical change. As we have seen in section 11.10, some attempt has been made, in the numerical applications of the model, to allow for technical change in the transitional period (i.e. before 1970) in so far as it affects the *current* input–output coefficients. This has been based either on observed rates of change in coefficients in the recent past or on special information, e.g. that during 1960–70 there will be a tendency for electricity and oil to be used more and more as fuel inputs and for coal and coke to be used less and less.[1] However, there has been no attempt as yet to make similar adjustments in the matrix of *capital* input–output coefficients; and while a method of allowing for changes in both A and K beyond the terminal year (1970) into the indefinite future has been suggested,[2] the implications of such adjustments for

[1] When change in the current input–output coefficients proceeds in an even way over the entire range of goods, it can be dealt with by multiplying the relevant row of the A matrix by a vector whose elements will be greater than 1 for 'expanding' items and less than 1 for 'declining' items. If, on the other hand, there are differential movements, i.e. if there are elements in the matrix whose movements over time are likely to be out of step with corresponding elements elsewhere, an *ad hoc* treatment becomes necessary.

[2] See Stone and Brown, *A Computable Model of Economic Growth*, p. 77.

the structure of output requirements have so far not been developed in quantitative terms.

The question of the nature of technical change underlies some of the most important as well as the most difficult issues in the theory of economic growth. The main theoretical advance in this field in recent years has been the idea that technical change is 'embodied', i.e. it affects the economic system through the creation of new capital equipment. Models based on the idea of embodied technical change – vintage models as they are called – have already made a major contribution to our understanding of the relationship of technical progress to capital accumulation on the one hand and to the level of employment on the other. The development of econometric work along these lines – reported to be already in progress – may enable a more integrated treatment of technical change to be achieved within the general analytical framework of the Cambridge growth model.

Our next comment concerns the way in which the problem of setting terminal conditions is handled in the Cambridge project. We encountered this problem earlier in discussing the theory of optimum economic growth and we pointed out that it was inherent in planning over a finite time horizon. In essence, the terminal conditions represent judgements about the nature of growth beyond the specified horizon which has been set; they indicate the extent to which planning over the specified horizon may be allowed to influence the possibilities of growth in the future beyond.

The Cambridge group attempt to set the appropriate terminal conditions by developing two separate models, viz. a 'steady-state' model and a 'transient' model, and trying to iterate between them. Stone himself describes this procedure as follows: 'One part is concerned with the rates at which the outputs of different products might grow after a transitional period ending, say, in 1970; this is the long-run or steady-state model. The other part is concerned with the problem of adapting the economy during the transitional period to meet the initial conditions of the steady state of growth; this is the short-run or transient model.'[1] The transient model in Stone's terminology corresponds to our finite-horizon planning model. Stone's method amounts to setting the terminal condition for this model in terms of a specified rate of growth, expressed in terms of consumption, from the terminal year on. Thus, in effect, Stone requires his solution to the finite-horizon model to satisfy the

[1] Stone, *The Model in its Environment*, p. 21.

condition that the various categories of consumption must grow from
the terminal year onwards at an exogenously given percentage rate
per annum.[1] Given the assumptions about technology, embodied in
the current and capital input–output matrices, this requirement is
readily translated into a condition about the minimum level of assets
required at the end of the terminal year. It then reduces to a terminal
capital stock requirement, the form in which it usually appears in the
literature on optimum growth. Indeed, in this particular formulation of
the finite-horizon planning model, the terminal capital requirement
can be expressed in terms of two parameters, namely the length of
the planning horizon and the postulated post-terminal rates of
growth.

Now the use of a vector of sustainable rates of growth of consumption as a terminal condition for a planning model has a good
deal to recommend it. In particular it bears a clear interpretation and
hence makes for meaningful political discussion. On the other hand
it involves a number of difficulties, two of which we shall now
discuss.

In the first place, the use of this form of terminal condition
involves an information problem. As we have seen earlier, one of the
important arguments in favour of using a finite, in preference to an
infinite, time horizon is that the infinite-horizon approach requires
information about technology and tastes extending into the indefinite future. Such information we do not, and indeed cannot, have.
This has been held to be an important, even a decisive, consideration in favour of a finite-horizon approach. Stone has used this
argument himself. For example, he points out that 'what we shall
want to do in the future, and what facilities we shall have to do it with,
becomes less and less clear as we try to imagine times which are
more and more remote. We cannot work forward into the future
without setting a target and we cannot derive this target from the
remote future because we have no information about it.'[2] However,
using a vector of rates of growth of consumption in a finite-horizon
model does not, as Stone appears to imply, eliminate this problem.
For what such a terminal condition requires is not simply that the
economy should remain capable at the end of the horizon in question
of providing specified rates of growth of consumption for evermore,
but that it should be capable of doing this on the basis either of

---

[1] We are referring here to the full model.
[2] Stone, *The Model in its Environment*, pp. 20–1.

existing technology or of what we *now* expect future technology to be. Assuming the present technology to continue into the indefinite future appears to be quite unreasonable. If, on the other hand, the terminal condition as to the rates of growth of future consumption is taken to be based on what we *now* expect future technology to be, we are faced with an information problem equivalent in content to that which occurs in the infinite-horizon formulation of the planning problem. Indeed, Stone's procedure effectively implies an infinite time horizon in the sense that the consumption programmes being compared extend over all future time. They are merely so constrained that they show the same growth rate for all $t \geq T$ where T stands for the finite horizon postulated and t denotes time. However, whereas in the traditional literature of optimum growth, based on infinite-horizon models the problem of information appears explicitly, in the Cambridge approach it is implicit and hence may escape attention.

Secondly, if, as Stone appears to suggest, the Cambridge exercise is meant not simply to test the consistency of multi-sectoral growth patterns (which, after all, any input–output analysis must do in some degree) but also as a preliminary step towards an optimising approach, the question of the sensitivity of the optimum programme to the terminal conditions becomes crucially important. Now if we regard the planning horizon as of given length T, the terminal conditions in Stone's formulation consist of the vector of growth rates applying to the different components of consumption in the post-terminal period. So far Stone's calculations have been confined to one particular vector of post-terminal growth rates. Hence it has not been possible for him to consider the sensitivity of the optimum programme to the terminal conditions. However, some work done by Chakravarty,[1] using an essentially similar model but with one consumption good (so that the post-terminal growth rate of consumption is a scalar rather than a vector), suggests that the optimum consumption programme may be relatively insensitive to the postulated post-terminal growth rate, provided that this growth rate is not set at an unreasonably high figure. In Chakravarty's model the postulated growth rate must not be higher than 20 per cent per year, which most people would regard as very high indeed! The problem is further

---

[1] S. Chakravarty, 'The Optimal Growth Path for Finite Planning Horizons', in Tapas Majumdar (ed.), *Growth and Choice* (Calcutta: Oxford University Press, 1969).

complicated by the fact that the maximum value of the post-terminal growth rate that ensures insensitivity may itself depend on T, the length of the horizon, and on whether or not decumulation is possible during the planning period. To this latter question we now turn.

There would be general agreement that guarding against the possibility of decumulation, i.e. preventing violation of the condition $\dot{K}(t) \geq 0$, $0 \leq t \leq T$, is a desirable property for a finite-horizon optimum growth model to have. It has been shown, however, that the standard optimum growth paths found in the literature may not necessarily satisfy such a requirement. Moreover, the question of the sensitivity of the optimum consumption path to the terminal condition may itself be tied up with the possibility of decumulation. Chakravarty's results, for example, show that the zone of parameter values for which the consumption path is relatively insensitive also tends to be the zone that allows decumulation to take place. In particular, he has shown that in models of optimisation using the post-terminal growth rate as the boundary condition, in which category the Stone model naturally belongs, it is not possible to rule out decumulation *a priori* without imposing further constraints on the system. At the present stage of the debate, the possibility of decumulation must be regarded both as a basic theoretical difficulty in using Stone-type models to investigate optimum growth paths for the British economy and as a major research area to be cleared up before further progress can be made along these lines.

Our final observation relates to the following question: what precisely is the contribution made by the Cambridge approach to the basic problem with which this chapter is concerned, namely the choice of an optimum growth path? We have repeatedly stressed our view that the real purpose of the Cambridge growth model is to give empirical content to alternative growth paths for the British economy and so help in choosing between them. How far does this objective seem likely to be achieved? An answer to this must necessarily be highly tentative, since the Cambridge model is a working model which is as yet in a relatively early stage of its development. Nevertheless, even on the basis of its performance so far, it seems fairly clear that its basic contribution lies in narrowing down the range within which the socially desired growth paths may be reasonably expected to lie. To take one example, the model shows that a sustainable rate of growth of consumption of 4 per cent per annum from

1970 onwards entails an increase in labour productivity during 1960–70 of the order of 8–9 per cent per annum in particular sectors. The attainment of higher steady-state rates of growth of consumption would require correspondingly higher rates of growth of productivity. This in itself may be regarded as prima facie evidence that the achievement of long-run rates of growth of much higher than 4 per cent might not be a sensible goal of policy for the British economy. One way of expressing this point would be to say that the model can help us to eliminate non-feasible growth paths from the choice set. However, at a deeper level, what is feasible is itself a question that cannot be resolved without introducing ethical judgements (see section 11.3). Thus, the concern that has recently been expressed in Britain about 'the high costs of growth' arises from the ethical judgement that the high rate of technical change (including changes in prevailing techniques of organisation) that is required to bring about a rapid change in the productivity of labour is a bad thing, e.g. because of the human cost involved. If such a value-judgement were widely shared in the community, this might itself result in a faster rate of growth becoming non-feasible! This is yet one more example of the difficulties in choosing a social welfare function. The Cambridge model – or any other model for that matter – cannot by itself resolve such difficulties which are inherent in the choice of an optimum rate of economic growth. However, it goes some way towards making informed, concrete and meaningful discussion of the issues involved possible.

While the Cambridge Project helps in specifying the nature of the desired growth rate for the British economy, on the question how best to achieve or maintain such a growth rate it offers relatively little guidance. Indeed, those concerned with the project have themselves pointed out that they are not, at the present stage, concerned with the question of how the transition from the current state of the economy to that state in 1970 which is appropriate for achieving a particular long-run rate of growth, should be brought about. As pointed out by Ball, this explicit denial of interest in the current growth path tends to limit the usefulness of the Cambridge model from a policy point of view.[1] Indeed it shares this characteristic with the literature on optimum economic growth in general. This leads us back to the point we made earlier, in discussing the treatment of the

[1] R. J. Ball, 'The Cambridge Model of Economic Growth', *Economica* (May 1963).

balance of payments constraint in the Cambridge model, that a wide
gap remains to be bridged between short-run models focusing
attention on specific instruments of policy and long-run models of
optimum growth. In this chapter we have been concerned with the
latter. In the next we shall take up some of the work that has been
done on the former.

11.12 Summary

We begin this chapter by pointing out some of the special difficulties
connected with the analysis of growth as an objective of economic
policy. The Ramsey theory of optimum economic growth, based on
the maximisation of a social welfare function over time, is developed
and some of the problems that arise in applying this approach to
macro-economic policy-making, in particular those involved in the
choice of the social welfare function and of the revelant time horizon,
are examined. It is stressed that, in order to be useful for decision-
making, the theoretical model must be capable of indicating in some
detail the consequences of adopting particular value judgements.
From this point of view, the inter-industry model of growth developed at Cambridge under the direction of Richard Stone is singled
out for attention and its assumptions, methods and conclusions are
discussed in the wider context of the theory of optimum economic
growth.

READING LIST

Chakravarty, S., 'The Existence of an Optimum Savings Program', *Econometrica*
    (Jan 1962).
——, 'The Optimal Growth Path for Finite Planning Horizons', in Tapas
    Majumdar (ed.), *Growth and Choice* (Calcutta: Oxford University Press,
    1969).
Dasgupta, A., 'A Note on Optimum Savings', *Econometrica* (July 1964).
Koopmans, T. C., 'Objectives, Constraints and Outcomes in Optimal Growth
    Models', *Econometrica* (Jan 1967).
Leitmann, G., *et al.*, *Optimization Techniques* (New York: Academic Press, 1962).
Pontryagin, L. S., *et al.*, *The Mathematical Theory of Optimal Processes* (New
    York and London: Interscience, 1962).
Ramsey, F. P., 'A Mathematical Theory of Saving', *Economic Journal* (Dec 1928).
Shell, K. (ed.), *Essays on the Theory of Optimal Economic Growth* (Cambridge,
    Mass.: M.I.T. Press, 1967).
Stevenson, C. L., *Ethics and Language* (New Haven, Conn.: Yale University Press,
    1944).
Stone, R. (ed.), *A Programme for Growth*, 1–6 (London: Chapman & Hall, for the
    Department of Applied Economics, University of Cambridge, 1962–5).

Appendix 11.1

EQUIVALENCE OF (11.11) AND (11.10)

Relationship (11.11) gives:

$$\dot{K} = \frac{B - u}{u'} \tag{11.1.1}$$

where $u(C)$, $u'(C)$ have been written more simply as u and u'. Using (11.2), (11.3) and (11.4), we can substitute in (11.1.1) for $\dot{K}$ to get:

$$f(K, L) - C = \frac{B - u}{u'}. \tag{11.1.2}$$

Differentiating both sides of (11.1.2) with respect to K, we have:

$$\frac{\partial f}{\partial K} - \frac{dC}{dK} = \frac{d}{dC}\left(\frac{B - u}{u'}\right) \cdot \frac{dC}{dK} = -\left[1 + (B - u)\frac{u''}{(u')^2}\right]\frac{dC}{dK}. \tag{11.1.3}$$

Substituting in (11.1.3) from (11.1.1) we get:

$$\frac{\partial f}{\partial K} = -\frac{dC}{dK}\,\dot{K}\frac{u''}{u'}. \tag{11.1.4}$$

This gives:

$$\frac{\partial f}{\partial K} = -\frac{dC}{dt} \cdot \frac{u''}{u'}.$$

Hence:

$$\frac{\partial f}{\partial K} = -\frac{du'}{dt}\bigg/ u'$$

which is (11.10).

Appendix 11.2

DERIVATION OF (11.41)

We begin by repeating the basic model:

$$q = B^{-1}e + B^{-1}v \tag{11.37}$$

$$v = K\Delta q \tag{11.38}$$

$$Ee = (I + \hat{r})e. \tag{11.39}$$

The simplest way to solve this model for q in terms of e and $\hat{r}$ is to solve for v in terms of e and $\hat{r}$ and then substitute the resulting expression in (11.37).

To solve for v in terms of e and $\hat{r}$ we make use of the following iterative procedure. We begin with a convenient initial 'estimate' of the solution vector, namely $v = 0$ where 0 is the null vector. Then using (11.37) and (11.39) we find the Δq which is implied by this initial estimate. Next, using (11.38), we find the v which is implied by this Δq. If this happened to be identical with the initial estimate, then the initial estimate would be consistent with the relationships as a whole, i.e. $v = 0$ would be the solution. In fact we find that the initial guess is wrong and we repeat the above procedure using the second estimate (the v which emerges on the first application of the procedure) as our starting-point. If the v which came out on the second trial happened to be identical with the v which went in (i.e. with the second estimate), then the second estimate would be the solution. Again, however, we find that the v which comes out differs from the v which went in and we repeat the procedure using our third estimate of v as a starting-point.

On examining the succession of v-estimates which emerge in this way, we find that the expression for the tth estimate is a sum of $(t - 1)$ terms. We also find that the sum converges, i.e. that the difference between the $(t - 1)$th estimate (the v that went in on the $(t - 1)$th repetition) and the tth estimate (the v that comes out on the $(t - 1)$th repetition) grows less and less as t increases. It follows that the solution emerges as t approaches infinity and that we can obtain as good an approximation to the solution as we choose simply by making t large enough, i.e. by repeating the procedure often enough.

We shall now consider the above in more detail. Denote the initial estimate of v by v_1, the q and Δq which are implied by this initial estimate by q_1 and Δq_1, the second estimate of v by v_2 and so on. Then we have:

$$v_1 = 0.$$

From (11.37) we get:

$$q_1 = B^{-1}e. \tag{11.2.1}$$

This gives:

$$Eq_1 = B^{-1}Ee.$$

Substituting in this expression from (11.39) we get:

$$Eq_1 = B^{-1}(I + \hat{r})e. \tag{11.2.2}$$

Using (11.2.1) and (11.2.2) we get:

$$\Delta q_1 = Eq_1 - q_1 = B^{-1}\hat{r}e. \tag{11.2.3}$$

Finally, substituting from (11.2.3) into (11.38) we get:

$$v_2 = KB^{-1}\hat{r}e.$$

The procedure is now repeated using v_2 as a starting-point. We have:

$$q_2 = B^{-1}e + B^{-1}v_2 = B^{-1}(I + KB^{-1}\hat{r})e$$
$$Eq_2 = B^{-1}(I + KB^{-1}\hat{r})(I + \hat{r})e$$
$$\therefore \quad \Delta q_2 = B^{-1}(I + KB^{-1}\hat{r})\hat{r}e$$
$$\therefore \quad v_3 = [(KB^{-1})\hat{r} + (KB^{-1})^2\hat{r}^2]e.$$

Continuing, we find that:

$$v_t = \sum_{i=1}^{t-1} [(KB^{-1})^i\hat{r}^i]e \qquad (t = 2, 3, \dots).$$

Now, in practice, the largest element of (KB^{-1}) will be about 5 and the elements of $\hat{r}$ will average about 0.05. Hence the elements of $(KB^{-1})^i\hat{r}^i$ will diminish as i increases. It follows that as we take the sum of more and more terms (i.e. as $t \to \infty$), we come closer and closer to the solution (make the difference between successive estimates smaller and smaller). Hence we say the solution is:

$$v = \sum_{i=1}^{\infty} [(KB^{-1})^i \hat{f}^i] e. \qquad (11.2.4)$$

Strictly speaking we never reach this solution but only approach it as t increases indefinitely. In practice a good approximation is obtained by summing the first four or five terms.[1] Substituting (11.2.4) into (11.37) we obtain (11.41).

[1] See Stone, *A Computable Model of Economic Growth*, pp. 75–6.

12 Growth Policy: The Pursuit of a High Growth Rate

12.1 The Choice of a Target Growth Rate

The widespread and continued concern about the rate of growth of the British economy in the period since the end of the Second World War is somewhat surprising in the light of Britain's past growth performance. The available statistical information suggests that the rate of growth of real gross domestic product per head in the United Kingdom was higher in this period than in any other period of comparable length in British history. Further, the growth rate was relatively stable; only twice since the end of the war did real G.D.P. per head actually decline (in 1952 and 1958). Business fluctuations occurred but mostly they took the form of higher than average or lower than average increases in output. The level of employment was sustained at a high level throughout the period. The percentage of the work force unemployed in any year never rose above 4 per cent; in most years it was considerably less.

Why, then, has Britain's failure to achieve 'rapid' growth caused so much concern, both at home and abroad? The reason is that the historical standard has not been deemed relevant. Britain's post-war growth performance has been judged by comparing the British growth rate in the post-war period with the growth rate of other Western European countries in the *same* period rather than with the British growth rate in an *earlier* period.

Since there are important similarities, in economic and social structure as well as in cultural background, between Britain and most other Western European countries, and since they also are Britain's main competitors in the international market, it has been argued that a comparison of British with European growth rates provides the only valid basis for judging how Britain has fared. Since such a comparison shows Britain to be consistently at, or near the bottom of, the European 'growth league', it is also suggested that a study of the factors that contributed significantly to the growth rate of the faster-growing countries should help in deciding how Britain could do better, i.e. increase her growth rate.

The 'comparative' approach has dominated the discussion of British post-war economic growth. Our discussion in the present chapter inevitably reflects this. This does not necessarily imply that we accept it. The adoption of European growth rates as a norm or objective for Britain, and equally the emulation of European policies to achieve them, involve value-judgements that may or may not be acceptable to the British people as a whole. This is a point to which we shall return towards the end of this chapter.

A discussion of the factors which influence the national growth rate must necessarily take some model of growth as its point of reference. Such a model may be implicit only. This has the disadvantage that it becomes difficult to relate conclusions to assumptions in any systematic way. Hence, in the recent literature on rates of economic growth, the growth model that provides the conceptual framework tends increasingly to be given an explicit formulation. Even if a particular model turns out to have little explanatory value, it is often possible to discover the specific ways in which it is deficient, and this may help to suggest the directions along which new and improved models could usefully be formulated and to pinpoint questions in need of further empirical research.

In the next section we shall give a brief outline of some of the models of the determinants of the growth rate which have played a prominent part in recent discussions of growth policy, and in section 12.3 we shall discuss various applications of these models to the problem of explaining the relatively slow growth of the British economy in the post-war period.

12.2 Models of the Determinants of the Growth Rate

To Harrod and Domar belongs the credit of constructing the first formal aggregative growth model, and we shall begin this section by presenting the Harrod–Domar model and considering its implications. For this purpose we shall use the following notation:

Y = realised real gross domestic product at time t

S = desired real saving at time t

I = realised real investment expenditure at time t

K^* = available stock of capital services at time t

K = utilised stock of capital services at time t

s, v, u = positive constants.

In terms of this notation the Harrod–Domar model consists of the following three relationships:

$$S = sY \tag{12.1}$$

(a) $K^* = K = vY$

(b) $I = \dfrac{dK}{dt} = v\dfrac{dY}{dt}$ $\Bigg\}$ (12.2)

$$S = I. \tag{12.3}$$

The first of these relationships is an aggregate saving function which makes desired real saving proportional to realised real G.D.P. at all points of time. Relationship (12.2) (a) consists of two parts. The first part ($K^* = K$) says, in effect, that the available capital stock is fully utilised, i.e. that there is no excess capacity. The second part ($K = vY$) is a fixed-technical-coefficients production function. Relationship (12.2) (b) is an alternative version of (12.2) (a) obtained by differentiating (12.2) (a) with respect to time. Finally (12.3), which equates desired saving and realised investment, is the saving–investment identity coupled with the assumption that desired and realised savings are equal.

Combining these relationships we get:

$$sY = v\frac{dY}{dt}$$

which gives the following formula for the proportional rate of growth of real G.D.P.:

$$\dot{Y} = \frac{dY}{dt} \Big/ Y = \frac{s}{v}. \tag{12.4}$$

Remembering that s and v are constants, we see from (12.4) that the growth rate generated by the Harrod–Domar model is an 'equilibrium' or 'steady-state' or 'warranted' growth rate.[1]

As we have seen, the Harrod–Domar growth formula (12.4) is based, in part, on the assumption of fixed factor proportions. An alternative formula which is free from this assumption can be derived from a continuously substitutable production function incorporating

[1] Note that throughout this chapter and the following chapters a dot above a variable will indicate 'proportional rate of increase' as in Chapters 9 and 10, not 'time derivative' as in Chapter 11.

'disembodied' technical progress. The production function of this type on which most attention has been concentrated is the Cobb–Douglas form:

$$Y = A(t)K^{\alpha}L^{1-\alpha}. \tag{12.5}$$

The notation is as follows:

K = capital input utilised at time t

L = labour input utilised at time t

$A(t)$ = index of technical progress satisfying: $A(t) = 1$ for $t = 0$; $A'(t) > 0$ for $t > 0$

α = constant satisfying: $0 < \alpha < 1$.

The following properties of the Cobb–Douglas production function (12.5) are particularly relevant when the function is applied to the analysis of the determinants of growth.

First, it assumes constant returns to scale. This is easily seen by multiplying both the capital and labour variables in (12.5) by a constant λ. The output variable then gets multiplied by $\lambda^{\alpha} \lambda^{1-}$, i.e. by λ.

Secondly, the exponent of the capital variable can be interpreted as the elasticity of output with respect to capital and similarly for the exponent of the labour variable. From (12.5) we have:

$$\log Y = \log A(t) + \alpha \log K + (1 - \alpha) \log L. \tag{12.6}$$

It follows that:

$$\frac{\partial Y}{\partial K} \frac{K}{Y} = \frac{\partial \log Y}{\partial \log K} = \alpha \tag{12.7}$$

$$\frac{\partial Y}{\partial L} \frac{L}{Y} = \frac{\partial \log Y}{\partial \log L} = 1 - \alpha. \tag{12.8}$$

Thus, α and $(1 - \alpha)$ are, respectively, the elasticity of output with respect to capital and the elasticity of output with respect to labour.

Thirdly, under the assumption of profit maximisation under perfect competition, (12.5) implies that the share of each factor in total output is constant and equal to the elasticity of output with respect to that factor. Under the stated assumptions the marginal physical product of each factor must equal its real reward. Hence if we denote the real reward of capital (real profit rate) by π and the real reward of labour (real wage rate) by w, we have:

$$\frac{\partial Y}{\partial K} = \pi \tag{12.9}$$

$$\frac{\partial Y}{\partial L} = w. \tag{12.10}$$

Using (12.9) and (12.10) in (12.7) and (12.8) we get:

$$\frac{\pi K}{Y} = \alpha \tag{12.11}$$

$$\frac{wL}{Y} = 1 - \alpha. \tag{12.12}$$

These relationships state that the share of profit in G.D.P. is α while the share of wages is $(1 - \alpha)$. The share of each factor in total income can thus be identified with the elasticity of output with respect to that factor.

Fourthly, the production function of (12.5) implies that the rate of growth of output can be expressed as the sum of a term representing the contribution of capital (the rate of growth of capital times the elasticity of output with respect to capital), a term representing the contribution of labour (the rate of growth of labour multiplied by the elasticity of output with respect to labour) and a residual item. This follows directly from the logarithmic form of the function given by (12.6). Taking derivatives with respect to time, we have:

$$\frac{1}{Y}\frac{dY}{dt} = \frac{1}{A(t)}\frac{dA(t)}{dt} + \alpha\frac{1}{K}\frac{dK}{dt} + (1 - \alpha)\frac{1}{L}\frac{dL}{dt}$$

or more simply:

$$\dot{Y} = \dot{A}(t) + \alpha\dot{K} + (1 - \alpha)\dot{L}. \tag{12.13}$$

As already shown, under the assumptions of profit maximisation and perfect competition, the share of profit in real G.D.P. is α and the share of wages is $(1 - \alpha)$. Hence, given these assumptions, the Cobb–Douglas production function (12.5) provides an imputation of the growth rate of real G.D.P. to the two inputs. Capital is credited with a contribution to growth equal to the growth rate of capital times the fraction of income which accrues as profit; a similar interpretation holds for labour. The part of growth which remains unexplained after the contributions of capital and labour have been taken into account (the first term in (12.13)) is attributed to 'technical change'.

In the Cobb–Douglas production function (12.5), technical change and capital accumulation are assumed to be mutually separable,

Hence the description of technical change as 'disembodied'. As against this, it has been argued that most, if not all, technical progress takes the form of new capital equipment; technical progress is 'embodied' in new equipment and in new equipment only. Accordingly, the rate of technical change is to be regarded as the rate of improvement in the *quality* of new capital goods. The implication of this view is that there will be distinct production functions for equipment built at different times (of different 'vintages'). Corresponding to (12.5) we will have:

$$Y_\phi = A(\phi)K_\phi^\alpha L_\phi^{1-\alpha} \qquad (12.14)$$

where the notation is as follows:

Y_ϕ = real gross domestic product at time t from machines of vintage ϕ

$A(\phi)$ = index of technical progress at time ϕ

K_ϕ = capital input at time t from machines of vintage ϕ

L_ϕ = labour input combined with machines of vintage ϕ at time t.

Total output at time t would be the sum of the outputs produced by machines of all vintages at time t.

The vintage view of technical progress allots a more important role to the rate of investment than does the 'disembodied' view. For, given the rate at which technical progress is proceeding (this rate is taken as exogenously determined in the vintage approach as in the disembodied approach), a higher rate of investment will tend to raise the proportion of the capital stock in use which is of the relatively newer vintages and hence to increase efficiency. On the other hand, it has been shown that, given certain assumptions, this effect is temporary only and that in a steady state the two types of model behave in exactly the same way.[1] Essentially this is because in both models the rate of technical progress is assumed to be independent of the rate of investment itself.

As against the vintage view, it has been emphasised in a class of growth models developed, in particular, by Arrow[2] that technical progress is a learning process and that learning depends on experience rather than on the passing of time as such. It follows that the higher the rate of investment (the more machines one produces),

[1] See D. W. Jorgenson, 'The Embodiment Hypothesis', *Journal of Political Economy* (Feb 1966).

[2] See K. J. Arrow, 'The Economic Implications of Learning by Doing', *Review of Economic Studies*, XXIX (1962) 155–73.

the more one learns, and hence the better the machines produced tend to get. Capital formation, apart from its direct effect on production through the increase of a particular input, also has an indirect effect via the induced change in the pace of technical advance.

While 'the Arrow effect' does not, strictly speaking, require the embodiment hypothesis – it is investment *per se* that provides the opportunity of learning by doing – it is likely to be more important in the context of embodied change. For embodiment itself is usually time-consuming. Since new technical processes or products in industry are almost inevitably beset by 'teething troubles', development tends to be a sequential learning process. The rate of learning depends crucially on the rate at which suggested improvements are tried out, which in turn involves new investment. In industries such as the aircraft or electricity industries where the pace of technical progress is rapid, the amounts of such investment can be quite substantial.

12.3 Empirical Analyses of Comparative Growth Rates

In this section we shall deal with a number of studies which attempt to explain the lower rate of growth in the United Kingdom in the post-war period compared with other countries in Western Europe. From the discussion of the previous section it will be clear that, in the theoretical literature concerned with the determinants of growth in advanced industrial countries, the central questions relate, in the main, to the role of capital formation as a determinant of growth. How investment and technical progress compare as regards their relative contributions to economic growth, and whether technical progress typically requires capital formation to become effective – these, and similar questions, are the ones on which attention has been focused and on which argument continues. Not surprisingly, these are also the questions which have received most attention in empirical analyses of comparative growth rates of the type to be discussed in the present section.

We shall begin by briefly considering a group of studies which attempt to explain the United Kingdom's relatively low rate of growth in terms of the investment–G.D.P. ratio. Typical of this type of approach are the studies of Maddison and Hill.[1]

[1] See A. Maddison, *Economic Growth in the West* (London: Allen & Unwin, 1964), and T. P. Hill, 'Growth and Investment According to International Comparisons', *Economic Journal*, LXXIV 294 (June 1964) 287–304.

Maddison uses pooled cross-section and time-series data to analyse comparative national growth rates in Western Europe and North America from this point of view. These data show that the rate of growth of gross domestic product, the rate of growth of the productivity of labour and the proportion of investment in gross domestic product are positively correlated between themselves. In particular, the time-series analysis for individual countries shows a particularly strong correlation between the proportion of G.D.P. devoted to investment in fixed-capital equipment, on the one hand, and the yearly rate of growth of productivity on the other.

In a similar study, Hill finds a strong positive correlation between the percentage share of gross investment in gross national product during 1953–61 and the rate of growth of gross national product in 1954–62 for a number of countries, viz. France, West Germany, Italy and the United Kingdom. A simple linear regression of the growth rate of G.N.P. on the share of fixed-capital investment in G.N.P. showed $r^2 = 0.96$. However, the correlation coefficient declines when the analysis is extended to include other countries in Western Europe as well. Essentially this is because, while no country achieved fast growth without a high share of investment in income, several countries which invested heavily failed to grow quickly. The conclusion is drawn that a high investment ratio is a necessary, though not a sufficient, condition for rapid growth.

A basic weakness of these and similar studies is the failure to link the statistical analysis to a well-defined theoretical framework. In the absence of such a framework, correlation coefficients can provide little guidance for policy.

The Harrod–Domar model discussed in the previous section constitutes one possible framework for empirical studies of comparative growth rates. From this standpoint one would ascribe a lower growth rate in country A than in country B during some given period to one or both of the following: a smaller investment ratio (smaller s) in country A than in country B; a higher capital–output ratio (higher v) in country A than in country B (cf. equation (12.4) above). Thus from the Harrod–Domar viewpoint, the relatively slow growth of the British economy in the post-war period would be explained in terms of a lower British investment ratio, together with a higher capital–output ratio (lower 'efficiency' of investment) in Britain than in the other countries of Western Europe. However, while the Harrod–Domar framework has the virtue of simplicity, it suffers from the extreme rigidity of its basic components: full utilisation of the capital stock; fixed factor proportions; and realisation of savings plans. Because of this limitation it has not been extensively used as a basis for empirical work on comparative growth rates.

An alternative theoretical framework is provided by the constant-returns, Cobb–Douglas production function with disembodied technical change, coupled with the assumption of profit maximisation under perfect competition. This forms the theoretical basis of Denison's study,[1] which is, perhaps, the most influential study of comparative growth rates to have emerged so far. Broadly speaking, Denison's object was to measure, for each of nine advanced industrial countries including the United Kingdom,[2] the contributions made to the observed rate of growth in real net national product (N.N.P.) in the post-war period by: (a) the growth of labour input; (b) the growth of capital input; (c) technical progress. Following (12.13), (a) and (b) were measured by determining the growth rate of the input concerned and multiplying the growth rate by the share of the input in N.N.P., while (c) was measured as a residual, i.e. by subtracting the sum of (a) and (b) from the observed rate of growth of real N.N.P.

We shall now attempt to give a brief summary of the main conclusions which emerge from Denison's work, especially as they bear on the question of why the United Kingdom's growth rate has been so much lower than that of other Western European countries in the post-war period.

1. Contribution made by Growth of Labour Input

Denison conceives of labour input as having four dimensions: (i) the number of employed workers; (ii) hours worked; (iii) age and sex distribution of employed workers; and (iv) education of employed workers. Of these four dimensions, the first two relate to the quantity of labour input and the second two to its quality. On this view, the growth in labour input which is observed over any period will be compounded from changes in each of these four constituents; and as well as measuring the contribution made by the growth of labour input as a whole, Denison attempts to measure the contribution made by each constituent separately. We shall begin by sum-

[1] See E. F. Denison, *Why Growth Rates Differ* (Washington: The Brookings Institution, 1967).
[2] The nine countries were the United Kingdom, the United States, Belgium, Norway, Netherlands, Denmark, France, West Germany, Italy.

marising the main findings of the study in relation to the constituents and then consider the findings in relation to labour input as a whole.

The main finding in relation to the constituents of labour input are as follows:

(i) The level of employment in the United Kingdom in 1962 exceeded its level in 1950 by 8·1 per cent. Both the rate of increase of employment per annum (0·65 per cent) and its contribution to the growth rate of real N.N.P. were lower than in West Germany but higher than in France. To some extent this was the result of a low initial degree of unemployment (only 1·3 per cent of the labour force in the United Kingdom as against 7·3 per cent in West Germany in 1950) and a slow rate of natural increase of population.

(ii) Hours worked per year by full-time non-farm wage and salary workers fell steadily over the period in all West European countries. In all of these except France, the rate of fall was greater than in the United Kingdom. In West Germany the fall was particularly large. This is presumed to have had a negative effect on growth rates except to the extent that lower hours helped increase the efficiency of work performed per hour.

(iii) Changes in the age and sex composition of the working force appear to have been only of marginal significance as a source of growth.

(iv) The level of education shows an upward trend in all the countries concerned, as new entrants to the labour force tend to be better educated on average than those leaving it. However, this cannot have been an important source of difference in growth rates since, both as regards the level of education and as regards its rate of increase, there was very little to choose between the various Western European countries.

Turning now to labour input as a whole, Denison finds that during the period 1955–62 the United Kingdom derived less growth from this source than any other country in Europe except Norway. Over the 1950–62 period as a whole, France, Denmark and Norway obtained less growth than the United Kingdom from increased labour input, while the other countries obtained more. However, by and large the differences are not substantial. Moreover, as far as British policy decisions are concerned, the labour supply is relatively less susceptible to control, with one major exception, namely immigration policy. However, immigration policy in Britain is predominantly a political issue and has probably been influenced more by such factors as racial prejudice than by the desire for higher growth rates. On the other hand, if our basic concern is with the growth rate of real output *per capita* rather than that of aggregate real output, an increase in the level of employment may not be helpful unless increases in employment and in productivity per man are mutually correlated (e.g. because of economies of scale).

On the whole, it is difficult to quarrel with Denison's finding that growth policies based on increasing the contribution of labour input have little significance for Britain. One possible reservation concerns the role of education. While Denison's measurement of the contribution of labour input is exceptionally painstaking, it neglects aspects of education other than the time spent in educational institutions and the school-leaving age, and some of these neglected aspects may have important implications for economic growth. Thus, it has been maintained, particularly by representatives of British industry, that the theoretical bias of university education in Britain tends to diminish the contribution that graduates might otherwise make in business. More recently, the possible harmful effects on economic growth of the swing away from science at both school and university levels has been widely commented on. Clearly, such questions cannot be resolved without quantitative research. An attempt to measure the effects of such factors by the use of proxy variables within the general framework of the production function approach could provide useful insights into the role of education in economic growth.

2. *Contribution made by Growth of Capital Input*

As far as the contribution to growth of changes in the capital input is concerned, Denison distinguishes between: (i) the capital of business enterprises (including government enterprises), which is further subdivided into (a) structures and equipment, and (b) inventories; (ii) capital in the form of dwellings; and (iii) capital in the form of international assets. His main finding is that industrial capital accumulation (increase in 'enterprise structures and equipment') contributed in lesser degree to economic growth in the case of the United Kingdom than in the case of any other European country included in the comparison except Belgium. This is ascribed in part to the lower rate of increase of the input itself, the faster growth of enterprise capital being a factor in the faster growth of output in other European countries; this is particularly important in the case of West Germany. In part, the lower contribution of capital formation to growth in the United Kingdom also reflects the lower weight applied to the rate of growth of capital input in the case of the United Kingdom, i.e. the smaller share of profit in the national income. This, in turn, is believed to be the result of a lower rate of return to capital in the United Kingdom. Here there is a link with explanations of Britain's poor growth performance of the Harrod–Domar type, which stress the lower incremental capital–output ratios that tend to prevail in the Continental countries as compared with the United Kingdom (see p. 433 above).

However, although his calculations show a lower contribution of capital formation to the growth rate in the United Kingdom than in the other countries, Denison does not conclude that greater emphasis on investment policy is called for as a means of accelerating British growth. There are two reasons for this. The first is that the magnitude of the contribution made by the capital input to growth appears to have been small in all the countries considered. All types of capital together contributed only about 0·8 percentage points to the growth rate during 1950–62 both in the United States and in the European countries as a group: and the highest figure, for West Germany, was only 1·4 points. Secondly, on more general grounds, he suggests that higher investment is a result, rather than a cause, of higher growth rates: 'Growth may be rapid for reasons unrelated to capital, but a rapid increase in capital is induced by rapid growth.'[1]

3. *Contribution made by Technical Progress*

Denison makes a systematic attempt to make the residual item less of a catch-all both by measuring the labour input in standardised efficiency units and by breaking down the residual into a number of different components. Thus the effect of education on the labour force is taken into account in measuring the labour input itself and hence is no longer (as in most previous studies) a part of the residual (see p. 434 above).

The residual remaining after the contributions of labour and capital to growth have been accounted for, is adjusted to take account of 'special sources', namely (i) differences between the years compared in respect of the pressure of demand; (ii) irregularities in farm output; (iii) balancing of capital stock; and (iv) differences in techniques of deflation used. None of these turns out to be important. Further, an

[1] See E. F. Denison, 'Economic Growth', in R. E. Caves and associates, *Britain's Economic Prospects* (London: Allen & Unwin, 1968) p. 273.

attempt is made to isolate the contribution made to the residual by important changes in resource allocation, in particular by the contraction of employment in agriculture and non-farm self-employment relative to employment in manufacturing industry. Such reallocation of resources is found to have been an important source of growth in countries other than the United Kingdom essentially because the proportion of agricultural employment and non-farm self-employment in total employment was much larger in the other countries than in the United Kingdom to start with. Next, an adjustment is made to take account of economies of scale. However, this adjustment is suspect since the estimation of scale effects within the framework of a model which assumes constant returns must be considered unsatisfactory.

The residual which still remains after these adjustments have been made is divided into two items, namely (i) advances of knowledge and (ii) changes in the rate of application of new knowledge and errors and omissions. However, this division is made on the basis of a comparison with the residual computed for the United States which is attributed to 'advances of knowledge' alone, lags in application as well as errors and omissions being assumed to be negligible. Since this is a highly arbitrary procedure, the analytic significance of the division would appear to be small. It seems preferable, therefore, to consider the final residual as consisting of the items (i) and (ii) together. This residual is found to be an important source of growth, particularly in the United Kingdom where it contributed a third of the observed growth rate of real N.N.P. during 1950–62. Denison attributes this to factors connected in some way with technological progress which were not isolated in the analysis itself.

It would appear, therefore, that from the point of view of British growth policy, the most important conclusion of Denison's study is that it is (disembodied) technical change which holds the key to faster growth. 'The future British growth rate will depend decisively on the group of income determinants whose effects are combined in the measure of "residual efficiency".'[1] Strictly speaking, this conclusion does not follow from Denison's statistical analysis, which shows that the rate of growth of residual productivity

$$\left(\frac{d \log A(t)}{dt} \right)$$

[1] See Denison, 'Economic Growth', p. 274.

in the post-war period has been about the same in Britain as elsewhere in Europe. To support his conclusion, Denison brings in the *level* of residual productivity (i.e. the difference in output as between different countries in the same time period which remain after adjustments have been made for differences in inputs and in scale and allocation effects). He finds that throughout the period this level was lower in Europe than in the United States and that the gap was wider in the case of the United Kingdom than in the case of the other Western European countries. He concludes that to 'catch up', Britain needs to achieve a higher rate of growth of 'residual productivity' than her European neighbours:

> Income per worker in the European countries cannot reach the United States level if the gap in residual productivity is not eliminated. On the other hand, any European country that could cut into the gap between itself and the United States could raise its growth rate substantially for a long time. The United Kingdom has a greater potential to do so than the other countries because the gap is greater. If residual productivity could even be raised to the level of France or Germany during the next decade or so, this would introduce a major break in the trend of British growth during this period.
>
> Although something might be done to raise the contribution from other growth determinants, there is no prospect that the growth rate of the United Kingdom will be as high as can reasonably be anticipated for most of the other countries unless it cuts the gap in residual productivity more than they do.[1]

Among the main suggestions which Denison makes for an improvement along these lines is the intensification of competition 'by whatever means are at hand' including major changes in the legal structure. It is suggested that a once-for-all recession of depth and duration sufficient to create a real fight for markets, and, through greater unemployment, to improve workers' performance, could also help.

12.4 Raising Britain's Growth Rate: Assessment of Policy Proposals

We now proceed to discuss the validity of the policy conclusions described in the preceding section. It seems appropriate to begin with an 'historical' comment. The production-function approach, in its

[1] Ibid., p. 275.

simple Cobb–Douglas form with 'disembodied' technical progress, was first applied empirically to estimate the relative contributions of capital accumulation and technological progress to the economic growth of the United States.[1] The conclusion which emerged was that technological progress – a rise in factor productivity – was the decisive source of U.S. growth. This result was thought to have implications for policy. Thus it was suggested that, in order to achieve higher growth rates, national policies should be focused not so much on movements along the production function as on movements of the production function itself. Inventiveness and entrepreneurial dynamism rather than austerity or the share of national output that was ploughed back to increase the stock of capital were held to be the keys to growth. Denison's study of economic growth in Western Europe is in essence based on the same growth model. His results, and the conclusions for British growth policy that he derived from them, are also largely similar.

It seems reasonable to say that one's assessment of policy conclusions must depend crucially one one's assessment of the model from which they are derived. As the controversy about models applying the production-function approach to the analysis of growth has centred on the interpretation of the residual (or, what comes to the same thing, on the treatment of technical change), we shall discuss this first.

Here the basic difficulty lies in interpreting, as the measure of technical progress, the residual left after the contribution to growth of all other sources included in the analysis has been estimated. In fact, however, this residual will reflect much else besides technical progress. In the first place it will reflect the effects of all omitted variables. Secondly it will incorporate the effects of errors of measurement. These may arise in a variety of ways. Thus they may be simply errors of observation. Again, and this is probably more important in the present context, they may arise through errors in specification, i.e. errors arising from the fact that the statistical data used as the basis for estimation correspond to concepts which are different from those required by the theory. Familiar examples of such specification errors in production-function analysis are errors in the measurement of inputs (differences in the intensity of work

[1] See E. F. Denison, *The Sources of Economic Growth in the United States and the Alternatives before Us* (New York: Committee for Economic Development, 1962).

would, for example, be included in the residual item) and errors of aggregation which are involved in combining different components of output and of labour and capital inputs into the corresponding national indices. Less obvious, but probably more significant in their effect, are specification errors which arise from complementarities between the different factors contributing to economic growth. We shall now discuss these in rather more detail.

The production-function analysis of growth rests on the assumption that the contributions of the individual factors are separable and mutually additive. This contrasts for example, with the approach to the study of growth normally adopted by economic historians who emphasise the mutual interactions between the different elements in the growth process. If such interactions are indeed substantial, neglecting them in the quantitative assessment of sources of growth may be misleading.

Complementarities may be of different types. Thus, as has been emphasised in some of the more recent models of growth, the rate of capital formation interacts with other elements in the growth process in a number of ways. First, as we pointed out in the previous section, capital formation is itself the vehicle of technical progress since it is often through new additions to the capital stock that technical change is introduced into the economic system. Technical change is then said to be of the 'embodied' form. A rise in the rate of investment, a reduction in the average age of equipment and a faster pace of technical progress thus tend to be correlated.

Secondly, capital formation tends to have a favourable effect on productivity by influencing the rate of learning. The learning effect of capital formation not only helps in keeping the technology used near the production frontier (in Denison's terminology, in reducing 'lags in application of knowledge'), but also in shifting the frontier itself outward (in contributing to 'advances of knowledge').

Thirdly, in addition to embodying technological progress and encouraging the learning effect, new capital is often essential for bringing about a redistribution of resources within the economy. This aspect is emphasised by the putty–clay type of vintage model developed by Johansen,[1] which allows unlimited substitutability between factors *ex ante* but zero substitutability once the capital is installed, i.e. perfect freedom in the choice of factor proportions at

[1] See L. Johansen, 'Substitution versus Fixed Production Coefficients in the Theory of Economic Growth: A Synthesis', *Econometrica* (Apr 1959).

P

the stage where equipment is designed, but fixed factor proportions over the working life of equipment once it is in use. To the extent that such models are a realistic description of the technology of manufacturing industry (and there is some evidence that they are), the achievement of increased output through the movement of labour from agriculture or retail trade to manufacturing industry, where the value of its marginal productivity is higher, will be limited by the rate at which new capital is being formed in the latter sector. The effect of the rate of investment is thus correlated with what has been described as 'the reallocation effect'.

So far we have been concerned with complementarities connected with the capital input. However, complementarities may also arise in the context of the labour input: education is a case in point. Thus, in statistical studies of the production function, the measured contribution of education refers only to its direct influence on the effective supply of the labour input. The indirect effects of the greater education of the working force in making possible wider and quicker adoption of new and improved technology may indeed be more important. At the same time the magnitude of the contribution made to output by educated people in general, and people engaged in research and development in particular, will itself depend on the pace of technological change.

The significance of complementarities for the production-function analysis of growth is that they give rise to an identification problem. Thus, if a Cobb–Douglas production function is being used as a basis for analysing growth in an economy in which capital formation is interacting with technical progress, a low measured output elasticity of capital together with a high residual may have the same interpretative significance as a high output elasticity of capital and a low residual. Policy conclusions based on the production-function analysis alone may then be seriously misleading.

So far, we have been concerned with the validity of interpreting the residual as a measure of technical progress. We now consider the nature of the causal relationship between technical progress and the rate of growth.

Even if one accepts the residual as a genuine measure of the 'improvement' factor, one cannot *a priori* rule out the possibility that it is the high growth rate that causes 'improvement' rather than the other way round. One element in 'improvement' relates to managerial efficiency or business dynamism in general. Economic historians have often ascribed periods of marked entrepreneurial dynamism to the experience of high and sustained growth rates in the economy. According to Beckerman,[1] the superior entrepreneurial performance of the French and Italians compared with the British in the recent past may be such a case. Thus, he argues that it is confident expectations, based on high rates of growth of demand, that have led to the recent striking improvements in the economic performance of French entrepreneurs who previously had been reputed to be anything but dynamic.

The core of truth in this argument, namely that the factors which tend to favour rapid economic growth are highly correlated among themselves, has already been emphasised above. However, in its specific application to the relative performance of the British economy in the post-war period, the argument fails to convince. First, the contention that the higher growth rate in France itself provides an incentive to greater entrepreneurial dynamism as compared with Britain requires not merely the assumption that growth rates, through creating confident expectations about future demand, influence economic performance directly, but also the far more questionable assumption that only *domestic* growth rates have this effect. The high and sustained expansion of the European economy, and indeed of the world economy as a whole, in the last two decades and the absence of a major recession have provided British no less than French entrepreneurs with opportunities. There is much independent evidence that the British have been slower to grasp them.

Secondly, the concept of dynamic entrepreneurship – 'animal spirits' as Mrs Robinson has described it[2] – has always been associated with the willingness to take risks, to seek out new markets and not merely follow existing ones, and in general to respond in all possible ways to the challenge of a new economic situation. It is in this respect that British business effort is alleged to be lagging behind. Beckerman's emphasis on demand projections, which is itself a necessary element in the total explanation, cannot provide an answer to this particular charge.

The most important conclusion which emerges from our discussion is that the variables, both 'economic' and 'non-economic', which are

---

[1] See W. Beckerman and Associates, *The British Economy in 1975* (Cambridge University Press, 1965) esp. chap. ii.

[2] See J. Robinson, *Collected Economic Papers*, vol. ii (Oxford: Basil Blackwell, 1964) p. 97.

involved in the process of economic growth are highly interrelated. This makes the quantitative estimation of their effects in terms of a Cobb–Douglas or any other form of production function a hazardous undertaking. Moreover, not merely do different elements in the growth process interact; a high growth rate itself has a feedback effect on the elements causing it. Hence, an attempt to distinguish between the 'supply' and the 'demand' factors – operating on the growth rate – gives rise to an identification problem of a particularly difficult kind. In an economy, such as the British, where a low growth rate has operated over a relatively long period, evidence for both supply and demand interpretations of slow growth is accordingly easy to come by. A more systematic attempt to identify the causal relationships involved by the use of appropriate econometric methods appears to be essential for deriving meaningful conclusions on growth policy.

Secondly, our discussion suggests that there is no single master-key to growth. While a faster pace of disembodied technical progress, including in particular an improvement in the quality of managerial performance, may indeed be necessary for a higher British growth rate, on the available evidence the role of capital formation seems no less important. This follows from our discussion above of the inter-relationship of technical progress and the rate of investment. It is also suggested by the fact that, in terms of structures and equipment other than housing, both the level of the capital stock per head in 1964 and the total quantity of investment per head over the period 1950–62 were lower for the United Kingdom than for any other country in Western Europe excepting Italy. The average British worker thus works with a smaller amount of capital than his counterpart elsewhere, which is clearly likely to have an unfavourable effect on productivity.

Finally, a higher growth rate is not to be valued as such but rather for the contribution it makes to social welfare. This indeed is the rationale of the welfare-maximising approach to economic growth discussed in the previous chapter. The welfare aspects of growth have received less attention in the recent debate on British economic growth, which has been concerned almost exclusively with relative growth rates. Thus, Britain's lagging behind in the rate of growth of productivity has been ascribed in large measure to certain long-standing features of British institutions and society which affect the performance of both management and workers. They relate to the degree of competitiveness, the extent of leisure-preference, restrictive practices, the nature of collective bargaining and so on. The persistence of such social–cultural patterns may, in part, simply reflect the force of inertia in a slow-growing economy. However, they may also partly reflect genuine social preferences which must be given due weight in deciding on policies.[1] Hence, Britain's relative slowness to change her methods of industrial organisation – even though, as Denison points out, 'the American model was available for imitation[2] – may not be due to incompetence alone: the desire to imitate may have been lacking.

There are two important difficulties in such an interpretation which one must guard against. First, value-judgements of different persons may be conflicting. It is only too easy to put forward one's own personal value-judgements in the guise of a social consensus which may not exist.[3] Secondly, the significant differences between value-judgements are likely to be essentially quantitative in character. Thus, for example, from the policy point of view, it is not very helpful to say that there should be a trade-off between extra output and pleasant working conditions unless one is also prepared to hazard an estimate of how large, approximately, the trade-off should be. It is such a spelling-out of what alternative value-judgements entail, in terms of quantifiable consequences, which along can provide a basis for informed decision-making by society. As our survey of the literature in the last two chapters shows, economics has started to move along this direction but it still has a long way to go.

12.5 Summary

While the previous chapter was concerned with the problems involved in choosing a desirable growth rate, this chapter considers

---

[1] This has recently been stressed by R. F. Harrod (*Economica*, Aug 1969, p. 325) in reviewing Denison's study: 'Nearly half a man's waking life – and perhaps more than half if we exclude routine occupations like dressing and tooth-brushing – is spent at work. Part of our objective should be to ensure that he is content and happy during the hours of work . . . . There should be a trade-off between extra output and pleasant working conditions. The latter are included in our total "way of life".'   [2] See Denison, *Why Growth Rates Differ*, p. 340.

[3] Thus, Harrod thinks that 'At our present rate of work, we have established, subject to bad patches, such as exist in all countries, a rather notably happy way of life' (op. cit., p. 325). This contrasts with Stone's view (*A Computable Model of Economic Growth*, p. 2) that the British rate of growth is too low: ' . . . But we are not satisfied: we strike for higher incomes; we worry about inflation; we grumble about taxes; we want to carry more weight in international affairs; some of us may even want to improve the living conditions of other races.'

how a chosen growth rate might in practice be achieved. Various growth models, in particular the Harrod–Domar model, the neoclassical model with disembodied technical change, and the neoclassical model with embodied technical change are explored in turn in order to build up a conceptual framework for analysing the determination of economic growth rates in advanced countries. The relative contribution of different factors, in particular of investment and technical progress, to the explanation of the relative growth performance of Western European countries in the post-Second World War period is then examined within this framework. The conclusion is drawn that there is no single master-key to growth and that disembodied technical progress as well as faster capital formation are essential if a higher growth rate of the British economy is to be achieved.

READING LIST

Arrow, K. J., 'The Economic Implication of Learning by Doing', *Review of Economic Studies* (June 1962).

Barna, T., *Investment and Growth Policies in British Industrial Firms* (Cambridge University Press, 1962).

Beckerman, W., and Associates, *The British Economy in 1975* (Cambridge University Press, 1965).

Johansen, L., 'Substitution versus Fixed Production Coefficients in the Theory of Economic Growth: A Synthesis', *Econometrica* (Apr 1959).

Solow, R. M., 'Technical Change and the Aggregate Production Function', *Review of Economics and Statistics* (Aug 1957).

——, 'Investment and Technical Progress', in Arrow, K. J., Karlin, S., and Suppes, P. (eds), *Mathematical Methods in the Social Sciences* (Stanford University Press, 1960).

Swan, T., 'Economic Growth and Capital Accumulation', *Economic Record* (Nov 1956).

PART FOUR

Interrelationships between Objectives

13 Internal Balance and Price Stability

13.1 Interdependence of Objectives

In Chapters 6–12 each of the four objectives of macro-economic policy dealt with in this book was considered in isolation, though the high degree of interdependence between the objectives was explicitly recognised. Thus in Chapter 6 we discussed the measures by which the authorities can pursue the internal balance objective without considering the significance of these measures for the remaining objectives, even though, as made clear in Chapters 7–10, they are highly relevant to external balance and price stability as well. Again, in discussing anti-inflation policy in Chapter 10 the question whether the attainment of the price-stability objective would help or hinder the attainment of the growth objective was not raised, though it has been much debated at various levels in recent years. This 'one-at-a-time' approach was adopted partly to simplify the exposition and also because it seemed clear to us that no proper discussion of the inter-relationship between objectives would be possible until each objective had been considered in detail by itself. However that may be, we shall now attempt to restore the balance by taking up the question of interdependence of objectives in the three remaining chapters of the book. In this chapter we shall deal with the interrelationship between the objectives of internal balance and price stability, in the next with the interrelationship between internal and external balance, and in the final chapter with the interrelationship between the price-stability and growth objectives.

The problem to be considered in the present chapter can be formulated in the following way. The empirical studies summarised in section 10.6 suggest that, at least as far as the British economy is concerned, internal balance and price stability may well be incompatible objectives. For what these studies show is that, if anti-inflationary policy consists of demand restriction alone, the achievement of price stability may require a level of unemployment of something like $2\frac{1}{2}$ per cent. This figure could be reduced somewhat if demand restriction were to be supported by a well-conceived and vigorous prices and incomes policy, but even the reduced figure is likely to be well above the figure (1 per cent has been suggested; see p. 358 above) which corresponds to internal balance. In short, it appears from the available empirical work that price stability and internal balance are likely to be incompatible in the sense that one or other is attainable but not both.

In these circumstances it will be necessary for the authorities to decide between the following three courses of action: (i) achievement of price stability whatever the consequent departure from internal balance; (ii) achievement of internal balance whatever the consequent departure from price stability; (iii) some compromise between (i) and (ii) such that, while neither objective is fully realised, the departure from internal balance is less than in (i) and the departure from price stability is less than in (ii). Under (i) price stability is made an over-riding objective, while under (ii) internal balance is given absolute priority. Under (iii) neither objective overrides the other; some departure from price stability (internal balance) is tolerated in the interests of a smaller departure from internal balance (price stability) than would otherwise be necessary, i.e. there is some 'trading-off' between the two objectives.

If the third course of action is decided on, the authorities will then face the problem of choosing the 'best' combination of price in-stability and demand deficiency, in some sense. Should the aim be a rate of price rise of, say, x per cent per annum coupled with a demand deficiency of £y per annum, or would a rate of price rise of r per cent per annum together with a demand deficiency of £s per annum be a better result? Is there some combination of the rate of price rise and the level of demand deficiency which would be better than either o the above? This is the problem which will occupy our attention in the present chapter. Two approaches to this problem have been developed in recent years: the 'static' approach and the 'dynamic' approach. The static approach, which is the simpler of the two, will be discussed in the next section. The more sophisticated dynamic approach will be dealt with in section 13.3. Section 13.4 will be concerned with some empirical work which is relevant to both approaches.

13.2 The Static Approach

The basis of the static approach[1] is a social utility function which shows the rate of social utility at time t as depending on: (i) the proportionate rate of increase of prices at time t; and (ii) the unemployment percentage at time t. Thus, if we denote the rate of social utility at time t by U, the proportionate rate of increase of prices[2] at time t by p and the unemployment percentage at time t by s, we have as our basic relationship:

$$U = \psi(p, s). \tag{13.1}$$

Various restrictions are imposed on this function. In particular it is assumed that: (i) $\psi_p < 0$; (ii) $\psi_s < 0$; (iii) $\psi_{ss} < 0$; (iv) $\psi_{ps} \geq 0$; (v) $\psi_{pp} < 0$; where ψ_p denotes $\partial\psi/\partial p$, ψ_s denotes $\partial\psi/\partial s$, ψ_{ss} denotes $\partial/\partial s(\partial\psi/\partial s)$, ψ_{pp} denotes $\partial/\partial p(\partial\psi/\partial p)$ and ψ_{ps} denotes $\partial/\partial s(\partial\psi/\partial p)$. Restrictions (i) and (ii) mean that for a fixed unemployment percentage (fixed rate of price increase) the rate of social utility declines as the rate of price increase (unemployment percentage) increases. The third (fifth) restriction implies that the rate of social utility declines at an increasing rate as the unemployment percentage (rate of price increase) increases, given the rate of price increase (unemployment percentage). Finally, restriction (iv) implies that the rate of decline of social utility with an increase in p, s given, does not increase as the given s increases. The combined effect of these restrictions is that the social utility function (13.1) can be represented graphically by means of a family of social indifference curves of the type shown in Fig. 13.1 by AB, CD and EF. That is, each member of the family is negatively sloped at all points and the slope becomes increasingly negative as one proceeds from left to right along the curve.[3]

---

[1] For examples of this approach see R. G. Lipsey, 'Structural and Deficient-Demand Unemployment Reconsidered', in R. M. Ross (ed.), *Employment-Policy and the Labor Market* (Berkeley: University of California Press, 1965), and F. Brechling, 'The Trade-off between Inflation and Unemployment', *Journal of Political Economy* (July/Aug 1968).

[2] In this chapter we propose to depart from the 'dot' notation for proportionate rates of increase which we have used in Chapters 9, 10 and 12 because we wish to keep our notation in line with the notation used in the basic literature on the inflation–unemployment interrelationship. We shall return to the dot notation in Chapter 15.

[3] From restrictions (i) and (ii) we have:

$$\frac{dp}{ds} = -\frac{\psi_s}{\psi_p} < 0.$$

To the social utility function of (13.1) is added the relationship:

$$p = f(s). \tag{13.2}$$

This is sometimes referred to as the 'quasi-Phillips' relationship because it emerges when the hypothesis: $p = h(w)$, where w denotes

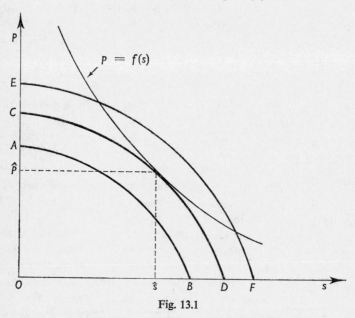

Fig. 13.1

the proportionate rate of increase of money wage earnings, is combined with the Phillips relationship: $w = g(s)$. The curve of (13.2) is assumed to be negatively sloped at all points ($f' < 0$), the justification being that the curve of $p = h(w)$ is positively sloped at all points and the curve of $w = g(s)$ negatively sloped at all points. It is also assumed

---

From restrictions (i)—(iv) and $dp/ds < 0$ we have:

$$\frac{d^2 p}{ds^2} = \frac{d}{ds}\left(-\frac{\psi_s}{\psi_p}\right)$$

$$= \frac{-\psi_p \dfrac{d}{ds}(\psi_s) + \psi_s \dfrac{d}{ds}(\psi_p)}{(\psi_p)^2}$$

$$= \frac{-\psi_p\left(\psi_{sp}\dfrac{dp}{ds} + \psi_{ss}\right) + \psi_s\left(\psi_{ps} + \psi_{pp}\dfrac{dp}{ds}\right)}{(\psi_p)^2} < 0.$$

that the slope becomes less negative as s increases ($f'' > 0$). Thus the quasi-Phillips curve is assumed to have the general form shown in Fig. 13.1.

In the static approach the 'best' unemployment percentage ($\hat{s}$) is found by maximising (13.1) subject to (13.2). The best rate of price increase ($\hat{p}$) is then found by substituting the best unemployment percentage into (13.2). Thus in the static approach, the solution of the problem of finding the best combination of price instability and demand deficiency proceeds as follows. Use (13.2) to write (13.1) as:

$$U = \psi(f(s), s). \tag{13.3}$$

Now take the derivative of ψ with respect to s and equate the resulting expression to zero:

$$\frac{d\psi}{ds} = \psi_p f'(s) + \psi_s = 0 \tag{13.4}$$

which gives:

$$f'(s) = -\frac{\psi_s}{\psi_p}. \tag{13.5}$$

Given the restrictions imposed on the functions ψ and f, the unemployment percentage which satisfies (13.5) must maximise social utility.[1] In terms of Fig. 13.1, the s which maximises social utility is given by the point at which the quasi-Phillips curve is tangential to an indifference curve, i.e. the maximising s is $\hat{s}$ with which is associated a rate of inflation $\hat{p}$.

As will be clear from the above discussion, the static approach is valid only if the quasi-Phillips curve does not shift over the planning interval. It is this limitation of the static approach which is stressed by the advocates of the dynamic approach. Their argument is that the quasi-Phillips curve is bound to shift with changes in the expected rate of inflation. Moreover, since the expected rate of inflation moves in response to the actual rate of inflation, the decision about the unemployment percentage which the authorities take today will help to determine the position of tomorrow's quasi-Phillips curve via today's rate of inflation, and hence, in part, will determine the constraints within which they must operate in deciding on tomorrow's unemployment percentage. This being so, the problem of choosing the best

[1] We have from (13.4):

$$\frac{d^2\psi}{ds^2} = \psi_p f''(s) + f'(s)[\psi_{pp} f'(s) + \psi_{ps}] + \psi_{sp} f'(s) + \psi_{ss} < 0.$$

combination of price instability and demand deficiency must be treated as a time-optimisation problem of a fairly complicated kind rather than as a conventional maximisation problem. So far the most notable contribution to the theoretical literature from this standpoint is that of Phelps,[1] and we shall devote the next section to an account of his work.

13.3 The Dynamic Approach

Our discussion of Phelps's path-breaking work will make use of the following notation which is close to, but not identical with, the notation which he uses.[2]

U = rate of social utility at time t

p = proportionate rate of increase of price level ('actual rate of inflation') at time t

x = expected proportionate rate of increase of price level ('expected rate of inflation') at time t

y = employment–capital ratio ('utilization ratio') at time t

r = real rate of interest at time t

i = money rate of interest at time t.

In terms of this notation Phelps's final formulation of the authorities' time-optimisation problem is as follows:[3]

To find a time path for y from time 0 onwards such that the sum of all future utilities, i.e.:

$$W = \int_0^\infty U(x, y)\, dt \qquad (13.6)$$

is maximised subject to:

$$\frac{dx}{dt} = G(y) \qquad (13.7)$$

$$x(0) = x_0. \qquad (13.8)$$

Our first task in the present section will be to explain the argument which underlies this particular formulation of the time-optimisation problem. Having completed this task we shall then proceed to consider how the problem can be solved once it has been set up in this

[1] See E. S. Phelps, 'Phillips Curves, Expectations of Inflation and Optimal Unemployment over Time', *Economica* (Aug 1967).

[2] In particular, it should be noted that Phelps uses x to denote the expected rate of *de*flation, i.e. Phelps's x is the negative of ours.

[3] The formulation which follows is for the case where there is no discounting of future utilities. Phelps also considers the case where future utilities are discounted. See Phelps, op. cit., pp. 278–81.

way. For this purpose we shall make considerable use of various restrictions which Phelps imposes on certain key functional relationships and which we shall introduce in the next subsection. On a first reading the reader may find it difficult to keep a hold on these restrictions, and to assist him we have collected them together in Appendix 13.1 in the form of a numbered list. This list will enable the reader who wishes to revise any particular restriction, in order to understand the argument fully, to locate quickly the page of the text on which that restriction was introduced.

1. The Formulation of the Problem

To explain the basis of the formulation of (13.6)–(13.8), one must explain the argument underlying the functions $G(y)$ and $U(x, y)$, since these, obviously, are the key elements.[1] This we shall now do.

(a) *The function* $G(y)$. The function $G(y)$, which gives the absolute rate of change of the expected rate of inflation in terms of the utilisation ratio, is derived from the following two relationships in which f and a are functions:

$$p = f(y) + x \qquad f'(y) > 0; f''(y) > 0 \qquad (13.9)$$

$$\frac{dx}{dt} = a(p - x) \qquad a(0) = 0; a' > 0. \qquad (13.10)$$

Substituting (13.9) into (13.10) we get:

$$\frac{dx}{dt} = a(f(y)).$$

Alternatively we have:

$$\frac{dx}{dt} = G(y) \qquad (13.11)$$

where $G(y) = a(f(y))$. To explain the function $G(y)$, therefore, it is necessary to present the reasoning underlying (13.9) and (13.10). Let us begin with (13.9).

To see the logic of relationship (13.9), first take the case where $x = 0$. We then have:

$$p = f(y) \qquad f'(y) > 0; f''(y) > 0. \qquad (13.12)$$

Relationship (13.12) defines a curve with the properties of the curve shown in Fig. 13.2. Essentially this is the quasi-Phillips curve of

---

[1] Relationship (13.8) merely specifies an initial value of x and hence requires no explanation.

Fig. 13.1. The latter shows p falling with increasing s. But increasing s means decreasing y. Hence the curve of Fig. 13.1 can be translated into a curve which shows p falling with decreasing y, as in Fig. 13.2.

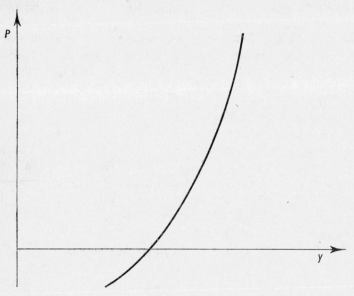

Fig. 13.2

Also, since the slope of the curve in Fig. 13.1 increases numerically (becomes more and more negative) as s decreases, the slope of the curve in Fig. 13.2 must also increase numerically (become more and more positive) as y increases, again as in Fig. 13.2. Thus we can say that, with $x=0$, relationship (13.9) defines the usual quasi-Phillips curve, albeit in an unfamiliar guise. It follows that relationship (13.9) is a generalisation of relationship (13.2) of the previous section in that it defines a *family* of quasi-Phillips curves, each member of which corresponds to a particular expected rate of inflation. The implication of (13.9) is that an increase of one point in the expected rate of inflation will cause a uniform vertical displacement of one point in the quasi-Phillips curve of Fig. 13.2.

In support of (13.9) it could be argued that an increase in the expected rate of inflation will cause workers and others to take protective steps and that these are bound to raise the actual rate of inflation even with no increase in the utilisation ratio. For example, an increase in the expected rate of inflation will cause the trade unions to seek larger wage increases than they would have done otherwise, even with no increase in the utilisation ratio; and, *ceteris paribus*, this will mean a higher actual rate of inflation quite apart from any increase in the utilisation ratio.

In Fig. 13.3 we show three members of the family of quasi-Phillips curves defined by (13.9) – those corresponding to $x = 0.01$, $x = 0$ and $x = -0.01$. The point y^*, where the curve corresponding to $x = 0$ cuts

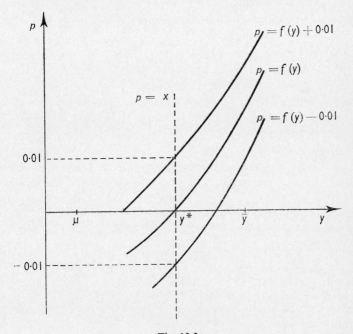

Fig. 13.3

the horizontal axis, is the unique value of y which makes $f(y) = 0$. In other words, y^* is that value of the utilisation ratio at which the actual rate of inflation and the expected rate are identical. In this sense it is the equilibrium utilisation ratio. Before leaving relationship (13.9) we must mention the two other special values of y which are shown in Fig. 13.3, namely μ and $\bar{y}$. These are, respectively, the lower and upper bounds on the utilisation ratio. Thus it is assumed that y cannot fall below some positive figure μ, nor rise above some positive figure $\bar{y}$. The justification for the finite upper bound is straightforward – the utilisation ratio (employment–capital ratio) must have an upper bound since at any point of time the labour force has an upper bound determined by the size of the population and the labour-force participation rate. The justification for making the lower bound positive rather than zero is rather more complicated. First it is assumed that the authorities take the necessary steps to ensure that real investment expenditure grows along some specified path. There will be some small utilisation ratio such that output is just sufficient to permit realisation of this investment programme, i.e. at which real consumption expenditure is zero. Call this particular utilisation ratio μ. Below μ consumption expenditure must be negative, given that the marginal productivity of labour is positive. But negative consumption is impossible. Hence the utilisation ratio cannot fall below μ.

We turn now to relationship (13.10), which embodies a mechanism for determining movements in the expected rate of inflation. According to this relationship the speed of change in the expected rate at any point of time is governed by the size of the discrepancy between the actual and the expected rates at that point of time. More precisely, the absolute rate of change of the expected rate of inflation is specified to be some increasing function of the excess of the actual rate of inflation over the expected rate such that there is no change in the expected rate when the actual rate and the expected rate are the same, i.e. when $p = x$ or when $y = y^*$. Thus the relationship will be of the type shown by the curve in Fig. 13.4.

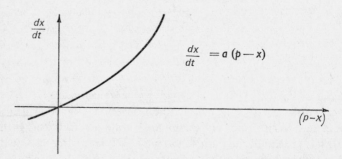

$$\frac{dx}{dt} = a\,(p - x)$$

Fig. 13.4

The curve shown in Fig. 13.4 implies $a'' > 0$. Actually the restriction which Phelps imposes on a'' is weaker than this; a'' can be zero, positive or negative provided it is not 'too negative' (see footnote below).

The restrictions imposed on the functions $a(p-x)$ and $f(y)$ imply certain restrictions on $G(y)$. Since $G(y)=a(f(y))$ and $a(0)=0$, it follows that $G(y)=0$ when $f(y)=0$, i.e. when $y=y^*$. Also, from the fact that a is an increasing function of f which is, in turn, an increasing function of y, it follows that $G'>0$. Finally, the restriction on a'' referred to in the previous paragraph, together with the restriction on f'', ensure that $G''>0$.[1]

(b) *The function* $U(x, y)$. Here Phelps's starting-point is a utility function in which the arguments are i and y:

$$U=\phi(i, y). \tag{13.13}$$

Various restrictions are placed on this function, and since these play an important part in the subsequent discussion, we shall begin by considering them in some detail.

First, certain restrictions are placed on $\delta\phi/\delta y$ to be denoted by ϕ_2. The nature of these restrictions can be seen from Fig. 13.5, which shows the variation of ϕ with y, for a fixed i ($\bar{i}$). The idea behind this curve is that as the utilisation ratio increases, so does output and hence consumption.[2] Consumption being one of society's 'basic desiderata', social utility will tend to rise as y increases. On the other hand, as y increases available leisure falls. Leisure being another social desideratum, social utility will tend to fall as y increases. For small values of y the first tendency is the more powerful of the two, so that at the lower end of the feasible y range social utility rises with increasing y. However, as y increases, the strength of the second tendency increases relative to that of the first and there will be some utilisation ratio less than $\bar{y}$ (say y^0) such that the gain in utility via increased consumption is exactly offset by the loss via reduced leisure at y^0, and more than offset beyond y^0. Thus the $\phi(\bar{i}, y)$ curve has a positive slope ($\phi_2>0$) up to y^0, reaches a maximum ($\phi_2=0$)

---

[1] From $G(y)=a(f(y))$ we have:

$$G'=a'f'.$$

Hence:

$$G''=a'f''+f'a''f'=(f')^2\left[\frac{a'f''}{(f')^2}+a''\right].$$

The restriction on a'' is:

$$a''>\frac{-a'f''}{(f')^2}.$$

This ensures that the square bracket in the above expression for G'' is positive and hence that $G''>0$.

[2] Recall that investment is regarded as a datum (see p. 458 above).

at y^0 and has a negative slope ($\phi_2 < 0$) beyond y^0. Further, it is postulated that y^0 exceeds the equilibrium utilisation ratio y^* and that

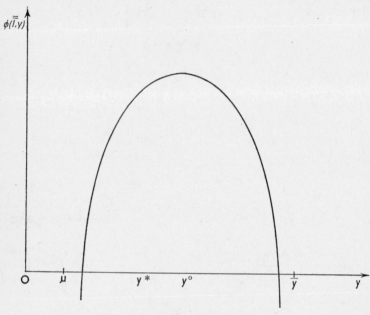

Fig. 13.5

disutility increases without limit both as y becomes increasingly small ($\phi(\bar{i}, y) \to -\infty$ as $y \to \mu$) and as y becomes increasingly large ($\phi(\bar{i}, y) \to -\infty$ as $y \to \bar{y}$). In short, the variation of ϕ with y for fixed i is as illustrated by the curve of Fig. 13.5. This curve implies the further restriction: $\phi_{22} < 0$, where ϕ_{22} denotes $\partial^2\phi/\partial y^2$.

Restrictions are also placed on $\partial\phi/\partial i$. Before we can explain these, we must refer to the bounds which are imposed on i. The lower bound is assumed to be zero on the ground that since money can be held without physical cost, no one will lend at a negative rate of interest. The upper bound is assumed to be some positive constant i_b. This is referred to as the 'barter point' and is defined as a rate of interest which is so high that money ceases to be held at that or any higher rate of interest because no one is prepared to tolerate the high opportunity cost involved. It is also necessary at this point to introduce $\hat{i}$. This is some low but positive interest rate such that at this or lower rates the incentive to economise on the stock of money held for transactions purposes is so weak that all transactions balances are held in the form of money. A situation characterised by $i \leq \bar{i}$ is described as a state of 'full liquidity'.

Turn now to the restrictions on $\partial\phi/\partial i$ to be denoted by ϕ_1. These can be followed with the help of Fig. 13.6, which shows the variation of ϕ with i for given y ($\bar{y}$). This curve is horizontal in the full-liquidity

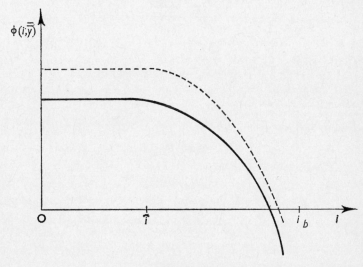

Fig. 13.6

range, $0 \leq i \leq \hat{i}$, has a negative slope in the range $\hat{i} \leq i \leq i_b$ and tends to $-\infty$ as i approaches its upper limit i_b. The idea here is that, by definition, there is no incentive to economise on the stock of money held for transactions purposes when i is in the full-liquidity range. Hence as the rate of interest increases between 0 and $\hat{i}$, there will be no loss of leisure from efforts to economise and hence, in turn, no loss of utility, i.e. when $0 \leq i \leq \hat{i}$ the $\phi(i, \bar{y})$ curve will be horizontal ($\phi_1 = 0$). As i increases above $\hat{i}$, however, leisure, and hence utility, will be increasingly lost through efforts to economise. Hence in the range $\hat{i} < i \leq i_b$ the curve will have a negative slope ($\phi_1 < 0$). Furthermore, the nearer i is to i_b, the greater is the loss of leisure, and hence utility, flowing from a further increase in i because the greater is the incentive to economise. Thus, between $\hat{i}$ and i_b the $\phi(i, \bar{y})$ curve will have an increasingly negative slope ($\phi_{11} < 0$ where ϕ_{11} denotes

$\partial^2\phi/\delta i^2$). In short, the $\phi(i, \bar{y})$ curve will have the general appearance of the curve shown in Fig. 13.6.

There is one further restriction on $\delta\phi/\delta i$ which can be explained by reference to the dotted curve in Fig. 13.6. This shows the variation of ϕ with i for a value of y which is higher than the value to which the unbroken curve relates. (We assume that both ys are between μ and y^0). It is required that the dotted curve should be horizontal in the full-liquidity range, like the original curve ($\phi_{12}=0$ in the full-liquidity range where ϕ_{12} denotes $\frac{\delta}{\delta y}(\frac{\delta\phi}{\delta i})$, and that its slope should not exceed that of the original curve outside the full-liquidity range ($\phi_{12} \le 0$ outside the full-liquidity range).

Having discussed the utility function: $U=\phi(i, y)$, we next consider its transformation into a function which has x and y as arguments. This transformation is based on the following new relationships:

$$i = r + x \qquad (13.14)$$

$$r = r(y) \qquad r(y) > 0; \; r'(y) > 0; \; r''(y) \ge 0. \qquad (13.15)$$

Relationship (13.14) is definitional in character; it arises from the definition of the real rate of interest as the money rate *less* the expected rate of inflation. Relationship (13.15) is based on the supposition that, for all practical purposes, the real rate of interest can be identified with the marginal product of capital, in which case it will be an increasing function of the utilisation ratio, given a well-behaved, linear-and-homogeneous production function.

The utility function with x and y as arguments is obtained from (13.13) with the help of (13.14) and (13.15). We have:

$$U = \phi(i, y) = \phi(r(y) + x, y) = U(x, y). \qquad (13.16)$$

The properties of this new function are deducible from those of the original function, as already specified. We shall refer to them at a later stage.

2. *The Solution of the Problem*

Having discussed Phelps's dynamic formulation of the inflation *versus* unemployment problem, we next consider the structure of his solution.

To pave the way we must first introduce two new symbols, namely $\tilde{y}$ and $\hat{x}$. Let us take them in turn. The symbol $\tilde{y}$ denotes the value of y which maximises the *current* rate of utility, given x. This is referred to as the 'static optimum' utilisation ratio. To determine $\tilde{y}$ on the basis of given x, one would equate to zero the derivative with respect to y of: $U = \phi(r(y) + x, y)$ and then solve for y. That is, one would seek the y which satisfied:

$$r'(y) = -\frac{\phi_2(i, y)}{\phi_1(i, y)} = -\frac{\phi_2(r(y) + x, y)}{\phi_1(r(y) + x, y)}. \tag{13.17}$$

Proceeding in this way one would find $\tilde{y} < y^0$. This follows from the restrictions already imposed on ϕ_1, ϕ_2 and r'. Since ϕ_1 is non-positive, the right-hand side of (13.17) can be positive (as it must be since $r' > 0$) only if $\phi_2 > 0$, which is the case only when $y < y^0$. One would also find that $\tilde{y}$ was a decreasing function of x.[1]

The above procedure for locating $\tilde{y}$ would break down if x, the expected rate of inflation, were so low that $i = r(y) + x < \hat{\imath}$ for all feasible y. For then we would have $\phi_1 = 0$ and (13.17) would give an indeterminate solution. The solution proposed for this situation is $\tilde{y} = y^0$. With y fixed at y^0 and with x fixed, i is determined and so, therefore, is the relevant Fig. 13.5 curve. With $y = y^0$ we shall be at the peak of this curve.

[1] To see this, consider the differentials of ϕ_2 and ϕ_1. We have:

$$\begin{aligned}
d\phi_2 &= \phi_{21}di + \phi_{22}dy \\
&= \phi_{21}(dr + dx) + \phi_{22}dy \\
&= \phi_{21}(r'dy + dx) + \phi_{22}dy \\
&= (\phi_{21}r' + \phi_{22})dy + \phi_{21}dx \\
d\phi_1 &= \phi_{11}di + \phi_{12}dy \\
&= (\phi_{11}r' + \phi_{12})dy + \phi_{11}dx.
\end{aligned}$$

Now suppose that (13.17) is satisfied by some y on the basis of some given x and allow x to be increased. Could (13.17) be satisfied by the *same* y? With $dx > 0$ and $dy = 0$, we would have $d\phi_2 \leq 0$ and $d\phi_1 < 0$ by virtue of the restrictions imposed on ϕ_{21} ($=\phi_{12}$) and ϕ_{11}. (These restrictions apply only outside the full-liquidity range, but this will be the range which is relevant. See the next paragraph of the text.) Hence the (negative) denominator of the right-hand side of (13.17) would increase in absolute value while the numerator would either remain the same or decrease. Consequently the right-hand side of (13.17) would be smaller than before for the value of y in question whereas the left-hand side would be the same as before by virtue of the restriction on r'. The particular value of y, therefore, could no longer satisfy (13.17), i.e. y could not be the same as it was with the lower x. Could y be *higher* than before? If it were (i.e. if $dy > 0$ and $dx > 0$), we would have $d\phi_1 < 0$ and $d\phi_2 < 0$ by virtue of the restrictions on ϕ_{21}, ϕ_{22}, ϕ_{11}, ϕ_{21} and r'. Hence the right-hand side of (13.17) would be smaller for any higher y whereas the left-hand side would be larger by virtue of the restriction on r'. It is not possible, therefore, that (13.17) could be satisfied by any higher y after the increase in x. The only possibility, therefore, is that y should decrease with the increase in x. This would mean a lower left-hand side for (13.17). However, it could mean a lower right-hand side also provided dy were sufficiently negative. A solution given a lower value of y for the higher x would therefore be a possibility and it would be the only possibility.

We turn now to $\hat{x}$. This is defined as that x (expected rate of inflation) which is sufficiently small, given y, to make $i = \hat{i}$, i.e. to permit full liquidity. Now the higher is y the higher is $r(r'(y) > 0)$. Hence from (13.14), the higher is y the lower is the x needed to make $i = \hat{i}$. It follows, therefore, that $\hat{x}$ is a decreasing function of y. A value of $\hat{x}$ which plays an important part in the ensuing discussion is the $\hat{x}$ which corresponds to $y = y^*$, i.e. the x which makes $i = \hat{i}$ when the utilisation ratio is at its equilibrium level. This is denoted by $\hat{x}(y^*)$.

Having introduced $\tilde{y}$ and $\hat{x}$, we proceed now to give a general account of the solution of the time-optimisation problem as formulated in (13.6)–(13.8).

The first step is to impose the condition:

$$U[\hat{x}(y^*), y^*] = \hat{U} = 0. \tag{13.18}$$

To see that this is legitimate, recall that the function U is determined only up to a monotonic increasing transformation, i.e. any monotonic increasing function of U will serve just as well as U since it will preserve the original ordering of utilities. This being so, if $\hat{U} = b$, say, where $b \neq 0$, we can apply the monotonic increasing transformation (linear transformation) $U - b$ to U to get the desired condition $\hat{U} = 0$.[1] Another way of putting the point is to say that we can ensure (13.18) by suitably changing the units in which utility is measured.

The next step in the solution is to derive a rule showing optimal utilisation at any point of time as a function of the expected rate of inflation at that point of time. To this end we use (13.7) to write $U(x, y)$, the integrand of (13.6), in an alternative form. Since $G'(y) > 0$ we can write (13.7) as:

$$y = g\left(\frac{dx}{dt}\right). \tag{13.19}$$

Hence:

$$U(x, y) = U\left[x, g\left(\frac{dx}{dt}\right)\right] = V\left(x, \frac{dx}{dt}\right) = V(x, G). \tag{13.20}$$

Using (13.20) we can now reformulate the time-optimisation problem as follows:

To find a time path for x from time 0 onwards such that:

[1] Cf. R. G. D. Allen, *Mathematical Economics* (London: Macmillan, 1960) p. 654.

$$W = \int_0^\infty V\left(x, \frac{dx}{dt}\right) dt$$

is maximised subject to:

$$x(0) = x_0.$$

This is the fundamental problem of the calculus of variations once again (see section 11.2). In this case the variable t does not appear explicitly in the function to be integrated and the necessary condition for a maximum is:

$$U(x, y) - G(y)\frac{U_y}{G'(y)} = k \qquad (13.21)$$

where k is some arbitrary constant and $U_y = \delta U(x, y)/\delta y$.[1] From (13.21) it follows that:

$$U[\hat{x}(y^*), y^*] - G(y^*)\frac{U_y[\hat{x}(y^*), y^*]}{G'(y^*)} = k. \qquad (13.22)$$

Using (13.18) and $G(y^*) = 0$, we find from (13.22) that $k = 0$. Hence the necessary condition for a maximum (relationship (13.21)) is:

$$U(x, y) - G(y)\frac{U_y}{G'(y)} = 0. \qquad (13.23)$$

This relationship defines the optimal utilisation ratio at time t as a function of the expected rate of inflation at time t.

The nature of the optimal time-path defined by (13.23) depends on the relationship between x_0, the initial expected rate of inflation, and $\hat{x}(y^*)$. There are three possibilities: (i) $x_0 > \hat{x}(y^*)$; (ii) $x_0 = \hat{x}(y^*)$; and (iii) $x_0 < \hat{x}(y^*)$. In case (i), i.e. when the initial expected rate of inflation is too large for full liquidity at $y = y^*$, optimal y is less than y^* at all points of time and converges on y^*. At the same time x, the expected rate of inflation, falls continuously and tends to $\hat{x}(y^*)$ in the limit. Thus in the limit, full-liquidity equilibrium is realised. In case (ii), $y = y^*$ is optimal for all t. Since $G(y^*) = 0$ there will be no change in x along the optimal time path, i.e. x will continue at the initial level $\hat{x}(y^*)$. In case (iii) no optimal time path exists.

We shall now develop a simple diagram which will help to illuminate these conclusions and at the same time give some idea of the argument which underlies them. To assist in the diagrammatic exposition, we first write (13.23) in an alternative form. We note

[1] Cf. R. G. D. Allen, *Mathematical Analysis for Economists* (London: Macmillan, 1967) p. 530.

from (13.20) that:

$$V_G = U_y \frac{1}{G'(y)} \tag{13.24}$$

where V_G denotes $\partial V / \partial G$. It follows that (13.23) can be written as:

$$V(x, G) - G V_G(x, G) = 0. \tag{13.25}$$

We now have a relationship giving the optimal *rate of change* of the expected rate of inflation as a function of the *level* of the expected rate.

Next we must deduce the character of the variation of the function $V(x, G)$ with G, for given x ($\bar{\bar{x}}$). This requires an investigation of the behaviour of V_G. As is evident from (13.24), this requires, in turn, a consideration of $G'(y)$ and U_y.

Take U_y first. From (13.16) it follows that U_y is given by:

$$U_y = \phi_1 r'(y) + \phi_2. \tag{13.26}$$

From (13.17) and the definition of $\tilde{y}$ (see p. 462 above) it follows that: $U_y = 0$ when $y = \tilde{y}$. It can also be shown that $U_{yy} < 0$ for all y, given the various restrictions placed on $\phi(i, y)$ and $r(y)$.[1] It follows that $U_y > 0$ for $\mu \le y < \tilde{y}$ and $U_y < 0$ for $\tilde{y} < y \le \bar{y}$.

Turning to $G'(y)$, it will be recalled that the restriction here is: $G'(y) > 0$. Using this, together with the results just obtained for U_y, we reach the conclusion that: $V_G > 0$ for $\mu \le y < \tilde{y}$, $V_G = 0$ for $y = \tilde{y}$, $V_G < 0$ for $\tilde{y} < y \le \bar{y}$. Now, when $\mu \le y < \tilde{y}$ we have $G(\mu) \le G < G(\tilde{y})$. Similarly, when $\tilde{y} < y \le \bar{y}$ we have $G(\tilde{y}) < G \le G(\bar{y})$. Finally, when $y = \tilde{y}$, $G = G(\tilde{y})$. Hence we have:

$$
\begin{aligned}
V_G > 0 \quad & G(\mu) \le G < G(\tilde{y}) \\
V_G = 0 \quad & G = G(\tilde{y}) \\
V_G < 0 \quad & G(\tilde{y}) < G \le G(\bar{y}).
\end{aligned}
$$

Our final conclusion, therefore, is that the variation of $V(x, G)$ with G for fixed x is of the character depicted in Fig. 13.7.

Our final preliminary step is to deduce the character of the variation of $V(x, G)$ with x for given G, i.e. to see how the curve of Fig. 13.7

[1] We have:

$$
\begin{aligned}
U_{yy} &= \phi_1 r''(y) + r'(y)[\phi_{11} r'(y) + \phi_{12}] + \phi_{21} r'(y) + \phi_{22} \\
&= \phi_1 r''(y) + \phi_{11}[r'(y)]^2 + 2\phi_{21} r'(y) + \phi_{22}.
\end{aligned}
$$

Given the restrictions on ϕ_1, ϕ_{11}, ϕ_{21}, ϕ_{22}, r' and r'' discussed above, the above expression must be negative for all y.

shifts when x changes. This requires an investigation of V_x where V_x denotes $\partial V/\partial x$.

Using (13.20) and (13.16), we see that:

$$V_x = U_x = \phi_1 \tag{13.27}$$

where U_x denotes $\partial U/\partial x$. Hence, using the restrictions already imposed on ϕ_1, we see that $V_x = 0$ when $x \leq \hat{x}$ and $V_x < 0$ for $x > \hat{x}$. This

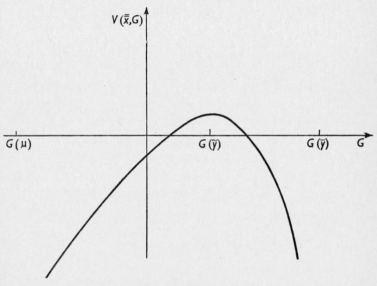

Fig. 13.7

means that the curve of Fig. 13.7 remains fixed when x increases in the range $x \leq \hat{x}$ and that it shifts downwards (upwards) when x increases (decreases) in the range $x > \hat{x}$.

We are now ready to consider in diagrammatic terms the conclusions presented earlier as to the nature of the optimal time path for the utilisation ratio defined by (13.23). First, consider case (i): $x_0 > \hat{x}(y^*)$. In this case the initial $V(x, G)$ curve will cut the vertical axis below the origin. For, given $x_0 > \hat{x}(y^*)$, it follows, using (13.18), that $U(x_0, y^*) < U(\hat{x}(y^*), y^*) = \hat{U} = 0$, since $U_x < 0$ for $x > \hat{x}$. Using (13.20) it follows, in turn, that $V(x_0, G(y^*)) < 0$, i.e. that $V(x_0, 0) < 0$, i.e. that initially the $V(x, G)$ curve passes under the origin in the manner of the unbroken curve of Fig. 13.8. The peak of the curve can be either to the right of the origin or to the left, depending on whether $\tilde{y}$ is greater or less than y^*. In Fig. 13.8 we show the peak of the curve to the right of the origin. Thus we assume that x_0 is small

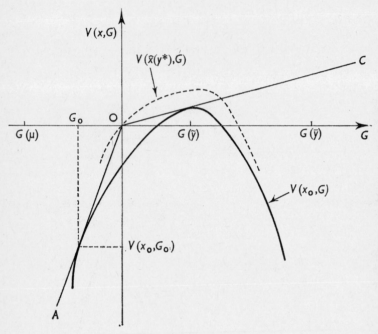

Fig. 13.8

enough to make the static optimum utilisation ratio greater than the equilibrium utilisation ratio ($\tilde{y}(x_0) > y^*$) but not small enough to permit full liquidity at $y^*(x_0 > \hat{x}(y^*))$.

The optimal value of G (and hence the optimal utilisation ratio) at time 0 is found by drawing a tangent (OA) from the origin to the initial $V(x, G)$ curve (see Fig. 13.8). At the point of tangency the slope of the tangent, i.e. $[V(x_0, G_0)]/G_0$, is equal to the slope of the $V(x_0, G)$ curve, i.e. $V_G(x_0, G_0)$. In other words, relationship (13.25) is satisfied at the point of tangency. Consequently G_0 must be the optimal G at time 0. Since $G(y^*) = 0$ and $G' > 0$, this means that the optimal y at time 0 is less than y^*, and hence less than the static optimum utilisation ratio, $\tilde{y}$.

Since optimal G is negative at time 0, x must be falling at time 0 (see relationship (13.11)) and hence the $V(x, G)$ curve must shift upwards, as already explained (see relationship (13.27)). Consequently the point of tangency must move upwards and to the right, i.e. optimal G must move closer to the origin, i.e. optimal y must move closer to y^*. This process will continue indefinitely under the influence of negative G, with optimal y continuing below y^* but converging on y^*. The limiting position of the $V(x, G)$ curve is shown by the broken curve of Fig. 13.8. This curve passes through the origin so that the origin becomes the point of tangency. Thus, in the limit, y^* is the optimal y while the limiting value of x is $\hat{x}(y^*)$.

Before turning to cases (ii) and (iii), we must consider three points relating to the argument just presented in relation to case (i). In the first place, the argument is valid only if the slope of the $V(x, G)$ curve diminishes as G increases from $G(\mu)$ to $G(y^*)$, i.e. only if $V_{GG} < 0$ in this particular range; otherwise no point of tangency will exist. However, examination of V_{GG} shows that, in fact, this condition is met.[1]

Secondly, the argument is valid only if the slope of the Fig. 13.7 family of curves at any value of G in the range $G(\mu) < G \leq G(y^*)$ does not decrease as one moves vertically up the diagram, i.e. only if $V_{Gx} \leq 0$ for all x and all G in the range in question; otherwise there is no guarantee that the value of G at the point of tangency will converge on zero. On examination of V_{Gx} we find this condition is also met.[2]

Thirdly, it will be noticed from Fig. 13.8 that there are two tangents through the origin to the $V(x_0, G)$ curve – OA and OC. Hence there are two possible values of G_0, i.e. two values of G which satisfy (13.25) given the initial $V(x, G)$ curve. One of these is negative; this is

---

[1] From (13.24) we have:

$$V_{GG} = \frac{G'(y)U_{yy}\dfrac{1}{G'(y)} - U_y G''(y)\dfrac{1}{G'(y)}}{[G'(y)]^2}$$

$$= \frac{G'(y)U_{yy} - U_y G''(y)}{[G'(y)]^3}.$$

Now, as already shown, $U_{yy} < 0$ for all y and $U_y > 0$ for $\mu \leq y < \bar{y}$, i.e. for $G(\mu) \leq G < G(\bar{y})$. Also we have $G'(y) > 0$ and $G''(y) > 0$ for all y. It follows that, in the range of G considered, $V_{GG} < 0$.

[2] From (13.24) we see that:

$$V_{Gx} = \frac{U_{yx}}{G'(y)}.$$

Now U_{yx} is given by:

$$U_{yx} = \phi_{11}r'(y) + \phi_{21}.$$

Given the restrictions imposed on ϕ_{11}, $r'(y)$ and ϕ_{21}, it follows that $U_{yx} < 0$ for all x and y and hence, given $G'(y) > 0$ for all y, that $V_{Gx} < 0$ for all x and all G.

the one on which the solution presented above is based. The other is positive. Does this mean that, in case (i), there is a second optimal time path for the utilisation ratio, starting with a positive G rather than a negative G? The answer is that the second time path cannot be optimal. For along this path the expected rate of inflation will be increasing at each point of time. Hence the $V(x, G)$ curve will be shifting downwards and the peak of the curve will be shifting closer to the vertical axis ($\bar{y}$ a decreasing function of x; $G'(y) > 0$). Hence the y corresponding to the point of tangency will converge on y^*, while x will converge on $\tilde{x}$ where $\tilde{x}$ is defined by: $\bar{y}(\tilde{x}) = y^*$, i.e. $\tilde{x}$ is that expected rate of inflation which equates the static-optimum y with the equilibrium y. This means that the rate of social utility will converge on $U(\tilde{x}, y^*)$. But since $\tilde{x} > x_0 > \hat{x}(y^*)$ and since $U_x < 0$ for $x > \hat{x}$, it follows that $U(\tilde{x}, y^*) < U(\hat{x}(y^*), y^*) = \hat{U} = 0$. Thus if the second path is followed, the integral to be maximised, $\int_0^\infty U(x, y)\, dt$, will diverge to $-\infty$ so that this path cannot be optimal.

Returning to the main argument we deal now with case (ii): $x_0 = \hat{x}(y^*)$. In this case we have: $U(x_0, y^*) = U(\hat{x}(y^*), y^*) = \hat{U} = 0$. From (13.20) it then follows that $V(x_0, G(y^*)) = V(x_0, 0) = 0$. In other words, in this case the initial $V(x, G)$ curve passes through the origin; it will, in fact, be the broken curve of Fig. 13.8. Thus, initially, the point of tangency is at the origin which means that $y = y^*$ is optimal for $t = 0$. Moreover, $y = y^*$ must remain optimal thereafter. For with $G = 0$ initially there is no pressure, upwards or downwards, on the $V(x, G)$ curve, which retains its initial position. Hence in this case $y = y^*$ is optimal for all t and along the optimal path the expected rate of inflation persists at its initial level.

Finally, we come to case (iii): $x_0 < \hat{x}(y^*)$. In this case the initial $V(x, G)$ curve is again the broken curve of Fig. 13.8, since $V_x = 0$ for $x \leq \hat{x}$. This suggests that the optimal time paths for y and x will be the same as in the previous case, i.e. $y = y^*$, $x = \hat{x}(y^*)$ for all t giving $U = \hat{U}$ for all t. However, the time path of case (ii) would not be optimal here because it would be possible to make $y > y^*$ for a time, thereby making $U > \hat{U}$, and still make $U = \hat{U}$ for ever after. By making $y > y^*$ the authorities would cause the expected rate of inflation to rise. But so long as the upward movement in x stopped short of $\hat{x}(y^*)$ (so long as the departure from $y = y^*$ were sufficiently short-lived), there would be no shift in the $V(x, G)$ curve ($V_x = 0$ when $x \leq \hat{x}$), i.e. the curve would still pass through the origin. Hence the return to $y = y^*$ would mean $\hat{U} = 0$ for all subsequent time as in case (ii).

On the other hand, while the time path of temporary $U > \hat{U}$, followed by permanent $U = \hat{U}$, would be superior to the optimal time path of case (ii), it would not itself be optimal because it would not satisfy the 'tangency condition' of relationship (13.25), which is a necessary condition of an optimum. Nor is there any other time path, apart from that of case (ii), which would do so. The conclusion therefore must be that, in case (iii), no optimum exists.[1]

13.4 Empirical Evidence on Inflation–Unemployment Relationship

For the *static* approach a key question is whether the curve of relationship (13.2) is steep or flat. For on this will depend the size of the optimum unemployment percentage. If the inflation–unemployment curve is close to the horizontal, the optimum unemployment percentage will be close to zero, as will be seen from Fig. 13.1. (Indeed, if the curve were a horizontal straight line[2] the optimum percentage would actually be zero because the point of tangency would then lie on the vertical axis.) On the other hand, if the curve is close to the vertical the point of tangency will lie well to the right of the origin and the optimum unemployment percentage will be well above zero. For the *dynamic* approach a critical question is what are the key determinants of shifts in the price–unemployment curve – in particular whether the emphasis given to the expected rate of inflation by Phelps and other proponents of the dynamic approach is, or is not, misplaced. Both of these questions are essentially empirical in character and the object of the present section is to give a brief review of some recent empirical research which bears on them. We shall take the questions one by one.

1. *The Slope of the Inflation–Unemployment Curve*

To throw light on the question of whether the inflation–unemployment curve is steep or flat, one must attempt an econometric estimate

---

[1] This conclusion could be avoided either by introducing a positive utility discount, i.e. by making the integral to be maximised:

$$\int_0^\infty e^{-\delta t} U(x, y) dt, \ \delta > 0,$$

or by introducing a finite time horizon. Cf. Phelps, op. cit., pp. 277–81.

[2] This would imply that the rate of price increase was determined entirely by variables other than the unemployment percentage, i.e. that the quasi-Phillips curve was non-existent.

of relationship (13.2). This can be approached in two main ways. One possibility is to begin by estimating the Phillips relationship and then to combine this with an estimated price–wage relationship to obtain an estimated price–unemployment relationship. The alternative procedure is to estimate the price–unemployment relationship directly, i.e. without estimating the Phillips relationship as an intermediate step. Perhaps the most noteworthy example of the first approach is to be found in the econometric work of Perry,[1] while the more recent work of Brechling[2] provides a good example of the second approach. Here we shall confine our attention to these two studies.

We begin by setting out the notation to be used, which closely resembles Brechling's notation and is also in line with the notation used in sections 13.2 and 13.3.

p = proportionate rate of increase in general price level

s = unemployment percentage

w = proportionate rate of increase in wage earnings per man-hour

ρ = proportionate rate of increase in output per man-hour

m = proportionate rate of increase in non-wage mark-up, defined as the ratio of G.D.P. to aggregate wage earnings

p^f = proportionate rate of increase in agricultural prices

R = profit rate.

We now consider Perry's study in terms of this notation. As already indicated, Perry begins by estimating a Phillips relationship and then combines this with a price–wage relationship to obtain a price–unemployment relationship. Perry's estimated Phillips relationship, which is arrived at after a considerable amount of experimentation, is as follows:

$$w_t = -4{\cdot}313 + 0{\cdot}367 p_{t-1} + 14{\cdot}711\ s_t^{-1} + 0{\cdot}424 R_{t-1} + 0{\cdot}729(R_t - R_{t-1}).$$
$$(13.28)$$

This relationship was obtained by applying ordinary least squares to quarterly data for the United States manufacturing sector for the post-war period.[3] Strictly speaking, it represents a family of Phillips relationships, each member of which corresponds to specified values for p_{t-1}, R_{t-1} and $(R_t - R_{t-1})$.

Perry's next step is to transform (13.28) into a price–unemployment

---

[1] See G. L. Perry, 'The Determinants of Wage Rate Changes and the Inflation-Unemployment Trade-off for the United States', *Review of Economic Studies* (Oct 1964).   [2] See Brechling, op. cit.   [3] See Perry, op. cit., p. 293.

relationship (more strictly a family of such relationships) by means of the relationship:

$$p_t = w_t - \rho_t. \tag{13.29}$$

This can be regarded as a crude form of our relationship (9.9) in which $\beta_1 = 1$, $\beta_2 = 0$ and $\dot{K}_t = 0$. Using (13.29), we can write (13.28) as:

$$p_t = -4 \cdot 313 + 0 \cdot 367 \, p_{t-1} + 14 \cdot 711 \, s_t^{-1} + 0 \cdot 424 \, R_{t-1}$$
$$+ 0 \cdot 729(R_t - R_{t-1}) - \rho_t. \tag{13.30}$$

Now in the context in which it is used in section 13.2, relationship (13.2) must be regarded as one which shows the *eventual* rate of price increase generated by a specified *steady* unemployment percentage. Hence, if (13.30) is to throw any light on the slope of the price–unemployment curve which features in the static approach, it must first be transformed into a 'steady-state' relationship. This can be done simply by suppressing time subscripts and using a bar over each variable to denote its steady-state value. Thus the steady-state version of (13.30) is:

$$\bar{p} = -4 \cdot 313 + 0 \cdot 367\bar{p} + 14 \cdot 711\bar{s}^{-1} + 0 \cdot 424\bar{R} - \bar{\rho}. \tag{13.31}$$

Solving for $\bar{p}$, we get:

$$\bar{p} = -6 \cdot 814 + 23 \cdot 324\bar{s}^{-1} + 0 \cdot 670\bar{R} - 1 \cdot 580\bar{\rho}. \tag{13.32}$$

The family of curves defined by this relationship has a pronounced negative slope, particularly for low values of $\bar{s}$. This can be seen from the four members of the family which Perry shows in his Figs 1A, 1B and 1C.[1] It can also be seen by examining the partial derivative of $\bar{p}$ with respect to $\bar{s}$. From (13.32), we have:

$$\frac{\partial \bar{p}}{\partial \bar{s}} = -23 \cdot 324(\bar{s})^{-2}. \tag{13.33}$$

This implies, for example, that when $\bar{s} = 2$ per cent $((\bar{s})^{-2} = 0 \cdot 25)$, the rate of increase of prices will rise by nearly six percentage points per one point decrease in the unemployment percentage, given the profit rate and the proportionate rate of increase of productivity. When $\bar{s} = 1 \cdot 5$, the rate of increase of prices will rise by a little over ten percentage points per one point decrease in the unemployment percentage, for a given profit rate and a given rate of productivity increase.

[1] Ibid., p. 298.

Q

We turn now to the study made recently by Brechling in which the price–unemployment relationship is estimated directly. Brechling's starting-point was an extension of (13.29), namely:

$$p_t = (w_t - \rho_t) + m_t \qquad (13.34)$$

which is our (9.9) with $\beta_1 = 1$, $\beta_2 = 0$. His procedure was to estimate the relationship between $(w - \rho)$ and s by least squares from quarterly United States data and then to estimate separately the relationship between m and s, using as explanatory variables in each case the unemployment percentage and the rates of increase of agricultural prices for the current quarter, the next quarter and the two preceding quarters.[1] He then added the resulting relationships (using (13.34)) to obtain the desired relationship between p and s. The steady-state versions of the component relationships and of the combined relationship are as follows:[2]

$$(\overline{w - p}) = 7{\cdot}7793 - 0{\cdot}9957\bar{s} + 0{\cdot}1772\bar{p}^f \qquad (13.35)$$

$$\overline{m} = -3{\cdot}2245 + 0{\cdot}5927\bar{s} + 0{\cdot}0156\bar{p}^f \qquad (13.36)$$

$$\bar{p} = 4{\cdot}5548 - 0{\cdot}4030\bar{s} + 0{\cdot}1928\bar{p}^f. \qquad (13.37)$$

For low values of $\bar{s}$ the curve of relationship (13.37) is much flatter than the corresponding Perry curve (relationship (13.32)). This can be seen from the following table.

TABLE 13.1

Value of $\bar{s}$ (per cent)	Rise in rate of increase of prices (percentage points) per one point decrease in $\bar{s}$	
	Perry	Brechling
1	23·324	0·4030
1·5	10·366	0·4030
2	5·831	0·4030
2·5	3·732	0·4030
3	2·592	0·4030
3·5	1·904	0·4030

Brechling argues, however, that the observed relationship between $\overline{m}$ and $\bar{s}$ (relationship (13.36)) must be regarded as strictly short-run in character. For it implies that, for any realistic value of $\bar{s}$, $\overline{m}$ will be negative;[3] and the implication of a continuously declining non-wage

[1] Regressions were also run with an excess demand variable replacing the unemployment percentage in the list of explanatory variables. See Brechling, op. cit., pp. 720–6.   [2] Ibid., p. 726, relationships (16) and (18).
[3] For example, if $\bar{p}^f = 0$, (13.36) implies that $m < 0$ for $\bar{s}$ below 5·4 per cent.

mark-up is not acceptable in a long-run context, since entrepreneurs, presumably, would not be content to allow the non-wage component of G.D.P. to disappear entirely. A more plausible long-run hypothesis, he argues, would be $\bar{m} = 0$ for all $\bar{s}$. This would mean that, in the long run, a decrease of one point in $\bar{s}$ would cause the rate of increase of prices to rise by nearly one point as compared with the short-run figure of less than half a point, assuming that relationship (13.35) holds both in the short run and in the long run. Thus Brechling's final conclusion is that, while the curve of $\bar{p} = f(\bar{s})$ is fairly flat in the short run, it is reasonably steep in the long run, though not as steep for low values of $\bar{s}$ as Perry's work would suggest.

2. The 'Expectations Hypothesis'

Having considered some empirical evidence relating to the slope of the $p = f(s)$ curve – a matter which is critical for the static approach – we turn now to some evidence bearing on the so-called 'expectations hypothesis' which is a key element in the dynamic approach.

The expectations hypothesis is derived from two separate hypotheses. The first hypothesis can be stated symbolically as:

$$p = f(s) + p^e \qquad f' < 0 \tag{13.38}$$

where p^e denotes the expected proportionate rate of increase in the general price level. The second hypothesis is that the expected rate of inflation (p^e) rises, stays constant or falls according to whether the actual rate of inflation (p) exceeds, equals or falls short of the expected rate. It will be observed that, apart from the use of s (the unemployment percentage) in place of y (the utilisation ratio) the above hypotheses constitute relationships (13.9) and (13.10), which are two of the key relationships of Phelps's model.

The first hypothesis implies that if s is held at that level (call it s^*) which makes $f(s) = 0$, p and p^e will be equal, in which case, by the second hypothesis, there will be no tendency for p^e to change and hence (by the first hypothesis) no tendency for p to change. In other words, when $s = s^*$ the actual rate of inflation will remain constant. On the other hand, if s is held at some level other than s^*, the rate of inflation will vary over time. If $s < s^*$, $f(s)$ will be positive and p will exceed p^e (first hypothesis). This will mean that p^e will rise (second hypothesis) and hence (first hypothesis) that there will be an equivalent rise in p. Consequently p will remain in excess of p^e so that p^e will continue to rise. Thus, if the unemployment percentage is held at any level in excess of s^* the rate of inflation will increase continuously, i.e. there will be explosive inflation. Conversely if $s > s^*$ the rate of inflation will decrease continuously, i.e. there will be explosive deflation. The 'expectations hypothesis' consists, in effect, of the conclusions just drawn and may be stated as follows: There exists some 'equilibrium' or 'natural' unemployment percentage (s^*) such that the rate of inflation decreases continuously, remains constant, or increases continuously according as s exceeds, equals or falls short of s^*.

Brechling has recently provided a test of the expectations hypothesis[1] which we shall now discuss. We begin by outlining the argument on which the test is based. It is assumed that the authorities

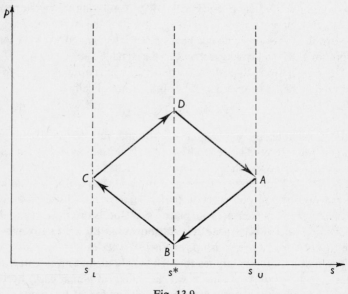

Fig. 13.9

aim to keep the unemployment rate within some specified range $s_L - s_U$ and that s^* falls in this range. When s rises to the upper limit, s_U, steps are taken to reduce s to s_L. Conversely when s falls to the lower limit, s_L, steps are taken to raise s to s_U. Suppose now that the economy is initially at point A, i.e. that the unemployment rate is initially at $s_U > s^*$ (see Fig. 13.9). Then, according to the expectations

[1] See Brechling, op. cit., pp. 717–19, 730–3.

hypothesis, p will fall; and since, by assumption, s will fall towards s_L, the (p, s) observations will move in a south-westerly direction as indicated by the arrow from A to B. Once point B is passed, i.e. once $s < s^*$, the expectations hypothesis predicts that p will rise. Since, by assumption, s will still be falling, the (p, s) observations will move in a north-westerly direction as indicated by the arrow from B to C. Once C is reached, s will begin to rise towards s_U. However, since $s < s^*$, p will continue to rise so that the (p, s) observations will move in a north-easterly direction as indicated by the arrow from C to D. Once point D has been passed, i.e. once $s > s^*$, the expectations hypothesis predicts that p will begin to fall. But since, by assumption, s will continue to increase up to s_U, the (p, s) observations must travel in a south-easterly direction as indicated by the arrow from D to A. Thus the conclusion to which the argument leads is that the expectations hypothesis predicts clockwise loops round the negatively sloping $p = f(s)$ curve. Brechling's test of the hypothesis consists, therefore, of observing whether the loops round the $p = f(s)$ curve are, in fact, clockwise or anti-clockwise in direction. In the first case the evidence would be held to support the hypothesis, in the second case to refute it.

To carry out the test, Brechling makes use of a quarterly regression based on United States data in which p_t is the dependent variable and s_{t+2}, s_{t+1}, s_t, s_{t-1}, s_{t-2}, p_{t+1}^f, p_t^f, p_{t-1}^f, p_{t-2}^f and t are the explanatory variables. A sequence of s observations with a time pattern of the type assumed in the development of the test is devised, namely one in which the $s_L - s_U$ range is 3 per cent to 9 per cent and in which s changes by one percentage point per quarter. This sequence is then fed into the regression equation in question and a sequence of p values is generated on the assumption that all four p^f variables are zero for all t. On examining the (p, s) observations which emerge in this way, Brechling finds that they display definite anti-clockwise loops and hence that they are inconsistent with the expectations hypothesis.

13.5 Summary

Empirical studies suggest that internal balance and price stability may well be incompatible objectives – in the British case that price stability can be achieved only at the cost of something like $2\frac{1}{2}$ per cent unemployment. If this is so, and if neither price stability nor internal balance can be regarded as an overriding objective, the authorities must find some means of choosing the 'best' combination of p (the rate of price increase) and s (the unemployment percentage). Two approaches to this problem have been proposed in recent years – the 'static' approach and the 'dynamic' approach.

In the case of the *static* approach the problem of choosing the best combination of p and s is treated as a conventional maximisation problem. The 'best' unemployment percentage is found by maximising a social utility function in which the arguments are p and s, subject to a relationship which shows p as a decreasing function of s (a 'quasi-Phillips' relationship). The best rate of price increase is then found by substituting the best unemployment percentage into the quasi-Phillips relationship.

The main limitation of the static approach is that it assumes that the quasi-Phillips curve remains fixed over the planning interval. This limitation is stressed by the proponents of the *dynamic* approach, who argue that the quasi-Phillips curve is bound to shift with changes in the expected rate of inflation and that this must be taken into account in choosing the optimum combination of p and s. Arguing along these lines, they are led to the conclusion that the problem must be treated as a time-optimisation problem requiring the use of calculus-of-variations techniques, rather than as a maximisation problem of the conventional kind.

For the static approach the slope of the quasi-Phillips curve is a matter of critical importance. If the quasi-Phillips curve is close to the horizontal the optimum unemployment percentage will be close to zero, whereas if the quasi-Phillips curve is close to the vertical the optimum unemployment percentage will be well above zero. In the final section of the chapter we review two recent empirical studies which throw some light on this question. These suggest that while the quasi-Phillips curve may well be fairly flat in the short run, it is likely to be quite steeply sloped in the long run.

For the dynamic approach the validity of the 'expectations hypothesis' is critical since this hypothesis is one of the main foundations on which the approach rests. The final section of the chapter also reviews some empirical work which is designed to test this hypothesis. The test in question is based on the argument that, if the expectations hypothesis is valid, one should find that the (p, s) observations form clockwise loops round the negatively sloping p–s relationship. Since the observed loops show an anti-clockwise rather than a clockwise pattern, it would appear that the expectations hypothesis is refuted by the data, at least in the form in which it is currently used by proponents of the dynamic approach.

READING LIST

Brechling, F., 'The Trade-off between Inflation and Unemployment', *Journal of Political Economy* (July–Aug 1968).

Lipsey, R. G., 'Structural and Deficient-Demand Unemployment Reconsidered', in Ross, R. M. (ed.), *Employment Policy and the Labour Market* (Berkeley: University of California Press, 1965).

Perry, G. L., 'The Determinants of Wage Rate Changes and the Inflation–Unemployment Trade-off for the United States', *Review of Economic Studies* (Oct 1964).

Phelps, E. S., 'Money-Wage Dynamics and Labor-Market Equilibrium', *Journal of Political Economy* (July–Aug 1968).

——, 'Phillips Curves, Expectations of Inflation and Optimal Unemployment over Time', *Economica* (Aug 1967).

——, 'Phillips Curves, Expectations of Inflation and Optimal Unemployment over Time: Reply', *Economica* (Aug 1968).

Williamson, J., 'Phillips Curves, Expectations of Inflation and Optimal Unemployment over Time: Comment', *Economica* (Aug 1968).

Appendix 13.1

RESTRICTIONS USED IN ARGUMENT OF SECTION 13.3

Restriction		*Page on which first introduced*
(a) $G(y)$		
1. $G(y^*)=0$		459
2. $G'>0$		459
3. $G''>0$		459
(b) $\phi(i, y)$		
4. $\phi_2>0$	$\mu \leq y < y_0$	459
5. $\phi_2=0$	$y=y^0$	460
6. $\phi_2<0$	$y_0 < y \leq \bar{y}$	460
7. $\phi_1=0$	$0 \leq i \leq \hat{\imath}$	461
8. $\phi_1<0$	$\hat{\imath} < i \leq i_b$	461
9. $\phi_{11}<0$	$\hat{\imath} < i \leq i_b$	461
10. $\phi_{12}=0$	$0 \leq i \leq \hat{\imath}$	462
11. $\phi_{12} \leq 0$	$\hat{\imath} < i \leq i_b$	462
12. $\phi_{22}<0$		460

14 Internal Balance and External Balance

14.1 Introduction

The discussion of Chapters 6 and 7 (see in particular sections 6.2 and 7.2) shows that a change in aggregate demand has consequences both for internal balance and for external balance. As regards the internal consequences, what emerges from these chapters is that a reduction in aggregate demand tends to drive the economy towards balance when demand is excess and away from balance when demand is deficient. Conversely, an increase in aggregate demand means a movement towards balance when demand is deficient and a movement away from balance when demand is excess. The external consequences of changes in aggregate demand arise from the short-run link between aggregate demand and real imports. A reduction in aggregate demand induces a fall in the quantity of imports (a movement down the short-run import function); and, given all the other elements in the external situation, this means a movement towards short-run external balance if international reserves are decreasing and away from balance if they are increasing. Conversely, an increase in aggregate demand induces a short-run increase in real imports and a movement towards external balance if the reserves are increasing and away from balance if they are decreasing.

Another conclusion which emerges from Chapters 6 and 7 is that both the internal situation and the external situation are affected by shifts in the short-run import function. An upward shift in this function, arising, for example, from an increase in the home–foreign price ratio, has the same implications for internal balance as a reduction in aggregate demand – both changes mean a decrease in $(D - M)$ – and a downward shift the same implications as an increase in aggregate demand. Moreover, an autonomous increase in real imports tends to restore short-run external balance if the reserves are increasing and to intensify the lack of balance if they are decreasing, and vice versa.

Given these conclusions, it seems natural to inquire whether it is possible for the authorities to achieve *simultaneous* internal and external balance by one type of policy manipulation only – by manipulating aggregate demand alone or by manipulating the import function alone; and if not, in what ways the two types of policy manipulation should be combined. The object of the present chapter is to consider these and other closely related questions in some detail. We shall begin, in the next section, by presenting a very simple diagram and using this diagram to exhibit a distinction which will play an important part in the subsequent argument.

14.2 Zones of Economic Unhappiness

The basis of our diagram is a very simple static model derived from relationships (3.2) and (3.4). The model is:

$$Y = D - M \tag{14.1}$$

$$M = \alpha + \beta D = \alpha + \beta(Y + M) = \frac{\alpha}{1 - \beta} + \frac{\beta}{1 - \beta} Y. \tag{14.2}$$

Here Y, D and M denote, respectively, a stationary equilibrium level of real gross domestic product, aggregate demand and real imports, and α and β are two positive constants. We treat aggregate demand as a datum, the implication being that the authorities are able to manipulate aggregate demand at will. Relationship (14.2) is regarded as being subject to shifts with changes in the variables incorporated in Z^2. In particular the import function will shift upwards with an increase in the home–foreign price ratio and vice versa.

We now proceed to show relationships (14.1) and (14.2) on a two-dimensional diagram in which Y is measured vertically and M horizontally. With D as a datum, relationship (14.1) can be shown on such a diagram as a family of negatively sloping straight lines with a vertical intercept of D and a numerical slope of unity. The line BC (Fig. 14.1) is a member of this family. A member corresponding to a higher value of D will be parallel to BC and further to the right, while a member corresponding to a lower value of D will be parallel and further to the left.

For given values of the 'import data' (variables incorporated in Z^2), relationship (14.2) appears on Fig. 14.1 as a straight line with a horizontal intercept of $\alpha/(1 - \beta)$ and a slope to the vertical axis of $\beta/(1 - \beta)$, a line such as LE. This line can also be regarded as one of a whole family of lines, each member of which corresponds to a given set of import data. For example, the member corresponding to the same relative delivery delay, the same intensity of import controls, etc., as LE but to a higher home–foreign price ratio will be represented by a line to the right of LE (larger M for given Y), while the member corresponding to a greater intensity of import controls and the same values of the other import data will appear as a line to the left of LE.

Given the level of aggregate demand underlying BC and the import data underlying LE, the equilibrium levels of Y and M will be given by the intersection of the two lines; they will be OF and OG respectively.

We now proceed to locate the point in Fig. 14.1 which represents equilibrium with simultaneous internal and external balance. Equilibrium with internal balance is defined by:

$$D - M = Y^p$$

where Y^p is some given equilibrium level of real potential gross domestic product. Using relationship (14.1) this can be written as:

$$Y = Y^p.$$

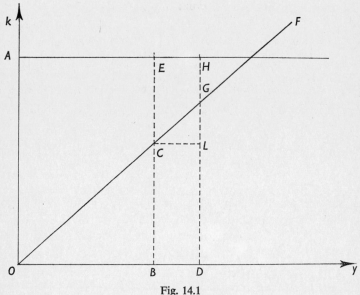

Fig. 14.1

Hence equilibrium with internal balance can be represented in Fig. 14.1 by a horizontal line which cuts the axis at Y^p, a line such as HK.

To show equilibrium with external balance on the diagram we treat all variables involved in the balance of payments, apart from M, as data. Thus we take as data import prices and export prices in terms of foreign currency, export volume, net capital outflow and so on. This enables us to define equilibrium with external balance in terms of a particular level of M and to represent this condition in Fig. 14.1 by a vertical line which cuts the M axis at the level of real imports in question, a line such as JN.

Equilibrium with *both* internal and external balance is then given by the point P where HK and JN intersect. Thus the equilibrium shown on the diagram ($Y = OF$ and $M = OG$) is not one characterised by simultaneous internal and external balance; Y is too small for internal balance and M too large for external balance.

Using the lines HK and JN we can now distinguish four distinct zones of economic unhappiness. These are set out in Table 14.1. It will be seen that the equilibrium given by the intersection of BC and LE falls in zone IV.

TABLE 14.1

Zone	Definition of zone	Location of zone in Fig. 14.1
I	Excess demand with balance of payments surplus	All points above HK and to the left of JN
II	Excess demand with balance of payments deficit	All points above HK and to the right of JN
III	Deficient demand with balance of payments surplus	All points below HK and to the left of JN
IV	Deficient demand with balance of payments deficit	All points below HK and to the right of JN

14.3 One Policy Variable or Two?

Using the diagram developed in the previous section we shall first consider the question: Can the authorities bring about simultaneous internal and external balance solely by manipulating aggregate demand? The answer is that they can do so only in rather special circumstances, the nature of which can be seen from Fig. 14.2. This shows an initial equilibrium falling in zone III. By raising aggregate demand from OB or OR and taking no other action, the authorities can clearly bring the economy from this initial equilibrium, in which neither internal nor external balance exists, to a new equilibrium in which both exist. This is so, however, only because the line *LE* passes through *P*. We conclude, therefore, that internal balance and external balance can be simultaneously achieved by demand manipulation alone only if, in the initial equilibrium, the import data happen to be set at levels which cause the import curve to pass through the point of economic happiness – the point *P*.

Can the two objectives be simultaneously achieved solely by manipulating one of the import data, say the home–foreign price ratio? Again this will be possible only in special circumstances, namely if aggregate demand in the initial equilibrium happens to be such that the line *BC* passes through the point *P*. This can be seen from Fig.

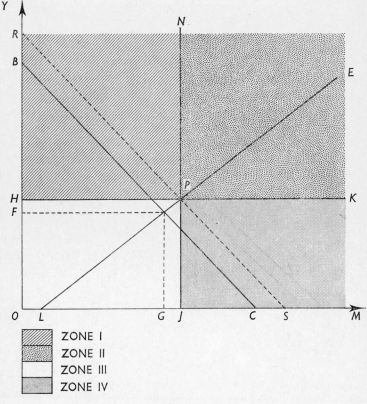

Fig. 14.2

14.3, which shows an initial equilibrium falling in zone I. It is clear that a new equilibrium, in which both internal and external balance exist, can be achieved by so altering the home–foreign price ratio that the import curve becomes *VW* rather than *LE*; no other action is required. It is also clear, however, that this possibility exists only because the aggregate demand curve passes through the point *P* in the initial equilibrium.

Our final conclusion, therefore, is that, except in rather special circumstances, it will not be possible for the authorities to bring about simultaneous internal and external balance by demand manipulation alone or by variation of the import data alone; in most situations both variables will have to be changed. This means that if manipulation of one or other of these variables is not practicable for

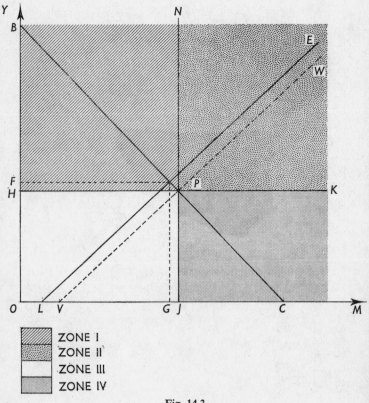

Fig. 14.3

some political or other reason, the two objectives of internal and external balance will normally be incompatible.

14.4 Zones and Sectors

In the previous section we saw that, in general, the two objectives of internal balance and external balance can be achieved simultaneously only if the authorities are in a position to manipulate both aggregate demand and the import data. The question which now arises is: Knowing only the zone in which the initial equilibrium falls, can we deduce the required direction of change for *both* variables? The broad answer is 'No'. We shall now consider this answer in detail. To simplify the discussion we shall treat manipulation of the import data as synonymous with manipulation of the home–foreign price ratio.

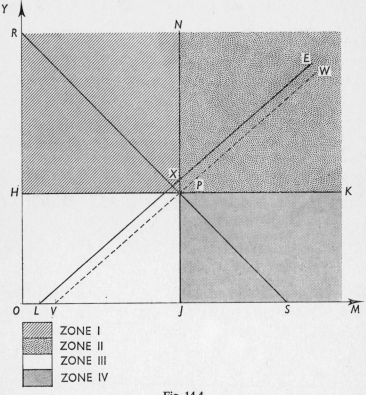

Fig. 14.4

Take first the case where the initial situation falls in zone I. If the starting-point is X (Fig. 14.4), no change is required in aggregate demand but the home–foreign price ratio must rise. If the starting-point is T (Fig. 14.5), the required directions of change are evidently an increase in aggregate demand coupled with a rise in the home–foreign price ratio. Finally, if the starting-point is U (Fig. 14.6), the required directions of change are clearly a decrease in aggregate demand coupled with a rise in the home–foreign price ratio. Thus we have found three points in the zone such that the required directions of change are the same for the home–foreign price ratio but different for aggregate demand. This shows that we cannot specify the required directions of change for both variables if we know only that the initial equilibrium falls somewhere in zone I.

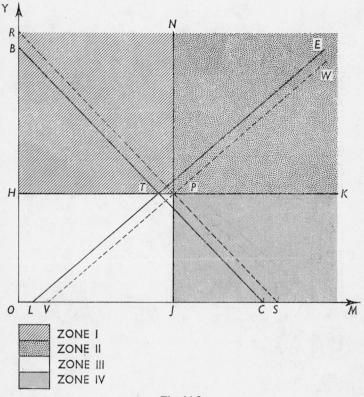

Fig. 14 5

It will be noticed that point X in Fig. 14.4 lies on RS, the aggregate demand line which is required for the attainment of economic happiness, that point T in Fig. 14.5 lies below RS and that point U in Fig. 14.6 lies above RS. Evidently the directions of change which we have deduced for X hold for *any* initial point in zone I falling on RS. Similarly the directions of change deduced for T hold for any initial point lying below RS and those deduced for U for any initial point lying above RS. This means that, while the required direction of change of the home–foreign price ratio is unambiguous for zone I (the ratio must rise), the required direction of change of aggregate demand varies according to whether the initial situation falls on RS (in this case aggregate demand must remain unchanged), falls below RS (in this case aggregate demand must be increased) or falls

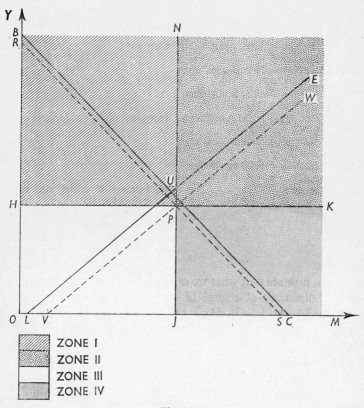

ZONE I
ZONE II
ZONE III
ZONE IV

Fig. 14.6

above RS (in this case aggregate demand must be reduced). In other words, before we can specify the directions of change of *both* variables we must know where the initial equilibrium falls in relation to RS.

The cases where the initial equilibrium falls in zones II, III and IV can be analysed along similar lines. The conclusions which emerge are summarised in Table 14.2.

TABLE 14.2

Required direction of change of:

Zone	Home–foreign price ratio	Aggregate demand
I	Increase	(a) Increase if initial equilibrium falls below RS (b) No change if initial equilibrium falls on RS (c) Decrease if initial equilibrium falls above RS
II	(a) Decrease if initial equilibrium falls below WV (b) No change if initial equilibrium falls on WV (c) Increase if initial equilibrium falls above WV	Decrease
III	(a) Decrease if initial equilibrium falls below WV (b) No change if initial equilibrium falls on WV (c) Increase if initial equilibrium falls above WV	Increase
IV	Decrease	(a) Increase if initial equilibrium falls below RS (b) No change if initial equilibrium falls on RS (c) Decrease if initial equilibrium falls above RS

We can now see that what we must know, if we are to specify the required directions of change of both variables, is not where the initial equilibrium falls in relation to HK and JN (not which zone it falls in) but rather where it falls in relation to RS and WV. In fact, using RS and WV we can divide the whole area of Fig. 14.6 into four parts such that, within each, the direction of change of both variables is quite unambiguous. These four parts, which overlap the zones, we shall call the four 'sectors'. They are summarised in Table 14.3.

TABLE 14.3

| | | Required direction of change of: | |
Sector	Location of sector in Fig. 14.7	Home–foreign price ratio	Aggregate demand
A	All points below RS and above WV	Increase	Increase
B	All points below RS and below WV	Decrease	Increase
C	All points above RS and below WV	Decrease	Decrease
D	All points above RS and above WV	Increase	Decrease

Every one of the policy prescriptions set out in Table 14.3 involves something of a paradox. This can be seen from Table 14.4, which is to be read in conjunction with Fig. 14.7. In each case, however, the paradox is easily resolved. Take, for example, the sector A paradox. This arises whenever the initial equilibrium falls in the zone I division of the sector, as in Fig. 14.7. In this situation the additional real imports required to eliminate the balance of payments surplus will exceed the initial excess demand. For example, QP in Fig. 14.7 is larger than TQ $(= QZ)$.[1] Hence an increase in real imports of the amount required for external balance accompanied by the *same* aggregate demand would convert the initial excess demand into a deficient demand : external balance would be attained but not internal balance. It follows, in turn, that the simultaneous achievement of both objectives requires that aggregate demand be increased as well as real imports, even though aggregate demand is excess in the initial equilibrium.

As a second example, take the sector B paradox. This is associated with an initial equilibrium which falls in the zone III division of sector B, as in Fig. 14.8. Whenever this happens the new aggregate demand line must intersect the old import line to the right of JN. Thus in Fig. 14.8, RS intersects LE at F. This means that if an increase of aggregate demand of the amount required for internal balance is accompanied by the same home–foreign price ratio, the initial balance of payments surplus would be converted into a balance of payments deficit : internal balance would be achieved but not external balance. Hence to achieve both objectives simultaneously it

---

[1] Recall that the slope of the aggregate demand line is numerically equal to 1 (see section 14.2 above).

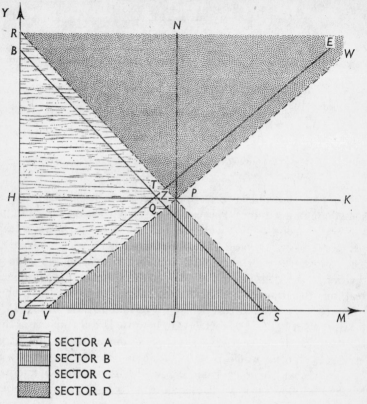

SECTOR A
SECTOR B
SECTOR C
SECTOR D

Fig. 14.7

is essential that the home–foreign price ratio be decreased even though the initial equilibrium is characterised by a balance of payments surplus.

TABLE 14.4

Sector	Paradox involved in prescription of Table 14.3
A	An *increase* in aggregate demand may be required when aggregate demand is initially *excess*
B	A *decrease* in the home–foreign price ratio may be required when the balance of payments is initially in *surplus*
C	A *decrease* in aggregate demand may be required when aggregate demand is initially *deficient*
D	An *increase* in the home–foreign price ratio may be required when the balance of payments is initially in *deficit*

The remaining paradoxes give no more trouble than the two just considered and their resolution will be left to the reader.

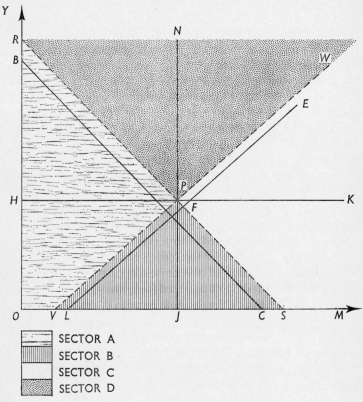

SECTOR A
SECTOR B
SECTOR C
SECTOR D

Fig. 14.8

14.5 Excess Demand and the Import Function

In the analysis so far we have tacitly assumed that the internal changes which are associated with the movement from the initial equilibrium to the point of economic happiness have no effect on the position of the import curve. As the discussion of Chapter 7 (see especially section 7.2) shows, this is unlikely to be the case. If the movement to the new equilibrium is associated with a smaller excess demand (if the initial situation lies anywhere above HK), both the overall delivery delay of home-produced importables relative to foreign-produced importables, and the rate of increase of home prices, will tend to fall. Both of these changes will tend to shift the import curve to the left. On the other hand, if the movement to the new equilibrium involves a smaller deficiency of demand (if the initial situation lies anywhere below *HK*), both the relative delivery delay and the rate of increase of home prices will tend to rise with the result that the import curve will tend to shift to the right. The question which arises is: How does this complication affect the validity of the policy prescriptions laid down in Table 14.3? Let us take them one by one.

The prescription for sector A remains valid if the initial equilibrium falls in the top part of the sector (above *HK*). In this case the movement to the new equilibrium will be associated with a reduction in excess demand and hence with a leftward shift in the import curve. The need for an increase in the home–foreign price ratio will therefore remain; in fact a larger increase will be required than would otherwise have been the case. If, however, the initial equilibrium falls in the bottom half of the sector (below *HK*), the movement to the new equilibrium will be associated with a rightward shift in the import curve. This may take the import curve beyond *P*. If it does, the appropriate manipulation of the home–import price ratio will be reversed: a decrease will now be called for rather than an increase.

The policy prescription for sector B remains entirely valid. In this case the initial equilibrium is always below *HK*. Consequently the move to the new equilibrium is accompanied by a reduction in the deficiency of demand and hence by a rightward shift in the import curve. A decrease in the home–foreign price ratio will therefore be even more necessary than before.

The prescription for sector C remains entirely valid as far as the zone IV portion of the sector (the bottom half) is concerned. If the initial equilibrium falls in zone IV, the movement to the point of economic happiness will be accompanied by a reduction in the deficiency of demand and, through this, by a rightward shift in the import curve. The need for a decrease in the home–foreign price ratio will therefore be intensified. As far as the top half of the sector is concerned, however, the prescription must be qualified. Here the move to the new equilibrium is associated with a leftward shift of the import curve via a reduction in excess demand. Should this take the import curve beyond *P*, an increase in the home–foreign price ratio will be called for, not a decrease.

Sector D resembles sector B; here, too, the policy prescription of Table 14.3 remains entirely valid. This follows from the fact that the move to the new equilibrium is always associated with a leftward shift of the import curve via a reduction in excess demand. Consequently there will be all the more need for an increase in the home–foreign price ratio. The position now reached is summarised in Table 14.5.

TABLE 14.5

Required direction of change of:

Sector	Home–foreign price ratio		Aggregate demand
A	Above *HK*:	Increase	Increase
	Below *HK*:	Uncertain	
B	Decrease		Increase
C	Below *HK*:	Decrease	Decrease
	Above *HK*:	Uncertain	
D	Increase		Decrease

14.6 Shifts in the External Balance Line

So far we have assumed that all variables affecting the balance of payments, other than import volume, are not only given, but fixed. On this assumption, the volume of imports required for external balance (the position of *JN*) is also fixed, which means that *P*, the point of economic happiness, is fixed, given the internal balance line, *HK*. In this section we shall continue to treat the variables in question as data; but we shall no longer require that they be fixed. In other words, we shall now allow for the possibility that the external balance line will shift from the position which it occupies in the initial equilibrium, either to the right or to the left.

Suppose, to begin with, that the initial equilibrium is disturbed by a once-for-all decline in export volume. Thus export volume falls in some period, say from the constant level of the initial equilibrium to some lower level, and remains fixed at this lower level throughout the movement to the new equilibrium. Assuming that the rest of the balance of payments data remain unchanged at their initial equilibrium levels, this once-for-all reduction in export volume will imply a leftward shift of the external balance line and, given the internal balance line, a leftward movement along *HK* of the point of economic happiness. In what directions will the two policy data now have to change if the economy is to be brought to a new equilibrium characterised by both internal and external balance? In particular, will the directions of change deduced on the basis of the *original* sector classification of the initial equilibrium, i.e. those set out in Tables 14.3 and 14.5, continue to apply?

The question is best approached in diagrammatic terms. In Fig. 14.9, the solid line *JN* is the external balance line in the initial equilibrium while the solid lines *RS* and *WV* are, respectively, the positions which the aggregate demand curve and the import curve must attain if internal and external balance are to be simultaneously achieved on the basis of *JN* and *HK*.[1] The broken line *J'N'* is the new external balance line, i.e. the external balance line corresponding to the postulated lower export volume, while the broken lines *R'S'* and *W'V'* represent the positions which the aggregate demand curve and the import curve must reach if both objectives are to be achieved on the basis of *J'N'* and *HK*.

Let us now return to our question: Will the directions of change

[1] These are the lines in terms of which the sectors of Tables 14.3 and 14.5 are defined.

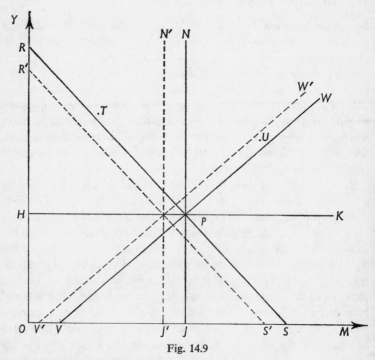

Fig. 14.9

which follow from the original classification of the initial equilibrium still apply in the face of the postulated autonomous decline in export volume? This will depend, obviously, on whether the new sector classification of the initial equilibrium is the same as the original classification; if it is, the prescriptions of Tables 14.3 and 14.5 will still hold and vice versa.

It is immediately clear from the diagram that an initial equilibrium originally classified as C will retain that classification, so that the decline in export volume can be disregarded in deciding on the appropriate directions of change of the two policy data. It is also clear that initial situations originally classified as A, B, or D may or may not retain their classification, depending on their exact position on the diagram. For example, an initial equilibrium at T which has an original classification of D will retain that classification so that a decrease in aggregate demand coupled with an increase in the home–foreign price ratio remain appropriate despite the decline in export volume. On the other hand, the classification of an initial equilibrium at U will change from D to C: as a result of the decline in export volume the appropriate policy changes will be a decrease in aggregate demand coupled with a decrease in the home–foreign price ratio rather than an increase.

The analysis has been conducted in terms of a leftward shift in the external balance line produced by a once-for-all decline in export volume, but it applies, obviously, to *any* leftward shift, e.g. to one produced by a once-for-all deterioration in the terms of trade. Obviously, too, it can be easily adapted to cover the case of a rightward shift in the external balance line due, say, to an improvement in the terms of trade.

14.7 Summary

The discussion of Chapters 5 and 6 shows that a change in aggregate demand has consequences both for internal balance and for external balance. It is also clear from these chapters that both the internal situation and the external situation are affected by shifts in the short-run import function. In the light of these conclusions it is natural to inquire whether it is possible for the authorities to achieve *simultaneous* internal and external balance by manipulating aggregate demand alone or by manipulating the home–foreign price ratio alone, and if not, in what ways the two data should be combined.

Using a simple comparative–statics analysis, it is shown that, in general, the authorities will not be able to achieve simultaneous internal and external balance by manipulation of one datum alone. The other major conclusion which emerges is that, in order to deduce the required direction of change of the two data, it is not enough to know the 'zone' in which the initial situation falls, i.e. whether the initial situation is one characterised by excess demand with balance of payments surplus, excess demand with balance of payments deficit, deficient demand with balance of payments surplus, or deficient demand with balance of payments deficit. The required direction of change of one of the two data is unambiguous for each zone, but the required direction of change of the other will vary according to the precise position in the zone of the initial situation. For example, if the initial situation is in 'zone I' (excess demand with balance of payments surplus), it will always be necessary to increase the home–foreign price ratio in order to achieve simultaneous internal and external balance. However, this increase in the home–foreign price ratio will need to be accompanied either by no change in the level of aggregate demand or by an increase, or by a decrease, depending on where in zone I the initial situation falls.

READING LIST

Corden, W. M., 'The Geometric Representation of Policies to Attain Internal and External Balance', *Review of Economic Studies* (Oct 1960).

Hemming, M. F. W., and Corden, W. M., 'Import Restriction as an Instrument of Balance-of-Payments Policy', *Economic Journal* (Sep 1958).

Swan, T. W., 'Longer-Run Problems of the Balance of Payments', in Arndt, H. W., and Corden, W. M. (eds), *The Australian Economy* (Melbourne: Cheshire, 1963).

15 Economic Growth and Price Stability

15.1 Introduction

Is there any reason to believe that a stable relationship exists between the rate of economic growth and the pace of inflation such that the more rapid the inflation the more rapid, *ceteris paribus*, the rate of economic growth? If so, is this because rapid inflation contributes to economic growth, or because rapid economic growth contributes to inflation, or both? One way of approaching these important questions, which has been followed in several recent studies,[1] is to correlate the percentage increase in real gross domestic product and the percentage increase in the general price level. This approach, however, is bound to be somewhat inconclusive. There are two main reasons for this. In the first place, whatever the country or period studied, it is likely that many important factors, apart from the rate of increase of prices, will have contributed to the observed rate of increase in real gross domestic product, and vice versa. As a result, the findings of the correlation analysis will usually be very difficult to interpret. For example, suppose we observe a high correlation between the percentage increase in the general price level and the percentage increase in real gross domestic product. Does this reflect the existence of a stable positive relationship between inflation and growth; or does it mean that the two were quite unconnected but that the effective determinants of growth and the effective determinants of inflation happened to be operating at just the intensity required to produce the observed high correlation? Both are possible. Secondly, even where a high correlation does provide clear evidence of the existence of a stable positive association between inflation and growth, it will not indicate the direction of causation; we shall still be ignorant about whether inflation promotes growth or whether growth promotes inflation.

[1] The main references are given in the reading list which appears at the end of the chapter.

The alternative to the empirical approach is the analytical approach. We shall adopt this approach in the present chapter. First we shall consider the mechanisms through which the pace of inflation may influence the rate of economic growth and attempt to form some judgement about their likely quantitative significance. We shall then discuss the ways in which the rate of economic growth may help to determine the pace of inflation.

15.2 Inflation and Realised Growth

In Chapter I we distinguished various possible meanings of the term *rate of economic growth*. In particular we made the distinction between the average percentage increase in real *realised* gross domestic product and the average percentage increase in real *potential* gross domestic product. In the present section we shall analyse the ways in which the pace of inflation may affect the rate of economic growth in the first of these two senses, which, for convenience, we shall call 'the *realised* growth rate'. The effect of inflation on the rate of economic growth in the second sense ('the *potential* growth rate') will be discussed in section 15.3.

We shall begin by developing a simple formula which gives the realised growth rate at time t in terms of its proximate determinants. Our starting-point is:

$$Y = D - M - U \tag{15.1}$$

where the symbols are defined as follows:

Y = real realised G.D.P. at time t

D = aggregate demand at time t

M = real realised imports at time t

U = undesired real disinvestment in inventories at time t.

This relationship will be recognised as the continuous-analysis version of relationship (3.2) – one of the relationships of the sequence of models developed in Chapters 3–5.

From (15.1), by taking logs and differentiating with respect to time, we obtain the following relationship:

$$\dot{Y} = \epsilon_1 \dot{D} - \epsilon_2 \dot{M} - \epsilon_3 \dot{U} \tag{15.2}$$

where $\qquad \epsilon_1 = \dfrac{D}{Y}; \quad \epsilon_2 = \dfrac{M}{Y}; \quad \epsilon_3 = \dfrac{U}{Y}$

and where the dot denotes 'proportional rate of increase'. This relationship suggests that the main routes alone which the pace of inflation can influence the realised growth rate at time t are $\dot{D}$, the proportional increase in aggregate demand at time t, and $\dot{M}$, the proportional increase in the volume of imports at time t. Let us take them in turn.

TABLE 15.1

	Case 1: stable prices	Case 2: price rise of 20 per cent
1. G.D.P. in constant prices	80	80
2. G.D.P. in current prices	100	120
3. Average rate of personal income tax (personal income tax as proportion of G.D.P.)	0·20	0·25
4. Personal income tax in current prices	20	30
5. Items in G.D.P., other than personal disposable income, in current prices	10	12
6. Personal disposable income in current prices	70	78
7. Personal disposable income in constant prices	56	52

It seems likely that, *ceteris paribus*, $\dot{D}$ will be lower the higher is the percentage increase in the price level. There are several reasons for this. The first is that, because of the progressiveness of the income-tax structure, a rise in prices leads, *ceteris paribus*, to a downward shift in the disposable-income function (relationship (2.26)) and hence to a lower level of real consumption expenditure (cf. relationship (2.24)), and hence, in turn, to a lower value of $\dot{D}$ than would have been the case with stable prices; and of course the larger the rise in prices, the more pronounced the downward shift in the disposable-income function and the more pronounced, therefore, the depressing effect on $\dot{D}$.

The simple arithmetical example set out in Table 15.1 may help to clarify this point. The table compares the relationship between real disposable income and real gross domestic product (G.D.P.) at a particular instant of time on two different assumptions about the movement in prices at that instant: (1) that prices are stable; and (2) that they are rising by 20 per cent per period. We start by supposing that G.D.P. is 80 in terms of constant prices and 100 in terms of current prices on assumption 1. On assumption 2 G.D.P. in terms of current prices will then be 120. Because G.D.P. in current prices is 20 per cent higher on assumption 2 than it is on assumption 1 and because of the progressive nature of the personal income-tax structure, the average rate of personal income tax will be higher on assumption 2 than on assumption 1 – we suppose it to be 25 per cent as compared with 20 per cent. We next take it, for simplicity, that the other items which intervene between G.D.P. and personal disposable income constitute the same proportion of G.D.P. on both assumptions, namely 10 per cent. This makes personal disposable income in current prices 70 on assumption 1 and 78 on assumption 2; and this, in turn, makes personal disposable income in constant prices 56 and 52 respectively. Thus, the real G.D.P. of 80 gives rise to a real personal disposable income of 56, on the assumption of stable prices, and of only 52 on the assumption of a 20 per cent price rise.

The second reason for postulating an inverse connection between $\dot{D}$ and the rate of increase in prices is that the higher the rate of increase in prices the lower, *ceteris paribus*, will be the real incomes of certain important groups of spenders and hence the lower will be their real expenditure. In developing countries, one such group are the exporters of primary products which are priced in world markets. The gross receipts of this group of producers will be independent of the rate of increase of domestic price levels, whereas their costs will rise as domestic prices rise. Consequently, their money incomes will be lower, *ceteris paribus*, the higher are domestic prices. In addition, of course, the real equivalent of any given money income will be lower the higher are domestic prices. For both these reasons there will be an inverse connection between the real incomes of primary-product exporters and the rate of inflation and hence between their real consumption, and investment, expenditure and the rate of inflation. Another group whose real incomes and real expenditure will be inversely related to the rate of inflation are retired people whose income consists of some form of pension, e.g. an old-age pension, payments from a superannuation fund, or an annuity purchased from lump-sum superannuation proceeds. In most cases the incomes of such people will be fixed or virtually fixed in money terms. Consequently the higher the general price level the lower will be their real incomes and hence the lower their real consumption expenditures. In short, rising prices will not only result in a *movement down* the consumption function via a downward shift in the disposable income function, but will also produce a *downward shift* of the consumption function. The faster the rise in the general price level, the more pronounced this downward shift and the more depressing the effect on $\dot{D}$.

Thirdly, rising prices may depress $\dot{D}$ by causing G (real government expenditure) to be lower than it would have been otherwise. This will happen if the machinery by which finance is made available to local governments (and, in the case of a federal system, to state or provincial governments) is such that the funds provided in any year are unaffected, or virtually so, by the pace of inflation. Such a situation appears to be quite common – it exists in Australia, for example.

Finally, the faster the pace of domestic inflation the worse the competitive position of price-makers (mainly producers of manufactured goods) in overseas markets. Hence the lower, *ceteris paribus*, the volume of their overseas sales. Thus a fourth reason for expecting an inverse connection between $\dot{D}$ and the percentage increase in prices is that the higher the price level the lower the variable E (exports in terms of constant prices). The significance of this point for any given economy depends, of course, on the proportion which real exports by price-makers bear to total real exports. In the case of the Australian economy, for example, this is still only about 20 per cent – primary exports which are priced in world markets (for which Australian producers are price-takers) still predominate and will almost certainly continue to do so in the foreseeable future, so that the point is of marginal significance. On the other hand, where exports consist almost exclusively of manufactured goods, as in the case of the British economy, the point is of considerable importance.

It must be recognised, of course, that inflation will have certain effects on $\dot{D}$ which will work against those just described. For example, while the real income and real expenditure of some groups will be reduced by rising prices, the real income and real expenditure of others will be increased; inflation will *redistribute* real income rather than reduce it in total. Again, as we shall see in the next section inflation will tend to stimulate $\dot{D}$ via fixed-capital investment expenditure. The arguments presented in the preceding paragraphs are therefore not quite as strong as they appear to be at first sight. Nevertheless, their combined weight is considerable.

We turn now from $\dot{D}$ to $\dot{M}$. According to (15.2), this is the second main channel through which the pace of inflation can influence the realised growth rate. Once again, the effect is likely to be adverse because the higher the percentage increase in domestic prices, the higher, *ceteris paribus*, will be the home–foreign price ratio and hence the greater will be the percentage increase of real imports. But, as is clear from (15.2), the higher is $\dot{M}$ the lower, *ceteris paribus*, will be $\dot{Y}$ and hence the lower will be the realised growth rate.

To sum up, it appears likely that the realised growth rate is inversely related to the pace of inflation because the higher the percentage increase in prices the lower, *ceteris paribus*, will be the percentage increase in aggregate demand and the higher the percentage increase in real imports. This does not mean, of course, that a target level of $\dot{Y}$ which would be achievable with price stability will not be achievable with inflation, but rather that the authorities will need to stimulate $\dot{D}$ more with inflation than with price stability (and/or depress $\dot{M}$ more) if they are to produce the particular level of $\dot{Y}$ which is required for the achievement of the desired growth rate. This will not matter very much if the authorities have ample fiscal and monetary means of influencing aggregate demand and import volume at their disposal and are uninhibited in their use, as in the British case. It could be significant, however, where government is weak and inexperienced, as it is in many of the developing countries, or where there is a strong ideological aversion to government intervention in economic affairs, as in the United States and Canada.

15.3 Inflation and Potential Growth

We turn now to a discussion of the ways in which the pace of inflation may affect the rate of economic growth in the sense of the average percentage increase in real *potential* gross domestic product. We shall refer to this for convenience as the potential growth rate. As in the previous section where we discussed the ways in which the pace of inflation influences the realised growth rate, we shall begin by developing a simple formula showing the potential growth rate in terms of its proximate determinants.

We take as our starting-point the continuously substitutable production function with disembodied technical progress:

$$Y^p = A(t)f(K^*, L^*) \qquad (15.3)$$

where Y^p denotes real potential G.D.P. at time t, K^* and L^* denote, respectively, available capital input at time t and available labour input at time t under 'normal full-employment conditions' (cf. section 1.5), and $A(t)$ denotes the index of technical progress (see section 12.2). This expression implies that there are two basic ways in which real potential gross domestic product can increase over time: as a result of increases in L^* and/or K^* at a given level of $A(t)$, and as a result of increases in $A(t)$ at given levels of L^* and K^*. In other words, real potential gross domestic product can increase over time either as a result of movements along f or as a result of shifts in f. Thus f can be thought of as an aggregate production function and $A(t)$ as some index which measures the effects of shifts in the function. Shifts in the aggregate production function can occur for a variety of reasons, but to ease the discussion we have lumped all these reasons under the heading 'technical progress' and have referred to $A(t)$ as the 'index of technical progress'.

It should also be noted that relationship (15.3) implies that technical progress is 'Hicks-neutral', meaning by this that shifts in the production function leave marginal rates of substitution between capital input and labour input unchanged – roughly that technical progress is not more closely associated with one of the two inputs than with the other. This simplifies the discussion without restricting it in any important way.

The differences between (15.3) and (12.5) are: (i) in (12.5) the production function is given the specific form: $f(K, L) = K^\alpha L^{1-\alpha}$; (ii) the input variables refer to 'utilised' rather than 'available' inputs; and (iii) the output variable is realised rather than potential output – as a consequence of (ii).

We now proceed to manipulate (15.3) to obtain the required expression for the potential growth rate in terms of its proximate determinants. Taking logs and differentiating with respect to time, we get:

$$\dot{Y}^p = \dot{A}(t) + \frac{1}{f}\frac{df}{dt} = \dot{A}(t) + \frac{1}{f}\left[\frac{\partial f}{\partial L^*}\frac{dL^*}{dt} + \frac{\partial f}{\partial K^*}\frac{dK^*}{dt}\right]. \qquad (15.4)$$

Since, from (15.3), $f = Y^p/A(t)$, we can write (15.4) as:

$$\dot{Y}^p = \dot{A}(t) + A(t)\left[\left(\frac{\partial f}{\partial L^*}\frac{L^*}{Y^p}\right)\left(\frac{dL^*}{dt}\frac{1}{L^*}\right) + \left(\frac{\partial f}{\partial K^*}\frac{K^*}{Y^p}\right)\left(\frac{dK^*}{dt}\frac{1}{K^*}\right)\right]. \qquad (15.5)$$

We now use:
$$\frac{\partial Y^p}{\partial L^*} = A(t)\frac{\partial f}{\partial L^*}; \quad \frac{\partial Y^p}{\partial K^*} = A(t)\frac{\partial f}{\partial K^*}$$

to write (15.5) as:

$$\dot{Y}^p = \dot{A}(t) + \left(\frac{\partial Y^p}{\partial L^*}\frac{L^*}{Y^p}\right)\dot{L}^* + \left(\frac{\partial Y^p}{\partial K^*}\frac{K^*}{Y^p}\right)\dot{K}^*. \qquad (15.6)$$

Denoting the two bracketed terms by ξ_1 and ξ_2, respectively, we have as our final expression:

$$\dot{Y}^p = \dot{A}(t) + \xi_1\dot{L}^* + \xi_2\dot{K}^*. \qquad (15.7)$$

R

Note that ξ_1 is the elasticity of real potential G.D.P. with respect to available labour input and similarly for ξ_2. Thus our argument shows, in effect, that (12.13) applies quite generally where technical progress is disembodied and Hicks-neutral and not merely to the special case where the production function is Cobb–Douglas of degree 1.

Relationship (15.7) enables us to identify the routes along which the pace of inflation may affect the potential growth rate. While there may well be some effects via the elasticities, ξ_1 and ξ_2, and the proportional increase in available labour input, $\dot{L}^*$, they are not likely to be particularly significant. It would seem that the main effects will be through $\dot{K}^*$ and $\dot{A}(t)$, and the ensuing discussion will concentrate exclusively on these two possibilities.

1. *Inflation and Capital Accumulation*

By definition we have:

$$\dot{K}^* = \frac{I^{nf}}{K^*} = \frac{I^{nf}}{Y} \frac{Y}{K^*}$$

where I^{nf} denotes real net investment in fixed-capital equipment. Assuming that the available capital input is fully utilised ($K = K^*$), it follows from the above that $\dot{K}^*$ is determined by the ratio of net fixed-capital investment to G.D.P., given the overall capital–output ratio. Thus to determine the effects of inflation on $\dot{K}^*$ we need to consider its likely effects on the ratio between net investment and gross domestic product. We saw in the previous section that inflation is likely to depress the denominator of this ratio and to this extent it will cause the ratio to rise. The question we have now to consider is whether or not the effects on the numerator are likely to work in the same direction. There are two main ways in which inflation may influence the level of real net fixed-capital investment expenditure, namely: (i) through the availability of resources for capital formation; and (ii) through the cost of finance. Let us consider these possibilities in turn.

Imagine a situation of *unsatisfied* demand and suppose that part of the total unsatisfied demand represents demand for fixed-capital equipment. In such a situation the level of real fixed-capital investment which is actually achieved is likely to be higher with inflation than with price stability, because inflation will reduce consumption demand and so release resources which can be used to meet some or all of the unsatisfied demand for fixed-capital equipment. This argument is supported by the analysis of Chapter 8 which relates to a situation of exactly the type we have in mind. It will be recalled that this analysis postulates an initial equilibrium and a disturbance which takes the form of the emergence of unsatisfied demand. Throughout the ensuing inflationary process, to which the disturbance gives rise, consumption demand is continually declining, being given by:

$$C_t = \frac{a}{P_{t-1}} + bY_{t-1}$$

in terms of initial equilibrium prices (see p. 277 above). As a result, unsatisfied investment demand is also continually declining. In any period subsequent to the disturbance, unsatisfied investment demand is given by the excess of the desired level of real investment expenditure over the realised level. From equation (8.3) this can be written, in terms of initial equilibrium prices, as:

$$\frac{I_t{}^*}{P_{t-1}} - \frac{I_t{}^*}{P_t} = I^*{}_t\left(\frac{P_t - P_{t-1}}{P_t P_{t-1}}\right).$$

As time passes, $(P_t - P_{t-1})$ will converge on zero,[1] which means that the unsatisfied investment demand will also converge on zero as consumption demand declines.

Once again the point appears to have little significance for an advanced industrial country because it assumes a condition of unsatisfied demand and, as stressed in Chapter 8, such a condition is not characteristic of advanced countries except, perhaps, in times of total war. On the other hand, the point may have considerable relevance for underdeveloped countries where unsatisfied demand seems to be a more general phenomenon and where, consequently, desired additions to the stock of fixed-capital equipment may frequently be prevented simply through lack of the necessary physical resources.

A second way in which rising prices may stimulate real net fixed-capital investment expenditure is through the cost of finance. The higher the percentage increase in prices the lower, *ceteris paribus*, will be the effective cost of borrowing to the individual firm and hence the higher its desired net fixed-capital investment expenditure (cf. sections 4.2, 4.3 and 5.5 above).

[1] This assumes that the inflationary process is convergent (cf. section 8.3).

That an inverse connection exists between the effective cost of finance and the percentage increase in prices can be seen from the following simple arithmetical example. Suppose that a firm borrows £100 for twelve months at a nominal rate of interest of 5 per cent per annum payable at the end of the loan period. Suppose, too, that the general price level is expected to rise by 3 per cent over the twelve months. Then in terms of the prices ruling at the beginning of the loan period, the net amount which the firm expects to pay to the lender is £[(105/1·03) – 100]. Thus the effective rate of interest (or the *real* rate of interest) is not 5 per cent per annum but $100[(1·05/1·03) – 1]$ per cent = 2 per cent. With a price rise of 5 per cent the real rate of interest would be zero and with a price rise of more than 5 per cent it would actually be negative. In general, when the interest is payable at the end of the loan period, as in the present example, the relationship between the nominal and the real rates of interest for any period is as follows:

$$\text{Real rate of interest} = 100\left(\frac{1+r}{1+\dot{P}} - 1\right) \text{ per cent.}$$

where r is the nominal interest payable on £1 (0·05 in the example) and $\dot{P}$ the expected proportional increase in prices (0·03 in the example).[1] This expression makes it clear that the effective cost of borrowing to the firm is inversely related to the pace of inflation. This point, unlike the first, may have more significance for an advanced country than for an underdeveloped country, because in the latter case fixed-capital investment is usually inhibited more by lack of available finance than by lack of incentive.

The conclusion which emerges from the discussion of this sub-section is, therefore, that inflation will tend to raise $\dot{K}^*$, and hence to raise the potential growth rate, by raising the ratio of net fixed-capital investment to G.D.P. It will raise this ratio both by raising the numerator and also by depressing the denominator.

2. *Inflation and Technical Progress*

There are three possible links between the proportional increase in the index of technical progress, $\dot{A}(t)$, and the pace of inflation which seem worth mentioning. In the first place, inflation is likely to stimulate real housing investment and in this way to make the average

---

[1] With interest payable in advance, the formula would be:

$$\text{Real rate of interest} = 100\left(r + \frac{1}{1+\dot{P}} - 1\right) \text{ per cent.}$$

quality of the housing stock better than it would otherwise be. To the extent that it does so, it will tend to improve the health, and hence to raise the quality, of the available labour input. This, in turn, will tend to raise $\dot{A}(t)$.

Inflation can be expected to stimulate real housing investment in two main ways. In the first place, as we have just seen, it will tend to lower the effective cost of borrowing; and, as the discussion of section 4.3 makes clear, this will tend to shift the housing investment function upwards.

The second effect is more subtle. The essential point here is that inflation reduces the liquidity of money and assets whose value is fixed in terms of money. Liquidity in the 'saleability' sense is not impaired unless the inflation is particularly rapid. However, liquidity in the 'store-of-value' sense definitely falls with inflation and falls, moreover, in proportion to the pace of the inflation. Consequently to maintain a *given degree* of liquidity in his asset holding, an individual will need to hold a smaller proportion of his wealth in the form of money with inflation than with price stability and a larger proportion in the form of assets whose liquidity is not reduced by rising prices. Now one such asset is a house: in the case of a house neither the saleability aspect of liquidity nor the store-of-value aspect is impaired by rising prices. It is to be expected, therefore, that, *ceteris paribus*, the demand for new houses will be stronger under inflationary conditions than when prices are stable and are expected to remain so. This conclusion would not necessarily hold if individuals normally required a *smaller degree* of liquidity under inflation than under price stability. In fact, however, the reverse is likely to be the case: since unforeseen opportunities for making advantageous purchases are likely to be more frequent under inflation than under price stability, the desired degree of liquidity is likely to be higher rather than lower.

A second possible link between $\dot{A}(t)$ and the pace of inflation is through I^{gf}, the level of gross real investment in fixed-capital equipment. As demonstrated in the preceding subsection, inflation will tend to stimulate I^{nf}. Hence it will tend to stimulate I^{gf} also.[1] To the extent that it does so, it will serve to narrow the gap between the existing and the best technology and in this way to raise the average quality of the available capital input. This in turn will tend to raise $\dot{A}(t)$.

---

[1] This assumes that there are no offsetting effects via replacement expenditure. These seem unlikely in the light of the discussion of pp. 98–9 above.

Finally, the pace of inflation may influence the rate of increase of the technical progress index via the *composition* of I^{gf}, as distinct from its level. It seems likely *a priori* that the composition of I^{gf} (and hence the composition of any given addition to the fixed-capital stock) will be different under conditions of inflation from what it will be under conditions of price stability. But unless all the relevant marginal output–capital ratios happen to be equal, this implies that the value of $\dot{Y}^p$ which corresponds to any given values of $\dot{K}^*$, $\dot{L}^*$, ξ_1 and ξ_2 will also be different. In other words it means, in view of (15.7), that the level of $\dot{A}(t)$ will vary with the pace of inflation. Whether this particular effect of inflation will tend to raise $A(t)$ or lower it depends, first of all, on what types of investment are likely to be stimulated in times of inflation and what types are likely to be depressed, i.e. on what type of redistribution of I^{gf} is likely to result from inflation. Unfortunately, nothing very definite can be said on this matter at the present time. One point that might be made is that as long as the real rate of interest is negative, the real rate will be lower the longer the period of loan.[1] Consequently fixed-capital investment by long-term borrowers, such as the public authority business undertakings, is likely to form a higher proportion of the total under conditions of fairly rapid inflation than under conditions of price stability. A second point, which might work against the first to some extent, is that because inflation increases the degree of uncertainty facing investors, it is likely to produce a bias in favour of fixed-capital investment which pays for itself in a reasonably short time. However, general points such as these do not take us very far; in this case hope seems to lie in empirical rather than in analytical investigation and the necessary empirical work has still to be done. Even if we knew something about the way in which inflation redistributes I^{gf}, we would still not be able to answer the question in hand (whether inflation is likely to raise $\dot{A}(t)$, via the composition of I^{gf}, or lower it) unless we also knew the relevant marginal output–capital ratios.

---

[1] This appears to hold fairly generally but can be demonstrated most easily for the case where the whole of the principal is repaid at the end of the loan period and the interest is compounded. Under these conditions, the real rate of interest on a loan for n years will be given by:

$$\text{Real rate of interest} = 100\left[\left(\frac{1+r}{1+\dot{P}}\right)^n - 1\right] \text{ per cent per annum}$$

where r is the nominal interest payable on £1 and $\dot{P}$ the expected proportional increase per annum in the general price level. Provided $r < \dot{P}$ (so long as the real rate of interest is negative), this will be a decreasing function of n.

We can sum up the discussion of the present section by saying that inflation appears likely to raise the potential growth rate in two main ways. The first is by raising $\dot{K}^*$ (in the case of an advanced industrial country like Britain mainly via the effective cost of borrowing) and the second is by raising $\dot{A}(t)$ (mainly through improving the average quality of the available labour input and the available capital input). Nothing definite can be said about the quantitative significance of these effects, but it seems unlikely that they would be substantial enough to warrant abandoning the price-stability objective in the interests of promoting faster economic growth.

15.4 Does Growth Cause Inflation?

So far in the present chapter we have been concerned with the question whether inflation makes for more rapid economic growth. We turn now to the opposite question: Does economic growth make for more rapid inflation?

One argument which can be advanced to support an affirmative answer is that in a growing economy it will be difficult for the authorities to maintain the special relationship between $\dot{D}$ and $\dot{Y}^p$ which is required for continuous internal balance.[1] Consequently in a growing economy one must expect frequent departures from the internal balance path in both directions. In particular one must expect growth to be accompanied by sporadic excess demand. But as the discussion of section 9.3 makes clear, the emergence of excess demand is one of the main ways in which an inflationary price rise can be started up. Hence one must expect growth to be accompanied by inflation.

A second argument in support of the view that economic growth intensifies the problem of inflation is one based on the hypothesis of 'sectoral inflation'. The changes in the pattern of aggregate demand and real potential G.D.P. which are an integral part of economic growth could conceivably be such that excess demand is zero at any

[1] This special relationship can be derived as follows. The condition for continuous internal balance is:

$$D = Y^p + M \text{ for all } t$$

where D, Y^p and M are, respectively, aggregate demand at time t, real potential G.D.P. at time t and real imports at time t. Taking logs and differentiating with respect to time, we get:

$$\dot{D} = \xi_1 \dot{Y}^p + \xi_2 \dot{M}$$

where ξ_1 denotes Y^p/D and ξ_2 denotes M/D.

point of time in every sector of the economy. However, there is no reason to believe that growth ever takes this very special form; on the contrary, we must expect that the normal growth pattern in the real world is one characterised by excess demand for commodities in some sectors and by deficient demand in others. If this is so, however, we must also expect that growth will have an inflationary impact even when it happens to occur with continuous internal balance – even when, by accident, the positive and negative excess demands exactly offset each other to give zero excess demand in the economy as a whole. The reason is that, while there will be a tendency for prices to rise in those sectors in which demand is excess, there will be little or no tendency for them to fall in the sectors in which demand is deficient. There will thus be a tendency for prices to rise in the economy as a whole, even when growth takes place along the internal balance path.

This reasoning can be carried one stage further. Just as one can conceive of a pattern of growth in real potential G.D.P. and aggregate demand which implies continuous zero excess demand in every sector, so one can envisage a situation in which the growth of real realised G.D.P. is distributed between sectors in such a way that the rate of increase of productivity is always exactly equal to the rate of increase in average earnings in every sector of the economy. Once again, however, there is no reason to believe that growth ever takes this perfectly balanced form; rather one must expect that a growing economy will be characterised by productivity increases in excess of wage increases (falling unit wage costs) in some sectors and wage increases in excess of productivity increases (rising unit wage costs) in others. If this is so, however, a growing economy will be prone to yet another form of sectoral inflation: there will be a tendency for prices to rise in response to rising unit labour cost in those sectors in which money wages are increasing faster than productivity, but little or no tendency for them to fall in the rest of the economy.

These arguments are persuasive but they are not completely decisive. The difficulty is that they apply not only to a growing economy but also to a stagnant economy and to a declining economy. For example, the authorities will find it difficult to maintain the special relationship between $\dot{D}$ and $\dot{Y}^p$ which is implied by continuous internal balance, not only when $\dot{D}$ and $\dot{Y}^p$ are typically positive (when the economy is growing), but also when they are typically zero (when the economy is stagnant) and when they are typically negative (when the economy is declining). Again it is undoubtedly true that a growing economy is likely to be unbalanced in the sense that there will normally be excess demand in some markets and deficient demand in others, even if there is no excess demand in the economy as a whole. But the same can be said of a declining economy: there is no more reason to believe in 'balanced decline' or 'balanced stagnation' as a real-world phenomenon than in 'balanced growth'. Now if the arguments for the view that a growing economy will be inflationary can be applied without difficulty to a stagnant or a declining economy also, it cannot be claimed that growth *as such* makes for inflation. To support such a position it would be necessary to show that there are sources of inflation in a growing economy which either do not exist in a stagnant or declining economy, or which are likely to be less prominent in the latter than in the former. It might well be possible to do this. For example, one might be able to show that changes in the pattern of aggregate demand and real potential G.D.P. are much more an integral part of economic growth than of stagnation or economic decline and hence that sectoral inflation of the excess demand variety is likely to be more pervasive in the growing economy than in the stagnant or declining economy. In the meantime, however, the question whether economic growth accentuates the problem of inflation must be regarded as a completely open one.

15.5 Summary

The interaction of economic growth and inflation has two aspects: the dependence of economic growth on the pace of inflation and the dependence of the pace of inflation on the rate of economic growth.

The rate of economic growth in the sense of the average percentage increase of real *realised* G.D.P. is likely to be adversely affected by inflation because the more rapid the price rise in any period, the lower, *ceteris paribus*, the percentage increase in aggregate demand and the higher the percentage increase in real imports. On the other hand, inflation appears to make for a higher rate of economic growth in the sense of the average percentage increase in real *potential* G.D.P. There are two reasons for this: the first is that the more rapid the rise in prices in any period, the larger, *ceteris paribus*, will be the percentage increase in the stock of available capital inputs. The second is that the more rapid the rise in prices in any period, the

R 2

larger, *ceteris paribus*, will be the percentage increase in the index of technical progress. Nothing definite can be said about the quantitative significance of these effects, but it seems unlikely that they would be substantial enough to justify abandoning the price-stability objective in the interests of a faster rate of economic growth.

The question whether economic growth intensifies the problem of inflation is difficult to settle because the arguments for believing that a growing economy will be inflationary apply equally to a stationary economy and to a declining economy. Thus, it is not easy to show that growth *as such* is an inflationary force.

READING LIST

Bhatia, R. J., 'Inflation, Deflation, and Economic Development', *International Monetary Fund Staff Papers* (Nov 1960).

Maynard, G., *Economic Development and the Price Level* (London: Macmillan, 1962).

Olivera, J. H. G., 'On Structural Inflation and Latin-American "Structuralism",' *Oxford Economic Papers* (Nov 1964).

Phelps Brown, E. H., and Browne, M. H., 'Distribution and Productivity under Inflation, 1947–57', *Economic Journal* (Dec 1960).

Seers, D., 'A Theory of Inflation and Growth in Under-Developed Economies Based on the Experience of Latin America', *Oxford Economic Papers* (June 1962).

U Tun Wai, 'The Relation between Inflation and Economic Development: A Statistical Inductive Study', *International Monetary Fund Staff Papers* (Oct 1959).

List of Main Symbols

Symbol	Meaning
C	Desired real consumption expenditure
D	Aggregate demand, i.e. aggregate desired real expenditure
E	Desired real expenditure by overseas entities / Actual level of employment (Chapter 9 only)
G	Desired real government expenditure
H	Excess demand for commodities
I	Desired real investment expenditure
I^{ci}	Desired real investment in inventories of finished goods
I^{gf}	Desired real gross fixed-capital investment
I^{gh}	Desired real gross housing investment
I^i	Desired real inventory investment
I^{nf}	Desired real net fixed-capital investment
I^{nh}	Desired real net housing investment
I^{ri}	Desired real investment in inventories of raw materials and work-in-progress
K	Aggregate stock of fixed-capital equipment (Chapter 9 only) / Index of the ratio of price to unit variable cost in the economy as a whole
K^c	Actual inventory of finished goods
$*K^c$	Desired inventory of finished goods
K^h	Actual stock of houses
$*K^h$	Desired stock of houses
K^r	Actual real inventory of raw materials and work-in-progress held by firms in the aggregate
$*K^r$	Desired real inventory of raw materials and work-in-progress held by firms in the aggregate
L	Actual level of liquid assets / Labour force (Chapter 9 only)
M	Realised real imports / Index of the cost of imported materials per unit of output in the economy as a whole (Chapters 9 and 10 only)
O	Index of output per man in the economy as a whole
P	Implicit deflator of gross domestic product at factor cost
$\hat{S}$	Expected sales
U	Undesired real disinvestment in inventories
U^c	Undesired disinvestment in inventories of finished goods
U^r	Undesired disinvestment in inventories of raw materials and work-in-progress

Symbol	*Meaning*
UD	Unsatisfied demand
W	Index of money wage earnings per man in the economy as a whole
W^r	Index of nationally negotiated wage rates per man
X	Real disposable income
Y	Real gross domestic product (real G.D.P.)

Index of Subjects

Index of Authors